Civil Litigation

Civil Litigation

Third Edition

Thomas F. Goldman, JD
Attorney at Law
Professor Emeritus
Bucks County Community College

Alice Hart Hughes, JD
Attorney at Law
Adjunct Professor
Bucks County Community College

PEARSON

Boston   Columbus   Indianapolis   New York   San Francisco   Upper Saddle River
Amsterdam   Cape Town   Dubai   London   Madrid   Milan   Munich   Paris   Montréal   Toronto
Delhi   Mexico City   São Paulo   Sydney   Hong Kong   Seoul   Singapore   Taipei   Tokyo

Editorial Director: Vernon Anthony
Product Manager: Gary Bauer
Editorial Assistant: Kevin Cecil
Director of Marketing: David Gesell
Senior Marketing Manager: Mary Salzman
Senior Marketing Coordinator: Alicia Wozniak
Program Manager: Megan Moffo
Project Management Team Lead: JoEllen Gohr
Project Manager: Jessica H. Sykes
Procurement Specialist: Deidra Skahill
Senior Art Director: Diane Ernsberger
Cover Art: David Graham
Media Project Manager: April Cleland
Full-Service Project Management: Christina Taylor/Integra Software Serices
Composition: Integra Software Serices
Printer/Binder: LSC Communications
Cover Printer: LSC Communications
Text Font: 11/13 Goudy Oldstyle Std

Library of Congress Cataloging-in-Publication Data

Goldman, Thomas F.
   Civil litigation: process and procedures/Thomas F. Goldman & Alice Hart Hughes.—3rd ed.
      p. cm.
   Includes bibliographical references and index.
   ISBN-13: 978-0-13-349386-3
   ISBN-10: 0-13-349386-5
   1. Civil procedure—United States.   2. Legal assistants—United States—Handbooks, manuals, etc.   I. Hughes, Alice Hart.   II. Title.
   KF8841.G65 2012
   347.73'5—dc22

                                                    2010045810

ISBN 10:   0-13-349386-5
ISBN 13: 978-0-13-349386-3

BRIEF CONTENTS

CONTENTS

CHAPTER 3

Litigation Management and
Technology   47

**UNIT TWO
PLANNING THE LITIGATION**

CHAPTER 4

The Court System, Settlement,
and Alternative Dispute
Resolution   79

UNIT THREE
DOCUMENTS IN CIVIL LITIGATION

UNIT FOUR
FORMAL DISCOVERY METHODS

CHAPTER 11
Introduction to Discovery   273

CHAPTER 12
Issues in Electronic Discovery   291

CHAPTER 15
Other Forms of Discovery   367

UNIT FIVE
TRIAL OF THE CASE

CHAPTER 16
Trial Preparation— Postdiscovery to Pretrial   381

CHAPTER 17
Trial   405

CHAPTER 18

The Electronic Courtroom and Trial Presentation   427

UNIT SIX
POSTTRIAL ISSUES

CHAPTER 19

Posttrial Procedures   443

CHAPTER 20

Enforcement of Judgments   465

ABOUT THE AUTHORS

THOMAS F. GOLDMAN, JD, is an experienced trial attorney who has represented nationally known insurance companies and corporations. He developed the Advanced Litigation Support and Technology Certificate Program at Thomas Edison State College, where he was a member of the Paralegal Studies Program Advisory Board and a mentor. He is Professor Emeritus at Bucks County Community College, where he was a professor of Law and Management, Director of the Center for Legal Studies, and Director of the ABA-approved Paralegal Studies Program.

Professor Goldman is an author of textbooks in paralegal studies and technology, including *The Paralegal Professional*, in its fourth edition; *Litigation Practice: E-Discovery and Technology*; *Accounting and Taxation for Paralegals*; *Technology in the Law Office*, in its third edition; *AbacusLaw: A Hands-On Tutorial and Guide*; and *SmartDraw: A Hands-On Tutorial and Guide*. In addition, he is the executive producer of the Paralegal Professional video series, in which he occasionally appears.

An accounting and economics graduate of Boston University and of Temple University School of Law, Professor Goldman has an active international law, technology law, and litigation practice. He has worked extensively with paralegals and has received the Boss of the Year award of the Legal Support Staff Guild. He was elected the Legal Secretaries Association Boss of the Year for his contribution to cooperative education by encouraging the use of paralegals and legal assistants in law offices. He also received the Bucks County Community College Alumni Association Professional Achievement Award.

He has been an educational consultant on technology to educational institutions and major corporations and a frequent speaker and lecturer on educational, legal, and technology issues. He was appointed to the American Association for Paralegal Education Board of Directors in October 2005; there, he served as the founding chair of the Technology Task Force, where he initiated the Train the Trainer program.

ALICE HART HUGHES, JD, is a practicing attorney and experienced litigator. She is a former Adjunct Professor of Paralegal Studies at Bucks County Community College, where she taught Civil Litigation, Legal Research and Writing, Accounting for Paralegals, Introduction to Paralegal Studies, Negligence, and Family Law. She is the author of *Real Estate Law Fundamentals* and participated in the production and script writing for the Video Law Office Experience. Mrs. Hughes holds a degree in real estate and finance from Temple University and graduated from Temple University School of Law. She has practiced civil litigation extensively, working in midsized, multi-office law firms. Her practice is limited to estate planning, administration, and litigation. In 2010, she was appointed to the Pennsylvania Board of Dentistry and lectures on ethical issues in the medical subspecialty of podiatry.

FROM THE AUTHORS

Few students taking a civil litigation class have ever had any actual contact with the courts or been involved in a lawsuit. As a result, most of their information and beliefs about courts and trials come from television dramas, where everything resolves itself in 30 to 60 minutes. In the real world, the process is slower and more complex; in addition, litigation can be a bit of a mystery because most of what happens goes on behind closed doors. We have tried, in both the text and the supplements, to open the doors of the law office and courthouse to present the process and the procedures of the real world of law.

One way we hope to reveal the mysteries of litigation is through the extensive use of video case studies. These videos follow the progress of a civil case from the factual setting that gives rise to the lawsuit to the preliminary interviews and investigations. The videos continue through the pretrial phases and conclude with the trial and appeal. These scenarios form a basis for discussion and help create an appreciation for the interconnection between professional ethics and actual practice and procedures.

In addition to presenting every stage of the litigation process on video, we have included a complete set of pleadings for a comprehensive case involving a school bus accident. This case is based on a real-life accident reported by the National Transportation Safety Board (NTSB). These pleading samples may be used to prepare one of the additional case studies provided in Appendix 2 or 3; in this way, students can gain practice and simulate the handling of a real case. All of the cases are based on actual incidents that may be further researched, if desired, using the Internet.

Successful civil litigation practice requires a skill set that includes both knowledge of legal concepts and the practical applications of that knowledge. You might think this statement applies only to litigation attorneys, but it also pertains to the lawyers, litigation support paralegals, and information technologists who form the heart of the civil litigation team. Litigation practice today calls on all of the knowledge and skills learned in formal courses of study and on the intangibles learned from life as well. Ethics, soft skills, technology, elements of substantive law, procedural rules, research, and writing skills are all part of the package of skills needed by the members of the litigation team.

This book can be used either as a reference or as a refresher course in the basics and the advanced knowledge needed to be successful in civil litigation. It has been written as a teaching text and as a practice reference manual, with a complete set of case documentation that may be used as a template in future assignments or real-life cases. As Albert Einstein said, "I don't need to know everything; I just need to know where to find it when I need it."

Civil litigation today is more complex than ever before. The pressures to be more efficient, more productive, and more cost effective require the legal team to make extensive use of technology when organizing and managing cases as well as when presenting evidence at trial. No civil litigation text can be complete today without an explanation of the impact and use of technology. Some of the most widely used software in the legal field is available for download from the Technology Resources Website at www.pearsonhighered.com/goldman. The selected software includes examples of each type of application program found in actual practice: office management, case management, electronic discovery, and trial presentation software.

The available software consists of actual programs used in today's litigation practices. Several demonstration versions of the full programs are valid for up to 120 days after installation to allow for their use over a complete semester. These versions are intended to offer a real-life work environment—a mini-internship—with printouts that can be included in a portfolio to demonstrate knowledge of the entire litigation process. In addition, the portfolio can be used for on-the-job reference in the future.

■ WHAT'S IN THE THIRD EDITION

We have updated law and procedural materials where applicable and have made a variety of changes to the presentation based on the feedback from a wide range of users of previous editions of the textbook. Here is a brief list of the most important major changes in the third edition:

- A new Causes of Action and Litigation Strategies (Chapter 5) has been added.
- Expanded end-of-chapter materials have been reorganized into concept review and skill-building sections.
- New case material has been added in the appendices, with new case documents online for use in assignments.
- New, assignable video case studies have been added at the ends of the chapters, fully illustrated with 46 video segments.
- New video interviews with experts have been added to the Advice from the Field feature.
- New Technology Resources Website replaces the Student DVD.

We hope that you enjoy using this textbook and the supporting videos and case material, and we encourage you to contact us with any concerns or suggestions.

Thomas F. Goldman, JD
Alice Hart Hughes, JD

KEY THEMES EXPLORED THROUGHOUT THIS TEXT

■ UNDERSTANDING THE LITIGATION PROCESS

Litigation is a process, not a single event. Each action taken is the result of some decision made by the client or the legal team. Each decision impacts the future direction of the case, which is a process with rules dictated by the courts. To demonstrate the process, a complete set of documents in this text follows a case from interview and investigation through trial and posttrial activity.

■ DEVELOPING CRITICAL THINKING AND PROCEDURAL SKILLS

End-of-chapter material focuses on developing critical thinking and hands-on skills. It includes exercises and assignments broken down into two sections:

Concept Review and Reinforcement

Key Terms
Chapter Summary
Review Questions and Exercises

Building Your Paralegal Skills

Internet and Technology Exercises
Civil Litigation Video Case Studies
Chapter Opening Scenario Case Study
Comprehensive Case Study

■ UNDERSTANDING HOW TO HANDLE ETHICAL SITUATIONS IN CIVIL LITIGATION

The text and resources are designed to build a strong foundational understanding of the ethical principles that apply to the members of the legal team in actual practice. Resources include references to national and individual state's codes of legal ethics and professional responsibility, Ethical Perspectives boxes integrated throughout the textbook, and 16 ethics-related video segments.

ORGANIZATION OF THE BOOK

The book is divided into six units:

- Introduction to Civil Litigation
- Planning the Litigation
- Documents in Civil Litigation
- Formal Discovery Methods
- Trial of the Case
- Posttrial Issues

UNIT ONE—INTRODUCTION TO CIVIL LITIGATION is a review of the concepts presented in Introduction to Paralegal Studies courses and emphasizes the specific applications, ethics, and skills required in civil litigation. For those students who have had any sort of Computers in the Law course, this unit offers a review and update on the use of technology in civil litigation. This unit also provides an introduction to litigation and the roles of the paralegal, the lawyers, and the office support personnel in the law firm. Each chapter begins with an Opening Scenario to draw the students' attention to the real world of a civil litigation law firm.

UNIT TWO—PLANNING THE LITIGATION reviews the organizational skills needed to develop and manage a case from the initial client interview through the use of the information at trial. The issues faced when conducting client and witness interviews and investigating the facts of the case are also covered. What makes our presentation of these materials unique is the inclusion and comparison of the specialty applications software used in the law office and the court system. Conducting electronic research, both factual and legal, as well as managing the case using specialty applications software are important functions of the paralegal.

UNIT THREE—DOCUMENTS IN CIVIL LITIGATION provides an overview of the rules of evidence and what information is admissible to establish the elements of the cause of action. This unit also covers the traditional areas of federal and state pleadings (including the complaint, summons, answers, and other responsive pleadings), with frequent examples of each document supplied for reference. References to specific Federal Rules of Civil Procedure and Federal Rules of Evidence are included for easy reference and further research.

UNIT FOUR—FORMAL DISCOVERY METHODS presents the traditional methods of discovery and also addresses the influence of technology in the courts and litigation. The unit prepares paralegals for traditional paper discovery methods and helps paralegals develop a sound understanding of the scope and methods of electronic discovery in this evolving area of civil litigation practice and court administration.

UNIT FIVE—TRIAL OF THE CASE presents the requirements in preparing for trial and offers guidance on how technology can be used to make better, more effective trial presentations. Court rules and individual judge's rules for the electronic courtroom and presentation are discussed and explained.

UNIT SIX—POSTTRIAL ISSUES focuses on post-litigation activities, including posttrial motions for relief and appellate procedures. This unit also gives practical advice on enforcing and collecting judgments.

CHAPTER PEDAGOGY AND FEATURES

Civil Litigation: Process and Procedures follows the same design used in the *Litigation Practice: E-Discovery and Technology* text to provide a consistent look and feel for those using both books. Chapter features include:

■ OPENING SCENARIOS: THE CIVIL LITIGATION TEAM AT WORK

Each chapter opens with a scenario designed to focus the reader on the relationship of the chapter's content to civil litigation practice. These scenarios offer insight into the operation of a civil litigation law firm and describe situations that a professional might encounter on the job. The scenarios revolve around activities in a fictional multi-location law office that is handling a major tort action through to the trial presentation.

■ ADVICE FROM THE FIELD ARTICLES AND VIDEO INTERVIEWS

These features present professional advice straight from the experts and cover such topics as interviewing skills, developing your portfolio, professional development, handling clients, and more.

■ ETHICAL PERSPECTIVES

This feature raises students' awareness of ethical issues encountered by the legal team and directs students to resources that will help them resolve those issues.

■ PRACTICE TIPS

The goal of this feature is to provide practical tips for the litigation team based on the authors' experience. Typical advice can incorporate the simple (*always check the local rules*), the practical (*call the courthouse to determine the electronic features available in the courtroom*), and the obtuse (*make sure the file formats are supported by the program you select*).

■ SKILL-BUILDING EXERCISES USING CASE RESOURCE MATERIALS

End-of-chapter practice materials, continuing case studies, and a comprehensive case study reflect the actual activities of professionals working in the civil litigation area. Samples are placed throughout the chapters for reference and guidance in preparing the assignments.

■ VIDEO CASE STUDIES

Civil Litigation: Process and Procedures is supported by 46 scenario-based video segments dealing with practice, procedures, and ethical issues in civil litigation practice, allowing instructors to bring the world of the practicing paralegal into the classroom. Thirty-one of the case videos are fact specific to the comprehensive case in Appendix 2 and the additional case studies in Appendix 3.

■ BUILDING YOUR PROFESSIONAL PORTFOLIO

One of the key outcomes of this course is the building of a professional portfolio of litigation documents that can be shown to prospective employers and will function as on-the-job reference material in the future. At the end of Chapter 1, you will find suggestions for organizing your portfolio. Then, as you move through the course, you will find specific assignments that require the production of documents to be included in the portfolio.

THE CIVIL LITIGATION VIDEO SERIES

The 46 video cases incorporated into this text illustrate each step of the litigation process and demonstrate a wide variety of practice and procedural scenarios. Students can view the cases at www.pearson-highered.com/careersersources.

A complete, 20-minute videotaped deposition of an expert witness and an accompanying written transcript (in both .TXT and .DOC formats) are provided for use in creating a deposition summary; they could also be used in conjunction with trial or deposition programs such as Sanction or CaseMap DocPreviewer.

Video Case Study List

1. Video Conferencing: Strategy Discussions
2. Confidentiality Issue: Family Exemption
3. UPL Issue: Interviewing a Client
4. Confidentiality Issue: Public Information
5. UPL Issue: When Friends Ask Friends for Legal Advice
6. Parent and Child Consult the Legal Team
7. Solicitation in the ER: Ethical Duties of the Profession
8. Fees and Billing Issue: Contemporaneous Time Keeping
9. Fees and Billing Issue: Using Time Effectively
10. Administrative Agency Hearing
11. Arbitration before Three-Member Panel
12. Settlement Conference with Judge
13. Preparing for Arbitration
14. Altercation on the School Bus
15. School Principal Reacts
16. Zealous Representation Issue: Handling Evidence
17. Zealous Representation Issue: When You Are Asked to Lie
18. UPL Issue: Working with a Witness
19. Zealous Representation Issue: Signing Documents
20. Zealous Representation Issue: Candor to the Court
21. Scheduling Conference with Judge: Discovery Issue Resolution
22. Court Hearing to Decide Who Represents a Minor: The Court's Duty to Protect the Child
23. Truck Driver's Deposition
24. Confidentiality Issue: Need-to-Know Circle
25. Attorney Meet and Confer: Electronic Discovery Issues
26. Confidentiality Issue: Disclosure of Damaging Information
27. UPL Issue: Improper Supervision
28. UPL Issue: Working with Experts—Deposition of a Medical Expert, Dr. Galo
29. Remote Videoconference: Taking Fact Witness Video Deposition
30. Real-Time Reporting Witness Testimony: Deposing a Minor
31. Video Deposition of a Treating Doctor: Deposition of Treating Doctor, Dr. Lee
32. Mechanic's Deposition
33. Final Pretrial Conference: Resolving Evidentiary Issues
34. Preparing for Trial: Preparing for Deposition and Trial
35. Fact or Expert: Resolving Objection in Videotaped Deposition Discussions
36. Jury Selection: Potential Juror Challenged for Cause
37. A Salesman's Courtroom Testimony
38. Trial: Direct and Cross-Examination of a Witness
39. Preliminary Jury Instructions before Trial
40. Closing Argument: A Lawyer's Last Chance
41. Judge Charges the Jury
42. Expert Witness Video Deposition
43. Three-Judge Appellate Panel
44. A Corporate Officer Seeks Legal Advice

CASE RESOURCES AVAILABLE IN TEXT AND ONLINE

A variety of case materials and documents is available for use as examples and for completing assignments throughout the course.

■ CHAPTER OPENING SCENARIO CASE STUDY

The chapter opening scenario case study sets the stage for the chapter topic. The scenarios revolve around activities in a fictional multi-location law office that is handling a major civil action through to the trial presentation. At the end of each chapter, an assignment revisits the scenario and poses questions involving procedural issues.

■ COMPREHENSIVE CASE STUDY: NTSB SCHOOL BUS ACCIDENT, MOUNTAINBURG, ARKANSAS

A sample case, based on a real-life accident as reported by the National Transportation Safety Board (NTSB), provides an overview of the litigation process from beginning to end, including a complete set of documents and pleadings. A brief synopsis of this case is presented in Appendix 2, and the full NTSB report (complete with related exhibits and photographs) is provided online.

A full set of all pleadings and related documents for cases discussed in the text is also provided online; these documents can be used as examples and templates in the completion of assignments in the text. The school bus accident case is presented as a comprehensive demonstration case; however, the pleadings and documents are meant to be used as examples and templates for completing assignments in the text that involve other cases assigned by the instructor.

At the end of each chapter is an assignment that involves analyzing a case and preparing the necessary documents for the attorney's review. The assignment is a task comparable to what an attorney might ask a paralegal to do. The resulting documents contribute to the student's professional portfolio as specific work samples.

The video case studies that are built into this textbook illustrate many of the steps in this sample case and the situations related to the shorter cases described below. The videos deal with scenarios arising from client interviews through to investigation, trial, and appeal.

■ ADDITIONAL, SHORT CASE STUDIES FOR USE IN ASSIGNMENTS

Additional, shorter case studies, including a simple property damage case, a personal injury case, and a civil assault case, are provided in Appendix 3. These case studies may be used for the completion of assignments within the text to provide students with hands-on experience preparing pleadings and working with case documents. Documents for these cases are provided online and include:

Simple Motor Vehicle Property Damage Claim Case
- Police incident report
- Estimate of repairs from Pope's Garage
- Notes of client interview
- Notes of witness interview

Personal Injury Claim (Injured Student) Medical Treatment Case

- School incident report
- Emergency room report
- Treating surgeon (Dr. Lee) report
- Dr. Lee's medical bill
- Medical records
- HIPAA release form signed by parent

Civil Assault on a School Bus Case

- School incident report
- Psychologist for attacker report (antisocial with psychotic tendency)
- Report of school nurse on search of student for knife
- HIPAA release form
- Notice to opposing counsel requesting medical records
- Medical records of victim, Davis Hilary

■ ADDITIONAL COMPREHENSIVE CASE STUDIES

We have provided two additional school bus accident cases and a major plane crash case. These case studies can be used in place of the Mountainburg case study to complete assignments in the Comprehensive Case Study section at the end of each chapter. Each of the complex cases is based on an NTSB report of an actual event and allows students to further develop their research skills as they find information on the cases through Internet searches. These full NTSB reports are provided online:

- **School Bus–Truck Case, Albany, New York**
- **School Bus–Truck Case, Arlington, Virginia**
- **Airplane Crash, Buffalo, New York**

LEGAL SOFTWARE RESOURCES

Students can download the latest (time-limited) versions of the most popular legal software from the Technology Resources Website at www.pearsonhighered.com/techresources. This website also contains links to software tutorials, video overviews, teaching notes, and a variety of other useful resources, including forms for faculty to request lab copies of software from vendors.

■ OFFICE MANAGEMENT AND ACCOUNTING SOFTWARE

Most law firms, from the sole practitioner to large, multi-office practices, use office management and accounting software extensively. This software is useful for keeping accurate calendars of appointments, schedules, and deadlines; for tracking time and billing information, client funds, and costs; and for preparing accurate billing records. One of the most popular and best-supported programs is **AbacusLaw.**

■ CASE ORGANIZATION AND MANAGEMENT SOFTWARE

Case management software can be used to organize the cast of characters in a case, the documents, the relevant timetables, the relevant issues, legal authority, and other desired information. Top programs useful here are **LexisNexis CaseMap** and **LexisNexis TimeMap.**

■ LITIGATION SUPPORT SOFTWARE

Litigation support software, such as **Summation** and **Concordance,** has the capability to manage electronic documents.

■ PRESENTATION AND TRIAL GRAPHICS SOFTWARE

Graphic creation programs, such as **SmartDraw,** can be used to create stand-alone presentations. They can also be used to create graphics for presentations created with other programs such as Microsoft PowerPoint. The obvious advantage of this type of software is that it gives the legal team the ability to create its own graphics, thus eliminating the need to hire graphic artists and outside consultants.

■ THE ELECTRONIC COURTHOUSE

Litigation support software, such as **Sanction II,** is used for in-court displays of documentary evidence, graphic presentations, and simulations of accident cases. Relevant portions of illustrations and documents can be displayed as a witness testifies, thus eliminating the need to distribute paper copies in court.

VIRTUAL LAW OFFICE EXPERIENCE
FOR CIVIL LITIGATION

The Virtual Law Office Experience is a multi-media program designed to allow students to apply their knowledge and skills in a workplace context. Throughout the course, students watch realistic video scenarios, work with case files and documents, and use the technology tools they will find in the law office to do the work a paralegal will be asked to do in practice. Throughout the course students build a portfolio of work that demonstrates that they have the training and experience employers are looking for.

- **Students engage in a workplace experience throughout the course as a law office intern**

- **Students see behind closed doors in practice and in the courts**

- **Students build a comprehensive portfolio of workplace products to show potential employers**

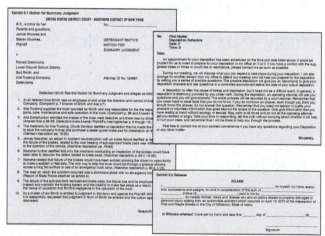

Within the Virtual law Office Experience program students can access a wealth of resources to complete assignments at any time including:

- **Ask the Law Librarian Instructional Videos** to answer student's research and writing questions
- **Ask Technical Support** for technology and legal software support
- **Forms File** contains examples of commonly used legal documents for the major legal specialties.

Contact your local representative for more information or a demonstration.

INSTRUCTOR RESOURCES

■ INSTRUCTOR'S MANUAL WITH TEST BANK

The Instructor's Manual, written by Thomas Goldman, Kathleen Smith, and David Freeman, contains sample syllabi, chapter outlines and summaries, answers to Web Resources questions and exercises, and teaching notes. This also contains a Word document version of the test bank.

■ MY TEST

This computerized test generation system gives you maximum flexibility in preparing tests. It can create custom tests and print scrambled versions of a test at one time, as well as build tests randomly by chapter, level of difficulty, or question type. The software also allows online testing and record-keeping and the ability to add problems to the database. This test bank can also be delivered formatted for use in popular learning management platforms, such as BlackBoard, WebCT, Moodle, Angel, D2L, and Sakai. Visit www.PearsonMyTest.com to begin building your tests.

■ POWERPOINT LECTURE PRESENTATION

Our presentations offer clear, straightforward outlines and notes to use for class lectures or study materials. Photos, illustrations, charts, and tables from the book are included in the presentations when applicable.

The Instructor's Manual, My Test, and PPT package can be downloaded from Pearson's Instructor's Resource Center. To access supplementary materials online, instructors need to request an instructor access code. Go to www.pearsonhighered.com/irc to register for an instructor access code. Within 48 hours of registering, you will receive a confirming email that includes your instructor access code. Once you have received your code, locate your text in the online catalogue and click on the Instructor Resources button on the left side of the catalogue product page. Select a supplement, and a log-in page will appear. Once you have logged in, you can access instructor material for all Pearson textbooks.

■ COURSECONNECT ONLINE CIVIL LITIGATION COURSE

Looking for robust online course content to reinforce and enhance your students' learning? We have the solution: CourseConnect! CourseConnect courses contain customizable modules of content mapped to major learning outcomes. Each learning objective contains interactive tutorials, rich media, discussion questions, MP3-downloadable lectures, assessments, and interactive activities that address different learning styles. CourseConnect courses follow a consistent, 21-step instructional design process, yet each course is developed individually by instructional designers and instructors who have taught the course online. Test questions, created by assessment professionals, were developed at all levels of Bloom's Taxonomy. When you buy a CourseConnect course, you purchase a complete package that provides you with detailed documentation you can use for your accreditation reviews. CourseConnect courses can be delivered in any commercial platform such as **WebCT, BlackBoard, Angel,** and **eCollege.** For more information, contact your representative or call 800-635-1579.

■ ALTERNATE VERSIONS EBOOKS

This text is also available in multiple eBook formats including Adobe Reader and CourseSmart. CourseSmart is an exciting new choice for students looking to save money. As an alternative to purchasing the printed textbook, students can purchase an electronic version of the same content. With a CourseSmart eTextbook, students can search the text, make notes online, print out reading assignments that incorporate lecture notes, and bookmark important passages for later review. For more information, or to purchase access to the CourseSmart eTextbook, visit www.coursesmart.com.

ACKNOWLEDGMENTS

Our appreciation to all the students over the years who have taught us lessons on presenting the material covered in this text. The tips and practice pointers are gleaned from many years of trying cases; for those, we thank opposing counsel everywhere and the judges before whom we have practiced.

To Charlie and Harry Hughes, Alice's son and husband, respectively, for the nights and weekends when the manuscript came first.

To all the reviewers for their thoughtful comments and suggestions, whose incorporation they will recognize on these pages:

Sandra Clawson
Cuyahoga Community College

Kathleen L. Daerr-Bannon
Temple University FSBM

Amy Feeney
Wilmington College

Jane Breslin Jacobs, Esq.
Community College of Philadelphia, Paralegal Studies Program

Brad Jansen
Roosevelt University

Reginia Judge
Montclair State University

Robert Ludditz
Nashau Community College

Kathleen Mack
Harrisburg Area Community College

Linda C. Marks
Pima Community College

Broderick E. Nichols
The University of Memphis

Beth R. Pless
Northeast Wisconsin Technical College

Tesha Poe
DeAnza College

Marshal "Patrick" Rake
Tarrant County College

Stefany Robinson
Wilmington College

Michael Sujecki
Milwaukee Area Technical College

Debbie Vinecour
SUNY Rockland Community College

Rhonda Weaver
University of Maryland–University College

Buzz Wheeler
Highline Community College

Karen M. Xander
Dusquesne University, Paralegal Institute

To the software companies who have generously provided software and support, a special thank you:

AbacusLaw
AD Summation
ALCoder
CaseCentral
Deadlines on Demand

LexisNexis CaseMap
LexisNexis Concordance
Sanction by Sanction Solutions
SmartDraw
Tabs3

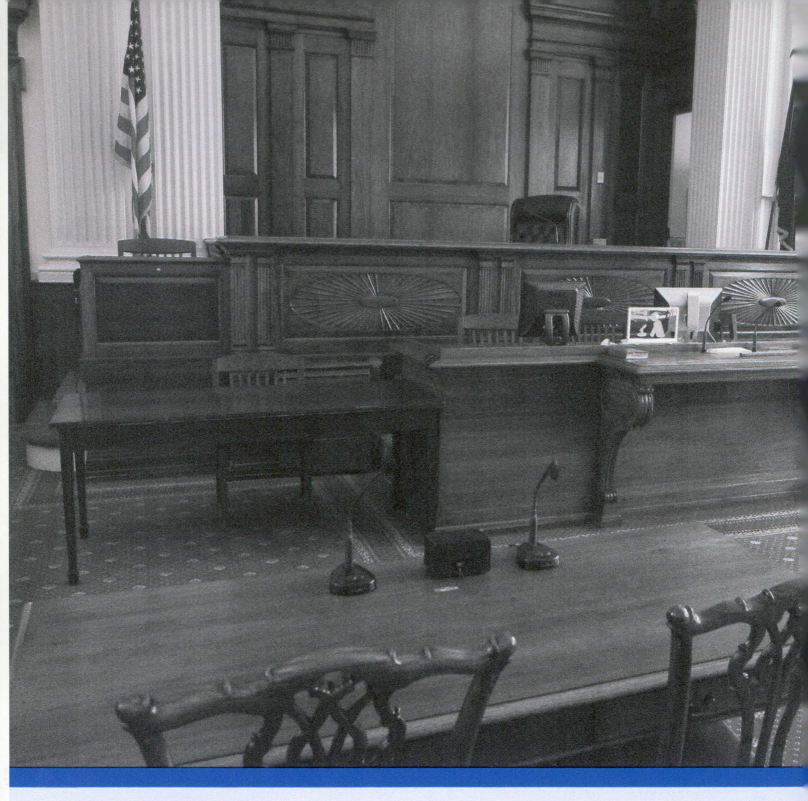

LEARNING OBJECTIVES

After studying this chapter, you should be able to:

1. Describe the role of the paralegal in civil litigation.

2. List and describe the necessary skills for a litigation paralegal.

3. List and describe the tasks performed by the civil litigation paralegal.

The Paralegal in Civil Litigation | CHAPTER 1

OPENING SCENARIO

 A growing litigation practice, new staff members, and an increased use of technology are causing some concerns for attorney Roy Saunders as he tries to set a correct path for a small, two-office law firm. With the offices at some distance apart, he has started to use technology in the form of videoconferencing to improve communication between the offices, the legal staffs, and his partners. He has committed the firm to the use of paralegals as members of the legal team. Unlike larger firms who have lawyers that are in the office to handle routine issues and lawyers specializing in litigation who spend most of their time in court, the small-firm partners must do everything, frequently finding themselves out of the office in court and depending on support staff for many office-based tasks and client interactions. With the eventual growth of the firm predicted, it is important to identify the organizational structure of the firm, define the roles of each partner and employee, and define the tasks to be assigned and who has the authority to act on each task.

OPENING SCENARIO LEARNING OBJECTIVE

Define the role of the paralegal in a litigation practice.

■ INTRODUCTION TO CIVIL LITIGATION

civil litigation
Resolution of legal disputes between parties seeking a remedy for a civil wrong or to enforce a contract.

criminal litigation
Government enforcement of laws or prosecution for breach of a law.

Civil litigation involves legal disputes between parties seeking a remedy for a civil wrong or to enforce a contract. Civil litigation differs from **criminal litigation,** where the government enforces a law or brings a prosecution for the breach of a law. Generally, the filing of a legal dispute with a court happens after the parties to the dispute have determined that they cannot resolve their differences amicably or through the use of alternative dispute resolution methods. In the United States, cases can be filed in federal court or state court. Within the state or federal court system, there may be multiple courts having the power to hear the same cause of action. The choice of a specific court may be made based on geographical convenience or trial strategy. One of the first steps in the civil litigation process is the analysis of in which courts the case could be filed.

■ THE ROLE OF THE PARALEGAL IN CIVIL LITIGATION

LEARNING OBJECTIVE 1
Describe the role of the paralegal in civil litigation.

legal team
The collective group of people working on a case or matter under the supervision of an attorney.

paralegal
A person qualified by education, training, or work experience who is employed or retained by a lawyer, law office, corporation, governmental agency, or other entity and who performs specifically delegated, substantive legal work for which a lawyer is responsible; equivalent term is *legal assistant.*

legal support staff
Members of the law office who provide support functions to the legal team; includes law librarians, legal secretaries, receptionists, information technologists, bookkeepers, and mailroom personnel.

Civil litigation is a process that requires the assembly of information and evidence, analysis of facts and law, preparation of material for trial presentation and posttrial appeals, and execution of judgments. One well-schooled, experienced lawyer could do it all, but more typically, these tasks are completed through a team effort. The **legal team** may include **paralegals,** litigation support staff, investigators, information technologists, and other **legal support staff** in varying roles. Law firms have structures that define everyone's function in the litigation process. In some law firms, that structure is formalized in a written office manual with detailed job descriptions. Other law firms are less structured, with more flexibility and loosely defined roles that frequently overlap. The members of the legal team in all working environments are ultimately accountable to the clients who hire and depend on them for competent legal representation. Each member of the team shares the total responsibility, performing other assigned functions and helping others on the team when the need arises. Successful legal teams allow for flexibility that will result in success in the litigation process. Some of the functions are defined by the permissible role the person can play in the courtroom. For example, only lawyers admitted to practice before a particular court may appear on behalf of clients. Paralegals and litigation support staff typically may sit at counsel table to assist the attorney, but some local rules may restrict even that activity, relegating the role to an associate attorney.

Managing Client Relationships

inside corporate counsel
Lawyer employed by a corporation to provide legal advice and counsel on corporate matters.

Clients involved in civil litigation may be individuals, small- or medium-sized businesses, or large corporate clients. The typical client contact with individuals and smaller businesses is directly with the individuals concerned. Working with corporate clients may be indirect—the client contact is the inside corporate counsel for the corporation. **Inside corporate counsel** generally selects the outside law firms and monitors the handling of civil litigation. Maintaining positive client relationships is a critical area of the practice of law. Clients want to be kept informed and have their inquiries answered promptly. In the inside counsel–outside law firm relationship, communication may occur via electronic sharing of information. With every client, minimizing the costs of litigation is important. It may be more important with inside counsel because of the need to budget the expenditures for senior management and justify the costs of every piece of litigation.

It is important that the legal team, and particularly the paralegal (who may be the person having the most direct and frequent contact with the client), understand the client's views and values. Corporate or business clients frequently refer to these views and values as the corporate culture. In some cases, clients are more concerned with the principles involved in the litigation than they are with the costs. In others, cost-consciousness dictates a very lean budget for litigation and a desire to do a cost-benefit analysis of the litigation decisions. In all cases, the paralegal becomes the eyes of the attorney and must keep counsel informed of the cost incurred—in effect, monitoring the litigation budget. Because it is often the paralegal on the legal team who hires the outside vendors or sees the time records, the paralegal is often in the best position to monitor the budgets.

Members of the Legal Team

The lawyers, paralegals, litigation support staff, investigators, information technologists, and other support staff handling a case are frequently referred to collectively as the legal team. **Lawyers** are law school graduates who have passed the bar examination and hold a license to practice law. Lawyers have met the minimum qualifications established by the individual jurisdictions or courts for obtaining a license to practice and represent clients. Because the standards for admission to the bar are unique to each state, a lawyer's license to practice the profession is generally limited geographically to a particular state. Within the law firm, lawyers may also have a title that refers to their status within the firm, such as managing partner, partner, or associate. Law firms are organized in many different ways from formal, with management committees; to informal, with one partner making the management decisions. Exhibit 1.1 shows organizational charts for typical small and

lawyers
Law school graduates who have passed the bar examination, hold a license to practice law, and have met the minimum qualifications established by the individual jurisdictions or courts for obtaining a license to practice and represent clients.

Exhibit 1.1 Organizational charts for typical midsized and small law firms

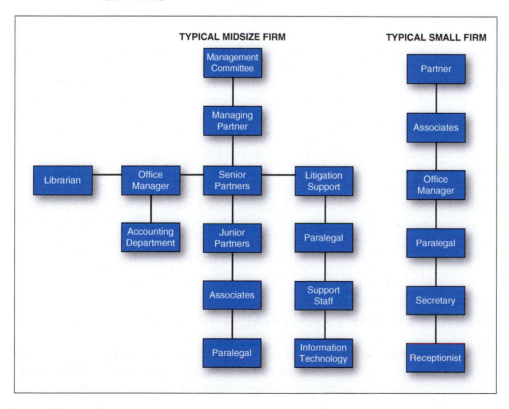

partners

Lawyers who have an ownership interest in a law firm and a stake in the firm's profits.

associates

Non-owner lawyers, usually salaried employees of the law firm.

managing partner

Partner responsible for managing the business operations of a firm, such as taking care of the facilities, management, human resources supervision, and public relations.

supervising attorney

Member of the legal team to whom all others on the team report and who has the ultimate responsibility for the actions of the legal team.

 **WEB RESOURCES**

Contrast and compare the ethical rules in your jurisdiction with the American Bar Association Model Rules of Professional Responsibility. See the ABA website.

midsized law firms. **Partners** are the lawyers who have an ownership interest and a stake in the profits of the law firm. **Associates** are non-owner lawyers, usually salaried employees of the law firm. The **managing partner** is the partner responsible for managing the business operations of the firm, such as taking care of the facilities, management, human resources supervision, and public relations.

Paralegals are generally not required to be licensed, except in a limited number of states. Ethical rules require paralegals to work under the supervision and control of a **supervising attorney.** Paralegals may report to and be supervised by one or more attorneys in a firm. The paralegal may have a permanent assignment to an attorney who always acts as the supervising attorney, or the paralegal may "float," working for different attorneys based on staffing needs, expertise, or availability to assist in a particular case.

The legal support staff consists of the other members of the law office who provide support functions to the legal team; these include litigation support staff, law librarians, legal secretaries, receptionists, information technologists, bookkeepers, and mailroom personnel.

Corporate Paralegals in Litigation

Most large corporations, and many smaller companies, have in-house counsel. In some companies, in-house counsel directs the activities of a large staff of attorneys, paralegals, and other legal support staff. Depending on the nature of the business and the needs of the corporation, in-house counsel staff may litigate cases or refer them to outside counsel and supervise the activities of the outside legal team where claims arise or rights need to be enforced. In-house paralegals may have a supervisory role in the litigation process, making sure deadlines are met, reviewing documents prepared by outside counsel, and monitoring the budgets for the litigation. When outside counsel is retained, the paralegals' primary role is the maintenance of the relationship among outside counsel, in-house counsel, and corporate officers and employees whose testimony may be required. When in-house counsel litigates cases, paralegals perform the same functions as those working in private legal practices.

Litigation Support Manager

One of the emerging opportunities for experienced paralegals is as the manager of litigation support—coordinating and facilitating the technology needs of the legal team. Contemporary litigation requires the use of technology for obtaining, organizing, and presenting evidence. All paralegals will have some level of responsibility with regard to technology. In large law firms the litigation support manager may serve to coordinate the technology for the entire firm. The lawyers on the team frequently delegate the technologic concerns to the litigation support manager so that the lawyers can concentrate on strategy, analysis, and preparation for trial. The paralegal must work with the technology support personnel and in-house or outside consultants. Paralegals have to explain the needs of the legal side while understanding the possibilities and limitations of the technical side. In this role, they must frequently educate the nonlegally trained IT staff on the ethical obligations of the legal profession.

LEARNING OBJECTIVE 2

List and describe the necessary skills for a litigation paralegal.

■ SKILLS OF THE PARALEGAL

The civil litigation paralegal may be called upon to perform any number of different tasks, including conducting legal research, typing a pleading or a court brief, scanning documents for electronic storage, making copies for litigation purposes, interviewing witnesses, and operating audiovisual equipment. Litigation can frequently be a fast-paced process with sudden deadlines and demands imposed by changing trial schedules, availability of witnesses, and changing trial strategy. Civil litigation can be exciting and stimulating; it can also test the stamina of the legal team. Everyone must be willing to pitch in to meet deadlines and must be ready to appear in court fully prepared after late nights spent researching and preparing for every alternative the other side may present. Obviously, the paralegal must have a basic knowledge of the law and of how the courts function. Depending upon the area of practice, additional knowledge may be required in areas of legal specialties such as intellectual property, medical malpractice, or estate law; knowledge of specialized court rules of practice such as those of bankruptcy, tax, or court of claims might also be necessary.

That does not mean that paralegals must know everything. However, they do need to know how to research new areas of the law, locate court rules, and find other information efficiently and effectively.

The skills needed by a paralegal are varied and depend, in some cases, on the size of the law firm and the nature of the legal specialty in which one works. All paralegals need certain basic skills and attributes, including resourcefulness, commitment, analytical skills, interpersonal skills, and communication skills. This is especially true for the civil litigation paralegal. Litigation attorneys come to depend on their civil litigation paralegals in the same way a surgeon depends on a scrub nurse in the operating room. While the lawyer is thinking through the strategy and preparing mentally, the paralegal is making sure everything comes together. Paralegals manage the scheduling; arrange the presence of clients, witnesses, exhibits, and audiovisual equipment; and complete last-minute research.

Soft Skills

Soft skills are sometimes called *people skills* or **human relations skills**—the ability to work successfully with others and handle oneself appropriately in the working environment. Paralegals must be able to work with people from all walks of life, economic backgrounds, and cultures. Paralegals should be sensitive to their fellow team members and be organized, prompt, and courteous. Those qualities are not only reserved for dealings with the legal team; they should also be exhibited when paralegals deal with clients and other people with whom they come in contact during their workday. For litigation paralegals, courthouse personnel play a crucial role and can make professional life easier or harder. Treating everyone in the courthouse courteously, even when they are not being helpful, will pay off in the long run for the legal team. You never know who is behind you or listening to you. Good behavior and courtesy may not always be reciprocated, but everyone in the courthouse hears about bad behavior and discourtesy. Always try to create friendly relationships.

Resourcefulness

Resourcefulness is the ability to meet and handle a situation and find solutions to problems. It is one of the most valuable skills anyone can have—and one that is not easily taught. A resourceful person in the office is sometimes referred to as the "can-do" person on the team. This is the person who usually finds some creative way to accomplish what everyone else has given up on. Certainly, creativity is involved—solving the problem by thinking outside the box and not limiting the solution to tried-and-true methods.

When everyone else says, "I can't find this witness," the resourceful person tries a new approach and finds the witness. When others use only standard

PRACTICE TIP

Continuing education courses offer the lawyer and the paralegal an opportunity to learn about new areas of law or update their knowledge of specialty areas. Many courses offer discounts for paralegals and special rates for lawyer–paralegal teams who attend together.

soft skills
Ability to work successfully with others and handle oneself appropriately in the working environment.

human relations skills
Soft skills; ability to work successfully with others and handle oneself appropriately in the working environment.

resourcefulness
Ability to meet and handle a situation and find solutions to problems.

telephone directories, the resourceful person uses the cross-reference or reverse phone directory. When local telephone directories do not yield results, resourceful people use online telephone directories and online social networking sites like Facebook to find information.

In the legal workplace, the person who gets noticed is the one who finds a way to get the job done in time for the hearing, meeting, or arbitration. This is the person who is willing to use unconventional ways to get the job finished, such as when the power goes out or the computer system crashes just before a deadline. Lawyers want resourceful people on their team and reward them to keep them on the team.

Commitment

commitment
Finishing what one starts out to do.

Commitment means finishing what one starts out to do. From our childhood we remember the story of the tortoise and the hare (rabbit), in which the tortoise wins the race by being "slow and steady." The tortoise wins in part because of commitment—putting everything into the race and not stopping until the job is done. Many people start jobs and don't finish them. Others start what seems to be an insurmountable task and—to their amazement, and maybe ours—finish, and finish well. Taking on an assignment in a law office requires commitment. Team members are expected to finish the task, whether it is researching a case, writing a brief, filing a pleading, or organizing a file.

As a professional, you are expected to finish the tasks within the assigned time frame. There is no excuse for not doing some tasks, such as filing a complaint with the court before the statute of limitations expires, or getting a brief to the court before the court-imposed deadline. Even a simple thing like getting to court on time requires commitment.

Not everyone has the necessary commitment or wants to take on the responsibility of meeting goals and deadlines. You have to decide whether you are willing to make the commitment. Others will be depending on you, and if you do not want to commit, admit it to yourself and to those who are depending on you, and then choose some other activity or profession. Choosing a profession, whether it is the legal profession, the paralegal profession, the medical profession, or the accounting profession, requires a commitment to serve others. As a professional, you are making a commitment to your clients that you will provide your best professional advice, skill, and effort. They depend on this **professionalism** and the necessary commitment.

professionalism
Conduct in accordance with the expectations of a profession.

Analytical Skills

analytical skills
Ability to follow a step-by-step process to solve a problem.

Analytical skills allow one to follow a step-by-step process to solve a problem. It could be finding a missing witness by looking in online directories or determining that the person is part of a group, such as a professional society or an organization that publishes a membership directory. Solving these types of problems requires analytical skills to figure out, for instance, what made a bottle explode, injuring a client. Determining the actual cause requires a step-by-step analysis of the potential reasons and the narrowing down of possible causes.

One of the basic skills that law students and paralegal students are taught is legal analysis, the ability to identify the facts and legal issues and contrast and compare them to the law and to other cases. This is a skill that develops with time. As you learn about various areas of law, you will learn the individual elements of each. In contracts law, for example, you will learn what conduct is a valid acceptance of a contract offer and, in tort law, what constitutes reasonable conduct under the circumstances.

Interpersonal Skills

Interpersonal skills, the ability to work with people, are vital to paralegal success, as well as to success in other endeavors. To categorize people, coworkers, colleagues, and employers might be unfair, but we all do it. We think—and sometimes say—things like, "He's a pleasure to work with" or "She has clients eating out of her hand." Conversely, we might say things like, "She's the most negative person I know" or "He's only out for himself." These comments reflect the other person's interpersonal skills (or lack thereof), the ability to work with and communicate with others. The true skill is the ability to maintain a positive attitude while working with different personalities to achieve the desired results.

interpersonal skills
Ability to work well with all types of people.

Creating an Impression

Unless you are intentionally trying to create a different impression, try to:

- have a positive attitude;
- be diplomatic;
- be flexible;
- establish good rapport with others;
- be a team player;
- be resourceful;
- be adaptable; and
- be thorough.

How we relate to others can make our job easier or harder. These "others" include not just coworkers as members of the legal team but also clients, witnesses, and opposing parties. Obviously, everyone in the firm or on the team must have a level of trust and confidence in their teammates. People who have a good working relationship accomplish more and enjoy their work. By contrast, conflict and tension make the job harder and can cause people to take shortcuts and avoid contact, which can result in poor performance and potential malpractice.

Not everyone has the personality to deal with every type of situation and every type of person—for example, not everyone can deal effectively with clients. But everyone on the legal team has to develop people skills and recognize when they may want to have someone else handle certain aspects of a case or client. The skill is in recognizing when and how the legal team can affect relationships and results. Some might call this *sensitivity*—to other people's needs, desires, wants, likes, and dislikes.

In the American culture, for example, people tend to be sensitive to odors—breath, body, environmental. We do not want to offend. Our use of language is another area of sensitivity. We try to avoid using words that we believe might offend another person in a specific circumstance, such as telling off-color jokes in a religious setting or in front of a member of the clergy.

The starting point in working with attorneys, paralegals, support staff, clients, opposing counsel, court personnel, and others is to be sensitive to issues such as these. What offends you probably offends others. Being sensitive to how others react to your words, conduct, and actions can provide good clues as to what is acceptable and what is not.

In the past, how we related to others and how others perceived us were measured by direct, face-to-face contact, telephone contact, and written communications. Today, we have to add to those forms of communication the way we write and use electronic communications: e-mail, text messages, etc. These technological advances make our communications more immediate. Too many happy faces and frowning faces, such as :) or :(in an e-mail, however, could be interpreted as overfamiliarity. The use of ALL CAPITAL LETTERS might be interpreted as shouting at the reader. Poor spelling and bad grammar in e-mails are likely to be seen as less than professional or the result of pure sloppiness or carelessness. In the past, letters were dictated, typed, proofread, and then signed, resulting in four opportunities to review before sending the letter. Today, we dash off an e-mail without much thought—and sometimes the e-mail reflects just that. How our clients view our capabilities and skills now might be measured by that quick e-mail response.

Communication Skills

communication skills
Ability to express ideas effectively in both spoken and written word.

Communication means expressing ideas effectively. The practice of law requires good **communication skills,** both oral and written. The lawyer and the paralegal who work together must be able to communicate assignments and information with clarity and, frequently, brevity. Over time, communication will improve as each person comes to understand what the other is really asking or saying.

Communication is made complex by subtleties, nuances, and expressions that may require interpretation or explanation. For example, older attorneys who are accustomed to using traditional methods of research may ask the new paralegal (who has a solid understanding of computer research methods but little traditional book experience) to "check the pocket parts." This means checking for the latest update or change to a statute in the booklet issued regularly to update a print volume; these booklets are inserted in a "pocket" in the back inside cover of the book. Asking a paralegal to "Shepardize" a case to find other references to where the case is mentioned may have no meaning to a paralegal who has learned only the Westlaw system (in which the method for checking other cases is called KeyCiting) or the Loislaw system (which refers to this task as GlobalCiting).

Communication can be a major problem in the fast-paced office—the litigation attorney might send a text message from court in the middle of trial to the support paralegal at the office, informing the paralegal that the other side has brought up an unexpected case in argument to the court. We rarely have the luxury of time to develop a common written and oral language base for communication among the paralegal, clients, opposing attorneys, and court personnel. Letters, pleadings, contracts, and other written documents must be clear and accurate. In many situations, there is only one document, and it must carefully communicate the idea, request, or demand.

Professionalism

Paralegals are professionals; they are expected to approach their jobs in a professional way and conduct themselves in a professional manner. Paralegals represent their law firms to the public. Professional appearance and attire are important in creating a level of comfort and confidence in others. Casual Fridays are common in today's workplace. Keep in mind that how you look even on casual Fridays is important to you and your career.

COMMUNICATION SKILLS

Do you

- read with comprehension?
- listen effectively and accurately?
- interpret nonverbal communication?
- write in clear, concise, and grammatically correct English?
- speak in clear, concise, and grammatically correct English?
- use language to persuade?
- tailor the nature of the communication to maximize understanding in the intended audience, taking into account people with different levels of education and different cultural backgrounds?

Source: American Association for Paralegal Education.

■ TASKS OF THE CIVIL LITIGATION PARALEGAL

The civil litigation paralegal may be called on to perform many tasks—interviewing clients and witnesses, investigating facts, organizing and managing case files, conducting factual and legal research, drafting pleadings and memos of law, scheduling and assisting in depositions, and even operating the trial presentation software in court. In addition to these tasks related to client representation, the paralegal should expect to be responsible for certain administrative tasks such as checking for conflicts of interest and maintaining time records for billing purposes.

LEARNING OBJECTIVE 3
List and describe the tasks performed by the civil litigation paralegal.

Interviewing Clients and Witnesses

The litigation paralegal is often the point of contact between the law firm and others, including clients, witnesses, opposing counsel, and the court. Paralegals with strong interpersonal and communication skills will be well suited to interview clients and witnesses and maintain personal contact during the case. During this important phase of civil litigation, the paralegal must encourage open communication to obtain information easily.

Investigating Facts

Another key component of the process of civil litigation is investigating the **facts** that have been described by the client. If at all possible, the legal team will attempt to verify through independent means the story the client has shared. It is human nature for people to relay events in such a way as to present themselves in the best possible light. It is not lying; it's perception and human nature. The resourceful civil litigation paralegal will know what records and information can be easily obtained and how to do so. Investigation of facts includes obtaining and reviewing records.

facts
Actual or alleged events and occurrences.

Conducting Discovery

Paralegals play an important role in the discovery process. Discovery is a step in the litigation process in which the parties share information relevant to their dispute. Successful discovery requires a familiarity with the rules of court and, increasingly, the rules relating to the discovery of electronically stored information (ESI) and files. The methods used to locate, preserve, and produce these electronically stored documents require a new set of skills and knowledge of specialty terminology.

Obtaining Records

In many litigation cases, paralegals will be asked to obtain copies of documents. Those documents relate in some way to the case on which the paralegal is working, and they will enable the legal team to better evaluate the strengths and weaknesses of the client's case. However, in this time of identity theft, privacy laws, and regulations, record keepers are understandably reluctant to freely provide copies of documents. The resourceful paralegal will know the procedures required to obtain these records. In fact, many paralegals have their own **reference manual** of information listing the procedures, agencies, web addresses, contact people, fees (if any), and forms necessary to obtain documents. Electronically stored document recovery may also require technical knowledge of accessing and opening documents stored in various electronic formats (such as PDF format) or those that have been compressed to save space and must be uncompressed using a specialty software program to unzip the files.

reference manual
A handbook of information updated and maintained by the paralegal.

Reviewing Records

Analytical skills developed by paralegals are essential to records review. When the paralegal reviews records, he or she should look for consistencies and inconsistencies with the client's story and that of other witnesses, noting these in the report to the supervising attorney. Medical records are particularly troubling for paralegals because they may contain many unfamiliar medical terms and symbols. Access to a good medical dictionary or website will help the paralegal to understand the nature of injuries and the cause of those injuries. Increased litigation involving technology, such as faulty computer modules in cars causing sudden acceleration, requires an understanding of the technical terminology or access to references like the medical dictionary in a personal injury case.

Paralegals need to be inquisitive and creative when reviewing records. Understanding terminology is not the sole object of a records review. Knowing what information is significant to the legal team (and potentially admissible as evidence) and finding facts in the records that support or contradict the client's case are examples of the art of being a paralegal.

Drafting Pleadings and Other Documents

Paralegals with good written communication skills can expect to be asked to draft pleadings and documents. The paralegal must be sure that the supervising attorney is actually supervising this task and ultimately signing the pleadings that are filed. Any document that affects a person's legal rights must be approved and signed by a person licensed to practice law in the particular jurisdiction or court, such as that required under federal rule 11, shown in Exhibit 1.2. A paralegal may assist by preparing drafts of these documents, but the supervising attorney must review, revise, correct, and sign them. To do otherwise may subject the paralegal to unauthorized practice of law charges.

Assisting at Trial

At trial, paralegals provide a wide variety of services to the attorney, such as ascertaining which electronic equipment is available in the courtroom (and which must be supplied by the legal team), ensuring that witnesses arrive at the appointed time, presenting exhibits, and keeping notes of what occurs daily during the trial.

Exhibit 1.2 Federal Rules of Civil Procedure Rule 11

Signing Pleadings, Motions, and Other Papers; Representations to the Court; Sanctions

(a) **Signature.**

Every pleading, written motion, and other paper must be signed by at least one attorney of record in the attorney's name—or by a party personally if the party is unrepresented. The paper must state the signer's address, e-mail address, and telephone number. Unless a rule or statute specifically states otherwise, a pleading need not be verified or accompanied by an affidavit. The court must strike an unsigned paper unless the omission is promptly corrected after being called to the attorney's or party's attention.

(b) **Representations to the Court.**

By presenting to the court a pleading, written motion, or other paper—whether by signing, filing, submitting, or later advocating it—an attorney or unrepresented party certifies that to the best of the person's knowledge, information, and belief, formed after an inquiry reasonable under the circumstances:

(1) it is not being presented for any improper purpose, such as to harass, cause unnecessary delay, or needlessly increase the cost of litigation;

(2) the claims, defenses, and other legal contentions are warranted by existing law or by a nonfrivolous argument for extending, modifying, or reversing existing law or for establishing new law;

(3) the factual contentions have evidentiary support or, if specifically so identified, will likely have evidentiary support after a reasonable opportunity for further investigation or discovery; and

(4) the denials of factual contentions are warranted on the evidence or, if specifically so identified, are reasonably based on belief or a lack of information.

Source: Federal Rules of Civil Procedure Rule 11

Administrative Tasks

Paralegals, as well as other members of the legal team, have certain administrative tasks they must perform. Two important tasks are conflicts checking and time keeping.

Conflicts Checking

Attorneys and members of the legal team have an ethical obligation to avoid situations wherein their interests or loyalties may be or may appear to be divided. A lawyer cannot represent both the defendant and the plaintiff in a lawsuit. This rule applies to the firm, the lawyer, and the paralegal. For the paralegal, it may mean not working on a case with parties who had been clients of the paralegal's former firm. Checking for the existence of **conflicts of interest** may fall on the paralegal. In most firms, conflicts checks are conducted with the aid of a database of the names of current and former clients and the types of cases handled. Based on the name of the new potential client, names of potential defendants, and the nature of the dispute, the firm's database will be checked for conflicts. Case management software can be employed for this function.

conflict of interest
Situations where the interests or loyalties of the lawyer and client may be or may appear to be adverse or divided.

Time Keeping

Time keeping is the lifeblood of the law firm. From time records, clients are billed for time and services provided to handle their claims. Lawyers and paralegals alike record their time for billing purposes. Time keeping becomes a written record of the activities performed on behalf of a client. The bills produced represent a form of communication with the client that advises the client regularly of

time keeping
Maintaining records of the time spent in performing tasks on a case or matter; may include the recording of costs or expenditures related to the performance of the tasks.

what work has been performed, when, and by whom. Typos and inaccuracies in billing can create client relation nightmares.

Not all time recorded, however, represents billable time. Ethical rules and court decisions prohibit billing clients for administrative activities, like typing, photocopying, and reviewing billing statements. Time spent drafting documents, interviewing witnesses, and investigating facts would be billable. While the paralegal will be required to account for all the hours in a day, not all the hours recorded will be billable. Time records are increasingly handled by software programs.

Organizing and Managing Case Files

The civil litigation paralegal will have primary responsibility for organizing and managing case files. The law firm and the supervising attorney may have a system in place for this task. The paralegal will be the person the supervising attorney asks for a document, the name and phone number of the opposing counsel, or a copy of the complaint. Crucial to case management is recording deadlines, such as the statute of limitations for filing a complaint, the due date of a pleading or motion, and the conference date with the assigned judge. Some law firms do this manually using a file card system; others use case management software that can automatically calculate deadlines based on the local rules of court.

The skill of organizing includes the abilities to:

- categorize;
- prioritize;
- coordinate; and
- utilize time efficiently.

Productivity and Cost-Effectiveness

The pressure is on everyone to become more productive in a working environment. The increased cost of litigation imposes additional demands upon the litigation team to accomplish the desired representation of clients in the most cost-effective manner. One of the methods for increasing productivity is the use of computers to eliminate some manual and repetitive functions. With increased scrutiny by clients and by the courts, accurate and detailed reporting adds to the burden of the litigation team.

For the litigation office representing corporate clients, an additional burden is imposed: the corporate in-house counsel demands the most cost-effective representation while expecting continual feedback and progress updates on the case and on the expenses incurred in the handling of the litigation. Many corporate clients utilize electronic communications for the interchange of information in the form of status reports, invoices, and documentation.

CONCEPT REVIEW AND REINFORCEMENT

KEY TERMS

civil litigation 4	legal support staff 4	associates 6
criminal litigation 4	inside corporate counsel 4	managing partner 6
legal team 4	lawyers 5	supervising attorney 6
paralegal 4	partners 6	soft skills 7

CHAPTER SUMMARY

THE PARALEGAL IN CIVIL LITIGATION

Introduction to Civil Litigation	Civil litigation involves real disputes between parties seeking a remedy for a civil wrong or to enforce a contract.
The Role of the Paralegal in Civil Litigation	Civil litigation is a process that requires the assembly of information and evidence, analysis of facts and law, preparation of material for trial presentation and posttrial appeals, and execution of judgments.
	Maintaining positive client relationships is a critical area of the practice of law.
	The paralegal is a member of a legal team. Lawyers supervise the team, which may be made up of law firm partners, associates, and legal support staff.
	Corporate paralegals typically serve in a supervisory role, coordinating between in-house counsel and litigation counsel.
	The increased use of technology has led to the paralegal serving as a litigation support manager, or coordinating and facilitating the technology needs of the legal team.
Skills of the Paralegal	Skills needed by a paralegal are varied and depend on the nature of the legal specialty. Skills common to all paralegals include resourcefulness, commitment, analytical skills, interpersonal skills, communication skills, professionalism, human relations skills, and soft skills.
Tasks of the Civil Litigation Paralegal	Civil litigation paralegals may be called upon to perform many tasks, including interviewing clients and witnesses, investigating facts, organizing and managing case files, drafting pleadings and other documents, and assisting at trial. Administrative tasks including conflict checking, time keeping, and organizing and managing case files.

REVIEW QUESTIONS AND EXERCISES

1. Describe the functions of the members of the legal team.
2. Why do lawyers in civil litigation rely upon the members of a legal team?
3. What are the skills required of the civil litigation paralegal?
4. What are the tasks the civil litigation paralegal can expect to perform?
5. Explain the relationship between the skills of the paralegal and the tasks assigned.
6. Does having family members working in separate offices of the same firm create any issues of client confidentiality?

BUILDING YOUR PARALEGAL SKILLS

INTERNET AND TECHNOLOGY EXERCISES

1. Use the Internet to find local area help-wanted postings for civil litigation paralegals. Explore opportunities from different areas of the country. What are the similarities and the differences in the qualifications, titles, and salaries?
2. Prepare a list of the websites used to locate help-wanted postings in question 1. Add these to the list of favorites or bookmarks in your Internet browser for future use.

3. Use the Internet to find information on the use and cost of videoconferencing in your area.
   a. What is the cost of in-office equipment to conduct videoconferencing?
   b. What facilities that provide videoconferencing by the hour or by the day are closest to your area? What do they charge?
   c. Add the information obtained to the Contacts and Resources section of your professional portfolio.

CIVIL LITIGATION VIDEO CASE STUDIES

Confidentiality Issue: Family Exemption

While having coffee with her mother, a paralegal discusses a case on which she is working.

After viewing the video at www.pearsonhighered.com/careersresources, answer the following question.

Is there an exemption that permits a member of the legal team to discuss cases with family members?

Videoconferencing: Strategy Discussions

The members of the litigation team are located in separate offices. To discuss the handling of a new case, they are meeting using videoconference technology.

After viewing the video at www.pearsonhighered.com/careersresources, answer the following questions.

1. What precautions should the team take in using videoconferencing?
2. Would an audio-only conference work as well?
3. Should there be a record kept of the discussion? If so, by whom and in what form?
4. Does videoconferencing replace the need for face-to-face meetings?
5. Is this an appropriate tool for use with clients?
6. What are the advantages for the law firm and the client in using videoconferencing to hold meetings when people are located in remote locations?
7. What are the disadvantages for the law firm and the client in using videoconferencing to hold meetings when people are located in remote locations? Who has the ultimate responsibility to ensure technology is used ethically?
8. How important is it for the staff to know to whom they report?

CHAPTER OPENING SCENARIO CASE STUDY

1. Keep a log of the time you spend in this course in tenths of an hour. You may do this using a manual system, such a notebook, or an electronic system, such as AbacusLaw (see the information below about free access to AbacusLaw).

Minutes	Tenths
6	1/10
12	2/10
18	3/10
24	4/10
30	5/10
36	6/10
42	7/10
48	8/10
54	9/10

Record the actual time spent (you can round to 1/10 of an hour) for:

a. Class attendance (show as "Conference with supervising attorney")

b. Travel to and from class (show as "Travel")

c. Time reading and researching material (show as "Research")

d. Time preparing assignments (show as "Drafting documents")

e. Time spent preparing for tests (show as "Preparation")

f. Time taking tests (show as "Trial")

g. Other miscellaneous items (show as "Miscellaneous")

2. A short-term-use version (120 days) of AbacusLaw may be downloaded from the Technology Resources Website for this course at www.pearsonhighered .com/techresources. Video tutorials are available to help you install and use the software.

Set up AbacusLaw to track the time spent in the course. Use your course's name as the Matter, and your instructor's name as the Client.

BUILDING YOUR PROFESSIONAL PORTFOLIO AND REFERENCE MANUAL

CIVIL LITIGATION TEAM AT WORK

Complete instructions for building your professional portfolio are immediately following Chapter 1. See page 18.

Policy Manual

1. Create a first draft of the table of contents for an operations manual for a small law firm including:

    a. Copies of all required local, state, and federal employee tax and employment forms.

    b. Telephone protocol or scripts such as answering the phone and referring potential clients.

    c. Software that should be installed on firm computers.

    d. Job descriptions for each member of the legal team including:

        i. Legal secretary
        ii. Paralegal manager
        iii. Civil litigation paralegal
        iv. Litigation support paralegal

Contacts and Resources

Contact information for your state and federal court-houses

1. Mailing address
2. Court clerk's office phone and fax numbers
3. Web and e-mail addresses

MYLEGALSTUDIESLAB

MyLegalStudiesLab Virtual Law Office Experience Assignments

Complete the pretest, study plan, and posttest for this chapter and answer the legal application questions as assigned. These will help you confirm your mastery of the concepts and their application to legal scenarios. Then complete the Virtual Law Office assignment as assigned by your instructor. These assignments are designed to develop your workplace skills. Completing the assignment will result in your producing the following documents for inclusion in your professional portfolio:

VLOE 1.1

BUILDING YOUR PROFESSIONAL PORTFOLIO AND REFERENCE MANUAL

■ OPENING SCENARIO

The paralegal staff met to discuss ways of saving time and providing consistent coverage and quality legal work product. Two of the more experienced paralegals had brought to the meeting large, tabbed binders that they carefully guarded. When they displayed the contents of the binders, the interns and new paralegals were amazed to see a carefully compiled collection of every type of legal document, and information on almost every procedure in and out of the office.

The office manager asked if anyone thought there were confidentiality issues in creating and keeping personal copies of legal documents and reference manual materials and sharing the contents among the members of the law office.

■ PORTFOLIO EXERCISES: LEGAL TEAM AT WORK

A professional portfolio is a collection of documents that demonstrate the mastery of a subject or a professional skill. The professional portfolio of documents may be used to show a prospective employer in the hiring process that you are the best-prepared candidate for the position. The same documents may also be included in your law office reference manual. As a student, your comprehensive professional portfolio should include sample documents from each of the legal courses or subjects studied. Initially, it may be more convenient to save the documents electronically on your personal computer, on a removable memory device, or in a cloud-based service like Dropbox. It is important to make backup copies on a regular basis on a separate memory device in case of loss or malfunction of a computer. Paper copies should be prepared for use in an interview. The presentation of printed documents is a good opportunity to demonstrate your attention to detail and organizational skills. It is suggested that a quality binder with carefully prepared dividers be used. A suggested list of dividers and subdividers is shown below.

1. CIVIL LITIGATION
   1. CLIENT FILES
   2. COMMUNICATIONS
   3. DOCUMENTS AND FORMS
   4. MEMORANDA OF LAW
   5. MISCELLANEOUS
   6. PLEADINGS
   7. FEE AGREEMENTS
   8. COVER LETTERS
2. CONTRACT LAW
3. CRIMINAL LAW
4. FAMILY LAW

5. LEGAL RESEARCH AND WRITING
6. PARALEGAL PROFESSIONAL
7. REAL ESTATE LAW
8. TECHNOLOGY IN LAW OFFICE
9. TORT LAW
10. WILLS, TRUSTS, & ESTATES
11. YOUR TIME RECORDS

■ REFERENCE MANUAL: CIVIL LITIGATION TEAM AT WORK

Over time, experienced members of the litigation team accumulate reference information: policy issues such as password policies; forms such as checklists for filing pleadings; procedural issues such as statute of limitation information; and contacts such as the phone numbers of the technology support person in the local courthouse. Many also add samples of pleadings and letters that can be used as references in the future.

The Building Your Reference Manual Exercises at the end of each chapter are designed to help you create your own personal law office and litigation practice reference manual. The main headings POLICY, FORMS, PROCEDURES, and CONTACTS AND RESOURCES are starting points. You may wish to further subdivide these by area of law or alphabetically to make finding a desired item easier. There are many different formats for the contents themselves. Policy statements may be in the form of formal or informal memos, and they may follow a specified format used by an organization. They may represent policy of the law firm, the courthouse, or an organization from which information is frequently requested. Forms may follow court requirements, or they may be checklists of your own design. Contacts and resources may use the format of address books, computerized contact forms, or preprinted forms. Samples of possible formats are shown below. Additional templates of memos and contacts may be downloaded from the samples provided in computerized office suites such as Microsoft Office or Corel WordPerfect.

Initially, set up a binder with a tab for each general category:

- POLICY,
- FORMS,
- PROCEDURES, and
- CONTACTS AND RESOURCES.

You may also want to set up an electronic file folder on your computer or a removable storage device entitled Reference Manual, with subfolders for the tab categories. For example:

Law Office Reference Manual

- Policy
- Forms
- Procedures
- Contacts and Resources

Most chapters suggest items to add to your manual. Add additional items that you may want to have for future reference.

Creating the Reference Manual

Information included in the manual will come from a variety of sources, such as the Internet, library reference materials, and textbooks. One of the most widely used sources of information today is the Internet. In some cases, the same website may be a source of information on a number of topics; for example, the American Bar Association website, www.americanbar.org, contains a copy of the Model Rules of Professional Responsibility and links to individual state's legal resources. The website of the Cornell University Law School, www.LII.edu, has online copies of cases, rules, and legal reference material.

An invaluable part of any portfolio is a current list of websites that provide necessary information. Be sure to add these Internet addresses (URLs) to your list of favorites or bookmarks on your computer and to keep a current list with you when your personal computer is not available. When you copy material from the Internet, always include the source in the same document and in your portfolio. This way, you can refer back to it when you want to update or confirm the information, such as when your colleague or a judge asks, "Where did you get that information?"

Your learning objective in doing the portfolio and reference manual exercises in each chapter is for you to gain real-world experience finding information frequently needed in the law office. With practice, the ability to locate desired information and complete assigned tasks becomes easier, helping you become the "go to person" that everyone relies on to answer legal questions.

When completing the assignments, use the text as your guide and starting point, but do not limit yourself to a single source. Think outside the box.

Policy

A policy is a set of guidelines; they may be voluntary or mandatory, formal or informal, such as everyone being asked to cover their coffee cups when walking in the halls, or, no one may bring any food or drinks into the courtroom. Exhibit 1A.1 is an example of an office policy.

Forms

Forms may include helpful checklists for completing tasks or for obtaining information, such as a new client interview form or a checklist to obtain documents needed to open a new case. They also may include a mandated form to file documents, such as a new case coversheet required to file a complaint in federal or state court. Exhibit 1A.2 is the Civil Cover Sheet form required by the Southern District of New York.

Procedures

Procedures are the required methods of completing tasks. Procedures include the required time frames for taking action, such as the procedural time limits within which to file an appeal, as well as the required documentation required to file an appeal. Exhibit 1A.3 is an example of a file closing procedure.

Contacts and Resources

Contacts and resources include everyone you will or may need to contact during any phase of the processing of a case, such as obtaining a client, setting up the case, investigating the facts, and trying the case in court. See Exhibits 1A.5 and 1A.6.

■ EXAMPLES OF A POLICY, FORM, PROCEDURE, AND CONTACT RECORD

Policy

Figure 1A.1 Panama City Real Estate and Property Management, LLC

Date: 8/17/2008   **Responsible Department:** Operations and Technology

- **Confidentiality**
  - All members are required to sign a Non disclosure form and are required to maintain a strict level of confidentiality for all customer and in house data and information.
  - Refer to Independent Contractors Agreement for details

- **Discrimination**
  - It is unlawful and unethical to engage in any form of discriminat[ion] based on race, creed, color or other criteria.

- **Education**
  - Training assistance is provided on an as needed basis.
  - Refer to Independent Contractors Agreement for details

- **Dress**
  - Members are required to dress appropriately for all occasions. Appropriate dress is defined as that appropriate for a given occasion. Business appropriate is standard dress however, business casual is permitted during non customer relations and functions.

- **Floor Time**
  - We do not require our members to take floor time.
  - Members make their own schedules and are required to be available on an as needed basis based on customer need.

- **Listings**
  - All listings are listed under Jennifer Mackay and as such will remain with Jennifer Mackay at all times, including agent contract expiration or agent dismissal.

- **Referrals**
  - Refer to Independent Contractors Agreement for details

- **Keys, Signs & Lockboxes**
  - Lockboxes are provided by Jennifer Mackay. Keys are to be provided by the agents. All signage must contain both the broker name and Jennifer Mackay.

Source URL: http://www.jennifermackay.com/images/team/Policy%20and%20Procedures%20Manual.pdf

Forms

Figure 1A.2

JS 44C/SDNY
REV. 5/2010

CIVIL COVER SHEET

The JS-44 civil cover sheet and the information contained herein neither replace nor supplement the filing and service of pleadings or other papers as required by law, except as provided by local rules of court. This form, approved by the Judicial Conference of the United States in September 1974, is required for use of the Clerk of Court for the purpose of initiating the civil docket sheet.

PLAINTIFFS   DEFENDANTS

ATTORNEYS (FIRM NAME, ADDRESS, AND TELEPHONE NUMBER   ATTORNEYS (IF KNOWN)

CAUSE OF ACTION (CITE THE U.S. CIVIL STATUTE UNDER WHICH YOU ARE FILING AND WRITE A BRIEF STATEMENT OF CAUSE)
(DO NOT CITE JURISDICTIONAL STATUTES UNLESS DIVERSITY)

Has this or a similar case been previously filed in SDNY at any time? No? ☐ Yes? ☐   Judge Previously Assigned

If yes, was this case Vol.☐ Invol. ☐ Dismissed. No☐ Yes ☐ If yes, give date _____ & Case No. _____

(PLACE AN [x] IN ONE BOX ONLY)   NATURE OF SUIT

ACTIONS UNDER STATUTES

TORTS

CONTRACT

[ ] 110 INSURANCE
[ ] 120 MARINE
[ ] 130 MILLER ACT
[ ] 140 NEGOTIABLE INSTRUMENT
[ ] 150 RECOVERY OF OVERPAYMENT & ENFORCEMENT OF JUDGMENT
[ ] 151 MEDICARE ACT
[ ] 152 RECOVERY OF DEFAULTED STUDENT LOANS (EXCL VETERANS)
[ ] 153 RECOVERY OF OVERPAYMENT OF VETERAN'S BENEFITS
[ ] 160 STOCKHOLDERS SUITS
[ ] 190 OTHER CONTRACT
[ ] 195 CONTRACT PRODUCT LIABILITY
[ ] 196 FRANCHISE

PERSONAL INJURY

[ ] 310 AIRPLANE
[ ] 315 AIRPLANE PRODUCT LIABILITY
[ ] 320 ASSAULT, LIBEL & SLANDER
[ ] 330 FEDERAL EMPLOYERS' LIABILITY
[ ] 340 MARINE
[ ] 345 MARINE PRODUCT LIABILITY
[ ] 350 MOTOR VEHICLE
[ ] 355 MOTOR VEHICLE PRODUCT LIABILITY
[ ] 360 OTHER PERSONAL INJURY

PERSONAL INJURY

[ ] 362 PERSONAL INJURY - MED MALPRACTICE
[ ] 365 PERSONAL INJURY PRODUCT LIABILITY
[ ] 368 ASBESTOS PERSONAL INJURY PRODUCT LIABILITY

PERSONAL PROPERTY

[ ] 370 OTHER FRAUD
[ ] 371 TRUTH IN LENDING
[ ] 380 OTHER PERSONAL PROPERTY DAMAGE
[ ] 385 PROPERTY DAMAGE PRODUCT LIABILITY

FORFEITURE/PENALTY

[ ] 610 AGRICULTURE
[ ] 620 OTHER FOOD & DRUG
[ ] 625 DRUG RELATED SEIZURE OF PROPERTY 21 USC 881
[ ] 630 LIQUOR LAWS
[ ] 640 RR & TRUCK
[ ] 650 AIRLINE REGS
[ ] 660 OCCUPATIONAL SAFETY/HEALTH
[ ] 690 OTHER

LABOR

[ ] 710 FAIR LABOR STANDARDS ACT
[ ] 720 LABOR/MGMT RELATIONS
[ ] 730 LABOR/MGMT REPORTING & DISCLOSURE ACT
[ ] 740 RAILWAY LABOR ACT
[ ] 790 OTHER LABOR LITIGATION
[ ] 791 EMPL RET INC SECURITY ACT

IMMIGRATION

[ ] 462 NATURALIZATION APPLICATION
[ ] 463 HABEAS CORPUS- ALIEN DETAINEE
[ ] 465 OTHER IMMIGRATION ACTIONS

BANKRUPTCY

[ ] 422 APPEAL 28 USC 158
[ ] 423 WITHDRAWAL 28 USC 157

PROPERTY RIGHTS

[ ] 820 COPYRIGHTS
[ ] 830 PATENT
[ ] 840 TRADEMARK

SOCIAL SECURITY

[ ] 861 HIA (1395ff)
[ ] 862 BLACK LUNG (923)
[ ] 863 DIWC/DIWW (405(g))
[ ] 864 SSID TITLE XVI
[ ] 865 RSI (405(g))

FEDERAL TAX SUITS

[ ] 870 TAXES (U.S. Plaintiff or Defendant)
[ ] 871 IRS-THIRD PARTY 26 USC 7609

OTHER STATUTES

[ ] 400 STATE REAPPORTIONMENT
[ ] 410 ANTITRUST
[ ] 430 BANKS & BANKING
[ ] 450 COMMERCE
[ ] 460 DEPORTATION
[ ] 470 RACKETEER INFLU- ENCED & CORRUPT ORGANIZATION ACT (RICO)
[ ] 480 CONSUMER CREDIT
[ ] 490 CABLE/SATELLITE TV
[ ] 810 SELECTIVE SERVICE
[ ] 850 SECURITIES/ COMMODITIES/ EXCHANGE
[ ] 875 CUSTOMER CHALLENGE 12 USC 3410
[ ] 890 OTHER STATUTORY ACTIONS
[ ] 891 AGRICULTURAL ACTS
[ ] 892 ECONOMIC STABILIZATION ACT
[ ] 893 ENVIRONMENTAL MATTERS
[ ] 894 ENERGY ALLOCATION ACT
[ ] 895 FREEDOM OF INFORMATION ACT
[ ] 900 APPEAL OF FEE DETERMINATION UNDER EQUAL ACCESS TO JUSTICE
[ ] 950 CONSTITUTIONALITY OF STATE STATUTES

ACTIONS UNDER STATUTES

CIVIL RIGHTS

[ ] 441 VOTING
[ ] 442 EMPLOYMENT
[ ] 443 HOUSING/ ACCOMMODATIONS
[ ] 444 WELFARE
[ ] 445 AMERICANS WITH DISABILITIES - EMPLOYMENT
[ ] 446 AMERICANS WITH DISABILITIES -OTHER
[ ] 440 OTHER CIVIL RIGHTS

PRISONER PETITIONS

[ ] 510 MOTIONS TO VACATE SENTENCE 20 USC 2255
[ ] 530 HABEAS CORPUS
[ ] 535 DEATH PENALTY
[ ] 540 MANDAMUS & OTHER
[ ] 550 CIVIL RIGHTS
[ ] 555 PRISON CONDITION

REAL PROPERTY

[ ] 210 LAND CONDEMNATION
[ ] 220 FORECLOSURE
[ ] 230 RENT LEASE & EJECTMENT
[ ] 240 TORTS TO LAND
[ ] 245 TORT PRODUCT LIABILITY
[ ] 290 ALL OTHER REAL PROPERTY

Check if demanded in complaint:

☐ CHECK IF THIS IS A CLASS ACTION UNDER F.R.C.P. 23

DO YOU CLAIM THIS CASE IS RELATED TO A CIVIL CASE NOW PENDING IN S.D.N.Y.? IF SO, STATE:

DEMAND $_____ OTHER _____   JUDGE _____ DOCKET NUMBER_____

Check YES only if demanded in complaint
JURY DEMAND: ☐ YES ☐ NO   NOTE: Please submit at the time of filing an explanation of why cases are deemed related.

Figure 1A.3

PROCEDURE

Closeout Letters

Closeout letters serve several purposes: 1) to document your work on a case; 2) to remind the client of the stages of the process you have gone through together; and 3) to provide the client with an accurate synopsis of what happened in his/her case. The following is a sample outline of a general closeout letter.

1) Subject line Re:

A subject line is the "Re:" in a letter and is typed between the inside address and the salutation. All business correspondence should include a subject line that identifies this case from all others. You may include the case name, case number, and court, i.e., Re: People v. Barney, 99-0567, Denver County Court.

2) First Paragraph: Synopsis

This paragraph contains a short summary, in lay terms—not legalese—of what happened in the case. [In criminal cases it should conclude with the violations originally charged, identified by name (e.g., battery) and appropriate citation (e.g., 42-4-1203(A) C.R.S. 1973). This paragraph also should include maximum penalties, either collectively or individually, to which the client would have been subjected. In civil cases, include the kind of problem presented and the client's goals.]

3) Details of Case and/or Resolution

This section contains what you did on the case such as negotiation and settlement (whether successful or not) and details of any and all court appearances. Identify the negotiating or opposing attorney, the court, the judge, and the date.

4) Explanation of Court Orders

Describe the outcome and remind the client of any obligations the court imposed and the consequences of failing to follow those obligations, such as making payments on a judgment. Be sure to explain all terms in simple, easy to understand diction. Be as clear as possible.

5) Shred Policy

Notify the client that the case will be destroyed without further notice after 10 years of the closing date. The client can contact us before that time period to receive a copy of her/his file.

6) Conclusion

End on a personal note if at all possible. Thank the clients for their cooperation, if applicable. Wish them well. Tell them to contact the office, not you, if they have any further questions on the case or if difficulties arise. Be careful not to give them the impression that we will handle future unrelated cases.

7) Closing

All closeout letters, as with all correspondence on cases, must be on SLO letterhead and reviewed by a faculty member. Every case is different so the letter must be tailored to the case. If a relevant event happened during the handling of the case, which is not covered in these instructions, it must be included. Consult with your supervisor.

Source: Closeout Letters from Student Law Office Policies and Procedures Manual. Used by permission of Sturm College of Law, University of Denver.

Procedures

Figure 1A.4

UNITED STATES DISTRICT COURT
SOUTHERN DISTRICT OF NEW YORK

CHIEF JUDGE LORETTA A. PRESKA
RUBY J. KRAJICK, CLERK OF COURT

| About the Court | Attorney | Cases | ECF | Fees | Forms | Judges | Jury Duty | Local Rules | Naturalization | Part 1 | Trial Support |

Welcome to the Southern District of New York

Forms Index

Forms Required to Start an Action

Misc. Pleadings and Motions

Transcripts

Judgments

Appeals

Criminal Justice Act (CJA)

Pro Se

Attorney Services

ECF Registration Only

Interpreters' Forms

Law Student Intern Appearance

All official Court forms must be used without modification.

Forms Required to Start an Action

Civil Cover Sheet
Contains Fields to Complete on-line (print out for filing)
JS 44C/SDNY (Rev. 05/10)

Summons in a Civil Case
Contains fields to complete on-line (print out for filing).
AO 440 (Rev. 12/09)

Fee Schedule

Waiver of Service of Summons
Contains Fields to Complete on-line (print out for filing)
AO 399 (Rev. 01/09)

Notice of Lawsuit and Request for Waiver of Service of Summons
Contains Fields to Complete on-line (print out for filing)
AO 398 (Rev. 01/09)

Consent to Proceed Before US Magistrate Judge
Contains Fields to Complete on-line (print out for filing)
AO 85 (Rev. 01/09)

Consent to Proceed Before US Magistrate Judge Over a Specific Motion
Contains Fields to Complete on-line (print out for filing)
AO 85A (Rev. 01/09)

Appearance
Sample PDF Form

Rule 7.1 Statement
Contains Fields to Complete on-line (print out for filing)

Getting Started

Starting an Action
24 Hour Filing   PACER

Attorney   Representing
Admission   Yourself (Pro Se)

Electronic Case Filing

Training Courses Schedules

Sign up to become a
Point of Contact (POC)

CJA

Revised Plan for Furnishing
Representation Pursuant to the
Criminal Justice Act
(18 U.S.C. § 3006A)

Individual Practices of Judges

U.S. District Judges
U.S. Magistrate Judges

Privacy and Security Notice | RSS Feeds

500 Pearl Street, New York, New York 10007-1312 ● 300 Quarropas Street, White Plains, New York 10601-4150

Source: http://www.nysd.uscourts.gov/forms.php

Contacts and Resources

Figure 1A.5

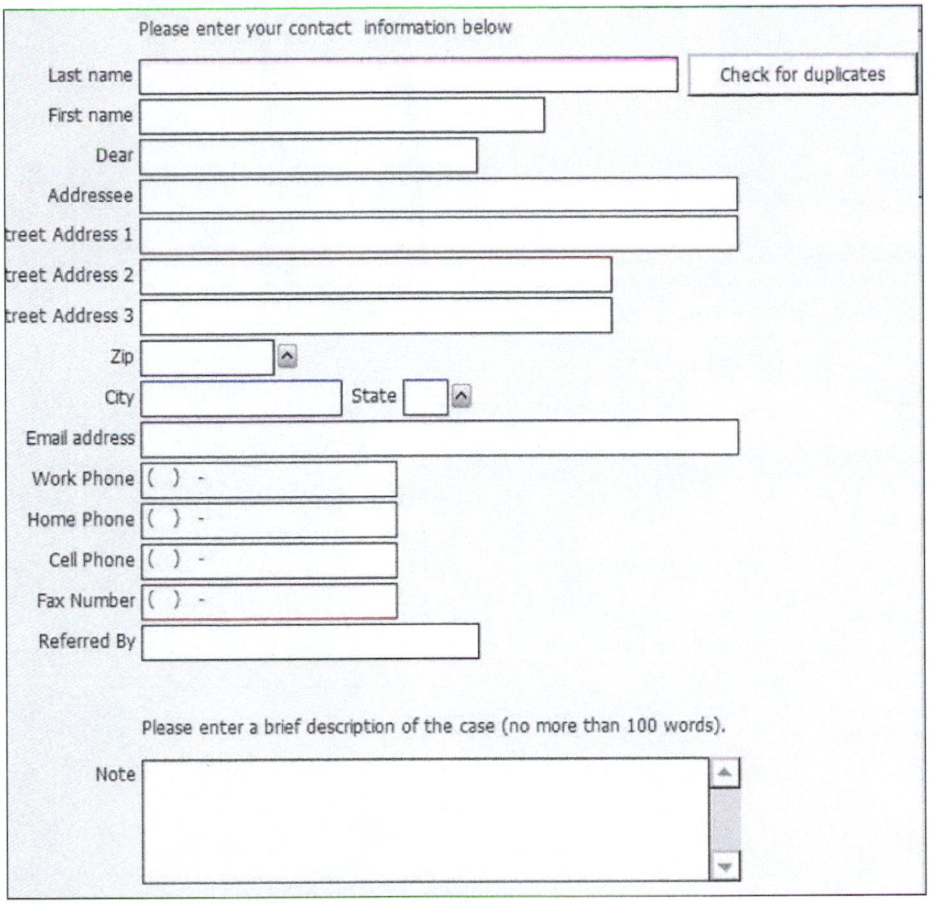

Please enter your contact information below

Last name	[ ] Check for duplicates
First name	[ ]
Dear	[ ]
Addressee	[ ]
Street Address 1	[ ]
Street Address 2	[ ]
Street Address 3	[ ]
Zip	[ ]
City	[ ] State [ ]
Email address	[ ]
Work Phone	( ) -
Home Phone	( ) -
Cell Phone	( ) -
Fax Number	( ) -
Referred By	[ ]

Please enter a brief description of the case (no more than 100 words).

Note [ ]

Figure 1A.6

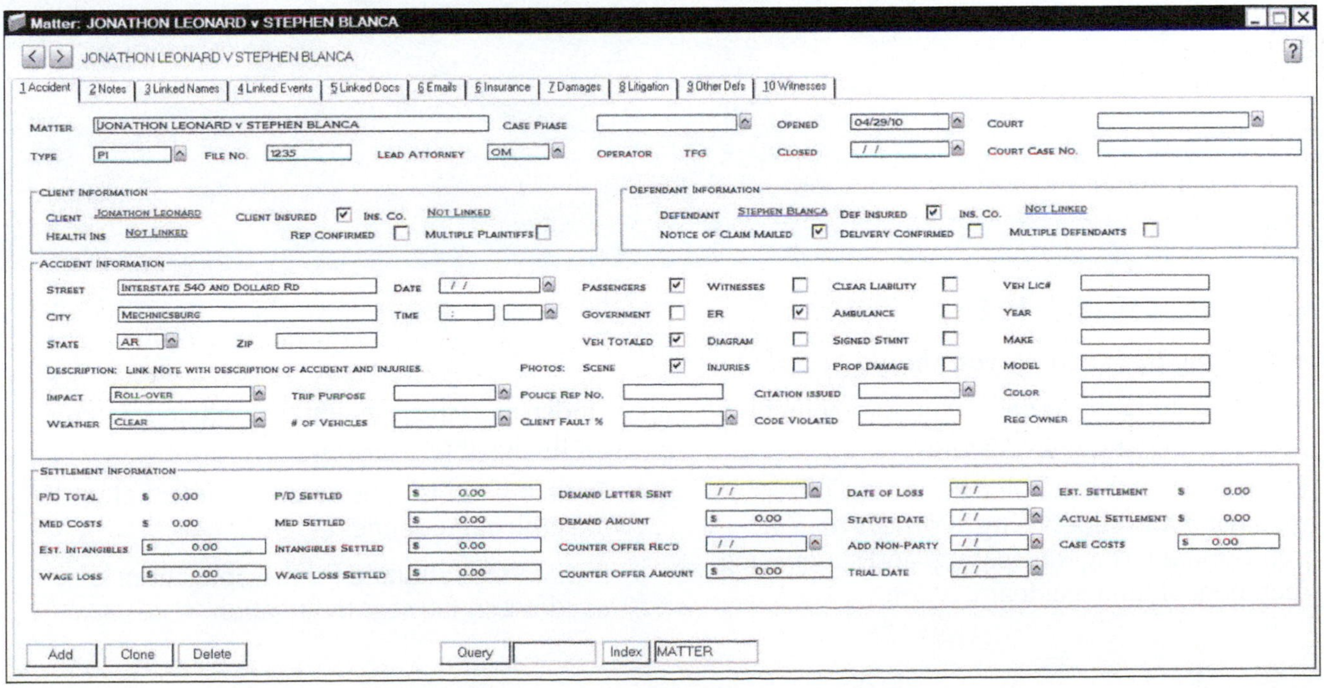

LEARNING OBJECTIVES

After studying this chapter, you should be able to:

1. Analyze situations to determine if they involve the unauthorized practice of law.

2. Describe the ethical obligation owed by managing and supervising attorneys of appropriate hiring, delegating, and supervising members of the legal team.

3. Understand the concept of conflict of interest for the legal profession.

4. Explain what is considered confidential under the ethical guidelines.

5. Explain the rationale for the obligations of candor and fairness in litigation.

Ethics and Professional Responsibility | CHAPTER 2

OPENING SCENARIO

 Ethan Benjamin and his associate Cary Eden were having coffee in the courthouse coffee shop during a break in a trial. At a nearby table, two paralegals from another firm were talking about a case that one of them was working on. The case had been the subject of an in-depth article in the morning newspaper; the article mentioned previously unreleased documents and facts. Ethan wondered aloud whether the reporting of the facts and evidence about a case in a newspaper removed the attorney or paralegal restriction on discussing details about a case. Cary reminded him about the ethical obligation of confidentiality under the lawyer's rules of ethics in their state and its application to members of the legal team. They agreed it was a topic that should be discussed at their firm's weekly meeting. They also agreed that this was something that should be a written policy guideline in the office and employee manual. Cary wondered to herself if she could still tell her friend (who was the opposing counsel in that case) what she had overheard that might help him to win the case.

OPENING SCENARIO LEARNING OBJECTIVE

Understand the duty of confidentiality.

■ INTRODUCTION TO ETHICS AND PROFESSIONAL RESPONSIBILITY

Professions such as law and medicine are regulated (by licensing or other means) for the protection of the public. The legal profession generally requires the passing of a written examination before admission to practice in the courts of a particular state. Unlike universal licensing of lawyers, the licensing of the paralegal profession is limited to a few states.

Every profession develops a set of guidelines for those in the profession to follow. These may be codes of conduct or ethical guidelines. National paralegal associations such as NALA (the National Association of Legal Assistants) and NFPA (the National Federation of Paralegal Associations) have ethics guidelines for members. These organizations require members to conduct themselves in accordance with these guidelines, observance of which is a condition of continued membership in the organization.

Ethics codes or rules typically set forth the minimum in ethical behavior—the very least each professional should do. In the field of law, these rules are referred to as "the rules of ethics" or "the rules of professional responsibility." Each state controls the right to practice law, and each state has adopted its own "rules of ethics." According to the American Bar Association, as of the spring of 2010, California was the only state not to have professional conduct rules that follow the format of the ABA **Model Rules of Professional Conduct** for lawyers. This wide-scale adoption provides a high degree of consistency in the ethical guidelines for the legal profession across the country.

The Supreme Court or legislature of each state has a committee or board that is authorized to enforce state rules of professional responsibility or ethics. States typically use a disciplinary board, which may be part of the state Supreme Court or part of a statewide bar association, to receive and investigate complaints against lawyers.

Among the ethical obligations of the attorney and the legal team acting as agent of the attorney are:

Rule 1.1, Competency,
Rule 1.6, Confidentiality of Information,
Rule 1.7, Conflicts of Interest: Current Clients,
Rule 3.3, Candor Toward the Tribunal,
Rule 3.4, Fairness to Opposing Party and Counsel, and
Rules 5.1 and 5.3, Duty to Supervise.

As more members are added to the legal team who do not fit within the traditional roles of lawyer, paralegal, legal assistant, clerk, or legal secretary, the concern broadens as to how the rules of confidentiality and privilege will be applied and enforced. The courts have recognized that the lawyer must engage others to help in the representation of clients, and numerous cases have explored the use of legal support staff like paralegals and investigators. The use of technology or computer consultants, however, may not be as clear. Certainly, computer consultants are essential where large volumes of e-discovery are involved. Most computer consultants, however, are not adequately educated in the ethical rules of the legal profession. Levels of technical ability and competency are important in choosing and using computer consultants and support staff. Also important are the confidentiality issues in adding computer and technology staff to the legal team; they are nonlegal personnel who may have access to files that contain privileged or confidential client information and trial strategy. Technology staff

WEB RESOURCES

Contrast and compare the **Rules Governing the Missouri Bar and the Judiciary Rules of Professional Conduct** at the Missouri State Courts website with the American Bar Association Model Rules of Professional Responsibility at the ABA website and the ethical rules in your jurisdiction.

ethics
Minimally acceptable standards of conduct in a profession.

Model Rules of Professional Conduct
The American Bar Association set of proposed ethical standards for the legal profession.

WEB RESOURCES

Contrast and compare the **Arkansas Rules of Professional Conduct** at the Arkansas Judiciary website with the American Bar Association Model Rules of Professional Responsibility at the ABA website and the ethical rules in your jurisdiction.

WEB RESOURCES

Information on state adoption of the model rules can be found at the ABA website.

WEB RESOURCES

The **ABA Model Rules of Professional Conduct** can be found at the ABA website.

WEB RESOURCES

Contrast and compare the **Oregon Rules of Professional Conduct** at the Oregon State Bar website with the American Bar Association Model Rules of Professional Responsibility at the ABA website and the ethical rules in your jurisdiction.

must understand the ethical obligations and the confidential nature of the files on which they are working.

> ### PRACTICE TIP
> Current ethical requirements for competency require a knowledge of technology and its use in the practice of law. The duty of supervision will logically require supervisors to have an understanding of the technology being applied by consultants and others.

LEARNING OBJECTIVE 1
Analyze situations to determine if they involve the unauthorized practice of law.

■ REGULATION OF THE PRACTICE OF LAW

Just as the practice of medicine and other professions is regulated, the practice of law is regulated by state government through legislation, regulation, and court rules in an attempt to protect the public from incompetent and unscrupulous practitioners. As a method of regulating and monitoring those who offer services to the public, certain occupations and professions such as law require one to obtain a license. Obtaining a license may be as simple as completing a form and providing proof that the required education and/or experience requirements have been satisfied. The profession of law, in most cases, requires taking a qualifying examination after proving that the required educational background has been obtained. This has not always been the case. In some states, reciprocal admission, that is, admission in another jurisdiction for a required period of time, granted admission to the second jurisdiction without the examination requirement. Today's rules generally require even seasoned attorneys who seek admission to states such as California and Florida to take the examination for that state as a condition for admission.

The Paralegal and Licensing

There are, with a few exceptions, no state licensing requirements for paralegals. Some states, such as California, Maine, and North Carolina, have enacted legislation establishing licensure to perform certain functions frequently performed by paralegals. Generally, these enactments seek to regulate the unsupervised performance of certain tasks by freelance or independent paralegals, such as document-completion services.

There is a fine line between lawful activity and unlawful practice of law. Recommending or selecting a form that may impact a person's legal rights is likely to be treated as practicing law and would therefore subject the unlicensed person to a charge of the unauthorized practice of law. The dilemma for the paralegal is to know when advising or helping someone fill in blank forms constitutes the **Unauthorized Practice of Law (UPL).**

At best, these laws carve out a small part of the practice of law that can be performed by nonlawyers for others without risking the performance of acts that constitute the unlawful practice of law. But none allow anyone other than a lawyer properly admitted to practice in the jurisdiction to give legal advice or opinions. Even the selection of the correct form is considered a lawyer's function.

Although each state is free to define the practice of law differently, the statutes have certain elements in common. Typical of the various states' definitions of the practice of law is that of *Rule 31, Rules of the Supreme Court of Arizona.*

    A. "Practice of law" means providing legal advice or services to or for another by:

        1. preparing any document in any medium intended to affect or secure legal rights for a specific person or entity;

        2. preparing or expressing legal opinions;

WEB RESOURCES
Contrast and compare the **Wisconsin Rules of Professional Conduct for Attorneys** at the Wisconsin State Legislature website with the American Bar Association Model Rules of Professional Responsibility at the ABA website and the ethical rules in your jurisdiction.

WEB RESOURCES
Contrast and compare the **Rhode Island Rules of Professional Conduct** at the Rhode Island Judiciary website with the American Bar Association Model Rules of Professional Responsibility at the ABA website and the ethical rules in your jurisdiction.

unauthorized practice of law (UPL)
Giving legal advice, if legal rights may be affected, by anyone not licensed to practice law.

WEB RESOURCES
Contrast and compare the **Arizona Ethics Rules** at the State Bar of Arizona website with the American Bar Association Model Rules of Professional Responsibility at the ABA website and the ethical rules in your jurisdiction.

3. representing another in a judicial, quasi-judicial, or administrative proceeding, or other formal dispute resolution process such as arbitration and mediation;

4. preparing any document through any medium for filing in any court, administrative agency or tribunal for a specific person or entity; or

5. negotiating legal rights or responsibilities for a specific person or entity. . . .

State Regulation

Individual states have used several techniques to set standards and regulate the profession. Some states control the profession by enacting a statute that defines who may identify themselves as a "paralegal." California's statute Cal. BPC §6450 defines a paralegal as someone qualified by education, training, or work experience who performs substantial legal work under the supervision and direction of an active member of the state bar. The code also defines a paralegal's duties, states minimum educational standards and continuing legal education requirements, and sets fines and jail time for anyone who violates the law.

In June 2012, the Supreme Court of Washington State authorized the issuance of a Limited License Legal Technician, which grants qualified paralegals a license to engage in certain defined legal functions.

While paralegals are not required to obtain the Limited License, only qualified paralegals may apply for it.

The state bar associations of some states have recognized the paralegal professional. A state bar association is not a governmental body; rather, bar associations are statewide professional organizations formed by attorneys to advance their profession. Florida and Ohio are among the states that have addressed the issue of paralegal certification.

Florida Registered Paralegal. A Florida Registered Paralegal is a person with education, training, or work experience who works under the direction and supervision of a member of The Florida Bar; who performs specifically delegated, substantive legal work for which a member of The Florida Bar is responsible; and who has met the requirements of registration as set forth in Chapter 20 of the Rules Regulating The Florida Bar. A Florida Registered Paralegal is not a member of The Florida Bar and may not give legal advice or practice law. Florida Registered Paralegal and FRP are trademarks of The Florida Bar. (*Source:* "Florida Registered Paralegal program," http://www.floridabar.org, Used by permission from Florida Registered Paralegal.)

Ohio State Bar Association Certified Paralegal. The Ohio State Bar Association offers a voluntary credentialing program for paralegals. An individual meeting the OSBA definition of "paralegal" who has satisfied the eligibility requirements and passed a written examination will be designated as an "OSBA Certified Paralegal." This credential, along with a logo provided for the purpose, may be used by the paralegal to the extent permitted by the Supreme Court of Ohio's Rules for the Government of the Bar and Rules of Professional Conduct. OSBA Paralegal Certification provides a valuable credential for paralegals in Ohio through the use of objective standards that measure the training, knowledge, experience, and skill of paralegals. It requires a commitment to excellence and will assist lawyers and law firms in identifying highly qualified paralegal professionals. (*Source:* http://www.ohiobar.org/pub/?articleid_785)

Whether a statutory definition or a certification recognized by the bar association, the goal is delivery of quality legal services at affordable prices with a reasonable standard of living for members of the legal profession and the paralegal profession. The traditional role of the attorney in advising and representing clients is limited to those who are admitted to practice as lawyers under the applicable state

---

SCOPE OF PRACTICE

Washington State

Legal Technicians are allowed to:

- explain facts and relevancy,
- inform the client of procedures and "anticipated course of the legal proceeding,"
- provide the client with self-help materials approved by the Board or prepared by a Washington state lawyer,
- review and explain the other side's documents and exhibits,
- select and complete forms approved by various groups,
- perform legal research and write legal letters and documents, but only if reviewed by a Washington lawyer,
- advise the client about other needed documents,
- assist the client in obtaining needed documents.

Source: Quote by Robert Mongue. Used by permission of Robert Mongue.

law. Some exemptions do exist that allow nonlawyers to perform certain services under state law, such as document preparation under California law.

Federal Practice

Under federal regulations, nonlawyers may represent parties before the U.S. Social Security Administration, the U.S. Patent and Trademark Office, and other government agencies. A conflict may arise between the federal law and the state law that limits the representation. For example, Florida sought unsuccessfully to enjoin a practitioner authorized to practice before the Patent Office, alleging UPL (*Sperry v. Florida*, 373 U.S. 379 (1963)).

Under federal regulation, a paralegal can, without supervision, represent individuals before the Social Security Administration and can appear before Administrative Law Judges on behalf of clients. Paralegals may appear as representatives of claimants for disability claims; Medicare parts A, B, and C; and cases of overpayment and underpayment. As representative of a claimant, the paralegal in practice before the Social Security Administration may obtain information, submit evidence, and make statements and arguments. The difference between the paralegal and the attorney is only in the matter of direct versus indirect payment for services. The Social Security Administration pays the attorney directly, whereas the paralegal must bill the client for services rendered. Within the Social Security Administration, paralegals are employed as decision writers and case technicians.

WEB RESOURCES
The complete version of the Formal Opinion is at the New York City Bar website.

Penalties for the Unauthorized Practice of Law

States such as Pennsylvania have specifically addressed the issue of unauthorized practice of law by paralegals and legal assistants. The Pennsylvania statute on the unauthorized practice of law makes it a misdemeanor for "any person, including, but not limited to, a paralegal or legal assistant who within this Commonwealth, shall practice law…" 42 Pa. C.S.A. § 2524.

The Pennsylvania statute seems to address concerns that the general public will misinterpret the title of paralegal or legal assistant as denoting a person admitted to practice law in the Commonwealth. An unresolved issue in Pennsylvania, and in other states, is to define what specific conduct the courts will hold to be the practice of law. Because the interpretation will vary from state to state, the paralegal must be aware of the local requirements and limitations that define the unauthorized practice of law within that jurisdiction.

In those states that have enacted legislation regulating paralegal activity, some guidance is offered by the defined activity that is permitted. For example, California has included within its Business and Professional Code the licensing of persons as "Unlawful Detainer Assistant" and "Legal Document Assistant" and defining the activity permitted.

> **Chapter 5.5. Legal Document Assistants and Unlawful Detainer Assistants**
> Article 1. General Provisions
> 6400(a) "Unlawful detainer assistant" means any individual who for compensation renders assistance or advice in the prosecution or defense of an unlawful detainer claim or action, including any bankruptcy petition that may affect the unlawful detainer claim or action. Cal. BPC §6400(a).

WEB RESOURCES
Contrast and compare Rule 1.6(c)(4) of the **Pennsylvania Rules** at the Disciplinary Board of the Supreme Court of Pennsylvania website with the American Bar Association Model Rules of Professional Responsibility at the ABA website and the ethical rules in your jurisdiction.

WEB RESOURCES
Read the entire article at the Disciplinary Board of the Supreme Court of Pennsylvania website.

Avoiding UPL: Holding Oneself Out

With so much uncertainty about what constitutes the unauthorized practice of law, the question every paralegal must ask is "How do I avoid UPL?" Some general guidelines should be followed. A common thread in the guidelines of how to avoid committing UPL is the prohibition of holding oneself out as a lawyer when one has not been admitted to practice law. The Florida statute was amended recently to read:

> Any person not licensed or otherwise authorized to practice law in this state who practices law in this state or holds himself or herself out to the public as qualified to practice law in this state, or who willfully pretends to be, or willfully takes or uses any name, title, addition, or description implying that he or she is qualified, or recognized by law as qualified, to practice law in this state, commits a felony of the third degree....

§454.23 Fla. Stat.

California, in the Business and Professional Code mentioned above, reinforces the concept of not misleading the public into thinking one is a lawyer when he/she provides limited service, by requiring the following statement to be made to prospective clients:

> (4) The statement: "I am not an attorney" and, if the person offering legal document assistant or unlawful detainer assistant services is a partnership or a corporation, or uses a fictitious business name, "(name) is not a law firm. I/we cannot represent you in court, advise you about your legal rights or the law, or select legal forms for you."

For the paralegal, the first rule is to inform the parties with whom they are dealing that they (paralegals) are not lawyers. Paralegals must not hold themselves out as being anything more than paralegals. Parties with whom the paralegal has contact must be aware of the limited role the paralegal plays on the legal team. Other lawyers, members of the legal team, and the courthouse staff are put on notice by being informed of the person's status as a paralegal. This may be by oral comment, written statement (such as a letter signed using the title "paralegal"), or presentment with a business card clearly showing the title of "paralegal."

Advising clients, witnesses, and other members of the general public of the paralegal's role is not as easy. Those who are not properly educated about the role of the paralegal may believe that a paralegal is someone with advanced training and knowledge who can perform some of the functions typically performed by lawyers, including giving legal advice and opinions. The safest course is to be certain the other party is not misled about the role of the paralegal. Use of the statement from the California Business and Professional Code above is a start: "I am not an attorney."..."I...cannot represent you in court, advise you about your legal rights or the law, or select legal forms for you."

Even this statement may not always be effective. Some members of the community may come from backgrounds where the distinctions among various members of the legal team are not clear—for example, those who come from countries where the legal systems are different or where different terms are used for those who perform legal functions such as notaries.

For non-native speakers of English, inaccurate translation also may play a role in the misunderstanding. To some clients, the paralegal is the "face" or main contact with the law firm. The paralegal may be the first point of contact and the one through whom all documents and information are communicated by the lawyers in the firm.

Paralegals must make it clear that they are paralegals and not lawyers. In a first meeting with anyone—client, witness, opposing counsel, or court personnel—the wisest course of action is to advise that person of your position as a paralegal. A short statement like "I am Ms. Attorney's paralegal" may be sufficient to put the other party on notice. Business cards and letterhead, where permitted, should clearly state the title of "paralegal." Correspondence always should include the title as part of the signature block.

Never allow the other party to think you are anything other than what you are—a professional who is a paralegal. For those who are not familiar with the role of the paralegal, you may have to clarify what a paralegal can and cannot do in your jurisdiction.

Avoiding UPL: Giving Advice

Every UPL statute or rule prohibits anyone other than a lawyer properly admitted to practice in the state or jurisdiction from preparing or expressing legal opinions. Clearly, then, a paralegal cannot give a legal opinion or give legal advice. It sounds simple, but the reality is that paralegals must constantly be on guard to avoid giving legal advice or rendering a legal opinion. Clients and those seeking "a little free advice" may not want to respect the limitations of the paralegal's role in the legal system. Certain conduct required or requested by an attorney or client should, at the very least, cause the paralegal to pause. A client's request to prepare a power of attorney "without bothering the lawyer" or to "go with me to the support conference" should raise a caution flag in the paralegal's mind. Even in a social setting, you may have to repeat the statement, "I am not an attorney."…"I/we cannot represent you in court, advise you about your legal rights or the law, or select legal forms for you."

When is giving advice an unauthorized practice of law? If legal rights may be affected, it probably is legal advice. The question of what advice is legal advice is not always easy to answer. Consider the seemingly innocent question, "How should I sign my name?" In most circumstances, the answer might be: "Just sign it the way you normally sign your name." But when a person is signing a document in a representative capacity—for example, as the officer of a corporation or on behalf of another person under a power of attorney—telling the client to "just sign your name" might be giving legal advice because the client's legal rights could be affected if he or she does not indicate the representative capacity.

Avoiding UPL: Filling Out Forms

Filling out forms for clients also can be a source of trouble. In some jurisdictions, paralegals are permitted to assist clients in preparing certain documents. Other courts, however, view this assistance as rendering legal advice.

> As a general matter, other courts have held that the sale of self-help legal kits or printed legal forms does not constitute the unauthorized practice of law as long as the seller provides the buyer no advice regarding which forms to use or how the forms should be filled out.

> *Fifteenth Jud. Dis. v. Glasgow*, M1996-00020-COA-R3-CV
> (Tenn.App. 12-10-1999)(FN4)

The Florida court addressed this issue in an unlawful practice of law case, holding that…

> a nonlawyer who has direct contact with individuals in the nature of consultation, explanation, recommendations, advice, and assistance in the provision, selection, and completion of legal forms engages in the unlicensed practice of law;…[W]hile a nonlawyer may sell certain legal forms and type up instruments completed by clients, a nonlawyer "must not engage in personal legal assistance

in conjunction with her business activities, including the correction of errors and omissions. . . ."

The Florida Bar, petitioner, versus We The People Forms and Service Center of Sarasota, Inc., et al., No. SC02—1675

Avoiding UPL: Representing Clients

Knowing when someone may represent a client before a judicial or quasi-judicial board, such as an administrative agency, is a difficult question to answer. The difficulty is in knowing what the individual courts allow or will permit in individual circumstances. Some jurisdictions and administrative agencies do permit those who are not licensed or admitted to practice to appear in court or before administrative law judges or referees on behalf of clients. (Typically, these are law students acting under the guidance and supervision of an attorney under limited circumstances, but they may include paralegals.) Depending upon the jurisdiction, nature of the action, and level of the court, the paralegal might be permitted to appear with or on behalf of a client—for example, before a Social Security Administration Administrative Law Judge.

Who may represent clients is not a simple question for lawyers or paralegals. Representation of parties has traditionally been the role of lawyers. But even lawyers are not always permitted to represent parties. Appropriate admission to practice in the jurisdiction is typically a requirement. A lawyer admitted to practice in one state may not necessarily be admitted to represent the same client in another state. Lawyers admitted to practice in one jurisdiction, however, may ask the court of another jurisdiction for permission to appear in order to try a specific case. This is a courtesy generally granted for a single case, and in these situations, the trial attorney usually retains local counsel who will appear as well to advise on local rules and procedures. But the issue of out-of-state counsel is not without other complications.

The complexity of the issue is raised in a portion of a report on the Unauthorized Practice of Law prepared by the Nevada Assistant Bar Counsel:

> The Bar has received complaints of out-of-state counsel participating in the pre[-]litigation mediation procedures. Writing notification letters, engaging in discovery, and appearing at pre-litigation mediations in a representative capacity is generally the practice of law. In Nevada there is no mechanism to obtain authority from the Supreme Court to appear in pre-litigation cases. Therefore, engaging in legal activities involving Nevada disputes and Nevada parties requires a licensed Nevada attorney. . . .

(Unauthorized Practice of Law, David A. Clark, Assistant Bar Counsel, September 20, 2001)

If the representation of clients is not clear for members of the bar, it certainly is not clear for members of the paralegal profession. Generally, however, only duly admitted lawyers in the jurisdiction may represent parties. But this rule has been modified to allow law students in some states to represent parties in certain situations, generally under appropriate supervision.

In some states, a nonlawyer employee may represent a business in some proceedings before administrative agencies or before the minor judiciary, such as small claims courts. There is no uniformity of rules that dictates when nonlawyers may represent parties or before which agencies or courts nonlawyers may appear. Any appearance before a court must therefore be approached carefully.

Even the presentation of a request for continuance of a case may be considered by some courts to be the practice of law. Appearance on behalf of clients before federal and state administrative agencies is no less lacking in uniformity than appearances before courts, but it frequently is easier to determine the ability to appear as a paralegal representing a client. Some federal agencies specifically permit nonlawyers to appear. Most notable is the Social Security Administration, which allows representation by nonlawyers with few differences from representation by lawyers. The U.S. Patent Office also specifically permits nonlawyer practice. Some states, by specific legislation or administrative rule, also permit representation by nonlawyers.

Avoiding UPL: Guidelines

The National Association of Legal Assistants, Inc. Model Standards and Guidelines for the Utilization of Legal Assistants provide guidelines on conduct that may prevent UPL.

Guideline 1

Legal assistants should:

Disclose their status as legal assistants at the outset of any professional relationship with a client, other attorneys, a court or administrative agency or personnel thereof, or members of the general public....

Guideline 2

Legal assistants should not:

Establish attorney–client relationships; set legal fees; give legal opinions or advice; or represent a client before a court, unless authorized to do so by said court; nor engage in, encourage, or contribute to any act that could constitute the unauthorized practice of law.

Guideline 3

Legal assistants may perform services for an attorney in the representation of a client, provided:

- The services performed by the legal assistant do not require the exercise of independent professional legal judgment;
- The attorney maintains a direct relationship with the client and maintains control of all client matters;
- The attorney supervises the legal assistant;
- The attorney remains professionally responsible for all work on behalf of the client, including any actions taken or not taken by the legal assistant in connection therewith; and
- The services performed supplement, merge with, and become the attorney's work product.

■ ETHICAL OBLIGATIONS

Ethical behavior is expected and required of every member of the legal team: attorneys, paralegals, litigation support staff, information technologists, and outside consultants.

What is sometimes not clear in the minds of nonlawyer members of the legal team is what ethical obligations they have and how the ethics rules are to be followed and enforced.

Duty to Supervise

The **supervising attorney** is ultimately responsible for the ethical conduct of everyone on the legal team. Under Rules 5.1 and 5.3, the supervising attorney is the one in charge of a case and those working on the case. The duty of

LEARNING OBJECTIVE 2
Describe the ethical obligation owed by managing and supervising attorneys of appropriate hiring, delegating, and supervising members of the legal team.

supervising attorney
The member of the legal team to whom all others on the team report and who has the ultimate responsibility for the actions of the legal team.

supervision is required of partners and lawyers with managerial authority in the firm to ensure that other lawyers' conduct conforms to the ethical code. Direct supervising attorneys with authority over nonlawyers have an ethical obligation to ensure that those persons' conduct is compatible with the obligations of the lawyer. What happens in the handling and processing of a case by the legal team is ultimately the responsibility of the supervising attorney. Any ethical breaches or lapses are ultimately the responsibility of the attorney under the ethical guidelines and under common law principles of agency law. Each person working for or supervised by the attorney is in fact the **agent** of the attorney. Under fundamentals of agency law, the agents (including paralegals, legal assistants, clerks and legal secretaries, and the **principal**—the attorney) have a **fiduciary relationship** to each other. The agent must obey the reasonable instructions of the principal, and the principal is presumed to know everything the agent learns in the ordinary course of working for the attorney on the case. The principal is responsible for the acts of the agent when the agent is acting within the scope of the agent's employment. The attorney is the one to whom the client looks for professional advice and a successful outcome of the case. The attorney will suffer any sanctions that result from members of the legal team failing to follow and enforce the ethical rules.

Ethical obligations of lawyers are enforced by the court in the jurisdiction where the attorney practices or where the case is being tried. The supervising attorney of every legal team must follow the ethics rules and ensure that the members of the legal team follow the same rules. The obligation to ensure ethical conduct is that of the supervising attorney under the ethical obligation to supervise all who work on the case for the attorney (under Rules 5.1 and 5.3).

These rules are as much a part of the administration of justice as the rules of civil or criminal procedure and the rules of evidence. The bigger issues are: who has the responsibility to instruct the nonlawyer members of the legal or trial team, and who is responsible for ensuring their compliance? While it is ultimately the responsibility of the lawyer to supervise the nonlawyers' support staff (such as secretaries, investigators, litigation support staff, and technical consultants), in many cases, this obligation falls to the paralegal or litigation manager on the legal team. Each person working for or supervised by the attorney is, in fact, the agent of the attorney. The attorney is ultimately responsible for the ethical conduct of the agent-paralegal, and therefore, the paralegal owes a duty to the supervising attorney similar to that of the traditional agent-servant relationship found in agency law—that of a fiduciary obligation. Among the fiduciary obligations of an agent are the duty to exercise reasonable care, skill, and diligence.

The agent also owes a duty of loyalty to the principal. This includes the obligation to act for the employer's benefit rather than for the agent's own benefit or the benefit of another whose interest may be adverse to that of the employer.

agent
A person authorized to act on behalf of another.

principal
One who authorizes another to act on his or her behalf.

fiduciary relationship
A relationship where one is under a duty to act for the benefit of another under the scope of the relationship.

WEB RESOURCES

The entire set of Michigan's proposed standards for imposing lawyer sanctions is at the Michigan One Court of Justice website.

Ethical Guidelines and Rules

Lawyers generally need to follow only one set of ethics guidelines. Although it may be a set enacted by the state legislature, it usually is one adopted by the Supreme Court of the state in which they practice.

Unlike the ABA for lawyers, no single source of ethical rules is set out for the legal assistant. Absent a single unified body of ethical rules, legal assistants must follow state statutes and conduct themselves in conformity with the rules of professional conduct applicable to attorneys and with the ethics opinions of their professional associations.

The two major legal assistant organizations that provide an ethical code for their members are the National Federation of Paralegal Associations (NFPA) and the National Association of Legal Assistants (NALA).

Although legal assistants are not governed directly by the American Bar Association ethical rules, there is an intertwined relationship among the lawyer, the client, and the paralegal. What the paralegal does or does not do can have a real impact on the lawyer's duty and obligation to the client. Under the Model Rules, the lawyer ultimately is responsible for the actions of the legal assistant.

Conflict of Interest

A **conflict of interest** exists if the representation of one client will be adverse to the interest of another client. Conflict of interest may best be explained by the adage that no one can serve two masters. If the master is entitled to complete loyalty, any conflict in loyalties presents a conflict of interest in which neither master can be certain of the loyalty of his or her servant. It's easy to see the conflict that would arise in a lawyer's going to court to represent both the plaintiff and the defendant.

Less obvious are situations in which the attorney represents two parties with a common interest, such as a husband and wife purchasing a new home. In most cases, the interests would be the same, and no conflict would exist. When these clients are seeking counseling for marital problems, however, the conflict becomes more obvious as one of them seeks a greater share of the common property (or other rights), and the lawyer is called upon to give legal advice as to the individual rights of one of the parties. Finally, lawyers clearly cannot represent both husband and wife in court in a marital dissolution trial.

The American Bar Association Model Rules of Professional Conduct provide a guideline in Rule 1.7, Conflict of Interest: Current Clients, which provides in part that a lawyer shall not represent a client if the representation of that client will be directly adverse to another client, unless the lawyer reasonably believes the representation will not adversely affect the relationship with the other client; and each client consents after consultation. The essence of the rule is that of loyalty to the client. The 1981 version of the American Bar Association Model Code of Professional Responsibility provides in Canon 5:

> A lawyer should exercise independent professional judgment on behalf of a client.

The ethical considerations comment to Canon 5 states:

> EC–1 The professional judgment of a lawyer should be exercised, within the bounds of the law, solely for the benefit of his client and free of compromising influences and loyalties. Neither his personal interests, the interests of other clients, nor the desires of third persons should be permitted to dilute his loyalty to his client.

Clearly, a lawyer should not accept the employment if the lawyer's personal interests or desires will (or if there is a reasonable probability that they will) adversely affect the advice to be given or services to be rendered to the prospective client. The information that may be considered to create a conflict of interest is not limited solely to that of the attorney representing a client. It also includes the information held by another member of the legal team, including the legal assistant.

The National Federation of Paralegal Associations Model Code of Ethics provides in Canon 8:

> A paralegal shall avoid conflicts of interest and shall disclose any possible conflict to the employer or client, as well as to their prospective employers or clients.

LEARNING OBJECTIVE 3
Understand the concept of conflict of interest for the legal profession.

conflict of interest
Situations where the interests or loyalties of the lawyer and client may be or may appear to be adverse or divided.

 **WEB RESOURCES**
Ethical Perspective
Review the most current version and comments to Rule 1.7 on Conflict of Interest of the American Bar Association Model Rules of Professional Conduct at the American Bar Association website.

The ultimate obligation to determine the conflict of interest of the paralegal or legal assistant rests with the supervising attorney. Standard procedure in law firms is to check for conflicts of interest within the law firm before accepting a new client or undertaking a new matter for an existing client. Just as other attorneys are asked to review lists of new clients and new matters, so must paralegals check to be certain they do not have a conflict of interest.

Conflicts of interest may arise for paralegals when they change from one employer to another. If the previous employer represented a client or handled certain matters for a client during the period in which the paralegal was employed, a conflict of interest may exist. A more difficult concern for the paralegal is the conflict of interest that can arise from a law firm's representation of the paralegal's family members and personal friends. Paralegals frequently refer family and friends to the attorney or the law firm where they work. The mere relationship or friendship itself might not create conflict, but in some cases could give rise to a claim of undue influence wherein the paralegal may stand to benefit from the action of the law firm. Examples are the drafting of wills and trusts in which the paralegal may be named as a beneficiary or instances in which the paralegal may be named as the executor of an estate or as a trustee receiving compensation.

Ethical Wall

ethical wall
An environment in which an attorney or a paralegal is isolated from a particular case or client to avoid a conflict of interest or to protect a client's confidences and secrets.

Law firms use the term **"ethical wall"**—also called a Chinese wall (after the Great Wall of China)—to describe an environment in which an attorney or a paralegal is isolated from a particular case or client to avoid a conflict of interest or to protect a client's confidences and secrets. By creating this boundary or wall, any potential communications, whether written or oral, are prevented between members of the legal team handling a particular matter or client and the person with whom there may be a conflict of interest.

In an age of consolidation of law firms in many areas, the number of individual employers has diminished while the number of clients has increased. As a result, professionals today may find themselves in firms that were on the opposite side of cases in the past. Creating an ethical wall permits the professional to accept employment with the other firm. It also permits greater mobility by professionals, as they can go to a new firm in which there may be a conflict.

Freelance or Independent Paralegal

Freelance or independent paralegals who work for more than one firm or attorney face the potential problem of conflict of interest. Special caution has to be taken to avoid accepting employment in cases where conflicts may exist. Freelance and independent paralegals are keenly aware of this and generally take precautions to prevent conflicts.

The law firms and attorneys for whom freelance paralegals work usually are also aware of the potential for conflicts. For example, a paralegal's acceptance of employment at the retail store the firm is suing presents a conflict of interest. Knowledge of the strategy of the case would be of interest to the retail store employer. But divulging the information would breach the confidence of the law firm and the confidence of the law firm's client. Failing to disclose information to the retail store that directly affects its business would breach the duty of loyalty to that employer.

■ CONFIDENTIALITY

For the attorney, the ABA Model Rules provide in Rule 1.6, Confidentiality of Information, that a lawyer shall not reveal information relating to representation of a client unless the client consents after consultation, except for disclosures that are impliedly authorized. What is confidential information is also defined in the ABA Model Rules: "all information, regardless of the source, gained in the representation of the client." Even information that may be published in the newspaper is confidential for the lawyer and paralegal working for the client and may not be discussed with others. The newspaper article may or may not be accurate, and any discussion with others could result in discussion of items not in the newspaper story; therefore, the lawyer or paralegal cannot confirm or deny anything.

The duty of **confidentiality** is just that for the legal team: a duty. It is a duty imposed on the attorney and each member of the legal team working under the supervision of the attorney. It enables clients to obtain legal advice by allowing them to freely and openly give the members of the legal team all the relevant facts without fear of disclosure of these facts (except in limited situations, such as to prevent commission of a crime or to defend against a client's suit).

Candor and Fairness in Litigation

Litigation is the practice of advocacy, advocating a legal position to the court or trying to persuade a **trier of fact** to accept the facts as presented. It is the duty of the advocate to avoid any conduct that undermines the integrity of the process. The duty to the client to persuasively present the case is a qualified duty, qualified by the ethical obligation of **candor** to not mislead the court or opposing counsel with false statements of law or of facts that the lawyer knows to be false. Without mutual respect, honesty, and fairness, the system cannot function properly. It is a simple ethical duty to competently research and present the current case and statutory law, even when the most current version is not favorable to the position taken. In the technology age, this duty requires making a complete search for ALL the law, both statutory enactments and case law, and not just the part that is favorable to the client's position. In an age of vast numbers of electronic cases, it is easy to lose track of a few laws or enactments or not run the search as professionally as possible. Not making the proper inquiry of the client's staff to find all of the law may lead to sanctions and even disbarment.

Fairness to Opposing Party and Counsel

Fairness in the practice of law has been an issue probably as long as there has been an adversarial justice system. A number of states have established professionalism commissions and committees. Attorneys are advocates for their clients, and they occasionally forget that the purpose of the legal system is justice for all. The ethical rule of fairness to opposing counsel and parties is an attempt to set the guidelines to ensure that justice is done even if one's client loses the case. Each side is expected to use its best skills and knowledge and to present fairly its position in the form of evidence for the trier of fact to determine where the truth lies. Destroying, falsifying, or tampering with evidence destroys the fabric of the system. If people lose confidence in the system because of these unfair tactics, the system breaks down. Just consider the criminal cases where the prosecutor does not turn over, as required, **exculpatory evidence** that might show the defendant innocent.

LEARNING OBJECTIVE 4
Explain what is considered confidential under the ethical guidelines.

WEB RESOURCES

Ethical Perspective
Review the most current version and comments to Rule 1.6 on Confidentiality of Information of the American Bar Association Model Rules of Professional Conduct at the American Bar Association website.

confidentiality
Ethical obligation to keep client information confidential (not disclose) founded on the belief that clients should be able to tell their attorneys everything about their case so the attorney can give proper legal advice to the client.

LEARNING OBJECTIVE 5
Explain the reasons for the obligations of candor and fairness in litigation.

trier of facts
The trier of facts decides what facts are to be accepted and used in making the decision. It is usually a jury, but may be a judge who hears a case without a jury and decides what the facts are and applies the law.

candor
Ethical obligation to not mislead the court or opposing counsel with false statements of law or of facts that the lawyer knows to be false.

exculpatory evidence
Evidence that tends to prove the innocence of the accused or prove the facts of the defendant's case.

WEB RESOURCES

Contrast and compare the **Colorado Supreme Court Rules of Professional Conduct** at the Colorado Bar Association website with the American Bar Association Model Rules of Professional Responsibility at the ABA website and the ethical rules in your jurisdiction.

ETHICAL Perspectives

COLORADO RULES OF PROFESSIONAL CONDUCT RULE 3.3. CANDOR TOWARD THE TRIBUNAL

a. A lawyer shall not knowingly:
1. make a false statement of material fact or law to a tribunal or fail to correct a false statement of material fact or law previously made to the tribunal by the lawyer;
2. fail to disclose to the tribunal legal authority in the controlling jurisdiction known to the lawyer to be directly adverse to the position of the client and not disclosed by opposing counsel; or
3. offer evidence that the lawyer knows to be false. If a lawyer, the lawyer's client, or witness called by the lawyer has offered material evidence and the lawyer comes to know of its falsity, the lawyer shall take reasonable remedial measures, including, if necessary, disclosure to the tribunal. A lawyer may refuse to offer evidence, other than the testimony of a defendant in a criminal matter that the lawyer reasonably believes is false.
b. A lawyer who represents a client in an adjudicative proceeding and who knows that a person intends to engage, is engaging or has engaged in criminal or fraudulent conduct related to the proceeding shall take reasonable remedial measures, including, if necessary, disclosure to the tribunal.
c. The duties stated in paragraphs (a) and (b) continue to the conclusion of the proceeding, and apply even if compliance requires disclosure of information otherwise protected by Rule 1.6.
d. In an ex parte proceeding, a lawyer shall inform the tribunal of all material facts known to the lawyer that will enable the tribunal to make an informed decision, whether or not the facts are adverse.

WEB RESOURCES

Review the current language of the Federal Rules of Civil Procedure Rule 26 (one source of the rule is the website of the Cornell Law School Legal Information Institute and the related Federal Rules of Criminal Procedure Rule 16 at the same website).

The obligation of the supervising attorney to the court and to the other side may not only extend to the legal team but also may ensure that the client and the client's staff fully comply with the rules of court. Sanctions for failure to properly supervise can come from two sources: the court hearing the underlying action (as in the *Qualcomm Attorney–Client* case below) and the attorney disciplinary agency. The court typically punishes this sort of misbehavior with monetary sanctions, the purpose of which is to compensate the other side for the time and effort they have expended or will expend because of the discovery abuse. The attorney disciplinary agency's punishment can include, in extreme cases, disbarment or suspension from practice before the court for a period of time, or in less extreme cases, public or private censure. In addition, under some circumstances, "unfair" litigation tactics may result in a suit for malpractice filed by the client against the attorney and the law firm.

As noted in the opinion of the magistrate judge in the *Qualcomm v. Broadcom* case:

> ...Producing 1.2 million pages of marginally relevant documents while hiding 46,000 critically important ones does not constitute good faith and does not satisfy either the client's or attorney's discovery obligations. Similarly, agreeing to produce certain categories of documents and then not producing all of the documents that fit within such a category is unacceptable. Qualcomm's conduct warrants sanctions....C. Sanctions

The Court's review of Qualcomm's declarations, the attorneys' declarations, and Judge Brewster's orders leads this Court to the inevitable conclusion that Qualcomm intentionally withheld tens of thousands of decisive documents from its opponent in an effort to win this case and gain a strategic business advantage over Broadcom.

Qualcomm could not have achieved this goal without some type of assistance or deliberate ignorance from its retained attorneys. Accordingly, the Court concludes it must sanction both Qualcomm and some of its retained attorneys....

QUALCOMM INCORPORATED, v. BROADCOM CORPORATION, and RELATED COUNTERCLAIMS. Case No. 05cv1958-B (BLM)

Duty to Report Unethical Conduct

Lawyers have an ethical duty under Rule 8.3 of the Model Rules of Professional Responsibility to report other lawyers' violations of the ethics rules to the appropriate professional authority in the state. Lawyers must have firsthand knowledge of the violation of the rules of ethics that raises a substantial question as to another lawyer's honesty, trustworthiness, or fitness as a lawyer. This does not mean that a lawyer may make a report of ethics violations to gain a competitive advantage in a civil case. A groundless accusation of unethical conduct to gain an advantage in a civil case would itself be unethical.

In practice, it may be a close call. A lawyer may have a duty to report an adversary who files a motion known to contain false factual allegations.

CONCEPT REVIEW AND REINFORCEMENT

KEY TERMS

ethics 28	supervising attorney 35	ethical wall 38
Model Rules of Professional Conduct 28	agent 36	confidentiality 39
unauthorized practice of law (UPL) 29	principal 36	trier of facts 39
	fiduciary relationship 36	candor 39
	conflict of interest 37	exculpatory evidence 39

CHAPTER SUMMARY

ETHICS AND PROFESSIONAL RESPONSIBILITY

Introduction to Ethics and Professional Responsibility	Ethics is the set of minimally acceptable standards of conduct in a profession. Ethical guidelines are enforced by the court in the jurisdiction where the attorney practices or where the case is being tried. The supervising attorney of every legal team must follow the ethics rules and ensure that the members of the legal team follow the same rules as the supervising lawyer.
Regulation of the Practice of Law	The practice of law is regulated to protect the public from incompetent and unscrupulous practitioners.

(continued)

The Paralegal and Licensing	With a few exceptions, there is no state licensing of paralegals.
State Regulations	Some states, such as California, have regulations defining who may identify themselves as a "paralegal." A recent development is the Limited License Legal Technician. In other states, such as Florida and Ohio, the state bar association has adopted rules defining who may use the title "paralegal."
Federal Practice	Under federal regulations, nonlawyers may in some areas, such as Social Security and patent law, represent individuals and appear before agencies.
Penalties for Unauthorized Practice	Most states provide criminal penalties for the unauthorized practice of law.
Avoiding UPL	A common thread of UPL is not holding oneself out as a lawyer or giving advice when legal rights may be affected. This includes prohibitions against filling out legal forms and representing clients in court.
Ethical Obligations	Every member of the legal or trial team has an obligation to act ethically.
Duty to Supervise	All lawyers and partners in law firms are required to supervise everyone over whom they have supervisory authority. All ethical breaches by members of the legal team are ultimately those of the supervising attorney.
Ethical Guidelines and Rules	For lawyers in most states, the ethical guidelines are based on the American Bar Association's Rules of Professional Conduct, which provide a fairly uniform set of rules across the country. There are no mandatory rules for paralegals except as an obligation of membership in national paralegal organizations.
Conflict of Interest	A lawyer should not accept an engagement (representation) if the lawyer's personal interests or desires will (or if there is a reasonable probability that they will) adversely affect the advice to be given or services to be rendered to the prospective client.
Ethical Wall	An ethical wall is an environment where a person is isolated from access to information about a client or case.
Freelance or Independent Paralegal	A freelance or independent paralegal may work for more than one firm or attorney, thereby creating the potential for a conflict of interest.
Confidentiality	Every member of the legal team must understand the ethical obligations of the legal profession to protect the communications received from clients.
Candor and Fairness in Litigation	A lawyer has an ethical duty (candor) to not mislead the court even when the most current version of the law is not favorable to the client's legal position. All members of the legal team are required to make accurate inquiry and present the most current information.
Fairness to Opposing Party and Counsel	Lawyers are expected to use their best skills when presenting a case but should avoid destroying or tampering with evidence or ignoring rules of court.
Duty to Report Unethical Conduct	Lawyers have an ethical duty to report other lawyers when they have first-hand knowledge of the violation of ethics rules.

REVIEW QUESTIONS AND EXERCISES

1. What is ethics?
2. What is the purpose of the confidentiality rule in the legal setting?
3. Can the confidentiality between attorney and client be lost?
4. What ethical guidelines, if any, does your state follow?
5. What is the ethical obligation of a paralegal to the firm's client?
6. What is the ethical obligation of a paralegal to the court?
7. What is the ethical obligation of a litigation support staff member to the client? To the court? Of a litigation support person from an outside firm or consultant? Explain.
8. Why is conflict of interest an issue for the legal team?
9. What are the ethical issues for a law firm using outside computer or technology consultants?
10. Do the ethical rules of fairness prevent lawyers from aggressively advocating a client's position?
11. Why would a partner in a law firm be required to supervise the other lawyers in the firm?
12. How can members of the legal team demonstrate that they have been adequately supervised?
13. Prepare a brief note to a supervising attorney on why a failure to properly supervise could result in a problem for the attorney and the firm.
14. Prepare a memo to the supervising attorney, who has just been admitted to practice in your jurisdiction. Write about the jurisdiction's continuing legal education requirements, including any ethical education elements.

BUILDING YOUR PARALEGAL SKILLS

INTERNET AND TECHNOLOGY EXERCISES

1. Find a copy of the most current version of the Model Rules of Professional Conduct published by the American Bar Association.
2. Use the Internet to locate the most current version of the ethical rules used in your jurisdiction. Save the website address for future reference.
3. Find ethics opinions or sources of information on ethics in your jurisdiction.
4. Use the Internet to locate your state's statute on the unauthorized practice of law. How is UPL treated in your state?

CIVIL LITIGATION VIDEO CASE STUDIES

Opening Scenario Video Case Study:
Confidentiality Issue: Public Information

 The law firm has a case that has received coverage by the local press. Two paralegals from the same firm are on a coffee break at a public coffee shop. One of the paralegals is working on the case; the other is not assigned to the case but has some interest in it.

After watching the video at www.pearsonhighered .com/careersresources, answer the following questions.

1. Does the legal team working on a case have a duty to remain silent, even when information about the case has been made public?
2. If incorrect information about a case has been made public, can the members of the legal team correct any misinformation?
3. Can confidential information about cases be shared among members of the same law firm?

4. What is the difference between confidentiality and attorney–client privilege?

Parent and Child Consult the Legal Team

A student accused of injuring a school bus driver and assaulting another student on the school bus is meeting with his parent and the lawyer supplied by their homeowner's insurance company. During the meeting, while the son is being interviewed by a paralegal in another room, the parent confides confidential information to the lawyer. The son also makes confidential statements to the paralegal.

After watching the video at www.pearsonhighered.com/careersresources, answer the following questions.

1. To whom does the attorney–client privilege belong?
2. Does a minor have an attorney–client privilege that requires withholding confidential information from his parent?

3. If the insurance company is paying for the defense, is it entitled to know the information the minor considers privileged?

Solicitation in the ER: Ethical Duties of the Profession

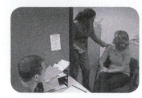

The mother of a child injured on a school bus is seeking information about her daughter from the emergency room clerk, who recommends and introduces her to a paralegal, who solicits the mother's case.

After watching the video at www.pearsonhighered.com/careersresources, answer the following questions.

1. What are the ethical guidelines on soliciting cases in the hospital setting?
2. Has the paralegal violated any ethical rules in asking the parent to meet with the attorney for whom the paralegal works?

CHAPTER OPENING SCENARIO CASE STUDY

Continue to maintain a time log of your activity in the course.

BUILDING YOUR PROFESSIONAL PORTFOLIO AND REFERENCE MANUAL

CIVIL LITIGATION TEAM AT WORK

See page 18 for instructions on Building Your Professional Portfolio and Reference Manual.

Policy

1. Prepare a script to use when a client, friend, or family member asks for legal advice.
2. Prepare a script to introduce yourself and define for the client or witness your role and limitations as a paralegal.
3. Compile supervising attorney contact information and notes on when he or she is available.
4. Compile procedures for determining who is the supervising attorney and when the supervising attorney is to be contacted.
5. Prepare a sample firm policy on discussion of cases among the litigation team, and others in the law firm not working on a particular case.
6. Prepare a sample firm policy for ethics training for the various members of the litigation team.

7. Prepare guidelines to ensure all staff members are properly supervised.
8. Describe procedures to protect confidential information and litigation work product.

Procedures

Obtain your local jurisdiction's continuing legal education requirements for:

1. Attorneys
2. Paralegals

Contacts and Resources

For your state and local bar association, obtain

1. Mailing addresses
2. Phone and fax numbers
3. Web and e-mail addresses
4. Web address of your jurisdiction's version of the Model Rules of Professional Conduct
5. Web address of ethics opinions for your jurisdiction

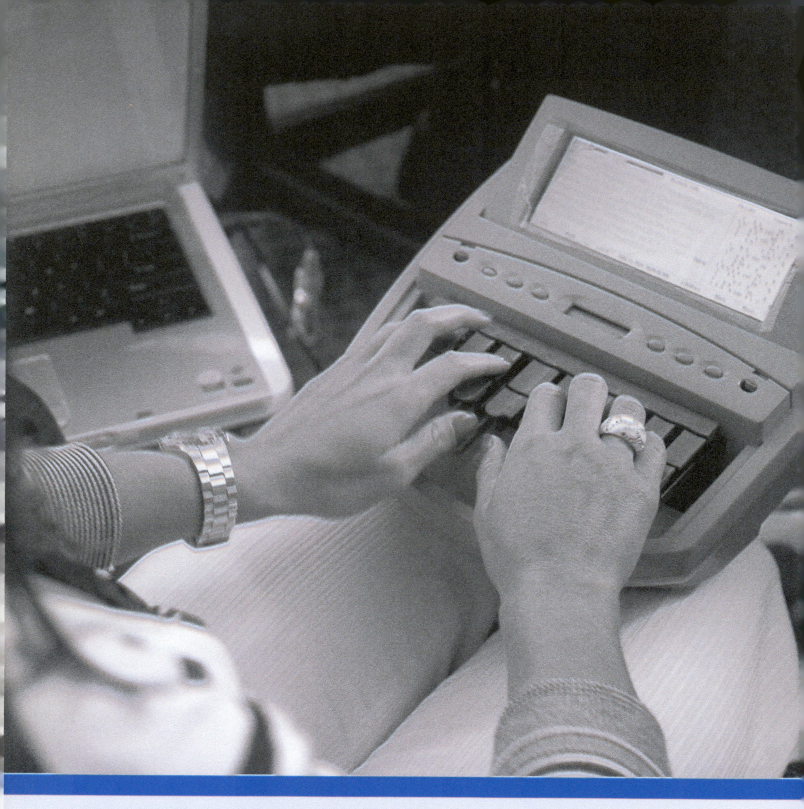

LEARNING OBJECTIVES

After studying this chapter, you should be able to:

1. Explain the use of technology in civil litigation and case management.

2. Describe the function and elements of electronic database software.

3. Explain how case management software systems can enable the legal team to work on cases more efficiently.

4. Explain the reasons for the use of software for managing litigation cases.

5. Explain the role of office management software in the operation of the law office.

Litigation Management and Technology

CHAPTER 3

OPENING SCENARIO

With two separate and growing offices, it was clear that a practices and procedures manual dealing with technology issues in civil litigation was essential. The two offices had to work together on many of the cases because each office, alone, lacked the resources to hire additional staff or attorneys. Managing the staff and office administration for both locations from the suburban office was a concern for the office manager/paralegal. She began to realize that everyone was depending on her to coordinate the activities and operations. When she returned to the office after attending an advanced paralegal education seminar, she understood what the speaker meant when he referred to people in her position as the critical "paralegal portal" in the firm. Her job was to maintain relationships with clients by keeping them informed; facilitate communication among the lawyers, opposing counsel, staff, and clients; and ensure that the litigation team collaborated in an efficient, effective manner.

Organizing information on cases and litigation was critical. With the remote operations, each member of the litigation team had to have a secure method to access critical confidential information at any time from either office—or even from the court or at home. Ethical issues of conflict of interest were also becoming a concern as new clients came in, the practice grew, and new consultants and legal staff from other law firms were hired to work on the cases. It was obvious that she could no longer rely on a paper system; going paperless in the offices and using software to manage the information and cases were now necessary, if for no other reason than the time and billing functions were now more essential to the firm's cash flow needs. Bills had to be accurately prepared and sent out on a regular basis.

OPENING SCENARIO LEARNING OBJECTIVE

Describe the use of technology in managing a legal practice efficiently and effectively.

■ INTRODUCTION TO LITIGATION MANAGEMENT AND TECHNOLOGY

Before the introduction of computers, litigation was defined by the ability to present cases using verbal communication skills, which were occasionally supported by hard-copy exhibit displays. As the world has changed and technology has become an integral part of daily life, those who litigate cases must also integrate computer technology into the handling and presentation of cases. Judges and juries have come to expect more than just classic legal oratory; they expect to see cases presented using computer monitors and video displays not unlike what they see on television. The underlying sources of evidence have shifted from a paper trail of letters and documents to an electronic trail of e-mails, electronically stored information, and Internet-available media. The tools and the skills necessary to be a successful litigator or litigation paralegal have changed. With the increased use of electronic devices for everything from communications to data storage and transmission, the volume of information has also increased exponentially. Paralegals are today charged with finding, protecting, storing, retrieving, and producing evidence and information with a few clicks of a computer keyboard and mouse. Whereas in the past, everything about a case could be found in the case file boxes in the office of the supervising attorney or his paralegal, today the case file information may be stored on a laptop, a file server in the office, or a remote data center. Success in the field of litigation requires an understanding of the tools and the process of using technology.

Older medical records and business records are still in paper form or are in photographic forms like microfilm and microfiche and have not been converted to electronic storage. However, these older storage methods are gradually being phased out in most cases in favor of electronic duplication and storage.

Until recently, uncertain that the "new" technology worked, many businesses and law offices kept both paper and electronic versions. The paper copy was the final version and the electronic file was a copy for use as a template or for making changes to the "final" paper document. Until recently, paper copies were the dominant items requested in discovery. Responses to interrogatories frequently came with paper records attached and only rarely with any electronic response. Many cases today still require access to paper records. For example, a medical malpractice action filed today may have its origins ten to eighteen years ago, when the plaintiff was a child and the statute of limitation extended until the minor reached the age of majority. At that time, hospitals and doctors kept records in paper form or converted them to a paper substitute, such as microfilm or microfiche. Other examples are the product-defect or liability cases such as the tobacco industry litigation, which started before records were routinely kept electronically.

LEARNING OBJECTIVE 1
Explain the use of technology in civil litigation and case management.

■ TECHNOLOGY IN CIVIL LITIGATION

The increased use of technology and computers in the law office, the court system, and the courtroom has changed the way many traditional law office functions and procedures are performed. The computer and the Internet are increasingly used, not just for traditional document preparation, but also for maintaining client databases, keeping office and client accounting records, communicating, legal and factual researching, filing documents with the court, sharing files with other counsel, producing documents in discovery, and presenting during trial.

Computers are being used with greater frequency to share information in digital format by the use of the Internet among remote offices, courthouses, government agencies, and clients. The trend is toward eliminating paper in the law office through the use of computer technology and software.

Online Data Storage and Collaboration

Members of the civil litigation team frequently find themselves working from locations outside the traditional office. In some cases, the legal team is composed of members who work from home, are located in different offices of the firm, or are members of different law firms located in different parts of the country or the world. Each member of the team, whether in the office, in depositions, or in court, may need access to the case data or electronic files. One solution is to have all of the files stored electronically in an **electronic repository** on a secure, protected file server to which everyone authorized has access over the Internet. The use of a secure repository that is accessible over the Internet by authorized users is sometimes referred to as **cloud computing.**

Members of the team may use the Internet to work collaboratively in real time, using **online collaboration** systems that allow each person to see the documents and, in some cases, each other, and to make on-screen notes and comments. A number of companies provide services and software for converting case documents to electronic format and storing them on a secure server. Collaboration software is provided for the individual members of the legal or litigation team. The litigation team must address technology and its impact on how documents are created, stored, and destroyed by clients. As a result of the rules on electronic discovery that were introduced in 2006 by the federal courts, the team must also address the impact that actual or potential litigation has on the rules for document retention and preservation in order to avoid claims of **spoliation of evidence.** State courts are also looking at these issues, and many have implemented or are implementing their own rules, frequently fashioned after the federal rules.

Among the important rules and case law decisions are those directing counsel to ensure, by putting a **litigation hold** on potential evidence, that clients do not destroy electronically stored documents. Courts are now imposing the obligation on the litigation team to ensure that clients preserve evidence.

electronic repository
A secure, protected file server to which everyone authorized has access over the Internet.

cloud computing
The access over the Internet of a secure repository by authorized users.

online collaboration
Members of the team using the Internet to work collaboratively using online software that allows each person to see the documents, and in some cases each other, and make on-screen notes and comments.

spoliation of evidence
Destruction of records that may be relevant to ongoing or anticipated litigation, government investigation, or audit. Courts differ in their interpretation of the level of intent required before sanctions may be warranted.

litigation hold
A process whereby a company or individual determines an unresolved dispute may result in litigation and, as a result, documents should not be destroyed or altered.

VIDEO ADVICE FROM THE FIELD

INTERVIEW: ROLE OF PARALEGAL IN LITIGATION

Charlotte Harris, Manager, Litigation Support, Hess Corporation.

A discussion of the role of litigation support personnel in the litigation process.

After watching the video at www.pearsonhighered.com/ careersresources, answer the following questions.

1. Why is it frequently necessary to have a third party at the meet and confer between the trial attorneys?
2. What is the role of the forensic expert in a trial?
3. What is the role of litigation support in educating others?

With the potentially massive delivery of documents in electronic form comes the concern that in delivering vast amounts of electronic documents, some confidential or attorney–client privileged material may inadvertently be produced to opposing counsel. These documents may be accidentally delivered to the opposing side even after review for privileged or confidential material. Because reviews are frequently performed by paralegals, it is important for them to know the rules of evidence and ethical responsibilities surrounding the issue of confidentiality and attorney–client privilege and the steps to take to retrieve the information and documents.

No longer can the legal team ignore the role of technology in use by clients or in litigation, whether the legal team is a sole practitioner with just a legal secretary or a mega-member international law firm with in-house technical support. Everyone on the legal team must understand the role of the various technologies in counseling and representing clients.

■ ELECTRONIC DATABASE BASICS

LEARNING OBJECTIVE 2
Describe the function and elements of electronic database software.

Databases are programs used to store information. After word processing programs, database programs are the most frequently used type of computer program. The advantage of a database program is its ability to search for individual or groups of words or numbers, to sort the results in some meaningful way such as by date, and then to show the results on a computer screen or in a hard-copy printout. For example, demographic data collected may be sorted by zip code, which by itself is not a very meaningful result. But adding to this result a search by zip code and income, sex, and number of children provides a good picture of the demographics of an area, such as the surveys conducted by the Census Bureau every ten years.

Electronic discovery software permits documents to be entered into a database and stored by key terms, phrases, or other criteria that then can be sorted to find patterns and connections. With a few keystrokes, lists of documents can be prepared for manual review, like an Internet search that produces a list of locations to check for desired content or products.

In addition to the obvious use of avoiding accepting representation of a client with a potential conflict of interest, the information in a database of contacts and clients may be used in firm public relations and marketing activities. Many firms use the information to send holiday, birthday, and anniversary greetings and to collect information on updates of specific changes in the law for which a client has previously consulted the firm.

Data Repositories

A database program is a repository of information of all types that can be sorted and presented in a desired, meaningful manner. The word "database" is just computer talk for a collection of information. For example, a Contact Database in a case management program is nothing more than a collection of information about people: their names, phone numbers, addresses, and maybe birthdays or other related information.

Besides basic contact information, other information can be collected such as occupation, children's names and dates of birth, or any other combination of information. In pre-computer days, databases were represented by a box or boxes of 3 × 5 cards with the information about clients or important dates. These were the heart of the conflict of interest or deadline databases. The date or calendar database was checked daily and a list made up for members of the legal team of such things as deadlines, statutes of limitations, and appointments. Conflicts of interest were checked in the same way, via a search of the cards maintained alphabetically in the boxes. In some offices, a card was prepared for all opposing parties. Each of these "decks of cards" was a database.

The electronic database is nothing more than a version of the cards in the boxes—except that more information can be automatically checked more quickly and more accurately—no more misfiled cards out of alphabetical order. A database is essentially an electronic card with information that can be searched using a set of things to look for and presented in a predefined manner or report. When information about a person is needed, the report showing the information is compiled by asking the database program to look up the person's information and show it on the computer screen, or in a printed format called a report. Any combination of information, or queries, can be requested for a report about a single person or a list of all people or contacts with the same information such as zip code; or a more detailed report can be prepared combining specific items, such as zip code and male or female, with a birthday before or after a certain date. Exhibit 3.1 shows an intake template and a contact form for the input of information into a contacts management database for one record. One of the advantages of the modern database is its ability to search across a number of different sets of information and sort the data according to a predefined set of criteria. Some have likened the World Wide Web to a big database that can be searched using a search engine. The database is the place where information is stored until a request is made for a report showing some or all of the information in a certain format or appearance.

Navigating Electronic Databases

Electronic databases use standard terminology to describe parts of the database: table, field, cell, and record, as shown in Exhibit 3.2.

Databases are collections of tables. Tables contain fields of information (data); a field is one type of information, like last name. A record is all the

Exhibit 3.1 An intake template and a contact form

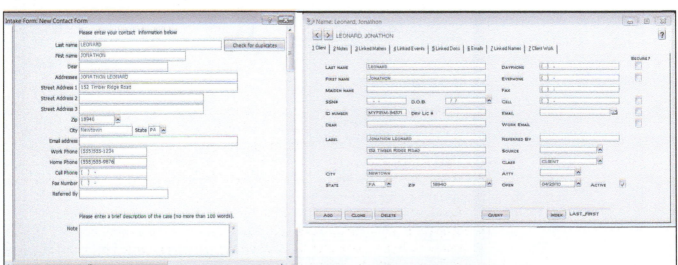

Exhibit 3.2 Parts of the database: table, field, cell, and record

This entire group of records represents the
SalesDeptContactInfo table

	ContactID	First Name	Last Name	CompanyName	Street Address	City	State	Business Phone
▶	1	Susan	Scantosi	eWidgetPlus	363 Rogue Street	St. Louis	MO	(612) 444-1236
	2	Thomas	Mazeman	BooksRUs	2165 Piscotti Ave	Springfield	IL	(888) 234-6983
	3	Douglas	Seaver	Printing Solutions	7700 First Ave	Topeka	KS	(888) 988-2678
	4	Amir	Ramiv	TechStands	1436 Riverfront Place	St. Louis	MO	(877) 867-7656
	5	Franklin	Scott	WorksSuite	8789 Ploughman Drive	Tulsa	OK	(800) 864-2390
	6	Ronald	Komeika	Creekside Financia	1264 Pond Hill Road	Toledo	OH	(343) 333-3333
	7	Barbara	Mitchell	Market Tenders	9823 Bridge Street	LaPorte	IN	(888) 238-2123
✱	(AutoNumber)							

The category First Name
is a field

A cell is the box containing
the information

All the information for Douglas
Seaver represents one record

Source: Screenshot "Electronic Databases Use Standard Terminology To Describe Parts Of The Database: Table, Field, Cell, And Record." Used by permission of Microsoft Corporation.

information about one item or person; for example, Exhibit 3.3 shows a record of information for one person. Think of the database as being a file cabinet; a table being a file drawer for a specific set of information like business contacts; the record being the individual file for each contact; and the field being individual pieces of information about the person.

Microsoft Access is a database widely used because of its inclusion with the Microsoft Office Suite. The Microsoft Access layout shown in Exhibit 3.4 is one

Exhibit 3.3 Contact details

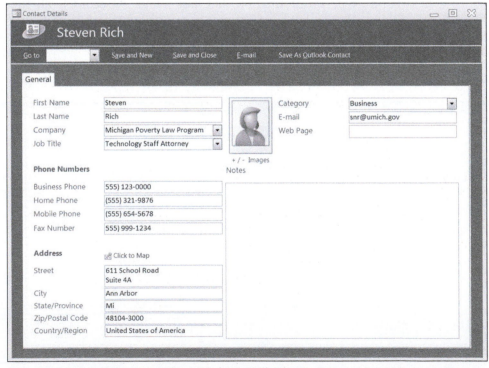

Source: Screenshot "A Record Is All The Information About One Item Or Person." Used by permission of Microsoft Corporation.

Exhibit 3.4 Record for business contact

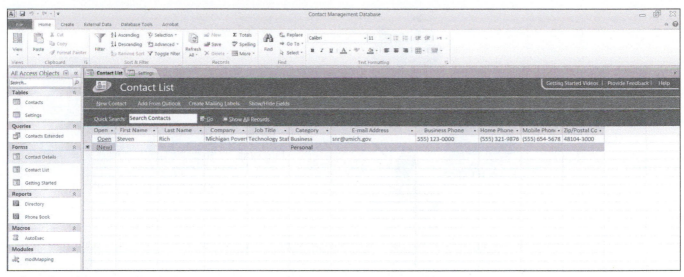

Source: Screenshot "Microsoft Access Layout." Used by permission of Microsoft Corporation.

way of presenting the basic elements of a database—the fields, records, and cells. The same elements may appear in a different layout, such as the Contact Details in Exhibit 3.2.

Tables

Databases can and frequently do contain two or more tables. For example, a database used in a legal office may have one table for employees of the firm, another for clients of the firm, a third for opposing attorneys, and a fourth for the opposing parties in cases the firm has handled.

Reports

Reports present the data from the database in an organized presentation. A report may present just the information from one table, such as employee birthdays. Frequently, a report shows the outcome of searching multiple tables and displays the relationships among the information and data from the different tables, such as a report of the employees that have ever worked for an opposing counsel in a case against a client.

Database Terminology Summary

Databases are collections of **tables.**
Tables contain **records.**
A **record** is all the information about one item or person; for example,
records contain **fields** of information (data).
Fields contain **cells.**
A **field** is one type of information.
A **cell** is the box containing the individual field information, like a last name.

database
A collection of similar records.

Database Example

One of the most significant legal cases in modern history was the Enron case, in which many individuals and institutions lost millions of dollars. The underlying case was built from an analysis of e-mails and other documents created and

Exhibit 3.5 Secure remote access

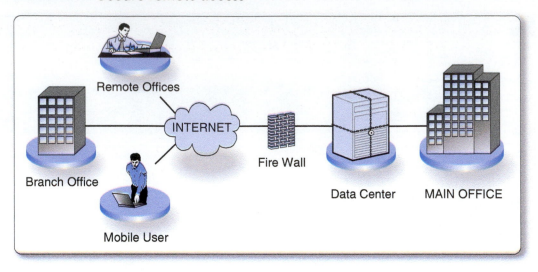

stored electronically at Enron. Databases were an important tool in accessing the information contained within the more than one million e-mails and documents in the investigation by the Federal Energy Regulatory Commission, or FERC, an independent agency that regulates the interstate transmission of natural gas, oil, and electricity. FERC made available the ESI by use of the Internet and the third-party electronic document review software called iCONECT nXT, as shown in the exhibit below. This is a good example of the use of the Internet and cloud computing, where information is made available for all those needing access over the Internet via a remote, hosted, secure electronic case review tool, as illustrated in Exhibit 3.5.

Exhibits 3.6 and 3.7 of iCONECT nXT show an example of access to a database, in this example, the case material in the investigation of Enron, with the results of searches of the e-mail database using selected terms.

Exhibit 3.6 FERC investigation material on a cloud-based system

Source: iCONECT Development, LLC. All rights reserved.

Exhibit 3.7 E-mails sorted by selected database fields

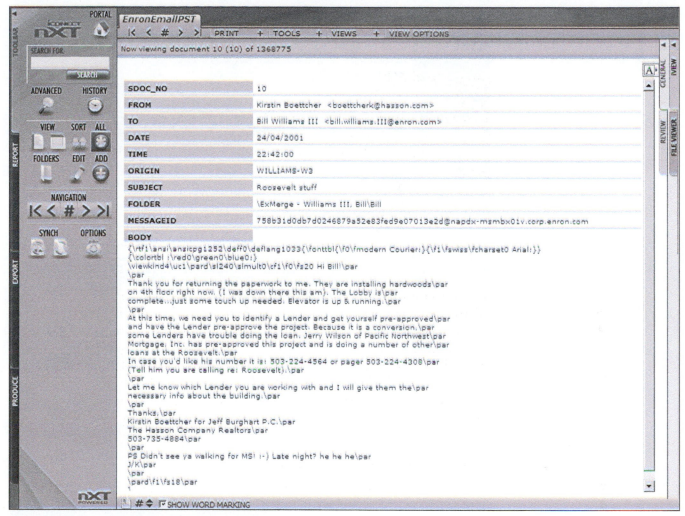

One of 1,368,775 e-mails is shown sorted by the following database fields:

SDOC_NO
FROM
TO
DATE
TIME
ORIGIN
FOLDER
ATTACHMENT

The results of a subsequent query using the name WILLIAMS from the initial search above is shown in Exhibit 3.8.

A summary **report** can be customized by the user to generate a comprehensive overview of relevant material, as shown in Exhibit 3.9.

Exhibit 3.8 Results of query using the name WILLIAMS

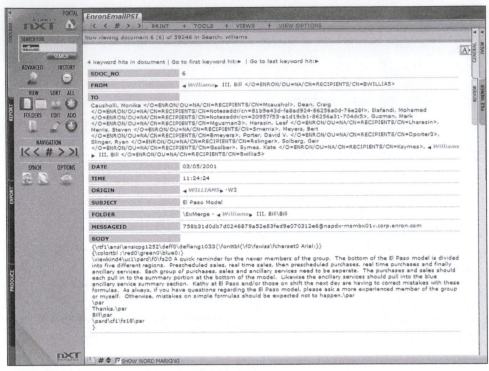

Exhibit 3.9 Custom summary reports

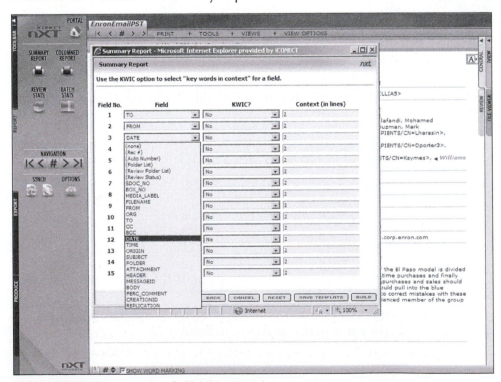

Database Issues in Litigation

The litigation team is the interface between the client, and the opposing side and the court. Discovery requests are filtered through counsel. It is the trial counsel's duty to obtain accurate responses to the legitimate discovery requests for electronic discovery. Trial counsel and the litigation team must know enough about the client's system for creating and storing and ultimately deleting electronically stored information to avoid claims of dilatory conduct and a lack of candor to the court.

Searches—Constructing the Query

Anyone who has ever conducted a search on the Internet using a single word or even a combination of a few words knows that such a search may not produce the desired results. Searching legal databases is also frequently frustrating if the exact, proper term is not entered as used in those databases. Searching electronically stored information when there are no universal, common terms or phrases such as the West Keywords can be difficult. For this reason, a number of new search methods have been developed and continue to be developed and refined to overcome the limitation of the traditional Boolean search using words and connectors like AND, OR, and NOT. Some database software search engines can isolate and identify previously unknown patterns or trends in large amounts of data. Conceptual searching, a type of search that looks for meaning, not specific letters in words, looks for information that is conceptually similar to the words in the search query. For example, a conceptual search for the phrase "breakfast foods" returns items of foods eaten for breakfast. One- or two-word conceptual queries rarely return good results, whereas more detailed queries, such as "what is eaten at a Sunday Mother's Day brunch," would result in additional, related items like "champagne," the mixed drinks served, and, potentially, all the other items served at a large buffet.

The Reality of Using Databases

The reality is that legal team members, lawyers, paralegals, and legal assistants rarely create their own databases. In some cases, a simple database of a single table might be used to sort or organize some information, such as the client list or conflict list.

So why do we need to learn about databases? While members of the legal team may not actually create their own databases, they do use them all the time. Virtually every law office's specialty application program for managing the office, cases, or documents in litigation is a database. Software vendors have created applications for the legal community. They have custom-designed the Form Views for input of information and the query forms for generating the desired reports, and set up the search and presentation algorithms (formulas for searching). When special applications are required, many of the software vendors will create custom tables and report generators, such as those for a particular area of practice, like estates.

Knowing what a database is and the associated terminology makes working with the software developer, in-house IT professional, or outside consultant easier and more effective in obtaining what is needed, wanted, and possible. Knowing how a database works and is organized makes the software applications that are based on database designs easier to use and work with. As electronic discovery becomes a more significant part of litigation, database programs will play an increasing role in the discovery process. In-house and electronic discovery vendor programs use databases to perform the functions of search, analysis, and reporting. Members of the litigation team must have a good basis in database operations and terminology to be able to communicate with the technical and litigation support members of the litigation team as well as to avoid claims by the court of lack of competency in the e-discovery process.

■ ORGANIZING AND MANAGING CASE FILES

LEARNING OBJECTIVE 3
Explain how case management software systems can enable the legal team to work on cases more efficiently.

tangible evidence
Physical objects.

trial notebook
Summary of the case, usually contained in a tabbed, three-ring binder with sections such as pleadings, motions, law, pretrial memo, and witnesses.

Effectively managing a case may involve reviewing, sorting, and marking for identification hundreds or even thousands of documents, photographs, and other graphics. Careful tracking and handling of evidence should start at the beginning of the case. Good case management requires a thoughtful process for storing, handling, examining, evaluating, and indexing every page. In the computer age, case management includes making decisions about the appropriateness and potential use of electronic display technologies (as well as traditional paper exhibit presentations) in court. **Tangible evidence**—physical items such as defective products in a strict liability action or an automobile in a motor vehicle accident—may have to be obtained and preserved for examination by expert witnesses or for use at trial.

There are almost as many different approaches to setting up case files and managing cases as there are legal teams. One of the traditional approaches includes the case notebook, or case **trial notebook.** Summary information about the case is maintained in a notebook with tabs for each major activity, party, expert, or element of proof needed, as shown in Exhibit 3.10.

With the use of a trial notebook comes the responsibility to maintain the case file and file boxes or file cabinets in which the hard copies of documents, exhibits, and physical evidence are maintained. If only one trial or case notebook is kept for the team, someone on the litigation team must take responsibility to be certain that there is no duplication of effort and that the most current information is entered. When multiple copies are used, each trial notebook must be updated regularly, again to be sure that there is no duplication of effort and that current activity information is made available to all members of the legal team.

Even in less complex litigation, the amount of paper that must be monitored and carried to court can be overwhelming. It is not unusual to see lawyers and their litigation support team using hand trucks to move file boxes to depositions or to court for trial. While there is a certain comfort in having the original paper copy, this is not always practical or realistic in contemporary cases; much of the documentation is in the form of electronically stored records for which there may not be an "original" hard copy. Even in simple traffic accident cases, much of the documentation is stored on a computer in electronic format, such as the accident report prepared by the investigating officers that is submitted electronically online to the police department and the state. Obtaining a hard copy of the report requires a computer and printer. In court, the report may be better shown to all by way of a computer presentation.

Exhibit 3.10 Tabs for the case notebook and the trial notebook

When there are hundreds or thousands of such documents, having a system for electronically storing, locating, and retrieving them becomes essential. For the litigation paralegal, the ability to quickly find the documents and then project them on the trial attorney's computer or the court computer screen in trial is a timesaver and stress reliever. No more scrambling through boxes of paper to find the specific item that is suddenly required as a result of unexpected testimony of a witness.

Every case starts with basic information in the form of interview notes and research by attorneys, paralegals, and investigators. Documents that may be used as evidence are gathered in paper or electronic form. Members of the legal team must analyze the facts and the documents to decide on the most appropriate course of action. Ultimately, pleadings and exhibits are prepared for use at trial. The question is how to organize everything in a meaningful way that allows access to those who need to know—when and where they need it. In the boxed paper file case, there is always the concern that someone has removed something without leaving a form or note to indicate that it has been taken it out of the file. Exhibit 3.11 shows the flow of information in a typical case, using CaseMap as a case management tool.

Exhibit 3.11 Case organization flowchart using LexisNexis CaseMap

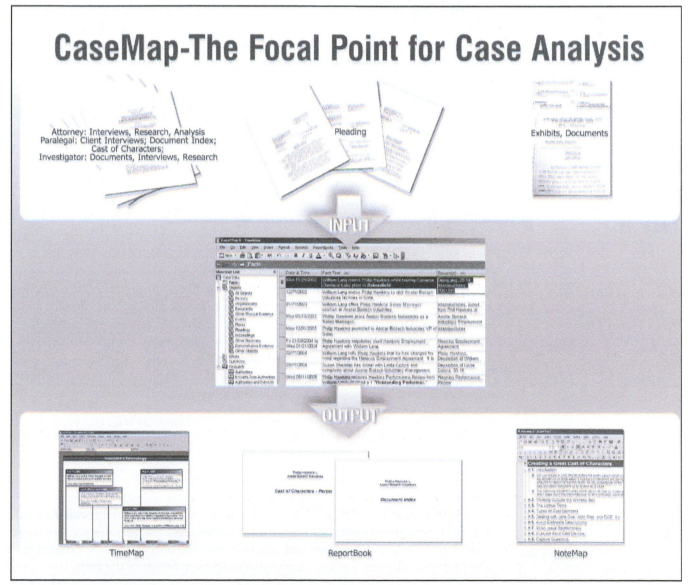

■ CASE AND PRACTICE MANAGEMENT SOFTWARE

LEARNING OBJECTIVE 4
Explain the reasons for the use of software for managing litigation cases.

Rarely do members of a legal team work on only one case. In some instances, different members of different teams may work on cases together. For example, a litigation support paralegal may work for different attorneys handling different cases in different areas of the law. The legal team may work on a number of cases at the same time, and each case may be in a different stage of preparation for trial. With the team approach to handling cases, each member of the team must be able to access case information and know what the other members of the team have done and what still needs to be done. In the traditional paper file case management approach, the physical file is the repository of everything from interview notes to pleadings and exhibits. As the team works on the case, members must locate the physical file and remove the needed folder. In the **paperless office,** everything, in theory, is available on the computer screen. Documents are stored electronically: pleadings and notes are saved as word processor files, and transcripts of depositions and court hearings might be scanned for electronic storage. For the case with voluminous paperwork and many days' or weeks' worth of deposition transcripts, the only way to access relevant documents or appropriate deposition notes quickly and efficiently is by use of computer software. The creation of documents in electronic format and the scanning of existing paper documents into electronic format allow the storage of shared documents from any data storage device. In some cases, the files are stored on remote file servers of outside consultants and vendors, sometimes called **e-repositories or online document repositories,** with remote access permitted only by authorization.

paperless office
Office where documents are created, stored, received, and sent electronically.

e-repository (online document repository)
An electronic data storage facility accessed using the Internet.

A number of software programs can be used to manage the law office and the cases within the office. These are generally called **case management** or **practice management systems.** Practice management programs have evolved out of the early programs that tracked time spent on cases, sometimes with a calendar component that could be used to track deadlines such as the statute of limitations for a case. Modern programs may include practice management functions such as time keeping, cost tracking, calendaring, conflict checking, scheduling, and contact management. Others allow for management of individual cases, including tracking of documents, parties, issues, and events.

case management system
Software for organizing the parts of a case in a central repository that can be shared by all members of the legal team.

practice management system
Programs for managing the daily operations and functions of an office.

There is a close relationship between office management and case management functions. Some of the functions overlap; for example, contact management (maintaining information for contacting clients, parties, and others, like mail and e-mail addresses and home, work, and cell telephone numbers) is a part of office management and of case management. Many of the specific specialty applications of software programs used to perform these functions duplicate the automation of these functions.

Case management programs typically store and index for quick access contact information, such as names and information on clients, parties, witnesses, opposing counsel, experts, judges, and anyone else associated with the case in any manner. They also provide links, in the form of a path, to the location where the document is stored. For example,

Server or Computer Drive	\Folder	\subfolder	\file name	.file format
C:	\clients	\Leonard	\police report	.pdf.

CaseMap

CaseMap™ from LexisNexis® is a case management and analysis software tool that acts as a central repository for critical case knowledge. As facts are gathered, parties identified, and documents and research assembled, they may be entered into the program, allowing for easy organization and exploration of the facts, the cast of

WEB RESOURCES
Find more information on central hosting servers at the IQwestIT website.

characters, and the issues by any member of the legal team. It also allows for creating specialty reports and documents including trial notebook information.

Cases (or matters, as they are sometimes called) are issues that a client has presented to a legal team to handle and resolve. Cases are sometimes referred to in the office as the "client file" or the "client file on the [name of topic] matter." A case file in a simple case like the "Gordon Power of Attorney file" or the "Leonard Will file" may consist of only a few pages of information obtained from the client, a copy of an old document, and the final document prepared for the client's signature. In a more complex case like a tort claim involving a building under construction, or an employment discrimination class action, the case file may consist of thousands of documents with hundreds of people involved as parties (plaintiffs and defendants), witnesses, and experts—and a dozen or more members of the legal team who will work on the case and need access to the information.

It is possible to handle a complex case without computers. For hundreds of years, lawyers have handled cases, pushed papers around, moved file boxes, and spent hours reviewing documents, creating indexes and catalogues, and writing notes to others working on the case.

Manual case management for the legal team may include the creation and use of a case notebook and a trial notebook. These are tabbed binders with a tab for each major element of the case. In some cases, an entire binder may be devoted to one topic, like witnesses or documents.

The following is a representative listing of tabs and a sample of the form that might be used.

cases
Issues that a client has presented to a legal team to handle and resolve.

■ Things to Do

Date Due	What	Responsible Party
6-30-2010	Obtain accident report	J L Investigator
7-15-2010	Interview investigating police officer	

■ Parties/Witnesses

Name	Address	Home Phone	Work Phone	Comments
Nancy Smith	333 Main St	123-456-7890	987-654-3210	Passenger in other car
K. Lombardo	222 South St	555-111-2222	555-333-4444	School bus driver letting off passengers facing accident scene

■ Documents

Bates #	Document Name	Date	Comments	Author
P001–P003	Police accident report	5-15-2010	Shows citations issued to Def.	Officer Hannah
P002	Repair record	4-20-2009	Shows brake problem in Def. car	Newtown auto repair mechanic Ed

■ **Research/Authorities**

Name	Jurisdiction	Type	Citation	Description
Bell v. Farmers Insurance Exchange	Cal. Super. Ct	Case law	234 Cal. 456	Compensation issue
Driving too fast for conditions	Cal	Statute	43 Ca. Code	Defines standards for...

A more complete list of tabs for the case notebook and the trial notebook is shown in Exhibit 3.10. Each of the pages in the case or trial notebook can be created using a word processing program and the table feature, with headings added as shown in previous samples. They could also be created using a spreadsheet or database program, depending on the need to sort information or extract information using database queries.

The manual method will work in smaller cases. In the days before computers, that was the only method available. Preprinted forms were used before forms were created with the word processing table feature. Database applications were accomplished by entering the information, such as witness contacts, on individual cards. In cases involving multiple members of the litigation team, constant questions heard in the offices were, "Who has the case file?" or "Who took home the evidence binder?" Similar pleas were heard regarding the location of a missing portion of a file needed by another member of the team to enter data, review information, or prepare documents.

However, the advent of the computer has been both a blessing and a curse. It has been, for some, a curse because it is so easy to create electronic documents that *may* be relevant to a case. Consider the number of e-mails generated each day in large organizations; these may need to be reviewed to find relevant documents to prove a large multinational financial institution created a hostile working environment or sexually harassed employees. The blessing is that computers can also be used to search for relevant terms in a document and can automatically eliminate duplicates of the same e-mail.

Case management software can be used to organize the cast of characters in a case—the documents, the relevant timetable, issues, legal authority, and other desired information. Good case management software organizes the data and provides it to everyone working on the case. Individuals are then able to input information on the portions for which they are responsible, and everyone has computer access to the information through a local network, a wide area network, or cloud computing.

The typical file or case starts with an interview with the client. In the precomputer days, in offices that had formalized their "paper system," this consisted of a client accident interview form, as shown in Exhibit 3.12, completed by the person who conducted the initial interview. The system may have also included the use of forms for gathering and organizing information from fact witnesses (Exhibit 3.13) and experts (Exhibit 3.14), and a summary system for recording and easy retrieval of key information on the outside of the file folder or on a paper data sheet on the inside cover.

The forms you see in Exhibit 3.15 and others like them are still used in many offices—not as a repository of the information, but as the input documents for

Exhibit 3.12 Paper-based interview form—Accident fact sheet

INVESTIGATION CHECKLIST

Client name

Phone (hm)   (wk)   (cell)

Current address

Prior address(es)

Date of birth   Place of birth

Social Security No.

VEHICLE CLIENT OPERATING/PASSENGER

Owner and type of motor vehicle

Insurance Co.   Policy number

Insurance company contact   Phone

Date of incident   Time of day   Weather conditions

Location of incident

City, State   County   Municipality

Opposing party

Address

Phone (hm)   (wk)   (cell)

Owner and type of motor vehicle

Insurance Co.   Policy number

FACT WITNESSES

Name   Address

Name   Address

Name   Address

Name of ambulance

Name of hospital

Police report issued   Copy ordered

Photographs of scene taken

Name of treating physicians

EXPERT WITNESSES

Name   Address

Name   Address

Summary of cause of action

Attach detailed accident/incident description, accident reports, and diagrams.

the computerized system used for case management. More impatient users can even bypass the paper input forms and enter the information directly using a smartphone, laptop, or tablet PC or by keyboarding directly into a workstation. Some case management programs have provisions for scanning in data directly from forms and templates. Exhibit 3.15 is a sample of the AbacusLaw form that is designed for importing information directly into the program database.

Exhibit 3.13 Paper-based interview form—Witness information

Witness Information

CLIENT PERSONAL DATA

Client Name	Case No.	File No.

Address	City, State, Zip	Phone

CASE DATA

File Label	Case issue	Date

Responsible Attorney(s)

WITNESS DATA

Witness Name

Aliases, if any	US Citizen ☐ Yes ☐ No

Current Address	City, State, Zip	Phone

Past Address(es)

Date & Place of Birth	Sex	Race	Age	Current Marital Status ☐ Single ☐ Divorced
Name of Spouse	Number/Former Marriages		Number/Children	☐ Married ☐ Widowed ☐ Separated

Name of Children (natural & adopted)	Age	Name	Age
_____	___	_____	___
_____	___	_____	___
_____	___	_____	___

Current Employer

Address	City, State, Zip	Phone

Job Title	Supervisor	From	To

Previous Employer

Address	City, State, Zip	Phone

Job Title	Supervisor	From	To

Education/Name of School	City/State	From	To	Degree
High School				
College				
Technical/Other				

Witness for ☐ Plaintiff ☐ Defendant	Type of Witness ☐ Expert ☐ Character ☐ Eye Witness	Have you ever been a party or witness in a court suit? ☐ No ☐ Yes

If yes, where & when

OTHER PERTINENT DATA

Form 8587 · 9/86 SYCOM Madison, WI Printed in U.S.A.

As the different members of the legal team—lawyers, paralegals, investigators, and secretaries—obtain the information, they can enter it into the case management software and update the case file as new information becomes available.

A typical case file contains documentation of the:

■ interview of the client;

■ interviews of fact and expert witnesses;

Exhibit 3.14 Expert witness interview form

EXPERT WITNESS CHECKLIST

BACKGROUND

| Full name | Date of birth |

Business address

| Business telephone number | Business fax number |

| Business email address | Business website |

Locations of prior offices

Home address

Home telephone number

EDUCATION

| Schools attended | Dates of attendance |

Degrees or honors awarded

Continuing education courses

WORK HISTORY

| Place of employment | Dates of employment |

Job description

Reasons for leaving

Specific area of expertise

Published articles and books

Professional affiliations

Professional magazines subscribed to

Licenses and jurisdictions

Litigations or disciplinary action

PRIOR LEGAL EXPERIENCE

Ratio of plaintiff/defense cases

Prior clients including date (plaintiff or defendant)

Types of investigations with dates

Deposition testimony given with dates

Court testimony with dates

Legal references

AVAILABILITY

| Vacation plans and dates | Potential meeting dates |

- investigation reports;
- expert reports;
- research memoranda;
- documents;
- evidence;
- pleadings; and
- trial preparation material.

Exhibit 3.15 AbacusLaw intake form

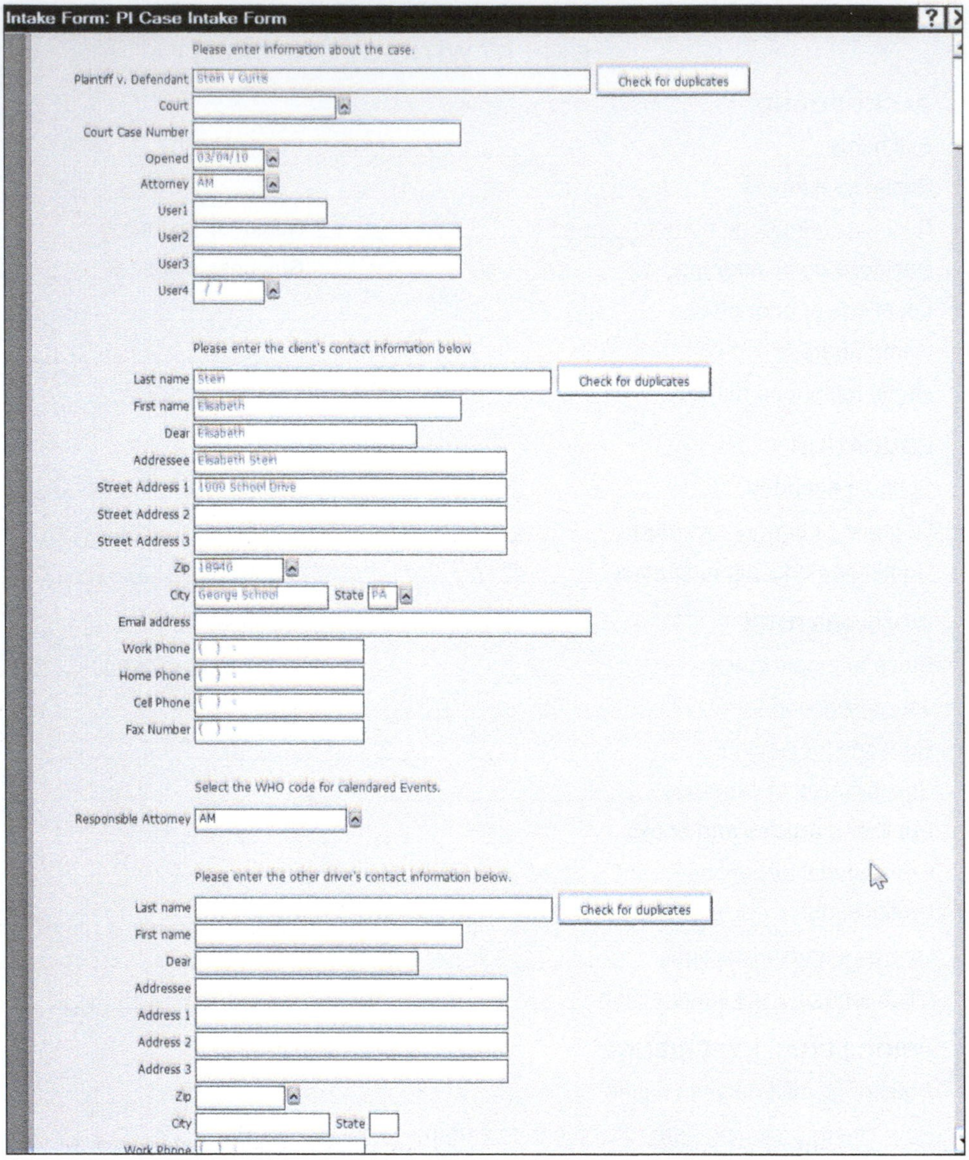

Source: Abacus Law Intake Form from Abacus Data Systems, Inc. Used by permission.

Using Case Management Systems

Efficient use of a case management system gives all authorized members of the legal team access to all of the case information, day or night. Effective case management, therefore, requires some central repository of the information gathered by each of the team members, as well as the ability of each to access the case information input by others. The Internet, networking, and cloud computing permit members of the legal team to access the repository from remote locations across town, across the country, and sometimes across the world.

A high level of collaboration among members of the legal team is becoming common practice, even in smaller law offices. In part, it is a result of increased complexity of cases, shortened time to prepare for trial (under court rules and procedures for getting the backload of cases reduced), and increased speed of

Exhibit 3.16 LexisNexis CaseMap Case Evaluation Screen

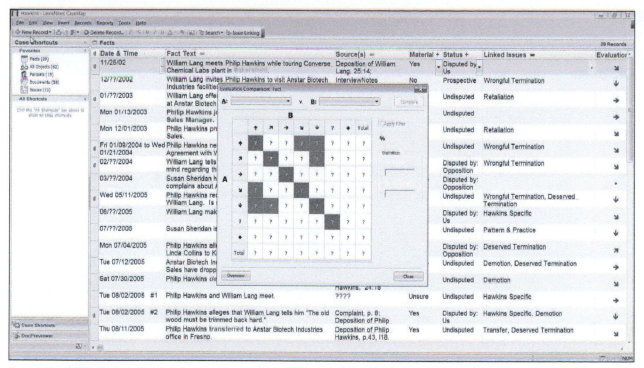

Source: One Of The Tools In Collaborative Situations Is The Individual Assessment Of The Importance Of Items In The Case. Used by permission of Lexis Nexis.

justice. In many smaller, specialized practices, the resources or the expertise may not be available to handle the occasional large or complex case. For example, a small firm of tax attorneys (with expertise in tax evasion issues but not much trial experience) may collaborate with a small trial or litigation boutique firm; each firm supplies the expertise in one area and shares all the case files and information to better serve the client. One of the tools in collaborative situations is the individual assessment of the importance of items in the case, as shown in Exhibit 3.16.

Litigation can be very expensive. Part of the cost is related to the time the litigation team must spend processing, organizing, and sharing information and documents. Where the organization can be handled by a team member whose time is billed at a lower rate, the client saves money, and the supervising attorneys and paralegals can work more productively. Clients and the courts prefer (or even require) members of the legal team, such as student law clerks and paralegals, to do work that does not require the skills of the higher-billing-rate attorney, as demonstrated in the *Berman v. Schweiker* case below.

In some courts, submitting a fee for work done by an attorney that could have been done more cost-effectively by a paralegal will result in the court denying or reducing that fee.

Sharing the responsibility of processing the information about a case requires collaboration. Each member of the team must have the ability to input and use information for the tasks assigned to him or her. For example, investigators input information on witness identifications and dates of importance, paralegals input information about parties and documentation, and lawyers evaluate the facts. To do their part, all must have the ability to share the information. Exhibit 3.17 shows a CaseMap facts display ready for entry of a new item. In pre-computer

Exhibit 3.17 CaseMap facts display screen

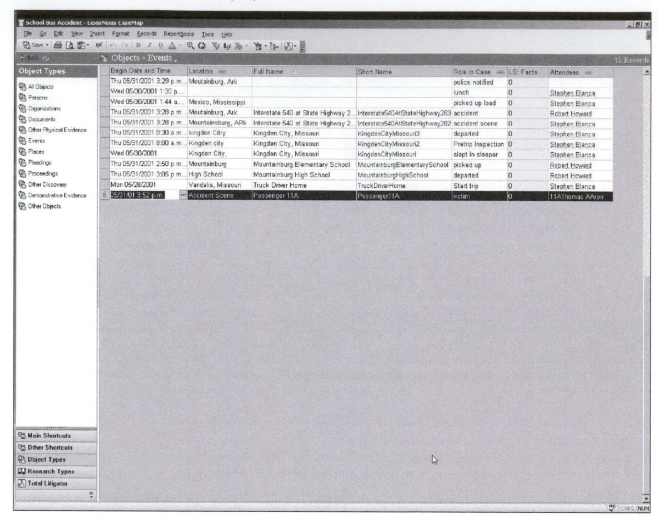

IN THE WORDS OF THE COURT...

Fee Calculation

Berman v. Schweiker,
531 F. Supp. 1149 at 1155 (N.D.Ill. 1982), aff'd,
713 F.2d 1290 (7th Cir. 1983).

"…The application states that counsel's firm actually paid the second year law student who worked on this case $14.00 per hour for his services. We believe these payments constitute reasonable expenses of counsel. Moreover, denying compensation for a student law clerk would be counter-productive. As plaintiff's counsel points out, law firms frequently employ student law clerks to perform tasks under attorney supervision as one way of controlling the spiraling costs of litigation. Excluding compensation for fees incurred by employing student law clerks will force attorneys to handle the entire case themselves, achieving the same results but at a much higher cost."

Exhibit 3.18 CaseMap document listing

Bates ...	Bates - End	Full Name	Short Name	Key	Date	Type +	Author(s)	Recipient(s)	Linked Is
P001232	P001232	Email from Phil Hawkins at 2002101...	P001232	■	Sat 12/28/2002 10...	E-mail	Philip Hawkins	William Lang	
P001233	P001233	Hawkins Letter of 8/2/2005	P001233	☑	Tue 08/02/2005	Letter	Philip Hawkins	William Lang	
P001234	P001234	Hawkins Letter of 9/19/2005	P001234	☑	Mon 09/19/2005	Letter	Philip Hawkins	William Lang	
P001235	P001235	Lang Letter of 11/11/2005	P001235	☑	Fri 11/11/2005	Letter	William Lang, Karen...	Philip Hawkins	Wrongful
P001267	P001268	Letter from William Lang to Carol Sa...	P001267	☐	Tue 09/27/2005	Letter	William Lang	Carol Sanders	
P001269	P001278	Reduction In Force Announcement	P001278	☐	Thu 11/10/2005	Internal memo	William Lang	Anstar Biotech...	
P001279	P001279	Lang Memo to Regan	P001279	☐	Fri 11/11/2005	Internal memo	William Lang	George Regan	
P001284	P001284	Varvaro Tip Letter	P001284	☑	Tue 05/03/2005	Letter	Frank Varvaro	George Regan	
P001334	P001356	Hawkins Employment Agreement	P001334	☑	06/??/2004	Contract	William Lang, Philip...		Wrongful
P001357	P001362	Hawkins Performance Review	P001357	☑	08/??/2005	Performance...	William Lang	Philip Hawkins, Karen...	
P001401	P001401	Email from Phil Hawkins at 2005092...	P001401	☐	Mon 09/19/2005 3:...	E-mail	Philip Hawkins	William Lang	
P001450	P001454	Thomas Memo to File	P001450	☐	Fri 06/17/2005	Internal memo	Karen Thomas		
P001554	P001560	Sheridan 2004 Performance Review	P001554	☐	Wed 03/17/2004	Performance...	Karen Thomas	Susan Sheridan	
P002000	P002000	Email from Phil Hawkins at 2005041...	P002000	☐	Mon 04/18/2005 1...	E-mail	Philip Hawkins	William Lang, Karen...	
P002001	P002001	Email from Phil Hawkins at 2005041...	P002001	☐	Tue 04/19/2005 9...	E-mail	Philip Hawkins	George Ny	
P002002	P002002	Email from Phil Hawkins at 2005041...	P002002	☐	Fri 04/15/2005 3:1...	E-mail	Philip Hawkins	Hank Randle	
P002003	P002003	Email from Phil Hawkins at 2005041...	P002003	☐	Fri 04/15/2005 3:1...	E-mail	Philip Hawkins	Hank Randle	
P002004	P002004	Email from Phil Hawkins at 2005041...	P002004	☐	Mon 04/18/2005 4:...	E-mail	Philip Hawkins	Karen Thomas, Frank...	
P002005	P002005	Email from Phil Hawkins at 2005041...	P002005	☐	Mon 04/18/2005 1...	E-mail	Philip Hawkins	Hank Randle	
P002006	P002006	Email from Phil Hawkins at 2005041...	P002006	☐	Mon 04/18/2005 1...	E-mail	Philip Hawkins	Karen Thomas	
P002007	P002007	Email from Phil Hawkins at 2005041...	P002007	☐	Mon 04/18/2005 1...	E-mail	Philip Hawkins	Hank Randle	
P002008	P002008	Email from Phil Hawkins at 2005041...	P002008	☐	Tue 04/19/2005 3:...	E-mail	Philip Hawkins	Frank Varvaro	
P002009	P002009	Email from Phil Hawkins at 2005041...	P002009	☐	Tue 04/19/2005 6:...	E-mail	Philip Hawkins	Karen Thomas	
P002010	P002010	Email from Phil Hawkins at 2005041...	P002010	☐	Mon 04/18/2005 4:...	E-mail	Philip Hawkins	Linda Collins, George...	
P002011	P002011	Email from Phil Hawkins at 2005041...	P002011	☐	Tue 04/19/2005 5:...	E-mail	Philip Hawkins	Karen Thomas	
P002012	P002012	Email from Phil Hawkins at 2005041...	P002012	☐	Tue 04/19/2005 2...	E-mail	Philip Hawkins	Linda Collins	
P002013	P002013	Email from Phil Hawkins at 2005041...	P002013	☐	Tue 04/19/2005 10...	E-mail	Philip Hawkins	Linda Collins	
P002014	P002014	Email from William Lang at 2005041...	P002014	☐	Tue 04/19/2005 10...	E-mail	William Lang	Philip Hawkins	
P002015	P002015	Email from Phil Hawkins at 2005041...	P002015	☐	Tue 04/19/2005 9:...	E-mail	Philip Hawkins	Susan Sheridan	
P002016	P002016	Email from William Lang at 2005042...	P002016	☐	Thu 04/21/2005 10...	E-mail	William Lang	Philip Hawkins	
P002017	P002017	Email from Phil Hawkins at 2005041...	P002017	☐	Tue 04/19/2005 9:...	E-mail	Philip Hawkins	Frank Varvaro	
P002018	P002018	Email from Phil Hawkins at 2005041...	P002018	☐	Tue 04/19/2005 5:...	E-mail	Philip Hawkins	Linda Collins	

Source: Case Map Document Listing. Used by permission of Lexis Nexis.

days, this task was accomplished by taking the file folder (an expandable folder), or a part of the file, from the file cabinet and working on it with an appropriate (paper) notice placed in the file or file cabinet to indicate who had the file.

The trial team frequently has to find a document or information on a specific issue from among potentially thousands of pages of documents. Exhibit 3.18 shows a list of the documents in a case in CaseMap. With a computer and the proper specialty software program, it is possible to locate the document quickly.

■ OFFICE MANAGEMENT SOFTWARE

There are certain administrative activities that are common to most, if not all, law offices. These are the functions that are necessary for the successful management of the business operation of the office. **Time keeping, calendar maintenance,** and accounting are all critical administrative activities in a law office. Without adequate time keeping, fees may be lost for hours worked and not billed. Missing a calendar date may result in missing a critical appointment, trial date, or worse, a statute of limitations. Tracking the expenses of any business is important. In a law office it is even more important because it may include the fiduciary responsibility of handling client funds in escrow accounts and accounting to the courts as well as to clients. In civil litigation cases, costs expended must be carefully tracked for recovery from any court verdict, settlement or from the client. In some cases, like class actions, fees for time properly documented by the legal team may be recovered in addition to the award to the injured parties.

LEARNING OBJECTIVE 5
Explain the role of office management software in the operation of the law office.

time keeping
Recording of all time spent performing activities during the workday.

calendar maintenance
Adding to the calendar critical deadlines, appointments, and reminders for each member of the legal team.

Most state disciplinary boards *require* that a separate account be maintained to hold client funds. Client funds are forbidden from being placed in the attorney business operating account.

The sole practitioner with only a secretary or paralegal and few clients can keep track of most important office information with a multiyear calendar and a checkbook. Appointments, deadlines, and statute of limitations dates can be entered and the calendar consulted on a daily basis. Any disbursements can be recorded in a checkbook; client funds can be deposited and disbursed using a separate checkbook.

When the number of clients increases and additional personnel are added, it becomes increasingly difficult to record and extract information. With busy schedules and the attorney spending more and more time out of the office, the communication of critical information may be delayed or lost. The manual paper system requires someone to physically look at "the book"—which is inconvenient to do if the offices are separated on different floors, and impossible if any of the legal team is out of the office in another town or courthouse. Electronic office management systems allow access from anywhere over a computer network or with an appropriate Internet connection. Important deadlines can be automatically sent to the responsible party by the software program without dependency on a staff person who might be out for the day.

In some states, each county court may have a different set of deadlines that must be tracked to avoid missing court dates. With rules-based software, these dates can be calculated automatically.

Office Management Program Functions

Most of the office functions can be divided into the following categories:

Calendar—keeping personal appointments, case deadlines, statutes of limitations, and important reminder dates.

Contacts—keeping a current list of names, addresses, phone numbers, e-mail addresses, and other information for clients, opposing counsel, vendors, networking contacts, and other people and firms.

Files—Keeping track of individual case files, projects, client matters, and related documents.

Accounting—Keeping track of time and billing information, client and firm funds, and escrow accounts; preparing bills, reports, and tax returns.

Office management software programs use a database or sets of databases to record information. These databases can then be searched for specific items; the information is assembled and reported as a response to a query, such as, "What are the appointments for today?" As previously described, a database is a collection of similar records such as your address book, which has a name, address, city, and phone number for each person in it. As an example, the AbacusLaw software program uses four main databases to store the information, as explained in its literature:

Names are the contents of your address book. This includes every person with whom your firm has contact: clients, prospects, vendors, defendants, judges, attorneys, expert witnesses, friends, relatives, and anyone you might want on your mailing list. Abacus gives you fast and easy access to information on anyone in your Names database. Notes for names are kept in a linked database so you can keep essentially unlimited notes about your contacts.

events
Any appointments, tasks, reminders, or things to do that are scheduled for specific dates.

Events are any appointments, tasks, reminders, or things to do that are scheduled for specific dates. Events can be entered into Abacus by many different methods. The Events window is the primary data window, while the Daily Organizer and various calendar windows give you different views of your events.

Matters are any matter, case, file, or project that you need to track. Once entered, matters can be attached to any number of names. Notes for matters are kept in a linked database so you can keep essentially unlimited notes about your files.

Documents in Abacus, are any previously saved word processing files, scanned images, pleadings, correspondence, or Web pages. They can be files on disk or just printed documents stored in a box. Abacus keeps a list of these documents in a database so you can find or edit them right from the client's Name or Matter window.

These databases can be searched individually, such as the Names database for a list of clients presented alphabetically, or across all databases; for example, a list of all documents for a client can sorted by individual matters being handled by the firm for the client and listing important dates and deadlines.

matters
Any item, case, file, or project that needs to be tracked.

documents
Word processing files, scanned images, pleadings, correspondence, or Web pages.

Calendar Maintenance Programs

The law office calendar is a source of information about:

appointments with clients;
litigation deadlines;
filing deadlines;
court appearance dates;
statute of limitations dates; and
routine reminders.

The more traditional approach to calendar issues was to maintain a master office calendar in paper form. In multiple-attorney offices, some of these calendars had multiple columns for the different attorneys. Frequently a task of the office assistant was to print out or photocopy the calendar on some regular basis, such as weekly, for each person in the office. Diary reminders, including the statute of limitations dates, were recorded on cards or multicarbon sets filed in a file box by date (usually a fixed period of time before the deadline to allow action on the file). The daily activities of the legal assistant or paralegal included pulling out the deadlines and reporting them to the responsible attorney, frequently with a reminder attached to the outside of the file.

 IN THE WORDS OF THE COURT...

Fee Calculation

Jean v. Nelson, 863 F. 2d 759 (11th Cir. 1988)

The 11th Circuit Court of Appeals has stated: "We have held that paralegal time is recoverable as part of a prevailing party's award for attorney's fees and expenses, [but] only to the extent that the paralegal performs work traditionally done by an attorney."

Quoting from *Allen v. United States Steel Corp.*, 665 F.2d 689, 697 (5th Cir. 1982): "To hold otherwise would be counterproductive because excluding reimbursement for such work might encourage attorneys to handle entire cases themselves, thereby achieving the same results at a higher overall cost."

The more contemporary approach to calendar matters is the use of a calendar database program. Calendar software is, at its basic level, a database of dates and related information. Preset reporting criteria allow for presentation of the data in a number of ways:

Office: daily, weekly, monthly, or annual calendars;

Individual: daily, weekly, monthly, or annual calendars; and

Reports: important dates—like statute of limitations—or reminders of deadlines

Calendar Program Overview

As with all technology, calendar programs are constantly being improved. A calendar system may consist of a paper calendar, an electronic calendar (such as Outlook), or a complex, rules-based calendaring program that automatically calculates deadlines based on the court rules of the selected jurisdiction, type of case, and event selected.

Using an automated rules-based system is highly recommended, especially due to the fact that calendar-related errors are the leading cause of malpractice claims. Both LawTool Box and AbacusLaw provide rules-based calendaring software with built-in court rules databases. Ideally, you want a system that is current, meaning the rules are updated with changes, and a system that takes into account holidays for the particular jurisdiction. Exhibit 3.19 shows AbacusLaw rules-based calendar calculation.

Exhibit 3.19 AbacusLaw rules-based calendaring

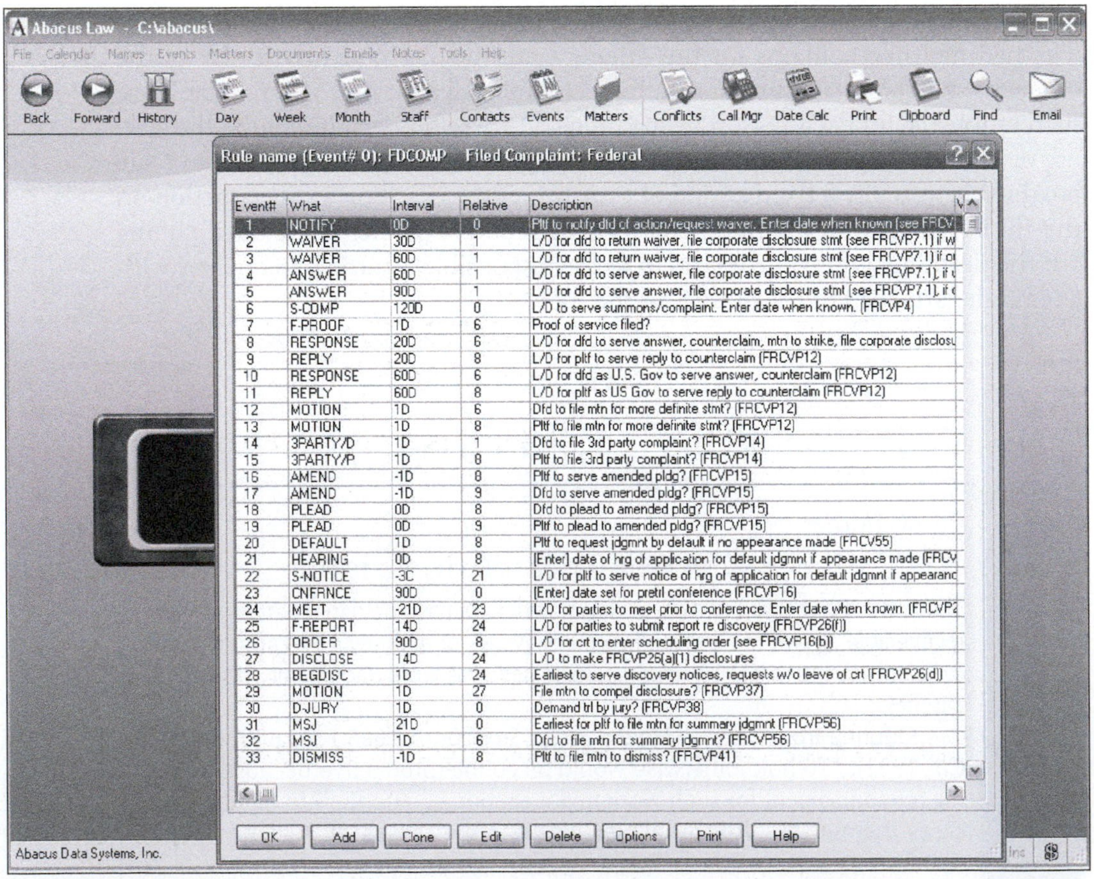

Source: Abacus law Rules-Based Calendaring from Abacus Data Systems, Inc. Used by permission.

Time-Keeping Software

Time keeping is one of the principal administrative functions in a law office. Time keeping includes the recording of all time spent performing activities during the workday. In some offices, only time spent doing work that may be billed to a client is recorded. In others, both billable and nonbillable time, such as pro bono work or client development, is also recorded. Keeping track of billable time becomes a critical function to ensure that the law firm will be properly compensated for its advice and efforts on behalf of clients. Time keeping is not limited to just the attorneys but usually includes paralegals and, in some cases, secretaries, information technologists, and file clerks. Fortunately, the task has been automated by the use of software, such as Tabs3 by STI (Software Technology Inc.), which accurately captures, stores, and processes this information and automatically prepares billing and time-keeping records; see the Tabs3 input screens in Exhibit 3.20.

ETHICAL Perspectives

PROOF OF SUPERVISION
Accurate, contemporaneously recorded time records for the paralegal and for the attorney may be used to show the supervising attorney's level of supervision of the paralegal.

Exhibit 3.20 Tabs3 from STI time entry screens

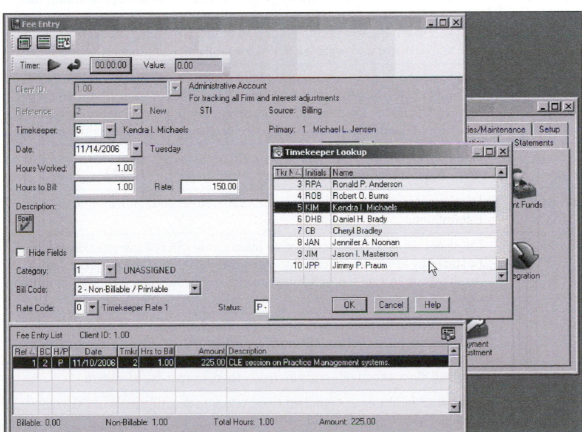

CONCEPT REVIEW AND REINFORCEMENT

KEY TERMS

electronic repository   49
cloud computing   49
online collaboration   49
spoliation of evidence   49
litigation hold   49
database   53
tables   53
record   53
fields   53

cell   53
reports   55
tangible evidence   58
trial notebook   58
paperless office   60
e-repository (online document repository)   60
case management system   60
practice management system   60

cases   61
time keeping   69
calendar maintenance   69
names   70
events   70
matters   71
documents   71

CHAPTER SUMMARY

LITIGATION MANAGEMENT AND TECHNOLOGY

Introduction to Litigation Management and Technology	Litigation is no longer defined by skilled oratory. Judges and jurors expect to see cases presented using video displays like they see on television. Office management and case management functions overlap. Early versions of some software programs were individual applications, like calendar creation and maintenance programs. There is a trend toward integrating all of the desired functions of office and case management and organization into a single master program.
Technology in Civil Litigation	The computer and the Internet are used for preparing documents, maintaining client databases, keeping office and client accounting records, communicating, legal and factual researching, filing documents with the court, sharing files with other counsel, and producing documents for discovery and trial presentations.
Online Data Storage and Collaboration	Use of an electronic repository to store all information online allows multiple users in remote multiple locations to work on the same case file.
Databases in Litigation	Databases are used in the litigation process to store, sort, and analyze information.
Electronic Database Basics	Databases are programs used to store information. Stored information may then be sorted by key terms, phrases, or other criteria. Among the frequent uses of databases are sorting through lists of names and performing a conflict of interest check.
Data Repositories	A data program is a repository of information of all types that can be sorted and presented in a desired, meaningful manner. Although a database is nothing more than an electronic version of cards and a card file, a database can be searched more effectively and efficiently than a paper-based system.

Navigating Electronic Databases	Electronic databases use standard terminology to describe parts of a database:
	    table, which contains fields of information
	    field, which is one type of information

record, all the information about one item

cell, which is the location of the field with one type of information

reports, which present the data from the database in an organized way.

Database Issues in Litigation	The litigation team, the interface between the client and the opposing party and the court, has the obligation to locate and produce the required or requested information from the client's databases.
Searches—Constructing the Query	The traditional method of searching databases is using the Boolean search method, which uses connectors such as AND, OR, and NOT.
The Reality of Using Databases	It is rare that the legal team creates its own database. Virtually every law office's specialty applications program for managing the office, managing cases, or managing presentations in litigation is a database, and the litigation team must understand the terminology to be able to communicate with those creating, maintaining, or working on the databases.
Organizing and Managing Case Files	Technology has facilitated the change from multiple boxes of paper to be culled through to the efficient use of software programs to store, retrieve, review, edit, share, and collaborate on the case file documents.

Case and Practice Management Software	Efficient use of a case management system provides all authorized members of the legal team with access to all of the case information, day or night.
	
	    Computer systems today even permit members of the legal team to access the same information from remote locations.
	
	    One of the tools in collaborative situations is the individual assessment of the importance of items in the case.
	
	    Clients and the courts prefer or even require members of the legal team, such as student law clerks and paralegals, to do work that does not require the skills of the higher-billing-rate attorney.
	
	    A fee submitted for court approval for work done by an attorney that could have been done by a paralegal will be denied or the fee reduced.
	
	    Each member of the team must have the ability to input and use information for the tasks assigned to him or her.

Using Case Management Systems	Complex litigation may involve millions of documents and hundreds of witnesses.
	
	    The use of computers for e-mail and document storage by businesses and government has caused a massive increase in the number of documents that may have to be reviewed, tracked, and made available.
	
	    Case management systems permit collaboration among the members of the legal team.

Office Management Software	Office management software programs use a database or sets of databases to record information about common office functions like calendar, contacts, files, and accounting.
Office Management Program Functions	These functions include calendars, contact lists, file management, and accounting.
Calendar Maintenance Programs	These programs track important deadlines, hearing dates, and appointments.
Time-Keeping Software	This software tracks and records time that may be billable to clients and documents the actions taken in a particular case.

REVIEW QUESTIONS AND EXERCISES

1. What are the tasks involved in managing a litigation case?
2. How is the trial notebook used in managing a case?
3. What are some of the issues for the litigation team in using a trial notebook?
4. How does the paperless office make it easier for members of the legal team to handle litigation?
5. What is the relationship between office management software and case management software?
6. How were documents in complex litigation processed before the use of computers in litigation?
7. What are some of the parts of a case file?
8. What is the relationship of law office administrative functions to civil litigation cases?
9. Why must the litigation team carefully track expenses and time spent on cases?
10. What are the main categories of functions for office management programs?
11. Why is the maintenance of calendaring dates critical to the litigation function?
12. How can the use of time records prove proper supervision of paralegals?
13. What are the organizational functions of a good case management program?
14. How does any case management system aid in the collaboration among the members of the legal team?
15. Explain the use of software for managing cases.
16. What are the steps that may be taken in organizing a new case file?
17. What are some of the advantages in using a case management software program?
18. What is the function of a database?
19. Identify the parts of a database record.
20. Give examples of the search terms that might be used to search e-mails.
21. Do members of the litigation team have to know how to create a database? Explain.
22. Why is it important for the litigation team to understand the terminology used in databases?

BUILDING YOUR PARALEGAL SKILLS

INTERNET AND TECHNOLOGY EXERCISES

1. Use a search engine to locate information on "case management software."
2. Prepare a list of the case management software programs that provide online tutorials for learning how to use the programs.
3. Visit the websites for the case management programs listed in this chapter. Determine the minimum operating requirements for a computer to run the software properly.
4. Locate information on companies that provide online document repository services.
5. Use Lexis Nexis CaseMap to set up a new file for the case in Appendix 1. List the legal team from the opening chapter scenarios and create a "cast" of characters.
6. After setting up the file using CaseMap, use LexisNexis TimeMap to create a timeline from the facts in the case study in Appendix 1.
7. Locate tutorial information on the Internet or in your office suite of programs on creating and using a database.
8. Use the instructions included in Microsoft Office Access or WordPerfect Office Quattro Pro to create a database of names, addresses, and phone numbers. Create separate fields for last, first, and middle names; number, street, city, state, and zip code; area code and phone number for your family, your classmates, or your study group. Sort the individual records by fields.

CIVIL LITIGATION VIDEO CASE STUDIES

Fees and Billing Issue: Contemporaneous Time Keeping

To prepare his billable time, a paralegal attempts to reconstruct the time he spent during the day.

After watching the video at www.pearsonhighered .com/careersresources, answer the following questions.

1. How can inaccurate time keeping be avoided?
2. Why are accurate time records important to the law firm?
3. What ethical issues arise when a member of the legal team fails to report time accurately?

4. What legal issues arise when a member of the legal team fails to report time accurately?

Fees and Billing Issue: Using Time Effectively

A paralegal finds she is spending a significant number of hours working on a project that might not be billable and might be completed more effectively.

After watching the video at www.pearsonhighered .com/careersresources, answer the following questions.

1. Who decides what does and does not get billed?
2. What is the paralegal's role in client billing?

CHAPTER OPENING SCENARIO CASE STUDY

Use the Opening Scenario for this chapter to answer the following questions.

1. Prepare an outline of the issues in handling a case with so many plaintiffs and potential witnesses.
2. Prepare a memo explaining how a case management program might be used to organize the case.
3. What are the items that will need to be tracked using the case management program?

4. Answer this question raised by one of the attorneys: "Can't we make our own database or spreadsheet to track the information and save money?"
5. How can using a program like CaseMap help in preparing for trial and during trial? Explain in a memo for the attorneys' review.

BUILDING YOUR PROFESSIONAL PORTFOLIO AND REFERENCE MANUAL

CIVIL LITIGATION TEAM AT WORK

See page 18 for instructions on Building Your Professional Portfolio and Reference Manual.

Policy Manual

Write a job description for:

1. Litigation support manager
2. Law office information technologist

Forms

1. Compile a set of tab titles for a trial notebook.
2. Create a checklist for setting up a new case file.

Contacts and Resources

Complete a list, with contact information, of companies that provide online document repository services for law firms in your jurisdiction.

LEARNING OBJECTIVES

After studying this chapter, you should be able to:

1. Identify and describe the sources of American law.

2. Understand the need to prove the elements of a cause of action and remedies available.

3. Describe the elements necessary to establish jurisdiction and venue for a particular court.

4. Describe the courts in the federal and state court systems.

5. Describe the advantages of settling a lawsuit before trial.

6. Create the documents for making a demand for settlement.

7. Prepare the documents for settling and terminating a lawsuit.

8. Describe the methods of alternative dispute resolution.

The Court System, Settlement, and Alternative Dispute Resolution

CHAPTER 4

OPENING SCENARIO

Roy Saunders, Esq., and his paralegal were discussing the new school bus versus dump truck collision case they had recently taken on with the partners and litigation staff on a conference call linking the two offices. The firm agreed to represent all the passengers and the families of the children injured in the accident. As part of the initial interview, they had obtained the initial state police investigation report with the names and addresses of all parties involved, as well as those of the potential defendants. It was clear to Mr. Saunders that there was a potential question of diversity of citizenship, and the damages were far in excess of the requirement under the federal rules for jurisdiction. The partners had to decide which of the potential courts was most desirable for bringing this action. One of the partners expressed concern as to whether the clients would be best served by filing suit in one of the state courts or in the federal court. The case strategy consumed much of the scheduled time for the conference. One of the most experienced personal injury paralegals asked if the young firm had the resources and ability to try a case of this magnitude against the combined resources of the insurance companies for the trucking company, school bus company, and school district. One of the partners rhetorically asked if they should try to quickly settle or maybe seek arbitration.

OPENING SCENARIO LEARNING OBJECTIVE

Explain the ethical obligations a law firm has in determining case strategy.

■ INTRODUCTION TO THE COURT SYSTEM, SETTLEMENT, AND ALTERNATIVE DISPUTE RESOLUTION

diversity of citizenship
Lawsuit permitted in the federal court where the plaintiffs are from states different from those of the defendants and the amount in controversy exceeds $75,000.

Courts are the ultimate place for the resolution of civil disputes, a neutral venue in which justice can be served. The federal and state courts are created and given their respective authority by the United States Constitution and the constitutions of the fifty state governments. Federal courts are given the power under the U.S. Constitution to hear and decide cases involving federal questions and matters involving **diversity of citizenship**—cases involving citizens from different states. In cases of diversity, both the state and the federal courts may have the power to hear the same dispute involving the same parties and subject matter. Although multiple courts may have the authority to hear a case, the choice of court for a particular case may be based on a strategic decision that one court is more convenient or more likely to be friendly in the particular subject matter or toward the parties. These are tactical decisions made by the legal team. Some courts have a reputation of being friendly to plaintiffs, where juries make generous awards after liability is found. Others may be more liberal or more conservative in matters of allowing expert testimony.

Only a small percentage of cases opened by law firms each year actually go to trial. Many are settled by informal negotiations between the attorneys for the parties or with an insurance company representative. Some cases are settled after submission of documentation to the other side that supports the client's claims. Others are resolved by alternative dispute resolution (ADR), including arbitration and mediation.

However, each case must be treated as if it were ultimately going to trial. Good case analysis and preparation may lead to pretrial settlement. With a proper evaluation and complete understanding of the strengths and weaknesses of the case, the legal team will be in a better position to advise the client of the economics of continuing toward trial, making an attempt at settlement, or using ADR. Proper preparation of the case includes evaluating the case realistically, making reasonable settlement demands, and responding to potential settlement offers.

■ SOURCES OF AMERICAN LAW

LEARNING OBJECTIVE 1
Identify and describe the sources of American law.

American law has four primary sources:

1. constitutions;
2. statutes;
3. administrative rules and regulations; and
4. case law.

The federal (national) or the state governments can create law in each of the four ways. People within each jurisdiction are required to obey all constitutionally created and permitted federal and state laws.

Constitutions

A **constitution** is a document that establishes the conception, character, and organization of a government. The American federal government and each of the fifty state governments have a constitution that creates a form of governance, defines its power, and defines the rights of its citizens. The Constitution of the United States serves that purpose for the federal government. Ratified in 1789, the U.S. Constitution created a unique form of government in which power is shared among three co-equal branches—**executive, judicial,** and **legislative**—and with the individual states. Along with the Constitution, those branches are the sources of our law. The U.S. Constitution leaves to the individual states all the powers not granted specifically to the three branches of federal government. It is the limited powers set forth in the Constitution against which all activities of government are measured as permitted by the Constitution. The Constitution also guarantees certain basic rights to the individual, such as freedom of speech, religion, and assembly.

Statutes

The legislative branch of the state and federal governments creates law by enacting statutes. **Statutes** include provisions to define and regulate the conduct of citizens, businesses, and professions.

Administrative Regulations and Adjudications

Administrative agencies enforce statutes. Both federal and state governments create administrative agencies by implementing statutes. Administrative agencies operate under the executive branch of the state and federal governments, administering the laws by creating and enforcing regulations to carry out the statutes. Administrative agencies create law in two ways. First, agencies issue rules and regulations that define rights and procedures in the areas that the agencies administer. For example, the Internal Revenue Service, an administrative agency under the governance of the Department of Treasury, issues rules and regulations that define what items are included as gross income for calculating income tax.

The second way administrative agencies create law is by conducting hearings to determine the rights and obligations of the parties subject to the agency's regulations. When a person seeks benefits under the Social Security law, the Social Security Administration conducts its own fact finding and hearing to render a decision to grant or deny benefits.

Some agencies operate solely on the federal level, such as the Internal Revenue Service and the Social Security Administration. Others operate solely on the state level, such as the Workers Compensation Board. Still others share concurrent authority, such as the Environmental Protection Agency (federal) and the Department of Environmental Resources (state).

Case Law

The judicial branch of the government is the source of **case law.** Case law is a written decision by a court that resolves a particular legal dispute before the court. Disputes that cannot be resolved amicably by the parties involved are presented to the courts for adjudication. Under our court system, written decisions serve as precedent to resolve similar disputes in the future. Courts review prior case decisions with facts similar to those in the current dispute. The system of using prior case law decisions for making current decisions is called *stare decisis. Stare decisis* allows for predictability and flexibility in our judicial system because courts

constitution
Document that establishes the conception, character, and organization of a government; the fundamental and organic law.

executive branch
One of the three co-equal branches of government; represented by the president and administrative agencies.

judicial branch
One of the three co-equal branches of government; represented by the court system.

legislative branch
One of the three co-equal branches of government; represented by Congress, the House of Representatives, and the Senate.

statutes
Enactments by the legislative branch that include provisions to define and regulate the conduct of its citizens; may also regulate the operation of a business or profession.

PRACTICE TIP

Some federal and state administrative agencies, such as the Social Security Administration, permit paralegals to represent clients in administrative hearings without the supervision of an attorney.

case law
Law created by written decisions issued by the judicial branch; decisions resolve the dispute before the court and serve as precedent or guidance for similar future disputes.

stare decisis
Legal principle that prior case law should apply unless there is a substantial change in society necessitating a change in the law.

VIDEO ADVICE FROM THE FIELD

Interviews with trial court Judge Chad F. Kenney, Court of Common Pleas of Delaware County, Pennsylvania

A. Meet the Courthouse Team:

The members of the courthouse team and their roles are described. Judge Kenney explains the role of the Judge, the roles of the plaintiff and defense and the expected decorum expected in a trial.

After watching the video at www.pearsonhighered.com/careersresources, answer the following questions.

1. What are duties and role of the different members of the courtroom team?
2. What are the limitations on the role of the paralegal in court?
3. What is expected by the court of the lawyers in a trial?

B. Difference Between Civil and Criminal Cases:

Judge Chad F. Kenney explains the differences between civil and criminal trials and the duties of the court in protecting the parties and the duties of the lawyers in each type of case.

After watching the video at www.pearsonhighered.com/careersresources, answer the following questions.

1. What is the burden of proof in a criminal case?
2. What is the burden of proof in a civil case?
3. Why is there a difference in the burden of proof?

C. Demeanor in Court:

Judge Chad F. Kenney explains what is expected of people appearing in court.

After watching the video at www.pearsonhighered.com/careersresources, answer the following questions.

1. What attire is expected and why?
2. Why is a paralegal not normally allowed to approach the bench?
3. Why is a lawyer not normally allowed to approach a witness in court?

---

negligence
Cause of action in which the plaintiff claims that another person's failure to act as a reasonable person would have acted under the same or similar circumstances caused injury for which the plaintiff should be awarded damages.

contract
Agreement entered by two parties for valid consideration.

LEARNING OBJECTIVE 2
Understand the need to prove the elements of a cause of action and remedies available.

cause of action
A wrong that is legally recognized as a basis for compensating one for the harms suffered.

torts
Civil wrongs that are not breaches of contract for which the court can fashion a remedy.

change prior case law decisions only when a significant societal change occurs that requires a reconsideration to meet contemporary needs. By reviewing prior case decisions with facts similar to those in the client's situation, the legal team can help the client plan how to proceed and predict how a dispute will be resolved. Where, however, the legal team can demonstrate to the court that the old decision is out of step with the demands of society, the court may change the law.

■ CAUSE OF ACTION AND REMEDIES

Not all wrongs committed result in civil litigation. Some wrongs are identified by the government as crimes that subject the wrongdoer to a fine and/or imprisonment. Other wrongs may be civil wrongs. A wrong that is legally recognized as a basis for compensating one for the harms suffered is called a **cause of action.** Legal recognition of a wrong can come from any of the four sources of law. In civil litigation, there are two main causes of action, torts and contracts, and within each are distinct causes of action, for example:

    Torts
        Product liability
        Negligence
        Discrimination
    Contracts
        Improper performance
        Failure to deliver

ADVICE FROM THE FIELD

ADAPTABILITY OF THE LAW

Judge Jerome Frank addressed the value of the adaptability of law (*Law and the Modern Mind*, 1930):

> The law always has been, is now, and will ever continue to be, largely vague and variable. And how could this be otherwise? The law deals with human relations in their most complicated aspects. The whole confused, shifting helter-skelter of life parades before it—more confused than ever, in our kaleidoscopic age.
>
> Men have never been able to construct a comprehensive, eternalized set of rules anticipating all possible legal disputes and formulating in advance the rules which would apply to them. Situations are bound to occur which were never contemplated when the original rules were made.

How much less is such a frozen legal system possible in modern times?

The constant development of unprecedented problems requires a legal system capable of fluidity and pliancy. Our society would be straightjacketed were not the courts, with the able assistance of the lawyers, constantly overhauling the law and adapting it to the realities of ever-changing social, industrial, and political conditions; although changes cannot be made lightly, yet rules of law must be more or less impermanent, experimental, and therefore not nicely calculable.

Much of the uncertainty of law is not an unfortunate accident; it is of immense social value.

Source: Adaptability of the Law by Jerome Frank, Law and the Modern Mind, Transaction Publishers, 1930.

Each cause of action is made up of **elements** that define that cause of action. To succeed in a civil lawsuit, the **plaintiff** must prove each element of the cause of action by **preponderance of the evidence.** For example, for the tort of negligence, the four elements are:

1. **Duty of care**—the **defendant** owed the plaintiff a duty of reasonable care to not be the cause of a risk of harm. For example, we all have the duty to operate our automobiles safely by observing traffic control devices and speed limits.
2. **Breach of the duty of care**—the defendant failed to observe the duty to use reasonable care as required of him. Running a stop sign is a breach of the duty of care.
3. **Causation**—the defendant's failure to observe the duty of care was the cause of an injury to the plaintiff. The defendant ran the stop sign, which resulted in his collision with the plaintiff's motorcycle.
4. **Damages**—the injury resulted in compensable damages. The collision with the motorcycle totaled the motorcycle, but fortunately, the plaintiff suffered no physical injury. Damages may be recovered for the motorcycle but not for physical injury to the plaintiff.

If any one of these elements is missing, the plaintiff's cause of action will fail.

Civil litigation is pursued when an individual believes he or she has been wronged, can establish all the elements of the cause of action, and, under the law, is entitled to some type of remedy to correct that wrong. There are two forms of remedies: monetary and equitable. **Monetary remedies** assign a financial value to the harm suffered by the plaintiff. In some cases, no amount of monetary damages will make the injured party whole. In those instances, an **equitable remedy** will be fashioned by the court to return the parties to the state they were in before the harm occurred. Specifically, the court may order someone to do or stop doing some particular act.

elements
Components of a legal claim that must be established by the burden of proof.

plaintiff
Party who files a lawsuit seeking relief for a harm suffered.

preponderance of evidence
Burden of proof in most civil litigation cases; where the amount of proof that tips the scales of justice ever so slightly in one direction or the other.

duty of care
Duty of individuals to use reasonable care to avoid causing harm.

defendant
Party who is sued in a lawsuit.

general damages
Damages related to the injury sustained that cannot be calculated with any particular formula or accuracy.

special damages
Damages that can be calculated with some level of accuracy.

monetary remedies
Form of damages that assigns a financial value to the harm suffered by a plaintiff.

equitable remedy
Remedy used where no amount of monetary damages can make the injured party whole.

■ JURISDICTION

Once it is determined that there is a cause of action, the legal team will have to prepare and file a lawsuit. There are a number of choices and important requirements to consider before filing. Courts will not entertain a case unless certain preliminary requirements are met. Collectively, these requirements may be referred to as **jurisdiction.** The requirements define who initiates an action, what types of disputes may be brought before the court, and what authority the court has to resolve disputes.

jurisdiction
Authority of a court to hear disputes and impose resolution of the dispute upon the litigants.

standing
Right to bring a lawsuit only where the plaintiff has a stake or interest in the outcome of the case.

Standing

Standing is the term used to describe the plaintiff's right to bring a lawsuit. A plaintiff has standing to bring a lawsuit only when he or she has a stake or interest in the outcome of the case. For example, Sharon's friend Nancy is injured when she slips and falls in a grocery store. Nancy refuses to sue. Sharon, however, cannot sue the grocery store on Nancy's behalf because Sharon does not have an interest in the result of the case.

Case or Controversy

The matter presented by the plaintiff must represent an actual dispute or controversy. Our courts do not issue advisory opinions or decisions based on hypothetical situations and will dismiss claims that are frivolous or lack foundation in a recognized legal principle. A court will only consider a real dispute that is brought by someone who has suffered a real harm.

Authority of the Court

In addition to the requirements of standing and real controversy, the court must have authority to hear and resolve the dispute presented. The court must also have the power to enforce its decision on the parties to the litigation. This authority of the court is called *jurisdiction*: subject matter jurisdiction and personal jurisdiction.

subject matter jurisdiction
Authority of a court to hear and decide a particular type of dispute.

Subject matter jurisdiction is the authority of a court to hear and decide a particular type of dispute. There are two types of subject matter jurisdiction a court may have: limited jurisdiction and general jurisdiction. If a court does not have subject matter jurisdiction, it cannot hear that particular type of case.

limited jurisdiction
Courts authorized to hear certain types of disputes such as divorce or bankruptcy.

Limited jurisdiction trial courts are authorized to hear certain types of disputes. Their jurisdiction may be limited as to the amount in controversy, such as small claims court, which hears disputes where the damages are less than a specific amount, like $2,000, $5,000, or $12,000. Jurisdiction may be based on summary criminal offenses, such as traffic court hearing motor vehicle violations. Other examples of limited jurisdiction courts include bankruptcy courts, landlord–tenant courts, juvenile courts, and justice of the peace courts.

general jurisdiction
Power of the court to hear all types of matters so long as the dispute does not fall within the limited jurisdiction of a particular court; it is subject to the court's general jurisdiction.

General jurisdiction courts have the power to hear all types of matters. So long as a dispute does not fall within the limited jurisdiction of a particular court, it is subject to the court's general jurisdiction. These are typically the trial courts that hear criminal and civil cases. Some states divide their general jurisdiction trial courts into specialized courts or divisions for efficiency. Some of these specialty courts are criminal division, domestic relations division, and complex litigation, such as asbestos cases.

personal jurisdiction
(*in personam*)
Authority of a court over persons as well as the subject matter of a lawsuit.

Personal jurisdiction, also known as *in personam* jurisdiction, requires the court to have authority over the persons as well as the subject matter of the lawsuit. Courts, to be effective, must have the power to enforce their orders and compel parties to obey them. Personal jurisdiction gives the court that power over the

IN THE WORDS OF THE COURT...

Case or Controversy

Lujan v. Defenders of Wildlife, 504 U.S. 555, 580, 581 (1992) 112 S.Ct. 2130

Lujan, Secretary of the Interior v. Defenders of Wildlife et al.

Certiorari to the United States Court of Appeals for the Eighth Circuit

No. 90-1424

Argued December 3, 1991

Decided June 12, 1992

...The Court's holding that there is an outer limit to the power of Congress to confer rights of action is a direct and necessary consequence of the case and controversy limitations found in Article III. I agree that it would exceed those limitations if, at the behest of Congress and in the absence of any showing of concrete injury, we were to entertain citizen suits to vindicate the public's nonconcrete interest in the proper administration of the laws. While it does not matter how many persons have been injured by the challenged action, the party bringing suit must show that the action injures him in a concrete and personal way.

This requirement is not just an empty formality. It preserves the vitality of the adversarial process by assuring both that the parties before the court have an actual, as opposed to professed, stake in the outcome, and that the legal questions presented...will be resolved, not in the rarified atmosphere of a debating society, but in a concrete factual context conducive to a realistic appreciation of the consequences of judicial action....

---

person appearing before it. Courts will not hear cases nor make decisions if they do not have the power to enforce their decisions.

In *rem* jurisdiction gives the court authority to hear and decide disputes over property located within the court's jurisdictional boundaries without necessarily having jurisdiction over the parties. The court may hear any dispute concerning property, such as title to real estate or ownership of personal property such as a painting, located within the geographic jurisdiction of the court.

in rem **jurisdiction**
Jurisdiction to hear a case because of jurisdiction over the property of the lawsuit.

Obtaining Personal Jurisdiction

Plaintiffs agree to be bound by the power of the court when they file suit. Simply by filing the complaint, the plaintiff consents to the personal jurisdiction of the court.

The court must also have jurisdiction over the defendant to the lawsuit. Defendants who reside or do business within the court's geographical area are subject to the personal jurisdiction of the court. Defendants may also be subject to the personal jurisdiction of the court where they are served with court papers while found within the geographic jurisdiction of the court.

Nonresident defendants may also be subject to a court's jurisdiction by virtue of a state's long arm statute. **Long arm statutes** are laws enacted by a state's legislative body to extend jurisdiction over parties who reside in other states but have utilized some state service or facility that subjects the parties to the jurisdiction of that state. For example, the driver from Georgia who causes an automobile accident while traveling in Texas will be subject to Texas personal jurisdiction via a long arm statute. Most states have a statute that provides that drivers must agree to submit to the state's jurisdiction to resolve any disputes that arise out of a traffic accident on state highways.

long arm statutes
Method of obtaining personal jurisdiction over a nonresident defendant based on a statute that extends a state's jurisdiction.

minimum contacts
Method of obtaining personal jurisdiction over a nonresident defendant based on the defendant having contacts within a state's jurisdiction.

Finally, the court may obtain jurisdiction over a defendant based on the concept of **minimum contacts** with the state. Here, a defendant has established contact with a state to the extent that it is not unreasonable to expect that the defendant might use that state's court or be required to defend a lawsuit in that jurisdiction—for example, a company that has no physical place of business in a state but solicits customers from within the state by use of the Internet and print advertisement. This company would have sufficient contacts with the state that it could reasonably bring a lawsuit within the state to enforce a contract for sale of its goods. Likewise, this company should expect to defend its activities within the state.

Today, with the advent of the Internet and the ability of persons and businesses to reach millions of people in other states electronically, applying the minimum-contacts standard can be difficult. In one case, Zippo Manufacturing Company (Zippo) sued Zippo Dot Com Inc. (Dot Com) in federal district court in Pennsylvania. Zippo manufactures its well-known line of Zippo tobacco lighters in Bradford, Pennsylvania, and sells them worldwide. Dot Com, a California corporation with its principal place of business and servers located in Sunnyvale, California, operates an Internet website that transmits information and sexually explicit material to its subscribers. Of Dot Com's 140,000 paying subscribers worldwide, 3,000 are located in Pennsylvania. Zippo sued Dot Com in federal district court in Pennsylvania for trademark infringement. Dot Com alleged that it was not subject to personal jurisdiction in Pennsylvania. The district court applied the *International Shoe* "minimum-contacts" standard and held that Dot Com *was* subject to personal jurisdiction under the Pennsylvania long arm statute and ordered Dot Com to defend itself there.

Venue

venue
Process of determining in which court to file a lawsuit when more than one court has subject matter and personal jurisdiction.

Jurisdiction refers to the power of the court to hear a case. In many instances, there will be more than one court with jurisdiction. **Venue** refers to which court will be selected for purposes of filing a lawsuit. The venue decision can be based on a number of factors. One factor is the geographical area that is the most convenient location in which to try the case. In most states, all of the county or parish trial courts have the same authority to hear the same types of cases. But it would not be convenient to try a case in northern California when the parties, witnesses, and counsel are all in San Diego, in southern California.

Other factors that may play a part in deciding venue, or in which court to file the lawsuit, include the following: (1) the speed with which matters reach trial; (2) the reputation of the judges; (3) historically high jury awards for damages; (4) the size and makeup of the jury pool; and (5) the attorney's familiarity with the court and judges. Convenience and these factors will be taken into account by the legal team when determining where to file the plaintiff's complaint. The process of selection is called *forum shopping* and results in filing the lawsuit in the court that will be most convenient and result in the most favorable treatment of the plaintiff.

There are times when a case may be tried in a court that is not the most convenient venue. The jurisdiction where the complaint has been filed may be inappropriate because pretrial publicity makes it impossible to find a fair and impartial jury. In these circumstances, the defendant may file a request for change of venue.

Removal and Remand

concurrent jurisdiction
Cases where the federal and state courts both have subject matter and personal jurisdiction.

In those cases where the federal and state courts both have subject matter and personal jurisdiction, there is **concurrent jurisdiction.** A lawsuit that includes state and federal claims or a diversity lawsuit might have concurrent jurisdiction.

The plaintiff has the opportunity to select where to file and may rightfully choose state court. Because of the existence of the federal jurisdiction, the defendant may petition for **removal** of the matter from state to federal court. So long as the issues that gave rise to the federal jurisdiction remain disputed and unresolved, the federal court will have jurisdiction to resolve both the state and federal claims. In the event the basis for the federal jurisdiction is dispensed with (by dismissal or summary judgment), the federal court has no authority to retain jurisdiction over the remaining claims based on state law. The federal court must release its jurisdiction over the state claims and remand the matter back to state court.

removal

Right of the defendant, in cases of concurrent jurisdiction, to have jurisdiction moved from state to federal court.

ORGANIZATION OF THE COURT SYSTEM

The federal and state courts have a similar system of trial and appellate courts. Exhibit 4.1 shows the typical state court system; Exhibit 4.2 shows the federal court system. Trial courts hear evidence and make findings of fact. Appeals courts do not take testimony or make findings of fact; instead, they review the lower court's application of the procedural and substantive law. **Procedural law** is the body of law that governs how a case is filed and tried. It includes the rules of court, like the Federal Rules of Civil Procedure, and the rules of evidence, like the Federal Rules of Evidence. **Substantive law** concerns the application of statutes and case law that determine the rights and obligations of the plaintiff and defendant.

LEARNING OBJECTIVE 4

Describe the courts in the federal and state court systems.

procedural laws

Laws that relate to how a trial is conducted and are usually based upon rules of court and rules of evidence.

substantive law

Law that relates to the law of a case, such as the law of negligence or contract.

Exhibit 4.1 Typical state court system

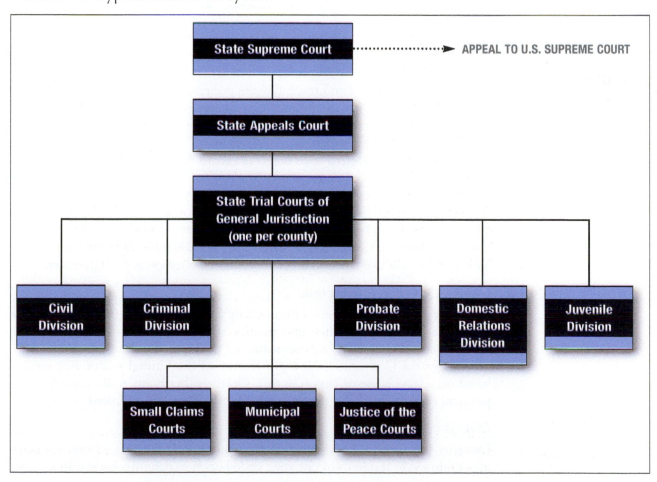

Exhibit 4.2 Federal court system

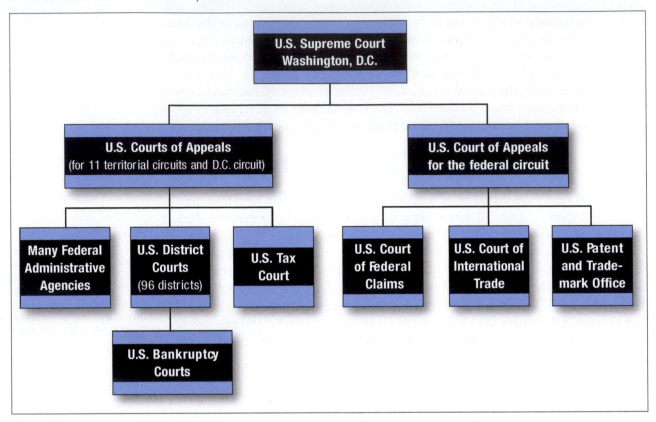

Trial Courts

In trial courts, evidence and testimony are presented to a finder of facts; the fact finder is frequently a jury. A trial in such a court is called a *jury trial*. When the judge sits and hears a case without a jury, the judge is the fact finder; such a trial is called a *bench* or *waiver trial*.

Trial courts are referred to as courts of record because the testimony and evidence presented are recorded and preserved.

Trial courts can have limited or general jurisdiction. In the federal court system, there are some specialized courts with limited subject matter jurisdiction, such as the bankruptcy court and the tax court. The trial courts in the federal court system are the federal district courts. Federal district courts are also courts of limited jurisdiction authorized to hear two types of disputes: (1) federal question and (2) diversity.

Federal Question Jurisdiction

The federal district courts are authorized by Congress to hear disputes that arise under the Constitution, laws, and treaties of the United States. An action to recover damages related to injuries sustained in an automobile accident does not arise under the Constitution, laws, or treaties of the United States. Recovery is based on a state cause of action in tort. On the other hand, a dispute about the payment of federal income taxes arises under the laws of the United States.

Diversity Jurisdiction

Diversity jurisdiction was devised by the Founding Fathers to address concerns about fairness to residents of one state called upon to defend a lawsuit in another

courts of record
Courts in which the testimony and evidence presented are recorded and preserved.

state. By giving the federal trial courts jurisdiction over these matters, the Founders hoped to achieve fairness in the federal and state judicial systems.

Today, diversity serves the same purpose. For diversity jurisdiction to exist, the plaintiff and the defendants must be citizens of different states *and* the amount in controversy must exceed $75,000. The federal court must use the appropriate state's law in deciding the case.

State trial courts include all those state courts that hear testimony, receive evidence, and render decisions. These include general jurisdiction courts (civil and criminal with specific divisions) and limited jurisdiction courts (the motor vehicle and small claims previously discussed).

Intermediate Appellate Courts

When a litigant is dissatisfied with the outcome of a trial, he or she may file an appeal to have the trial reviewed by an appellate court. This review is usually to an intermediate appellate court. Where there is an intermediate-level appellate court, the litigant is said to have the right to appeal. In the federal court system, the circuit court of appeals is the intermediate appellate court. There are eleven federal circuits or geographic regions in the U.S.; for example, the 7th Circuit Court of Appeals hears appeals from the federal district courts located in Wisconsin, Illinois, and Indiana. Exhibit 4.3 shows the various federal circuit courts of appeals. There are two specialized circuit courts: the Federal Circuit, which has limited subject matter jurisdiction over certain government suits, such as patent and trademark cases, and the D.C. Circuit, which is given the responsibility of directly reviewing the decisions and rule making of many federal independent agencies of the United States government and is based in the nation's Capital.

Most states also have an intermediate appellate court, which hears appeals from the state trial courts. A few states do not, and in those states, the appeal is heard by the highest court of the state.

WEB RESOURCES

Contrast and compare the Colorado Rules of Professional Conduct at the Colorado Bar Association website with the American Bar Association Model Rules of Professional Responsibility at the ABA website and the ethical rules in your jurisdiction.

Exhibit 4.3 Federal circuit courts of appeals

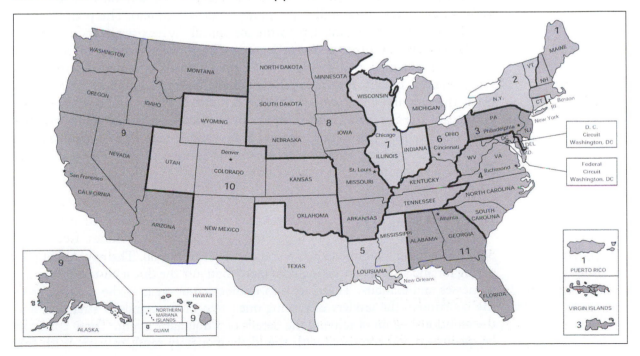

appellate courts
Courts that review the record from the trial court to determine if the trial judge made an error in applying the procedural or substantive law.

Appellate courts review the record from the trial court to determine if the trial judge made an error in applying the procedural or substantive law. Errors in procedural law relate to how the trial was conducted and are usually based upon rules of court and rules of evidence. A typical error is the admission of hearsay testimony that does not fall within the listed exceptions to hearsay under the rules of evidence. Errors in substantive law relate to the law of the case, such as the law of negligence or contract. A typical substantive error would be if the judge gave the jury the wrong instructions.

Appeals courts do not hear any additional testimony but rely upon the written record from the trial court, the legal briefs filed by the parties, and the oral arguments made by counsel before a panel of appeals court judges. Appellate courts may agree with the trial court and **affirm** the decision of the trial court, or they may disagree and **reverse** the decision made at the trial or **remand** the case, sending the case back to the trial court to take further testimony and either make new findings of fact or make new applications of law.

affirm
Ruling of appellate court that agrees with the outcome of a trial and can find no error.

reverse
Ruling of appellate court that disagrees with the outcome of a trial and finds that error was made.

remand
Appellate court disagrees with the outcome of a trial court but sends the matter back to the trial court for further proceeding in accordance with its opinion.

Highest Appellate Court or the Supreme Court

In both the federal and the state court systems, there is an ultimate court of appeals; in the federal system, it is the Supreme Court of the United States. In many states, it is also referred to as the Supreme Court; in some states it is referred to as the Superior Court. The function of these courts is generally to act as a court of last resort, hearing appeals from the intermediate appellate court; reviewing the decisions made; ensuring that laws passed by the legislative branch and the actions of the executive branch of government comply with the provisions of the Constitution; and ensuring that the Constitutional rights of the parties have been properly observed. Cases from a state's highest appellate court may be appealed to the United States Supreme Court when there is a question involving the application of one of the rights afforded under the United States Constitution.

Appeals to the Supreme Court of the United States are rare and subject to the willingness of the Court to review the case. Those seeking United States Supreme Court review must file a petition for writ of certiorari. This petition seeks the Supreme Court's permission to file an appeal. When certiorari is granted, the appeal may be filed with the Supreme Court. When certiorari is denied, the appeal is denied, and the decision of the circuit court stands. Certiorari is rarely granted, usually only in cases involving important Constitutional issues or issues that are unresolved among the thirteen circuit courts. Just as in the court of appeals, the Supreme Court does not hear evidence but instead reviews the record of the trial proceeding, reviews briefs, and listens to oral arguments of counsel. Oral argument is conducted before the entire court of nine justices. The Court will affirm, reverse, or remand a case.

■ SETTLEMENTS

LEARNING OBJECTIVE 5
Describe the advantages of settling a lawsuit before trial.

Settlements eliminate the expense and uncertainty of trial. The expense of preparing for and attending trial includes more than just the direct costs of preparing witnesses and exhibits. There are also indirect costs, such as the time spent in the courtroom, the anxiety of placing one's fate in the hands of strangers, and the emotional strain of reliving the details of a traumatic event. These costs can be quantified and compared with the likely monetary result of trial. With this information, the client is able to make a cost-benefit analysis to decide if a potential settlement is acceptable.

No matter how thoroughly a legal team prepares for trial, there is always the potential for surprise. In litigation, the unexpected can and does happen. Witnesses fail to appear, evidence gets lost, and judges make unfavorable evidentiary rulings that admit harmful (or bar the introduction of helpful) evidence at trial. Juries are always an unknown factor. How individual jurors will view the evidence or the credibility of parties or witnesses can never be known with certainty beforehand. A formal or informal settlement eliminates the uncertainty of a jury verdict or judge's decision in a non-jury case. What constitutes an acceptable settlement offer is ultimately the decision of the client. The lawyer can provide direction and recommendations, but it is the client who ultimately must accept the offer to settle the case. Keeping clients fully informed about their case is important when it is time to discuss settlement options.

Cases that have been valued by the legal team at higher amounts may be settled for much less if the defendant has limited assets, such as limited personal assets and minimal available insurance coverage to pay a judgment. People with limited personal assets also tend to purchase limited amounts of insurance because they have less to protect in the event of a claim against them. For example, many people purchase the minimum amount of automobile liability coverage required by state law to lawfully operate a motor vehicle. People with limited savings who rent their residence have little to lose see no value in paying for more coverage than necessary.

Lawyers representing plaintiffs injured in accidents by a defendants with limited financial resources and minimum insurance coverage must sometimes advise clients that although they have a good case, their recovery will be limited and will be less than the true value of the case because there is limited insurance coverage and few, if any, other assets from which to pay a judgment that might be obtained at trial.

Clients who themselves have limited resources may need funds to compensate them for the time lost from work or for other financial obligations. These clients cannot afford to wait months or years for the case to go to trial even if the potential verdict is greater than that offered to settle the case immediately. For some, the idea of settling the case by accepting a lesser amount now is more attractive than risking it all on the chance a jury might award a higher amount. This is particularly true where there are unsettled issues of law involved and the potential for a protracted trial followed by posttrial motions and an appeal.

Settlements are favored by judges. Judges pride themselves on being able to quickly dispose of cases so that there is no backlog of cases showing on their **docket,** their personal list of pending cases. Trying cases does not clear the docket as quickly as settling cases; therefore, a frequent reason behind a successful settlement is the negotiating skills of the judge. Clients should be advised of the role of the judge in trying to settle the case during the pretrial conferences, when the judge and lawyers meet to discuss issues involved in the pending trial. Because it is always the client's decision to accept or reject the settlement offers, many judges require each attorney to have the clients available by phone or in person in the courthouse during these meetings in order to facilitate settlement discussions. It is not unheard of for some judges to actually discuss the settlement issue with the client in front of counsel. The paralegal may frequently be called upon to sit with the client during these times to ensure client availability and, where appropriate, to relay information between counsel and the client.

docket
A particular judge's list of cases pending.

When to Settle

Defendants, especially corporate defendants and insurance carriers that insure defendants, generally want a quick settlement. For them, it is an economic decision. They would rather pay the plaintiff a little more to settle the case than pay a greater sum in legal fees to defense counsel. Individual defendants and plaintiffs should prepare a cost-benefit analysis just as they are prepared by the insurance companies and corporate parties. For the corporate defendant and insurance carrier, it is a matter of the total dollars required. Rarely does it matter to them if more goes to the plaintiff or to the defense counsel; they just want to settle within the amount they set aside for the case. This amount is called the **reserve**—an amount the companies must show as a contingent or potential liability on their corporate financial statements. If they can settle the case for less than the amount of the reserve, they get to reduce the liability and return any excess saved to the general corporate fund—effectively a profit to them. For many companies, there is a concerted effort to clear these reserves (pay the claims) near the end of the corporation's fiscal year.

Negotiations during the early stages of the processing of the case may not result in a settlement, but there is nothing lost in trying. Important information about the opposing party's strategy and witnesses can be gained during the negotiations. How the opposing party intends to present the case is sometimes disclosed during settlement discussions as a way of showing the strength of the party's case. That information is invaluable when preparing for trial or later settlement discussion, possibly with the help of the trial judge. Paying attention to how the other side views the evidence of the case may help in preparing trial strategy.

Negotiation of a Settlement

There is no one way to conduct **settlement negotiations.** Each lawyer develops a personal style. Some take the approach of presenting their cases with "shock and awe," loud, blustering threats and intimidation, trying to show their personal ability to try the case with much bravado. Others follow a more traditional approach, demonstrating quiet confidence and carefully explaining the strengths of their case. There is no way to predict how a particular lawyer might conduct settlement discussions. In part, the strategy depends not just on the strength of the case, in law and fact, but also the experience and reputation of the opposing counsel. Trial lawyers gain reputations, and having a good, solid reputation for being well prepared and skillful goes a long way in how the other side will react to settlement negotiations. If the opposing counsel has a reputation for never bluffing and always being well prepared, a less-skilled attorney or one with a weak case may want to settle to avoid the inherent risks of trial or resolution through ADR.

■ SETTLEMENT DOCUMENTS

Settlement Letters

In many cases, an informal settlement demand is made in a letter prepared by the plaintiff's lawyer. Exhibit 4.4 is a sample settlement demand letter in an accident case. It clearly and concisely sets out the facts and the law, which places liability on the defendant. It also includes a calculation of special damages.

reserve
An amount of insurance companies set aside for damages in a claim or lawsuit.

LEARNING OBJECTIVE 6
Create the documents for making a demand for settlement.

Exhibit 4.4 Sample settlement demand letter in an accident case

MASON, MARSHALL AND BENJAMIN
ATTORNEYS AT LAW

Owen Mason

Ariel Marshall

Ethan Benjamin

Cary Eden

July 28, 2015

Mary Smith

Claims Adjuster

Any Insurance Carrier

Ivytown, PA 00000

Re: Our client: Samuel James

    Your Insured: Suzanne Lincoln

    Your claim No. ZZZ1234

Dear Claims Adjuster

In regard to your claim captioned above enclosed please find the following:

1. Police Accident Report
2. Report of Speedy Emergency Rescue Ambulance
3. Records of Mercy Hospital Emergency Room
4. Records of Mercy Hospital
5. Records of Full Range Physical Therapy
6. Report of Treating Physician Dr. Miller
7. Record of ABC Trucking Company
8. Schedule of Damages

This letter is issued solely for the purposes of facilitating settlement negotiations. Nothing contained herein is admissible in court for any purpose. Nothing contained herein is an admission of liability on the part of the plaintiff.

The report of the investigating police officer, who is also a certified accident reconstructionist, leaves no doubt that your client was responsible for the accident. Not only is fault determined based upon the finding of the report but your insured also received traffic citations for exceeding the speed limit by more than 25 miles, failure to stop at a traffic control device, and careless driving. A review of the court records reveals that your insured has pleaded guilty to all of these charges. Under the laws of our state, once a driver pleads guilty to a moving violation that resulted in a traffic accident, the driver's liability for the accident and damages arising therefrom is conclusively established. Liability being established, the issue remains for us to determine the appropriate level of damages to compensate our client.

A review of the medical records and schedule of damages reveals the nature and extent of our client's injuries, the lengthy hospital stay following surgery, the grueling physical therapy program, and the permanent nature of the injuries sustained. Our client was ejected from his seat simultaneously with the car overturning, which resulted in the car landing on its side on top of our client's legs. Our client remained conscious throughout the extrication process suffering great pain, shock, and horror at the sight of his legs being pinned under the car.

The six-week hospital stay was necessitated by four surgeries to repair severed nerves, veins, and arteries as well as stabilization of broken bones. Following this lengthy hospitalization our client participated in physical therapy to regain the use of his legs. Although he has regained the ability to walk, one leg is now shorter than the other, resulting in a limp that requires him to use a cane. Additionally, our client has limited sensation in his lower extremities and is at risk for infection because of peripheral vascular disease related to damaged veins and arteries.

These permanent physical limitations have impacted on our client's ability to work as a truck driver. He is unable to support his family in the manner they are accustomed financially. He is also unable to perform the duties he customarily provided around the house such as repairs, maintenance, and home improvement projects.

In light of your insured's liability, the nature, extent, and permanency of the injuries, the pain and suffering experienced and the loss of life's pleasures, we assert a demand of $1,500,000 is appropriate to compensate our client.

Very truly yours,

Mason, Marshall & Benjamin

by_____

Settlement Brochures

The **settlement brochure** contains the same information as the demand letter but is presented as a more formal statement of the plaintiff's case. It starts with an introduction that describes the basic facts of the case. As with all written documents, the introduction sets the tone for the remainder of the brochure. In cases involving serious injuries and damages for large sums of money, the settlement brochure may be prepared professionally by a media consultant. The usual order of presentation is:

1. description of the basic facts,
2. damages, and
3. demand.

The facts may be a chronology of an accident or the commercial transaction or other foundation establishing the liability. With liability clearly laid out, it is then a matter of presenting the damages and the reasons for the amount demanded. Inclusion of the components, described below, in a settlement brochure affects its impact and credibility.

Photographs

The right photograph can convey the seriousness of an accident or of an injury sustained that words cannot convey. Selected photographs that would be used as evidence in trial should be included in the settlement brochure. Photographs may show an accident scene, the damaged motor vehicles, and the plaintiff's physical condition before and after an accident and during medical treatment. Such photographs should be integrated into the settlement brochure along with the plaintiff's medical records. High-definition copies should be made so that the defendant's lawyer can readily see what a trier of fact would see—injury caused by the conduct of the defendant. Adding captions or short explanations about each photograph can direct the viewer's attention to the desired focus of the items. For ease of identification, each photograph should be given an exhibit number so that references to each photograph can be made throughout the settlement brochure.

Bills and Reports

A summary of the bills and expenses should be placed at the beginning of the section containing the medical bills, expenses, and related reports. Medical bills and reports, employment documentation, or other pertinent records are included to support the demand and also to demonstrate the evidence that may be introduced at trial. As with the photographs, each item should be marked with an appropriate exhibit number.

Day in the Life

To better visualize how a plaintiff's life has changed as a result of the accident, a "day-in-the-life" video may be prepared and sent with the settlement brochure. Whether illustrated by a video or with still photographs, a day in the plaintiff's life is an important part of any settlement brochure. The documents and the video should show all of the dramatic changes in the plaintiff's life as a result of the injuries he or she sustained. Those changes, and the fact that the medical records indicate that the plaintiff will live that way without any realistic expectation of recovery, can be important arguments in favor of a sizeable settlement demand.

Evaluation of the Plaintiff's Case

The demand for settlement purposes is a combination of the special and general damages computed by the legal team as part of the case valuation. Damages are designed to compensate the plaintiff for bodily injuries, the resulting pain and suffering, and the loss of life's pleasures.

Frequently, plaintiff's lawyers set forth a summary of the plaintiff's damages; these are then mathematically totaled to determine the settlement demand. Those itemized damages should include all of the previously discussed items of damage. This list must contain both the bills paid on behalf of the plaintiff and those damages that are not documented by an invoice and may include the actuarially determined future costs of treatment and loss of income.

The chart in Exhibit 4.5 shows the future damages a child will suffer as a result of a brain injury sustained at the age of four years. It is noteworthy that no dollar amounts are listed; instead, a compelling description of the physical, mental, and psychological limitations is given. This approach focuses on the totality of the injury instead of on the individual special damages.

Final Caution

A final caution on the creation of a settlement brochure: There is a careful balance between making a persuasive case and giving away trial strategy and **attorney work product**—material prepared for litigation. Disclosing too much about the plaintiff's case will enable the defense legal team to rebut any creative

Exhibit 4.5 Damage analysis of brain injury in child

AGE	DEGREE OF IMPACT	DESCRIPTION
4–5 yrs.	Catastrophic (90%)	Hospitalization; major operation; unable to attend school; inability and difficulty in caring for self; practical activities and social life completely disrupted; anxiety, fear, and concern over physical condition.
6–13 yrs.	Mild to moderate (24–45%)	Some interference with academic performance and school activities, increasing awareness of limitations; increased anxiety due to inappropriate behaviors.
13–18 yrs.	Moderate (50%)	Increasing interference with academic performance and school activities as academic demands increase; increasing awareness by self and others of inappropriate behaviors; increased frustration due to inability to meet expectations and goals.
18–25 yrs.	Moderate to Severe (33–67%)	Substantial reduction of potential enjoyment in engaging in preferred occupation; frustration from inability to effectively manage college-level academic work; reduced opportunity for marriage partners due to organic personality disorder; some limitation in social activities. Possible depression as a result of inability to meet life goals.
26–55 yrs.	Moderate (40%)	The quality of Brittany's life will depend upon the degree to which she will be able to meet normal life goals of marriage, family (children), and occupational/vocational enjoyment. Possibility of continued bouts of depression, which may be severe at times if unable to meet her life goals.
55–71 yrs.	Moderate to Severe (33–70%)	As Brittany grows older she will be more prone to physical trauma from medical complications, particularly from early degenerative joint disease/arthritis in left hip. Risk of early development of dementia due to closed head injury, which may require placement in institution.

Source: Courtesy Charles G. Monnett III & Associates, www.Carolinalaw.com

or imaginative legal arguments the plaintiff legal team has developed. The rules of discovery will ultimately require the disclosure of documents, photographs, and witnesses' statements. However, the legal team's legal research and trial strategy are not discoverable under the **work product doctrine.** Be wary of disclosing too much in a settlement brochure or letter, but be comprehensive and convincing.

Ethical Considerations

There are several important ethical considerations that should guide paralegals during the settlement process. Paralegals may not make settlement offers or demands or agree to a settlement on behalf of a client. Paralegals also cannot advise clients on the acceptability of a settlement offer or demand. Such activities would constitute the unauthorized practice of law. Settlement discussions and the advisability of accepting settlement are the lawyer's responsibility. Paralegals are frequently asked to play an active role in settlement negotiations by their supervising lawyer. Paralegals should seek authorization for all negotiation activities, being especially careful about releasing confidential information about the case during any discussions. The ethical obligation of confidentiality applies to paralegals, and all confidential information must be protected.

Clients should be kept informed of all developments, including settlement offers and demands. Paralegals commonly interact with clients, and clients rely on paralegals for such information; but paralegals may communicate only information that is authorized by the supervising attorney.

■ DOCUMENTS FOR SETTLING AND TERMINATING A LAWSUIT

LEARNING OBJECTIVE 7
Prepare the documents for settling and terminating a lawsuit.

As noted previously, in civil litigation, a settlement agreement is a contract between the parties to resolve or end a lawsuit. Both the plaintiff and the defendant give consideration to make the contract valid. The plaintiff gives up the right to sue the defendant in exchange for the payment of a sum of money paid by the defendant.

Each party's reason for settling may be different, and it is unlikely one knows what brought the other to the settlement table. Because you can never predict if a case will settle or if it will proceed to trial, information about a legal team's settlement strategy must be kept confidential. While the terms of a possible settlement will be fully discussed, the reasons or motives for settlements are not.

Either side may start the settlement discussions. The plaintiff may demand a specific sum to settle the case, or the defendant may offer an amount to settle. **Settlement demands** and **settlement offers** are usually far apart, and the negotiation process attempts to bring the parties' figures closer together. In those rare instances where the demand and the offer are close, settlement occurs quickly. Exceptionally high demands or unreasonably low offers rarely result in further negotiations. The offer-demand must be within a range of possibility if the legal teams are serious about a potential for settlement. Whatever the amount offered or demanded, the legal team must be able to verbally justify it as reasonable.

It is no secret that the first demand made by the plaintiff's lawyer is usually much greater than the amount of authority granted by the plaintiff as acceptable for settlement. Clients are always happy when the legal team announces that the

settlement demand
Amount demanded by plaintiff to settle a case.

settlement offer
Amount offered by defendant to settle a case.

settlement amount is greater than what the client expected. Clients will always be happy with the legal team's efforts if it recovers more money than authorized. The same can be also said of offers. If the defense legal team can settle a case for less than its settlement authority, then the legal team is successful in saving the client money. During the negotiations, efforts are made to reduce the plaintiff's demand and raise the defendant's offer.

The speed of settlement negotiations will be governed by the ability of the legal team to respond quickly to offers or demands from the opposing party. If the legal teams are prepared and have thoroughly evaluated their client's case, then settlement negotiations should quickly determine if the case can be settled. Sometimes settlement negotiations are delayed because of the necessity of communicating with the client. All settlement offers or demands must be communicated to the client, even when the legal team knows the amount is outside the client's authorization. In all cases, the client is entitled to consider the offer or demand.

Sometimes a demand and an offer do not involve a monetary settlement. In those cases, the dispute is over the right to do or not do something or over ownership of property where the remedy sought is a specific performance—an equitable remedy as opposed to a monetary remedy.

Minors' Settlements

If a lawsuit has not been filed and the settlement is reached prior to any litigation, the parties to the settlement usually do not have to concern themselves with any judicial involvement. However, there is an exception to this general rule: when one of the parties is a minor, or under a mental disability, the court must approve the settlement. The rules of many courts mandate that judges approve the settlement of a minor's claims for the settlement to be effective. Exhibit 4.6 is a sample Petition for Minors Compromise for California and Exhibit 4.7 is one from Pennsylvania.

Approval of such settlements can be obtained by filing a petition in which the details of the liability and damages are reviewed. Legal fees and costs to be paid from the minor's recovery are also subject to the scrutiny of the court. Some courts limit the amount to a percentage that is less than what would be charged an adult plaintiff. Understandably, judges seek to give the minor the greatest possible recovery. Many jurisdictions have specific rules governing the investment of minors' funds. Speculative investments are discouraged in favor of safe investments in insured accounts to protect the principal sum and generate income until the minor reaches adulthood. Some jurisdictions also require court approval for settlements involving claims by the estate of decedents and other similar plaintiffs. Part of the evaluation of a client's case should include a thorough knowledge of the rules and practices applicable to the settlement of cases in your local court. Do not fail to overlook the possibility that any settlement may first need the court's approval.

Settlement Documents

Settlement agreements, like many contracts, must be reduced to writing. The skillful preparation of accurate and appropriate settlement documents will prevent problems and guarantee conclusion of the client's claim as agreed.

The **release** is the document, signed by the plaintiff, in which the plaintiff states that the defendant is released from all possible claims arising out of a

release
Written document in which plaintiff releases claims against defendant.

Exhibit 4.6 Petition for Minor's Compromise—California

MC-350

ATTORNEY OR PARTY WITHOUT ATTORNEY *(Name, State Bar number, and address):*	*FOR COURT USE ONLY*

TELEPHONE NO.:   FAX NO. *(Optional):*

E-MAIL ADDRESS *(Optional):*

ATTORNEY FOR *(Name):*

SUPERIOR COURT OF CALIFORNIA, COUNTY OF

    STREET ADDRESS:

    MAILING ADDRESS:

    CITY AND ZIP CODE:

    BRANCH NAME:

CASE NAME:

CASE NUMBER:

PETITION TO APPROVE: ☐ COMPROMISE OF DISPUTED CLAIM	HEARING DATE:

☐ **COMPROMISE OF PENDING ACTION**

☐ **DISPOSITION OF PROCEEDS OF JUDGMENT**

    ☐ **Minor**   ☐ **Person With a Disability**

DEPT.:   TIME:

NOTICE TO PETITIONERS:

Except as noted below, you must use this form to request court approval of (1) the compromise of a disputed claim of a minor, (2) the compromise of a pending action or proceeding in which a minor or a person with a disability (including a conservatee) is a party, or (3) the disposition of the proceeds of a judgment for a minor or person with a disability. (See Code Civ. Proc., § 372; Prob. Code, § 3600 et seq.) You and the minor or disabled person must attend the hearing on this petition unless the court for good cause dispenses with a personal appearance. The court may require the presence and testimony of witnesses, including the attending or examining physician, and other evidence relating to the merits of the claim and the nature and extent of the injury, care, treatment, and hospitalization. The court may consider on an expedited basis without a hearing requests for approval of the compromises of certain claims and actions or the disposition of the proceeds of certain judgments. If your claim, action, or judgment qualifies for expedited consideration and you want to request it, you must use form MC-350EX for your request. See Cal. Rules of Court, rule 7.950.5.

1. **Petitioner** *(name):*

2. **Claimant** *(name):*
   a. Address:

   b. Date of birth: c. Age: d. Sex: e. ☐ Minor   ☐ Person with a disability

3. **Relationship** Petitioner's relationship to the claimant *(check all applicable boxes):*
   a. ☐   Parent   g. ☐   Other relationship *(specify:)*
   b. ☐   Guardian ad litem
   c. ☐   Guardian
   d. ☐   Conservator
   e. ☐   Disabled adult claimant is a petitioner. *(See instructions for items 3e and 3f below.)*
   f. ☐   Disabled adult claimant's express consent to the relief requested in this petition is provided on Attachment 3f.

   (If you checked item 3e or 3f, state facts on Attachment 3e or 3f showing that the claimant has capacity under Probate Code section 812 to petition or consent to a petition. Only an adult claimant who has sufficient capacity and who does not have a conservator of the estate may petition or consent to a petition. See Probate Code section 3613.)

4. **Nature of claim** The claim of the minor or adult person with a disability:
   a. ☐   Has not been filed in an action or proceeding. *(Complete items 5–23.)*
   b. ☐   Is the subject of a pending action or proceeding that will be compromised without a trial on the merits of the claim.
        Name of court:

        Case no.:   Trial date: *(Complete items 5–23.)*

Page 1 of 10

Form Adopted for
Alternative Mandatory Use
Judicial Council of California
MC-350 [Rev. January 1, 2010]

PETITION TO APPROVE COMPROMISE OF DISPUTED CLAIM OR PENDING ACTION OR DISPOSITION OF PROCEEDS OF JUDGMENT FOR MINOR OR PERSON WITH A DISABILITY
(Miscellaneous)

Code of Civil Procedure, § 372 et seq.;
Probate Code, § 3500 et seq.;
Cal. Rules of Court, rules 3.1384,
7.101, 7.950, 7.951
www.courtinfo.ca.gov

Exhibit 4.7 Petition for Minor's Compromise—Pennsylvania

PETITION FOR LEAVE TO SETTLE OR COMPROMISE MINOR'S ACTION

To The Honorable, the Judges of the Said Court:

The Petition of _____, a minor, by his Guardian, by his attorney, _____, Esquire respectfully requests:

1. Petitioner is :_____.

2. The minor was born on _____.

3. The minor resides with _____ at the following address: _____.

4. A guardian (was) (was not) appointed for the minor as follows: _____. A copy of the Order is attached.

5. The minor's mother is _____ who resides at the following address: _____.

6. The minor's father is _____ who resides at the following address: _____.

7. The defendant is _____ who resides or whose principal place of business at all relevant times was _____.

8. On _____ the minor sustained the following injuries at the following location (set forth in detail):_____.

   (If additional space is needed, please continue on separate page).

9. A Complaint was filed against defendant(s) as follows: _____.

10. Attached hereto is a report by Dr. _____ dated _____ which sets forth the present condition of the minor.

11. Attached hereto is a statement, under oath, of the minor's parents and/or guardian and/or guardian ad litem certifying the physical and/or mental condition of the minor, as well as the parents' and/or guardian's and/or guardian ad litem's approval of the proposed settlement and distribution.

12. Attached hereto is the written approval of the proposed settlement and distribution by the minor, who is sixteen (16) years of age or older.

13. The following settlement has been proposed: _____

    (If additional space is needed, please continue on separate page).

14. Counsel is of the professional opinion that the proposed settlement is reasonable due to the following:_____

    (If additional space is needed, please continue on separate page).

15. Counsel has incurred the following expenses for which reimbursement is sought (please set forth in detail)_____

    (If additional space is needed, please continue on separate page).

16. The following costs have been incurred by or on behalf of the minor and must be paid from the proceeds of the settlement:_____

    (If additional space is needed, please continue on separate page.)

17. The Department of Public Welfare, or any other entity, does (not) have a claim or lien against the plaintiff(s) as follows _____

    (If additional space is needed, please continue on separate page.)

(continued)

Exhibit 4.7 *(continued)*

18. Counsel requests a fee in the sum of $_____ which is _____% per cent of the net settlement payable to the minor. A copy of the retainer agreement is attached.

19. Counsel (has) (has not) and (will) (will not) receive collateral payments as counsel fees for representation involving the same matter from third parties (i.e. subrogation).

20. The net settlement payable to the minor (after deduction of costs and attorneys fees) is $_____.

WHEREFORE, Petitioner requests that he/she be permitted to enter into the settlement recited above and that the Court enter an Order of Distribution as follows:

    a. To _____ $_____ Reimbursement for Costs

    b. To _____ $_____ Reimbursement for Costs

    c. To _____ $_____ Counsel Fee

    d. To: Adult Plaintiff(s) $_____ (if applicable)

    e. To _____, a $_____ minor, in restricted accounts not to be withdrawn before majority or upon prior leave of Court.

OR

    e. To _____, the Guardian $_____ of the Estate of _____, A Minor, appointed or to be appointed by the Orphans' Court of _____ County, after posting appropriate security.

---

mutual release
Written document in which both plaintiff and defendant agree to release one another from claims.

certain contract, accident, or other occurrence in exchange for the payment of a sum of money. Exhibit 4.8 is a release prepared for the plaintiff.

Sometimes the release is drafted as a **mutual release,** with both the plaintiff and defendant agreeing to release each other from any and all claims arising from the transaction or occurrence that gave rise to the dispute. Mutual releases are preferable because they conclude all disputes between the two parties. Without a mutual release, defendants can pursue counterclaims against plaintiffs if there is a settlement prior to the filing of any lawsuits. A mutual release precludes any future litigation by either side of the dispute. Exhibit 4.9 is a mutual release for the plaintiff and the defendant.

The supervising attorney must review and approve the release before it is sent to opposing counsel for review or for the client's signature. Normally, it is the defendant's legal team that prepares the release and other settlement documents and submits them to plaintiff's counsel for signature. Local practice may vary, and paralegals should become familiar with the custom in the jurisdictions where they are working.

Exhibit 4.8 Release

RELEASE

I, _____ for myself, my heirs, executors, successors and assigns, for and in consideration of the sum of _____ dollars ($_____) _____ paid to me by _____ _____do hereby remise, waive and release any and all claims related to property damages or personal injury arising from an automobile accident which occurred on December 25, 2015 at the intersection of First and Maple Streets in the City of Millstown, State of Idaho.

    In Witness whereof I have set my and and seal this _____ day of _____, 20_____.

                                              _____
                                            Signature

Exhibit 4.9 Mutual release

SETTLEMENT AGREEMENT AND MUTUAL RELEASE

This Settlement Agreement and Mutual Release ("Agreement") is entered into this _____ day of _____, 20_____, by and between _____ ("passenger"), and _____ ("driver")

WITNESSETH:

WHEREAS, the Passenger was a passenger in an automobile owned and operated by Driver on July 15, 2014;

WHEREAS, Driver and Passenger were arguing over control over the stereo CD player in the car;

WHEREAS, Driver then lost control of the vehicle and struck a tree resulting in injury to Passenger ("Accident");

WHEREAS, Driver and Passenger seek to resolve any disputes between them arising out of the Accident

NOW, THEREFORE, in consideration of the premises set forth above, which are fully incorporated herein by reference thereto, and in consideration of the mutual promises and agreements contained herein, the sufficiency of which is hereby acknowledged, the parties do hereby agree as follows:

AGREEMENT

1. **Incorporation by Reference.** The above premises and recitals are expressly incorporated into the parties' Agreement herein by this reference.

2. **Driver's Obligations.** Driver agrees to pay to Passenger the sum of $50,000.

3. **Passenger's Obligations.** Passenger agrees to waive any further right to recovery as a result of the Accident.

4. **General Release.** Driver and Passenger for themselves and each of their spouses, heirs, executors, administrators, successors and assigns hereby irrevocably and unconditionally release, acquit and forever discharge the other, their heirs, executors, administrators, successors and assigns to the fullest extent permitted by law, from any charges, complaints, claims, liabilities, grievances, obligations, promises, agreements, contracts, covenants, duties, controversies, damages, actions, suits, proceedings, rights, demands, costs, losses and expenses (including attorneys' fees and costs actually incurred) of any nature whatsoever, known or unknown, suspected or unsuspected, in law or in equity, whether statutory or common law, whether federal, state, local or otherwise, which the parties now have, own, hold or claim to have from the date of this Agreement to the end of time and arising out of the Accident.

5. **Parties Fully Advised.** The parties acknowledge that they have read and, having had an opportunity to seek the advice of counsel, understand the provisions of this Agreement and represent that their execution of this Agreement constitutes their knowing and voluntary act made without coercion or intimidation. The parties further acknowledge that this Agreement is binding upon them, their heirs, executors, administrators, successors and assigns.

6. **Interpretation.** This Agreement has been prepared after negotiation between the parties, with each contributing equally to its content and the final written expression thereof. If any ambiguity is contained herein then in resolving such ambiguity no weight shall be given in favor of or against any party solely on account of its drafting this Agreement. This Agreement shall be interpreted and governed in all respects by the laws of the State of Illinois.

7. **Execution.** Each signatory hereto further personally and separately represents and warrants that she/he is duly authorized to enter into this Agreement and bind the party on whose behalf she/he is acting.

8. **Integration/Amendment.** This two (2) page Agreement, with all signature lines appearing on the second (2nd) page, incorporates all prior discussions and negotiations among the parties, and constitutes the full and entire agreement between and among the parties with respect to the subject matter hereof. No amendment hereto shall be effective unless it is in writing and signed by all of the parties.

9. **Headings.** The headings used herein are for ease of reference only and have no legal purpose or effect.

10. **Counterparts/Facsimile.** This Agreement may be executed in one or more counterparts and by facsimile, each of which shall be deemed an original, but all of which together shall constitute one and the same instrument.

IN WITNESS HEREOF, the parties have caused this Agreement to be duly executed and delivered under seal, dated as of the day and year first written above:

_____

(Print Name: _____)

_____

(Print Name: _____)

Checklist

- Correctly identify the parties.
- Correctly identify the transaction, accident, or occurrence from which the dispute arose.
- If a lawsuit has been started, include the identification of the suit by court and docket number.
- Correctly identify the settlement terms and payout method.
- If a lawsuit has been filed, include provisions for withdrawing or dismissing the case.
- Be certain the appropriate release language is present.
- Include a confidentiality clause to protect the client's privacy.
- Include signature lines.

Confidentiality and Settlements

Because most settlements actually occur out of court, the terms of the settlement do not pass through the court. The release is not filed with most courts, and settlements are frequently confidential. Some releases even condition the settlement on the parties keeping the terms of the settlement confidential. The parties are specifically forbidden in those cases from speaking with the media or anyone else about the outcome of the case. But not all confidentiality agreements are enforceable. Where the agreement fails to state a penalty, there is no sanction for not keeping the terms confidential.

Termination of Lawsuits

When settlement occurs after the lawsuit is filed, the agreement of the parties settling the action must be prepared and executed, as well as the appropriate documentation to have the case marked as settled in the court records. In federal court, an action may be terminated by **notice of dismissal, stipulation**, or a **consent judgment.**

A notice of dismissal might be used when no answer to the complaint was filed, and only the plaintiff signs the notice of dismissal. By contrast, a stipulation of dismissal is signed by all parties to the lawsuit. Exhibit 4.10 is a stipulation of dismissal. The advantage of this method of termination is that the details of the settlement agreement of the parties are not made public; only the information contained in the original pleadings and the fact that the action has been dismissed are part of the public record.

With the entry of a consent judgment, the defendant agrees to a judgment being entered on the court docket for a particular sum. The consent judgment might be used when the agreed sum is expected to be paid out over an extended period of time. The judgment becomes a matter of public record. If the defendant fails to make payment, the plaintiff has the ability to execute on the judgment. The plaintiff has a priority claim over other claims entered against the defendant after the judgment. Exhibit 4.11 is a consent judgment.

State court systems have different procedures for officially terminating a lawsuit. All courts require litigants to notify the court of a settlement. The form that a local court uses is specified in the local court's rules of civil procedure. Most law offices have a template form available in their word processing files; the form may also be available from the court's online services. All lawsuits that are settled must be terminated by filing the necessary documents so that the information is entered on the official court docket.

Exhibit 4.10 Notice of stipulation of dismissal

UNITED STATES DISTRICT COURT
NORTHERN DISTRICT OF NEW YORK

B.K., a minor by her   No.: _____
Parents and Guardians,   **STIPULATION OF**
Janice Knowles and   **DISMISSAL**
Seven Knowles,   Plaintiff   **CIVIL ACTION—NEGLIENCE**

v

Harry Hart,
Kinnicutt Bus Company,
Charles Stanley, and
MVF Construction Company, Defendant   Attorney ID No. 124987

On this _____ day of _____, 20___, it is stipulated and agreed between counsel for Plaintiff and

counsel for Defendant that this action be dismissed, with/without prejudice regarding all claims and

counterclaims of the parties and without costs to the parties and that an order consistent with the

stipulation be entered without further notice.

                                                    _____
                                                            Attorney for Plaintiff
                                                    _____
                                                            Attorney for Defendat

SO ORDERED
_____, Judge,
United States District Court for the Northern District of New York this _____ day of _____, 20___.

■ ALTERNATIVE DISPUTE RESOLUTION

Alternative dispute resolution, commonly referred to as **ADR,** plays an important role in the American legal system. ADR is an alternative to resolution of disputes using the traditional court system. In many jurisdictions, alternative dispute resolution has become part of the judicial system. In an effort to clear backed-up court dockets, local rules may require all matters with damages less than $50,000.00 to participate in court-sponsored arbitration or mediation before a trial can be held. Where there is no court rule requiring ADR, parties may find that a contract provision requires it or they may voluntarily submit to ADR. In any event, cases are heard and decisions or recommendations are made by individuals who are selected by the parties, or in some judicial ADR systems, appointed by the court. These individuals may or may not be lawyers. The judge or jury is replaced by independent individuals outside of the courtroom who resolve the dispute.

Lawyers and clients frequently choose ADR because it is less costly than a trial, and the dispute is resolved more quickly. Where the parties do not want the information or dispute made public, as it would become with the filing of a lawsuit and accompanying open court proceeding, ADR provides confidentiality.

Unlike traditional trials, ADR generally does not have formal discovery, nor are the rules of evidence strictly applied. Depending on the facts of the case, less formal procedures may be an advantage or a detriment. Arbitrators and mediators in ADR are less likely to be swayed by the emotion or

LEARNING OBJECTIVE 8
Describe the methods of alternative dispute resolution.

alternative dispute resolution (ADR)
Resolution of disputes without utilizing the court system; may include arbitration, mediation.

Exhibit 4.11 Consent judgment

UNITED STATES DISTRICT COURT
NORTHERN DISTRICT OF NEW YORK

_____

B.K., a minor by her
Parents and Guardians,
Janice Knowles and
Seven Knowles, Plantiff

v

Harry Hart,
Kinnicutt Bus Company,
Charles Stanley, and
MVF Construction Company, Defendant

No.: _____

JUDGMENT
CIVIL ACTION—NEGLIENCE

Jury Trial Demanded

Attorney ID No. 124987

On this _____ day of _____, 20___, it is stipulated and agreed between counsel for Plaintiff and counsel for Defendant that this action be dismissed, with/without prejudice regarding all claims and counterclaims of the parties and without costs to the parties and that judgment be entered in the amount of $_____ in favor of the plaintiff and against the defendant and an order consistent with the stipulation be entered without further notice.

_____
Attorney for Plaintiff

_____
Attorney for Defendant

SO ORDERED

_____, **Judge, United States**
District Court for the Northern District of New York this _____ day of _____, 20____.

sympathy that a jury might have for a party. In addition, without the authority of a judge to impose procedural law (or in extreme cases, to compel attendance with subpoenas and hold attorneys and parties in contempt), ADR must be a mutually desirable method with which both sides feel comfortable. Strategically, some attorneys may feel that a particular opposing counsel does not conduct him- or herself well without the power of the judge to control courtroom behavior and tactics.

Frequently with ADR, parties may stipulate to the use of reports and evidence without the need to bring in custodians of the records or experts. For example, both sides may agree to the admission of all the medical records in a motor vehicle accident case without bringing in or deposing the treating doctors.

One final consideration on the use of ADR is the limited right of appeal. By agreement of the parties, the decision may be binding, with no right of appeal of an adverse decision. Most courts limit appeals from ADR decisions to those cases where the decision maker(s) had a conflict of interest not previously disclosed, were corrupt, or were guilty of misconduct. In some cases, parties in their original contractual dealing have agreed to arbitration, such as when opening a stock brokerage account or signing a real estate agreement of sale. Where there is no requirement to use ADR, the ultimate decision to use ADR to resolve the dispute is a strategic one that the legal team must make after full and complete disclosure of the advantages and disadvantages to the client.

ADVICE FROM THE FIELD

BY HELEN I. BENDIX—JUDGE, LOS ANGELES
Former Editor-in-Chief of the Los Angeles County Bar Association's *ADR Section Newsletter*

Overview

With the increase in litigation costs and court congestion, individuals and business entities are turning to alternative dispute resolution or "ADR" to resolve their disputes. While ADR denotes a variety of techniques to resolve disputes outside the courtroom, the following proceedings typically come within the rubric of "ADR": negotiation, **mediation**, **neutral fact finding**, early neutral evaluation, mini-trials, summary jury trials, **arbitration** and private judging. Although each of these ADR methods has its own characteristics, they generally enable the parties to:

1. Resolve their dispute in a confidential setting;
2. Establish deadlines and procedural rules governing the proceedings;
3. Select the presiding official or "neutral"
4. Contain litigation costs; and
5. Maintain on-going business and personal relationships.

ADR may not be appropriate in all settings, for example, where:

1. The parties want a jury trial;
2. The dispute turns on witness credibility;
3. Public resolution of a novel legal issue (e.g. legal precedent) is needed to discourage similar claims;
4. One wants to preserve full rights of appeal; or
5. The possibility of settlement is so slim that ADR may only achieve educating the other side about the weaknesses of one's case.

ADR Methods

NEGOTIATIONS

In the context of ADR, the term "negotiations" refers to negotiations to settle pending disputes. Negotiations are the most common form of ADR, and are, by definition, voluntary and non-binding. Negotiations are generally conducted by the parties and sometimes their attorneys as well. While negotiations generally do not involve intervention of third-party presiding officials, independent third-parties can aid settlement negotiations by helping participants focus not on the assignment of fault, but instead on what caused the dispute and how it can be remedied.

MEDIATION

Mediation is a non-binding structured process in which the mediator helps the participants reach a negotiated settlement of their differences. The mediator...does not have the power to render a decision.... [T]he mediator acts as a facilitator in helping the participants themselves arrive at a solution.

Although mediation is generally voluntary, it may be required in certain substantive cases. For example... where the amount in controversy does not exceed $50,000....

Mediation allows the parties to preserve their business relationship and provides the parties a neutral, non-adversarial forum for evaluating the strengths and weaknesses of their respective positions. Mediations are confidential and can afford a more creative resolution of problems because the parties control the process. Sometimes mediation is combined with other ADR techniques. For example, the parties can agree to "med-arb." Med-arb typically involves an agreement first to mediate a dispute and then to arbitrate the dispute before the same neutral who served as the mediator if the mediation is unsuccessful.

Mediation, however, may not be advantageous where the parties are of substantially unequal bargaining strength because the stronger party may force a compromise on the weaker party. Where there is no genuine possibility of settlement, mediation may just educate one's "adversary" without resolving the dispute....

NEUTRAL FACT FINDING

Where a dispute involves an issue requiring expertise, and that issue is a stumbling block to settlement, the parties may agree on a neutral third-party to decide that issue. The parties may make the neutral's decision binding or not....

EARLY NEUTRAL EVALUATION

Early neutral evaluation is an ADR technique developed by the courts—notably the United States District Courts for the Southern and Northern Districts of California—to assist parties in settling their cases early on in the litigation. Generally, these programs require the parties to appear before an expert voluntary attorney selected by the court, and to provide written statements setting forth a description of the dispute and the legal and factual issues whose early resolution would reduce the scope of the suit or contribute to settlement negotiations....

MINI-TRIALS

To some extent, the term "mini-trial" is a misnomer because mini-trials are not trials. More accurately, they are a form of non-binding settlement proceeding developed to resolve disputes between business entities. In a mini-trial, each side

(continued)

(continued)

presents its case to a panel comprising the parties' decision-makers with settlement authority. The goal of the mini-trial is to settle the dispute through negotiation by the parties' decision-makers. The parties may appoint a neutral with expertise in the substantive law at issue to advise the decision-makers. Generally, the parties also stipulate to staying pending litigation until the mini-trial is concluded.

The mini-trial is confidential and typically is scheduled after an opportunity for limited discovery. The proceedings consist of each side's presentation of a summary of evidence and testimony that they would produce at trial and argument of counsel.

At a minimum, mini-trials narrow issues, and if settlement is reached, they also reduce litigation costs....

SUMMARY JURY TRIAL

A summary jury trial is an ADR technique under court auspices aimed at promoting settlement. It has been called the jury equivalent of a mini-trial in that it involves the presentation, before a six or eight member mock jury, of counsel's opening and closing statements, as well as a narrative of each side's evidence. Typically, there is no live testimony. After brief instruction from the presiding judge or magistrate, the jury returns an advisory verdict. Thereafter, the presiding judge or magistrate will meet with the parties and their counsel to attempt to forge a settlement....

ARBITRATION

Arbitration is perhaps the most well-known ADR technique and generally denotes submission of a dispute to a third-party for binding or non-binding resolution after a hearing in which each side presents evidence and argument of counsel. In this way, arbitration differs from mediation and other structured settlement techniques, which are far less adversarial. Arbitration can be voluntary or mandatory as, for example, in a fee dispute between an attorney and his client where the client requests arbitration.

In voluntary arbitration such as where the parties contractually agree to arbitrate disputes arising under a contract, the parties are able to define the procedures that will govern the arbitral proceedings, including what, if any, discovery will be allowed or whether traditional evidentiary rules will apply to the arbitral proceedings. If the parties fail to define the procedures governing the arbitration, the procedures set forth in any applicable arbitration statute govern. Typically, an arbitrator is not bound to follow substantive law, but may also employ concepts of equity and justice, business practice and whatever technical expertise he or she brings to the process. If confirmed by the court, an arbitration award is enforceable like any court judgment, but unlike a judgment rendered by a court, appeal from an arbitral award is generally not available for errors of law.

Arbitration can have distinct advantages. It allows the parties to select the decision-maker(s) as well as the procedural rules governing resolution of their dispute. Unlike many other ADR techniques, credibility of witnesses can be adjudicated....In addition, arbitrations are typically confidential.

Arbitration may also have disadvantages. Some argue that arbitrators tend to "split the baby" in trying to give something to all parties. Discovery is generally limited, which may disadvantage a party needing compulsory process to obtain information to support his case. Arbitration will not be desirable if one wants a jury trial. Finally, as noted above, arbitral awards are usually not appealable except for fraud, corruption and defects aimed at the process that rendered the award as opposed to the substance of the award.

PRIVATE JUDGING

Broadly described, private judging refers to adjudication of all or part of a case by a judge selected by, and paid by, the parties. The parties may also define the procedures governing the proceedings before the private judge, and control the time and place of the proceedings. In contrast to any other presiding official in an ADR proceeding, a temporary judge has full judicial power, including the contempt power. If the parties so desire, the temporary judge may also preside over a jury trial. In further contrast to other ADR techniques, a judgment rendered by a temporary judge enjoys the same right of appeal as afforded to judgments rendered by sitting judges....

Source: "Advice From The Field" by Helen I Bendix. Used by permission of Honorable Helen I Bendix, State of California, Los Angeles County Superior Courthouse.

Types of ADR

There are a number of alternative dispute resolution options, as discussed in the Advice from the Field reading. Judge Bendix prepared the article when she was Editor-in-Chief of the Los Angeles County Bar Association's *ADR Section Newsletter*.

Private ADR

Even with the advent of court-annexed ADR programs, most ADR is done privately. Many contracts for consumer goods, real estate sales, cell phone service, or cruise line tickets have a clause that requires disputes to be resolved through arbitration, frequently binding arbitration. Many business transactions include similar provisions. These provisions define the selected method of ADR, typically arbitration in accordance with the Federal Arbitration Act or the rules of the **American Arbitration Association (AAA)** (Exhibit 4.12). The AAA is a private, nonprofit organization providing lists of potential arbitrators for the parties to select from and a set of rules for conducting the private arbitration.

The acceptance and growth of ADR is directly the result of the **Federal Arbitration Act,** which provides that arbitration agreements in commercial contracts are valid, irrevocable, and enforceable unless some legal or equitable grounds (fraud, duress) exist to invalidate them. Roughly half the states have adopted a **Uniform Arbitration Act,** similar to the Federal Arbitration Act. The Act describes the procedures that must be followed for arbitration to be initiated, how the panel of arbitrators is to be selected, and the procedures for conducting arbitration hearings.

In those instances where there is no mandatory, court-annexed ADR or a contract provision requiring ADR, the parties to the dispute may opt for ADR. By agreement, the parties may submit their dispute to ADR. The agreement will include terms for the type of ADR, and will explain how the arbitrator, mediator, or judge will be selected. The agreement will also indicate whether the decision will be binding on the parties (see Exhibits 4.13 and 4.14).

Exhibit 4.12 The American Arbitration Association website

Source: Reprinted with permission from the American Arbitration Association. All Rights Reserved.

Exhibit 4.13 Request for arbitration through the AAA

American Arbitration Association
Dispute Resolution Services Worldwide

_____**ARBITRATION RULES**
(ENTER THE NAME OF THE APPLICABLE RULES)
Demand for Arbitration

MEDIATION: *If you would like the AAA to contact the other parties and attempt to arrange mediation, please check this box. ☐*
There is no additional administrative fee for this service.

Name of Respondent	Name of Representative (if known)
Address:	Name of Firm (if applicable):
	Representative's Address

City	State	Zip Code	City	State	Zip Code

Phone No.	Fax No.	Phone No.	Fax No.

Email Address:	Email Address:

The named claimant, a party to an arbitration agreement dated _____, which provides for arbitration under the _____ Arbitration Rules of the American Arbitration Association, hereby demands arbitration.

THE NATURE OF THE DISPUTE

Dollar Amount of Claim $	Other Relief Sought: ☐ Attorneys Fees ☐ Interest ☐ Arbitration Costs ☐ Punitive/ Exemplary ☐ Other _____

Amount Enclosed $_____ In accordance with Fee Schedule: ☐Flexible Fee Schedule ☐Standard Fee Schedule

PLEASE DESCRIBE APPROPRIATE QUALIFICATIONS FOR ARBITRATOR(S) TO BE APPOINTED TO HEAR THIS DISPUTE:

Hearing locale_____ (check one) ☐ Requested by Claimant ☐ Locale provision included in the contract

Estimated time needed for hearings overall: _____hours or _____days	Type of Business: Claimant _____ Respondent_____

Is this a dispute between a business and a consumer?   ☐Yes ☐No
Does this dispute arise out of an employment relationship?   ☐Yes ☐No

If this dispute arises out of an employment relationship, what was/is the employee's annual wage range? Note: This question is required by California law. ☐Less than $100,000 ☐ $100,000 - $250,000 ☐ Over $250,000

You are hereby notified that a copy of our arbitration agreement and this demand are being filed with the American Arbitration Association with a request that it commence administration of the arbitration. The AAA will provide notice of your opportunity to file an answering statement.

Signature (may be signed by a representative) Date:	Name of Representative
Name of Claimant	Name of Firm (if applicable)
Address (to be used in connection with this case):	Representative's Address:

City	State	Zip Code	City	State	Zip Code

Phone No.	Fax No.	Phone No.	Fax No.

Email Address:	Email Address:

To begin proceedings, please send a copy of this Demand and the Arbitration Agreement, along with the filing fee as provided for in the Rules, to the AAA. Send the original Demand to the Respondent.
Please visit our website at www.adr.org if you would like to file this case online. AAA Case Filing Services can be reached at 877-495-4185

Exhibit 4.14 Request for mediation through the AAA

American Arbitration Association
Dispute Resolution Services Worldwide

Please visit our website at www.adr.org if you
would like to file this case online.
AAA Customer Service can be reached at 800-778-7879

SUBMISSION TO DISPUTE RESOLUTION

The named parties hereby submit the following dispute for resolution, under the rules of the American Arbitration Association.

To be completed and signed by all parties (attach additional sheets if necessary).

Rules Selected: ☐Commercial ☐Construction ☐Employment ☐Other (please specify) _____

Procedure Selected: ☐Binding Arbitration ☐Mediation ☐Other (please specify)_____ .

NATURE OF DISPUTE:

Dollar Amount of Claim $ _____

Other Relief Sought: ☐Attorneys Fees   ☐Interest

☐Arbitration Costs ☐Punitive/ Exemplary ☐Other _____

PLEASE DESCRIBE APPROPRIATE QUALIFICATIONS FOR ARBITRATOR(S) TO BE APPOINTED TO HEAR THIS DISPUTE:

Amount Enclosed $_____ In accordance with Fee Schedule: ☐Flexible Fee Schedule ☐Standard Fee Schedule

HEARING LOCALE REQUESTED: _____

Estimated time needed for hearings overall:
_____ hours or _____ days

We agree that, if arbitration is selected, we will abide by and perform any award rendered hereunder and that a judgment may be entered on the award.

Name of Party	Name of Party
Address:	Address:
City: State Zip Code	City: State Zip Code
Phone No. Fax No.	Phone No. Fax No.
Email Address:	Email Address:
Signature (required): Date:	Signature (required): Date:
Name of Representative:	Name of Representative:
Name of Firm (if applicable)	Name of Firm (if applicable)
Address (to be used in connection with this case)	Address (to be used in connection with this case)
City: State Zip Code	City: State Zip Code
Phone No. Fax No.	Phone No. Fax No.
Email Address:	Email Address:

To begin proceedings, please send a copy of this Demand and the Arbitration Agreement, along with the filing fee as provided for in the Rules, to: American Arbitration Association, Case Filing Services, 1101 Laurel Oak Road, Suite 100 Voorhees, NJ 08043. Send the original Demand to the Respondent.

Source: Reprinted with permission from the American Arbitration Association. All Rights Reserved.

CONCEPT REVIEW AND REINFORCEMENT

KEY TERMS

diversity of citizenship   80
constitution   81
executive branch   81
judicial branch   81
legislative branch   81
statutes   81
case law   81
stare decisis   81
cause of action   82
elements   83
plaintiff   83
preponderance of evidence   83
torts   82
contracts   82
negligence   82
duty of care   83
defendant   83
monetary remedies   83
equitable remedy   83
jurisdiction   84
standing   84
subject matter jurisdiction   84

limited jurisdiction   84
general jurisdiction   84
personal jurisdiction (*in personam*)   84
in rem jurisdiction   85
long arm statutes   85
minimum contacts   86
venue   86
concurrent jurisdiction   86
removal   87
procedural law   87
substantive law   87
courts of record   84
appellate courts   90
affirm   90
reverse   90
remand   90
settlements   90
docket   91
reserve   92
settlement negotiations   92
special damages   83

preliminary value   96
settlement brochure   94
damages   83
general damages   83
attorney work product   95
work product doctrine   96
settlement demand   96
settlement offer   96
release   97
mutual release   100
notice of dismissal   102
stipulation   102
consent judgment   102
alternative dispute resolution (ADR)   103
mediation   105
neutral fact finding   105
arbitration   105
American Arbitration Association (AAA)   107
Federal Arbitration Act   107
Uniform Arbitration Act   107

CHAPTER SUMMARY

THE COURT SYSTEM, SETTLEMENT, AND ALTERNATIVE DISPUTE RESOLUTION

Introduction to the Court System, Settlement, and Alternative Dispute Resolution	Courts are the ultimate place for the resolution of civil disputes in a neutral location.
Sources of American Law	There are four primary sources of American law: constitutions, statutes, administrative rules and regulations, and case law.
Cause of Action and Remedies	A cause of action is a wrong that is legally recognized as a basis for compensating a person for harm caused by another. The two main areas of the civil causes of action are torts and contracts.

Jurisdiction	Jurisdiction is the power of the court to hear a case when a person has standing to bring a lawsuit in an actual dispute or controversy for which the specific court has subject matter jurisdiction to hear and decide the particular type of dispute.
	Some courts have limited jurisdiction; they are authorized to hear only certain types of disputes. Other courts have general jurisdiction, which gives them the power to hear all types of matters.
	Before a court will act, it must have personal jurisdiction—authority over the person—as well as subject matter jurisdiction.
	Long arm statutes give the courts power over parties who reside in other states but had utilized some state service or facility, which subjects them to the jurisdiction of that court.
	Venue refers to the choice of court (of all of the courts that have jurisdiction over the persons involved and the subject matter) that is the most convenient for the witnesses or parties involved.
Organization of the Court System	State and federal court systems have trial courts, where evidence and testimony are presented to a finder of fact; intermediate appellate courts that review the procedural and substantive issues raised in the trial court; and an ultimate court of appeals, which in the federal system is the Supreme Court of the United States.
Introduction to Settlements and Alternative Dispute Resolution	Most cases are settled in informal negotiation or through the use of alternative dispute resolution (ADR).
Settlements	Settlements eliminate the expense, both monetary and psychological, and the uncertainty of trial. Judges favor settlements before trial and frequently help to negotiate a settlement between the parties.
	A settlement may occur at any time prior to or after the initiation of the lawsuit.
	There is no single method of negotiation used; therefore, every case must be properly prepared for trial if a settlement cannot be reached.
Damages	Special damages are those damages that can be easily calculated; they include expenses for out-of-pocket costs associated with the injury and lost wages.
	General damages are losses, noneconomic in nature, that the law presumes follow from the type of injuries sustained and are not subject to easy calculation.
	Liability is the legal responsibility for the plaintiff's damages. Without proof of liability, there can be no recovery of damages.
Settlement Documents	Settlement letters are informal demands to settle a case.
	Settlement brochures are more formal presentations detailing the facts of the case, the injuries sustained, the damages, and a demand for settlement.
	Settlement brochures will frequently contain photographs, day-in-the-life representations (either in still photographs or in video) of how the injury has affected the plaintiff, and an evaluation of the case, which is the basis for the demand to settle.
	Only the attorney may make a recommendation to the client with regard to settlement. Paralegals must have specific authorization for any actions they take during the negotiation process.

Documents for Settling and Terminating a Lawsuit	A settlement is a contract between the parties to resolve or end the lawsuit.
	Plaintiffs frequently demand an amount substantially higher than they will be willing to accept in settlement, and defendants' offers are substantially lower than they are willing to pay to settle the case. Some of the negotiation involves agreeing to a number somewhere between the original offer and the original demand.
	Occasionally the settlement may be nonmonetary and involve performing (or refraining from performing) some act.
	Settlements involving minors and other incapacitated persons may need to be approved by the court even when settled through adult court methods.
	Releases are documents used to settle cases where one or both parties agree to release the other from any and all claims arising from the transaction or occurrence. They may be individual or mutual releases.
	Cases settled prior to suit frequently include a confidentiality clause in which the parties agree to keep the terms of the dispute and settlement confidential.
	Where a case has been settled after the institution of suit, it must be marked in the court records as settled. In the federal courts, this is done by filing a notice of dismissal or a stipulation signed by all the parties or by the entry of a consent judgment. A notice of dismissal may be used where no answer has been filed to the complaint and only the plaintiff need sign. A stipulation of dismissal may be used where the parties desire the details not be made public. A consent judgment may be entered upon agreement of the defendant, giving the plaintiff a priority standing against others to maintain judgments against the same defendant.
Alternative Dispute Resolution	Alternative dispute resolution (ADR) is a method of resolving disputes without using the traditional court system. Cases are heard by independent, neutral parties.
	Arbitration involves the use of a neutral third party or parties who hear the case and make a decision, called an award.
	Mediation is a form of negotiation where the parties to the dispute use a neutral third party to assist them in reaching a settlement.
	A mini-trial is a voluntary, private proceeding where an abridged version of the case is presented to representatives of the parties who have authority to settle the case.
	Neutral fact finding involves a third party hired to investigate technical facts and report their findings.
	In some jurisdictions the courts impose ADR in the form of arbitration, which is usually mandatory, although the parties have the right to appeal.
	Most ADR is done privately. The largest private ADR organization is the American Arbitration Association.
	The Federal Arbitration Act provides that arbitration agreements in commercial contracts are valid, irrevocable, and enforceable, except under very limited circumstances. Many states have adopted the Uniform Arbitration Act, which is similar to the Federal Arbitration Act at the state level.

REVIEW QUESTIONS AND EXERCISES

1. What is the source of authority for the federal and state courts?
2. What is diversity of citizenship?
3. If both a federal court and a state court have the power to hear a particular case, why would one be selected over the other?
4. What are the sources of American law?
5. What are statutes?
6. What is the rule of administrative agencies?
7. How do administrative agencies create law?
8. What is meant by *case law*?
9. What is the concept of *stare decisis*?
10. What is meant by the term *cause of action*?
11. What is the difference between special damages and general damages?
12. What is the difference between compensatory damages and punitive damages?
13. What is meant by *standing to sue*?
14. Why do the courts insist that there be "case or controversy" before hearing any case?
15. What is meant by *subject matter jurisdiction*?
16. What is the difference between limited jurisdiction and general jurisdiction?
17. How can a court obtain personal jurisdiction over a person?
18. What is the difference between jurisdiction and venue?
19. What is the function of a trial court?
20. What is the function of an intermediate appellate court?
21. What is a *writ of certiorari*?
22. How are most cases resolved? Explain.
23. What is the obligation of the legal team in preparing a case that the team expects will be settled?
24. What is the advantage of a settlement?
25. Why would a client want to settle a case that she believes has greater value than that offered in settlement?
26. What are some of the surprises that can occur during a trial?
27. Who has the ultimate decision-making power with regard to a settlement?
28. Why might a plaintiff settle a case for less than the desired amount?
29. Does the defendant's having insurance always ensure a proper recovery?
30. Why do judges favor settlements?
31. What is the advantage of negotiating a case settlement?
32. What is the standard method for negotiating any settlement?
33. What are special damages? Give an example.
34. What are general damages? How are they computed?
35. How is the preliminary value of the case determined?
36. What are some of the damages that a plaintiff might be seeking in a contract dispute?
37. Why does the issue of liability determine the plaintiff's recovery?
38. What is the difference between a settlement letter and a settlement brochure?
39. What is the purpose of a day-in-the-life video?
40. What authority does a paralegal have in settling a case?
41. How may the parties keep the terms of the settlement confidential?
42. What is the advantage of using the mutual release over any simple release form?
43. What are the methods that may be used for terminating a lawsuit on the court docket?
44. What is the advantage to the plaintiff in obtaining a consent judgment?
45. What is the advantage of alternative dispute resolution?
46. How does arbitration differ from mediation? What is the impact of the Federal Arbitration Act or the Uniform Arbitration Act on an arbitration agreement in a contract?

BUILDING YOUR PARALEGAL SKILLS

INTERNET AND TECHNOLOGY EXERCISES

1. Supplement your list of favorites or bookmarks with the web addresses for the courts in your state.
2. Locate the rules for electronic filing and find any online forms, if any, for the courts in your

state. Bookmark or save the locations in your web favorites.

3. Locate the state and federal courts in your local jurisdiction. Prepare a checklist of resources for accessing forms, rules, judges' personal information and chamber rules, and state and local ethics rules and opinions.

4. Use the Internet to obtain the forms needed to request arbitration or mediation with the AAA.

5. Use the Internet to determine the local or state rules on ADR in your jurisdiction.

CIVIL LITIGATION VIDEO CASE STUDIES

CHAPTER OPENING SCENARIO CASE STUDY

Use the Opening Scenario for this chapter to answer the following questions.

1. What are the potential courts in which the case might be filed? Explain the basis for jurisdiction and venue in each.

2. What factors should be considered in determining which court should be selected for filing suit?

3. Are there any ethical issues in deciding whether to try or settle cases?

Preparing for Arbitration

The lawyer representing the student assaulted by the school bully on the school bus is meeting with his paralegal to get ready for presentation of the civil case before a three-attorney court-appointed arbitration panel.

After viewing the video at www.pearsonhighered.com/careersresources, answer the following questions.

1. Why are the rules of evidence more informal in an arbitration than in a trial?

2. What are the advantages and disadvantages in stipulating to the admission of exhibits?

3. Can the same stipulation be agreed to for introduction of exhibits in the trial?

Arbitration Before Three-Member Panel

A student assaulted on a school bus seeks recovery in a civil action before a board of arbitrators.

After viewing the video at www.pearsonhighered.com/careersresources, answer the following questions.

1. Why might the legal team use an arbitration proceeding rather than go to trial?

2. What differences are there in preparing for and presenting evidence at an arbitration instead of at a trial?

3. Do you think a panel of three practicing attorneys can decide a case with more skill and common sense than a jury or a judge?

COMPREHENSIVE CASE STUDY

SCHOOL BUS–TRUCK ACCIDENT CASE

Review the assigned case study in Appendix 2.
- Identify areas of law that might impact this case, including statutes, administrative regulations, and issues for further case law research.

BUILDING YOUR PROFESSIONAL PORTFOLIO AND REFERENCE MANUAL

Procedures

1. Local court voluntary and mandatory arbitration procedures
2. American Arbitration Association rules and procedures

Contacts and Resources

1. American Arbitration Association
   a. Mailing address
   b. Phone and fax numbers
   c. Web address and e-mail address
2. Local private arbitration or mediation services in your jurisdiction
   a. Mailing address
   b. Phone and fax numbers
   c. Web address and e-mail address

CIVIL LITIGATION TEAM AT WORK

See page 18 for instructions on Building Your Professional Portfolio and Reference Manual.

Forms

The forms for filing a case online for the courts in your state

Procedures

The rules for electronic filing for the courts in your state

Contacts and Resources

For each court in your jurisdiction, from lowest-level minor judiciary to the highest appeals courts:

1. Prepare a list of contact information including:
   a. Web address,
   b. Physical locations,
   c. Telephone number, and
   d. Hours of operation.
2. Prepare a list of the courts in your jurisdiction from the lowest to the highest, identifying the jurisdictional requirements of each and the venue, if applicable.
3. For each court, prepare a list of contact information including web address, physical locations, telephone number, and hours of operation.

LEARNING OBJECTIVES

After studying this chapter, you should be able to:

1. Describe the litigation strategies and options for recovering damages.

2. Describe the elements that must be proven in tort litigation and potential defenses.

3. Describe the elements necessary to prove a breach of contract claim and potential defenses.

4. Describe the purpose and proof necessary to recover monetary damages or equitable relief.

Causes of Actions and Litigation Strategies | CHAPTER 5

CHAPTER 5

OPENING SCENARIO

Roy Saunders, Esquire, was delayed in court. Rather than reschedule a meeting with a new client, he asked his paralegal to meet with the client and obtain the necessary information to set up the new matter in the office case management system, complete the conflict of interest check, and draft a fee agreement for his review. The client, a retired police officer, told the paralegal that after he had retired from the police force, he took a job as a school bus driver to keep active and to supplement his pension. He explained that he was injured during his regular afternoon run taking students home when he was struck by a student as he separated two students who were fighting on the bus. He added that he had become aware of the fight when a third student shouted that one of the students had a knife. He quickly stopped the bus and went toward the back of the bus, where he pulled one student, whom he identified as Bobby, off the other student and forcibly situated Bobby in a seat across the aisle. As the driver was trying to restrain Bobby during the scuffle, the driver was hit in the face. He wants to know his options and how to recover for his injuries and loss of time from work.

OPENING SCENARIO LEARNING OBJECTIVE

Describe the options and strategies in pursuing civil litigation remedies for clients.

■ INTRODUCTION TO CAUSES OF ACTIONS AND LITIGATION STRATEGIES

Civil litigation is the last resort for individuals seeking a remedy for injuries to themselves and their property. Remedies may be sought for physical and emotional injuries, breach of contract, or other damage to property interests. In some cases, there may be multiple causes of action and alternative remedies arising from the same set of facts. State or federal law determines what causes of action and remedies are available. Injuries may be caused by the conduct of another person or as a result of conduct of others involving a defective product. The conduct may be intentional or negligent. Causes of action may also be available under theories of strict liability or product defect against the manufacturer or seller of the original product that caused the injury or loss. Additional remedies may be available under applicable state law such as the Uniform Commercial Code. The issue for the legal team is to determine all of the potential causes of actions and remedies available for their client to maximize the likelihood of obtaining the remedy for the injury or loss suffered.

Interviewing clients and investigating potential claims require an understanding of the options for recovery or compensation available and the elements that must be proven to win a case in court.

■ LITIGATION STRATEGY AND OPTIONS

LEARNING OBJECTIVE 1
Describe the litigation strategies and options for recovering damages.

cause of action
A fact or set of facts, sometimes referred to as the elements of the cause of action, that is the basis for a lawsuit and an award of a judicially enforceable remedy.

specific performance
Something that the court orders someone to do or not to do.

A **cause of action** is a fact or set of facts (also referred to as elements) that is the basis for a lawsuit and an award of a judicially enforceable remedy. The most commonly desired remedy is monetary damages, that is, compensation in dollars for physical and emotional injuries suffered as a result of the wrongful actions of another. For some clients, however, money is not the desired remedy; instead, they want to compel or prevent some form of action or conduct by another. For example, they want **specific performance** to enforce a promise in a contract, such as a person's agreement not to compete when that person leaves the company, or the delivery of a unique item such as a work of art or a family heirloom.

Selecting the specific cause of action depends on a careful consideration of:

- The *source of law* of the cause of action: state or federal law or both;
- The *facts* of the cause of action that must be proven;
- The *evidence* available to prove each fact; and
- The *procedure* that must be followed.

Whether based on state or federal statutory or common law (case law), each cause of action is defined by certain facts or elements. Successful litigation requires the legal team to be able to prove each of the elements. Use of a chart like the one depicted in Exhibit 5.1 can assist the legal team in determining the potential causes of action and the necessary elements for each. For example, a common law cause of action in contract and/or tort may exist under state law for injuries received from the use of a defective product sold by a manufacturer or retailer. There may also be a set of remedies available under the version of the Uniform Commercial Code adopted by an individual state that allows guests and members of a household to also obtain recovery. Further, there may be a federal statute or regulatory scheme that dictates minimum industry standards such as the automobile standards requiring airbags.

Exhibit 5.1 Causes of action and affected parties checklist

POTENTIAL CAUSES OF ACTION	POTENTIAL PLAINTIFFS	POTENTIAL DEFENDANTS
Tort of Negligence 　Elements: 　　■ Duty 　　■ Breach 　　■ Causation 　　■ Damages	Plaintiff Spouse Children Family or household Guests Invitee	
Tort of _____ 　Elements: 　　■ Duty 　　■ Breach 　　■ Causation	Plaintiff Spouse Children Family or household Guests Invitee	
Breach of Contract 　Elements: 　　■ Valid contract existed 　　　• Agreement 　　　• Offer & Acceptance 　　　• Meeting of the minds 　　　• Consideration 　　　• Legality 　　　• Capacity 　　■ Breach of the terms 　　　without excuse 　　■ Damages	Plaintiff Spouse Children Family or household Guests Invitee	
UCC Article 2 Sales Breach of Express Warranty	Plaintiff Spouse Children Family or household Guests Invitee	
UCC Article 2 Sales Breach of Implied Warranty	Plaintiff Spouse Children Family or household Guests Invitee	
UCC Article 2 Sales Breach of Implied Warranty of Fitness for a Particular Purpose	Plaintiff Spouse Children Family or household Guests Invitee	
Strict Liability	Plaintiff Spouse Children Family or household Guests Invitee	
Product Liability	Plaintiff Spouse Children Family or household Guests Invitee	

tort
A civil wrong.

contract
An agreement between two or more competent parties supported by consideration for a lawful purpose.

Uniform Commercial Code (UCC)
A recommendation of law covering the sale and lease of goods, negotiable instruments, and secured transaction; was written by a group of legal scholars as part of the American Law Institute and the National Conference of Commissioners on Uniform State Laws.

preponderance of the evidence
The burden of proof in most civil litigation cases; the amount of proof that tips the scales of justice ever so slightly in one direction or the other.

Multiple causes of action may arise out of the same set of facts, including:

tort—negligence,
contract—breach of contract, and
Uniform Commercial Code (UCC)—breach of warranty.

Courts require more than the simple assertion that someone was injured from the action or inaction of another. Each element or fact of the cause of action must be established by a **preponderance of the evidence**, that is, sufficient **relevant evidence** to tip the scales of justice ever so slightly in one direction or another. Relevant evidence may come in the form of written documents, photographs, witness testimony, or the defective product itself. The availability of documentary evidence, the defective product, or an independent witness may dictate the cause of action selected. Lack of sufficient relevant evidence may limit the ability to prove the case to a judge or jury. On the other hand, overwhelming volumes of evidence such as e-mails and other correspondence may clearly prove the facts alleged in the cause of action and the damages that resulted.

Exhibit 5.2 Tort evidence checklist

TORT	ELEMENTS	FACTS	PROOF—EVIDENCE
TYPE: Negligence	DUTY BREACH CAUSATION DAMAGE		

relevant evidence
Evidence that tends to prove the existence of facts important to the resolution of the case.

PRACTICE TIP

Set up a checklist, such as that shown in Exhibit 5.2, of all potential remedies, each item of evidence available to prove each required element of proof, and which witness can be used to introduce the evidence.

Procedural requirements may in some cases limit the available causes of action and potential remedies. For example, state law may place caps or limits on monetary damages for certain types of injuries such as those due to medical malpractice. Or, a statute of limitations period may require lawsuits to be brought within very short periods of time, such as those imposed in certain states for injuries claimed in recreational activities (one year instead of two years).

IN THE WORDS OF THE COURT...

The Vermont Statutes Online
Title 12: Court Procedure
Chapter 23: LIMITATION OF TIME FOR COMMENCEMENT OF ACTIONS
12 V.S.A. § 513. Skiing, injuries sustained while participating in sport of

An action to recover for injuries sustained while participating in the sport of skiing shall be commenced within one year after the cause of action accrues, and not after.

Source: http://www.leg.state.vt.us/statutes/fullsection.cfm?Title=12&Chapter=023&Section=00513

Individual **statutes of limitations** may, in some cases, limit the available causes of action and potential remedies. For example, a client injured by a defective product waits three years before seeking the advice of a law firm. A cause of action in tort for negligence in most states typically has a two-year statute of limitations. However, state law may provide a four-year statute of limitation for claims under the Uniform Commercial Code, or a four- or six-year statute of limitations for breach of contract. It is important to note that while a cause of action may still exist and litigation may still be pursued under one of the alternative causes of action, the remedies available under those actions may be limited or significantly different. Thus the legal team must always consider other options such as the available causes of actions and statutes of limitations in other state or federal courts having jurisdictions over the subject matter and the parties.

statute of limitations
A procedural time limit for filing suit or taking action.

PRACTICE TIP

As soon as a potential client contacts the firm, the legal team must determine the potential statute of limitation deadline in order to avoid a potential claim for malpractice for failure to act within the time limits. The statute of limitation on a desired cause of action may expire the same day the client calls for an appointment. A potential client may think he or she is represented after the initial phone contact to make an appointment and hold the law firm liable for missing the limitation deadline. Initial screening contacts have been held to create an attorney–client relationship.

The court where the lawsuit is filed must have **jurisdiction** over the subject matter and over the parties. In some cases, such as those involving parties residing in different states, both the state and the federal courts will have jurisdiction. In those cases, the selection of a particular court can be based upon a number of factors: (1) the preference of the attorney, who may be more comfortable trying the case in a particular court; (2) the attorney's belief that one court or another, based on prior experience or reputation, is friendlier to the plaintiff or the defendant; (3) the speed with which cases come to trial; (4) the reputation for high or low jury awards; (5) the convenience for the witnesses who may be called to testify.

jurisdiction
Judicial authority to hear a case.

Initial investigation of the facts of a case includes determining what state or federal courts have jurisdiction. For example, jurisdiction may be appropriate in Maryland, Alabama, or California state or federal courts concerning a motor vehicle accident that occurs on an interstate highway in Maryland involving a driver from Pennsylvania and a professional truck driver from Alabama operating a tractor-trailer truck owned by a company in California. Jurisdiction may be appropriate where the case occurred or where one of the defendants resides.

WEB RESOURCES

Where the plaintiff has filed in state court, the defendant may be able to remove the case to federal court where there is diversity of jurisdiction or a federal question involved. 28 USC 1441

■ TORTS

Torts are those civil wrongs that are not breaches of contract for which the court can fashion a remedy. Most tort claims involve some level of conduct that fails to meet the norms of society but does not rise to the level of a criminal act. These acts are referred to as negligent conduct. **Negligence** is a cause of action in which the plaintiff claims that another person's failure to act as a reasonable person would have acted under the same or similar circumstances caused injury for which the plaintiff should be awarded damages.

LEARNING OBJECTIVE 2
Describe the elements that must be proven in tort litigation and potential defenses.

negligence
Failure to exercise a reasonable duty of care under the circumstances.

duty of care
Requirement that everyone conform to a recognized minimum standard of care. The minimum standard of care will depend on the circumstances.

breach of the duty of care
Failure to use reasonable care to avoid causing harm to another.

causation
The link between the injury suffered by the plaintiff and the action or inaction of the defendant, includes causation in fact (actual cause) and proximate cause (legal cause).

damages
A calculation, usually financial, of harm suffered.

reasonable person standard
The hypothetical legal standard describing how a reasonable person acts and does things sensibly and without serious delay and taking ordinary but not excessive care.

intentional torts
Wrongs against individuals or against another person's property in which an individual acts intentionally.

battery
The unauthorized or offensive touching or contact with another person.

assault
The immediate threat of offensive or harmful contact or any other action that causes a person to have a reasonable apprehension of immediate harm; actual physical contact is not necessary.

The four elements of a cause of action in negligence are:

1. **Duty of care**—the defendant owed the plaintiff a duty of reasonable care to not be the cause of a risk of harm. For example, the duty to operate automobiles safely by observing traffic control devices and speed limits is a duty of reasonable care.
2. **Breach of the duty of care**—the defendant failed to observe the duty to use reasonable care as required. For example, running a stop sign is a breach of the duty of care.
3. **Causation**—the defendant's failure to observe the duty of care was the cause of an injury to the plaintiff. The defendant ran the stop sign, which resulted in his collision with the plaintiff's motorcycle.
4. **Damages**—the injury resulted in compensable damages. The collision with the motorcycle totaled the motorcycle, but fortunately, the plaintiff suffered no physical injury. Damages may be recovered for the motorcycle but not for physical injury to the plaintiff.

All four of these elements must exist in order for the plaintiff to have a valid cause of action for negligence. If any one of these elements is missing, the plaintiff's cause of action will fail.

The duty of care requires that everyone conform to a recognized minimum standard of care. The minimum standard of care depends on the circumstances. Breach of the duty of care is based upon the individual circumstances using a **reasonable person standard**. The reasonable person standard asks: What would a reasonable person under the same set of circumstances do? An automobile driver is held to the standard of care of other automobile drivers. If the harm is foreseeable, failure to do what is required to avoid the harm may be negligence. In addition, professionals are held to the standard of other professionals; for example, a surgeon is held to the standard of care of other surgeons.

Intentional Torts Against Persons

Intentional torts include wrongs against individuals or against another person's property. Intentional torts against persons occur when an individual acts intentionally and, as a result, another person is injured. It is not required that the individual intended the harm that resulted, only that the individual intended the action. For example, carelessly throwing a rock that hits a car driving below on a high-speed roadway is an intentional tort. The person did not intend to hit a particular car, but did intentionally throw the rock.

Two intentional torts against persons are **battery** and **assault**. Battery is the unauthorized or offensive touching or contact with another person. There must be some physical or actual contact between the parties. For example, a nursing home administering a pneumonia vaccination to a patient who has not agreed to have the vaccination or who lacks the ability to consent to that vaccination has committed battery. The intention to vaccinate the patient is a good intention. But because it is an unauthorized touching of the patient, it is battery.

Assault is the immediate threat of offensive or harmful contact or any other action that causes a reasonable person to have a reasonable apprehension of immediate harm. For assault, actual physical contact is not necessary. For example, a tall, muscular person stands within a few feet of a smaller, frail person and makes a threat by verbal or physical actions. The smaller person reasonably believes the threat will result in being physically harmed. This is assault. If actual physical violence in the form of a punch or touching occurs, a separate tort claim may be made for the tort of battery. In addition, there may be criminal conduct separate from the civil wrong. Typically in criminal law, an assault is an attempted battery, the battery being the completed act of wrongful or physical touching of another.

Intentional Torts Against Property

The most common intentional tort against property is **trespass to land.** Trespass to land is the intentional and unlawful violation of an owner's right to exclusive possession of land. There does not have to be interference with the owner's right of enjoyment or use of his or her land; it is enough that the tortfeasor unlawfully enters onto the other person's land without permission. It may also occur when a person who otherwise had permission to be on the land refused to leave after being asked to do so.

Defenses to Tort Actions

A **defense** is a legal reason why the person should not be held legally responsible and serves to bar the plaintiff's claim. Even if everything the plaintiff alleges is true, the plaintiff is not entitled to recovery because of some legal principle. The most common affirmative defenses in a tort action are the expiration of the statute of limitations, the assumption of risk, and, depending on individual state law, contributory negligence.

The statute of limitations is a time frame within which a plaintiff must file a complaint, or the right to recovery is barred. For example, the statute of limitations for most negligence actions is two years under common law. Failure to bring the action within two years of the occurrence will bar the right to recovery. There are some exceptions; where the negligence or injury could not be reasonably discovered within two years, the statute is extended. For example, in the class action lawsuit against the manufacturers of asbestos, many of those seeking recovery were diagnosed with mesothelioma, a rare form of lung cancer directly related to asbestos exposure, exposure that may have occurred as long as 70 years ago, during World War II. But recovery is permissible when a suit is instituted within two years of when the disease was discovered.

The **assumption of risk** doctrine states that the plaintiff knew the risks involved with a particular activity and voluntarily proceeded with that activity. The fan at the baseball game cannot sue for being struck by a foul ball because foul balls entering the stands are common at a baseball game. The plaintiff thus assumed the risk that he might be struck by a foul ball when he purchased a ticket and attended the game. Exceptions may include someone completely unfamiliar with the game, such as a visitor from a country in which baseball is not played.

Contributory and **comparative negligence** doctrines are closely related, and most jurisdictions have adopted one or the other. These doctrines state that where the plaintiff's actions were also negligent and contributed to the occurrence that resulted in injuries, the plaintiff's recovery may be denied or limited. Suppose someone fell on the stairs and was injured, but because he had two armfuls of groceries, he was not holding onto the banister. This individual, by carrying too many bags of groceries and not holding onto the banister, contributed to his own injury. In a contributory negligence jurisdiction, there is no recovery where the plaintiff contributed to his injuries. Because this result is harsh, in those states that use contributory negligence, they also recognize the last clear chance doctrine. Under this doctrine, if the plaintiff's own actions contributed to injury, he may still be able to recover. If the defendant had the last opportunity to prevent the harm and failed to do so, the plaintiff can still recover. In the

trespass to land
The intentional and unlawful violation of the owner's right to exclusive possession of land.

defense
A legal reason why the person should not be held responsible and the claim should be denied.

assumption of risk
Plaintiff knew the risks involved with a particular activity and voluntarily proceeded with that activity.

contributory negligence
An affirmative defense that bars any recovery if the plaintiff was in any way at fault.

comparative negligence
Damages apportioned according to fault.

liability
Legal responsibility for another's damages.

products liability
A cause of action against the designer, manufacturer, or seller of a product. The injured person must establish that there was a breach in the standard of care in the manufacturing, inspection, packaging, and/or instructions and warnings for the product's use.

strict liability
Liability without fault.

stairwell case, whether the landlord had properly maintained the staircase could represent the last clear chance and permit the plaintiff to recover.

Because of the harsh results under contributory negligence, many states have opted instead for comparative negligence. Under comparative negligence, the jury will be asked to assign percentages of **liability** to the plaintiff and to the defendant and to determine damages without regard to fault. In the stairwell fall, the jury may find the plaintiff 15 percent negligent and the defendant 85 percent negligent. If the jury awards plaintiff damages of $100,000, the plaintiff will recover $85,000, the 85 percent amount of liability assigned to the defendant.

Products Liability and Strict Liability

Products liability and **strict liability** are specially recognized causes of actions against manufacturers and sellers of goods. In products liability cases, someone who is injured by an unsafe product may have a cause of action against the designer, manufacturer, or seller of the product. The injured person must establish that there was a breach in the standard of care in the manufacturing, inspection, packaging, and/or instructions and warnings for the product use. Establishing the breach of the standard of care can be difficult for an individual plaintiff. Thus, the concept of strict product liability has evolved. Under strict liability theory, a cause of action may also exist for anyone else harmed by the defect, such as family members or guests. The plaintiff is thus not required to prove a breach of duty of care because the proof is solely within the possession of the defendant, or the defect that caused injury is unreasonably dangerous to the user of the product.

Cases of defectively manufactured products may require proof of the internal operations of a factory, something that the average plaintiff cannot obtain through traditional discovery. Employees and owners may be reluctant to admit anything or allow access. Strict product liability laws are thus a solution to the burden of proof problem. These laws take the position that, but for some wrongdoing or negligence, the product would not have been defective and caused injury. However, one social theory states that even the best manufacturing practices will result in some defects that will cause injury. Society should therefore spread the cost of the injury to one person over the rest of the purchasing and using public, as insurance does.

The Restatement of the Law Second, Torts provides a recommended definition for strict liability that has been adopted by most states either through legislative enactment or through judicial decisions.

Restatement § 402A provides:

1. One who sells any product in a defective condition unreasonably dangerous to the user or consumer or to his property is subject to liability for physical harm thereby caused to the ultimate user or consumer, or to his property, if
   a. the seller is engaged in the business of selling such a product, and
   b. it is expected to and does reach the user or consumer without substantial change in the condition in which it is sold.
2. The rule stated in Subsection (1) applies although
   a. the seller has exercised all possible care in the preparation and sale of his product, and
   b. the user or consumer has not bought the product from or entered into any contractual relation with the seller.

Defenses to Product Liability

Just as there are defenses to tort actions, there are defenses to strict and product liability actions, including the running or tolling of the statute of limitations and assumption of the risk. Further, where the product has been misused, or used in a way that was not foreseeable by the manufacturer, there will be no liability—for example, a pressure cooker that explodes when used as a bomb. If the plaintiff misuses the product in an abnormal way such as the pressure cooker bomb, and it is not reasonable for the manufacturer to foresee that misuse, there is no liability. However, once the misuse becomes known, the manufacturer must make efforts, such as including warning labels and instructions for proper use, to protect itself from future liability. Some products, such as guns and knives, are commonly known to be dangerous, and there is no liability assigned to the manufacturer. Finally, where the product has been altered after it left the hands of the manufacturer, the supervening event may cut off the manufacturer's liability.

■ CONTRACTS

A common area of dispute that results in civil litigation involves a breach of contract. The two main sources for contract law in the United States are the **common law** and the Uniform Commercial Code. The common law is the result of court decisions primarily in the individual states. Because of the variations among the 50 states' interpretations of contract terms and provisions, an attempt to apply a nationally accepted, uniform set of laws resulted in the adoption of the Uniform Commercial Code by most states. Article 2, which governs sales, was the original article describing a uniform set of rules for the creation and enforcement of contracts for the sale of goods. The subsequent adoption of article 2A extended the provisions to leases of goods, such as a lease of automobiles.

Common law contract principles still apply in those cases not covered under the provisions of the Uniform Commercial Code for the sales or leases of goods. Therefore, state law and federal contract law where applicable must be consulted.

Elements of Common Law Contracts

A contract is an agreement that is enforceable by a court of law or equity. A valid contract contains:

a. **Agreement** between the parties. An agreement requires an offer by one party that is accepted by the other party. The Restatement (Second) Of Contracts defines an offer as "the manifestation of willingness to enter into a bargain, so made as to justify another person in understanding that his ascent to that bargain is invited and will conclude it."

b. **Consideration** for the promises made by the parties. Consideration is the giving of something of legal value in exchange for a promise. Consideration can, but is not required to be, financial. A promise to do or refrain from doing something the individual has a right to do or not do is consideration. A promise to do something that the person must do anyway is not consideration.

c. **Contractual capacity** of the parties. The parties to the contract must have contractual **capacity**. This means that they must be of lawful age within the jurisdiction to enter into a contract and not be under any disability by virtue of mental impairment. Contracts by intoxicated persons, for example, may be voided if the intoxication prevented the person from understanding the nature of the transaction. On the other hand, persons who have been

LEARNING OBJECTIVE 3
Describe the elements necessary to prove a breach of contract claim and potential defenses.

common law
The law found in court decisions in the individual states.

agreement
The manifestation by two or more persons of the substance of a contract.

consideration
Something of legal value given in exchange for a promise.

contractual capacity
In contract law, the legal ability to enter into a contract.

capacity
In contract law, the legal ability to enter into a contract.

declared mentally incompetent by a court may not enter into any contracts, and any attempt to enter into a contract is considered void.

lawful objective
Subject of a contract that a court will enforce.

d. **Lawful objective**. Courts will not enforce contracts to perform illegal acts

A contract cause of action requires:

- A valid contract,
- A situation in which one of the parties failed to meet his/her obligation under the terms of the valid contract and there is no excuse, and
- The other party suffered damages.

Exhibit 5.3 is a good starting point in a contracts case.

Exhibit 5.3 Contracts Checklist

ELEMENT	DETAILS	PROOF—EVIDENCE
AGREEMENT	Offer Acceptance	
CONSIDERATION	Form	
COMPETENT PARTIES	Age Disability	
LAWFUL PURPOSE	Subject Matter	
STATUTE OF FRAUDS	Writing Signed by Plaintiff Defendant	

Defense to Contracts

If there is no relevant evidence supporting any of the elements of a contract, there is no contract, only an agreement, and there can be no recovery for a breach of contract. The statute of limitations will bar actions not brought in a timely manner. In contracts, there is generally a longer statute of limitations period than in torts. It is critical for the legal team to know their state's rules because contracts for different types of matters may have different time limitations.

Statute of Frauds

statute of frauds
A law that requires certain types of contracts to be in writing to be enforced by courts.

Every state has a **statute of frauds** that requires certain types of contracts to be in writing to be enforced by their courts. These generally are contracts of such importance that relying on one person's word or memory is not sufficient. Typically, the following contracts must be in writing to be enforceable in a court of law:

- Contracts involving interests in real estate, such as a lease or a sales agreement
- Contracts that cannot be completed in year, such as a multiyear employment contract
- Contracts to pay the debts of another, such as parents agreeing to pay student loans
- Contracts of a value beyond a certain amount

Under the Uniform Commercial Code where written contracts are required, they are enforceable against the party who signed the contract. For example, the buyer need not sign the contract to enforce the terms against a seller, if the seller has signed the contract. As for the seller, he or she has no right of enforcement against a buyer who did not sign.

If a landlord seeks to enforce a rent provision for which there is no written contract, the court will not enforce it. There may be a valid agreement, but the courts will not enforce the rights of the parties because of the concern of potential fraud due to the lack of a written document to support the existence of the contract.

Fraud and misrepresentation are also defenses to a breach of contract claim. When one of the parties to a contract has made a false representation of a material fact with the intention of deceiving the other, innocent party, and the innocent party justifiably relied on the representation in entering the contract, fraud and misrepresentation have occurred. There can be no recovery against the innocent party.

The Uniform Commercial Code

The Uniform Commercial Code (UCC) is a statute covering the sale and lease of goods, negotiable instruments, and secured transactions that was written by a group of legal scholars from the American Law Institute and the National Conference of Commissioners on Uniform State Laws. The law was a recommendation to state legislators, who could adopt it in its original form or as changed or amended by the state legislature during the adoption process. The UCC was presented to the legislatures of the states as a replacement for the common law of the 50 states that impacted the sale and lease of goods. Modern commercial transactions typically involve cross–state border transactions between individual citizens and commercial enterprises. Prior to the almost universal adoption of the UCC, each state sought to protect the interests of its citizens, frequently to the detriment of the interests of businesses in other states. Farm states, for example, sought to protect agricultural goods sellers, while manufacturing-centered states, such as those in the northern United States, favored buyers of their raw materials. As commerce among the states grew during the Industrial Revolution and expanded after the Second World War, it was clear that states had to have a common set of laws to resolve disputes and avoid litigation from the increased commercial activity.

WEB RESOURCES
American Law Institute information can be found at the ALI website, www.ali.org, and information on the National Conference of Commissioners on Uniform State Laws can be found at the NCCUSL website, www.nccusl.org.

Recognizing the significant need for guidance for sellers and buyers and a standard set of rules for the courts to apply when all else failed, the framers of the UCC sought to create a level commercial playing field for business. In an attempt to eliminate states objecting to the uniform set of laws, the UCC was limited to coverage of issues that involve primarily interstate transactions. For example, Article 2 deals only with the sale of goods and Article 2A deals only with the lease of goods.

Article 2-102 provides "…this Article applies to transaction in goods," which are defined in Article 2-105 as "…all things which are movable at the time of identification to the contract for sale …[,]" and to satisfy the farm states includes "…unborn young of animals and growing crops…."

Articles 2 and 2A of the UCC provide a number of remedies designed to reflect the potential issues that might arise during the process of a transaction for the sale or lease of goods. Unlike the rigid rules of the common law of contracts, the UCC is more flexible. For example, in the rules of formation and execution of a transaction, the UCC provisions eliminate some of the technical elements used to avoid formation or execution, such as strict offer and acceptance rules under the common law. The obligation of the parties is spelled out in Article 2 as "…seller is to transfer and deliver and…buyer [is] to accept and pay in accordance with the contract." As a general guide to using and determining rights and obligations, the UCC provides a set of definitions to be used within the application of the UCC, eliminating the reliance on state common law definitions when the UCC applies to a transaction.

The UCC also recognizes the reality of commercial transactions, where things sometimes go wrong, such as when perishable goods are destroyed due to unexpected excessive heat or a breakdown in a refrigeration unit on a delivery truck. In these cases, the seller is given the right to replace the nonconforming goods or, in the words of the UCC, to "cure the defect."

Formation of Contracts Under the UCC

The UCC deviates from the rigidity of the common law of contracts by providing a flexible system for contract creation. For example, unless otherwise unambiguously indicated, acceptance in any manner and by any medium reasonable to the circumstance is permissible under UCC 2-206. Whereas the common law of contracts declares an offer rejected if even the slightest change is made in the acceptance, the UCC recognizes negotiations as part of the contract process under UCC 2-207. Each change proposed becomes part of the agreement under the UCC unless specifically rejected. All of the back-and-forth changes and proposals become the agreement when the last change is proposed and not rejected. Even the existence of an open term does not invalidate the contract, as it would under the common law.

> Article 2-204(3) states: "Even though one or more terms are left open[,] a contract for sale does not fail for indefiniteness if the parties have intended to make a contract…."

Custom and Usage

The UCC makes a distinction between **merchants**, those who deal in goods of a particular kind (UCC 2-104(1)) contracted for, and laypeople, who may not understand the customs and ways of doing business in a particular field, such as quality grades like prime, commercial, and cutter in the meat business. The first step in a case involving goods, as defined in the UCC, is to determine the status of the buyer and the seller—whether either or both are merchants as defined in the UCC.

Warranties

Buyers of goods expect certain minimum promises from the seller; under the UCC, these are called **warranties**. First, Under UCC 2-312, is the Warranty of Title, where the seller guarantees that he/she has the right and the authority to sell the particular goods. Buyers want to buy goods, not engage in lawsuits to determine who owns the goods.

Expressed warranties are included without the need for the use of formal words like "warranty" or "guarantee" and are based on the seller's expressed affirmations, promises, stated description, and samples shown to the buyer (UCC 2-213). If the seller is a merchant as defined in the UCC, the sale includes, unless specifically excluded or modified properly, the **implied warranty of merchantability** (UCC 2-314) that the goods will be fit for the ordinary purpose for which such goods are used. The **warranty of fitness for a particular purpose** (UCC 2-315) arises when the seller knows the particular purpose for which the goods are required and selects the goods for the buyer. A layperson is not held to the same standard as a merchant who regularly deals in good of a particular kind.

> ### PRACTICE TIP
>
> The warranty of fitness for a particular purpose is a warranty based on the skill of the seller to select appropriate goods for the need as defined by the lay buyer. It does not apply when the buyer makes the selection without input from the seller or when the buyer is also a merchant.

Selecting Appropriate Causes of Action

The UCC may provide additional remedies than the common law remedies of breach of contract and tort. Different statutes of limitations may apply to each potential cause of action. Use of an alternative remedy may be necessary when the statute of limitation for filing a civil action has expired, such as a two-year statute of limitation for a tort claim for injury. The UCC may allow a claim for the injuries under a breach of warranty with a longer, four-year statute of limitations.

> ### PRACTICE TIP
>
> The UCC proposal provided to the state legislatures contained alternative clauses that could be selected by the state in enacting its version of the code, specifically 2-318, which has three alternative selections of application of warranties to third parties such as family members, guests in a home, or anyone else likely to be affected. Check your state's adoption to clarify the coverage available before filing suit.

■ DAMAGES

Civil litigation is pursued when an individual believes he or she has been wronged and, under the law, is entitled to some type of remedy to correct that wrong. There are two forms of remedies: monetary damages and equitable remedies.

Monetary Damages

Monetary damages assign a financial value to the harm suffered by the plaintiff. Monetary damages can take a number of forms, depending on whether the recovery is based on a tort or a breach of contract.

The first is **compensatory damages**, which seek to calculate a monetary value for the actual loss suffered by the plaintiff. In tort, there are two types of compensatory damages: **special damages** and **general damages**. Special damages are those that can be calculated with some level of accuracy. For example, knowing how much a plaintiff earns per week, we can calculate the wages lost as a result of not working for a week following an injury in an auto accident. We can also calculate his or her medical bills. General damages are related to the

---

implied warranty of merchantability
A warranty that the goods will be fit for the ordinary purpose for which such goods are used.

warranty of fitness for a particular purpose
A warranty on the skill of the seller to select appropriate goods when the seller knows the particular purpose for which the goods are required and makes the selection for the buyer.

LEARNING OBJECTIVE 4
Describe the purpose and proof necessary to recover monetary damages or equitable relief.

monetary damages
A financial value assigned to the harm suffered by the plaintiff.

compensatory damages
A monetary value for the actual loss suffered by the plaintiff.

special damages
Damages that can be calculated with some level of accuracy.

general damages
Damages related to the injury sustained that are not calculated using any particular formula or accuracy.

injury sustained but are not calculated with any particular formula or accuracy. The award for pain and suffering or loss of life's pleasures is an example of general damages.

In contract cases, the plaintiff will be compensated through **consequential damages** or **liquidated damages**. Consequential damages are forseeable damages that arise from circumstances outside the contract, such as obtaining replacement goods or services and loss of profits caused by the delay in receiving the goods when promised. Liquidated damages are provided for in the contract. In anticipation of a potential breach of contract, the parties agree that damages will be limited to some amount.

Monetary damages also include **punitive damages**, which are designed to punish the defendant for behavior that shocks the conscience of the finder of fact. Consider a corporation's decision to forego installing a 25-cent safety device that could have prevented hundreds of fatal accidents. That decision might shock the conscience of the finder of fact to the extent that the corporation, in addition to having to pay compensatory damages, also has to pay a punitive damage amount.

Finally, monetary damages also include **statutory damages** that are defined or ordered under the scheme of a particular statute. In employment discrimination cases, for example, the judge must, under the terms of the statute, order the employer found in violation of the statute to pay a specified amount of the damages and attorney's fees and costs.

Both tort and contract cases may give rise to punitive and statutory damages.

Equitable Remedies

In some cases, the amount of monetary damages cannot make the injured party whole—for example, a breach of contract for the sale of unique, irreplaceable items such as a famous painting like the *Mona Lisa*, or a dispute between neighbors (an intentional tort—trespass to land) where a fence was placed three feet beyond the property line. The property owner is not adequately compensated by a monetary award of the value of a strip of land three feet wide. The **equitable remedy** is to order the neighbor to remove the fence or relocate it to the actual boundary line. This remedy is called specific performance—the court orders someone to do something. Another form of equitable relief is an **injunction**—the court orders someone to stop doing something.

Calculating Damages

The paralegal may assist with identifying and itemizing all of the damages suffered by the plaintiff. Calculating damages should begin early in the representation of the client. Armed with an early and accurate calculation of damages, the legal team can assess the costs and benefits of settling a case or proceeding to trial.

First, a listing of special damages, which are readily calculable and include lost wages, medical bills, and the cost of hiring a cleaning service to perform the plaintiff's regular household duties, will be completed. To that is added an estimate of general damages, those damages that do not need to be specifically claimed or proven. These are the damages the law presumes follow from the type of injury sustained, such as those for pain and suffering. Although general damages are not calculated by reference to some formula, many jurisdictions customarily use an unwritten rule of thumb (for example, three times the special

---

consequential damages
Foreseeable damages that arise from circumstances outside the contract.

liquidated damages
Damages to which parties to a contract agree in advance should be paid if the contract is breached.

punitive damages
Damages that are designed to punish the defendant for behavior that shocks the conscience of the finder of fact.

statutory damages
Damages provided by statute as distinguished from those provided by common law.

equitable remedies
A court order to do (specific performance) or not do (injuction) something when monetary damages cannot make the injured party whole.

injunction
The court ordering someone to stop doing something.

damages). The amount of general damages may be speculative. Reference to reports of case awards published in local legal newspapers or in specialty damage reporters should be consulted for those unique cases where the local rule of thumb is not appropriate. The total of the special and estimated general damages is the preliminary value of the case.

The preliminary value of the case may then be adjusted after carefully reviewing the strengths and weaknesses of the evidence in the case. Defense counsel will certainly claim that any personal injury was preexisting, or one with which the plaintiff was born. The jury may view the lack of substantial physical damage to the vehicle in which the plaintiff was riding as an indication there was not as much harm caused as claimed. Each of these issues is likely to be a point of discussion between the attorneys in settlement negotiations. Causation-of-injury issues may warrant a review of pre-accident medical records by a medical expert who is familiar with litigation and is available to testify that any preexisting injury was aggravated in the current case.

Most plaintiffs seek compensation tied to the loss suffered. The easiest cases are those where recovery is sought for something lost or damaged that has an easily determined value, such as the price of a new or used automobile. The more difficult cases are those seeking recovery for speculative injuries, such as pain and suffering. In all cases the fact finder must determine the equivalent monetary value for the loss. Occasionally, the plaintiff may also seek, through punitive or exemplary damages, to punish or deter the defendant from repeating the same conduct or actions, such as the punitive damages sought in the following case.

IN THE WORDS OF THE COURT...

BMW of North America, Inc v Gore 517 US 559 (1996)
Justice Stevens delivered the opinion of the Court.

In January 1990, Dr. Ira Gore, Jr. (respondent), purchased a black BMW sports sedan for $40,750.88 from an authorized BMW dealer in Birmingham, Alabama. After driving the car for approximately nine months, and without noticing any flaws in its appearance, Dr. Gore took the car to "Slick Finish," an independent detailer, to make it look "'snazzier than it normally would appear.'" 646 So. 2d 619, 621 (Ala. 1994). Mr. Slick, the proprietor, detected evidence that the car had been repainted. [n.1] Convinced that he had been cheated, Dr. Gore brought suit against petitioner BMW of North America (BMW), the American distributor of BMW automobiles. [n.2] Dr. Gore alleged, *inter alia,* that the failure to disclose that the car had been repainted constituted suppression of a material fact. [n.3] The complaint prayed for $500,000 in compensatory and punitive damages, and costs....

The jury returned a verdict finding BMW liable for compensatory damages of $4,000. In addition, the jury assessed $4 million in punitive damages, based on a determination that the nondisclosure policy constituted "gross, oppressive or malicious" fraud. [n.6] See Ala. Code §§6-11-20, 6-11-21 (1993)....

Perhaps the most important indicium of the reasonableness of a punitive damages award is the degree of reprehensibility of the defendant's conduct. As the Court stated nearly 150 years ago, exemplary damages imposed on a defendant should reflect "the enormity of his offense." *Day* v. *Woodworth*, 13 How. 363, 371 (1852)....

(continued)

The second and perhaps most commonly cited indicium of an unreasonable or excessive punitive damages award is its ratio to the actual harm inflicted on the plaintiff. See *TXO*, 509 U. S., at 459; *Haslip*, 499 U. S., at 23. The principle that exemplary damages must bear a "reasonable relationship" to compensatory damages has a long pedigree....

The sanction imposed in this case cannot be justified on the ground that it was necessary to deter future misconduct without considering whether less drastic remedies could be expected to achieve that goal. The fact that a multimillion dollar penalty prompted a change in policy sheds no light on the question [of] whether a lesser deterrent would have adequately protected the interests of Alabama consumers. In the absence of a history of noncompliance with known statutory requirements, there is no basis for assuming that a more modest sanction would not have been sufficient to motivate full compliance with the disclosure requirement imposed by the Alabama Supreme Court in this case....

The fact that BMW is a large corporation rather than an impecunious individual does not diminish its entitlement to fair notice of the demands that the several States impose on the conduct of its business. Indeed, its status as an active participant in the national economy implicates the federal interest in preventing individual States from imposing undue burdens on interstate commerce. While each State has ample power to protect its own consumers, none may use the punitive damages deterrent as a means of imposing its regulatory policies on the entire Nation....

...we are fully convinced that the grossly excessive award imposed in this case transcends the constitutional limit....

Proving Damages

It is necessary to convince the fact finder of the extent and monetary loss suffered by the plaintiff. This may be the most difficult part of the case. However, one way to portray how someone's life has changed is to present a **"Day in the Life" video**, which documents the permanently injured individual's efforts to do everyday things like getting dressed, making a pot of coffee, or folding laundry. Proving the extent of pain and suffering draws upon the emotions of the fact finder. In these difficult cases, it is necessary to be able to "place" the fact finder in a similar situation and have him or her imagine what would be acceptable when one is involuntarily forced into that situation. For example, among the horrendous losses in the Boston Marathon bombing was the loss of arms and legs. What is the monetary value that adequately compensates a healthy, athletic, 20-year-old individual for the loss of both legs?

In tort action there are rights of recovery granted to the spouse and family members of the injured party. Family members such as spouses and children depending on the person for emotional and financial support suffer compensable losses. A spouse may suffer from loss of consortium, the affection and companionship of his or her spouse. A dependent child or elderly parent may suffer the loss of financial resources for support, including housing, health care, and education.

Less speculative than loss of consortium and pain and suffering are losses a business suffers from physical damages. It is easier to calculate the cost of replacing windows, doors, and furniture. It may be more difficult, however, to calculate lost business from when streets were closed, preventing customers from entering the store. In that case, historical sales information such as business records and receipts may be used to show average daily business.

"Day in the Life" video
A video which documents the permanently injured individual's efforts to do everyday things.

CONCEPT REVIEW AND REINFORCEMENT

KEY TERMS

agreement   125

assault   122

assumption of risk   123

battery   122

breach of duty of care   122

capacity   125

causation   122

cause of action   118

common law   125

comparative negligence   123

compensatory damages   129

consequential damages   130

consideration   125

contracts   120

contractual capacity   125

contributory negligence   123

damages   122

"Day in the Life" video   132

defense   123

duty of care   122

equitable remedies   130

expressed warranties   128

fraud and misrepresentation   127

general damages   129

implied warranty
   of merchantability   129

injunction   130

intentional torts   122

jurisdiction   121

lawful objective   126

liability   124

liquidated damages   130

merchants   128

monetary damages   129

negligence   121

preponderance of the
   evidence   120

products liability   124

punitive damages   130

reasonable person
   standard   122

relevant evidence   120

special damages   129

specific performance   118

statute of frauds   126

statutes of limitations   121

statutory damages   130

strict liability   124

tort   120

trespass to land   123

Uniform Commercial Code
   (UCC)   120

warranties   128

warranty of fitness for a particular
   purpose   129

CHAPTER SUMMARY

Introduction to Causes of Action and Litigation Strategies	In some cases there are multiple causes of action arising from the same set of circumstances and alternative remedies that may be available. Interviewing clients and investigating potential claims requires an understanding of the options for recovery, the compensation available, and the necessary elements that must be proven.
Litigation Strategy and Options	The choice of the specific cause of action depends upon consideration of: The source of law of the cause of action; The elements of the cause of action that must be proven; The evidence available to prove each fact; and The procedures that must be followed.
Jurisdiction in Civil Litigation	Jurisdiction may exist in multiple federal or state courts. Suits may be instituted in those courts in whose territorial jurisdiction the cause of action arose or in which the courts have jurisdiction over the defendant or in federal court where there is a diversity of citizenship or involving a federal question.

(continued)

Torts	Torts are civil wrongs that are not breaches of contract for which the court can fashion a remedy. Most tort claims involve some level of conduct that fails to meet the norms of society but does not rise to the level of a criminal act. Negligence is a tort cause of action that requires proof of four elements: 1. Duty of care 2. Breach of the duty of care 3. Causation 4. Damages
Intentional Torts Against Persons	Intentional torts against individuals occur when a person acts intentionally and the action results in harm to another. It is not required that the harm be intentional but the action must be intentional. Two common intentional torts are battery and assault.
Intentional Torts Against Property	The most common intentional tort against property is that of trespass to land.
Unintentional Torts—Negligence	The tort of negligence is a result of a person not acting as a reasonable person would act under the same or similar circumstances, causing another person injury.
Defenses to Tort Actions	Defenses are legal reasons why a person should not be held responsible and the claim denied, and include the statute of limitations, assumption of the risk, contributory negligence, and comparative negligence.
Products Liability and Strict Liability	Products liability and strict liability provisions of state laws does not require plaintiffs to prove a breach of duty.
Defenses to Product Liability	Parties will not be held liable where the product was used in a way that was not foreseeable or the product was altered after leaving the possession of the manufacturer.
Contracts	Contract actions may be governed by the common law of contracts in a particular state, and may include statutory enactments including the Uniform Commercial Code.
Elements of Common Law Contracts	Under the common law, the elements of a contract are: Agreements between the parties Consideration for the promises made by the parties Contractual capacity Lawful purpose
Defense to Contracts	The statute of frauds is a requirement under state law that contracts be in writing to be enforceable in the courts. Under the Uniform Commercial Code, contracts are enforceable against the party who has signed the contract even when the other party has not signed the contract. Fraud and misrepresentation are also defenses to contact actions.
The Uniform Commercial Code	The UCC is more flexible than the common law with regard to the formation and execution of transactions and facilitating the delivery of goods that conform to the agreement of the parties as a primary remedy.

Formation of Contracts Under the UCC	The UCC deviates from the rigidity of the common law of contracts, providing a flexible system that allows for modification of offers and incorporation of proposed changes in the final agreement unless rejected by the other party. Unless specifically and properly disclaimed, each sale of goods includes express warranties based upon the affirmations or promises made by the seller and implied warranties that the goods will be suitable for the intended purpose and properly packaged, and where the buyer relies upon the superior skill of the seller in selecting appropriate goods for a particular purpose, a warranty of fitness for that particular purpose.
Damages	Monetary damages assign a financial value to the harm suffered by the plaintiff. They may be special damages or general damages. The court may also award punitive damages when appropriate to punish the defendant for behavior that shocks the conscience of the court. The court may award statutory damages where required under a particular statutory scheme.
Equitable Remedies	When monetary damages are not a sufficient remedy, the court may order, by way of an injunction, specific performance, which compels someone to perform a specific act or to refrain from performing a specific act.
Calculating Damages	Calculating damages should begin early in the representation of the client so that the legal team can assess the costs and benefits of settling a case or proceeding to trial.

REVIEW QUESTIONS AND EXERCISES

1. How is a cause of action the basis for litigation? Explain.
2. What are the factors that will determine the selected cause of action in a particular case?
3. What are some of the forms of evidence that may be used to prove a cause of action?
4. What is the level of evidence necessary to win a civil case?
5. How can the statute of limitations determine the specific cause of action selected in a particular case?
6. What dangers does the statute of limitations impose upon the attorney in dealing with a new client or new matter?
7. What are the requirements for a court to have jurisdiction over a case? How might different courts each have jurisdiction?
8. What are some of the considerations in selecting the court in which to institute litigation?
9. What options does the defendant have in the selection of the court to hear a case?
10. What are the elements necessary to prove a cause of action in negligence?
11. Is the duty of care the same for all persons? Explain and give an example.
12. What is the difference between compensatory damages and punitive damages?
13. What is meant by intentional torts? Give an example.
14. What are some defenses to tort actions?
15. What is meant by assumption of the risk? Give an example of an assumption of the risk.
16. What is the difference between comparative and contributory negligence?
17. What is meant by products liability?
18. How does strict liability differ from ordinary liability in torts?
19. What are some defenses that a defendant may use in a products liability case?
20. What are the elements that must be proven in a breach of contract case?

21. What are the main sources of contract law in United States?

22. How is the statute of frauds a defense to a contract case?

23. When will the court award an equitable remedy? Give an example.

24. How is the preliminary value of a case determined?

25. What are the remedies provided for under the Uniform Commercial Code?

26. How does the formation of a contract differ under the Uniform Commercial Code than under common law?

27. What are warranties under the Uniform Commercial Code?

28. Why is the warranty of fitness for a particular purpose not a warranty on the quality of the goods?

BUILDING YOUR PARALEGAL SKILLS

INTERNET AND TECHNOLOGY EXERCISES

Locate the Online State Version

1. Locate your state version of the UCC.

2. Use the internet to find your state statutes of limitation for sports injuries.

3. Find a web resource location for the U.S.C.

4. Use the internet to find a copy of the case of BMW of North America, Inc, v. Gore 517US559(1996).

CIVIL LITIGATION VIDEO CASE STUDIES

Parent and Child Consult the Legal Team

A father and his son, who is accused of assaulting another student on a school bus, seek representation.

After viewing the video at www.pearsonhighered.com/ careersresources, answer the following questions.

1. Is there a conflict of interest in representing the father and the son?

2. Is information provided to a paralegal privileged information?

3. What is the difference between privileged information and confidential information?

4. Is information received from one client privileged and unable to be disclosed to the other client or other attorney?

CHAPTER OPENING SCENARIO CASE STUDY

Administrative Agency Hearing

A school bus driver injured in a work-related incident seeks advice from an attorney.

After viewing the video at www.pearsonhighered.com/ careersresources, answer the following questions.

1. Are there alternatives to traditional litigation in seeking recovery for a client's injuries?

2. In your jurisdiction, is workers' compensation the exclusive remedy, or may action be brought in contract or tort for injuries suffered on the job?

3. May a paralegal represent a client before an administrative agency in your jurisdiction?

BUILDING YOUR PROFESSIONAL PORTFOLIO AND REFERENCE MANUAL

1. Prepare a memorandum that answers the question: May a paralegal represent a client in workers' compensation administrative hearings in your jurisdiction?

2. Prepare a standard paragraph that might be included in a letter to a client on the difference between confidential information and privileged information.

LEARNING OBJECTIVES

After studying this chapter, you should be able to:

1. Define *evidence* and explain why some evidence is not used in trial.

2. Use the Federal Rules of Evidence to find relevant rules of evidence.

3. Describe and distinguish admissible from inadmissible evidence.

4. Distinguish among the types of tangible evidence.

5. Describe witness testimony and how credibility of a witness is challenged.

6. Identify types of hearsay evidence and the important exceptions to the hearsay rule.

Evidence

OPENING SCENARIO

The law firm of Mason, Marshall, and Benjamin, with co-counsel Roy Saunders, had divided up the work on the personal injury case so that both offices could be as efficient as possible. Ethan Benjamin and his associate, Cary, were heading up the legal team concerned with proving the defendants were negligent. Owen Mason and Ariel Marshall took on the task of proving the extent of the injuries and the issue of damages. The initial problem was proving the cause of action and avoiding a motion for summary judgment. If the case had sufficient proof of negligent conduct, then showing the extent of the injuries and getting as much sympathy from the jury as possible was the path to achieving a major monetary verdict. Emily, the paralegal in the suburban office, expressed some concerns about the graphic nature of the photographs, rhetorically asking if they might bias the jury and make jurors less sympathetic. She had shared with her sister Caitlin, the paralegal working on the negligence side of the case, the evidence her team had and was thinking of using. It was the disagreement on the impact of the photos that raised the question of admissibility. The lawyers had to decide on a strategy.

OPENING SCENARIO LEARNING OBJECTIVE

Explain the issues in allowing or not allowing photographs to be used at trial.

■ INTRODUCTION TO EVIDENCE

The attorney must weigh the value of the evidence and decide what evidence best presents the client's legal position. Trial strategy requires attorneys to plan the presentations of their cases. Included in the trial strategy is an evaluation of the available evidence. Does a particular piece of evidence support or hurt the client's case? What does the attorney really want a jury or judge to hear? What effect might a particular piece of evidence have on the jury's deliberations? In gathering information and preparing the case, the legal team must keep in mind the ultimate goal—the impact of the courtroom presentations on the decision by the trier of fact.

■ EVIDENCE

LEARNING OBJECTIVE 1
Define *evidence* and explain why some evidence is not used in trial.

evidence
Testimony, documents, and tangible items that tend to prove or disprove a fact.

Evidence includes testimony, documents, and tangible things that tend to prove or disprove a fact. To begin, evidence is either direct or circumstantial. Direct evidence proves the existence of a fact or event. Examples include the surveillance video that shows the driver running a red light and the resulting crash, testimony from the scrub nurse who saw the doctor cut the artery in the patient's leg, or the original contract with a forged signature. Direct evidence is best but rarely available. Instead, most cases are established by circumstantial evidence. Circumstantial evidence is a group of facts that, when considered as a whole, tend to prove a fact or event. Rather than the testimony of the scrub nurse, the circumstantial evidence might be: (1) the patient's testimony of his condition before and after surgery; (2) the examination and testing performed by another doctor, who says the patient's condition is a result of artery damage; and (3) the report from the corrective surgery that states the condition of the artery could have only been the result of it being cut. The inference is that the patient had a problem as result of the first surgery. Using circumstantial evidence takes longer to reach the conclusion, but the result is similar in that there is negligence on the part of the first surgeon.

admissible evidence
Evidence that is relevant to the case and from a reliable source.

relevant
In litigation, a fact that, if changed, would change the outcome of the case.

What is actually presented at the trial of a case is frequently different from what an attorney *could* present. Not all evidence is usable in a trial—to be usable, the evidence must be *admissible*. **Admissible evidence** must be **relevant** to the case for the court to allow it to be presented. Just as there are rules of court governing the procedures that must be followed in civil actions, there are also rules of evidence. The federal court evidence rules are found in the Federal Rules of Evidence.

Fact

fact
Event or occurrence.

A **fact** is an event or occurrence. "The plaintiff was driving a motor vehicle" is a fact, as is the time of day when the accident occurred and that the plaintiff was a passenger in a motor vehicle.

Early in the investigation of a client's case, the legal team should identify all of the facts that will be needed to prove the case. To do that, the team will need to research the law and determine the elements of the client's cause of action. In a lawsuit based on negligence, it is necessary for the plaintiff to show that the defendant owed the plaintiff a duty of care. That duty of care may be based on case law or found in a statute. Consider a tavern owner being sued for damages resulting from the acts of an intoxicated patron. Most states have a law, commonly referred to as a *dram shop statute,* that requires those who serve liquor to stop serving visibly intoxicated patrons—a duty imposed by the law. Proof of the breach of this duty is found in the existence of facts showing the patron was visibly intoxicated, the tavern owner knew or should have known of the intoxication, and the tavern owner nonetheless served the patron.

■ INTRODUCTION TO THE RULES OF EVIDENCE

The purposes of the rules of evidence are to promote fairness in the courtroom, eliminate unnecessary expense and delay, and ensure that proceedings are justly decided (Fed. R. Evid. 102). The **Federal Rules of Evidence** were enacted in 1975. These rules, and the amendments enacted since, apply to proceedings in all federal courts. Prior to the enactment of the Federal Rules of Evidence, in federal court cases evidentiary principles had to be extracted from federal court decisions. These evidence principles were not available in an organized rule format, and legal research of court decisions had to be done in order to determine the latest evidentiary rulings of the federal courts.

> **LEARNING OBJECTIVE 2**
> Use the Federal Rules of Evidence to find relevant rules of evidence.

Federal Rules of Evidence
Enacted in 1975, rules that apply to proceedings in all federal courts to determine what evidence will be admissible in court.

PRACTICE TIP

Keep a current edition of the Federal Rules of Evidence (Fed. R. Evid.) and your jurisdiction's rules of evidence readily available. In all phases of case preparation and trial, paralegals will increase their value to the legal team if they are familiar with the rules that govern evidence in both the federal and state jurisdictions. Time can be saved if potentially objectionable evidence is identified early in the investigation.

Each of the rules of evidence is identified by a number, starting with number 101. They are identified as the Federal Rules of Evidence, and cited as Fed. R. Evid., **for example Fed. R. Evid. 504**.

States have also enacted rules of evidence that are applicable to proceedings in courts within their jurisdiction. Generally, the rules of evidence do not apply to administrative agency proceedings. Nevertheless, lawyers frequently refer to the applicable state rules of evidence and argue that these rules should serve as a guide on evidence issues in proceedings before administrative law judges.

■ ADMISSIBILITY OF EVIDENCE—RELEVANT, RELIABLE, AND REAL

All evidence, regardless of the form, must satisfy certain requirements to be admissible at trial. To be admissible, the evidence must be relevant, reliable, and real.

> **LEARNING OBJECTIVE 3**
> Describe and distinguish admissible from inadmissible evidence.

Relevant Evidence

Relevant evidence tends to prove the existence of facts that are important to the resolution of a case (Fed. R. Evid. 401 and 402). In a civil action, the color of an automobile involved in a traffic accident, and whether its headlights were on, are two facts. On a clear, sunny day, those facts would be irrelevant to the outcome of the lawsuit. However, if the accident occurred at night, those facts could be relevant. Relevant facts are those that, if changed, would change the outcome of the lawsuit. For example, a traffic light is reported as green for southbound traffic. That fact is relevant because traffic controls for cross traffic (westbound) would show a red light. If this fact were not true, it would change the outcome. If both

relevant evidence
Evidence that tends to prove the existence of facts important to the resolution of a case.

parties had a green light, neither may be negligent. Other relevant evidence that is contradictory may also be presented, such as that the traffic light was malfunctioning and as a result, the traffic light was green for both intersecting streets. It is for the trier of fact—judge or jury—to decide which piece of relevant evidence to believe. The legal team must be prepared to present relevant evidence, hoping that it will be convincing.

Reliable Evidence

reliable evidence
Evidence that is trustworthy; for example, testimony from a witness who observed an accident is reliable.

Evidence in all forms must also be reliable. **Reliable evidence** is that which is trustworthy. For witness testimony to be reliable, it must be based on personal observations (Fed. R. Evid. 602). With regard to documents or photographs, they are reliable when someone testifies about the authenticity of the record (Fed. R. Evid. 901(a)). It is possible to question the weight that the trier of fact should give to any evidence, even if it is admitted into evidence. Reliable evidence is not binding evidence. However, it can serve as a basis for the ultimate decision in any civil case. Court decisions should not be based on information that does not form a solid foundation for the court's resolution of a case.

Real Evidence

physical evidence
Any tangible physical evidence; usually an item directly related to the litigation.

real evidence
Testimony that is based on real facts, not some imaginary or hypothetical situation.

Finally, evidence must be real. The testimony must be based on real facts, not some imaginary or hypothetical situation. For **physical evidence, real evidence** is an object that is pertinent to the issues in the lawsuit.

Probative Value

probative value
The tendency of the evidence to demonstrate a fact important to the resolution of a case outweighs any prejudice it might create.

prejudice
In evidence, the probative value must outweigh prejudice that might mislead or confuse the jury, creating an emotional reaction.

Even evidence that meets the three tests—relevant, reliable, and real—may still be inadmissible. The final test is whether the **probative value** of the evidence is outweighed by the **prejudice.** If the evidence is relevant, reliable, and real—but may mislead or confuse the jury, create some emotional reaction, or result in unfair prejudice—then the evidence may be inadmissible (Fed. R. Evid. 403).

The judge, acting as the arbiter of procedural law, might say the item's value as evidence, which tends to prove a central issue in the case, is outweighed by any damage it may cause. It is almost as if the evidence is weighed on an imaginary scale, with the probative value of the evidence on one side and the prejudice on the other. Whichever side is weightier determines if the evidence will be admitted. A typical example is a color photograph of a bloody accident scene. The graphic details of how the plaintiff was thrown from the car and her leg severed at the knee are one thing to hear and yet another to see in a color photo. Viewing the picture may result in too much sympathy for the plaintiff, and the picture may be ruled inadmissible evidence by the judge.

Judicial Notice

judicial notice
A court's acceptance of a fact without requiring the party's proof.

Certain facts may be admitted as evidence without being formally subjected to the tests of admissibility. The doctrine of **judicial notice** allows the court to establish or accept as true a particular fact, usually a commonly known fact. Because the fact is one that is commonly known or can be easily verified, it speeds the judicial process along to take notice of the fact rather than have a witness testify. Under Fed. R. Evid. 201, the fact must be one that is not subject to dispute; it must be generally known or capable of accurate confirmation from a source that is virtually unquestionable. That Barack Obama is the first African

American elected President of the United States is a commonly known fact. By contrast, that February 15, 1962, was a Thursday may not be generally known but can be easily determined by referring to a calendar. Both would be appropriate facts for the court to take judicial notice of rather than requiring a witness to testify. Either party to the litigation may ask the court to take judicial notice of a particular fact, or the court may do so on its own.

Inadmissible Evidence

Certain types of evidence are not admissible at trial because the underlying facts have a high probability of creating a negative inference in the mind of the jury. Some of the **inadmissible evidence** is about conduct that we, as a society, wish to encourage. If the jury were informed about it, jurors might misinterpret it as an admission of wrongdoing, leading the jury to make an award or finding that is not based on the facts. In these special circumstances, the prejudice created outweighs the probative value and the evidence is not admissible.

inadmissible evidence
Evidence that either the rules or the court determines is not admissible at trial.

Subsequent Remedial Measures

It is common sense to encourage others to make repairs rather than neglect their property. If someone fell and was injured on the sidewalk in front of someone's property, the building owner might repair the cause of the injury—whether it was a crack in the sidewalk, raised tree roots, or a patch of ice—in order to prevent future incidents. However, the evidence of the repair is not admissible and may not be revealed to the jury. If it were revealed, the jury might be inclined to think that making the repair represents admission of fault. If the sidewalk had been previously corrected, the plaintiff would not have been injured, and the jury would hold the landowner liable based on the evidence of the repair. This assignment of liability for making repairs might discourage landowners from correcting and repairing their properties. Thus, the court has determined that the prejudice to those who make repairs outweighs the probative value of the repair.

Offers of Compromise or Settlement

Parties to a lawsuit make offers to settle the case for a number of reasons. Economics is one reason—the cost of a trial versus the cost of a settlement. Where there are multiple defendants, one defendant may wish to conclude his involvement with the litigation by settling with the plaintiff. However, offers of settlement or settlement of one or more claims is not admissible at trial. The jury might be inclined to think the party would not have made the offer to settle if he or she was not guilty. Rather than considering the facts of the case, the jury would likely be prejudiced by the existence of settlement discussions. Most cases that are filed are settled before trial. From a judicial efficiency standpoint, litigants should be encouraged to settle and not try cases. If defendants thought the settlement discussion would be revealed to the jury, defendants might be less inclined to participate in settlement discussions and in resolving cases by settlements (Fed. R. Evid. 408).

Payment of Medical Expenses

As with settlement discussions, evidence of the voluntary payment of the injured party's medical expenses is not admissible at trial. Again, because of the more than likely prejudicial inference the jury would draw from the evidence, it is inadmissible (Fed. R. Evid. 409).

Existence of Liability Insurance

The existence of liability insurance to pay the claims from an accident or other incident creates the impression that the defendant will not be personally harmed by an award to the plaintiff. In some circles, this is referred to as the "deep pocket" theory—that is, where there is a large corporation or insurance company involved, the jury may feel that the money would not be coming from the defendant's pocket. It is just some big company that can afford it, so why not give the plaintiff something? This preconceived notion can make the weighing of the actual facts and the assessment of true wrong secondary to giving the plaintiff some award (Fed. R. Evid. 411).

■ TYPES OF TANGIBLE EVIDENCE

LEARNING OBJECTIVE 4
Distinguish among the types of tangible evidence.

Evidence can take several forms. The most common type of evidence is the testimony of witnesses. However, physical objects, diagrams, and business records can also be evidence. All of the various types of evidence tell a piece of the plaintiff's or defendant's story, somewhat like the pieces of a jigsaw puzzle. When all the pieces fit together, they make a complete picture.

Tangible Evidence

tangible evidence
Physical items that may be presented at trial for the jury to consider.

Tangible evidence refers to physical items that may be presented at trial for the jury to consider. Tangible evidence includes documents and business records, demonstrative evidence, and physical items that are part of the litigation.

Documentary Evidence

documentary evidence
Writings, recordings, and photographs; includes X-ray films, electronic recordings, or any other data compilation.

Documentary evidence can be writings, recordings, and photographs, as well as X-ray films, electronic recordings, or any other data compilation. Although most lawyers and courts think about documents as being on paper, documents can take many forms, including those that are stored electronically (Fed. R. Evid. 1001).

Regardless of the method used to create or store them, documents are commonly the source of information that is relevant to the issues before the court. Medical records are usually introduced into evidence in personal injury cases because they contain pertinent information about the injuries and treatment of the plaintiff. In lawsuits involving the sale of real estate, the deed and agreement of sale are relevant documents for the court's review.

Documents need to be authenticated by a witness as being true and correct and that they were kept in the usual course of business (Fed. R. Evid. 901). Records librarians or custodians are the witnesses who examine documents in front of the jury and confirm they are the true and correct documents and that they were maintained in the ordinary course of business of a business, hospital, or office.

best evidence rule
Court preference for original writings, recordings, and photographs.

The **Best Evidence Rule** represents the court's preference for original writings, recordings, and photographs (Fed. R. Evid. 1002). Whenever possible, the original of all evidence should be obtained and preserved for use at time of trial. The original is the best evidence possible. However, the rules of evidence allow the court to admit a copy of a document to the same extent as the original. If a genuine question is raised as to the authenticity of the document copy, then the court may insist on the original (Fed. R. Evid. 1003).

There are also some circumstances in which the original is not required and other evidence of the contents is admissible. Unless the original is intentionally lost or destroyed in bad faith, a party may offer a copy as admissible evidence. Testimony is still necessary to establish what the original document said and whether the record being offered into evidence accurately reflects the contents of the missing original.

Self-authenticating documents eliminate the requirement of extrinsic evidence of authenticity as a condition to admissibility (Fed. R. Evid. 902). Those documents that are self-authenticating include **domestic public documents.** Records that are on file with any domestic government are admissible evidence if they bear the seal of the office and a signature attesting to their authenticity. Similarly, foreign public documents can be self-authenticating as long as they have been identified as genuine by an appropriate official of the government.

Certified copies of official business records are also self-authenticating as long as the business record is of a regularly conducted activity and was made at or near the time of the recorded occurrence.

Demonstrative Evidence

Demonstrative evidence is a tangible item that depicts, displays, or demonstrates a fact. A photograph is an example of demonstrative evidence. A medical model of the spinal column that shows a herniated disc is demonstrative evidence. A magnetic board that depicts an accident site and has magnetized cars for a witness to use to demonstrate the movement of the automobiles before, at, and after impact is demonstrative evidence.

Demonstrative evidence, like documentary evidence, must be authenticated. The witness must be able to testify that the photo, model, or other item is a fair and accurate representation of the thing it depicts. Typically, the witness called to testify using the demonstrative evidence will authenticate the evidence. For example, before evidence such as a photo is shown to the jury, the witness must identify it as a fair and accurate depiction of the item described; or, the witness must testify that the magnetic board is an accurate depiction of the intersection, with lane indicators and traffic control devices.

Physical Evidence

Physical evidence generally refers to physical items that are the subject matter of the lawsuit. It could be the brake pads and rotors that failed, causing the car accident; the remains of an electric appliance that caused a house fire; or a toy on which a small child choked. These types of physical evidence must be preserved for potential testing by expert witnesses and for presentation at trial.

The two main concerns related to physical evidence are:

1. preserving the item in its original state after the incident, and
2. creating records establishing that the item, when presented at trial, is in the same condition it was in at the time of the accident.

Much has been written about the failure of the plaintiff and/or defendant to preserve critical evidence directly related to the litigation. Failure to preserve the evidence, or spoliation, can result in a jury charge—jurors may infer from the destruction of the evidence that it would have had a negative effect on the party's case.

In determining the proper penalty for spoliation of evidence, courts are most likely to consider:

1. the degree of fault of the party who altered or destroyed the evidence;
2. the degree of prejudice suffered by the opposing party; and
3. the availability of a lesser sanction that will protect the opposing party's rights and deter future similar conduct (*Schroeder v. Department of Transportation*, 710 A2d 23 (1998)).

self-authenticating documents
Because of the nature of the document or the circumstances under which it is created or stored, an original is not required.

domestic public documents
Type of self-authenticating document; these records are on file with any domestic government office and are admissible evidence if they bear the seal of the office and a signature attesting to their authenticity.

demonstrative evidence
Tangible item such as a photograph or map that depicts, displays, or demonstrates a fact.

PRACTICE TIP

Documents should be analyzed as they are collected to determine whether they are originals or copies. An effort should be made to obtain the originals and determine what certifications will be required for their introduction into evidence. Lack of proper authentication or certification may prevent the "smoking gun" from being admitted into evidence at trial.

chain of custody
Written record showing the identity of everyone accessing evidence and showing that the evidence was not altered while in possession of the law firm.

Related to spoliation is record keeping that establishes that the item has been preserved in its original state and was not subject to tampering. All potential tangible evidence, including original documents, that comes into the possession of the legal team must be properly identified and cataloged for future reference.

The storage of physical evidence in the law firm is crucial to maintaining the integrity of the evidence. If the object or document is not kept securely, its value as evidence can be seriously compromised. Brake pads and other vehicle parts that are casually left lying around the office may not be in their original condition when needed for inspection or at trial. The law office should maintain a secure evidence locker with access limited to the members of the legal team who must have access. A log should also be maintained so the **chain of custody** can be established to show the identity of everyone who accessed the evidence and to show that the evidence was not altered since its arrival at the law firm.

Documents present less of a problem than objects because documents can readily be copied. Identifying marks should not be added to an original document. The original document should be kept in a secure location such as a locked file drawer. In order to maintain the integrity of the original document, only one member of the team should have access to that drawer. Again, such a filing system establishes the chain of custody of each document from the time it arrived in the law office until it is used as evidence. Such a system eliminates any possible questions at trial.

■ TESTIMONY OF WITNESSES

LEARNING OBJECTIVE 5
Describe witness testimony and how credibility of a witness is challenged.

testimony evidence
Evidence given by witnesses who usually appear live in the courtroom to testify.

Testimony evidence is given by witnesses, who usually appear live in the courtroom to testify. Parties to the lawsuit and other individuals can appear as lay or expert witnesses, but only if they have been called to testify by one of the parties. When people are called as witnesses, they are sworn to "tell the truth, the whole truth, and nothing but the truth." That oath may be taken with a hand placed on a holy book, such as the Bible or Koran. Witnesses who do not want to swear can affirm to tell the truth. All witnesses must affirmatively state that they will tell the truth before they will be allowed to testify. The purpose of the oath or affirmation is to awaken the conscience of witnesses to the serious nature of the event they are about to participate in and to impress on their minds the duty to be truthful (Fed. R. Evid. 603).

Giving Testimony

hostile witness
A witness who does not cooperate with the party who called him to testify; a reluctant witness who demonstrates some hostility to the case presented or toward the party who called him to testify.

Although many witnesses would prefer to spontaneously tell their story, witnesses are generally not allowed to testify by way of a monologue. Testimony is directed by the trial attorneys, who examine the witnesses by asking questions. Procedurally, the party with the burden of proof calls its witnesses first. Questioning the witness to prove one's case is called *direct examination*. By calling a witness, the attorney is in effect vouching for the credibility of the witness. Exceptions occur when a reluctant witness is called who demonstrates some hostility to the case presented. In these cases, the attorney advises the court that the witness is a **hostile witness.** The lawyer is not vouching for the hostile witness, but is using the witness to present testimony that only that witness can offer, even if done so reluctantly. The lawyer may ask the hostile witness leading questions, a tactic normally reserved for use in cross-examination of the other party's witnesses, instead of the normal open-ended questions asked on direct examination of one's own friendly witnesses. The opposing party will ask questions to test or challenge the witness; this is called *cross-examination*. Witnesses will then be asked additional questions by the party that called them in order to clarify the answers given on cross-examination; this is called *redirect examination*. The opposing party may, by recross examination, challenge any new points brought out on redirect examination.

Form of Questions

On direct and redirect, witnesses are questioned using open-ended questions that call for a short narrative response. These types of questions allow the witness to tell the story of the case. On cross and recross examination, questions will be leading questions, which, by their nature, suggest an answer—usually *yes* or *no*. On direct, the question might be, "Where were you headed on the morning of August 21?" On cross, the same question might be, "You were rushing because you were late for work on the morning of August 21?"

Lay Witnesses

A **lay witness** or **fact witness** is a person who has personal knowledge about the matter before the court. Such witnesses are commonly called *eyewitnesses* because they observed something pertinent to the case. However, witnesses' other senses could also be the source of evidence—they heard, touched, or smelled something relevant to the dispute.

lay witness
Person who has personal knowledge about the matter before the court.

fact witness
A witness who testifies about facts based upon his observation or has personal knowledge about the matter before the court.

> ### PRACTICE TIP
>
> Paralegals are frequently called on to interview clients and witnesses and prepare them for deposition and trial. Paralegals should ask the witness practice questions in preparation for deposition or trial to give the witness confidence in his ability to answer questions. Witnesses should be instructed to answer only the question asked and to wait for the question to be completely asked before beginning their answer. Witnesses will sometimes have annoying habits or mannerisms, which should be pointed out to them in a respectful way to help them avoid embarrassment before a judge or jury. Explaining the courtroom procedures is another way to put the witness at ease.

There is no special training or qualification to be a lay witness. Anyone, anywhere, can become a lay witness if he or she was present at the time something pertinent to the case occurred. Being a lay witness does not limit the witness to testifying only about facts; lay witnesses may give opinion testimony if the opinion is based on the witness's personal knowledge and observations. The opinion of a lay witness is permitted where it is based upon firsthand knowledge, is helpful to jurors in understanding the testimony, and is not based upon some scientific or specialized knowledge. For example, if the lay witness is familiar with the handwriting of another person, such as a parent or spouse, then the lay witness is allowed to offer an opinion about the authenticity of a signature. Lay witnesses can also testify about the speed of a motor vehicle if they saw the vehicle and are familiar with the speeds of automobiles. Note that lay witnesses cannot offer opinions except in those unique situations in which their opinion testimony is based on their personal perception, and not on technical or specialized knowledge (Fed. R. Evid. 701).

Sometimes the issue of using lay versus expert witnesses depends on whether the issue before the court truly requires an expert opinion because it is outside the realm of common knowledge.

There are some basic criteria to keep in mind when interviewing potential lay witnesses. First, lay witnesses must have personal knowledge of an event in question. Do the witnesses have firsthand knowledge, or are they repeating what they were told happened by someone else?

Second, lay witnesses must be physically and mentally capable of understanding the duty to tell the truth. The oath taken by all witnesses requires each witness to acknowledge that he pledges to completely tell the truth during his subsequent testimony. That oath is meaningful only if the witness is physically and mentally able to understand its requirements.

Third, witnesses must have the ability to recollect and communicate. Even if a witness has firsthand knowledge, she must be physically and mentally able to testify. Occasionally a witness can no longer communicate what she observed. Unless some alternative method of communication is available, she will not be able to testify in court.

Checklist ✔   QUALIFYING A FACT WITNESS

1. Personal knowledge
2. Competency of witness
   a. Physical and mental capacity to understand oath
   b. Capacity to recollect and communicate

Expert Witnesses

expert witness
Person qualified by education, training, or experience to render an opinion based on a set of facts that are outside the scope of knowledge of the fact finder.

There is frequently a need to use **expert witnesses** to offer evidence needed to prove a case. Expert witnesses are a special type of witness used to explain to the fact finder an area that is outside the scope of the average individual's training or learning experiences (Fed. R. Evid. 702). For example, most people are not knowledgeable about high-voltage electrical transmission on the power lines that run along highways or near homes and businesses. An expert who does not have personal knowledge of the event giving rise to the litigation may be called to explain this type of technical information to the jury so they can better understand the facts. Expert witnesses are those who have special knowledge, training, or experience that qualifies them to offer expert opinions pertinent to the issues in the case on trial. The offered opinion must assist the judge or jury in reaching the ultimate decision in the case. The opinion cannot answer the ultimate question of fact in the case. For example, in a negligence lawsuit, an expert cannot offer the opinion that "the defendant was negligent." However, an expert witness who is an accident reconstructionist can offer an opinion about the speed the defendant's vehicle was traveling immediately prior to the impact—based on the skid marks, point of impact, and location where the vehicles came to rest. It is then for the judge or jury to decide if the defendant was driving at a speed that, under the circumstances, constituted negligent operation of the motor vehicle.

In order for witnesses to be qualified as experts, they must have some special knowledge, training, or experience, which is frequently based on academic and professional credentials—degrees earned, positions held, and treatises written. However, an expert's qualification can also be in the form of on-the-job training. Opinions relevant to the trial of a case may involve car repairs or home construction. Experts in those fields will have on-the-job experience, rather than formal schooling, that qualifies them as experts. To offer an expert opinion, the witness must be qualified in that field. Unless the lawyers stipulate in advance that a person is an expert, he must be qualified and accepted by the court as being an expert before offering his opinion. This is done by a series of questions asked by the side offering the expert. These questions bring out the qualifications and experience that the court accepts as sufficient background, training, and skill to allow the person to give an expert opinion. Without qualifications, a witness would be considered a lay witness, and lay witnesses cannot offer expert opinions.

Prerecorded Testimony

There will be situations when a witness is unavailable to appear in the courtroom during trial. It may be a medical expert whose schedule will not permit time away from the hospital or medical practice, or an elderly or disabled person who cannot physically appear. In those situations, rules of the court may allow **prerecorded testimony** to be used at trial. The Federal Rules of Civil Procedure permit deposition testimony to be used in the courtroom in lieu of live testimony if the witness is dead or unable to attend the trial because of age, illness, infirmity, or imprisonment. State courts have similar rules, which seek to promote the interest of justice. The Federal Rules of Civil Procedure also allow the deposition to be recorded by sound, sound-and-visual, and stenographic means. If the legal team anticipates a potential problem with getting a witness to the courtroom for trial, the applicable rules of court should be reviewed to determine the best available method to present the testimony of an absent witness. Court reporting services that offer video deposition services can usually provide the necessary technical assistance and advice on local rules (Fed. R. Civ. P. 32).

prerecorded testimony
Testimony that is recorded in advance of trial that may be used at trial in the event the witness is unavailable to testify.

Challenging the Credibility of Witnesses

One of the uses of cross-examination of a witness is to raise doubts as to the accuracy, **credibility,** or truthfulness of the testimony given in direct examination. Showing a history of dishonesty, or prior conduct or statements inconsistent with the testimony, may cause the jury to have doubts about the testimony given under direct examination (Fed. R. Evid. 607).

credibility
Truthfulness and believability of the testimony given.

Out-of-Court Statements

During the questioning at trial, witnesses sometimes make statements that are inconsistent with their prior statements. Before a friendly witness or client testifies at a hearing or at a deposition, there should be a meeting during which the anticipated testimony is reviewed. That discussion should include a review of all of the witness's prior statements. In a motor vehicle accident case, for example, there may be prior statements recorded on a police accident report or in a signed statement given to an investigator, or perhaps oral comments were overheard and reported by another witness at the accident scene. Whether or not they were recorded, such **prior inconsistent statements** can be used by the other side of the case for the purpose of attacking the credibility of the witness when the prior statements are inconsistent with the testimony given in court (Fed. R. Evid. 613).

prior inconsistent statement
Prior statement given by a witness that is inconsistent with the testimony the witness gives at trial.

When weighing the evidence, the judge and jury consider the credibility of the witness. Credibility of the witness can be based on whether the witness has told the same version of the observed events. Prior inconsistent statements undermine the credibility of the witness and the value that a judge or jury might attach to the testimony.

Attacking the Credibility of a Witness

Criminal History. The credibility of a witness can also be attacked by use of the witness's criminal history (Fed. R. Evid. 609). Evidence that a witness had been convicted of a crime involving dishonesty or making false statements can be used to cast doubt on the credibility of the witness in the present civil action. However, the Federal Rules of Evidence impose a ten-year limit. If the conviction is more than ten years old, evidence of the crime is not admissible. The rules do provide that a ten-year-old conviction is admissible as long as the proponent of the evidence gives the adverse party notice of her intention to use such evidence so that a fair opportunity exists to prepare to contest this evidence.

Religious Beliefs. Religious beliefs can never be used to impeach the credibility of a witness in a civil action nor used to enhance the believability of testimony (Fed. R. Evid. 610). No attempt should be made to influence the judge and jury to give greater value to the testimony of a witness with profound religious beliefs.

Character and Habit. As a general rule, the character of a party or witness is not admissible at trial to show that he acted in a particular way. For example, Mary may not be called to testify that Dave is a safe driver in order to prove that he was not negligent in an automobile accident (Fed. R. Evid. 404). However, Mary can testify about Dave's habits with regard to driving. Perhaps Mary carpools to work with several people and Dave is the driver. After riding for years with Dave, Mary is aware of his driving habits, including the fact that he comes to a full, three-second stop at all stop signs. The testimony of Dave's habit has the same effect as character evidence, but it is more reliable because it is based on Mary's personal observation (Fed. R. Evid. 406).

Character evidence will be admissible when it relates to the witness's reputation for truthfulness (Fed. R. Evid. 608). This narrow exception to the general rule is limited to those circumstances where the credibility of a witness has been attacked. The character evidence must refer to the witness's reputation for truthfulness. The character witnesses should be people from the witness's community who know his reputation for telling the truth. Specific instances of the conduct of the witness are not admissible as evidence; rather, the character witnesses' testimony should be limited to describing the reputation of the witness.

IN THE WORDS OF THE COURT…

Hearsay

Crawford v. Washington 541 U.S. 36 (2004).

Where nontestimonial hearsay is at issue, it is wholly consistent with the Framers' design to afford the States flexibility in their development of hearsay law—as does *Roberts,* and as would an approach that exempted such statements from Confrontation Clause scrutiny altogether. Where testimonial evidence is at issue, however, the Sixth Amendment demands what the common law required: unavailability and a prior opportunity for cross-examination. We leave for another day any effort to spell out a comprehensive definition of "testimonial."

Whatever else the term covers, it applies at a minimum to prior testimony at a preliminary hearing, before a grand jury, or at a former trial; and to police interrogations. These are the modern practices with closest kinship to the abuses at which the Confrontation Clause was directed.

■ THE HEARSAY RULE

Hearsay is an out-of-court statement made by someone (declarant) other than the witness testifying, and that statement of the declarant is offered for the truth of its contents (Fed. R. Evid. 801). The statement can be oral, nonverbal, or written.

> *Example:* Mary said to me that John was taken by the ambulance to Jefferson Hospital.

In this example, the out-of-court statement is about John being taken to the hospital; Mary is the declarant, or the person whose statement is being presented at trial for its truth.

The general rule is that hearsay is not admissible evidence because it is not reliable (Fed. R. Evid. 802). Hearsay is not reliable because it is the statement of another who is not available for testing through cross-examination. Written documents are also considered hearsay, as the author typically is not available to testify about the statements made in his writing. The hearsay rule is a rule of evidence in every court. In some courts, the rule has been codified, as with the Federal Rules of Evidence; in others, the rules are founded on a series of legal opinions or precedent.

For the legal team, hearsay is sometimes like a puzzle or a game. When interviewing witnesses and clients, it is important to listen for the "she said/he told me" statements. The first reaction should be, "That is a hearsay statement that we won't be able to use at trial." Then comes the puzzle—is there some rule or exception that will permit the hearsay statement? In the example above, perhaps Mary should be interviewed and consideration given to whether she should be available to testify at trial. Perhaps the statement is not hearsay because it won't be offered for the truth that John went to the hospital, but rather to show the reason the witness went to the hospital immediately.

Statements That Are Not Hearsay

Two types of statements are deemed by the Federal Rules as **non-hearsay.** The first is a prior inconsistent statement. This is a prior statement of a witness that is inconsistent with the testimony that he is now giving at trial. The prior statement must have been a recorded statement made under oath (Fed. R. Evid. 801(d)(1)). It is these inconsistencies that opposing counsel will look for to undermine the credibility of the witness who is testifying. The second is an **admission of a party opponent.** This is an out-of-court statement made by one of the parties of the litigation wherein she admits liability (Fed. R. Evid. 801(d)(2)). Because the person is a party to the lawsuit, she is in court and available for cross-examination. The statement is subject to the testing inherent to our adversarial system.

In both these instances of non-hearsay, the witness who is testifying is being tested or cross-examined about a statement he/she previously made. Therefore, in both cases, the testimony about the prior statement is not hearsay.

Exceptions to the Hearsay Rule

As with most legal principles, there are exceptions to the hearsay rule. Hearsay evidence is not admissible unless the legal team can find at least one exception to the rule that is applicable to the hearsay statement. **Hearsay exceptions** acknowledge that there are certain times people say things when they are not likely to lie or fabricate information. These statements made by a declarant are reliable because of the circumstances under which they were made.

LEARNING OBJECTIVE 6

Identify types of hearsay evidence and the important exceptions to the hearsay rule.

hearsay
Out-of-court statement made by someone (declarant) other than the witness testifying; the statement of the declarant is offered for the truth of its contents.

non-hearsay
Items that are not hearsay because the declarant, while presently not testifying, is available to be cross-examined about the statement.

admission of a party opponent
A form of non-hearsay; an admission of fact made by one of the parties to the lawsuit.

hearsay exceptions
Hearsay statements that are admissible because they are made under circumstances in which they are likely to be true.

The federal rules list twenty-seven exceptions to the basic hearsay rule that prohibits a statement's introduction into evidence. Exhibit 6.1 contains the list of exceptions.

If the hearsay falls within one of those exceptions, the hearsay evidence is admissible. The job of the legal team is to fit the hearsay statement into one of these exceptions so that the testimony may be admitted at trial. The following discussion describes the exceptions encountered most frequently at trial.

Present-Sense Impression

present-sense impression
Hearsay exception in which a statement made describes an event that the declarant was then perceiving.

An exception to the hearsay rule has been carved out for **present-sense impressions.** An example of a present-sense impression is a statement made describing an event as the declarant perceived it. The witness, who heard the statement, would then testify to what the declarant said, provided of course that the court would be satisfied that the statement was indeed a present-sense impression. Even if the declarant is available, the witness could relate to the judge and jury what was said.

Exhibit 6.1 Exceptions to the Hearsay Rule Under the Federal Rules of Evidence

1. Present-sense impression
2. Excited utterance
3. Then-existing mental, emotional, or physical condition
4. Statements for purpose of medical diagnosis
5. Recorded recollection
6. Records of regularly conducted activity
7. Absence of entry in records kept in accordance with provision of paragraph 8
8. Public records and reports
9. Records of vital statistics
10. Absence of public record or entry
11. Records of religious organizations
12. Marriage, baptismal, and similar certificates
13. Family records
14. Records of documents affecting an interest in property
15. Statements in documents affecting an interest in property
16. Statements in ancient documents
17. Market reports, commercial publications
18. Learned treatises
19. Reputation concerning personal or family history
20. Reputation concerning boundaries or general history
21. Reputation as to character
22. Judgment of previous conviction
23. Judgment as to personal, family or general history, or boundaries
24. Former testimony
25. Statement under belief of impending death
26. Statement against interest
27. Statement of personal or family history

The usual justification for allowing such hearsay evidence is that a present-sense impression is reliable because the declarant had no opportunity to shade or fabricate a story about the events as they happened. Consequently, it is generally thought that present-sense impressions are reliable evidence and are not subject to the usual weaknesses of hearsay evidence (Fed. R. Evid. 803(1)).

Excited Utterances

An **excited utterance** is a statement by a declarant about a startling event. In order to satisfy the hearsay exception, the declarant must have made the statement during the stress of the excitement caused by the startling event or condition. Startling or shocking events commonly cause people to blurt out a statement about what they saw. That testimony can be presented for the purpose of proving the truth of anything said by the declarant. Of course, the judge must be satisfied that the statement is indeed an excited utterance. The circumstances precipitating the excited utterance thus need to be explained to the court by the proponent of the evidence (Fed. R. Evid. 803(2)).

excited utterance
Hearsay exception in which the statement by a declarant about a startling event is admissible.

Then-Existing Mental, Emotional, or Physical Condition

These are statements by the declarant concerning his mental, emotional, or physical condition at the time those conditions were experienced. These are not what the declarant later remembers about the event. Statements that one was in excruciating pain or frightened at the time he was thrown from the motorcycle struck by the car would be examples (Fed. R. Evid. 803(3)).

Statements for Purposes of Medical Treatment

Any information supplied by a patient for the purposes of receiving medical treatment and describing medical history is admissible. Past or present symptoms, pain, or medical problems are examples of medical information patients commonly supply to medical personnel. That information is frequently used to treat and diagnose medical conditions.

In civil actions where bodily injuries are alleged, pertinent medical information can be admitted into evidence. Even if the patient who supplied the information is available to be a witness, the medical witness can testify about such statements, which are usually recorded in the patient's medical records (Fed. R. Evid. 803(4)).

Recorded Recollection

Witnesses are permitted to consult writings to refresh their recollections. It is common for people to refer to personal, contemporaneous records to refresh their recollections about what happened on a particular day. The courts recognize this common human practice and allow witnesses to refresh their memories using **recorded recollection.**

As a hearsay exception, a recorded memorandum concerning a matter about which a witness once had knowledge may be read into the record. However, there are some conditions that must first be met. The matter must have been fresh in the witness's memory at the time it was recorded, and the record must reflect that memory accurately. Consequently, even if the witness does not presently remember, the recorded memorandum can be used as evidence as a hearsay exception (Fed. R. Evid. 803(5)).

recorded recollection
Hearsay exception that allows a personal, contemporaneously made statement in order to refresh a witness's recollection about what happened on a particular day.

Records of Regularly Conducted Activity

Any record kept in the regular course of business falls within this hearsay exception. Business records made contemporaneously with the recorded events are considered reliable and worthy of being admitted as evidence. Ledgers or logbooks are commonly used by businesses to document their daily activities. Many of these records are presently kept electronically. Nevertheless, in order for the court to admit the records as evidence (as an exception to the hearsay rule), a records custodian needs to testify to the fact that the records were indeed kept in the ordinary course of business. With such supporting testimony, all information in the records constitutes proof of the proposition before the court (Fed. R. Evid. 803(6)).

Public Records

A similar exception to the hearsay rule is made for records kept by public officials or government agencies. Records of vital statistics such as birth, death, and marriage are admissible if the records are kept in a public office. Any reports of matters related to the activities of a public office or records maintained pursuant to law are admissible as evidence. Deed records filed in county courthouses can also be evidence in spite of the hearsay rule prohibition. Such records are kept in the usual course of a government agency's business and therefore are considered trustworthy (Fed. R. Evid. 803(8)).

Family and Ancient Records

Family records, genealogies, family photographs, and the like can be evidence of facts concerning family history. Occasionally, a person's lineage is at issue, and the only source of such information may be an old family record. A statement in such a document may be relevant to an issue before the court. In addition, if a document can be authenticated as an ancient document, it can then be admitted to prove a statement in the document (Fed. R. Evid. 803(13)).

Exceptions to Hearsay—Declarant Unavailable

Sometimes the declarant will not be available to testify, and the only way for the jury to learn the declarant's testimony is through hearsay evidence. A witness may assert one of the privileges and therefore refuse to testify. An individual may be out of the country, perhaps as a member of the armed forces overseas on active duty. The person may have developed an illness that prevents him from communicating, such as a stroke that affects speech or Alzheimer's disease, which affects memory. Finally, the witness may have passed away. Despite the unavailability of the witness, the testimony may be crucial to the case. In the event someone is unavailable, there are special exceptions that allow hearsay statements of that individual to be used at trial.

Former Testimony. Prior recorded testimony of the now unavailable witness made under oath at another hearing or proceeding, including a deposition, may be admitted at trial. It is not required that it be from the same or even a proceeding related to the one now before the court. However, to fit into the exception, the testimony now being offered must have been subject to cross-examination (Fed. R. Evid. 804(b)(1)).

dying declaration
Hearsay exception for a deathbed statement.

Dying Declaration. A deathbed statement, or **dying declaration,** made by an individual is believed to be reliable. Due to the psychological and physical stresses of the situation, it is unlikely that in one's final moments, a person would lie or fabricate anything said (Fed. R. Evid. 804(b)(2)).

Statement Against Interest. Human nature decrees that persons do not make statements that are harmful to themselves or against their own best interests. Thus,

statements against interest are reliable and admissible evidence as an exception to the hearsay rule (Fed. R. Evid. 804(b)(3)).

Statements of Personal or Family History. Statements one makes concerning family history, such as birth, adoption, marriage, and death, are considered reliable. These statements made by a closely related family member or someone with personal and intimate knowledge of the family history are admissible even if the declarant is not available to testify (Fed. R. Evid. 804(b)(4)).

Residual Exception

There is one final exception to the hearsay rule. When all else fails, this is the wild card for the legal team. That is, if the legal team cannot find any other exception that will allow the hearsay to be admitted, this exception can be used. Called the **residual exception,** this exception allows hearsay where the hearsay statement being offered is a material fact of the case and there is no better evidence or testimony available to establish that fact. Permitting the hearsay statement must best serve the interest of justice without unduly prejudicing the opposing party. This catch-all exception is available at the judge's discretion and will be granted where the probative value outweighs the possible unreliability of the hearsay statement.

Raising Objections

There is one cardinal rule of evidence to remember—if a timely objection is not raised on the record of the proceeding, the erroneous admission of evidence cannot be the basis of a later motion (Fed. R. Evid. 103(a)). The underlying basis of this rule is that lawyers must preserve their objections to the introduction of evidence at the time the evidence is offered. An orderly trial requires that evidence issues be argued and decided in a timely manner, not after the witness has left the courtroom or after the trial is over. Fairness requires that lawyers raise timely objections so that judges can promptly decide what evidence will or will not be heard or seen by the jury.

statement against interest
Hearsay exception that recognizes that human nature dictates that people do not make statements that are harmful to themselves or against their own best interests.

residual exception
Allows hearsay where the hearsay statement being offered is a material fact of the case and there is no better evidence or testimony available to establish the fact.

CONCEPT REVIEW AND REINFORCEMENT

KEY TERMS

CHAPTER SUMMARY

EVIDENCE

Introduction to Evidence	Trial strategy requires planning the presentation of the case, including evaluating admissible evidence and deciding which particular pieces will have the most positive impact on the jury.
Evidence	Evidence includes testimony, documents, and tangible things that tend to prove or disprove a fact. Only admissible evidence may be offered in a trial.
Introduction to the Rules of Evidence	What constitutes evidence in federal cases is determined under the Federal Rules of Evidence.
Admissibility of Evidence—Relevant, Reliable, and Real	To be admissible, evidence must be: relevant (tending to prove the existence of facts that are important to the resolution of a case); reliable (trustworthy); and real (not based on imaginary or hypothetical situations). To be admissible, evidence must also have probative value that outweighs any prejudicial value the evidence may have, such as pictures that are particularly bloody or gory. Some evidence is not admissible because it will likely prejudice the decision of the jury in situations in which the social benefit accomplished by the action outweighs the value, such as making repairs, paying medical expenses, and having liability insurance.
Types of Tangible Evidence	Tangible evidence refers to the physical items that may be presented at trial, including writings, recordings, photographs, X-rays, and other electronic recordings or compilations. Generally, to be offered, documentary evidence must be the original writing, recording, or photograph under the best evidence rule. Where the original documents are not available, copies may be used under appropriate authentication, such as use of documents that are self-authenticating like public documents or certified copies of official business records. Physical evidence is those tangible items that give rise to the cause of action. Precautions to preserve the chain of custody and prevent spoliation are required.
Testimony of Witnesses	Witness testimony is given in an organized manner, with first the party calling the witness asking questions on direct examination and then the opposing party cross-examining the witness in an attempt to raise questions about the credibility of the witness. Redirect examination follows the cross-examination to allow the party calling the witness to rehabilitate the witness, who is subject to recross examination from the opposing party if any new areas of testimony are offered. Lay witnesses present testimony about personal knowledge and are sometimes called eyewitnesses because they may have observed something related to the case. Anyone who has in some way observed, heard, or otherwise sensed some fact relevant to the case may be called as a lay witness. Expert witnesses are used to guide the finders of fact in areas that are beyond the usual expertise or knowledge of the finders of fact (judge or jury). Each witness who testifies will have the truthfulness and reliability of his/her testimony challenged on cross-examination. Challenges to credibility include use of prior contradictory statements, convictions of crimes related to truthfulness (such as perjury or embezzlement), and the truthfulness of prior testimony.

The Hearsay Rule	Hearsay is an out-of-court statement offered for the truth of a statement in court that was made by someone not in court. Hearsay is generally not admissible because it is not reliable; in addition, the party who made the statement is not available to be examined or cross-examined. However, some hearsay is admissible—where the utterance or statement was made under specific circumstances in which people tend to tell the truth. Examples include an excited utterance made after a startling event or statements made to a doctor or other medical provider for treatment. Documents that are created in the regular course of business by public officials or government agencies and documents in the form of family or ancient records are admissible.
Raising Objections	Unless objections are made in trial (contemporaneously with the offer of evidence), the objection to the introduction is waived and may not be raised in the future.

REVIEW QUESTIONS AND EXERCISES

1. What is the difference between evidence and admissible evidence? Explain and give examples of each.
2. What is considered a fact for the purposes of evidence at a trial? Give an example.
3. Why is knowledge of the elements of a claim important in determining the evidence necessary for presentation and trial?
4. Prior to the enactment of the Federal Rules of Evidence, how were evidentiary principles determined?
5. What are the three Rs of admissible evidence?
6. How do the Federal Rules of Evidence define *relevant evidence*?
7. What makes a witness's testimony reliable?
8. What is *physical evidence*?
9. What is meant by the term *probative value of evidence*?
10. Why is some evidence not admissible?
11. Why is evidence of subsequent repairs not admissible in a negligence action?
12. Why might payment of an injured person's medical bills not be admissible in a case?
13. What is the danger in allowing a jury to know that there is insurance coverage available for the defendant?
14. Why are witnesses asked to take an oath or make an affirmation before testifying?
15. What is the difference between a lay witness and an expert witness?
16. When should an expert witness be used?
17. When may a lay witness or a fact witness give an opinion?
18. When is prerecorded testimony desirable in civil litigation?
19. How can out-of-court statements be used by the litigation team?
20. What is the purpose of attacking the credibility of a witness?
21. Give examples of documentary evidence. Explain any authentication required for admission as evidence.
22. What are the circumstances under which evidence of character is admissible?
23. What is the purpose of the best evidence rule?
24. Under what circumstances may copies of original documents be entered into evidence?
25. Explain and give examples of self-authenticating documents.
26. What are the evidentiary issues in spoliation of physical evidence?
27. Why is knowledge of the chain of custody important with regard to the use of physical evidence in trial?
28. What is the hearsay rule?
29. Why are some exceptions to the hearsay rule allowed? Explain and give examples.
30. What is the effect of not objecting to the introduction of evidence at the time it is offered?

BUILDING YOUR PARALEGAL SKILLS

INTERNET AND TECHNOLOGY EXERCISES

1. On the Internet, locate a copy of the Federal Rules of Evidence and the rules of evidence for your jurisdiction. Bookmark the web addresses for future reference and use.
2. Prepare a timeline of the assigned case in Appendix 1.

3. Locate any newspaper articles about the accident.
4. Using the Internet, locate any relevant information about the defendants in the case in Appendix 1.

CIVIL LITIGATION VIDEO CASE STUDIES

Altercation on a School Bus

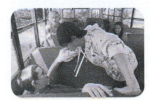

A student is attacked by another student on a school bus.

After viewing the video at www.pearsonhighered.com/ careersresources, answer the following questions.

1. Can the school bus video be used as evidence in arbitration or at trial?
2. What evidence would be needed to prove a case of civil assault and failure of the school to protect the student?

School Principal Reacts

The school principal reacts to the assault on the school bus.

After viewing the video at www.pearsonhighered.com/ careersresources, answer the following questions.

1. Are there records that should be requested for use in arbitration or at trial?
2. What records (besides the school records) might be available that might be of use in arbitration or at trial?

Final pretrial conference to resolve evidentiary issues

Attorneys meet with the trial judge to resolve evidentiary issues before trial, including the use of photographs of injured children.

After viewing the video at www.pearsonhighered.com/ careersresources, answer the following questions.

1. What are the standards a judge must consider in allowing or denying the use of photographs?
2. How important are photographs in proving a case to a jury?
3. Why would the defense object to any photographic evidence?

CHAPTER OPENING SCENARIO CASE STUDY

Use the Opening Scenario for this chapter to complete the following tasks.

1. Prepare an electronic discovery plan for use in the school bus case with the potential claims for

liability that includes a product defect or negligent truck maintenance.

2. Prepare a discovery plan for use in a complex litigation case like the airplane crash.

COMPREHENSIVE CASE STUDY

SCHOOL BUS–TRUCK ACCIDENT CASE

Review the assigned case study in Appendix 2.

1. Prepare a set of interrogatories for use in this case.

2. Prepare a rule 30 deposition notice for use in this case.

BUILDING YOUR PROFESSIONAL PORTFOLIO

See page 18 for instructions on Building Your Professional Portfolio.

Forms

1. Web address for the Federal Rules of Evidence
2. Web address for the rules of evidence for your jurisdiction

Procedures

Your local rules for issuing a subpoena to a witness, how service of the subpoena should be made, and whether a witness fee must be included at the time the subpoena is served. If so, how is the fee calculated?

Contacts and Resources

Locate the professional organizations in your area that could assist you in finding experts in the field of stress disorder.

LEARNING OBJECTIVES

After studying this chapter, you should be able to:

1. Explain the importance of the initial contact with clients and witnesses.

2. Explain the considerations and steps in preparing for an interview of any client or witness.

3. Describe the skills needed to successfully conduct a client or witness interview.

4. Explain how expert witnesses are used in litigation.

5. Explain the steps in conducting an investigation of a claim.

Interviews and Investigation in Civil Litigation

CHAPTER 7

OPENING SCENARIO

 The firm's paralegals, Caitlin and Emily, raised concerns about interviewing the injured children and the parents of the deceased children who had been in the bus. They wanted to be certain that each client was properly interviewed and all the necessary investigations were concluded before filing suit. The nature of the claims and potential damages led the partners in the firm to decide that the federal court offered the best place to try the case. Mr. Mason, the partner most familiar with the federal courts, was concerned about the time limitations for additional investigation after the suit was filed and the defendants were served. Staff resources were not unlimited, as they were in some of the bigger firms, and it was certain that a large litigation firm with virtually unlimited resources would be representing the individual and corporate defendants. To the extent possible, everything had to be completed before commencing suit.

OPENING SCENARIO LEARNING OBJECTIVE

Describe the types of questions that should be asked to be certain all information has been obtained and information that may impeach a witness.

■ INTRODUCTION TO INTERVIEWS AND INVESTIGATIONS

Any contact that a paralegal has with a client, prospective client, or witness constitutes an interview. It may involve limited contact, such as a screening interview or an initial contact with a client or prospective client; or it may be an in-depth, initial fact-gathering interview. The paralegal is usually the firm's first point of contact with the new client or witness. The impression the paralegal makes is the impression the firm makes. As someone once said, we have only one opportunity to make a good first impression.

It is important to note that depending on the experience of the paralegal and the size and culture of the law firm, paralegals may conduct interviews on their own, without the supervising attorney being present. This has the potential to turn off the client or witness, who might be inclined to think, "I'm not important enough for the attorney to meet with me." On the other hand, many attorneys want the first opportunity to view and assess the client or witness and the story being told. In those instances, the paralegal will be present to take notes and assist in the interview process.

■ INITIAL CONTACTS

LEARNING OBJECTIVE 1
Explain the importance of the initial contact with clients and witnesses.

Paralegals frequently conduct the initial investigation of a client's case and make the initial contact with potential witnesses. This may be a telephone call to set up a meeting or a telephone interview. The initial meeting with potential witnesses may be in the office or at the witness's home or place of business. The initial contact with a potential witness, as with a potential client, may set the tone for the interview and can influence the willingness of the person to cooperate.

It is never too soon to start preparing for trial. Trial preparation starts with the first client contact and gathering the first document. Good preparation for trial includes an assessment of how well clients and witnesses will react in depositions or in court under the pressure of cross-examination and how they will be perceived by opposing counsel, the judge, or the jury. Will they come across as being truthful and likeable? Or will they appear sneaky, unpleasant, and deceptive? Observational notes may be of great importance when the legal team must decide whether to settle or try the case.

A practical consideration in deciding whether to try a case before a jury is how the parties will appear to the jury. If the client appears to be sympathetic and deserving and the opposing party unsympathetic but having adequate financial resources, a jury may try to reward the client with a finding unsupported by the facts or evidence.

The Screening Interview

Many clients come to a law firm or lawyer from a referral, such as a current or former client. This source of clients acts as a potential screening mechanism. The referring source tells the new client about the nature of the practice, the attorney who will handle the referred client's case, and the perceived reputation or ability of the lawyer or law firm. Other potential clients find the law firm's name in the telephone book, on a website listing of attorneys, or from another legal referral source such as a Bar Association listing. Finally, some people simply appear at the office door and ask for an appointment or for basic information about the firm's

IN THE WORDS OF THE COURT...

Implied Attorney–Client Relationship

Pro Hand Services Trust v. Monthei, 49 P.3d 56, 59 (Mont. 2002).

"...An implied attorney–client relationship may result when a prospective client divulges confidential information during a consultation with an attorney for the purpose of retaining the attorney, even if actual employment does not result...."

ability or interest in taking a case. In smaller law offices, a paralegal often takes these calls, doubling as receptionist/phone operator.

The initial contact, or **screening interview,** is filled with potential landmines. If the paralegal solicits too much information or the prospective client volunteers too much information, an **implied attorney–client relationship** may be created. An implied attorney–client relationship has been found to exist, even if no fee is paid, if the party believes he or she is divulging confidential information for the purpose of obtaining legal advice. If too little information is obtained, the attorney will not have enough information to decide if he or she wants to talk to the potential client. Therefore, the paralegal or receptionist has to decide how much information to take and how much information to give.

Once the decision is made to represent a client, the legal team must immediately start to gather all of the relevant information about the client's case. The initial investigation may reveal information indicating that the client does not have a valid cause of action or that the applicable statute of limitations has expired, barring the use of the courts for maintaining the cause of action. For example, what appears at first to be a case of medical malpractice may, after the records are analyzed by a medical expert who indicates the treatment received was within appropriate medical practice and procedure, turn out not to be such a case. In those jurisdictions requiring a certification by a medical expert, the inability to obtain such a certification would act as a bar to the institution of a suit. This determination is one that must be made by the supervising attorney.

Good practice requires that the client be appropriately notified in writing of the decision of the law firm to accept or decline the representation. If the representation is accepted, a fee agreement should accompany the cover letter. Exhibit 7.1a is sample hourly fee engagement letter, and Exhibit 7.1b is a contingent fee engagement letter. If representation is declined, the paralegal may draft a letter summarizing the facts as related by the client and the facts as determined by the firm, including the reason for the non-representation. A recommendation to clients concerning the next step in their cause of action should be made as soon as possible. Quick action is particularly necessary if your client is a defendant who is mandated by the court's rules to file a timely, responsive pleading to the complaint served on the client.

Letters of Engagement and Termination of Engagement

One of the leading causes of lawyer malpractice is missing deadlines (like the statute of limitations deadlines in civil litigation), which then bars court actions. Many other causes of friction between lawyers and their clients are related to fees and costs. In many states, a written fee agreement is required; this must be signed by the lawyer and the client. Also called an engagement letter,

screening interview
Limited first contact with a prospective client.

implied attorney–client relationship
Relationship that may result when a prospective client divulges confidential information during a consultation with an attorney for the purpose of retaining the attorney, even if actual employment does not result.

WEB RESOURCES

Sample engagement, non-engagement, and termination letters are available at the ABA website.

Exhibit 7.1a Sample Hourly Fee Engagement Letter

January 29, 2015

Mr. and Mrs. Thomas Daniels

12 Route 189

Your town, State

RE: *Employment of Mason, Marshall and Benjamin by Mr. and Mrs. Thomas Daniels*

Dear Mr. and Mrs. Daniels:

Thank you for selecting Mason, Marshall and Benjamin to represent you with respect to the breach of contract action against Honey Bee Pollintors, Ltd. This letter will confirm our recent discussion regarding the scope and terms of this engagement.

Our firm has agreed to represent you in this lawsuit. I personally will supervise the case. However, it is anticipated that other lawyers and legal assistants in the firm also will work on the case.

We will attempt to obtain compliance with the provisions of the contract to have fruit trees on your property pollinated as agreed or, in the alternative, to seek damages for breach of the contract.

You have agreed to pay for our services based on the time we spend working on the case. My current hourly rate is $250 per hour. The rates of our associates currently range between $125 and $225 per hour. Paralegals, who will be utilized where appropriate to avoid unnecessary attorney fees, currently are charged at $75 per hour. These rates are subject to change once a year, usually in December. Generally, you will be billed for all time spent on your matter, including telephone calls.

As discussed, our current estimate for this engagement is $5,000, not including any out-of-pocket expenses for experts, court reporter fees, or court fees. This estimate is imprecise as my knowledge of the facts at this time is limited. We will advise you if fees will be significantly higher than this estimate. At such time, you may decide to restrict the scope of our efforts or we may make other adjustments. This estimate does not include cost items.

You have paid us the sum of $3,000 as an advance against fees and costs, which we have deposited to our trust account. After your receipt of monthly statements, we will pay the amount of the statement from the trust account. If any portion of the advance is unexpended at the conclusion of the case, it will be refunded to you. If the advance is expended, you have agreed to pay subsequent monthly statements on receipt. An interest charge of one and one-half percent per month is charged on statement balances not paid within 30 days of billing.

You will appreciate we can make no guarantee of a successful conclusion in any case. However, the attorneys of this firm will make their best efforts on your behalf.

My objectives are to provide you with excellent legal services and to protect your interests in the event of my unexpected death, disability, impairment, or incapacity. To accomplish this, I have arranged with another lawyer to assist with closing my practice in the event of my death, disability, impairment, or incapacity. In such event, my office staff or the assisting lawyer will contact you and provide you with information about how to proceed.

If this letter fairly states our agreement, please so indicate by signing and returning the enclosed copy in the enclosed business reply envelope. If you have any questions or concerns, please call me to discuss them. We greatly appreciate the opportunity to represent you on this case and look forward to working with you.

Sincerely,

Owen Mason, Esq.

Mason, Marshall and Benjamin

Exhibit 7.1b Sample Contingent Fee Engagement Letter

RE: *Employment of Mason, Marshall and Benjamin by Jonathan Leonard*

Dear Mr. Leonard:

Thank you for selecting our firm to represent you with respect to the personal injury action against Acme Trucking Company. This letter will confirm our recent discussion regarding the scope and terms of this engagement.

Our firm has agreed to represent you in this lawsuit. I personally will supervise the case. However, it is anticipated that other lawyers and legal assistants in the firm also will work on the case.

We will represent you in the investigation, preparation and civil trial of your claim against Acme Trucking in the U.S. District Court or Local Trial Court to the rendering of a verdict. Our engagement at this time does not cover any appellate activity or post trial work on your behalf.

We will be compensated on a contingent fee basis. We will receive for our services 25% of any recovery plus all out of pocket costs for service and filing fees, expert witness fees, court reporter fees, and charges for investigation, travel and accommodation, telephone long distance, photocopies. These out of pocket costs will be billed to you on a monthly basis itemizing the monies we have advanced on your behalf.

As discussed, our current estimate cost for out of pocket expenses for this engagement is $5,000. This estimate is imprecise as my knowledge of the facts at this time is limited.

You have paid us the sum of $1,000.00 as an advance against costs, which we have deposited to our trust account. After your receipt of monthly statements, we will pay the amount of the statement from the trust account. If any portion of the advance is unexpended at the conclusion of the case, it will be refunded to you. If the advance is expended, you have agreed to pay subsequent monthly statements on receipt.

You will appreciate we can make no guarantee of a successful conclusion in any case. However, the attorneys of this firm will use their best efforts on your behalf.

You understand that we represent other plaintiffs involved in the same case and where possible will prorate costs. You have agreed that our firm representing the other plaintiffs is acceptable to you.

If this letter fairly states our agreement, will you please so indicate by signing and returning the enclosed copy in the enclosed business reply envelope. If you have any questions or concerns, please call me to discuss them. We greatly appreciate the opportunity to represent you on this case and look forward to working with you.

Sincerely,

Owen Mason

Mason, Marshall and Benjamin

---

this agreement is addressed to the client and sets out the specific duties the law firm agrees to undertake for the client—in other words, what the firm will or will not do for the client. It may also spell out the specific obligations the firm will undertake, the basis of the fee (contingent fee, hourly fee, flat fee, or a combination), and the terms of payment. In litigation cases, the engagement letter may include clarification on payment for costs and expenses related to investigation and deposition costs.

Non-Engagement

A non-engagement letter may be more important than the engagement letter; it tells the person—the would-be client—that the firm will not represent him or

Exhibit 7.2 Non-Engagement Letter

Dear Mr. Wilkins:

Thank you for consulting our firm about your case against the Acme Trucking Company. After reviewing the facts we regret that we cannot represent you in this matter.

I strongly recommend that you contact another lawyer immediately. Failure to act immediately may result in the barring your ability to file suit. If you do not have another lawyer in mind, I suggest you call the Bar Association Referral service at 218-555-1000.

Thank you for contacting me. I hope to be of service to you in the future.

Very truly yours,

_____

Ethan Benjamin

Mason, Marshall and Benjamin

LEARNING OBJECTIVE 2
Explain the considerations and steps in preparing for an interview of any client or witness.

PRACTICE TIP

Investigation checklists, such as Exhibit 7.3, are starting points in gathering information. Be alert to additional information that may be available based on the responses of clients and witnesses. Update and modify the checklist to keep it dynamic.

Do not allow yourself to become so preoccupied with filling in the blanks that you miss important clues to additional information.

her. This is important when a statute of limitations deadline is approaching and the engagement is declined. The potential client must be clearly advised that the firm is not representing him or her and that he or she should seek counsel immediately. If a person believes that he or she is represented and the lawyer does not clearly express that the firm is *not* taking the representation, an implied attorney–client relationship may arise.

A sample non-engagement letter is shown in Exhibit 7.2.

■ PREPARING FOR THE INTERVIEW

The first step in preparing for an interview or conducting an investigation is to understand the outcome desired. One of the desired outcomes in an initial interview with a new client is to instill in the client confidence in the firm and its personnel. The fundamental desired outcome of any interview is to obtain all of the relevant facts for the case. Exhibit 7.3 is a sample client interview checklist. Understanding the goals of the interview or investigation, the background or cultural issues of the individual, and the nature of the situation will help in structuring a successful interview. Occasionally, an interview has to be conducted without time for preparation, such as when the paralegal is asked to fill in for someone else at the last moment.

Physical surroundings, clothing, and appearance are important in preparing for interviews and investigations. They merit your attention.

Investigation Checklists

The investigation checklist should not be viewed as a static document. The checklist should start with a listing of all of the parties involved who should be interviewed, including initial **fact witnesses** (Exhibit 7.4). As additional parties and witnesses are interviewed, more people may need to be added to

Exhibit 7.3 Sample Client Interview Checklist

CLIENT INTERVIEW CHECKLIST

CLIENT PERSONAL INFORMATION

Name _____

Address _____

City _____ State _____ Zip _____

Phone (hm) _____ (wk) _____ (cell) _____

How long at this address _____

Date of birth _____ Place of birth _____

Social Security No. _____

Prior address _____

City _____ State _____ Zip _____

Dates at this address _____

Employer: _____

Job description _____

Marital status _____ Maiden name _____

Spouse's name _____ Date of birth _____

Child's name _____ Date of birth _____

Child's name _____ Date of birth _____

Child's name _____ Date of birth _____

CASE INFORMATION

Case referred by _____

Case type: ☐ Appeal   ☐ Business   ☐ Corporate   ☐ Estate   ☐ Litigation
            ☐ Municipal   ☐ Real Estate   ☐ Tax   ☐ Trust   ☐ Other

Opposing party(ies) _____

Opposing party _____

Address _____

Opposing attorney _____

Address _____

Date of incident _____ Statute of limitation date _____

Summary of facts _____

_____

_____

_____

---

the list. Exhibit 7.5 is a witness information form. Investigation of locations and physical evidence may result in the need to examine additional locations and evidence. Initial interviews also may result in the need to add one or more expert witnesses to the investigation checklist.

A checklist can be a valuable tool in ensuring that all the information required for a case or other legal matter is obtained during the initial interview.

fact witness
A witness who testifies about facts based upon his observation or personal knowledge about the matter before the court.

Exhibit 7.4 Investigation Checklist for Auto Accident

INVESTIGATION CHECKLIST

Client name

Phone (hm)   (wk)   (cell)

Current address

Prior address(es)

Date of birth   Place of birth

Social Security No.

VEHICLE CLIENT OPERATING/PASSENGER

Owner and type of motor vehicle

Insurance Co.   Policy number

Insurance company contact   Phone

Date of incident   Time of day   Weather conditions

Location of incident

City, State   County   Municipality

Opposing party

Address

Phone (hm)   (wk)   (cell)

Owner and type of motor vehicle

Insurance Co.   Policy number

FACT WITNESSES

Name   Address

Name   Address

Name   Address

Name of ambulance

Name of hospital

Police report issued   Copy ordered

Photographs of scene taken

Name of treating physicians

EXPERT WITNESSES

Name   Address

Name   Address

Summary of cause of action

Attach detailed accident/incident description, accident reports and diagrams.

The same checklist offers a good foundation for developing a more detailed interview plan when there is time for preparation. A caution: Never let the checklist prevent you from listening and responding to the information a client or witness is sharing. Being too concerned about filling in the blanks on the checklist can leave the client or witness feeling as though you have no interest in his or her story.

Exhibit 7.5 Witness Information Form

Witness Information

CLIENT PERSONAL DATA

Client Name	Case No.	File No.

Address	City, State, Zip	Phone

CASE DATA

File Label	Case issue	Date

Responsible Attorney(s)

WITNESS DATA

Witness Name

Aliases, if any	US Citizen ☐ Yes ☐ No

Current Address	City, State, Zip	Phone

Past Address(es)

Date & Place of Birth	Sex	Race	Age	Current Marital Status ☐ Single ☐ Divorced

Name of Spouse	Number/Former Marriages	Number/Children	☐ Married ☐ Widowed ☐ Separated

Name of Children (natural & adopted)	Age	Name	Age

Current Employer

Address	City, State, Zip	Phone

Job Title	Supervisor	From	To

Previous Employer

Address	City, State, Zip	Phone

Job Title	Supervisor	From	To

Education/Name of School	City/State	From	To	Degree
High School				
College				
Technical/Other				

Witness for ☐ Plaintiff ☐ Defendant	Type of Witness ☐ Expert ☐ Character ☐ Eye Witness	Have you ever been a party or witness in a court suit? ☐ No ☐ Yes

If yes, where & when

OTHER PERTINENT DATA

Form 8587 · SJPE SYCOM Madison, WI Printed in U.S.A.

Physical Surroundings

The physical surroundings of the interview location can set the tone for the interview. Depending upon the purpose of the interview and the person being interviewed, the paralegal may wish to create either a formal or an informal environment. You probably can remember a situation in which someone interviewed you from across a desk. Did the formality make you feel subservient to the interviewer? Contrast that situation with an informal setting with a low coffee table and living-room-style chairs. This setting gives the meeting a more personal tone. Beware of interviewing a client or witness in a cluttered office, which can give the impression that the paralegal is too busy or too disorganized.

Putting a client at ease may be easier in an informal setting, whereas dealing with opposing counsel might be better handled in a formal, "across-the-desk" setting. In most cases, the paralegal will want to convey the impression of being a competent professional, although in some situations, it might be beneficial to convey a more casual and less professional image. Some witnesses are more cooperative and helpful when they feel as if they are in charge and are helping the paralegal.

Dress and Appearance

Remember the old saying, "First impressions count"? The impression a paralegal makes when walking into a room for the initial interview may set the tone for the entire relationship with the client or witness and can either enhance or destroy one's credibility. Clothing, posture, and manner of greeting create the first impression.

Clothing sends a nonverbal message about the person and the firm or business. In the practice of law, or in a corporate law department, the unexpected can become the norm. Many attorneys, male and female alike, keep a "going-to-court suit" in the office just in case they need to have a more professional appearance at a moment's notice. When the new client comes in, the attorneys can change clothes quickly; the receptionist or secretary can buy them time to change into the "power" outfit.

A client may be offended by a paralegal's "casual Friday" appearance, believing that the paralegal is not taking his case seriously. The working paralegal, however, usually doesn't have time to change when the unexpected arises, and is often the one who has to "buy time" for the attorney. Therefore, paralegals always must be prepared to make a good impression and tailor their appearance appropriately as the situation warrants. When the paralegal conducts field interviews, however, a casual appearance may put the potential witness at ease.

Communication Skills in a Multicultural Society*

Those with whom paralegals communicate can be addressed in many ways. Clients, witnesses, and others with whom the paralegal comes into contact should never be stereotyped. At the same time, paralegals should be aware of the gender, religious, and ethnic sensitivities of people. Paralegals' skills as interviewers depend on their abilities to appreciate the differences in how and why individuals act and react differently. They must not assume that everyone in a certain category believes and acts the same. They must be sensitive to issues that may cause a person not to communicate, which might have been anticipated from first impressions of them. We will point out some general differences in the way men and women communicate and give some cultural background considerations.

---

*This section on communication skills is adapted from *Crosstalk: Communicating in a Multicultural Workplace*, by Sherron Kenton and Deborah Valentine, 1997. Reprinted with permission of the authors.

Gender Differences

A man is more likely to:

- have been socialized to perform more aggressively and boast of his successes;
- have learned from childhood games that winning is desirable;
- be motivated by competition;
- view conflict as impersonal, a necessary part of working relationships;
- be impressed by power, ability, and achievement;
- hear only the literal words and miss the underlying emotion;
- not express his true feelings through facial expressions; and
- have a more direct communication style.

A woman is more likely to:

- have been socialized to work cooperatively and to be modest about her success;
- have learned from childhood games to compromise and collaborate and to be motivated by affiliation;
- compete primarily with herself—with her own expectations of what she should be able to accomplish;
- take conflict personally;
- be impressed by personal disclosure and professional courage;
- have the ability to focus on several projects at the same time;
- be proficient at decoding nonverbal meanings and likely to display her feelings through facial expression and body language; and
- have an indirect style, except with other women of equal rank.

There may also be gender differences in the receiver's attitudes about the paralegal:

- Paralegal man to man: Male receiver may afford the male paralegal instant credibility based on their same gender.
- Paralegal woman to woman: Female receiver may expect the female paralegal to be friendly, nurturing, and concerned and may afford the paralegal instant credibility based on same-gender assumptions.
- Paralegal man to woman: Female receiver may expect that the male paralegal will not really listen to her based on the different gender.
- Paralegal woman to man: Male receiver may expect the female paralegal to be friendly and nurturing, even passive-dependent. Any aggressive behavior or deviation from his expectation could cause him discomfort and confusion or produce negative responses. He may simply disregard the female paralegal.

Cultural Sensitivity

The culturally sensitive person is aware of how other people's religious and ethnic backgrounds and their belief systems influence their behavior. As the cultural makeup of the United States has become more diverse, the need for **cultural sensitivity** in the legal and paralegal professions has grown. Just as men and women are said to be different in some ways, so are Europeans, Asians, Latinos, and Africans who have not fully assimilated into the culture of the country.

Interviewing a Latino male, for example, may require a different approach than when interviewing an Asian female. Even subtleties of eye contact can affect an interview. Whereas Americans view eye contact as a sign of sincerity, some Asian cultures view this as aggressive. In developing their communication skills, paralegals must become sensitive to how they are perceived and learn to fashion their approach to maximize accuracy of communication.

cultural sensitivity
Awareness of and sensitivity to the reasons for differences in the way people behave based on religious and ethnic backgrounds and belief systems.

The effectiveness of paralegals also is influenced by how well they "read" the cultural backgrounds of those with whom they interact. Cultural norms involve the manner of speaking, dressing, and acting and can differ for men and women in a particular culture. Cultural differences can affect the interpretation of words and body language: What is heard may not be what was intended, and what one person perceives may not be what another person perceives. We will briefly highlight some general characteristics of four cultural groups.

European Background.   Generally, the countries of Western Europe, including Scandinavia, comprise the group of those with a European background. This group is extraordinarily large and complex, which limits attempts to make cultural generalities. In terms of gender differences, men and women with roots in the European culture may have different initial reactions and attitudes to the paralegal. Male and female listeners alike tend to perceive men as having more credibility than women of equal rank, experience, and training. Men tend to be more credible to other men, and women may be more credible to other women.

Now consider the cultural implications of graphic pictures of physical injuries from car crashes. These photos are acceptable in the United States, but Germans tend to dislike the sight of blood and the British are likely to be offended by violence.

According to Kenton and Valentine, if the paralegal appears to be European-American, receivers of communication may be concerned that the paralegal will:

- reject their opinions;
- take advantage of them or hold them back;
- consider them different in a negative way; or
- deny them equal opportunities.

Latino Background.   Collectively, Latin America encompasses fifty-one countries generally considered to be those south of the U.S. border: Mexico and the countries of Central America, South America, and the Caribbean islands. With so vast an area, many differences can be expected from country to country and even from city to city. The languages spoken within Latin American countries, too, are not the same. Portuguese is spoken in Brazil, and the Spanish that is spoken in South America differs from the Spanish spoken in Puerto Rico. The Latino-American population has moved closer to becoming the largest minority group in the United States. According to Kenton and Valentine, individuals with roots in the Latino culture tend to:

- value family and loyalty to family;
- honor nationalism;
- exhibit a strong sense of honor;
- have a fatalistic view of the world; and
- express passion in speech, manner, and deed.

Asian Background.   More than thirty countries can be considered Asian, among them China, Malaysia, Japan, the Philippines, India, and Korea. They, too, demonstrate vast differences from culture to culture. Some generalizations may be made, however.

- Asian cultures generally consider being direct and to the point rude, and relationships are considered top priority.

ETHICAL Perspectives

NATIONAL FEDERATION OF PARALEGAL ASSOCIATIONS, INC, MODEL CODE OF ETHICS AND PROFESSIONAL RESPONSIBILITY AND GUIDELINES FOR ENFORCEMENT

1.7 A Paralegal's Title Shall Be Fully Disclosed.

Ethical Considerations

Ec-1.7

(a) A paralegal's title shall clearly indicate the individual's status and shall be disclosed in all business and professional communications to avoid misunderstandings and misconceptions about the paralegal's role and responsibilities.

Source: Used by Permission from NFPA.

■ The Japanese, for example, tend to prefer an indirect style of communication. In communicating with people who have an Asian background, then, it might be best to begin with pleasantries about the weather or sports, or inquire about the well-being of the individual and his or her family.

Roots in the African Culture. African Americans represent the largest ethnic group in the United States. A distinction should be made between African Americans of recent immigration, with strong cultural ties to the African culture, and African Americans with extensive family ties and cultural roots within the United States. According to Kenton and Valentine, some of the African core beliefs and cultural values that may influence attitudes and behavior are:

■ a holistic worldview;
■ emotion and expressiveness; and
■ a keen sense of justice or fairness.

■ CONDUCTING THE INTERVIEW

In the first meeting, the paralegal must make clear that he or she is not an attorney and that only an attorney can give legal advice. During the first few minutes of the interview, paralegals must build a relationship with their interviewees, explaining the reason for the interview and eliminating any barriers that might prevent them from obtaining the necessary information. Sometimes interviewees seem to be fully cooperative when, in fact, they are not cooperating. The subject matter may be embarrassing, or interviewees may have a fear of authority figures or might be uncomfortable using certain terms necessary to describe the situation.

Effective interviewers learn the verbal and nonverbal cues that will help them understand the reasons for interviewees' reluctance to answer questions. In some situations, the solution is first to ask easy questions, such as the person's name and address. Once interviewees start speaking, they have less trouble answering well-thought-out questions that build logically on the previous information.

LEARNING OBJECTIVE 3
Describe the skills needed to successfully conduct a client or witness interview.

This is not always the case, though. In times of great stress, clients have been known to read the name from a nameplate in the office and state it as their own name! The interviewer must be careful to avoid embarrassing the interviewee and have questions prepared that can be answered easily, such as, "My records show that you live at 123 South Main Street. Is that correct?" or "How do you spell your name?," thereby helping the person gain composure.

Listening Skills

A good interviewer must master the skill of listening. Most of us hear the words being said but may not be listening to *what* is being said. Instead of concentrating on what is being said, listeners may be more concerned with the next question they want to ask, emotionally influenced by the speaker's message, or distracted by the speaker's behavior. The professional interviewer must listen to what is really being said in a nonjudgmental, impartial manner.

Interviewing clients and witnesses requires listening to what is being said in the context of the speaker's cultural makeup. It also requires an understanding of the type of witness—friendly, hostile, or expert—and the witnesses' bias toward the client or the type of case for which they are being interviewed. Fact witnesses may not want to get involved, or they may be **hostile witnesses,** saying either what they think you want to hear or what will move their own agenda along. Fact witnesses in criminal matters involving members of different races or religions may not be as concerned for the truth as they are for someone "paying" for committing the crime. Bias and cultural identity may thus influence what is said.

hostile witness
A witness who does not cooperate with the party who called him to testify; a reluctant witness who demonstrates some hostility to the case presented or toward the party who called him to testify.

The paralegal must focus on what is said, not on how it is said. Some people are not articulate, and the facts may be lost if a paralegal doesn't listen carefully. Others may try to shock or put off the paralegal by using buzzwords designed to get a reaction. In sports, this is referred to as "trash talk"—saying things to get the listener to react emotionally and lose concentration.

Good listeners disregard distractions. They do not allow themselves to lose focus because of environmental distractions, such as noise or activity in the area of the interview, or a speaker's annoying physical habits, such as tapping fingers or legs, or speech impediments, such as stuttering. Think about how hard it is to concentrate on what is being said in a large classroom. Good listeners focus on the message and block out distractions.

In addition, good interviewers do not make assumptions about the facts of the case. They listen with an open mind. Making assumptions about people or facts can lead to attempts to make the facts fit the interviewer's preconceived notions. Sometimes the facts are not what they first seem to be. Look at the number of people released from jail after DNA evidence proved they did not do the crime everyone assumed they had committed. In some instances, fact witnesses may have been interviewed and may have given a version of the incident that, after DNA testing, is proven incorrect, and the person turns out to be innocent.

A good listener must also be a good observer. Good listeners are able to detect when the person they are speaking with is having difficulty understanding the question. It may be an elderly client who has a hearing loss, or a client for whom English is a second language, or a client who is functionally illiterate. Not recognizing these signs will hinder the paralegal's goal of obtaining accurate, complete information. The clients who claim to have forgotten their glasses and ask you to read the information to them or tell you they trust that whatever you've done is correct may actually be unable to read the documents. Functional illiteracy might be related to the fact that English is not a client's first language.

Checklist ☑️

- Empathize with the person. Try to put yourself in his or her place to help you see the point.
- Don't interrupt. Allow time for the person to say what he or she is trying to say.
- Leave your emotions behind and control your anger. Emotions will prevent you from listening well.
- Get rid of distractions.
- Don't argue mentally.
- Don't antagonize the speaker. This could cause someone to conceal important ideas, emotions, and attitudes.
- Avoid jumping to conclusions. This can get you into trouble. For example, don't assume that the speaker is using the words in the same way that you are interpreting them. If you are unsure, ask for clarification.

Source: Reprinted with permission from the Student Counseling Service at Texas A&M University.

Leading Questions

Leading questions are questions that suggest the desired answer. In conducting a cross-examination, lawyers in trial frequently use leading questions to force the witness to answer in a desired manner. An obvious example is "Have you stopped kicking your dog?" On direct examination, an attorney might ask a more direct and neutral question: "Have you ever kicked your dog?"

Leading questions do not lead to open-ended answers but are intended to elicit a desired answer: "You ran the red light, didn't you?"

leading questions
Questions that suggest the answer calls for a "yes" or "no" response.

Open-Ended Questions

Open-ended questions are designed to give interviewees an opportunity to tell their stories without being limited to yes-or-no answers. Open-ended questions create a **narrative opportunity** for the witness; for example, "Tell me about your life" or "Tell me about your life since the accident."

In fact-gathering interviews, the witness should have the opportunity to give open-ended, narrative answers. By asking a question to solicit an answer that you desire, you may cut off the possibility of discovering information that is essential to your case. For example, you may want to know whether your client was at the scene of an accident, and therefore you ask the witness, "Did you see my client at the scene of the accident?" The answer to this question may be "yes" or "no." A better question would be, "Who was present at the scene of the accident?" This kind of question may lead to information regarding additional witnesses you may want to interview.

Similarly, the question, "How fast were the cars going prior to the impact?" is much better than "Were the cars speeding before the impact?" In this context, the term "speeding" may be interpreted as exceeding the speed limit instead of going too fast for the conditions.

With the witness's statements from the interview in hand at the time of trial, the trial attorney might appropriately ask a leading question such as, "My client wasn't present at the scene of the accident, was she?" or, "Isn't it true that the defendant was speeding before the impact?" With the attorney's knowledge of the prior statement, there should be no surprise in the answer at trial. If there is, the prior statement can be used to impeach the credibility of the witness, if desired, as part of the trial strategy.

At times, the interviewer may want to guide clients or witnesses by asking questions that give them a perspective of time or place, such as, "What did you observe

open-ended questions
Questions that usually do not have a "yes" or "no" answer but call for a short narrative response.

narrative opportunity
Question that encourages an answer requiring a full explanation.

at noon on Saturday?" or "Tell me what happened on September 11, 2001." Or, "What you were doing on the day of the bombing at the Boston Marathon in 2013?" The tragedy of those days will haunt the memories of Americans and most of the rest of the world, so little stimulus will be needed to elicit where they were and what they observed. This is true of most traumatic events in people's lives—the loss of a loved one, the birth of a child, or a serious accident in which they were injured. Other days and periods of time tend to blur and have to be brought to the consciousness of the witness by making statements such as, "Let's think back to August 19, 2013" and asking, "What happened to you that day?"

Privileged Communication

privileged communication
Communication to be kept confidential based on a relationship with another party, such as attorney and client.

Certain forms of communication are considered privileged and are not usable at trial unless the privilege is waived. Forms of **privileged communication** are:

1. attorney–client communications;
2. doctor–patient communications;
3. priest–penitent communications; and
4. spousal communications during marriage.

Each of these privileges can be waived, but the waiver must come from the client, the patient, the penitent, or the spouse making the statement with the belief that it is privileged. Changes in some of the rules of ethics, and by statute, may permit certain, otherwise privileged communications to be revealed to prevent harm or injury to another. The spouse, the priest, or the doctor may have a moral issue in revealing what was communicated.

When the paralegal is acting on behalf of the attorney, communications between a client and the paralegal have the same privilege as those between the client and the attorney. Information gathered from the client as part of representation of the client and necessary for rendering competent legal advice is privileged. The paralegal, therefore, is in the same position as the attorney, the doctor, the priest, or the spouse to whom the confidential information has been communicated. Each must carefully guard the confidential information and not inadvertently or intentionally reveal the information. In some cases, such as when another person's life may be in danger, these people may be compelled by a court to testify even when they believe it is a violation of their moral duty to another person from whom they have received information.

Moral versus Ethical Obligations

moral obligation
An obligation based on one's own conscience.

At times in the investigation of a case, it is necessary to consider the difference between a moral obligation and an ethical obligation. A **moral obligation** is based on one's own conscience or a person's perceived rules of correct conduct,

WEB RESOURCES

Contrast and compare The Delaware Lawyers' Rules of Professional Conduct at the Delaware State Courts website, http://courts.delaware .gov/Rules/?DLRPCwithComments_ Oct2007.pdf, with the American Bar Association Model Rules of Professional Responsibility at the ABA website, http://www.abanet .org/cpr/mrpc/mrpc_toc.html, and the ethical rules in your jurisdiction.

ETHICAL Perspectives

THE DELAWARE LAWYERS' RULES OF PROFESSIONAL CONDUCT RULE 1.6 CONFIDENTIALITY OF INFORMATION

(a) A lawyer shall not reveal information relating to the representation of a client unless the client gives informed consent, the disclosure is impliedly authorized in order to carry out the representation, or the disclosure is permitted by paragraph (b)....

generally in the person's own community. Some communities, for instance, may consider it to be morally improper to ask someone to give information about another person. An **ethical obligation** for members of the legal team, including those acting on behalf of a supervising attorney, is the ethical responsibility of the legal profession under the ABA Model Rules of Professional Conduct, including thoroughness in representing a client.

Is it ethically improper to ask someone to tell the truth surrounding the facts of a case if those facts may lead to a neighbor, relative, or friend being subjected to liability for his or her actions? The primary ethical obligation for the paralegal and the legal team is the duty to the client. Some members of the legal team, for example, may be distressed if they were told to ask a mother to testify against her child in a case involving negligence and personal injury. This is a moral issue for the mother—the results may cause her child financial hardship or ruin. Ethics, however, may require this unpleasant course of conduct from the paralegal.

ethical obligation
A minimum standard of conduct, usually within one's profession.

■ EXPERT WITNESSES

Expert witnesses are individuals whose backgrounds, educations, and experiences are such that courts recognize them as qualified to give opinions based on a set of facts. The expert witness may be a doctor certified by a board of medical experts or a scientist or engineer specializing in an area of science such as flammability of fabrics. The reports of these experts may be based on the facts of a potential case and may determine whether there is sufficient evidence to believe that a wrong has occurred or malpractice has been committed. Without this report, the lawyers may be obligated to advise clients that they have no actionable cause of action.

There is no clear rule on whether information revealed to an expert in the preparation of a case is protected as part of the attorney–client privilege in the same manner as that revealed to a member of the trial team, including other attorneys, paralegals, and secretarial staff working on the case with the primary trial attorney. Almost certainly, anything revealed to an expert who is listed as an expert witness on the list of witnesses to be called at trial is discoverable.

Some law firms retain an expert to advise them but do not use that expert to testify. The advice and information provided by these experts to help in the preparation for trial may come under the privilege. Although the privilege is the client's, the paralegal and others on the legal team must be careful not to divulge privileged or confidential material without authorization.

The expert retained for background trial advice must have as much confidence in the legal team as the legal team has in the expert's advice and integrity. Some experts fear that the legal team will give them only selected information. With the limited information provided, they might give an expert opinion that is not what they would have given if they had received the complete set of facts.

Exhibit 7.6 indicates factors to be considered in arranging for an expert witness.

LEARNING OBJECTIVE 4
Explain how expert witnesses are used in litigation.

expert witness
Person qualified by education, training, or experience to render an opinion based on a set of facts that are outside the scope of knowledge of the fact finder.

PRACTICE TIP
TIMING OF EXPERT DEPOSITION
FEDERAL RULES OF CIVIL PROCEDURE 26 FRCP 26(B) (4)

(4) Trial Preparation: Experts

  (A) A party may depose any person who has been identified as an expert whose opinions may be presented at trial. If a report from the expert is required under subdivision (a) (2) (B), the deposition shall not be conducted until after the report is provided.

Checklist ✔

Ask an expert witness these ten questions at deposition, even if you don't have time to ask anything else:

- What opinions have you formed in this matter?
- What did you do to reach those opinions?
- How did you do that?
- Why did you do that?
- What results did you get?
- How did the results affect your opinion?
- Are there reliable authorities in this field?
- What assumptions did you make in your work?
- What tasks didn't you do?
- Is this your current and accurate resume?

Source: Reprinted with permission from Expert Rules: 100 (and More) Point You Need to know About Your Expert Witnesses, 3d Ed. by David M. Malone and Paul J. Swire. Copyright owned by the National Institute for Trial Advocacy. A full copy of this publication may be purchased at http://www.lexisnexis.com.

■ INVESTIGATING CLAIMS

LEARNING OBJECTIVE 5
Explain the steps in conducting an investigation of a claim.

Restatement of the Law Third, Torts: Product Liability
A legal treatise with suggested rules of laws relating to torts.

The legal team must gather all of the relevant information about a cause of action before making a recommendation to a client to file a lawsuit or respond to a claim of wrongdoing. In most cases, the paralegal has some indication of the area of law or the nature of the claim before the first interview with the client is conducted. The paralegal may have gotten this idea from a telephone interview (when the client called for an appointment) or from the referral from the supervising attorney to the paralegal to conduct the interview and investigation. If paralegals specialize in certain areas of law, they are likely to understand the underlying elements of the claims or rights the client wishes to assert. Those in general practice and those entering a new area have to understand the rules of law as they apply to that issue.

For example, in a product liability case, understanding the common law of negligence is not enough. One also must understand the law of strict liability for product defect cases as found in the **Restatement of the Law Third, Torts: Product Liability.** Whereas negligence requires a breach of duty, strict liability is without fault in cases in which the doctrine applies. An interview conducted considering negligence as the only basis for legal action could improperly result in the client's being advised that he or she does not have a claim when, under the no-fault, strict liability concept for defective products, an action might exist.

The first step is to determine the elements that underlie the cause of action and that arise from the client's claim. With an understanding of the legal basis of the claim and the applicable law, an investigative plan can be prepared to obtain the necessary witness statements, locate physical evidence, and obtain photographs, reports, and other evidence for use in preparation for and at trial. Where a claim of negligence is to be made, photographic evidence may be essential in demonstrating the nature of the hazard.

For example, when a client has injured himself or herself as result of a fall in a store, photographs showing the hazardous condition should be obtained as

Exhibit 7.6 Expert Witness Checklist

EXPERT WITNESS CHECKLIST

BACKGROUND

Full name _____ Date of birth _____

Business address _____

Business telephone number _____ Business fax number _____

Business email address _____ Business website _____

Locations of prior offices _____

Home address _____

Home telephone number _____

EDUCATION

Schools attended _____ Dates of attendance _____

Degrees or honors awarded _____

Continuing education courses _____

WORK HISTORY

Place of employment _____ Dates of employment _____

Job description _____

Reasons for leaving _____

Specific area of expertise _____

Published articles and books _____

Professional affiliations _____

Professional magazines subscribed to _____

Licenses and jurisdictions _____

Litigations or disciplinary action _____

PRIOR LEGAL EXPERIENCE

Ratio of plaintiff/defense cases _____

Prior clients including date (plaintiff or defendant) _____

Types of investigations with dates _____

Deposition testimony given with dates _____

Court testimony with dates _____

Legal references _____

AVAILABILITY

Vacation plans and dates _____ Potential meeting dates _____

---

quickly as possible. In the case of strict liability involving a product defect that caused injury or loss, preservation of the defective product or photographic documentation of the defect is essential as a matter of proof. Knowing what elements of the cause of action must be proven dictates what evidence must be located in the form of witnesses, photographs, and physical evidence. Knowing the elements of the cause of action will ensure that the proper questions are asked in the interview, which then will dictate the necessary investigation steps.

One of the most useful tools in the gathering of information about a case is a digital camera or a smartphone with a good camera feature. Digital photographs are easily shared on computer networks or by Internet transfer to other members of the legal team, clients, and possible witnesses. It also is useful to take pictures of potential witnesses so other members of the legal team may recognize them later at the time of depositions and trial. If the photographs are going to be used at trial, keep in mind that the photographer may be called to authenticate them.

A Defense Perspective

Most people quite naturally think of a lawsuit from the plaintiff's perspective and in terms of the violation of rights and resulting injury. In a perfect world, only legitimate actions would be filed, and the law would provide a perfect remedy for all wrongs. But not every plaintiff is in the right, and some have been known to file frivolous or even fraudulent lawsuits.

The balance in the American legal system is achieved by a vigorous defense on behalf of the defendant. A plaintiff may claim, for example, that she slipped and was injured as a result of the negligence of a store owner. The defendant store owner might be innocent of any wrongdoing or breach of any duty. Remember that for every plaintiff, there is a defendant, and for each party, there is a law firm, an attorney, and a paralegal. Anticipating the potential defenses will help the legal team evaluate the client's case.

Obtaining Official Reports

Most incidents giving rise to litigation have associated official reports. In the negligence action, it may be a police accident or incident report, emergency medical services report, fire department call report, or incident reports of safety violations by federal, state, or local authorities. These reports are filed in a central repository as public records. A useful starting point, then, is to obtain any official reports associated with the case. These reports frequently indicate time, place, and the names of fact witnesses. In some cases, detailed diagrams or photographs may accompany the reports. Exhibit 7.7 is an example of a police accident report form.

Fact Analysis

Analyzing the facts starts with interviewing the clients to obtain their recollections of the time, place, circumstances, and other people involved as participants or witnesses. A complete analysis usually requires further field investigation of the location, the object involved (such as an automobile), and interviews of the parties and witnesses. Keep in mind that one person's perception may not be reality. A client's recollection and description of the physical surroundings may not be confirmed when the investigator visits the location. What one person describes as a narrow, congested walkway may actually be a standard-width, open sidewalk.

The ultimate trier of fact will be a jury, a panel of arbitrators, or a judge acting as the trier of fact. Therefore, analysis of the facts must be sufficient to justify the position taken and the presentation made in pursuing a client's claim or the legal team's defense in **arbitration** or in trial.

arbitration
Form of ADR in which the parties choose an impartial third party to hear and decide a dispute.

Locations

Careful analysis of a claim includes verification of the physical aspects of the actual location where the cause of action occurred. Ask any group of people to describe a location, and you're likely to get as many different descriptions as there are people in the group. How the person viewed the location—from the south, north, east, or west—may influence his or her description. Or, a driver's view

Exhibit 7.7 Sample Police Accident Report Form

COMMONWEALTH OF PENNSYLVANIA
POLICE ACCIDENT REPORT

(XX) REFER TO OVERLAY SHEETS

REPORTABLE ☐ NON - REPORTABLE ☐

PENNDOT USE ONLY

POLICE INFORMATION

1. INCIDENT NUMBER
2. AGENCY NAME
3. STATION/ PRECINCT — 4. PATROL ZONE
5. INVESTIGATOR — BADGE NUMBER
6. APPROVED BY — BADGE NUMBER
7. INVESTIGATION DATE — 8. ARRIVAL TIME

ACCIDENT INFORMATION

9. ACCIDENT DATE — 10. DAY OF WEEK
11. TIME OF DAY — 12. NUMBER OF UNITS
13. # KILLED — 14.# INJURED — 15. PRIV. PROP. ACCIDENT Y ☐ N ☐
16. DID VEHICLE HAVE TO BE REMOVED FROM THE SCENE? UNIT 1 Y ☐ N ☐ UNIT 2 Y ☐ N ☐ — 17. VEHICLE DAMAGE 0 - NONE 1 - LIGHT 2 - MODERATE 3 - SEVERE UNIT 1 ☐ UNIT 2 ☐
18. HAZARDOUS MATERIALS Y ☐ N ☐ — 19. PENNDOT PROPERTY Y ☐ N ☐

ACCIDENT LOCATION

20. COUNTY — CODE
21. MUNICIPALITY — CODE

PRINCIPAL ROADWAY INFORMATION

22. ROUTE NO. OR STREET NAME
23. SPEED LIMIT — (24) TYPE HIGHWAY — (25) ACCESS CONTROL

INTERSECTING ROAD:

26. ROUTE NO. OR STREET NAME
27. SPEED LIMIT — (28) TYPE HIGHWAY — (29) ACCESS CONTROL

IF NOT AT INTERSECTION:

30. CROSS STREET OR SEGMENT MARKER
31. DIRECTION FROM SITE N S E W — 32. DISTANCE FROM SITE FT. MI.
33. DISTANCE WAS MEASURED ☐ ESTIMATED ☐
(34) CONSTRUCTION ZONE ☐ — (35) TRAFFIC CONTROL DEVICE PRINCIPAL ☐ INTERSECTING ☐

UNIT # 1

36. LEGALLY PARKED ? Y ☐ N ☐ — 37. REG. PLATE — 38. STATE
39. PA TITLE OR OUT-OF-STATE VIN
40. OWNER
41. OWNER ADDRESS
42. CITY, STATE & ZIPCODE
43. YEAR — 44. MAKE
45. MODEL - (NOT BODY TYPE) — 46. INS. Y ☐ N ☐ UNK ☐
(47) BODY TYPE — (48) SPECIAL USAGE — (49) VEHICLE OWNERSHIP
(50) INITIAL IMPACT POINT — (51) VEHICLE STATUS — (52) TRAVEL SPEED
(53) VEHICLE GRADIENT — (54) DRIVER PRESENCE ☐ — (55) DRIVER CONDITION
56. DRIVER NUMBER — 57. STATE
58. DRIVER NAME
59. DRIVER ADDRESS
60. CITY, STATE & ZIPCODE
61. SEX — 62. DATE OF BIRTH — 63. PHONE
64. COMM. VEH. Y ☐ N ☐ — 65. DRIVER CLASS — 66. DRIVER SS #
67. CARRIER
68. CARRIER ADDRESS
69. CITY, STATE & ZIPCODE
70. USDOT # — ICC # — PUC #
(72) VEH. CONFIG. — (73) CARGO BODY TYPE — 74. GVWR
75. NO. OF AXLES — (76) HAZ ARDOUS MATERIALS — 77. RELEASE OF HAZ MAT Y ☐ N ☐ UNK ☐

UNIT # 2

36. LEGALLY PARKED ? Y ☐ N ☐ — 37. REG. PLATE — 38. STATE
39. PA TITLE OR OUT-OF-STATE VIN
40. OWNER
41. OWNER ADDRESS
42. CITY, STATE & ZIPCODE
43. YEAR — 44. MAKE
45. MODEL - (NOT BODY TYPE) — 46. INS. Y ☐ N ☐ UNK ☐
(47) BODY TYPE — (48) SPECIAL USAGE — (49) VEHICLE OWNERSHIP
(50) INITIAL IMPACT POINT — (51) VEHICLE STATUS — (52) TRAVEL SPEED
(53) VEHICLE GRADIENT — (54) DRIVER PRESENCE ☐ — (55) DRIVER CONDITION
56. DRIVER NUMBER — 57. STATE
58. DRIVER NAME
59. DRIVER ADDRESS
60. CITY, STATE & ZIPCODE
61. SEX — 62. DATE OF BIRTH — 63. PHONE
64. COMM. VEH. Y ☐ N ☐ — 65. DRIVER CLASS — 66. DRIVER SS #
67. CARRIER
68. CARRIER ADDRESS
69. CITY, STATE & ZIPCODE
70. USDOT # — ICC # — PUC #
(72) VEH. CONFIG. — (73) CARGO BODY TYPE — 74. GVWR
75. NO. OF AXLES — (76) HAZ ARDOUS MATERIALS — 77. RELEASE OF HAZ MAT Y ☐ N ☐ UNK ☐

AA-45 (1/92) PAGE: CENTER FOR HIGHWAY SAFETY

(continued)

Exhibit 7.7 (continued)

78. RESPONDING EMS AGENCY	INCIDENT #:
79. MEDICAL FACILITY	ACCIDENT DATE:

80. PEOPLE INFORMATION

A	B	C	D	E	F	G	NAME	ADDRESS	H	I	J	K	L	M

86. DIAGRAM

o

81. ILLUMINATION ☐   82. WEATHER ☐
83. ROAD SURFACE ☐

84. PENNSYLVANIA SCHOOL DISTRICT (IF APPLICABLE)

85. DESCRIPTION OF DAMAGED PROPERTY

OWNER

ADDRESS

PHONE

87. NARRATIVE - IDENTIFY PRECIPITATING EVENTS, CAUSATION FACTORS, SEQUENCE OF EVENTS, WITNESS STATEMENTS, AND PROVIDE ADDITIONAL DETAILS. LIKE INSURANCE INFORMATION AND LOCATION OF TOWED VEHILCES, IF KNOWN.

INSURANCE INFORMATION	COMPANY		INSURANCE INFORMATION	COMPANY
UNIT 1	POLICY NO		UNIT 2	POLICY NO

88. WINTESSES	NAME	ADDRESS	PHONE
	NAME	ADDRESS	PHONE

	89. VIOLATIONS INDICATED	90. SECTION NUMBERS (ONLY IF CHARGED)	TC NTC
UNIT 1			☐ ☐
UNIT 2			☐ ☐

	91. PROBABLE USE	92. TYPE TEST	93. RESULTS		91. PROBABLE USE	92. TYPE TEST	93. RESULTS		94. INVESTIGATION COMPLETE ?
UNIT 1			0.___ __%	☐ NO TEST ☐ REFUSE ☐ UNK	UNIT 2			0.___ __% ☐ NO TEST ☐ REFUSE ☐ UNK	YES ☐ NO ☐

AA-45 (1/92)   PAGE: **CENTER FOR HIGHWAY SAFETY**

from behind the wheel of a large tractor-trailer might be different from the view from behind the wheel of a small sports car.

Investigation of a case should involve a trip to the location where the incident occurred. The trier of fact relies upon the plaintiff's and defendant's counsels to describe in their presentations the characteristics of the physical location. He or she looks at the location from an impartial, neutral point of view, usually without prior familiarity with the location. The diagrams usually presented at trial are those of an aerial view, with its sterile, one-dimensional perspective. Photographs from the points of view of all the participants can make the difference in understanding the duties and responsibilities of the litigants. Unlike diagrams of the location, these photographs more typically will be from the point of view of the plaintiff, defendant, or witness at ground level, from behind the wheel of a vehicle, or looking out of a building window.

Satellite photos are available of locations around the world. Google Earth™ offers web access to images that may be modified to add desired descriptions such as street names and points of interest, including lodgings, restaurants, schools, churches, and many other places, with the click of the computer mouse. Images taken before a loss, such as Super Storm Sandy in 2012, combined with images taken after the devastation may be helpful in submitting claims for damages.

Tangible Evidence

Tangible evidence consists of the physical objects that may have caused an injury. These may include items as small as a giveaway toy from a fast food restaurant swallowed by a two-year-old, to a bottle that exploded, to a large automobile whose brakes failed or whose seatbelts snapped. In some cases, the tangible evidence is essential to proving negligence or an element of strict liability in tort.

Much has been written about the effects of plaintiffs' and defendants' failures to preserve critical evidence of this type. Failure to preserve evidence has resulted in loss of cases by both plaintiffs and defendants.

It is important to understand the local rules with regard to the loss or destruction of evidence, or **spoliation of evidence,** and its effect on a cause of action. In determining the proper penalty for spoliation of evidence, courts are most likely to consider:

1. the degree of fault of the party who altered or destroyed the evidence;
2. the degree of prejudice suffered by the opposing party; and
3. the availability of a lesser sanction that will protect the opposing party's rights and deter future similar conduct (*Schroeder v. Department of Transportation*, 710 A2d 23 (1998).

tangible evidence
Physical evidence that one can see and inspect may be presented at trial for the jury to consider.

spoliation of evidence
Destruction of records that may be relevant to ongoing or anticipated litigation, government investigation, or audit. Courts differ in their interpretations of the level of intent required before sanctions may be warranted.

Timelines

Causes of action should be viewed from the events leading up to the incident to the events and occurrences following the incident. (See Exhibit 7.8 for a comparison of conflicting accounts.) Few things in life that give rise to a potential claim occur in a vacuum. Usually, some facts lead up to the incident and others follow the incident. The question may be "Given the time in which the parties allege this happened, could this really have happened?" For example, could the parties have driven the thirty miles in twenty minutes through crowded rush-hour traffic on city streets? In a food-poisoning case, could ingestion of the food at noon have caused the reaction claimed by 1:00 P.M.? The claimant might have been negligent, or the first perceived wrongdoer perhaps was not the correct person, as most food-poisoning cases require six to twelve hours from ingestion of the tainted food until onset of symptoms of the illness.

The starting point is the time of the alleged injury. Also important from a fault standpoint or a defense standpoint is what happened that led up to the incident. From the damages standpoint, what happened after the incident, including treatment and subsequent changes in the person's life or lifestyle, is important to know.

Exhibit 7.8 Conflicting Accounts Comparison Timeline

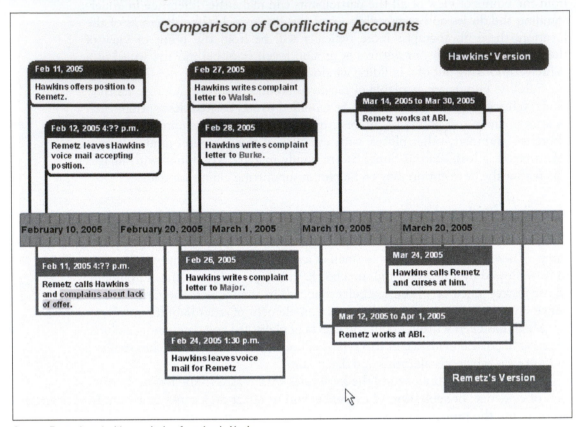

Source: Reproduced with permission from Lexis Nexis.

Freedom of Information Act

The **Freedom of Information Act (FOIA)** is a federal statute designed to make accessible to the public the information possessed by the federal government and its agencies. The federal government is a good source of information. Many of the documents required to be filed are available through the government, and are frequently online, such as corporate filings with the Securities and Exchange Commission. Other information may be available by request, under the provisions of the FOIA, 5 U.S.C. § 552. However, note that some limitations apply to what information is available. The general exceptions, as found in the statute, are:

1. classified documents concerning national defense and foreign policy;
2. internal personnel rules and practices;
3. exemptions under other laws that require information to be withheld, such as patent applications and income tax returns;
4. confidential business information and trade secrets;
5. intra-agency and inter-agency internal communications not available by law to a party in litigation;
6. protection of privacy of personnel and medical files and private lives of individuals;
7. law enforcement investigatory files;
8. examination, operation, or condition reports of agencies responsible for the regulation and supervision of financial institutions; and
9. geological and geophysical information and data including maps concerning wells.

Many federal agencies do not require a formal FOIA request. Some federal agencies, such as the National Transportation Safety Board, make information available online (Exhibit 7.9) or by online request (Exhibit 7.10). Other agencies, such as the Consumer Product Safety Commission (CPSC), permit requests to be made on the CPSC website (Exhibit 7.11). The CPSC site also is helpful in finding information about defective products that may be a cause of a client's

Exhibit 7.9 NTSB Freedom of Information Act Website

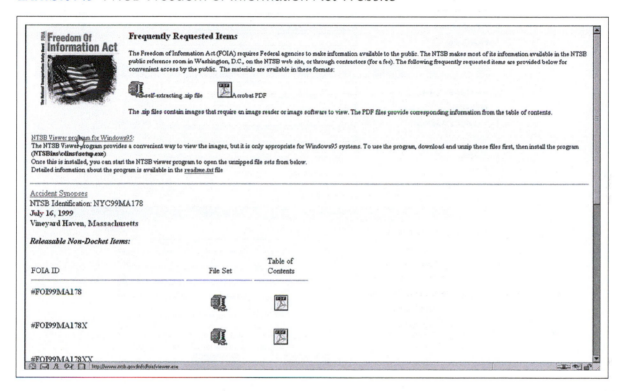

Exhibit 7.10 NTSB FOIA request form

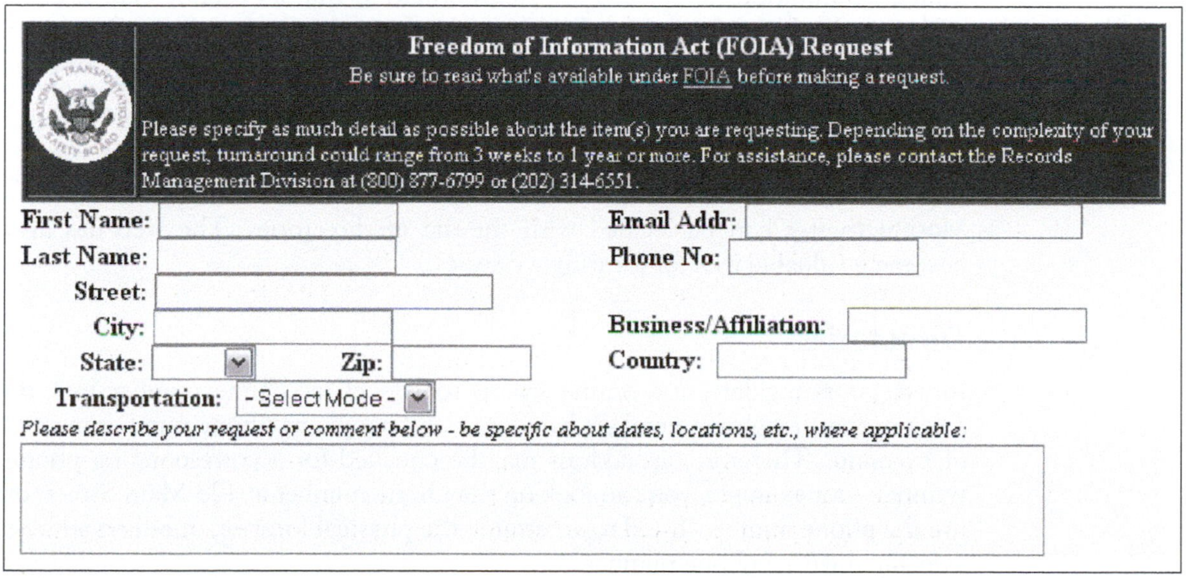

Exhibit 7.11 U.S. Consumer Product Safety Commission FOIA Internet Request Form

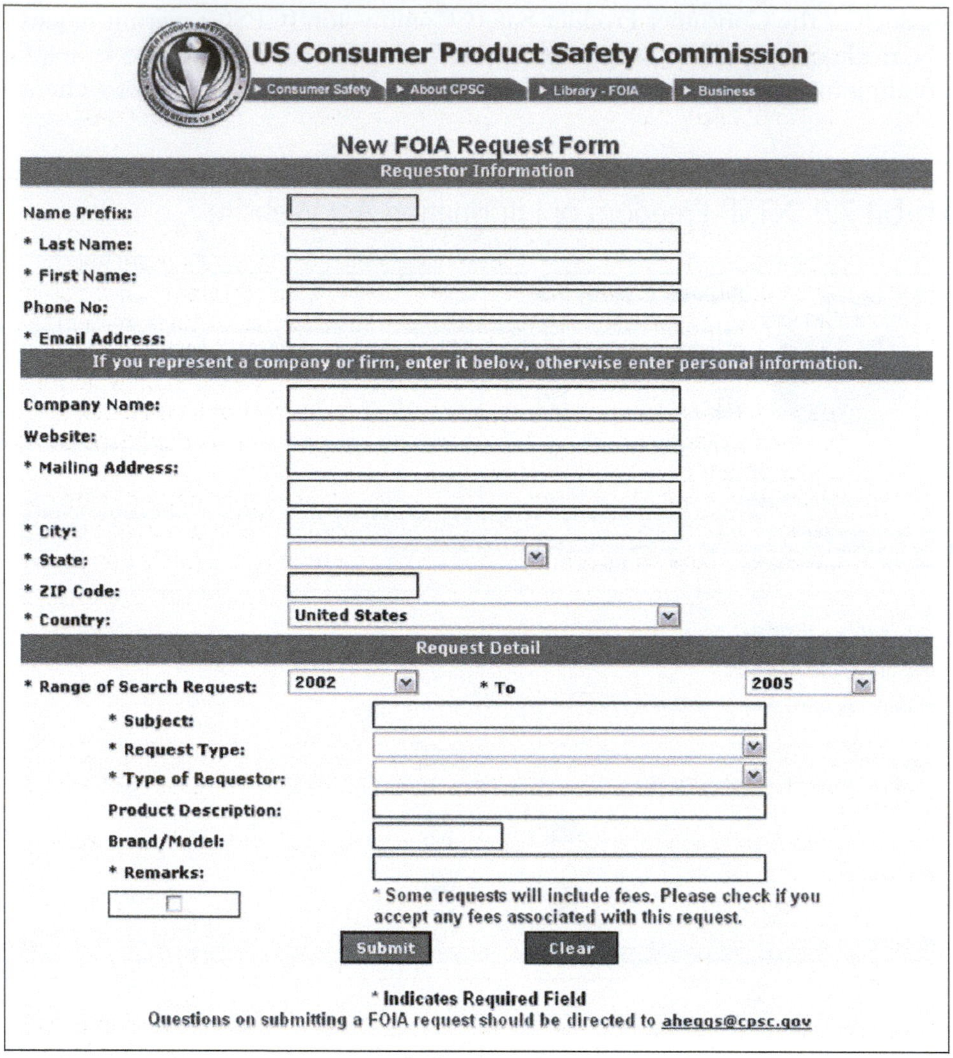

US Consumer Product Safety Commission

▸ Consumer Safety ▸ About CPSC ▸ Library - FOIA ▸ Business

New FOIA Request Form

Requestor Information

Name Prefix:

* Last Name:

* First Name:

Phone No:

* Email Address:

If you represent a company or firm, enter it below, otherwise enter personal information.

Company Name:

Website:

* Mailing Address:

* City:

* State:

* ZIP Code:

* Country: United States

Request Detail

* Range of Search Request: 2002 * To 2005

* Subject:

* Request Type:

* Type of Requestor:

Product Description:

Brand/Model:

* Remarks:

* Some requests will include fees. Please check if you accept any fees associated with this request.

Submit Clear

* Indicates Required Field

Questions on submitting a FOIA request should be directed to ahegqs@cpsc.gov

injuries. Limitations are placed on the information that an agency may disclose under applicable federal law. For example, limitations placed on Consumer Product Safety Commission information are shown in Exhibit 7.12 and those for National Transportation Safety Board information are shown in Exhibit 7.13.

Locating Witnesses

Most witnesses can be located with the aid of directories. The web has also become a valuable tool for locating witnesses.

Directories

Investigators regularly use online search tools such as phone number look-up services that list phone numbers by address and people by phone number instead of by name. Therefore, an address may be checked for a corresponding phone number—for example, you can look up the phone number at 123 Main Street, or use the phone numbers listed to determine the physical location or billing address associated with a phone number.

Exhibit 7.12 Consumer Product Safety Commission FOIA Limits

CONSUMER PRODUCT SAFETY COMMISSION

LIMITATIONS OF FOIA DISCLOSURE

15 U.S.C. § 2055. Public disclosure of information release date: 2005-08-01

"(a) Disclosure requirements for manufacturers or private labelers; procedures applicable

    (1) Nothing contained in this Act shall be construed to require the release of any information described by subsection (b) of section 552 of title 5 or which is otherwise protected by law from disclosure to the public.

    (2) All information reported to or otherwise obtained by the Commission or its representative under this Act which information contains or relates to a trade secret or other matter referred to in section 1905 of title 18 or subject to section 552 (b)(4) of title 5 shall be considered confidential and shall not be disclosed.

    (3) The Commission shall, prior to the disclosure of any information which will permit the public to ascertain readily the identity of a manufacturer or private labeler of a consumer product, offer such manufacturer or private labeler an opportunity to mark such information as confidential and therefore barred from disclosure under paragraph (2).

    (4) All information that a manufacturer or private labeler has marked to be confidential and barred from disclosure under paragraph (2), either at the time of submission or pursuant to paragraph (3), shall not be disclosed, except in accordance with the procedures established in paragraphs (5) and (6)...."

Exhibit 7.13 National Transportation Safety Board Exemptions

NATIONAL TRANSPORTATION SAFETY BOARD EXEMPTIONS LIMITATIONS OF FOIA DISCLOSURE

The four most common exemptions under which the NTSB withholds information are:

    (1) 5 USC 552 (b)(5), draft reports and staff analyses (see 49 CFR 801.54);

    (2) 5 USC 552 (b)(6), personal information, where a personal interest in privacy outweighs a public interest in release; this includes graphic photographs of injuries in accidents and autopsy reports (see 49 CFR 801.55);

    (3) 5 USC 552 (b)(4), Trade Secrets and/or confidential financial/commercial information submitted by private persons or corporations to the NTSB in the course of an investigation (see 49 CFR 801.59); and

    (4) 5 USC 552 (b)(3), information protected from release by another statute (see 49 CFR 801.53). This includes information such as:

- Cockpit Voice Recorder (CVR) tapes. Release of the tapes is prohibited by 49 USC 1114(c). However, the Board will release a CVR transcript [edited or unedited], the timing of such release is also controlled by statute—49 USC 1114(c)(B);

- Voluntarily provided safety-related information. 49 USC 1114(b)(3) prohibits the release of such information if it is not related to the exercise of the Board's accident or incident investigation authority and if the Board finds that the disclosure would inhibit the voluntary provision of that type of information; and

- Records or information relating to the NTSB's participation in foreign aircraft accident investigations. 49 USC 1114(e) prohibits the release of this information before the country conducting the investigation releases its report or 2 years following the accident, whichever occurs first.

Online directories are not limited to just the United States but typically are available for most parts of the world in one form or another. Companies and businesses also can be located by use of online commercial or industrial directories and trade association website listings of members, both domestic and international.

These listings may be limited to membership but can be useful in cases where the name and the association are known but the geographic location is unknown.

Search engines can also help locate individuals, businesses, and organizations on the Internet. Communications companies and other private firms offer a number of online white pages for individuals and yellow pages for businesses. Many organizations and publishers of professional directories offer their directories online. An example is the web version of Martindale-Hubbell shown in Exhibit 7.14. These companies may change or cancel their web-based products and others may be added, so the list of websites has to be kept up to date.

Exhibit 7.14 Web Version of Martindale-Hubbell Directory

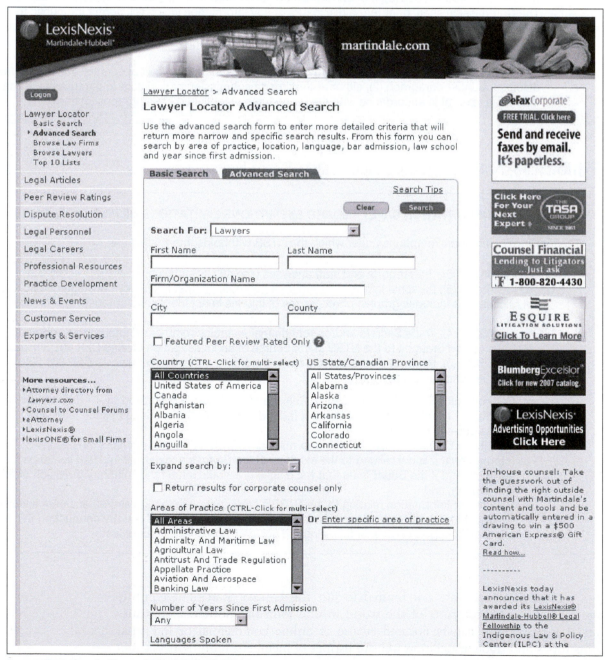

Source: Reproduced with permission from Lexis Nexis.

Common Sense Analysis

The results of an investigation should also be analyzed using common sense. Jurors will be told to apply their collective common sense to the evidence during their deliberations. The legal team should do the same.

The events that gave rise to the client's claim did not occur in a vacuum. The paralegal should evaluate the chronology of events to see if it withstands common sense analysis. For example, is it possible for the plaintiff to have traveled across town at rush hour in just ten minutes? Does it really make sense that the plaintiff's inability to work was the result of a minor automobile accident that caused no damage to either vehicle?

There can always be unforeseen explanations for what at first appears to be unusual or impossible. The paralegal should identify such inconsistencies in the early stages of the investigation and do the additional research or investigation needed to resolve such discrepancies. Successfully investigating and analyzing the client's case will make the paralegal's job rewarding and the legal team's job easier.

Checklist ✔   INVESTIGATION INFORMATION SOURCES

Information Source	Web Address	Physical Location	Comments
Police Records—Local	www.		
Police Records—State	www.		
Birth Records	www.		
Death Records	www.		
Driver's Licenses	www.		
Vehicle Registration	www.		
Corporate Records	www.		
Real Estate—Recorder	www.		
Real Estate—Tax	www.		
Real Estate—Land Mapping	www.		
Register of Wills	www.		
Trial Court	www.		
Federal District Court—Clerk's Office	www.	Room Federal Court House	
Federal Bankruptcy Court	www.		
Occupational License	www.		
Weather Reports	www.		

Complete this list by adding the local or regional office web address, mailing addresses, and room numbers for personal visits; add comments and note any applicable contact people, costs, or hours of operation.

CONCEPT REVIEW AND REINFORCEMENT

KEY TERMS

screening interview   163
implied attorney–client
    relationship   163
fact witness   167
cultural sensitivity   171
hostile witness   174
leading questions   175

open-ended
    questions   175
narrative opportunity   175
privileged communication   176
moral obligation   176
ethical obligation   177
expert witness   177

Restatement of the Law Third,
    Torts: Product Liability   178
arbitration   180
tangible evidence   183
spoliation of evidence   183
Freedom of Information Act
    (FOIA)   184

CHAPTER SUMMARY

INTERVIEWS AND INVESTIGATION IN CIVIL LITIGATION

Introduction to Interviews and Investigations	Trial preparation starts with the first client contact and the gathering of the first document. The initial contact with a client or potential witness may set the tone for the interview and willingness of the person to cooperate.
Preparing for the Interview	Investigation checklists should not be viewed as static documents. Physical surroundings in the interview location can set the tone for the interview. Dress and appearance, including clothing, posture, and manner of greeting, create the first impression. Communication skills in a multicultural society require that interviewers develop an ability to appreciate differences in how and why individuals act and react differently.
Conducting the Interview	The paralegal must, in the first meeting, make it clear that he or she is a paralegal and not an attorney, and that only an attorney can give legal advice. Listening skills include the ability to listen to what is being said and not just the words being used. Good listening skills include the ability to disregard distractions and not make assumptions about the facts of the case. Leading questions are those that suggest the desired answer. Open-ended questions are designed to give interviewees an opportunity to tell their stories without the limitation of a yes-or-no answer. Moral obligations are based on one's own conscience or perceived rules of correct conduct. Ethical obligations for the paralegal are based upon the Model Rules of Professional Conduct.
Expert Witnesses	Experts are individuals whose backgrounds, educations, and experiences are such that the court recognizes them as qualified to give an opinion based on a set of facts. Some law firms retain an expert to advise them but do not use that expert to testify.

Investigating Claims	The legal team must gather all of the relevant information about a cause of action before making a recommendation to a client about whether to file a lawsuit or respond to a claim of wrongdoing. Considering the defense's perspective allows the legal team to anticipate the potential defenses.
	Official reports associated with all litigation must be obtained and analyzed. This analysis includes verification of the physical aspects of the case.
	Tangible evidence consists of physical objects that may have caused the injury. Loss or destruction of physical evidence may lead to a claim of spoliation of evidence and an adverse inference or sanctions from the court.
	Timelines can be used to view the physical events leading up to and following from the incident and offer a graphic representation.
	The Freedom of Information Act (FOIA) is a federal statute designed to make accessible to the public information possessed by the federal government and its agencies.
	Individual agencies may not make available certain types of information.
	Witnesses may be located from official reports, directories, and the web.

REVIEW QUESTIONS AND EXERCISES

1. What is a screening interview? How is it different from any other interview?
2. Describe how to prepare for an interview.
3. Why are the physical surroundings and appearance of the interviewer important?
4. Explain the impact our multicultural society has on the interview process.
5. Why is paying attention to nonverbal cues as important as listening to the words spoken?
6. Define *leading* and *open-ended questions*. When are they best used?
7. Explain the difference between moral and ethical obligations of the paralegal.
8. What communications are privileged?
9. How are experts used by the legal team? Are all communications with an expert protected by the doctrine of privilege or work product? Why or why not?
10. What is the purpose of investigating the client's claim?
11. Why should the legal team consider the defense perspective when conducting its investigation?
12. Define *tangible evidence*. What penalties might be imposed on a party that destroys tangible evidence?
13. How is the preparation of a timeline helpful in investigation of claims?
14. What is FOIA? How does FOIA help the legal team investigate a client's claims?
15. Describe how the use of the interent and computer technology can assist in the investigation and organization of the client's claim.

BUILDING YOUR PARALEGAL SKILLS

INTERNET AND TECHNOLOGY EXERCISES

1. Find an aerial photograph that depicts your county courthouse.
2. Use three search engines to search for your name, and record or print the results. If you were a witness to an accident, would the search engines help a legal team find you?
3. Locate a witness with expertise in the use of Botox for medically necessary treatment rather than as a cosmetic procedure.
4. Enter data into a case management software program.
5. Create a database using Microsoft Access with information from the Appendix 1 case.

CIVIL LITIGATION VIDEO CASE STUDIES

Zealous Representation: When You Are Asked to Lie

 The supervising attorney asks the paralegal to lie to obtain information needed in a case.

After viewing the video at www.pearsonhighered .com/careersresources answer the following questions.

1. Is misrepresenting yourself to obtain needed information in a case ethical?
2. May information obtained by misrepresentation be used as part of the case?

UPL Issue: Working with a Witness

 A paralegal, while investigating an accident, asks a witness to come to the office to give a statement and then offers to compensate the witness for his time.

After viewing the video at www.pearsonhighered .com/careersresources answer the following questions.

1. Under what circumstances may a witness be paid a fee for testifying?
2. What are the ethical issues of paying a fact witness a fee?
3. Did the paralegal create the wrong impression by failing to identify himself?
4. Might the amount of the fee have any impact on the truth of the statements made by the witness?

CHAPTER OPENING SCENARIO CASE STUDY

Use the Opening Scenario for this chapter to answer the following questions.
1. Prepare an investigation plan for the opening scene scenario or the assigned case study. Start by preparing a timeline.
2. Design an investigation checklist.

COMPREHENSIVE CASE STUDY

SCHOOL BUS–TRUCK ACCIDENT CASE

Review the assigned case study in Appendix 2.
1. Enter the assigned case study data into AbacusLaw or another case management software program.

2. Prepare a list of questions to ask the parents of the children killed in the accident. What special methods or techniques should be considered?

BUILDING YOUR PROFESSIONAL PORTFOLIO

CIVIL LITIGATION TEAM AT WORK

See page 18 for instructions on Building Your Professional Portfolio.

Forms

1. Interview and investigation forms for:
   a. Client
   b. Fact witness
   c. Expert witness
   d. Accident investigation

2. Document requests
   a. Police report in your jurisdiction
   b. State police reports
   c. Medical records under local rules of court
   d. Newspaper articles and photographs
3. Freedom of Information Act (FOIA) requests
   a. National Transportation Safety Board (NTSB) reports
   b. Consumer Product Safety Commission reports

Contacts and Resources

Complete the investigation information sources checklist from this chapter.

Information Source	Web Address	Physical Location	Comments

1. Design a client information sheet that will focus the paralegal on the information that must be obtained from the client.

2. Prepare a list of ten open-ended questions to obtain the information needed to complete the client information sheet you have designed.

LEARNING OBJECTIVES

After studying this chapter, you should be able to:

1. Select the appropriate court rules for preparing pleadings in civil litigation.

2. Describe the impact of the statute of limitations on the commencement of a lawsuit.

3. Draft a complaint and a summons.

4. Determine the rules for filing and serving the initial pleadings.

5. Create a timeline for litigation.

6. Determine when amended or supplementary pleadings may be required.

Pleadings: Complaint, Summons, and Service

CHAPTER 8

OPENING SCENARIO

The legal team had broken down the work on the case into two parts: the downtown office handled the liability issues; and the suburban office handled the damage issues. The paralegals gathered all the information and were asked to prepare a draft of the complaint. Over dinner they discovered they were doing some of the same work. They needed a single complaint for filing in federal court. To save time, they asked to work out of the same office while preparing the complaint and related documents. The partners thought it was time for the entire team to get together and review the case. While each was handling a specific portion of the case, they would all be bound by the same pleadings and, ultimately, preparation for one trial.

OPENING SCENARIO LEARNING OBJECTIVE

Draft a complaint.

■ INTRODUCTION TO PLEADINGS

pleadings
Documents filed to commence and respond to a lawsuit.

Pleadings are the documents filed with a court to commence or respond to a lawsuit. In the initial pre-filing phase, it is important to be familiar with the applicable rules of the court in which the action is to be filed and tried. The form of the pleadings and the procedures for filing and serving the pleadings are dictated by the court rules for the court in which the action will be filed. The rules vary between federal and state courts. Within the same court system, there may also be local practice rules that amend or supplement the standard rules.

The initial pleading is designed to give the party being sued notice of the filing of the lawsuit. The initial responsive pleading answers the claims made by the plaintiff or adds other parties that the responding party believes are responsible for the plaintiff's losses.

Pleadings define the case by establishing, in the complaint, the alleged wrong and the claims for relief, and in the answer filed by the defendant, the defenses to the plaintiff's claims.

WEB RESOURCES

Using one of the following state trial court websites, determine whether there is a requirement for page size, margins, and font type. Also find your state court's website.

New York http://www.courts.state.ny.us/courts/trialcourts.shtml

Pennsylvania Courts http://www.courts.state.pa.us/default.htm

Illinois Courts http://www.state.il.us/court/SupremeCourt/Rules/Art_II/default.asp

Texas Courts http://www.courts.state.tx.us/

California Courts http://www.courtinfo.ca.gov/courts/trial/

LEARNING OBJECTIVE 1

Select the appropriate court rules for preparing pleadings in civil litigation.

Rules of Civil Procedure
A set of rules and procedures in each court that must be followed in all litigation.

Federal Rules of Civil Procedure
Rules and procedures that control all litigation filed in the federal court system.

■ RULES OF COURT

Rules of Civil Procedure establish the procedures that must be followed in all civil actions. There are federal rules that govern civil proceedings in the federal court system and state rules for the state courts. These rules have been written to provide a level playing field so that civil litigation is conducted fairly and produces a just result. The use of standard rules permits everyone to know the required procedures for instituting and processing a case from beginning to end. In the American system, it also means that there is a body of case law available that demonstrates how the courts have interpreted the procedural rules and how they are likely to rule on the procedural aspects of current cases.

The **Federal Rules of Civil Procedure** (Fed. R. Civ. P.) provide the basic set of rules for civil litigation in federal court. State courts have their own set of rules of civil procedure. Exhibit 8.1 shows a sample of a set of state court procedural rules. The basic federal and/or state rules are frequently modified by the addition of local rules that must also be followed. For example, some local courts have specific rules on electronic filing of pleadings. Exhibit 8.2 shows an example of local rules defining how documents should be signed for filing in the Federal District Court for the District of Utah. Some of the local rules are as basic as requiring a specific location and method of stapling documents, the allowable paper size, and the requirements for using or not using backers on documents filed with the court. Rules that may seem unimportant ("What difference does it make if the document is stapled on the top or the side?") are important to the court, and failure to follow them will, at the very least, irritate courthouse staff, who have to take the time to unstaple and restaple the pleading. At the worst, in those courts that have transitioned to mandatory electronic filing, failure to check the most current rules and obtain the necessary training for electronic filing may result in a rejection of a filing and missing an important deadline. The rules of court also provide the timetable within which the parties must act—for example, the time for the defendant to deny the allegations before a default judgment may be entered or a motion for dismissal of the lawsuit may be filed.

PRACTICE TIP

The December 2007 and 2009 Amendments to the Federal Rules of Civil Procedure have been approved, and some sections have been renumbered. Be sure you have the latest version.

Exhibit 8.1 Uniform Rules for New York State Trial Courts

New York State Unified Court System

Rules

Part & Title:

200
Uniform Rules for
Courts Exercising
Criminal Jurisd.

201
[Reserved]

202
Uniform Civil Rules
for the Supreme
Court and County
Court

203
[Reserved]

204
[Reserved]

205
Uniform Rules for
the Family Court

206
Uniform Rules for
the Court of Claims

207
Uniform Rules of
the Surrogate's
Court

208
Uniform Rules for
the New York City
Civil Court

209
[Reserved]

210
Uniform Civil Rules
for the City Courts
Outside of NYC

211
[Reserved]

212
Uniform Civil Rules
for the District
Courts

213
[Reserved]

214
Uniform Civil Rules
for the Justice

Uniform Rules for N.Y.S. Trial Courts

PART 202. Uniform Civil Rules For The Supreme Court And The County Court

202.01 Application of Part; waiver; additional rules; . . .
202.02 Terms and parts of court
202.03 Individual assignment system; structure
202.04 County Court judge; ex parte applications in Sup. Court . . .
202.05 Papers filed in court
202.05a Filing by facsimile transmission
202.05b Filing by electronic means
202.06 Request for judicial intervention
202.07 Calendaring of motions; uniform notice of motion form; . . .
202.08 Motion procedure
202.09 Special proceedings
202.10 to 202.11 [Reserved]
202.12 Preliminary conference
202.13 Removal of actions without consent to courts of Ltd. jurisdiction
202.14 Special masters
202.15 Videotape recording of civil depositions
202.16 Matrimonial actions; calendar control of financial disclosure . . .
202.17 Exchange of medical reports in pers. injury and wrongful death
202.18 Testimony of court-appt expert witness in matrimonial action
202.19 Differentiated case management
202.20 [Reserved]
202.21 Note of issue and certificate of readiness
202.22 Calendars
202.23 [Reserved]
202.24 Special preferences
202.25 Objections to applications for special preference
202.26 Pretrial conference
202.27 Defaults
202.28 Discontinuance of actions
202.29 to 202.30 [Reserved]
202.31 Identification of trial counsel
202.32 Engagement of counsel
202.33 Conduct of the voir dire
202.34 [Reserved]
202.35 Submission of papers for trial
202.36 Absence of attorney during trial
202.37 to 202.39 [Reserved]
202.40 Jury trial of less than all issues; procedure
202.41 [Reserved]
202.42 Bifurcated trials
202.43 Ref. of triable issues and proceedings to judicial hearing . . .
202.44 Motion to confirm or reject judicial hearing officer's report . . .
202.45 Resched. after jury disagreement, mistrial or order for new trial
202.46 Damages, inquest after default; proof
202.47 Transcript of judgment; receipt stub
202.48 Submission of orders, judgments and decrees for signature
202.49 [Reserved]
202.50 Proposed judgments in matrimonial actions; forms
202.51 Proof required in dissolution proceedings
202.52 Deposit of funds by receivers and assignees
202.53 Trust accountings; procedure
202.54 Proceedings relating to appts. of guardians w respect . . .
202.55 Procedure for perfection of civil appeals to the County Court
202.56 Medical, dental and podiatric malpractice actions; special rules
202.57 Judicial review of orders of the State Division of Human Rights
202.58 Small claims tax assessment review proceedings

COURTS

LITIGANTS

ATTORNEYS

JURORS

JUDGES

CAREERS

SEARCH

Source: Reprinted with permission from the New York State Office of Court Administration.

■ STATUTE OF LIMITATIONS

The first time limit that must be determined in every potential civil action is when the **statute of limitations** will expire for the particular cause of action. With the exception of the crime of murder, every wrong, whether civil or criminal, has a time frame within which a party must bring suit or lose his right to utilize the courts to enforce his rights. This is referred to as the statute of limitations. The statute of limitations in civil cases may be as short as thirty or sixty days, such as the time within which notice must be given, under a state's law protecting its primary tourist business, to a potential defendant for an injury sustained on a ski slope. More typical is the statute of limitations requiring commencement of a lawsuit for a cause of action,

LEARNING OBJECTIVE 2
Describe the impact of the statute of limitations on the commencement of a lawsuit.

statute of limitations
Time frame within which an action must be commenced, or the party will lose his or her right to use the courts to seek redress.

Exhibit 8.2 Administrative Procedures that Modify the Federal Rules of Civil Procedure in the Utah District Court

---

II. PREPARING PAPERS FOR COURT FILING

A. SIGNATURES

1. Filing Attorney's Signature. Each attorney who files electronically shall be issued a login name and password by the Court. The attorney is responsible for maintaining the security of that login and password. The submission of a document that is (i) signed with an "/s/attorney name" or electronic image of the attorney's signature, and (ii) filed under that attorney's login and password, shall constitute an original signature for purposes of Federal Rule of Civil Procedure 11. CM/ECF presently cannot accommodate documents which have been digitally signed using Adobe Acrobat's Digital Signature feature.

2. Signatures of Other Attorneys. When a document to be filed requires the signature of attorneys other than that of the filing attorney, such as a stipulation, the attorney may obtain approval from any other attorney to state that the other attorney has authorized the filing attorney to electronically sign the document. Such approval shall be indicated by any of the following:

   a. Verbal Approval for Electronic
      Signature /s/ Other Attorney
      (Signed by Filing Attorney with permission of Plaintiff Attorney)
      Electronic Signature or /s/ Filing Attorney
      The filing attorney is responsible for maintaining a record of when and how permission was obtained to sign the other attorney's name until all appeals have been exhausted or the time for seeking appellate review has expired.

   b. Approval by Signature. The filing attorney may obtain and maintain a paper copy of the document signed by the other attorney. Possession of a signed copy shall be indicated as follows:
      /s/ Other Attorney
      (Signed copy of document bearing signature of Other Attorney is being maintained in the office of the Filing Attorney)
      Electronic Signature or /s/ Filing Attorney
      The filing attorney shall maintain the signed copy of the document until all appeals have been exhausted or the time for seeking appellate review has expired.

ADMINISTRATIVE PROCEDURES   **7**   **D-UTAH VERSION 09-22-06**

---

like one for personal injuries, within one to two years of the injury itself, or when the plaintiff became aware or should have become aware of the injury, such as a claim for medical malpractice for a foreign object left inside the person during an operation. A patient may not be aware of the medical malpractice committed by a surgeon for an extended time, sometimes years, until persistent pain is finally diagnosed as being caused by a medical sponge or instrument left inside the person's body during an earlier surgery. It would not be fair for the time limit to start when the injury was caused—the date of the original surgery. Fundamental fairness requires that the time frame begin when the patient learns the cause of the injury/pain.

In other cases, the time limit may begin at a point in the future. Societal concepts of justice allow those injured as **minors** (children) to bring an action after they reach the **age of majority** (usually eighteen years of age) for an injury suffered during their minority. In these cases, the statute of limitations starts on the birthday on which the individual reaches the age of majority in the applicable jurisdiction.

In contract cases, there may be various statutes of limitations, depending upon the particular cause of action pursued. For example, a contract dispute may come under the common law and be subject to a six-year statute of limitations; it might at the same time be a violation of the Uniform Commercial Code (UCC), which imposes a four-year statute of limitations (or such other time frame as

minors
Individuals who have not reached the legal age, or age of majority, usually 18 years old.

age of majority
Age at which an individual is recognized as an adult, usually 18.

specified under state law). Bringing the cause of action under the appropriate statute may give new life to a case for which the UCC limitation is less than the common law time frame permitted.

■ PLEADINGS

Lawsuits are commenced by the plaintiff filing an initial pleading with the appropriate court that has jurisdiction. Depending on the applicable rules of that court, the lawsuit may be commenced by the filing of a writ of summons, a summons and a complaint, a complaint alone, or some other combination of pleading and supporting documents. In some jurisdictions, a civil action is commenced by filing with the civil clerk of court a summons and a **Notice to Plead,** in Spanish and English, as well as additional court procedural documentation such as a fact cover sheet or document processing form. An example of a dual-language notice to plead is shown in Exhibit 8.3 and a fact cover sheet in Exhibit 8.4.

LEARNING OBJECTIVE 3
Draft a complaint and a summons.

Notice to Plead
Document containing the same information as a summons but often issued in dual languages.

Exhibit 8.3   Required Bilingual Notice to Defend for the Court of Common Pleas for the City of Philadelphia

NOTICE

You have been sued in court. If you wish to defend against the claims set forth in the following pages, you must take action within twenty (20) days after the complaint and notice are served, by entering a written appearance personally or by attorney and filing in writing with the court your defenses or objections to the claims set forth against you.
You are warned that if you fail to do so the case may proceed without you and a judgment may be entered against you by the court without further notice for any money claimed in the complaint or for any other claim or relief requested by plaintiff. You may lose money or property or other rights important to you.

YOU SHOULD TAKE THIS PAPER TO YOUR LAWYER AT ONCE. IF YOU DO NOT HAVE A LAWYER OR CANNOT AFFORD ONE, GO TO OR TELEPHONE THE OFFICE SET FORTH BELOW TO FIND OUT WHERE YOU CAN GET LEGAL HELP.

PHILADELPHIA BAR ASSOCIATION
Lawyer Referral and Information Service
1101 Market Street, 11th Floor
Philadelphia, Pennsylvania 19107
(215) 238-1701

AVISO

Le han demandado a usted en la corte. Si usted quiere defenderse de estas demandas expuestas en las páginas siguientes, usted tiene veinte (20) dias de plazo al partir de la fecha de la demanda y la notificatión. Hace falta asentar una comparencia escrita o en persona o con un abogado y entregar a la corte en forma escrita sus defensas o sus objeciones a las demandas en contra de su persona. Sea avisado que si usted no se defiende, la corte tomará medidas y puede continuar la demanda en contra suya sin previo aviso o notificación. Además, la corte puede decidir a favor del demandante y requiere que usted cumpla con todas las provisiones de esta demanda. Usted puede perder dinero o sus propiedades u otros derechos importantes para usted.

LLEVE ESTA DEMANDA A UN ABOGADO INMEDIATAMENTE. SI NO TIENE ABOGADO O SI NO TIENE EL DINERO SUFICIENTE DE PAGAR TAL SERVICIO, VAYA EN PERSONA O LLAME POR TELEFONO A LA OFICINA CUYA DIRECCION SE ENCUENTRA ESCRITA ABAJO PARA AVERIGUAR DONDE SE PUEDE CONSEGUIR ASISTENCIA LEGAL.

ASOCIACIÓN DE LICENCIADOS DE FILADELFIA
Servicio De Referencia E Información Legal
1101 Market Street, 11th Floor
Filadelfia, Pennsylvania 19107
(215) 238-1701

Exhibit 8.4 Sample Civil Case Cover Sheet

CM-010

ATTORNEY OR PARTY WITHOUT ATTORNEY *(Name, State Bar number, and address)*:

FOR COURT USE ONLY

TELEPHONE NO.:   FAX NO.:

ATTORNEY FOR *(Name)*:

SUPERIOR COURT OF CALIFORNIA, COUNTY OF

STREET ADDRESS:

MAILING ADDRESS:

CITY AND ZIP CODE:

BRANCH NAME:

CASE NAME:

CIVIL CASE COVER SHEET		Complex Case Designation	CASE NUMBER:
☐ Unlimited (Amount demanded exceeds $25,000)	☐ Limited (Amount demanded is $25,000 or less)	☐ Counter ☐ Joinder Filed with first appearance by defendant (Cal. Rules of Court, rule 3.402)	JUDGE: DEPT:

Items 1–6 below must be completed (see instructions on page 2).

1. Check one box below for the case type that best describes this case:

Auto Tort
☐ Auto (22)
☐ Uninsured motorist (46)

Other PI/PD/WD (Personal Injury/Property Damage/Wrongful Death) Tort
☐ Asbestos (04)
☐ Product liability (24)
☐ Medical malpractice (45)
☐ Other PI/PD/WD (23)

Non-PI/PD/WD (Other) Tort
☐ Business tort/unfair business practice (07)
☐ Civil rights (08)
☐ Defamation (13)
☐ Fraud (16)
☐ Intellectual property (19)
☐ Professional negligence (25)
☐ Other non-PI/PD/WD tort (35)

Employment
☐ Wrongful termination (36)
☐ Other employment (15)

Contract
☐ Breach of contract/warranty (06)
☐ Rule 3.740 collections (09)
☐ Other collections (09)
☐ Insurance coverage (18)
☐ Other contract (37)

Real Property
☐ Eminent domain/Inverse condemnation (14)
☐ Wrongful eviction (33)
☐ Other real property (26)

Unlawful Detainer
☐ Commercial (31)
☐ Residential (32)
☐ Drugs (38)

Judicial Review
☐ Asset forfeiture (05)
☐ Petition re: arbitration award (11)
☐ Writ of mandate (02)
☐ Other judicial review (39)

Provisionally Complex Civil Litigation (Cal. Rules of Court, rules 3.400–3.403)
☐ Antitrust/Trade regulation (03)
☐ Construction defect (10)
☐ Mass tort (40)
☐ Securities litigation (28)
☐ Environmental/Toxic tort (30)
☐ Insurance coverage claims arising from the above listed provisionally complex case types (41)

Enforcement of Judgment
☐ Enforcement of judgment (20)

Miscellaneous Civil Complaint
☐ RICO (27)
☐ Other complaint *(not specified above)* (42)

Miscellaneous Civil Petition
☐ Partnership and corporate governance (21)
☐ Other petition *(not specified above)* (43)

2. This case ☐ is ☐ is not complex under rule 3.400 of the California Rules of Court. If the case is complex, mark the factors requiring exceptional judicial management:
   a. ☐ Large number of separately represented parties
   b. ☐ Extensive motion practice raising difficult or novel issues that will be time-consuming to resolve
   c. ☐ Substantial amount of documentary evidence
   d. ☐ Large number of witnesses
   e. ☐ Coordination with related actions pending in one or more courts in other counties, states, or countries, or in a federal court
   f. ☐ Substantial postjudgment judicial supervision

3. Remedies sought *(check all that apply)*: a. ☐ monetary b. ☐ nonmonetary; declaratory or injunctive relief c. ☐ punitive
4. Number of causes of action *(specify)*:
5. This case ☐ is ☐ is not a class action suit.
6. If there are any known related cases, file and serve a notice of related case. *(You may use form CM-015.)*

Date:

_____
(TYPE OR PRINT NAME)

▶

_____
(SIGNATURE OF PARTY OR ATTORNEY FOR PARTY)

NOTICE
- Plaintiff must file this cover sheet with the first paper filed in the action or proceeding (except small claims cases or cases filed under the Probate Code, Family Code, or Welfare and Institutions Code). (Cal. Rules of Court, rule 3.220.) Failure to file may result in sanctions.
- File this cover sheet in addition to any cover sheet required by local court rule.
- If this case is complex under rule 3.400 et seq. of the California Rules of Court, you must serve a copy of this cover sheet on all other parties to the action or proceeding.
- Unless this is a collections case under rule 3.740 or a complex case, this cover sheet will be used for statistical purposes only.

Page 1 of 2

Form Adopted for Mandatory Use
Judicial Council of California
CM-010 [Rev. July 1, 2007]

CIVIL CASE COVER SHEET

Cal. Rules of Court, rules 2.30, 3.220, 3.400–3.403, 3.740;
Cal. Standards of Judicial Administration, std. 3.10
www.courtinfo.ca.gov

Exhibit 8.5 Minnesota Civil Practice Notice-Pleading Rules From the LexisNexis Total Litigator Service

Source: Reproduced with permission from Lexis Nexis.

The common information in all initial pleadings identifies the parties and the subject matter of the lawsuit. In some courts, the process is to file a complaint, and the court issues the summons to the defendant. The parties who have been sued and served copies of the pleadings usually file responsive pleadings stating their legal position, denying any wrongdoing, claiming others are responsible, or claiming that the defendant is the innocent party and the plaintiff the wrongdoer. Defendants who fail to respond in a timely manner as determined by court rule run the risk of having a judgment entered against them by default.

In the federal court system, there is only one way to commence a civil action: by filing a complaint (Fed. R. Civ. P. 3). In the complaint, the plaintiff must set forth all of the allegations that support a claim for relief. Federal pleadings are **notice pleadings,** designed to put the parties on notice of the claims. Some states are also notice-pleading jurisdictions. Exhibit 8.5 shows the Minnesota notice-pleading rules as shown in a search using LexisNexis Total Litigator. Other jurisdictions use **fact pleading.** Exhibit 8.6 shows a representative rule of civil procedure requiring fact pleading in a state court.

notice pleading
Pleading required to include sufficient facts to put the parties on notice of the claims asserted against them.

fact pleading
Pleadings required to include all relevant facts in support of all claims asserted.

Exhibit 8.6 Pennsylvania Fact-Pleading Requirement Under the Pennsylvania Rules of Civil Procedure

---

RULE 1019. CONTENTS OF PLEADINGS. GENERAL AND SPECIFIC AVERMENTS

(a) The material facts on which a cause of action or defense is based shall be stated in a concise and summary form.

(b) Averments of fraud or mistake shall be averred with particularity. Malice, intent, knowledge, and other conditions of mind may be averred generally.

(c) In pleading the performance or occurrence of conditions precedent, it is sufficient to aver generally that all conditions precedent have been performed or have occurred. A denial of such performance or occurrence shall be made specifically and with particularity.

(d) In pleading an official document or official act, it is sufficient to identify it by reference and aver that the document was issued or the act done in compliance with law.

(e) In pleading a judgment, order or decision of a domestic or foreign court, judicial or administrative tribunal, or board, commission or officer, it is sufficient to aver the judgment, order or decision without setting forth matter showing jurisdiction to render it.

(f) Averments of time, place and items of special damage shall be specifically stated.

(g) Any part of a pleading may be incorporated by reference in another part of the same pleading or in another pleading in the same action. A party may incorporate by reference any matter of record in any State or Federal court of record whose records are within the county in which the action is pending, or any matter which is recorded or transcribed verbatim in the office of the prothonotary, clerk of any court of record, recorder of deeds or register of wills of such county.

(h) When any claim or defense is based upon an agreement, the pleading shall state specifically if the agreement is oral or written.

Note: If the agreement is in writing, it must be attached to the pleading. See subdivision (i) of this rule.

(i) When any claim or defense is based upon a writing, the pleader shall attach a copy of the writing, or the material part thereof, but if the writing or copy is not accessible to the pleader, it is sufficient so to state, together with the reason, and to set forth the substance in writing.

Adopted June 25, 1946, effective Jan. 1, 1947. Amended April 12, 1999, effective July 1, 1999; Nov. 28, 2000, effective Jan. 1, 2001.

 # IN THE WORDS OF THE COURT…

Notice Pleading

Conley v. Gibson, **355 U.S. 41, 47–48 (1957) 78 S.Ct. 99.**

…The respondents also argue that the complaint failed to set forth specific facts to support its general allegations of discrimination and that its dismissal is therefore proper. The decisive answer to this is that the Federal Rules of Civil Procedure do not require a claimant to set out in detail the facts upon which he bases his claim. To the contrary, all the Rules require is "a short and plain statement of the claim" that will give the defendant fair notice of what the plaintiff's claim is and the grounds upon which it rests. The illustrative forms appended to the Rules plainly demonstrate this. Such simplified "notice pleading" is made possible by the liberal opportunity for discovery and the other pretrial procedures established by the Rules to disclose more precisely the basis of both claim and defense and to define more narrowly the disputed facts and issues. Following the simple guide of Rule 8(f) that "all pleadings shall be so construed as to do substantial justice," we have no doubt that petitioners' complaint adequately set forth a claim and gave the respondents fair notice of its basis. The Federal Rules reject the approach that pleading is a game of skill in which one misstep by counsel may be decisive to the outcome and accept the principle that the purpose of pleading is to facilitate a proper decision on the merits. Cf. *Maty v. Grasselli Chemical Co., 303 U.S. 197.…*

Individual court rules dictate the layout and contents of pleadings and must be consulted before attorneys file any document with the court. The diagram below shows some of the common elements that local court rules frequently address.

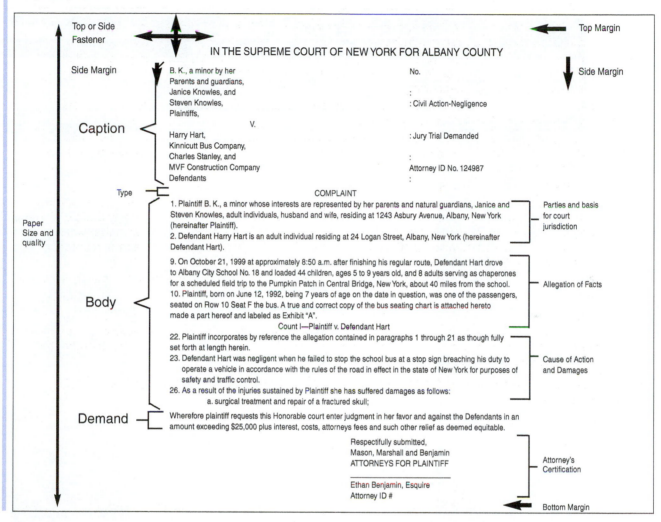

Notice pleading requires that enough information be included to give defendants notice of events and claims against them arising from those events. Fact pleading requires that all relevant facts that support each claim be included in the complaint.

In the state courts, state rules of civil procedure direct how a case must be commenced. Most states require the filing of a complaint as the initial pleading in a case. However, some state rules allow actions to be started by a petition in which the plaintiff must identify the exact basis of the civil lawsuit. The court, the legal team, and the defendants will rely on the allegations contained in the initial pleading. Those allegations will serve as the basis for all future court proceedings in the civil case.

Preparing the Summons

In the federal court system, the complaint must be accompanied by a summons and a civil cover sheet. Both forms are obtained from the court in which the complaint is filed. Most courts have forms available on their website that are easily downloaded, copied, and prepared. These forms request factual information about the litigants and the case.

Exhibit 8.7a Front of a PDF Form of Summons for the Federal District Court for the Southern District of Florida, with Highlighted Fields that can be Completed Online

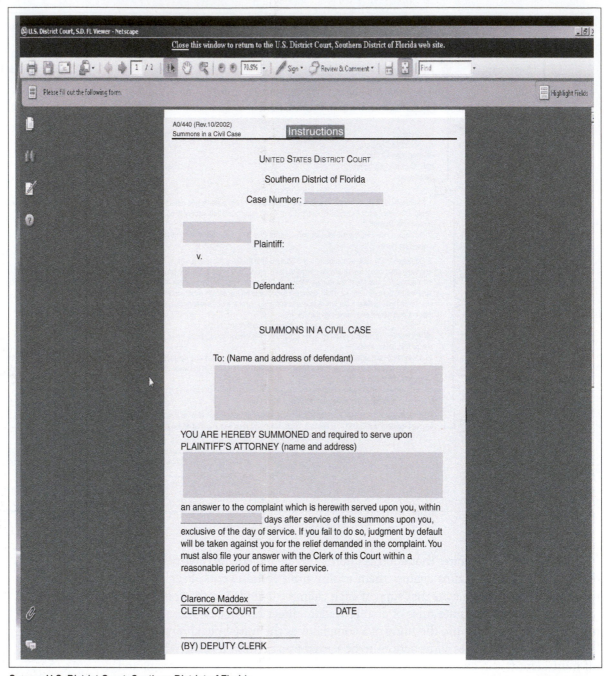

Source: U.S. District Court, Southern District of Florida.

summons

Document that advises the defendant he has been sued and gives the time frame within which he must respond; alerts him that a failure to respond may result in a loss of rights.

The **summons** advises the defendant of the suit and the time within which a response must be filed. It states that failure to respond will result in the loss of important rights, and it also explains how to obtain a lawyer. Exhibit 8.7a shows a summons in a federal court civil action. This form is available online from the court website in PDF format, allowing the form to be completed online and then printed. Exhibit 8.7b shows the second page of the summons, the Proof of Service form.

Exhibit 8.7b Back of a PDF Form of Summons for the Federal District Court for the Southern District of Florida, with Highlighted Fields that can be Completed Online

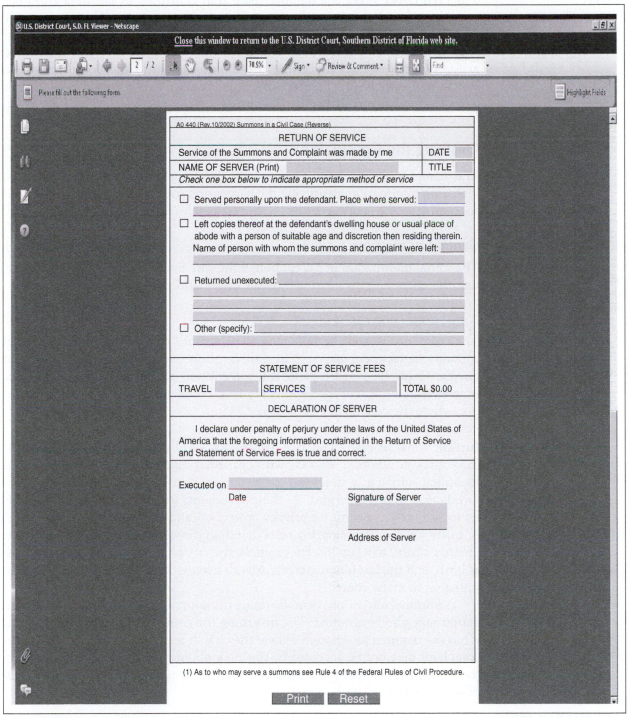

Source: U.S. District Court, Southern District of Florida.

The form is completed by the legal team filing the complaint. The clerk of court adds the court filing information, including court number and assigned judge, and finally, the summons is issued to the defendant.

The plaintiff's legal team makes arrangements for the summons and a copy of the complaint to be served on the defendant.

WEB RESOURCES

Forms for filing in federal court may be obtained online at http://www.uscourts .gov/FormsAndFees/Forms/ CourtFormsByCategory.aspx

Civil Cover Sheet

civil cover sheet
A summary page of information about a case.

Most courts also require that a civil cover sheet be attached to the complaint. The **civil cover sheet** is a summary page that is utilized by the data entry personnel in the clerk of court's office. These forms provide all the basic information on a single sheet and include the names and addresses of parties, trial counsel's contact information, and the types of claims asserted. This sheet assists court personnel in getting the information into the court's computer system more efficiently. Exhibit 8.8 is a civil cover sheet for the federal district court for the Eastern District of Michigan.

Drafting the Complaint

complaint
Initial pleading filed by the plaintiff designed to give notice to the defendant of the claims against her.

The **complaint** must have certain basic information dictated by court rule, including information identifying the parties and the cause of action, in a format acceptable to the court as defined in the court rules.

Caption of the Case

caption
Identity of the parties, the court, and the court-identifying information on the complaint.

The initial information in the **caption** of the case includes the identity of the parties, the court, and the court identifying information.

Numbered Paragraphs

The complaint is made up of numbered paragraphs that, to the extent practical, contain one fact per paragraph. In reality, it is rare that a paragraph will contain one fact; more likely, each paragraph will contain a group of facts that are inextricably related, such as the identification and residence of the defendant or location where the defendant can be served.

jurisdictional facts
Allegations demonstrating the court's jurisdiction over the persons and subject matter required in a complaint.

Jurisdictional Facts.   The first paragraphs of the complaint must establish the court's jurisdiction, also known as **jurisdictional facts.** The parties must be identified sufficiently to allow for a determination by the court whether it has jurisdiction over the persons. As these documents will become a part of the public record, new concerns for privacy protection and identity theft have resulted in many local courts adopting rules describing what information will suffice to identify a party to a lawsuit. For example, the city and state of residence, the year of birth, and the last four digits of a driver's license or Social Security number are sufficient in many courts.

Additional allegations demonstrating the court's jurisdiction over the subject matter may also be required. The first thing the court wants to determine is that it has the required jurisdiction to hear the case. If the court lacks jurisdiction, the complaint may not be accepted by the clerk of courts, or it may be dismissed by the court on motion of the defendant without any further inquiry into the cause of action of facts alleged.

> **PRACTICE TIP**
>
> Jurisdictional limits on the amount in controversy vary from court to court. Be sure to check the rules for the court where you intend to file the complaint to determine its jurisdictional limit.

> **WEB RESOURCES**
>
> Find the Judicial Conference Committee on Court Administration and Case Management on Privacy and Public Access to Electronic Case Files at the United States Courts website.

Background of the Cause of Action

The allegations in the complaint tell the client's story. This is usually accomplished by allegations of fact set forth in chronological order. The complaint sets out the facts that are the basis of the dispute. Some courts refer to this as the background section of the complaint because it contains the facts that are applicable to all the legal claims that arise from the transaction or occurrence.

Exhibit 8.8 Civil Cover Sheet for the Eastern District of Michigan (Online Form with Fillable Fields Highlighted)

JS 44 (Rev. 11/04)   **CIVIL COVER SHEET**   County in which this action arose _____

The JS 44 civil cover sheet and the information contained herein neither replace nor supplement the filing and service of pleadings or other papers as required by law, except as provided by local rules of court. This form, approved by the Judicial Conference of the United States in September 1974, is required for the use of the Clerk of Court for the purpose of initiating the civil docket sheet. (SEE INSTRUCTIONS ON THE REVERSE OF THE FORM.)

I. (a) PLAINTIFFS

DEFENDANTS

(b) County of Residence of First Listed Plaintiff _____
(EXCEPT IN U.S. PLAINTIFF CASES)

County of Residence of First Listed Defendant _____
(IN U.S. PLAINTIFF CASES ONLY)

NOTE: IN LAND CONDEMNATION CASES, USE THE LOCATION OF THE LAND INVOLVED.

(c) Attorney's (Firm Name, Address, and Telephone Number)

Attorneys (If Known)

II. BASIS OF JURISDICTION (Select One Box Only)

☐ 1 U.S. Government Plaintiff
☐ 3 Federal Question (U.S. Government Not a Party)
☐ 2 U.S. Government Defendant
☐ 4 Diversity (Indicate Citizenship of Parties in Item III)

III. CITIZENSHIP OF PRINCIPAL PARTIES (Select One Box for Plaintiff and One Box for Defendant)
(For Diversity Cases Only)

	PTF	DEF		PTF	DEF
Citizen of This State	☐ 1	☐ 1	Incorporated *or* Principal Place of Business In This State	☐ 4	☐ 4
Citizen of Another State	☐ 2	☐ 2	Incorporated *and* Principal Place of Business In Another State	☐ 5	☐ 5
Citizen or Subject of a Foreign Country	☐ 3	☐ 3	Foreign Nation	☐ 6	☐ 6

IV. NATURE OF SUIT (Select One Box Only)

CONTRACT	TORTS		FORFEITURE/PENALTY	BANKRUPTCY	OTHER STATUTES
☐ 110 Insurance	**PERSONAL INJURY**	**PERSONAL INJURY**	☐ 610 Agriculture	☐ 422 Appeal 28 USC 158	☐ 400 State Reapportionment
☐ 120 Marine	☐ 310 Airplane	☐ 362 Personal Injury - Med. Malpractice	☐ 620 Other Food & Drug	☐ 423 Withdrawal 28 USC 157	☐ 410 Antitrust
☐ 130 Miller Act	☐ 315 Airplane Product Liability	☐ 365 Personal Injury - Product Liability	☐ 625 Drug Related Seizure of Property 21 USC 881		☐ 430 Banks and Banking
☐ 140 Negotiable Instrument	☐ 320 Assault, Libel & Slander	☐ 368 Asbestos Personal Injury Product Liability	☐ 630 Liquor Laws	**PROPERTY RIGHTS**	☐ 450 Commerce
☐ 150 Recovery of Overpayment & Enforcement of Judgment	☐ 330 Federal Employers' Liability		☐ 640 R.R. & Truck	☐ 820 Copyrights	☐ 460 Deportation
☐ 151 Medicare Act	☐ 340 Marine	**PERSONAL PROPERTY**	☐ 650 Airline Regs.	☐ 830 Patent	☐ 470 Racketeer Influenced and Corrupt Organizations
☐ 152 Recovery of Defaulted Student Loans (Excl. Veterans)	☐ 345 Marine Product Liability	☐ 370 Other Fraud	☐ 660 Occupational Safety/Health	☐ 840 Trademark	☐ 480 Consumer Credit
☐ 153 Recovery of Overpayment of Veteran's Benefits	☐ 350 Motor Vehicle	☐ 371 Truth in Lending	☐ 690 Other	**SOCIAL SECURITY**	☐ 490 Cable/Sat TV
☐ 160 Stockholders' Suits	☐ 355 Motor Vehicle Product Liability	☐ 380 Other Personal Property Damage	**LABOR**	☐ 861 HIA (1395ff)	☐ 810 Selective Service
☐ 190 Other Contract	☐ 360 Other Personal Injury	☐ 385 Property Damage Product Liability	☐ 710 Fair Labor Standards Act	☐ 862 Black Lung (923)	☐ 850 Securities/Commodities/ Exchange
☐ 195 Contract Product Liability			☐ 720 Labor/Mgmt. Relations	☐ 863 DIWC/DIWW (405(g))	☐ 875 Customer Challenge 12 USC 3410
☐ 196 Franchise			☐ 730 Labor/Mgmt.Reporting & Disclosure Act	☐ 864 SSID Title XVI	☐ 890 Other Statutory Actions
REAL PROPERTY	**CIVIL RIGHTS**	**PRISONER PETITIONS**	☐ 740 Railway Labor Act	☐ 865 RSI (405(g))	☐ 891 Agricultural Acts
☐ 210 Land Condemnation	☐ 441 Voting	☐ 510 Motions to Vacate Sentence	☐ 790 Other Labor Litigation	**FEDERAL TAX SUITS**	☐ 892 Economic Stabilization Act
☐ 220 Foreclosure	☐ 442 Employment	**Habeas Corpus:**	☐ 791 Empl. Ret. Inc. Security Act	☐ 870 Taxes (U.S. Plaintiff or Defendant)	☐ 893 Environmental Matters
☐ 230 Rent Lease & Ejectment	☐ 443 Housing/ Accommodations	☐ 530 General		☐ 871 IRS—Third Party 26 USC 7609	☐ 894 Energy Allocation Act
☐ 240 Torts to Land	☐ 444 Welfare	☐ 535 Death Penalty			☐ 895 Freedom of Information Act
☐ 245 Tort Product Liability	☐ 445 Amer. w/Disabilities - Employment	☐ 540 Mandamus & Other			☐ 900 Appeal of Fee Determination Under Access to Justice
☐ 290 All Other Real Property	☐ 446 Amer. w/Disabilities - Other	☐ 550 Civil Rights			☐ 950 Constitutionality of State Statutes
	☐ 440 Other Civil Rights	☐ 555 Prison Condition			

V. ORIGIN (Select One Box Only)
☐ 1 Original Proceeding
☐ 2 Removed from State Court
☐ 3 Remanded from Appellate Court
☐ 4 Reinstated or Reopened
☐ 5 Transferred from another district (specify)
☐ 6 Multidistrict Litigation
☐ 7 Appeal to District Judge from Magistrate Judgment

VI. CAUSE OF ACTION
Cite the U.S. Civil Statute under which you are filing (Do not cite jurisdictional statutes unless diversity):

Brief description of cause:

VII. REQUESTED IN COMPLAINT:
☐ CHECK IF THIS IS A CLASS ACTION UNDER F.R.C.P. 23
DEMAND $ _____
CHECK YES only if demanded in complaint:
JURY DEMAND: ☐ Yes ☐ No

VIII. RELATED CASE(S) IF ANY (See instructions):
JUDGE _____
DOCKET NUMBER _____

DATE _____
SIGNATURE OF ATTORNEY OF RECORD _____

FOR OFFICE USE ONLY

RECEIPT # _____ AMOUNT _____ APPLYING IFP _____ JUDGE _____ MAG. JUDGE _____

Elements of the Cause of Action

The elements of the cause of action must be sufficiently alleged that the defendant has notice of the wrong claimed. Each cause of action will appear in the complaint as a separate count. For example, separate counts would be required in a suit alleging negligence and strict liability; each must be alleged in its own separate count. The defendant must be given sufficient information so that a response can be filed or others joined in the suit who may actually be responsible for the alleged harm that caused the injury or loss. Under federal rules, the complaint must contain "a short, plain statement of the claim showing that the pleader is entitled to relief..." (Fed. R. Civ. P. Rule 8). This rule has been interpreted to mean that the plaintiff must not plead every fact or element of the cause of action. In notice-pleading jurisdictions, as in federal court, the plaintiff must set forth just enough information that the claims against the defendant are discernible from the face of the complaint. Exhibit 8.9 shows an example of a federal notice pleading.

In fact-pleading jurisdictions, all facts relevant to establish all elements of the causes of action must be pleaded. Exhibit 8.10 shows an example of a fact-pleading complaint for the same notice-pleading complaint that appears in Exhibit 8.9.

Damage Allegation

The plaintiff must also be sure to include a statement setting out the damages alleged to have been caused by the defendant's wrongful conduct. This may include the allegation of personal physical injury, property damage, or other losses related to the harm caused by the defendant, including loss of wages or earning capacity.

prayer for relief
Also known as a wherefore clause, a paragraph that ends each count of the complaint and asks the court for the specific relief the plaintiff seeks.

wherefore clause
Also known as a prayer for relief, a paragraph that ends each count of the complaint and asks the court for the specific relief the plaintiff seeks.

Prayer for Relief.   The **prayer for relief,** also called the **wherefore clause,** is directly related to the statement of damages. This "WHEREFORE" paragraph ends each count of the complaint, asking the court for the specific relief the plaintiff seeks, such as:

"Wherefore the plaintiff demands judgment against the defendant in a sum exceeding $75,000.00 plus interests, costs, attorney's fees, and such other relief as the court deems reasonable."

Signatures

Each pleading in the federal system and, generally, in all state courts must be signed by the attorney filing the pleading. Under the federal rules, by signing the pleading, the attorney certifies that:

1. The attorney is familiar with the facts and claims presented;
2. There exists a basis in law for the claims asserted;
3. There is no improper purpose, such as harassment, for the filing;
4. An investigation into the facts has been conducted; and
5. To the best of the attorney's knowledge, the information contained in the complaint is true and accurate.

sanctions
Penalties imposed to punish wrongful behavior of litigants and their counsel; can include a monetary fine paid into court, dismissal of a claim, or payment of the reasonable attorney's fees.

Attorneys may be subject to sanctions if they file a frivolous claim or a claim unsupported by the facts (Fed. R. Civ. P. 11). **Sanctions** are designed to punish wrongful behavior of litigants and their counsel. Sanctions can include a monetary fine paid into court, dismissal of a claim, or payment of the reasonable attorney's fees for the one who was injured by the violation of the rule. Investigating facts and doing legal research before signing a pleading is thus an important step in civil litigation. Failure to take this step can result in charges of malpractice and sanctions imposed by the court. In some jurisdictions, a similar statement called a **verification** is prepared for the plaintiff to sign. The difference between a client's signature on a verification and an attorney's signature on a pleading is that the verification is signed by the client and is usually subject to criminal penalties related to perjury.

verification
Statement attached to the end of a pleading that is signed by the client and states that the information contained therein is true.

Exhibit 8.9 Notice-Pleading Complaint

UNITED STATES DISTRICT COURT - NORTHERN DISTRICT OF NEW YORK

B.K., a minor by her Parents and guardians,	:	No.: _____
Janice Knowles and	:	COMPLAINT
Steven Knowles, Plaintiff	:	CIVIL ACTION - NEGLIGENCE
v.	:	
Ronald Clemmons,	:	Jury Trial Demanded
Lower Council School District,		
Bud Smith, and	:	Attorney ID No. 124987
Ace Trucking Company, Defendants	:	

Plaintiff in the above captioned action alleges as follows:

JURISDICTION

1. Plaintiff and defendants are residents of different states and the amount in controversy exceeds $75,000.00, exclusive of interest and costs as specified in 28 U.S.C.§1332.

PARTIES

2. Plaintiff is B.K. a minor whose interests are represented by her parents and natural guardians, Janice and Steven Knowles, adult individuals, husband and wife, residing at 1243 Asbury Avenue, Bennington, Vermont (hereinafter Plaintiff).

3. Defendant, Ronald Clemmons is an adult individual residing at 24 Logan Street, Albany, New York (hereinafter Defendant Clemmons).

4. Defendant Lower Council School District is a governmental unit duly authorized and existing under the laws of the State of New York with its principal place of business being 701 Wilkes Road, Albany, New York (hereinafter Defendant School).

5. Defendant Bud Smith is an adult individual residing at 332 S. Hearn Lane, Pittsfield, Massachusetts (hereinafter Defendant Smith).

6. Defendant Ace Trucking Company is a corporation duly organized and existing under the laws of the State of New York with its principal place of business being 2501 Industrial Highway, Center Bridge, New York (hereinafter Defendant Ace).

7. At all relevant times, Defendant Clemmons, a 69 year old, duly licensed school bus driver, was employed by and under the direction, supervision and control of Defendant School.

8. At all relevant time Defendant Smith, a 46 year old, duly licensed truck driver, was employed by and under the direction, supervision and control of Defendant Ace.

9. On October 21, 2013, after finishing his regular route, Defendant Clemmons drove to Albany City School No. 18 and loaded 44 children, ages 5 to 9 years old, and 8 adults for a scheduled field trip.

10. Plaintiff, who was 7 old on the date in question, was a passenger on the bus, seated on Row 10 Seat F. A true and correct copy of the bus seating chart is attached hereto, made a part hereof and labeled as Exhibit "A".

11. At approximately 10:30 a.m., the bus was traveling north on SR-30A between 15 and 25 mph as it approached the intersection with SR-7. The north- and southbound traffic on SR-30A was controlled by an advance warning sign that indicated a stop ahead, a stop sign, flashing red intersection control beacons, pavement markings that included the word "STOP", and a stop bar.

12. Defendant Clemmons, who was looking for SR-7, saw the posted stop sign, slowed, but did not stop the bus, which then entered the intersection.

13. Upon entering the intersection, the bus was struck on the right side behind the real axel by a dump truck operated by Defendant Smith.

14. Defendant Smith was driving the dump truck with utility trailer, owed and operated by Defendant Ace. Defendant Smith was traveling about 45 mph westbound on SR-7. East- and westbound traffic on SR-7 at the intersection with SR-30A was controlled by flashing yellow intersection control beacons.

(continued)

Exhibit 8.9 (*continued*)

Count I – Plaintiff v. Defendant Clemmons

15. Plaintiff incorporates by reference the allegations contained in paragraphs 1 through 14 as though fully set forth at length herein.

16. Defendant Clemmons was negligent when he failed to stop the school bus at a stop sign.

17. As a result, Plaintiff was injured when the impact of the dump truck with the school bus she was thrown about the interior of the school bus striking her head and shoulders on the side and roof of the bus resulting in a fractured skull and fractured vertebra at C3 and 4, contusions and abrasions suffering damages, as follows:

   a. surgical treatment and repair of a fractured skull;

   b. placement of a halo brace upon her head and shoulders for stabilization and healing of vertebra fractures as C3 and 4;

   c. physical therapy to rehabilitate and restore the normal use of her head and neck;

   d. medical expenses related to the treatment and rehabilitation for the injuries sustained;

   e. time lost from school while hospitalized and unable to attend school;

   f. arranging and paying for private tutors to come to her home for missed school instruction;

   g. inability to participate in soccer, Daisy Scouts and other of life's pleasures, and;

   h. such other damages as will be proved at trial of this matter

Wherefore plaintiff requests this Honorable court enter judgment in her favor and against the Defendants in an amount exceeding $75,000 plus interest, costs, attorneys fees and such other relief as deemed equitable.

Count II – Plaintiff v. Defendant School

18. Plaintiff incorporates by reference the allegations contained in paragraphs 1 through 14 as though fully set forth at length herein.

19. Defendant School failed to properly supervise, control and direct its employee Defendant Clemmons

20. As a result of Defendant School negligence in employing and supervising Defendant Clemmons the collision of October 21, 2013 occurred causing plaintiff to suffer, as follows:

   a. surgical treatment and repair of a fractured skull;

   b. placement of a halo brace upon her head and shoulders for stabilization and healing of vertebra fractures as C3 and 4;

   c. physical therapy to rehabilitate and restore the normal use of her head and neck;

   d. medical expenses related to the treatment and rehabilitation for the injuries sustained;

   e. time lost from school while hospitalized and unable to attend school;

   f. arranging and paying for private tutors to come to her home for missed school instruction;

   g. inability to participate in soccer, Daisy Scouts and other of life's pleasures, and;

   h. such other damages as will be established at the trial of this matter.

Wherefore plaintiff requests this Honorable court enter judgment in her favor and against the Defendants in an amount exceeding $75,000 plus interest, costs, attorneys fees and such other relief as deemed equitable.

Count IV - Plaintiff v. Defendant Smith

21. Plaintiff incorporates by reference the allegations contained in paragraphs 1 through 14 as though fully set forth at length herein.

22. Defendant Smith was negligent in the operation and control of a dump truck driving too fast for conditions while approaching an intersection with flashing yellow lights.

23. As a result, Plaintiff was injured upon the impact of the dump truck with the school bus she was thrown about the interior of the school bus striking her head and shoulders on the side and roof of the bus resulting in a fractured skull and vertebra at C3 and 4 and suffered damages as follows:

   a. surgical treatment and repair of a fractured skull;

   b. placement of a halo brace upon her head and shoulders for stabilization and healing of vertebra fractures as C3 and 4;

   c. physical therapy to rehabilitate and restore the normal use of her head and neck;

   d. medical expenses related to the treatment and rehabilitation for the injuries sustained;

   e. time lost from school while hospitalized and unable to attend school;

   f. arranging and paying for private tutors to come to her home for missed school instruction;

Exhibit 8.9 *(continued)*

g. inability to participate in soccer, Daisy Scouts and other of life's pleasures, and;

h. such other damages as will be established in the trial of this matter.

Wherefore plaintiff requests this Honorable court enter judgment in her favor and against the Defendants in an amount exceeding $75,000 plus interest, costs, attorneys fees and such other relief as deemed equitable.

Count V – Plaintiff v. Defendant Ace

24. Plaintiff incorporates by reference the allegations contained in paragraphs 1 through 14 as though fully set forth at length herein.

25. Defendant Ace was negligent in failing to inspect and correct mechanical deficiencies to the brake system, the air hose linking the truck and the trailer, permitting use of a dump truck to pull a trailer, allowing its driver to operate a vehicle not designed to pull a trailer, and failed to properly supervise and train employee Smith concerning the rules of the road.

26. As a result of Defendant Ace's negligence the dump truck struck the school bus in which Plaintiff was a passenger, injuring her when upon impact she was thrown about the interior of the school bus striking her head and shoulders on the side and roof of the bus resulting in a fractured skull and vertebra at C3 and 4 and suffered the following damages:

a. surgical treatment and repair of a fractured skull;

b. placement of a halo brace upon her head and shoulders for stabilization and healing of vertebra fractures as C3 and 4;

c. physical therapy to rehabilitate and restore the normal use of her head and neck;

d. medical expenses related to the treatment and rehabilitation for the injuries sustained;

e. time lost from school while hospitalized and unable to attend school;

f. arranging and paying for private tutors to come to her home for missed school instruction;

g. inability to participate in soccer, Daisy Scouts and other of life's pleasures, and;

h. such other damages as will be established at the trial of this matter.

Wherefore plaintiff requests this Honorable court enter judgment in her favor and against the Defendants in an amount exceeding $75,000 plus interest, costs, attorneys fees and such other relief as deemed equitable.

Respectfully submitted,
Mason, Marshall and Benjamin
ATTORNEYS FOR PLAINTIFF

_____

Ethan Benjamin, Esquire
Attorney ID #
Mason, Marshall and Benjamin
Address
Albany, New York
Phone
Fax
Email

VERIFICATION

I, JANICE KNOWLES, verify that I am authorized to make this verification. I verify that the Complaint is true and correct to the best of my knowledge, information and belief. I understand that false statements herein are made subject to the penalties of perjury relating to unsworn falsification to authorities.

Date: _____   _____

JANICE KNOWLES

I, STEVEN KNOWLES, verify that I am authorized to make this verification. I verify that the Complaint is true and correct to the best of my knowledge, information and belief. I understand that false statements herein are made subject to the penalties of perjury relating to unsworn falsification to authorities.

Date: _____   _____

STEVEN KNOWLES

Exhibit 8.10 Fact-Pleading Complaint

IN THE SUPREME COURT OF NEW YORK FOR ALBANY COUNTY

B.K., a minor by her Parents and guardians, Janice Knowles and Steven Knowles, Plaintiff	: : :	No.: _____
	:	Civil Action - Negligence
v.	:	
Ronald Clemmons, Lower Council School District, Bud Smith, and Ace Trucking Company, Defendants:	: :	Jury Trial Demanded Attorney ID No. 124987

COMPLAINT

NOW comes the plaintiff, by her attorneys, Mason, Marshall and Benjamin and brings this complaint alleging as follows:

1. Plaintiff is B.K. a minor whose interests are represented by her parents and natural guardians, Janice and Steven Knowles, adult individuals, husband and wife, residing at 1243 Asbury Avenue, Albany, New York (hereinafter Plaintiff).

2. Defendant, Ronald Clemmons is an adult individual residing at 24 Logan Street, Albany, New York (hereinafter Defendant Clemmons).

3. Defendant Lower Council School District is a governmental unit duly authorized and existing under the laws of the State of New York with its principal place of business being 701 Wilkes Road, Albany, New York (hereinafter Defendant School).

4. Defendant Bud Smith is an adult individual residing at 332 S. Hearn Lane, Albany, New York (hereinafter Defendant Smith).

5. Defendant Ace Trucking Company is a corporation duly organized and existing under the laws of the State of New York with its principal place of business being 2501 Industrial Highway, Center Bridge, New York (hereinafter Defendant Ace).

6. At all relevant times, Defendant Clemmons, a 69 year old, duly licensed school bus driver, was employed by and under the direction, supervision and control of Defendant School.

7. At all relevant time Defendant Smith, a 46 year old, duly licensed truck driver, was employed by and under the direction, supervision and control of Defendant Ace.

8. On October 21, 2013 at approximately 7:20 a.m. Defendant Clemmons began transporting students to school on his regular morning route driving a 2005 full size school bus owned and operated by Defendant School.

9. On October 21, 2013 at approximately 8:50 a.m., after finishing his regular route, Defendant Clemmons drove to Albany City School No. 18 and loaded 44 children, ages 5 to 9 years old, and 8 adults serving as chaperons for a scheduled field trip to the Pumpkin Patch in Central Bridge, New York, about 40 miles from the school.

10. Plaintiff, born on June 12, 2006, being 7 years of age on the date in question, was one of the passengers, seated on Row 10 Seat F of the bus. A true and correct copy of the bus seating chart is attached hereto, made a part hereof and labeled as Exhibit "A".

11. Although familiar with the Central Bridge area, Defendant Clemmons had never been to the Pumpkin Patch.

12. Defendant School did not provide its driver, Defendant Clemmons with directions or a map to the site.

13. Defendant Clemmons asked a chaperone for directions which were obtained from a secretary in the school office.

14. Each school bus passenger seat was equipped with three color-coded lap belts, one color coded belt for each passenger in a seat. Each child was seated and restrained with a lap belt before the trip began for purposes of safety and supervision.

15. Departing the school about 9:20 a.m., Defendant Clemmons took the New York State Thruway west to exit 25A onto Interstate-88 (I-88) and then traveled west on I-88 toward exit 23, the intended exit.

Exhibit 8.10 *(continued)*

16. Defendant Clemmons was confused about the directions to the Pumpkin Patch and exited at exit 24, the wrong exit. Clemmons stopped the bus on the exit 24 ramp, turned the bus around, returned to I-88, and continued traveling to exit 23, the correct exit.

17. At the end of the exit ramp for exit 23, Defendant Clemmons turned right onto State Route 30A (SR-30A) and started looking for State Route 7 (SR-7).

18. At approximately 10:30 a.m., the bus was traveling north on SR-30A between 15 and 25 mph as it approached the intersection with SR-7. The north- and southbound traffic on SR-30A were controlled by an advance warning sign that indicated a stop ahead, a stop sign, flashing red intersection control beacons, pavement markings that included the word "STOP", and a stop bar.

19. At the same time, Defendant Smith was driving a dump truck towing a utility trailer owed and operated by Defendant Ace. Defendant Smith was traveling about 45 mph westbound on SR-7. East- and westbound traffic on SR-7 at the intersection with SR-30A was controlled by flashing yellow intersection control beacons.

20. As the school bus approached the intersection, several children on board saw the sign for the Pumpkin Patch that was beyond the intersection and yelled.

21. Defendant Clemmons, who was looking for SR-7, saw the posted stop sign, slowed, but did not stop the bus, which then entered the intersection where the dump truck struck it on the right side behind the rear axle.

Count I – Plaintiff v. Defendant Clemmons

22. Plaintiff incorporates by reference the allegations contained in paragraphs 1 through 21 as though fully set forth at length herein.

23. Defendant Clemmons was negligent when he failed to stop the school bus at a stop sign breaching his duty to operate a vehicle in accordance with the rules of the road in effect in the state of New York for purposes of safety and traffic control.

24. Defendant Clemmons breached the duty of care owed to the passengers of the bus when he violated the rules of the road failing to stop at the traffic control device.

25. As a direct result of Defendant Clemmons' negligence in the operation of the school bus, Plaintiff was injured when upon impact of the dump truck with the school bus she was thrown about the interior of the school bus striking her head and shoulders on the side and roof of the bus resulting in a fractured skull and fractured vertebra at C3 and 4, contusions and abrasions.

26. As a result of the injuries sustained by Plaintiff she has suffered damages as follows:

    a. surgical treatment and repair of a fractured skull;

    b. placement of a halo brace upon her head and shoulders for stabilization and healing of vertebra fractures as C3 and 4;

    c. physical therapy to rehabilitate and restore the normal use of her head and neck;

    d. medical expenses related to the treatment and rehabilitation for the injuries sustained;

    e. time lost from school while hospitalized and unable to attend school;

    f. arranging and paying for private tutors to come to her home for missed school instruction;

    g. inability to participate in soccer, Daisy Scouts and other of life's pleasures, and;

    h. such other damages as will be proved at trial of this matter

Wherefore plaintiff requests this Honorable court enter judgment in her favor and against the Defendants in an amount exceeding $25,000 plus interest, costs, attorneys fees and such other relief as deemed equitable.

Count II – Plaintiff v. Defendant School

27. Plaintiff incorporates by reference the allegations contained in paragraphs 1 through 21 as though fully set forth at length herein.

28. Defendant School failed to properly supervise, control and direct its employee Defendant Clemmons as follows

    a. failure to obtain proper medical certification of a bus driver known to have a heart condition, hypertension, and Type I Diabetes in violation New York Department of Motor Vehicles Article 19-A;

(continued)

Exhibit 8.10 *(continued)*

    b. failure to provide map and directions for drivers destination;

    c. failure to establish a policy to limit the eligibility of senior drivers known to be easily confused, distracted and unable to focus on multiple stimuli, and;

    d. such other negligence as may be discovered in preparation of the trial of this matter.

29. As a result of Defendant School negligence in employing and supervising Defendant Clemmons the collision of October 21, 2010 occurred causing plaintiff to suffer, as follows:

    a. surgical treatment and repair of a fractured skull;

    b. placement of a halo brace upon her head and shoulders for stabilization and healing of vertebra fractures as C3 and 4;

    c. physical therapy to rehabilitate and restore the normal use of her head and neck;

    d. medical expenses related to the treatment and rehabilitation for the injuries sustained;

    e. time lost from school while hospitalized and unable to attend school;

    f. arranging and paying for private tutors to come to her home for missed school instruction;

    g. inability to participate in soccer, Daisy Scouts and other of life's pleasures, and;

    h. such other damages as will be established at the trial of this matter.

Wherefore plaintiff requests this Honorable court enter judgment in her favor and against the Defendants in an amount exceeding $25,000 plus interest, costs, attorneys fees and such other relief as deemed equitable.

Count IV - Plaintiff v. Defendant Smith

30. Plaintiff incorporates by reference the allegations contained in paragraphs 1 through 21 as though fully set forth at length herein.

31. Defendant Smith was negligent in the operation and control of a dump truck driving too fast for conditions while approaching an intersection with flashing yellow lights.

32. As a direct result of Defendant Smith's negligence the dump truck he was operating struck the school bus in which Plaintiff was a passenger.

33. Plaintiff was injured when upon impact of the dump truck with the school bus she was thrown about the interior of the school bus striking her head and shoulders on the side and roof of the bus resulting in a fractured skull and vertebra at C3 and 4.

34. As a result of the injuries sustained by Plaintiff she has suffered damages as follows:

    a. surgical treatment and repair of a fractured skull;

    b. placement of a halo brace upon her head and shoulders for stabilization and healing of vertebra fractures as C3 and 4;

    c. physical therapy to rehabilitate and restore the normal use of her head and neck;

    d. medical expenses related to the treatment and rehabilitation for the injuries sustained;

    e. time lost from school while hospitalized and unable to attend school;

    f. arranging and paying for private tutors to come to her home for missed school instruction;

    g. inability to participate in soccer, Daisy Scouts and other of life's pleasures, and;

    h. such other damages as will be established in the trial of this matter.

Wherefore plaintiff requests this Honorable court enter judgment in her favor and against the Defendants in an amount exceeding $25,000 plus interest, costs, attorneys fees and such other relief as deemed equitable.

Count V – Plaintiff v. Defendant Ace

35. Plaintiff incorporates by reference the allegations contained in paragraphs 1 through 21 as though fully set forth at length herein.

36. Defendant Ace was negligent in failing to inspect and correct mechanical deficiencies to the brake system, the air hose linking the truck and the trailer, and permitting use of a dump truck to pull a trailer.

37. Defendant Ace was negligent in allowing its driver to operate a vehicle not designed to pull a trailer and failed to properly supervise and train employee Smith concerning the rules of the road.

Exhibit 8.10 (*continued*)

38. As a result of Defendant Ace's negligence the dump truck struck the school bus in which Plaintiff was a passenger.

39. Plaintiff was injured when upon impact of the dump truck with the school bus she was thrown about the interior of the school bus striking her head and shoulders on the side and roof of the bus resulting in a fractured skull and vertebra at C3 and 4.

40. As a result of the injuries sustained by Plaintiff she has suffered damages as follows:

   a. surgical treatment and repair of a fractured skull;

   b. placement of a halo brace upon her head and shoulders for stabilization and healing of vertebra fractures as C3 and 4;

   c. physical therapy to rehabilitate and restore the normal use of her head and neck;

   d. medical expenses related to the treatment and rehabilitation for the injuries sustained;

   e. time lost from school while hospitalized and unable to attend school;

   f. arranging and paying for private tutors to come to her home for missed school instruction;

   g. inability to participate in soccer, Daisy Scouts and other of life's pleasures, and;

   h. such other damages as will be established at the trial of this matter.

Wherefore plaintiff requests this Honorable court enter judgment in her favor and against the Defendants in an amount exceeding $25,000 plus interest, costs, attorneys fees and such other relief as deemed equitable.

Respectfully submitted,
Mason, Marshall and Benjamin
ATTORNEYS FOR PLAINTIFF

_____

Ethan Benjamin, Esquire
Attorney ID #
Mason, Marshall and Benjamin
Address
Albany, New York
Phone
Fax
Email

VERIFICATION

I, JANICE KNOWLES, verify that I am authorized to make this verification. I verify that the Complaint is true and correct to the best of my knowledge, information and belief. I understand that false statements herein are made subject to the penalties of perjury relating to unsworn falsification to authorities.

Date: _____   _____

JANICE KNOWLES

I, STEVEN KNOWLES, verify that I am authorized to make this verification. I verify that the Complaint is true and correct to the best of my knowledge, information and belief. I understand that false statements herein are made subject to the penalties of perjury relating to unsworn falsification to authorities.

Date: _____   _____

STEVEN KNOWLES

Checklist ☑

- Caption
- Body of the complaint
- Identification of parties
    - Jurisdictional facts
    - Background facts or those facts that apply to all causes of action
- Element of causes of action
    - Negligence
    - Breach of contract
    - Professional malpractice
    - Class actions
- Allegation of damages
- Prayer for relief (wherefore clause)
- Signature of attorney
- Affidavit or verification

PRACTICE TIP
UTAH DISTRICT COURT ADMINISTRATIVE GUIDE
PRIVACY

1. All counsel should carefully review proposed pleadings and attachments with regard to the inclusion of personal information. Certain types of sensitive information should not be included in documents filed with the Court. Personal information not protected will be available on the Internet via CM/ECF. If sensitive information must be included, the personal data identifiers must be redacted in the document.
   a. Social Security numbers—show only the last four numbers;
   b. Names of minor children—show only the initials;
   c. Dates of birth—show only the year;
   d. Financial account numbers—show only the last four numbers; and
   e. Home addresses—show only the city and state.
2. In addition, counsel shall carefully consider whether the following types of information should be redacted in court filing:
   a. Personal identifying numbers such as driver's license number;
   b. Medical records including treatment and diagnosis records;
   c. Employment history;
   d. Proprietary or trade secret information;
   e. Information regarding an individual's cooperation with the government;
   f. Information regarding the victim of criminal activity;
   g. National security information; and
   h. Sensitive security information described in 49 U.S.C. 114(s).
3. It is the sole responsibility of counsel and the parties to redact personal identifiers; the Clerk will not review any e-filed document to determine whether it includes personal information. All e-filers should review the Judicial Conference Privacy Policy and applicable court rules before entering documents on the CM/ECF system: *http://www.privacy.uscourts.gov*

Administrative Procedures 6 D-Utah Version 09-22-06

■ FILING AND SERVING THE COMPLAINT

Filing the complaint with the court is not a particularly difficult process. Most of the offices where the pleadings are filed use a checklist to be certain everything that is required is part of the filing—for example, the proper format, paper size, required number of copies, signatures of responsible counsel, affidavits (if required) of the parties, and filing fees. Filing requirements for courts with mandatory electronic filing can be located at the court's website.

Filing Fees

Filing fees must be paid at the time of filing of the complaint or summons to start the lawsuit, unless waived by the court. Most rules provide that the action is not considered commenced until the applicable fees have been paid to the court. In most cases, this is not an issue. However, it may be an issue if the person filing the pleading does not have the required fees and the applicable statute of limitations is going to expire unless the action is properly commenced by the deadline. Most court offices are open during specific business hours and expect that normal business, including the filing of pleadings, will occur during those hours. However, there is usually a procedure that provides an after-business-hours method for filing time-critical documents. It may involve a clerk or deputy who is on call or a judge who is available to accept documents. It is not that unusual for a potential client to appear with a claim on the day the statute of limitations will expire. The person who first learns of this deadline is the person conducting the initial interview, usually a paralegal conducting a screening interview. Therefore, paralegals must be alert to the issue and ask questions to determine the possible claims and dates of the alleged wrong. If a statute of limitations issue appears to be imminent, the paralegal must immediately contact his or her supervising attorney.

filing fees
Fees charged by the court system that must be paid at the time of filing the complaint.

PRACTICE TIP
Always know who the backup is for your supervising attorney in case he or she cannot be contacted. Be sure you have sufficient contact information including office numbers, home numbers, and cell phone numbers. Have a backup for the backup—if a statute of limitation is missed, the firm may be subject to a malpractice action.

Electronic Filing

Increasingly, jurisdictions require **electronic filing** of pleadings and documents. Some jurisdictions permit rather than require electronic filing. In either event, the requirements for electronic filing are not uniform or standardized. Each court has its own set of rules and requirements. The specific state or federal rules *and* local court rules for each court must be checked. The rules are constantly being changed as technology allows and experience requires. Some courts permit but do not require electronic filing of all pleadings; others allow filings that do not add or change named parties. Typically, the complaint accompanied by the civil cover sheet will be the document that causes the creation of a file in the court's computer system. Some courts require that a request for permission to use electronic filing be submitted with the complaint. Other forms, such as that from a California court shown in Exhibit 8.11, seek permission of the litigants for consent to electronic filing. Exhibit 8.12 shows a form for the United States District Court Waiver of the Service of Summons. Always consult the current local rules for the requirements for electronic filing, including the necessary format of the submitted files (Microsoft Word, Corel WordPerfect, PDF, or other file format). The importance of following the local rules cannot be underestimated with regard to electronic filing requirements.

electronic filing
Filing court documents by electronic means, such as e-mail.

Exhibit 8.11 California Consent to Electronic Service

(New, 12-01-02)

Form 13.
Consent to Electronic Service
Pursuant to Ninth Circuit Rule 25-3.3

I agree that _____,
(law firm or name of unrepresented litigant)

who represents _____ may electronically serve me
(name of party)

with copies of all documents filed with the court.

Electronic service shall be accomplished by (*check all that apply*):

_____   facsimile transmission to _____ (facsimile number)

_____   electronic mail at _____ (electronic mail address)
limited to documents created in the following word proceeding
formats: _____

_____   both facsimile transmission to _____ (facsimile number) and electronic
mail at _____ (electronic mail address) limited to documents created in the
following word processing formats_____

_____   Electronic service must be accompanied by simultaneous service by mail or
commercial carrier of a paper copy of the electronically served document.

DATED: _____   _____

Attorney for _____

(name of party)
Or Pro Se Litigant

Service of Process

service of process
Delivery of the complaint and summons to the defendant as required under the rules of civil procedure.

In federal district court cases, once the complaint is filed and the clerk issues the summons, the plaintiff has 120 days to arrange for **service of process**—delivery of the complaint and summons to the defendant. The purpose of service of process is to make sure the defendant receives notice of being sued and knows the time within which to respond or lose important rights. The Federal Rules of Civil Procedure provide the rules for effective service of process and provide a variety of methods to ensure that the defendant receives actual notice of the action filed against him or her (Fed. R. Civ. P. Rules 4 and 5).

The preferred method of service is personal service of the complaint and summons on the defendant. Generally, effective service is completed by an adult individual, not a party to the lawsuit, who hand-delivers the summons and a copy of the complaint to the defendant at his or her residence or usual place of business. The federal rules adopt the rules for service of the state court system in which the district court is located. If state rules permit leaving a copy of the complaint with any adult who appears to be in charge at the defendant's residence or place of business, that rule is valid for purposes of the federal district court.

On the reverse side of the federal court summons is an affidavit that is to be completed by the person serving the defendant and filed with the clerk of court

Exhibit 8.12 Consent to Electronic Service for Ninth Circuit Court of Appeals

---

AO 399 (01/09) Waiver of the Service of Summons

UNITED STATES DISTRICT COURT
for the

_____ ▾

_____	)	
Plaintiff	)	
v.	)	Civil Action No. _____
_____	)	
Defendant	)	

WAIVER OF THE SERVICE OF SUMMONS

To: _____

(Name of the plaintiff's attorney or unrepresented plaintiff)

I have received your request to waive service of a summons in this action along with a copy of the complaint, two copies of this waiver form, and a prepaid means of returning one signed copy of the form to you.

I, or the entity I represent, agree to save the expense of serving a summons and complaint in this case.

I understand that I, or the entity I represent, will keep all defenses or objections to the lawsuit, the court's jurisdiction, and the venue of the action, but that I waive any objections to the absence of a summons or of service.

I also understand that I, or the entity I represent, must file and serve an answer or a motion under Rule 12 within 60 days from _____, the date when this request was sent (or 90 days if it was sent outside the United States). If I fail to do so, a default judgment will be entered against me or the entity I represent.

Date: _____

	_____
	Signature of the attorney or unrepresented party
_____	
Printed name of party waiving service of summons	_____
	Printed name
	_____
	Address
	_____
	E-mail address
	_____
	Telephone number

Duty to Avoid Unnecessary Expenses of Serving a Summons

Rule 4 of the Federal Rules of Civil Procedure requires certain defendants to cooperate in saving unnecessary expenses of serving a summons and complaint. A defendant who is located in the United States and who fails to return a signed waiver of service requested by a plaintiff located in the United States will be required to pay the expenses of service, unless the defendant shows good cause for the failure.

"Good cause" does *not* include a belief that the lawsuit is groundless, or that it has been brought in an improper venue, or that the court has no jurisdiction over this matter or over the defendant or the defendant's property.

If the waiver is signed and returned, you can still make these and all other defenses and objections, but you cannot object to the absence of a summons or of service.

If you waive service, then you must, within the time specified on the waiver form, serve an answer or a motion under Rule 12 on the plaintiff and file a copy with the court. By signing and returning the waiver form, you are allowed more time to respond than if a summons had been served.

(see Exhibit 8.7b). The service affidavit lists the particulars of how service of the complaint and summons were completed—when, how, and on whom served. That information becomes part of the **docket entries** maintained in the clerk's office.

The federal rules also provide a procedure that waives formal or personal service of process and allows service by regular mail. This form of service is best utilized in cases where the litigants have been in contact prior to the institution of the lawsuit. Exhibit 8.13 shows the Notice of Lawsuit and Request to Waive Service of a Summons. Exhibit 8.14 shows the Federal District Court form for Waiver of the Service of Summons form AO 399. This optional procedure is designed to save costs and time for litigants. The defendant, if he or she agrees, will sign the waiver of service of process. The complaint is then served by mail. The signed waiver and an affidavit of service by mail are then filed with the clerk for inclusion in the docket entries. There are two benefits for the defendant: The defendant avoids the embarrassment of being personally served with legal documents at home or at the office, and the defendant receives an automatic extension of time for filing an answer to the complaint—sixty days rather than twenty days. There is also a financial incentive: If the defendant refuses to accept service by mail, the defendant will be responsible for the costs of personal service. These costs can be related to the costs of the U.S. Marshall, a sheriff, or a private process server traveling to the defendant's physical location and serving the defendant.

Finding the proper address for serving a pleading on a defendant may present difficulty. A defendant may have relocated or changed his business location, and finding a valid address will test the resourcefulness of the paralegal. Information on forwarding addresses can be obtained from the U.S. Postal Service, professional association directories, and online phone directories. Voter registration, driver's license, and automobile registrations are also good sources for locating a change of address. When all else fails, certain state rules (which are incorporated into the Federal Rules, Fed. R. Civ. P. 4(e)(1)) provide a mechanism for service of process by publication of a notice in a local newspaper. A motion seeking permission to use publication must be filed with the court, and the facts contained in the motion must demonstrate that reasonable efforts were made to determine the physical location of the defendant's home or place of business.

■ DEADLINES AND TIME CONSTRAINTS

After filing the complaint and having the summons issued, the plaintiff must serve the defendant within 120 days. Failure to serve the complaint within the 120 days can result in the complaint being dismissed. Alternatively, the plaintiff may file a motion seeking the court's permission to reinstate the complaint and reissue the summons.

The time for the defendant to file a responsive pleading begins when the complaint is served, not on the last day the complaint could have been served. If served with the traditional means—by U.S. Marshall, county sheriff, or private process server—the defendant has twenty days to respond to the complaint. If served by **notice and waiver**, the defendant has sixty days to respond. Failure to respond in a timely fashion permits the plaintiff to obtain a default judgment against the defendant. Default is not an automatic procedure but a right the plaintiff may enforce. Calculating for the due date is important for the plaintiff as well as the defendant, who must properly calculate the due date to avoid a **default judgment** for inaction.

docket entries
Written record maintained in the clerk of court's office listing documents filed with the court.

WEB RESOURCES
Learn more about selecting an investigator or process server at www.ServeNow.com and www.PInow.com

LEARNING OBJECTIVE 5
Create a timeline for litigation.

notice and waiver of service
Under the Federal Rules of Civil Procedure, a procedure in which formal service of process is waived and service by regular mail is acceptable.

default judgment
Judgment obtained by the plaintiff against the defendant in which the defendant has failed to respond in a timely fashion to the complaint.

Exhibit 8.13 Federal District Court Form AO 398

AO 398 (Rev. 01/09) Notice of a Lawsuit and Request to Waive Service of a Summons

UNITED STATES DISTRICT COURT
for the

_____ ▾

_____	)	
Plaintiff	)	
v.	)	Civil Action No. _____
_____	)	
Defendant	)	

NOTICE OF A LAWSUIT AND REQUEST TO WAIVE SERVICE OF A SUMMONS

To: _____

(Name of the defendant or - if the defendant is a corporation, partnership, or association - an officer or agent authorized to receive service)

Why are you getting this?

A lawsuit has been filed against you, or the entity you represent, in this court under the number shown above. A copy of the complaint is attached.

This is not a summons, or an official notice from the court. It is a request that, to avoid expenses, you waive formal service of a summons by signing and returning the enclosed waiver. To avoid these expenses, you must return the signed waiver within _____ days *(give at least 30 days, or at least 60 days if the defendant is outside any judicial district of the United States)* from the date shown below, which is the date this notice was sent. Two copies of the waiver form are enclosed, along with a stamped, self-addressed envelope or other prepaid means for returning one copy. You may keep the other copy.

What happens next?

If you return the signed waiver, I will file it with the court. The action will then proceed as if you had been served on the date the waiver is filed, but no summons will be served on you and you will have 60 days from the date this notice is sent (see the date below) to answer the complaint (or 90 days if this notice is sent to you outside any judicial district of the United States).

If you do not return the signed waiver within the time indicated, I will arrange to have the summons and complaint served on you. And I will ask the court to require you, or the entity you represent, to pay the expenses of making service.

Please read the enclosed statement about the duty to avoid unnecessary expenses.

I certify that this request is being sent to you on the date below.

Date: _____

_____
Signature of the attorney or unrepresented party

_____
Printed name

_____
Address

_____
E-mail address

_____
Telephone number

Exhibit 8.14 Form AO 399 Notice of Waiver of Service

AO 399 (01/09) Waiver of the Service of Summons

UNITED STATES DISTRICT COURT
for the

_____ ▼

_____	)
Plaintiff	)
v.	) Civil Action No. _____
_____	)
Defendant	)

WAIVER OF THE SERVICE OF SUMMONS

To: _____.
      (Name of the plaintiff's attorney or unrepresented plaintiff)

I have received your request to waive service of a summons in this action along with a copy of the complaint, two copies of this waiver form, and a prepaid means of returning one signed copy of the form to you.

I, or the entity I represent, agree to save the expense of serving a summons and complaint in this case.

I understand that I, or the entity I represent, will keep all defenses or objections to the lawsuit, the court's jurisdiction, and the venue of the action, but that I waive any objections to the absence of a summons or of service.

I also understand that I, or the entity I represent, must file and serve an answer or a motion under Rule 12 within 60 days from _____, the date when this request was sent (or 90 days if it was sent outside the United States). If I fail to do so, a default judgment will be entered against me or the entity I represent.

Date: _____

                                                                                         Signature of the attorney or unrepresented party

_____
Printed name of party waiving service of summons

                                                                        Printed name

                                                                                      Address

                                                                           E-mail address

                                                                       Telephone number

---

Duty to Avoid Unnecessary Expenses of Serving a Summons

Rule 4 of the Federal Rules of Civil Procedure requires certain defendants to cooperate in saving unnecessary expenses of serving a summons and complaint. A defendant who is located in the United States and who fails to return a signed waiver of service requested by a plaintiff located in the United States will be required to pay the expenses of service, unless the defendant shows good cause for the failure.

"Good cause" does *not* include a belief that the lawsuit is groundless, or that it has been brought in an improper venue, or that the court has no jurisdiction over this matter or over the defendant or the defendant's property.

If the waiver is signed and returned, you can still make these and all other defenses and objections, but you cannot object to the absence of a summons or of service.

If you waive service, then you must, within the time specified on the waiver form, serve an answer or a motion under Rule 12 on the plaintiff and file a copy with the court. By signing and returning the waiver form, you are allowed more time to respond than if a summons had been served.

All pleadings after the initial complaint and answer have a twenty-day response time. This includes the plaintiff's response to counterclaims or affirmative defenses asserted by the defendant and the response to any motion.

Calculating Deadlines

The rules of civil procedure governing the court in which the complaint has been filed will include a provision describing how time is calculated. Generally, counting begins with the day after receipt of a pleading. For example, for a complaint served today, day 1 is tomorrow, and the twenty calendar days that follow, including Saturdays, Sundays, and holidays, are counted to arrive at a due date. If the twentieth day falls on a Saturday, Sunday, or holiday, then the due date is the next regular business day of the court (Fed. R. Civ. P. 6). Under applicable court rules, when the number of days is less than eleven, Saturdays, Sundays, and intervening holidays may not be included in the calculation of days.

The paralegal generally will be responsible for entering the due dates and reminder dates into the firm's central calendaring system.

■ AMENDMENT OR SUPPLEMENT TO THE COMPLAINT

Sometimes counsel for the plaintiff discovers new information important to the complaint after it has been filed. The information could be the correct identification of a party to the lawsuit, an additional count seeking relief on alternate grounds, or the correction of erroneous material. As long as no responsive pleading has been filed, the plaintiff may freely amend his or her complaint. This rule holds true for all forms of pleadings—as long as no response has been filed, an amendment can be made without seeking court permission (Fed. R. Civ. P. 15).

Once a response has been filed, however, a motion must be filed requesting the court's permission to amend or supplement the pleading. The rationale for amending or supplementing the pleading is the same—to correct an error or add information previously unknown. The pleading may also be amended to make it match the evidence and claims submitted at trial.

LEARNING OBJECTIVE 6
Determine when amended or supplementary pleadings may be required.

CONCEPT REVIEW AND REINFORCEMENT

KEY TERMS

CHAPTER SUMMARY

PLEADINGS: COMPLAINT, SUMMONS, AND SERVICE

Introduction to Pleadings	Pleadings are the documents filed to commence and respond to a lawsuit. Initial pleadings are designed to give the responding party notice of the filing of the suit, the alleged wrong, and the claims for relief.
Rules of Court	Each court has a set of rules of civil procedure that establish the procedures that must be followed in all litigation. In the federal courts, it is the Federal Rules of Civil Procedure. The Federal Rules of Civil Procedure, as well as state rules of civil procedure, may be and frequently are amended by specific local rules, which attorneys must consult before preparing pleadings.
Statute of Limitations	The statute of limitations is a critical date that must be determined at the early stages in interviews with clients or potential clients. It is the time frame within which an action must be commenced, or the party will lose his or her right to use the courts to seek redress. Clients frequently appear at the law office on the day the statute of limitations will expire, and the paralegal must be alert to that possibility and always have a supervising attorney readily available to process the claim.
Pleadings	The initial pleading filed by the plaintiff is designed to give notice to the defendant of the claim(s) against him or her. It may be in the form of a writ of summons, a summons, or a complaint. Pleadings in federal court are typically notice pleadings designed to give the parties notice of the claims. Some states utilize fact pleadings, in which more details are provided of the alleged wrong and exact basis of the lawsuit. In the federal courts, the complaint is accompanied by a summons and a civil cover sheet. The summons, when completed by the clerk of court, advises the defendant of the suit, states the time within which response must be filed, and alerts him or her that a failure to respond may result in a loss of rights. The complaint consists of: 1. a caption 2. numbered paragraphs 3. jurisdictional facts 4. background of the cause of action 5. elements of the cause of action 6. damage allegation 7. prayer for relief 8. signature
Filing and Serving the Complaint	Filing the complaint includes paying the applicable fees to the clerk of court and submitting all of the documentation required under local court rules. Many courts permit electronic filing under specific local rules recognizing the technology available to the court and the particular resources available. The pleadings must be served effectively upon the defendant to give him or her notice of the institution of a lawsuit. In the federal courts, the complaint and summons must be served within 120 days of the date it is filed, or a motion must be filed to extend the date.

Deadlines and Time Constraints	Following the filing and service of every pleading, there is a time frame within which a responsive pleading must be filed. After the initial complaint and answer, additional pleadings typically must be responded to within twenty days of service.
Amendment or Supplement to the Complaint	If new information important to the pleading is discovered before the responding party has filed a response, an amended pleading may be served without seeking court permission. Once a response has been filed, a motion seeking court approval must be filed to amend any pleading.

REVIEW QUESTIONS AND EXERCISES

1. Which rules determine the form in which a civil action may be commenced?
2. What is the function of the initial pleading in a civil lawsuit?
3. What is the theory behind having rules of civil procedure?
4. What is the name of the rules used in federal courts? Where can a current copy of the federal rules be found on the Internet?
5. What is the effect of local rules on the Federal Rules of Civil Procedure?
6. What is the worst possible outcome if the local rules of civil procedure are not followed?
7. What is the purpose of a summons in a civil suit?
8. What is the statute of limitations?
9. What is the biggest danger for the paralegal with regard to the statute of limitations?
10. How is the statute of limitations extended for minors?
11. What is the purpose of the civil cover sheet?
12. What is included within the caption of the case?
13. How many facts may be alleged in a paragraph of a complaint under the federal rules?
14. Why are jurisdictional facts required to be alleged at the beginning of a complaint?
15. How much detail must be included in the paragraphs on the cause of action alleged by the plaintiff?
16. What types of damages may the plaintiff allege?
17. What is included in the wherefore clause?
18. How important are local rules for filing a complaint?
19. When will the court accept a filing as complete without the requisite filing fee?
20. What cautions should parties use when filing electronically with the court?
21. What is the time frame within which the plaintiff must serve the complaint on the defendant in federal court?
22. What methods may be used to serve a complaint on the defendant in federal court?
23. What is the purpose of the informal service of process in federal cases?
24. What conduct may result in a default judgment against the defendant?
25. Why would Saturdays, Sundays, and holidays be ignored when calculating the due date for responsive pleading under the federal rules?
26. When may an amendment to the complaint or other pleading be made without leave of court?

BUILDING YOUR PARALEGAL SKILLS

INTERNET AND TECHNOLOGY EXERCISES

1. Obtain the web addresses, physical addresses, and telephone and fax numbers for your state court and federal district court.

2. Using the web addresses obtained in number 1, obtain a listing of filing fees for complaints and other pleadings and the requirements for electronic filing in your state and federal courts.

3. Using an online legal research database, determine your state's statute of limitations for:
   a. personal injury sustained in an automobile accident
   b. breach of contract
   c. medical malpractice
4. Find the Judicial Conference Committee on Court Administration and Case Management on Privacy and Public Access to Electronic Case Files at http://www.privacy.uscourts.gov/requestcomment.htm.

5. Find your state court's website.
6. Using your state trial court website, determine whether there is a requirement for page size, margins, and font type.
7. Prepare and save a template for a complaint for use in your jurisdiction for state and federal courts.
8. Prepare the complaint for the case in Appendix 1 in proper format for your local and federal courts.
9. Calculate a timeline of case deadlines in your jurisdiction for the case in Appendix 1.

CIVIL LITIGATION VIDEO CASE STUDIES

Zealous Representation Issue: Signing Documents

A paralegal signs a pleading for the attorney so that the pleading can be filed before the statute of limitation expires.

After viewing the video at www.pearsonhighered.com/careersresources, answer the following questions.

1. May a paralegal ever sign a pleading for an attorney?
2. What procedures should the paralegal follow before taking any documents to the courthouse for filing?
3. What are your local court rules for signing pleadings? Federal court rules?

CHAPTER OPENING SCENARIO CASE STUDY

Use the Opening Scenario for this chapter to answer the following questions.
1. What policies and procedures should be set up to avoid duplication of efforts by the two offices working on the same case?
2. What solutions can be used to coordinate better where multiple parties are working on the same cases in different locations?

3. Who is responsible for tracking statutes of limitations for individual cases?
4. Who must sign the pleadings filed with the court? May a paralegal sign for an attorney when the attorney is not available?

COMPREHENSIVE CASE STUDY

SCHOOL BUS–TRUCK ACCIDENT CASE

Review the assigned case study in Appendix 2.
1. Prepare a summons and complaint for filing in your local federal district court.
2. For your local court:
   a. Prepare the necessary pleadings to initiate a lawsuit in your state court;
   b. determine the filing fees required;
   c. determine the location of the office where the complaint may be filed;
   d. determine whether the complaint may or must be filed electronically, and the procedure to follow if electronic filing is available or required;
   e. determine the hours during which the court accepts pleadings for filing.

BUILDING YOUR PROFESSIONAL PORTFOLIO AND REFERENCE MANUAL

CIVIL LITIGATION TEAM AT WORK

See page 18 for instructions on Building Your Professional Portfolio.

Policy Manual

Research the policy and procedure for the filing of pleadings after usual business hours in both the federal and state courts within your local jurisdiction. Include the information necessary for someone to file the initial pleadings to avoid the statute of limitations expiring, including phone numbers, addresses, and other contact information.

Forms

1. Forms for commencing a civil action in your jurisdiction including civil cover sheet, summons or notice to defend, and complaint.
2. Requirement for page size, margins, and font type.

Procedures

1. Checklist of documents, signatures, and fees for commencing a civil action.
2. Web addresses for:
   a. Federal Rules of Civil Procedure
   b. Local Rules of Civil Procedure
3. Determine whether your jurisdiction is a notice-pleading or fact-pleading state.
4. Procedure for service of a summons and complaint in your jurisdiction.
5. Method for calculating days and deadlines in your jurisdiction.

Contacts and Resources

Physical location of office for filing civil action, with hours of operation:
a. In your jurisdiction
b. Federal court

LEARNING OBJECTIVES

After studying this chapter, you should be able to:

1. Prepare a motion in proper format.

2. Explain how lawyers may use motions during the pleading phase of a case.

3. Explain how lawyers may use motions to compel opponents to comply with rules of court and evidence.

4. Describe the use of motions to terminate a case before trial.

5. Explain how motions may be used at the end of a trial.

CHAPTER 9

Motions Practice

OPENING SCENARIO

The litigation team at the law firm of Mason, Marshall and Benjamin was holding its weekly case review meeting. Ethan reported on his problems getting an expert examination of the truck that had been involved in the accident. They had notified the opposing counsel of their desire to have the vehicle and potentially defective parts preserved for examination by an expert witness. The defendant had refused to allow them the access they needed to make the inspection. Attorney Saunders suggested they prepare appropriate motions to compel inspection (and in the alternative, a motion for sanctions for spoliation that could be submitted, depending on what the judge indicated he would sign).

OPENING SCENARIO LEARNING OBJECTIVE

Prepare a motion to compel.

■ INTRODUCTION TO MOTIONS

motion
Formal request to the court seeking some type of relief during the course of the litigation.

Motions are used by the parties to the lawsuit to ask the court to intervene or act during the course of the litigation. Motions are not pleadings. Pleadings set forth the facts and the legal basis for recovery, and demand damages. Motions seek relief from certain actions or inactions that arise during the process of the litigation itself. Motions may be used at various times during the litigation to compel or restrain action of a party and the way the case proceeds through the court system. The requests made in a motion can be as simple as a request to extend time to respond to a complaint; or, they can be as complex as a request to end the litigation by the entry of summary judgment after a determination by the court that there is no genuine case or controversy to take to trial. Finally, motions may seek punishment of one of the parties to the lawsuit or his/her counsel.

■ FORM OF MOTIONS

LEARNING OBJECTIVE 1
Prepare a motion in proper format.

The form of all motions is the same as the form of pleadings (Fed. R. Civ. P. 7(b)). Motions include the caption of the case and a descriptive title that clearly identifies the nature of the motion, such as Motion for Summary Judgment. Under Fed. R. Civ. P. 10, the identity of the parties, issue presented, and action requested of the court are listed in individually numbered paragraphs, as shown in Exhibit 9.1.

It is good practice to attach to the motion a proposed form of the court order for the relief requested for the judge to sign, as shown in Exhibit 9.2. In some jurisdictions under local court rules, a proposed form of order is required to be attached as the first page or on top of the motion itself. This saves the judge from having his staff prepare the order, and it also saves the moving party from having to spend additional time in getting the relief sought. With the proposed order attached, the judge will usually sign the order immediately after hearing the legal argument of counsel. It also ensures that the **movant** (party filing the motion) receives the relief requested.

movant
The party who files a motion.

certificate of service
Form required by the court certifying the manner and method in which service is made; used after personal service of the complaint for all other pleadings.

Like pleadings, motions must be served on all parties to the lawsuit, even if they are not affected by the relief requested. The filing of a **certificate of service** indicating that the motion was served may be required with the motion or within a specified time after filing as set by local court rule. See Exhibit 9.3.

Under federal court rules, service by using the U.S. Mail is sufficient. In the federal court system, the motion is accompanied by a **notice of motion,** which briefly describes the nature of the motion and lists the hearing date and the time within which a response to the motion should be filed. See Exhibit 9.4.

notice of motion
Form required by the court that the movant sends with the motion to the responding party; it usually provides a summary of the motion and a hearing and response date.

While members of the legal team may refer to *Motions Practice* as though it is a separate area of the law, it is actually a part of the procedure of every lawsuit that is filed.

■ MOTIONS IN THE PLEADING PHASE

LEARNING OBJECTIVE 2
Explain how lawyers may use motions during the pleading phase of a case.

In the initial phases of a case, a motion may be filed with the court requesting that the time to respond to a pleading be extended, requesting default be entered for failure to respond to a complaint in a timely manner, or requesting that the lawsuit be terminated for failing to allege a proper basis in law or fact.

Exhibit 9.1 Motion for Summary Judgment

UNITED STATES DISTRICT COURT - NORTHERN DISTRICT OF NEW YORK

B.K., a minor by her
Parents and Guardians,
Janice Knowles and
Steven Knowles,
Plaintiff

v.

Ronald Clemmons,
Lower Council School District,
Bud Smith, and
Ace Trucking Company,
Defendants

No.: _____

DEFENDANT SMITH'S
MOTION FOR
SUMMARY JUDGMENT

Attorney ID No. 124987

Defendant Smith files this Motion for Summary Judgment and alleges as follows:

1. At all relevant time Smith was an employee of and under the direction and control of Ace Trucking Company. (Complaint p. 7 Answer of Smith and Ace p. 7).

2. Ace Trucking supplied the truck operated by Smith and was responsible for the the replacement parts, care, maintenance and safe operation of the truck. (Complaint p. 36 and Answer of Ace p. 36).

3. Ace Construction admitted the brakes of the truck were defective and there was no driver error (Answer Ace pp. 36–38, Defendant Ace's Answer to Plaintiff's Interrogatories q. 8 through 10).

4. The mechanic for Ace Trucking, Chuck Dentson, testified at deposition that he made the decision to save the company money and purchase a lesser grade brake pad for installation on the truck. (Dentson deposition pp. 15–20)

5. James Kaercher, an expert in accident reconstruction with air brake failure, testified at deposition that the failure of the brakes, related to the over heating of sub-standard brake pads, was without warning to the operator of the vehicle. (Kaercher deposition pp. 78–83)

6. Kaercher further testified that only the mechanic conducting an inspection of the brakes would have been able to discover the defect related to brake pads. (Kaercher deposition p. 85 ll. 15–25).

7. Kaercher stated that failure of the brakes would have been sudden, allowing the driver no opportunity to make a sudden or fast stop. The only way to stop the truck would be through a gradual slowing across a long flat surface or use of an emergency truck ramp. (Kaercher deposition p. 90 ll. 1–13).

8. The road on which the accident occurred was a downward slope with no emergency truck ramps. (Report of State Police attached as exhibit A).

9. The failure of the sub-standard replacement brake pads, the failure of Ace and its employees to properly inspect and maintain the braking system and the inability to make fast stops as a result, serve to cut the nexus of causation that Smith was negligent in the operation of the truck.

10. As a matter of law Smith is entitled to judgment in this favor and against the Plaintiff.

WHEREFORE it is respectfully requested that judgment in favor of Smith be entered and the action against him be dismissed.

Respectfully submitted,

Motion to Enlarge Time to Respond

Upon receipt of the complaint, the defendant and counsel have critical decisions to make with little time to investigate and prepare the Answer. If the complaint has been personally served on the defendant, there are just 20 days to respond. A **motion to extend the time to respond** (Fed. R. Civ. P. 6) may be required. It is

motion to extend the time to respond
A request for a court order allowing additional time to respond.

Exhibit 9.2 Order for Summary Judgment

UNITED STATES DISTRICT COURT - NORTHERN DISTRICT OF NEW YORK

B.K., a minor by her Parents and Guardians, Janice Knowles and Steven Knowles, Plaintiff	: : :	No.: _____
v.	:	DEFENDANT SMITH'S MOTION FOR SUMMARY JUDGMENT
Ronald Clemmons, Lower Council School District, Bud Smith, and Ace Trucking Company, Defendants	: :	Attorney ID No. 124987

ORDER

AND NOW, this _____ day of _____, 20__, upon consideration of the within Motion for Summary Judgment, the responses thereto, the Pleadings and the items of Record presented it is hereby ORDERED that judgment is entered in favor of the defendant Bud Smith and against the plaintiff and the counts of the complaint against him are dismissed with prejudice.

_____
J.

Exhibit 9.3 Certificate of Service

UNITED STATES DISTRICT COURT - NORTHERN DISTRICT OF NEW YORK

B.K., a minor by her Parents and Guardians, Janice Knowles and Steven Knowles, Plaintiff	: : :	No.: _____
v.	:	DEFENDANT SMITH'S MOTION FOR SUMMARY JUDGMENT
Ronald Clemmons, Lower Council School District, Bud Smith, and Ace Trucking Company, Defendants	: :	Attorney ID No. 124987

CERTIFICATE OF SERVICE

The undersigned certifies that the document described below was served on the parties listed below by first class mail postage prepaid delivered at the post office in Albany, New York 05432 on October 15, 2014.

Document served: Defendant Smith's Motion for Summary Judgment with Proposed Order and Notice of Motion

Parties Served: Ethan Benjamin, Esquire
                         Roy Saunders, Esquire
                         Counsel for plaintiff
                         Mason, Marshall and Benjamin
                         Street address
                         Albany New York

                         William Buchter, Esquire
                         Counsel for Defendants Clemmons and Lower Council School District
                         Street Address
                         Albany, New York

Exhibit 9.4 Notice of Motion in Federal Court

UNITED STATES DISTRICT COURT - NORTHERN DISTRICT OF NEW YORK

B.K., a minor by her Parents and Guardians, Janice Knowles and Steven Knowles, Plaintiff v. Ronald Clemmons, Lower Council School District, Bud Smith, and Ace Trucking Company, Defendants	: : : : : : :	No.: _____ DEFENDANT SMITH'S MOTION FOR SUMMARY JUDGMENT Attorney ID No. 124987

NOTICE OF MOTION

PLEASE TAKE NOTICE that upon attached Motion for Summary Judgment the supporting material referred to therein and the Memorandum of Law in support thereof Defendant Bud Smith, will move this court, before the honorable Judge Raleigh Newsome, U.S.D.J., in Court room ____ United States Courthouse, _____ , on the day of 21st day of November 2014 at 10:00 a.m. or as soon thereafter as counsel can be heard, for an order pursuant to Rule of the Federal Rules of Civil Procedure granting Judgment in favor of the Defendant Smith and against the plaintiff and dismissing those counts of the complaint relevant to him with prejudice.

Dated: October 15, 2014

_____
John Morris, Esquire
Attorney for Defendant Smith

---

common to informally request from opposing counsel an extension of time to file a responsive pleading. If that request is granted, the legal team must prepare and file a **stipulation** with the court. Exhibit 9.5 is a stipulation for extension of time to respond.

stipulation
An agreement of the parties.

PRACTICE TIP

Granting an extension is a courtesy that firms hope to have reciprocated. At some point, everyone has an emergency or other obligation that requires asking for an extension. Attorneys remember those who have extended that courtesy and those who have not.

If opposing counsel refuses, a motion for enlargement of time to respond to the complaint should be prepared and filed. These motions are granted liberally by the court so long as there is no indication of bad faith or undue delay on the part of the movant. Exhibit 9.6 is a motion for enlargement of time.

Motion for Default Judgment

When the defendant fails to file a timely response to a complaint, including an answer or motion to enlarge time to respond, the plaintiff may request a **default judgment** be entered (Fed. R. Civ. P. 55). Entry of default judgment is not automatic; rather, the plaintiff's counsel must file a motion for a default judgment with the court. In most state courts, the entry of the default judgment on the record terminates the lawsuit. In the federal court system, this is a multistep process.

default judgment
Judgment obtained by the plaintiff against the defendant where the defendant has failed to respond in a timely fashion to the complaint.

Exhibit 9.5 Stipulation for Extension of Time to Respond

UNITED STATES DISTRICT COURT - NORTHERN DISTRICT OF NEW YORK

B.K., a minor by her Parents and Guardians, Janice Knowles and Steven Knowles, Plaintiff	:	No.: _____
	:	
	:	STIPULATION FOR EXTENSION OF TIME TO ANSWER COMPLAINT
	:	
v.	:	CIVIL ACTION - NEGLIGENCE
Ronald Clemmons, Lower Council School District, Bud Smith, and Ace Trucking Company, Defendants	:	Jury Trial Demanded
	:	
		Attorney ID No. 124987

STIPULATION FOR EXTENSION OF TIME TO ANSWER COMPLAINT

On this ____ day of _____, 2014, it is stipulated and agreed between counsel for Plaintiff and counsel for Defendant Smith, that Defendant Smith's Answer to the Complaint shall be filed within 90 days of the service of the complaint but in no event shall the Answer be filed later than August 30, 2014, and that an order consistent with this Stipulation be entered without further notice.

Respectfully submitted,

_____
Ethan Benjamin, Attorney for Plaintiff

_____
John Morris, Attorney for Defendant Smith

SO ORDERED
THIS ____ DAY OF _____, 2014

_____
JUDGE

Entry of Default on the Docket

docket
The clerk of court's official record of action on a case.

In federal court, the process begins with filing a request for entry of default. Along with an affidavit describing the facts of default, the plaintiff asks the clerk of the court to enter the defendant's default on the **docket.** Entry of default on the docket prevents the clerk of court from accepting an answer from the defendant after the due date for the Answer. Exhibit 9.7 shows the request for entry of default and supporting affidavit.

Entry of Default Judgment

The next step is to request entry of default judgment, which has two variations, depending upon whether the damages are ascertainable.

Judgment can, in some cases, be entered for a specific sum simply by referring to the information contained in the complaint; for example, a default judgment is entered for failure to make payments under the terms of a mortgage. The complaint should show the amount due and the daily interest rate; the judgment

Exhibit 9.6 Motion for Enlargement of Time

UNITED STATES DISTRICT COURT - NORTHERN DISTRICT OF NEW YORK

B.K., a minor by her Parents and Guardians, Janice Knowles and Steven Knowles, Plaintiff	: : : : :	No.: _____ **MOTION TO ENLARGE TIME TO ANSWER COMPLAINT**
v.	:	CIVIL ACTION - NEGLIGENCE
Ronald Clemmons, Lower Council School District, Bud Smith, and Ace Trucking Company, Defendants	: :	Jury Trial Demanded Attorney ID No. 097531

MOTION OF DEFENDANTS BUD SMITH AND ACE TRUCKING TO ENLARGE TIME TO ANSWER COMPLAINT

Defendants Bud Smith and Ace Trucking file this Motion for relief and allege as follows:

1. On May 12, 2014, Plaintiff personally served a Summons and Complaint upon Defendant Bud Smith by hand delivering to him at his home address.

2. On May 16, 2014, Plaintiff personally served a Summons and Complaint upon Defendant Ace Trucking by hand delivering a copy to Ace's local office.

3. An Answer to the Complaint was due on June 1, 2014, from Smith and June 5, 2014, for Ace.

4. At the time the Complaint was served, Defendant Ace's employee, Smith, who was operating a company vehicle on the date of the accident, was on vacation and not scheduled to return to work until May 31, 2014.

5. Under ordinary circumstances, twenty days would be insufficient time for Defendants Smith and Ace to properly investigate, prepare a response and raise defenses to the multiple claims set forth in the Plaintiff's Complaint.

6. The fact that Defendant Ace's key employee in unavailable until six days before the response is due makes the enlargement of time to respond a necessity.

7. On May 18, 2014, Counsel for Defendants Smith and Ace attempted to contact Plaintiff's counsel to arrange for a stipulation to extend time. To date Plaintiff's counsel has not replied.

8. To promote fairness, Defendants Smith and Ace seek an enlargement of sixty days from the date of this Motion to respond to the Complaint.

WHEREFORE, it is respectfully requested this Honorable court enter an order granting Defendants Smith and Ace an enlargement of time of sixty days to respond to the complaint.

Respectfully submitted,

_____

John Morris, Esquire
Attorney for Defendants

(continued)

Exhibit 9.6 (continued)

UNITED STATES DISTRICT COURT - NORTHERN DISTRICT OF NEW YORK

B.K., a minor by her Parents and Guardians, Janice Knowles and Steven Knowles, Plaintiff v. Ronald Clemmons, Lower Council School District, Bud Smith, and Ace Trucking Company, Defendants	: No.: _____ : : MOTION TO ENLARGE : TIME TO ANSWER : COMPLAINT : CIVIL ACTION - NEGLIGENCE : Jury Trial Demanded : Attorney ID No. 124987

ORDER

AND NOW this _____ day of _____, 2014, the matter having been brought before the court on Defendants Smith and Ace's Motion to Enlarge Time to Answer Complaint and after consideration of the Reply and the hearing on this matter is it hereby ORDERED that Defendants Smith and Ace shall within sixty (60) days of the date hereof file their responses to the Plaintiff's Complaint.

BY THE COURT:

_____
J.

Exhibit 9.7 Request for Entry of Default and Supporting Affidavit

---

UNITED STATES DISTRICT COURT - NORTHERN DISTRICT OF NEW YORK

B.K., a minor by her Parents and Guardians, Janice Knowles and Steven Knowles, Plaintiff v. Ronald Clemmons, Lower Council School District, Bud Smith, and Ace Trucking Company, Defendants	: No.: _____ : : REQUEST FOR ENTRY : OF DEFAULT : CIVIL ACTION - NEGLIGENCE : : Jury Trial Demanded : Attorney ID No. 124987

REQUEST FOR ENTRY OF DEFAULT ON THE DOCKET
WITH AFFIDAVIT IN SUPPORT

TO THE CLERK OF COURT:

Defendant Bud Smith, having failed to answer or otherwise respond or appear in the above captioned action, and the time for appearance having expired, kindly enter his default upon the docket pursuant to Rule 55(a) of the Federal Rules of Civil Procedure. An affidavit in support of the within written request appears on the following page.

Dated _____

Respectfully submitted,
Mason, Marshall and Benjamin
Attorneys for the Plaintiff

(continued)

Exhibit 9.7 (*continued*)

UNITED STATES DISTRICT COURT - NORTHERN DISTRICT OF NEW YORK

B.K., a minor by her Parents and Guardians, Janice Knowles and Steven Knowles, Plaintiff	: : :	No.: _____ REQUEST FOR ENTRY OF DEFAULT - Affidavit
v.	: :	CIVIL ACTION - NEGLIGENCE
Ronald Clemmons, Lower Council School District, Bud Smith, and Ace Trucking Company, Defendants	: :	Jury Trial Demanded Attorney ID No. 124987

AFFIDAVIT IN SUPPORT OF REQUEST FOR ENTRY OF DEFAULT

State of New York
County of _____

Ethan Benjamin being duly sworn says:

1. I am the attorney for the plaintiff in the above captioned matter.
2. A copy of the Summons and Complaint were served on Defendant Bud Smith on May 16, 2014, and return of service of Dennis Hall, Process Server has been filed with the clerk.
3. Defendant Smith has not answered or otherwise appeared in the action and the time to respond has expired.

_____

Ethan Benjamin, Esquire

Sworn and subscribed before me, a notary public
This _____ day of _____, 2014.

_____
NOTARY PUBLIC

---

amount can be calculated and entered. If the damages requested in the plaintiff's complaint represent a sum certain or a sum easily ascertainable by referring to the complaint, the clerk may enter judgment in that amount against the defendant upon a request to enter judgment accompanied by an affidavit of counsel. Exhibit 9.8 is a motion to enter default judgment.

In many cases, the damages cannot be calculated by referring to the face of the complaint. A personal injury action will seek damages for some items that can be calculated (lost wages and medical bills) and some that are not easily calculated (pain and suffering). Where damages cannot be reliably calculated, a motion to enter default judgment and request for hearing on damages must be submitted to the court for approval. The clerk will enter default judgment as to liability of the defendant on the docket of the court. Then a hearing will be held to determine the damages.

Setting Aside Default

A defendant who has a default judgment entered against him is not without recourse. In the interests of promoting justice, every jurisdiction has a mechanism that permits a default to be set aside as long as the defendant can demonstrate good cause for failure to file his answer in a timely manner. It could be that a defendant was prevented from meeting with an attorney because of health

Exhibit 9.8 Motion to Enter Default Judgment

UNITED STATES DISTRICT COURT - NORTHERN DISTRICT OF NEW YORK

B.K., a minor by her Parents and Guardians, Janice Knowles and Steven Knowles, Plaintiff	:	No.: _____
	:	
	:	**MOTION FOR ENTRY OF DEFAULT JUDGMENT**
v.	:	**CIVIL ACTION - NEGLIGENCE**
	:	
Ronald Clemmons, Lower Council School District, Bud Smith, and Ace Trucking Company, Defendants	:	Jury Trial Demanded
	:	Attorney ID No. 124987

MOTION FOR ENTRY OF DEFAULT JUDGMENT

The plaintiff in the above entitled action requests that judgment by default be entered against the Defendant Bud Smith in the amount of $ _____ plus interest and costs.

Respectfully submitted,
Mason, Marshall and Benjamin
ATTORNEYS FOR PLAINTIFF

or family reasons. It could be that the attorney hired to answer the complaint failed to do so. So long as the defendant can establish a reason other than simple neglect, the court will permit the default to be set aside.

In the federal court system, setting aside a default judgment requires filing a motion clearly describing the reason. The sooner a motion to set aside a default is filed, the better for the defendant. Length of delay in notifying the court can play a part in the court's decision to grant or deny the motion. It is not unusual to file a motion to extend time to respond combined with the motion to set aside default.

subject matter jurisdiction
The authority of a court to hear and decide a particular type of dispute.

personal jurisdiction
Requires the court to have authority over the persons as well as the subject matter of the lawsuit.

venue
Process of determining in which court to file a lawsuit when more than one court has subject matter and personal jurisdiction.

insufficiency of process
Failure to properly serve process, such as a complaint, on another party.

indispensable party
A party whose interest would be affected by a court's ruling.

PRACTICE TIP

A motion to extend time to answer a complaint should be filed simultaneously with the motion to set aside default. The combination of the two motions shows the court due diligence on the part of the defendant to correct his earlier oversight.

Rule 12(b) Motions

Under Federal Rule 12, defenses to any complaint must be included in the defendant's answer to the complaint. In some cases, where those defenses could result in the swift conclusion of the litigation, the defendant will file a motion to dismiss the complaint rather than filing an answer. The grounds for dismissing an action include lack of **subject matter jurisdiction,** lack of **personal jurisdiction,** lack of **venue, insufficiency of process,** defect in the service of process, failure to state a claim upon which relief can be granted, and failure to join an **indispensable party.** These grounds to dismiss the complaint are found under federal Rule 12(b). The defense team must first read and analyze the complaint for a possible motion to dismiss under the Rule. If there are no grounds to dismiss

Exhibit 9.9 Federal Rules of Civil Procedure Rule 12(b) Grounds for Dismissal of Complaint

Fed. R. Civ. P. Rule 12 Grounds for Dismissal

1. Lack of subject matter jurisdiction
2. Lack of personal jurisdiction
3. Lack of venue
4. Insufficiency of process
5. Defect in the service of process
6. Failure to state claim upon which relief can be granted
7. Failure to join an indispensable party

the complaint under Rule 12, the defendant must file an answer to the complaint (Fed. R. Civ. P. 12(a)(1)(A)).

A Rule 12(b) Motion to Dismiss is related to the type of defect for which the complaint may be dismissed.

Some of the grounds for dismissal are easily cured by the plaintiff. Exhibit 9.9 provides a summary of the grounds for dismissal.

If the defendant files a motion to dismiss, assuming the **statute of limitations** is not close to expiring, the plaintiff may easily cure most of these defects. If the complaint was filed in the wrong court for purposes of subject matter or personal jurisdiction, the plaintiff may simply withdraw the complaint and file it in the correct court. If the jurisdiction is correct but the venue is wrong, the plaintiff may simply request the court to transfer the case to the court that has proper venue. Where the complaint or summons incorrectly identifies a party, or the service of process is defective, the plaintiff can make the necessary corrections and arrange for service of the revised complaint. Where a party necessary to the lawsuit had not been included, the complaint can be amended to include that indispensable party.

A fatal flaw in the plaintiff's complaint is the failure to state the facts or law necessary to grant the plaintiff the relief requested. Under these circumstances, the plaintiff has stated a group of facts that fail to support any legal claim; for example, failure to allege that the defendant was the cause of an auto accident. The accident and damages sustained by the plaintiff are clearly stated in the complaint, but with no allegation that the defendant's actions caused the harm, the complaint is deficient. Alternatively, the facts may not give rise to a legally recognized cause of action, such as a claim for emotional distress because of hurt feelings over criticism from a teacher. In essence, the complaint fails to set forth a recognized legal claim for which the plaintiff is entitled relief. Exhibit 9.10 shows a sample motion to dismiss under Fed. R. Civ. P. 12(b)(6), Failure to State a Claim Upon Which Relief Can Be Granted.

Courts tend to be liberal in hearing and ruling on motions to dismiss. They don't want to deny a remedy on a technicality, particularly when it is one that can easily be corrected. For those that are easily curable, the court will order the plaintiff to make the correction within a short period of time, usually ten to twenty days. For the failure to state a claim upon which relief can be granted, the court will likely grant the plaintiff the right to amend the complaint. Thereafter, the complaint is served and the defendant must file an answer.

From a strategic standpoint, the defense legal team will evaluate how to proceed when any of these grounds exist. A simple telephone call and a request that an amended complaint be filed could be an appropriate response, confirmed in writing for the record. Grounds for dismissal could be included

statute of limitations
The time frame within which an action must be commenced or the party will lose his/her right to use the courts to seek redress.

Exhibit 9.10 Motion to Dismiss

UNITED STATES DISTRICT COURT - NORTHERN DISTRICT OF NEW YORK

B.K., a minor by her Parents and Guardians, Janice Knowles and Steven Knowles, Plaintiff	: : : :	No.: _____ MOTION TO DISMISS UNDER RULE 12(b)(6)
v.	:	CIVIL ACTION - NEGLIGENCE
Ronald Clemmons, Lower Council School District, Bud Smith, and Ace Trucking Company, Defendants	: :	Jury Trial Demanded Attorney ID No. 124987

DEFENDANT BUD SMITH'S RULE 12(B)(6) MOTION TO DISMISS COMPLAINT

Defendant Bud Smith moves this court pursuant to Rule 12(b)(6) of the Federal Rules of Civil Procedure to dismiss Count IV of the Complaint as it fails to state claim against him upon which relief can be granted.

Respectfully submitted,

_____

John Morris, Esquire
Attorney for Defendant Smith

---

in the answer to the complaint and left for resolution until the time of trial. In certain circumstances, filing a separate motion before answering the complaint might be the right tactic to let opposing counsel know that the defendant intends to hold the plaintiff to a strict level of proof in prosecuting the claims.

Making use of the Rule 12 Motion to Dismiss does not mean the defendant will not have to answer the complaint. Because the courts are liberal in granting plaintiffs the right to cure the defects or amend the complaint, the defendant may just be delaying the inevitable or gaining additional time within which to investigate the facts and prepare an answer to the complaint.

Motion for Judgment on the Pleadings

motion for a judgment on the pleadings
A request for judgment as a matter of law based only on the contents of the pleadings.

undisputed facts
Failure to deny material facts in a pleading.

After the conclusion of the pleadings phase of the litigation, either the plaintiff or the defendant may file a **motion for a judgment on the pleadings** (see Exhibit 9.11), claiming they are entitled to judgment as a matter of law (Fed. R. Civ. Pro. 12(c)). The motion asks the court to consider everything contained in the pleadings, and not any outside matters, in the light most favorable to the non-moving party (the opposing party). If there are no disputed material facts, then, when applying the law to those facts, the moving party is entitled to judgment. "**Undisputed facts**" in this context means that any fact denied by the opposing party is considered as not true, and all of the opposing party's allegations are treated as true. Because either party can bring the motion, judgment may be entered in either's favor.

Exhibit 9.11 Motion for Judgment on the Pleadings

UNITED STATES DISTRICT COURT - NORTHERN DISTRICT OF NEW YORK

B.K., a minor by her Parents and Guardians, Janice Knowles and Steven Knowles, Plaintiff	: : :	No.: _____ **MOTION FOR JUDGMENT ON THE PLEADINGS**
v.	:	**CIVIL ACTION - NEGLIGENCE**
Ronald Clemmons, Lower Council School District, Bud Smith, and Ace Trucking Company, Defendants	: :	Jury Trial Demanded Attorney ID No. 124987

MOTION OF DEFENDANT SMITH FOR JUDGMENT ON THE PLEADINGS

Defendant Smith files this Motion for Judgment on the Pleadings and alleges as follows:

1. At all relevant time Smith was an employee of and under the direction and control of Ace Trucking Company. (Complaint p. 7 Answer of Smith and Ace p. 7).
2. Ace Trucking supplied the truck operated by Smith and was responsible for the care, maintenance and safe operation of the truck. (Complaint p. 36 and Answer of Ace p. 36).
3. Ace Trucking admitted the brakes of the truck were defective and there was no driver error (Answer Ace pp. 36–38).
4. There is no allegation in the pleadings that Smith was negligent.
5. Viewing the allegations of the complaint and the responses of Defendant Ace in the light most favorable to the plaintiff, the pleadings fail to state a claim for which Smith may be found liable.

WHEREFORE it is respectfully requested that judgment in favor of Smith be entered and the action against him be dismissed.

Respectfully submitted,

UNITED STATES DISTRICT COURT - NORTHERN DISTRICT OF NEW YORK

B.K., a minor by her Parents and Guardians, Janice Knowles and Steven Knowles, Plaintiff	: : :	No.: _____ **MOTION FOR JUDGMENT ON THE PLEADINGS**
v.	:	**CIVIL ACTION - NEGLIGENCE**
Ronald Clemmons, Lower Council School District, Bud Smith, and Ace Trucking Company, Defendants	: :	Jury Trial Demanded Attorney ID No.

ORDER

AND NOW, this _____ day of _____, 2014, upon consideration of the within Motion for Judgment on the Pleadings, the responses thereto and the Pleadings it is hereby ORDERED that judgment is entered in favor of the defendant Bud Smith and against the plaintiff and the counts of the complaint against him are dismissed.

_____

J.

■ DISCOVERY MOTIONS

LEARNING OBJECTIVE 3
Explain how lawyers may use motions to compel opponents to comply with rules of court and evidence.

After the pleadings are closed, the parties begin the process of discovery. This process includes the exchange of documents and statements of witnesses that will potentially be used as evidence or could lead to evidence that will be utilized at trial. In theory, discovery should be accomplished in a cooperative fashion without court intervention. Often, that is not the case. When attempts by counsel at informally encouraging compliance fail, the legal team must seek the assistance of the court via a motion. Responses to opposing party discovery requests may be delayed while information for the response is gathered; worse, the response may be forgotten while the legal team attends to other cases or matters. Therefore, the legal team must have a system in place to comply with discovery deadlines—that means establishing an internal calendaring system and obtaining client cooperation. There are times when it is not possible to comply within the deadlines under court rules for discovery; at those times, steps must be taken to obtain an extension of time to comply.

Most judges do not want to be involved in the discovery process. Judges feel that trial counsel should be able to resolve these issues without court intervention. Many lawyers find court intervention is like a trip to the principal's office after a disagreement on the school bus—it's unpleasant and leaves a bad impression on the person in charge. The litigation teams should thus anticipate problems that might arise in the discovery process and resolve them in federal court during the Rule 26(f) conference, documenting their agreement as to discovery issues via the **scheduling order.**

scheduling order
A pretrial discovery order.

Motion to Compel

When a discovery request's deadline passes with no response, opposing counsel's office should be contacted as a matter of professional courtesy. The goal of this initial contact is to determine the cause of the delay and to determine a date when the responses will be completed. Typically, the attorneys will agree to an extension, which should be memorialized with a stipulation filed with the court.

If opposing counsel fails to provide responses in accordance with the terms of the stipulation, a follow-up telephone call or letter may be appropriate to encourage compliance. When the amicable attempts at encouraging compliance fail, the legal team must seek the assistance of the court via a **motion to compel** (Fed. R. Civ. Pro. 37(a)). Under this motion, the moving party must demonstrate the good faith efforts made to obtain the opposing party's cooperation and compliance. Thus, the phone contact and stipulation for extension serve to establish both professional courtesy and the required good faith efforts to obtain compliance from the opposing party. Typically, the motion will be heard by the judge, sometimes in court and sometimes in the judge's chambers. The result is an order compelling the party to respond to the discovery request within a certain time period (usually twenty days from the date of the order) and to pay the costs of the moving party. Exhibit 9.12 is a Motion to Compel Discovery with the proposed form of order.

motion to compel
Motion seeking the opposing party's cooperation and compliance in responding to discovery requests.

Motion for Sanctions

If opposing counsel fails to comply with the court-ordered deadline, a **motion for sanctions** may be the next step (Fed. R. Civ. Pro. 37(b)). This motion will seek the court's intervention for failure to comply with the court order and instruct that responses be completed in twenty days. Often, a motion for sanctions is

motion for sanctions
Where an order compelling a party to cooperate is not complied with, the next step is to request that the court impose a penalty against the noncompliant party.

treated as a petition for contempt of court and will raise the judge's level of irritation and displeasure with the litigants. A typical sanction imposed by the court is to prohibit the introduction of any materials that the non-compliant party may want to use and that would have been contained in the response to the discovery request. A more serious sanction would be an entry of judgment against the non-compliant party or the dismissal of any claims they might raise. In either event, the court will frequently order the non-compliant party to pay costs and counsel fees associated with the motion.

Exhibit 9.12 Motion to Compel Discovery with the Proposed Form of Order

---

UNITED STATES DISTRICT COURT - NORTHERN DISTRICT OF NEW YORK

B.K., a minor by her Parents and Guardians,	:	No.: _____
Janice Knowles and Steven Knowles, Plaintiff	:	PLAINTIFF'S MOTION TO COMPEL DEFENDANT LOWER COUNCIL SCHOOL DISTRICT'S ANSWERS TO INTERROGATORIES
v.	:	
	:	CIVIL ACTION - NEGLIGENCE
Ronald Clemmons, Lower Council School District,	:	Jury Trial Demanded
Bud Smith, and	:	
Ace Trucking Company, Defendants		Attorney ID No. 124987

Plaintiff in the action files this Motion for relief and alleges as follows:

1. On July 15, 2014, Plaintiff served by first class mail Interrogatories addressed to the Defendant Lower Council School District.

2. Answers to the Interrogatories were due on August 15, 2014.

3. On August 18, 2014, counsel for plaintiff contacted defense counsel by telephone and confirming letter to ascertain the reason for the delay in response and to obtain a time frame within which answers would be provided. Defense counsel indicated an additional 30 days was required. A true and correct copy of the confirming letter dated August 18, 2014, is attached as Exhibit A.

4. On September 20, 2014, more than 30 days had passed and still the answers to Interrogatories were outstanding. Plaintiff's counsel attempted to telephone and left numerous messages for defense counsel, none of which were returned.

5. On September 25, 2014, Plaintiff's counsel issued a letter advising defense counsel of the intention to file the within Motion to Compel. A true and correct copy of the letter dated September 25, 2014, is attached as Exhibit B.

6. To date, Defendant has neither answered nor objected to the Interrogatories.

7. To date, Defendant has filed neither a Motion for Enlargement of Time to Respond nor a Motion for Protective Order.

8. Plaintiff has incurred costs in conjunction with seeking the compliance of Defendant Lower Council School District. Attached as Exhibit C is an affidavit of the time expended in informal means of contacting Defendant as well as for the preparation, filing and service of the within Motion.

WHEREFORE, it is respectfully requested this Honorable court enter and order compelling Defendant Lower Council School District to issue answers to Interrogatories within 10 days, prohibiting Defendant from raising any objection to answer and awarding attorneys fees and costs in a reasonable sum.

Respectfully submitted,

(continued)

Exhibit 9.12 *(continued)*

UNITED STATES DISTRICT COURT - NORTHERN DISTRICT OF NEW YORK

B.K., a minor by her Parents and Guardians, Janice Knowles and Steven Knowles, Plaintiff	:	No.: _____
	:	PLAINTIFF'S MOTION TO COMPEL DEFENDANT LOWER COUNCIL SCHOOL DISTRICT'S ANSWERS TO INTERROGATORIES
v.	:	
	:	CIVIL ACTION - NEGLIGENCE
Ronald Clemmons, Lower Council School District, Bud Smith, and Ace Trucking Company, Defendants	:	Jury Trial Demanded
	:	Attorney ID No. 124987

ORDER

AND NOW this _____ day of _____, 2014, the matter having been brought before the court on Plaintiff's Motion to Compel and after consideration of the Reply and hearing on this matter it is hereby ORDERED that Defendant Lower Council School District shall within ten (10) days of the date hereof answer completely, fully and without objection the Interrogatories served upon it by the Plaintiff on July 15, 2014. Failure to comply with the terms of this Order will result in the imposition of sanctions in accordance with Fed.R.Civ.P. 37;

FURTHER ORDERED, Defendant Lower Council School District shall within ten (10) days of the date hereof pay to Plaintiff the sum of $1,500.00, the reasonable attorney's fees and costs associated with obtaining compliance with the discovery requested.

BY THE COURT:

_____
J.

Motion for Protective Order

In some instances, the information or documents sought through discovery may be inappropriate for disclosure. The questions may be duplicative in nature, request information that is within the possession or control of another party, or be unduly burdensome or harassing. Questions that ask for attorney notes would be protected under the **work product doctrine.** Although called a **motion for protective order,** the motion actually serves the purpose of presenting an objection to supplying the requested information to the court for a ruling (Fed. R. Civ. Pro. 26(c)). The court considers the request and the claimed objection (such as attorney–client privilege or work product privilege) and then determines whether the discovery request should be answered or if an order protecting the material from discovery is appropriate. Exhibit 9.13 is a Motion for a Protective Order with a Proposed Form of Order.

work product doctrine
A limited protection for material prepared by the attorney, or those working for the attorney, in anticipation of litigation or for trial.

motion for protective order
Motion that asks the court to determine whether certain information must be disclosed in discovery.

■ PRETRIAL MOTIONS

LEARNING OBJECTIVE 4
Describe the use of motions to terminate a case before trial.

Motions may be filed before the trial starts in order to test the sufficiency of the pleadings, asking the court to determine if the opposing party has stated a cause of action with sufficient information to allow the case to go to trial. Also prior to trial, motions will be filed related to the admissibility of evidence.

Motion for Summary Judgment

During discovery, but more likely after discovery is completed and before trial, the legal team will usually file a **motion for summary judgment** (Fed. R. Civ. P. 56). This motion forces the legal team to focus on the legal issues and the elements required to prove them and to compare those elements with the facts developed through discovery. If the legal teams have thoroughly and properly investigated their clients' claims and defenses, there should be few surprises. When filing the motion for summary judgment, the legal team tells the court there are no disputed material facts; all that remains is the application of the law to the facts and a

motion for summary judgment
A motion by which a party seeks to terminate the lawsuit prior to trial, alleging there are no disputed material facts and all that remains is the application of the law to the facts.

Exhibit 9.13 Motion for a Protective Order with a Proposed Form of Order

---

UNITED STATES DISTRICT COURT - NORTHERN DISTRICT OF NEW YORK

B.K., a minor by her Parents and Guardians,	:	No.: _____
Janice Knowles and Steven Knowles, Plaintiff	:	DEFENDANT CLEMMONS' MOTION FOR PROTECTIVE ORDER
	:	
v.	:	CIVIL ACTION - NEGLIGENCE
Ronald Clemmons, Lower Council School District, Bud Smith, and	:	Jury Trial Demanded
Ace Trucking Company, Defendants	:	Attorney ID No.

Defendant Clemmons files this Motion for Protective Order and alleges as follows:

1. On July 15, 2014, Defendant Clemmons was served with Interrogatories from Plaintiff.

2. On August 15, 2014 Defendant Clemmons' Answers to Interrogatories were served in a timely fashion upon Plaintiff. A true and correct copy of the Interrogatories with Answers is attached as Exhibit A.

3. Simultaneously with serving the Answers to Interrogatories, Defendant Clemmons files this Motion for Protective Order seeking determination of the objections raised in his Answers to Interrogatories.

4. In his Answers to Interrogatories Defendant Clemmons objected as follows:

   a. Interrogatory No. 7: The information requested is protected from disclosure by the physician-patient privilege, is not likely to lead to admissible evidence and to the extent discoverable has already been provided in the materials produced through mandatory disclosure.

   b. Interrogatory No. 15: The request is overly broad, vague and unduly burdensome, serving no purpose but to harass the Defendant.

   c. Interrogatory No. 20: The information requested has been provided through mandatory disclosure.

5. Defendant seeks the court's order sustaining the objections aforesaid and protecting him from revealing information protected from disclosure based upon the physician-patient privilege and duplicative requests for information already having been provided through mandatory disclosure under Fed.R.Civ.P. 26.

WHEREFORE, it is respectfully requested this Honorable court enter an order sustaining Defendant Clemmons' objections to Interrogatories 7, 15 and 20, protecting him from disclosing the information requested and from sanctions for failing to respond

Respectfully submitted,

_____

(continued)

Exhibit 9.13 (*continued*)

UNITED STATES DISTRICT COURT - NORTHERN DISTRICT OF NEW YORK

B.K., a minor by her Parents and Guardians, Janice Knowles and Steven Knowles, Plaintiff	: : :	No.: _____ DEFENDANT CLEMMONS' MOTION FOR PROTECTIVE ORDER
v.	:	CIVIL ACTION - NEGLIGENCE
Ronald Clemmons, Lower Council School District, Bud Smith, and Ace Trucking Company, Defendants	: :	Jury Trial Demanded Attorney ID No.

ORDER

AND NOW this _____ day of _____, 2014, the matter having been brought before the court on Defendant Clemmons' Motion for Protective Order and after consideration of the Reply and hearing on this matter it is hereby

ORDERED that the objections to Interrogatory 7, 15 and 20 are sustained and a protective order is issued such that Defendant Clemmons is relieved from answering or suffering sanctions for failure to answer the aforesaid Interrogatories.

BY THE COURT:

_____
J.

---

representation that, when the law is applied to the facts, there can be just one outcome—in the client's favor.

Few lawsuits involve only a single legal issue. For example, in a construction contract lawsuit, there may be multiple claims, each having separate legal issues—for example, claims based on breach of contract, breach of warranties related to the workmanship or goods used, or fraud and misrepresentation as to quality of workmanship and goods provided. The facts developed through discovery may disclose a work change order signed by the client's spouse that authorizes the use of substitute goods of a lesser quality. With that document, the legal issues and claims related to fraud (or breach of warranty as to the quality of goods) would be appropriate for a motion for summary judgment. Because a successful motion for summary judgment will resolve one or more legal issues presented to the court for consideration, the evaluation of the legal claims for purposes of preparing a motion for summary judgment is a crucial element of trial preparation. Those issues, along with the witnesses and evidence necessary to prove the claim, will not need to be part of the trial presentation. Exhibit 9.14 is a Motion for Summary Judgment.

Motion in Limine or Pretrial Motion

Most courts require pretrial motions or motions in limine prior to trial to streamline the operation of the trial itself. This goal of smooth trial operations is achieved through the use of a motion filed shortly before trial that lists the areas of agreement, such as stipulated facts and exhibits, and areas of disagreement, such as use of gruesome photographs. The judge will rule on the disputed items prior to trial.

Exhibit 9.14 Motion for Summary Judgment

UNITED STATES DISTRICT COURT - NORTHERN DISTRICT OF NEW YORK

B.K., a minor by her Parents and Guardians, Janice Knowles and Steven Knowles, Plaintiff	: NO. _____
	: DEFENDANT STANLEY'S MOTION FOR SUMMARY JUDGMENT
v.	:
Harry Hart, Kinnicutt Bus Company, Charles Stanley and MVF Construction Company, Defendants	: Attorney ID No. 387431

Defendant Stanley files this Motion for Summary Judgment and alleges as follows:

1. At all relevant times, Stanley was an employee of and under the direction and control of MVF Construction Company (Complaint p. 7 Answer of Stanley and MVF p. 7).

2. MVF Construction supplied the truck operated by Stanley and was responsible for the care, maintenance, and safe operation of the truck (Complaint p. 36 and Answer of MVF p. 36).

3. MVF Construction admitted the brakes of the truck were defective and there was no driver error (Answer MVF pp. 36–38, Defendant MVF's Answer Plaintiff's Interrogatories q. 8 through 10).

4. James Kaercher, an expert in accident reconstruction involving air brake failure, testified at deposition that the failure of the brakes was without warning to the operator of the vehicle (Kaercher deposition pp. 78–83).

5. Kaercher further testified that only the mechanic conducting an inspection of the brakes would have been able to discover the defect (Kaercher deposition p. 85 ll. 15–25).

6. Kaercher stated that failure of the brakes would have been sudden, allowing the driver no opportunity to make a sudden or fast stop. The only way to stop the truck would be through a gradual slowing across a long flat surface or use of an emergency truck ramp (Kaercher deposition p. 90 ll. 1–13).

7. The road on which the accident occurred was a downward slope with no emergency truck ramps (Report of State Police attached as exhibit A).

8. The failure of the brakes, the failure of MVF to properly inspect and maintain the braking system, and the inability of the driver to make fast stops as a result all serve to cut the nexus of causation that Stanley was negligent in the operation of the truck.

9. As a matter of law, Stanley is entitled to judgment in his favor and against the Plaintiff.

WHEREFORE it is respectfully requested that judgment in favor of Stanley be entered and the action against him be dismissed.

Respectfully submitted,

(continued)

Exhibit 9.14 (continued)

UNITED STATES DISTRICT COURT - NORTHERN DISTRICT OF NEW YORK

B.K., a minor by her Parents and Guardians, Janice Knowles and Steven Knowles, Plaintiff	: : :	NO. _____ DEFENDANT STANLEY'S MOTION FOR SUMMARY JUDGMENT
v.	:	
Harry Hart, Kinnicutt Bus Company, Charles Stanley and MVF Construction Company, Defendants	: :	Attorney ID No. 387431

ORDER

AND NOW, this _____ day of _____, 2014, upon consideration of the within Motion for Summary Judgment, the responses thereto, the Pleadings and the items of Record presented, it is hereby ORDERED that judgment is entered in favor of the defendant Charles Stanley and against the plaintiff, and the counts of the complaint against him are dismissed.

_____

J.

■ POSTTRIAL MOTIONS

LEARNING OBJECTIVE 5
Explain how motions may be used at the end of a trial.

Posttrial motions are made following the conclusion of a trial. The jury will be excused and the attorneys offered an opportunity to make any oral motions for relief to the trial court. These motions must also be made in writing within ten days from the entry of judgment. When put in writing, the motion will include references to the trial testimony and evidence that supports the claims asserted and the relief sought. It is possible that trial transcripts will be available to assist with this process. More likely than not, the legal team will need to rely on notes made during trial.

Motion for Judgment as a Matter of Law

motion for a judgment as a matter of law
Asks the trial judge to review and overturn the jury verdict.

A **motion for a judgment as a matter of law** (also known as a judgment notwithstanding the verdict, or judgment n.o.v.), asks the trial judge to review and overturn the jury verdict (Fed. R. Civ. P. 50(b)). This motion is used when error is found in the jury's decision, such as when the evidence or the law has been disregarded. The moving party asserts (1) the jury's decision is against the weight of evidence and/or (2) the jury has disregarded the law as instructed by the judge. After reviewing the record, no reasonable minds could disagree about the outcome of the case. However, the jury did not rule in that manner. The movant basically says, "There is no way the jury could have reached that verdict given the evidence presented in this trial and/or the law that is applicable. Your Honor, please correct what that jury has done." Exhibit 9.15 is a Motion for Judgment as a Matter of Law.

Exhibit 9.15 Motion for Judgment as a Matter of Law

UNITED STATES DISTRICT COURT - NORTHERN DISTRICT OF NEW YORK

B.K., a minor by her Parents and guardians,	:	No.: _____
Janice Knowles and Steven Knowles,	:	DEFENDANT SMITH'S MOTION FOR
Plaintiff	:	JUDGMENT AS A MATTER OF LAW
	:	
v.		
	:	CIVIL ACTION - NEGLIGENCE
Ronald Clemmons,	:	Jury Trial Demanded
Lower Council School District,		
Bud Smith, and	:	
Ace Trucking Company,		Attorney ID No.
Defendants		

Defendant Smith files this Motion for Judgment as a Matter of Law as follows:

1. Trial in the above matter was held and a jury verdict was issued in favor of the plaintiff and against the defendant on November 15, 2014.

2. At the conclusion of trial, counsel for Defendant Smith requested a judgment as a matter of law and/or judgment not withstanding the verdict as the jury disregarded the judge's instruction concerning the requirements of negligence.

3. Specifically the judge instructed the jury on the elements of duty of care owed to the plaintiff, breach of that duty which was the cause of injury to the plaintiff that resulted in damages.

4. No evidence was presented at trial that Defendant Smith was negligent in the operation of truck he was driving.

5. The evidence and testimony stated that nothing Smith did resulted in the accident. Any other operator of that truck would have had the same result.

6. The judge's instruction on causation included relieving an individual of any liability where there are intervening causes that serve to cut off the liability.

7. The jury disregarded the video tape deposition of John Kaercher stating the cause of the accident was the result of brake failure that the driver could not perceive, anticipate or avoid once it occurred.

8. The jury disregarded the weight of the evidence and the law as instructed by the judge.

9. The verdict slip prepared by the jury answered NO to the following question: "Do you find the negligence of Defendant Smith was the cause of the harm suffered by the Plaintiff?"

WHEREFORE, it is respectfully requested that the jury verdict as to Defendant Smith be stricken and a judgment as a matter of law in favor of Smith be entered.

Respectfully submitted,

Motion to Mold the Verdict

A **motion to mold the verdict** asks the court to take the jury verdict and calculate the amount that the defendant is obligated to pay the plaintiff. This motion is necessary where the defendant is successful on his counterclaim or the plaintiff has been assigned some portion of negligence in a **comparative negligence** jurisdiction. Exhibit 9.16 shows a jury verdict slip that would require a motion to mold the verdict. Exhibit 9.17 shows how the verdict might be molded.

motion to mold the verdict
Asks the court to take the jury verdict and calculate the amount that the defendant is obligated to pay the plaintiff.

comparative negligence
An affirmative defense that reduces an award to the plaintiff by the percentage his own negligence contributed to his injuries.

Exhibit 9.16 Jury Verdict Slip

UNITED STATES DISTRICT COURT - NORTHERN DISTRICT OF NEW YORK

JURY VERDICT SLIP

ON THE FIRST COUNT

1. Do you find that the Defendant's actions were negligent?
   ___x___ Yes   _____ No

2. Do you find that the negligent actions of the Defendant caused the accident?
   ___x___ Yes   _____ No

3. Do you find that the Plaintiff was injured as a result of the accident?
   ____x__ Yes   _____ No

4. Do you find that the Plaintiff was negligent?
   ___x___ Yes   _____ No

5. Do you find the negligence of the Plaintiff caused the accident?
   ___x___ Yes   _____ No

6. If you answered YES to both questions 4 and 5 above please determine the percentage of liability
   __30___% Plaintiff
   __70___% Defendant

7. Please assess a dollar value as to the damages sustained by the Plaintiff
   $___300,000.00_____

ON THE SECOND COUNT

1. Do you find that the Plaintiff breached the contract?
   ___x___ Yes   _____ No

2. Do you find the Defendant suffered damages as a result of the breach?
   ___x___ Yes   _____ No

3. Please assess a dollar value as to the damages sustained by the Defendant
   $ ___30,000.00_____

Exhibit 9.17 Molded Verdict

MOLDED VERDICT

ON THE FIRST COUNT
Judgment in favor of the Plaintiff in the sum of $210,000.00

ON THE SECOND COUNT
Judgment in favor of the Defendant in the sum of $30,000.00

FINAL judgment is entered in favor of the Plaintiff and against the Defendant in the sum of $180,000.00.

Motion for a New Trial

A **motion for a new trial** asserts that an error was made in a trial, either by the judge or by the jury. The error can be related to the admission of evidence, the instructions to the jury, or a verdict unsupported by the law or evidence. Often the error is related to something that occurred at trial that is so prejudicial that it would be a denial of justice to let the jury verdict stand. An example might be jurors meeting and discussing the case with reporters while the trial is still ongoing.

motion for a new trial
Request for a new trial because an error was made in the trial by the judge or jury.

CONCEPT REVIEW AND REINFORCEMENT

KEY TERMS

motion   230

movant   230

certificate of service   230

notice of motion   230

motion to extend the time to respond   231

stipulation   233

default judgment   233

docket   234

subject matter jurisdiction   238

personal jurisdiction   238

venue   238

insufficiency of process   238

indispensable party   238

statute of limitations   239

motion for a judgment on the pleadings   240

undisputed facts   240

scheduling order   242

motion to compel   242

motion for sanctions   242

work product doctrine   244

motion for protective order   244

motion for summary judgment   245

motion for a judgment as a matter of law   248

motion to mold the verdict   249

comparative negligence   249

motion for a new trial   251

CHAPTER SUMMARY

MOTIONS PRACTICE

Introduction to Motions	Motions are used by the parties to the lawsuit to ask the court to intervene or act during the course of the litigation. Motions are not pleadings.
Form of Motions	Like pleadings, the motion begins with the caption and title of the document, which clearly identify its purpose. Numbered paragraphs include the identification of the parties, the issue presented, and the action requested of the court.
Motions in the Pleading Phase	A motion may be used to extend the time to respond, terminate the lawsuit, or test the sufficiency of the pleadings to allege a proper basis in law or fact to allow the case to proceed.
Motion to Enlarge Time to Respond	This motion is a request for a court order allowing additional time to respond.

(continued)

Motion for Default Judgment	The plaintiff may request a default judgment be entered (Fed. R. Civ. P. 55) when the defendant fails to file a timely response to a complaint.
Entry of Default on the Docket	In federal court, the plaintiff asks the clerk of the court to enter defendant's default on the docket by affidavit describing the facts of default.
Entry ot Default Judgment	Default judgment may be entered on the docket by the clerk for a specific amount where the damages can be readily determined from the face of the pleadings. When damages cannot be determined, default judgment can be entered but a hearing will be conducted to determine damaged.
Setting Aside Default	Upon affidavit of good cause or motion to set aside, a default judgment may be opened to allow the defendant to file an answer.
Rule 12(b) Motions	This motion is made by the defendant to dismiss the complaint because of a defect on the face of the pleading or a defect in service of process.
Motion for Judgment on the Pleadings	This motion made by the plaintiff or defendant stating either is entitled to judgment as a matter of law.
Discovery Motions	When attempts at encouraging compliance fail, the legal team must seek the assistance of the court via motion.
Motion to Compel	When the amicable attempts at encouraging compliance fail, the legal team must seek the assistance of the court via motion to compel.
Motion for Sanctions	This motion will seek the court's intervention for failure to comply with the court order instructing that discovery responses be completed.
Motion for Protective Order	This is a motion for an order that the question need not be answered based on an objection to supplying the requested information.
Pretrial Motions	Motions may be filed before the trial starts to test the sufficiency of the pleadings.
Motion for Summary Judgment	This motion states that there are no disputed material facts, and that all that remains is the application of the law to the facts and a representation that when the law is applied to the facts, there can be just one outcome.
Posttrial Motions	Posttrial motions are made following the conclusion of a trial.
Motion for Judgment as a Matter of Law	Also known as judgment notwithstanding the verdict, or n.o.v., this motion asks the trial judge to review and overturn the jury verdict. This motion is used when error is found in the jury's decision, such as when the evidence or the law has been disregarded.
Motion to Mold the Verdict	This motion asks the court to take the jury verdict and calculate the amount that the defendant is obligated to pay the plaintiff.
Motion for a New Trial	This motion asserts that an error was made in a trial, either by the judge or by the jury, which was so prejudicial a new trial must be granted.

REVIEW QUESTIONS AND EXERCISES

1. What is a motion?
2. How is a motion similar to a complaint? How is it different?
3. What is a default judgment?
4. How is a default judgment obtained in federal court?
5. Is a default judgment final? Can it be overturned?
6. What is the purpose of a motion to enlarge time?
7. What are the grounds for a federal Rule 12(b) motion?
8. Why would the legal team use or decide not to use a Rule 12(b) motion?
9. When is a motion for judgment on the pleadings appropriate?
10. What is the purpose of a motion to compel?
11. What are the sanctions that may be imposed for failure to comply with a motion to compel?
12. What is the purpose of a protective order and how is it obtained?
13. What is a judgment n.o.v.? When is it appropriate?
14. What is a molded verdict and where and how is it obtained?
15. What is the purpose of a motion for a new trial, and why would a new trial be necessary?
16. Why might a court still have a hearing after a default judgment has been entered?
17. What remedy is available for the defendant who has a valid excuse for not filing a responsive pleading that resulted in a default judgment?

BUILDING YOUR PARALEGAL SKILLS

INTERNET AND TECHNOLOGY EXERCISES

1. Use your state court's website to find the requirements and procedure to enter a default judgment.
2. Use your state court's website to find the procedure to compel compliance with discovery requests and to obtain a protective order.
3. Use your state court's website to find what sanctions can be imposed for failure to comply with an order to compel.

CIVIL LITIGATION VIDEO CASE STUDIES

Zealous Representation Issue: Candor to the Court

A paralegal appears before a judge when her supervising attorney is not available, requesting an order be signed. She uses a copy of a motion previously presented to the court without checking the current status of the law.

After viewing the video at www.pearsonhighered.com/ careersresources, answer the following questions.

1. When may a paralegal appear before the court?
2. What is the ethical obligation to verify the currency of the law cited in a petition or motion?

Scheduling Conference with Judge: Discovery Issue Resolution

 At a scheduling conference in the judge's chambers, the attorneys and the judge discuss discovery issues in the case and motions for sanctions. The plaintiffs' attorney has been denied access to the truck involved in the collision, including the brake parts that may have failed, in order to inspect them. There is concern that the evidence needed by the plaintiffs to prove their case has been disposed of and no longer exists.

After viewing the video at www.pearsonhighered.com/careersresources, answer the following questions.

1. Are there legitimate reasons to deny the opposing party access to an item relevant to the litigation?

2. What is the impact of ignoring the judge's order on the litigants? On the members of the legal team?

Court Hearing to Decide Who Represents a Minor: The Court's Duty to Protect the Child

 The case concerns an injured minor whose mother is denying treatment based on religious belief. The court must decide who will represent the child.

After viewing the video at www.pearsonhighered.com/careersresources, answer the following questions.

1. What standard does a court use to determine who represents a minor?
2. Why would the court bring in a third-party attorney for the minor?

CHAPTER OPENING SCENARIO CASE STUDY

Use the Opening Scenario for this chapter to answer the following question.

1. Review the complaint prepared in the previous chapter assignments. Would that complaint survive challenges based on Rule 12(b) grounds?

COMPREHENSIVE CASE STUDY

SCHOOL BUS–TRUCK ACCIDENT CASE

Review the assigned case study in Appendix 2.

1. Prepare a Motion to Dismiss on behalf of one of the defendants.

BUILDING YOUR PROFESSIONAL PORTFOLIO AND REFERENCE MANUAL

CIVIL LITIGATION TEAM AT WORK

See page 18 for instructions on Building Your Professional Portfolio.

Procedures

1. Requirements and procedure to enter a default judgment.

2. Procedure for the filing of motions in both the federal and state courts within your local jurisdiction; include the forms to be used, amount of filing fees, location where it might be filed and if it may be or must be filed electronically, and requirements for notice to the other parties.

LEARNING OBJECTIVES

After studying this chapter, you should be able to:

1. Determine what pleadings the defendant can file in response to the complaint.

2. Draft an answer to the complaint with affirmative defenses, a counterclaim, and a cross claim.

3. Prepare, file, and serve a third-party complaint and summons.

4. Explain the result of not properly responding to the complaint.

Pleadings: Responses to Complaint

CHAPTER 10

OPENING SCENARIO

 The paralegal in the downtown office had been given the responsibility for filing and arranging service of the complaint on the defendants in the school bus accident. It was her responsibility to enter the dates when the defendants were required to have their responses filed and to prepare for filing the default judgment documentation if they did not respond on time. The attorney for one of the defendants had agreed to voluntarily accept service and submit whatever paperwork was necessary. The other defendants had to be served personally. Under court rules, this meant there were different dates for the defendants to file a responsive pleading. The defense attorney who had agreed to accept service for his client indicated that he would, in all likelihood, be adding an additional defendant whom his client claimed was responsible for the brake failure. Anticipating the need to respond to this new pleading, Caitlin quickly consulted the rules to be certain that the time frames were properly followed.

OPENING SCENARIO LEARNING OBJECTIVE

Prepare an answer to the complaint.

■ INTRODUCTION TO RESPONSES TO COMPLAINT

defendant
The party who is sued in a lawsuit.

The party sued is called the **defendant.** This designation is not any indication of guilt or wrongdoing—it simply means that the person was named as the one to respond to the claims of the plaintiff. The defendant may be the innocent party, the one who should have filed the lawsuit seeking redress, or there may be another person or company that is responsible for the wrong alleged in the plaintiff's complaint, such as the manufacturer of a product sold in a sealed container.

responsive pleading
A pleading filed in response to a prior filed pleading.

Rules of court impose an obligation to file a **responsive pleading** or risk having a default judgment entered for not responding. Because the result of not answering is so serious, the legal team representing the defendant must act promptly. The time limits for filing the response after the service of the complaint on the defendant can be very short, typically twenty to thirty days. To the extent the defendant has any defenses to plaintiff's claims or has claims against the plaintiff, they must be included as part of the response.

■ RESPONSIVE PLEADINGS

LEARNING OBJECTIVE 1
Determine what pleadings or motions the defendant can file in response to the complaint.

answer
Document by which the defendant responds to the allegations contained in the plaintiff's complaint.

An **answer** to the complaint is a response to the complaint, but it is not the only form of responsive pleading. A responsive pleading may be one that includes claims against the plaintiff such as might have been the basis of a lawsuit by the defendant against the plaintiff. It may also include claims that someone else is responsible for the harm alleged by the plaintiff. Equally appropriate as a response to the complaint is a Rule 12(b) motion to dismiss the action. In an effort to move the case forward, the plaintiff's counsel may want to limit the response to only an answer to the complaint. Defense counsel will want to keep all options open and may ask for an extension of time to file a responsive pleading, which would include the filing of motions to dismiss, counterclaims, cross claims, and joinders of others.

In some cases, when asked for an extension of time, the alert plaintiff counsel may agree to an extension "only to file an answer to the complaint and no other responsive pleading." By doing so, plaintiff counsel eliminates the delay that may be associated with 12(b) motions. Defense counsel should be certain that the extension of time is documented to allow the extension of time for any responsive pleading allowed under court rules. If the extension to file any responsive pleading is denied by opposing counsel, prompt action of the court to obtain an extension to file any responsive pleading should be filed, usually by way of a motion.

Pleadings Allowed by Federal Rules of Civil Procedure

The pleadings permitted are:

- Complaint
- Answer, which may include affirmative defenses, counterclaims, and cross claims
- Reply to cross or counterclaim
- Third-party complaint
- Third-party answer
- Reply to cross and counterclaims asserted in a third-party answer

Time Deadlines and Entry into Tickler System

The time for the defendant to file a responsive pleading begins to run when the complaint is properly served as required by court rule. If personally served by traditional means (U.S. Marshall, county sheriff, or private process server), the defendant, under the Federal Rules of Civil Procedure, has twenty days to respond. If served by Notice and Waiver of Service, the defendant has sixty days to respond to the complaint. Failure of the defendant to respond in a timely fashion permits the plaintiff to obtain a default judgment against the defendant. The defendant also must know the rule and properly calculate the due date to avoid a **default judgment** for inaction.

All pleadings after the initial complaint and answer have a twenty-day response time. This includes the plaintiff's response to counterclaims or affirmative defenses asserted by the defendant and the response to any motion.

Calculating Deadlines

The rules of civil procedure of the court in which the complaint has been filed will include a provision describing how the time limits are calculated. Generally, counting begins on the day after receipt of a pleading. If served with a complaint today, day 1 is tomorrow, and the counting includes all calendar days that follow, including Saturdays, Sundays, and holidays. The due date is the twentieth day. If the due date falls on a Saturday, Sunday, or holiday, the due date is the next regular business day of the court. The paralegal generally is responsible for entering the due dates and sufficient reminder dates into the firm's central calendaring system.

Software for Calculating Deadlines

Calculating the important dates in a case requires a careful review of the specific court rules of the jurisdiction in which the case is filed. Within the same state, there may be variations in the timetable for civil litigation proceedings. Some software programs provide rules-of-court-based automatic calendaring. In these programs, such as Abacus (Exhibit 10.1), the calendar dates for those jurisdictions selected are built into the program. Automatic calculation is based on the required interval (in days) after specific events, or a customized date calculation can be created.

The custom date calculation can be used to set deadlines or reminders based on a set of days after selected events, such as the time for sending reminders or follow-up letters or dates for routine case status conferences in the office. Where local rule books are available, the deadlines and timetables can be determined by consulting the court rules. Where the case is in a jurisdiction for which the rule book is not readily available, such as a case being handled by outside or out-of-state counsel, dates can be determined by online reference to the specific court or by use of an automated, online, rules-based calendaring service such as LawToolBox, as shown in Exhibit 10.2.

Responses to the Complaint

Upon receipt of the complaint, the defendant and counsel have some critical decisions to make. In many instances, defendants know that a lawsuit may be filed against them. Being served with a complaint may not be a surprise, but the quickly approaching deadlines can be intimidating for the legal defense team if it is not promptly advised by the client. If served personally, the defendant

default judgment
Judgment obtained by the plaintiff against the defendant where the defendant has failed to respond in a timely fashion to the complaint.

 **WEB RESOURCES**
Learn more about Abacus and the Law Tool Box on the Technology Resources website at www.pearsonhighered.com/techresources.

Exhibit 10.1 AbacusLaw Rules-Based Calendaring

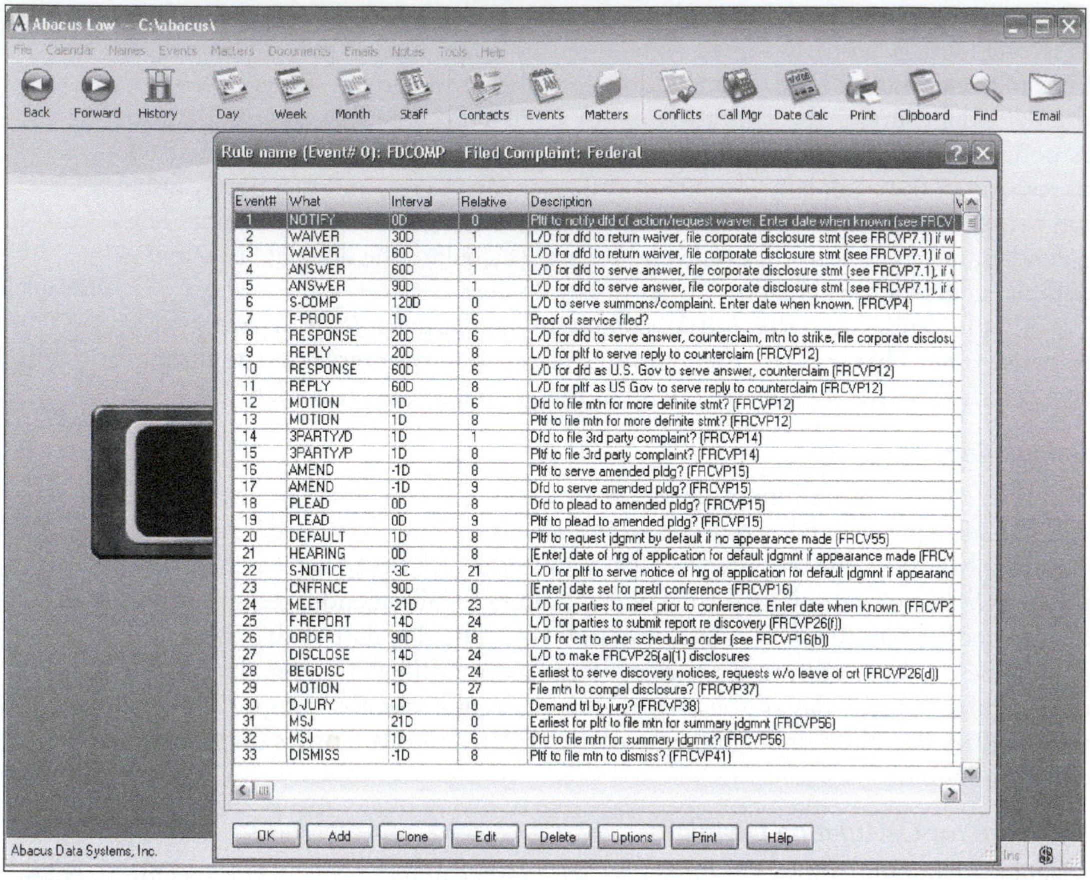

Source: Reprinted with permission from Abacus Data Systems, Inc.

has twenty days to respond, which is probably insufficient time to thoroughly investigate and respond. Just as plaintiffs frequently wait to file suit until the last date before the statute of limitations, defendants frequently wait to meet with an attorney until the date the response is due to be filed in court. Thus, for the defense team, the first step may be to request an **extension of time to respond** from opposing counsel. If that request is granted, the team must prepare and file a stipulation with the court.

If opposing counsel refuses, a motion for enlargement of time to respond to the complaint should be prepared and filed. These motions are granted liberally by the court so long as there is no indication of bad faith.

The better situation for a defendant is to have agreed to a waiver of service, which includes sixty days to answer or respond to the complaint.

The next step for the defense team is to review and evaluate the complaint to determine whether there is a basis to file a Rule 12(b) Motion to Dismiss the complaint. In some jurisdictions this process may be referred to as raising preliminary objections to the complaint; that is, without waiving any rights associated with answering the complaint, the defendant may object to the matters set forth in the complaint. The goals of judicial economy and efficiency are served when lawsuits are terminated at the earliest stage possible.

The grounds for dismissing a complaint action include (1) lack of subject matter jurisdiction, (2) lack of personal jurisdiction, (3) lack of venue, (4) insufficiency of process, (5) defect in the service of process, (6) failure to state a

extension of time to respond
Request by the defendant to enlarge the time to respond to the complaint beyond that which is permitted under the rules.

Exhibit 10.2 Sample Court Dates Report

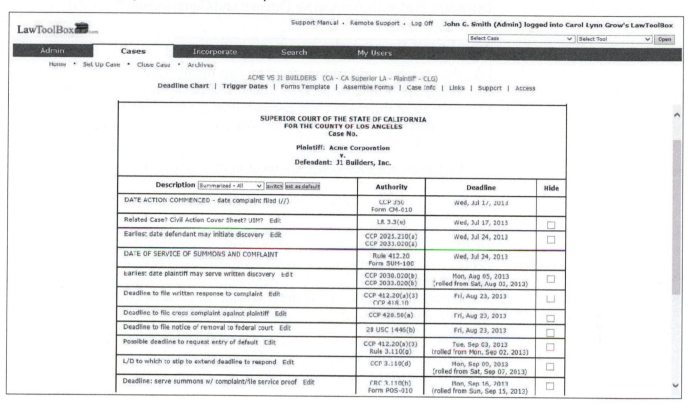

claim upon which relief can be granted, and (7) failure to join an indispensable party. These grounds are the lenses through which the complaint should first be read. With the exception of number 6 (failure to state a claim upon which relief can be granted), the grounds for dismissal are procedural and easily corrected by the plaintiff. A motion to dismiss filed Rule 12(b)(6) is more serious, as it states the plaintiff has failed to allege facts that support a legal claim or has asserted a legal claim that is not recognized by our courts. Courts are generous in the review of these motions, often granting the plaintiff the opportunity to correct the procedural mistake or file an amended complaint restating the facts to support the claim or restating the legal claims. After an amended complaint is filed pursuant to a Rule 12 motion, or if there are no grounds to file the motion, the defendant must file his answer to the complaint (Fed. R. Civ. P. 12).

■ ANSWER TO THE COMPLAINT

The defendant is required to respond to the allegations contained in the plaintiff's complaint. This is done by preparing, filing, and serving an Answer to the complaint. An answer is made up of the same sections as in a complaint, whether in federal or state court: caption, numbered paragraphs, prayer for relief, and affirmative defenses.

LEARNING OBJECTIVE 2
Draft an answer to the complaint with affirmative defenses a counterclaim, and a cross claim.

Caption

The answer begins with the caption identifying the court, the parties, the number assigned to the case by the court, and identification of the document as "Answer." If there are multiple defendants, there is an indication of which defendant is answering, such as "Answer of Defendant Hart." And if defenses or new claims are being asserted they must also be identified, such as "Answer of Defendant Hart with Affirmative Defenses and Counterclaim."

Numbered Paragraphs

Like the complaint, the answer must contain numbered paragraphs. Each numbered paragraph will correspond to a numbered paragraph of the complaint. So, paragraph 10 of the answer will respond directly to the averments, or facts, set forth in paragraph 10 of the complaint. When responding to the averments of the complaint, there are two basic choices:

admit
A possible response of the defendant to the complaint that accepts the facts of the averment are true.

1. **Admitted**—the facts of the averment in the complaint are acknowledged as true, or
2. **Denied**—the facts of the averment in the complaint are not true.

deny
A possible response of the defendant to the complaint that asserts the facts of the averment are not true.

In some jurisdictions, simply denying averments of the complaint is not sufficient. In those jurisdictions, the word "Denied" with nothing more is a **general denial.** A general denial is one that has no effect and is treated as if the answer was "Admitted."

general denial
In some jurisdictions, the word "Denied" alone is insufficient and the averment of the complaint is treated as if it were "Admitted."

In those jurisdictions where the reason for the denial is crucial to any defense, the reasons for the denial must be listed and include:

1. Denied, as the facts are not as stated by the plaintiff in the complaint. The defendant claims that there is a different set of facts than those the plaintiff has stated in the complaint and the defendant must specifically state those alternate facts.
2. Denied, as after reasonable investigation, the defendant lacks adequate knowledge to determine whether the information contained in the plaintiff's averment is true. This response is usually for facts that are within the sole knowledge of the plaintiff such as the nature and extent of the plaintiff's injuries, medical treatment, recovery, pain, and suffering. Thus, the defendant states that after reasonable investigation, he lacks knowledge of those facts and typically will include a statement demanding proof of those items at trial.
3. Denied, as the averment represents a conclusion of law to which no response is required. The plaintiff's allegation that the defendant's actions were negligent is a conclusion of law. While the plaintiff must allege this element of the cause of action, the defendant has no obligation to respond since it is a conclusion of law; that is for the finder of fact to determine at trial.
4. No answer is required, as the averments are addressed to another defendant. In some instances, particularly when there are multiple defendants to whom the complaint is directed, there may be paragraphs to the complaint that do not require an answer because they are addressed to another defendant.

Prayer for Relief

Just as the plaintiff asks the court for relief, so too will the defendant. Following the averments responding to the complaint, the defendant's prayer is generally that the complaint be dismissed and may include a request for counsel fees and costs.

Affirmative Defenses

affirmative defense
Those legal theories asserted by the defendant that bar the plaintiff's claim.

After answering the averments contained in the plaintiff's complaint, the defendant may make claims against the plaintiff. This section of the answer will begin with the title **Affirmative Defenses** to the plaintiff's complaint. Affirmative defenses are those legal theories that serve to bar the plaintiff's claim. Affirmative defenses claim that even if everything the plaintiff alleges is true, the plaintiff is not entitled to recovery because of some legal principle. Affirmative defenses have a "use it or lose it" character. If the defendant fails to raise the affirmative defense in the Rule 12(b) Motion or in the Answer to the complaint, he loses the right to later raise those defenses. Depending on the local rules, this may be true even if facts that support the affirmative defense are learned during the discovery process. For many practitioners, an answer to a complaint will have a set of all affirmative defenses related to a particular cause of action included whether they are applicable or not. The most common affirmative defenses are the statute of limitations, statute of frauds, assumption of risk, and contributory and/or comparative negligence.

The statute of limitations is a time frame within which a plaintiff must file a complaint, or the right to recovery is barred. For example, the statute of limitations for written contracts is six years in many states under the common law.

The statute of frauds requires certain types of contracts to be written, such as a contract involving an interest in real estate. Someone who sues to enforce a sale of real estate when there is no written contract will be barred from recovering under the statute of frauds.

The **assumption of risk** doctrine states that the plaintiff knew the risks involved with a particular activity and voluntarily proceeded with that activity. The fan at the baseball game cannot sue for being struck by a foul ball because foul balls entering the stands are common at a baseball game. The plaintiff assumed the risk that he might be struck by a foul ball when he purchased a ticket and attended the game. Exceptions may include someone completely unfamiliar with the game, such as a visitor from a country in which baseball is not played.

assumption of risk
An affirmative defense that states the plaintiff knew the risks involved with a particular activity and voluntarily proceeded with that activity.

Contributory and **comparative negligence** doctrines are closely related, and most jurisdictions have adopted one or the other. These doctrines state that where the plaintiff's actions were also negligent and contributed to the occurrence that resulted in injuries, the plaintiff's recovery may be denied or limited. Suppose someone fell on the stairs and was injured, but because he had two armfuls of groceries, he was not holding onto the banister. This individual, by carrying too many bags of groceries and not holding onto the banister, contributed to his own injury. In a contributory negligence jurisdiction, there is no recovery where the plaintiff contributes to his injuries. This result is harsh and many states have opted instead for comparative negligence. Under comparative negligence, the jury will be asked to assign percentages of liability to the plaintiff and to the defendant and to determine damages without regard to fault. In the stairwell fall, the jury may find the plaintiff 15 percent negligent and the defendant 85 percent negligent. If the jury awards plaintiff damages of $100,000, the plaintiff will recover $85,000, the amount of liability assigned to the defendant (85 percent).

contributory negligence
An affirmative defense that states there is no recovery where the plaintiff's negligence contributed to his injuries.

comparative negligence
An affirmative defense that reduces an award to the plaintiff by the percentage his own negligence contributed to his injuries.

Causes of Action

After stating those grounds for which the plaintiff's claims should be denied, the defendant must assert any claims he has against the plaintiff, or **counterclaims,** that arise out of the same incident, transaction, or occurrence. In the typical automobile accident, both drivers are injured, and both cars are damaged. In responding to the complaint, the defendant may first assert the affirmative defense claim of comparative negligence and then include a separate count claiming that the plaintiff's negligence alone caused the defendant

counterclaim
Claims the defendant has against the plaintiff.

to suffer injuries that resulted in damages. Claims that arise from the same event must be included in the answer to the complaint, or the defendant loses the right to bring them. These are **mandatory counterclaims** against the plaintiff.

The defendant may also include **permissive counterclaims,** those claims against the plaintiff that don't arise from the same event but, in the interests of justice, make sense to include. If the plaintiff who fell in the stairwell was a tenant who owed the defendant back rent, the claim for the rent could be included as a permissive counterclaim. It makes sense to include the claim for back rent; it can be used to offset the damages the defendant owes the plaintiff.

The final cause of action that may be included as a separate count in the answer to the complaint is a **cross claim.** Cross claims are those claims that one defendant may have against another defendant. A passenger injured in an automobile accident sues the driver of the car in which he was a passenger and the driver of the other vehicle. In the answer, the driver of the other vehicle may assert a cross claim against the driver of the car the passenger was riding in, claiming he was totally at fault.

Whether the defendant files cross claims, mandatory counterclaims, or permissive counterclaims, he must plead sufficient information to put the other party on notice of the claim against him. Just as in the complaint, the defendant must include the elements of the cause of action, the damages sustained, and a prayer for relief in any counterclaim or cross claim.

Prayer for Relief

Following the count that includes affirmative defenses and the counts that include counter- and cross claims, the defendant must include his requested relief:

> Wherefore defendant respectfully requests this honorable court dismiss the plaintiff's complaint and enter judgment in favor of the defendant in an amount exceeding $75,000 plus interest, costs, and attorney's fee and such other relief as this court deems equitable.

Exhibit 10.3 and 10.4 provide Answers to the Complaints set forth in Chapter 8.

Exhibit 10.3 Answer to Fact-Pleading Complaint

IN THE SUPREME COURT OF NEW YORK FOR ALBANY COUNTY		
B.K., a minor by her Parents and Guardians, Janice Knowles and Steven Knowles, Plaintiff	: : : : :	No.: 2007–19743–N–11
		Civil Action - Negligence
v.	:	
Ronald Clemmons, Lower Council School District, Bud Smith, and Ace Trucking Company, Defendants	: : :	Jury Trial Demanded Attorney ID No. 097531

Exhibit 10.3 *(continued)*

ANSWER OF DEFENDANT CLEMMONS TO PLAINTIFFS COMPLAINT
WITH AFFIRMATIVE DEFENSES

NOW comes Defendant Clemmons, by his attorneys, Li and Salva, and answers the complaint alleging as follows:

1. Admitted.

2. Admitted.

3. Admitted.

4. Admitted upon information and belief.

5. Admitted upon information and belief.

6. Admitted.

7. Admitted upon information and belief.

8. Admitted.

9. Admitted.

10. Admitted upon information and belief.

11. Admitted.

12. Admitted.

13. Denied that defendant Clemmons asked a chaperone or anyone else for directions to the Pumpkin Patch. Although Clemmons had never been to the Pumpkin Patch he was familiar with the location and knew where it was and how to get there. A chaperone did provide a map and directions but it is specifically denied that this was at the request of defendant Clemmons.

14. Admitted in part and denied in part. It is admitted that the each bus seat was equipped with three colorcoded lap belts, one for each passenger in a seat. It is specifically denied that each student on the bus was belted. After reasonable investigation, answering defendant lacks adequate knowledge, information or belief as to the truth of the allegations concerning each child being belted or the reasons therefore. Strict proof thereof is demanded at trial.

15. Admitted.

16. Admitted in part and denied in part. It is admitted that Clemmons exited at the wrong exit, exit #24, reentered the Highway and continued to the correct exit, #23. The remaining allegations of the paragraph are denied. It is specifically denied that Clemmons was confused about the directions or the exit number. To the contrary, Clemmons was not confused when he exited at Exit 24. There was a traffic accident on the highway with police diverting thru-traffic around the accident by use of the exit and entrance ramps of Exit 24. It is specifically denied that Clemmons turned the bus around on the exit ramp for Exit 24. To the contrary, Clemmons was following the directions of state police diverting traffic from the highway to the ramp and back onto the highway to go around an accident blocking the lanes.

17. Admitted.

18. Admitted.

19. Admitted based upon information and belief.

20. Denied as stated. The yelling and screaming of the children was not limited to the approach of the intersection. The children were uncontrolled, jumping about and switching seats, and loudly singing, yelling, and screaming throughout the ride from Public School No. 18. After reasonable investigation, answering defendant is unable to determine whether this behavior was attributable to seeing signs for the Pumpkin Patch or simply the uncontrolled behavior of the children.

21. Denied as stated. It is true that answering defendant slowed as he approached the intersection, which was accomplished by removing his foot from the accelerator of the vehicle. Upon attempting to apply the brakes to further slow and stop the vehicle, the defendant discovered the brakes were not operating properly, thus causing the vehicle to enter the intersection without stopping. It is admitted that the vehicle was then struck by a dump truck.

(continued)

Exhibit 10.3 *(continued)*

Count I
Plaintiff v. Defendant Clemmons

22. No answer is required to the averments set forth in this paragraph. To the extent an answer is required Defendant Clemmons incorporates paragraphs 1 through 21 hereof as though fully set forth at length.

23. Denied as a conclusion of law. Further denied that Defendant Clemmons was negligent or failed to observe the rules of the road. To the contrary, Clemmons complied with all rules of the road including following the instructions of the police officers controlling traffic patterns around an accident scene. Failure to bring the vehicle to a stop was a result of mechanical failure of the brakes not the action or inaction of Clemmons.

24. Denied as a conclusion of law and for the reasons set forth in paragraph 23 which are incorporated herein by reference.

25. Denied as a conclusion of law and for reasons set forth in paragraph 23 which are incorporated herein by reference. Further denied, as after reasonable investigation, answering defendant lacks adequate knowledge as to any of the injuries suffered by the plaintiff. Strict proof thereof is demanded at the trial of this matter.

26. Denied as a conclusion of law. Further denied, as after reasonable investigation, answering defendant lacks adequate knowledge as to any of the injuries suffered by the plaintiff. Strict proof thereof is demanded at the trial of this matter.

WHEREFORE, Defendant respectfully requests that plaintiff's complaint be dismissed with prejudice.

Paragraphs 27–40. No answer is required as they are addressed to defendants other than Clemmons.

AFFIRMATIVE DEFENSES

41. Defendant Clemmons incorporates by reference his answers to paragraphs 1 through 40.
42. Plaintiff's claims are barred by the statute of limitations.
43. Plaintiff's claims are barred by the doctrine of sovereign immunity.
44. Plaintiff's claims are barred by the doctrine of contributory negligence.
45. Plaintiff's claims against the answering defendant are barred by the doctrine of respondeat superior.

WHEREFORE, Defendant respectfully requests plaintiff's complaint be dismissed.

Exhibit 10.4 Answer to Notice-Pleading Complaint

UNITED STATES DISTRICT COURT - NORTHERN DISTRICT OF NEW YORK

B.K., a minor by her Parents and Guardians, Janice Knowles and Steven Knowles, Plaintiff	: : :	No.: _____ ANSWER OF DEFENDANT CLEMMONS TO COMPLAINT
v.	:	CIVIL ACTION - NEGLIGENCE
Ronald Clemmons, Lower Council School District, Bud Smith, and Ace Trucking Company, Defendants	: :	Jury Trial Demanded Attorney ID No. 097531

Exhibit 10.4 (*continued*)

ANSWER OF DEFENDANT CLEMMONS TO PLAINTIFFS COMPLAINT
WITH AFFIRMATIVE DEFENSES

NOW comes Defendant Clemmons, by his attorneys, Li and Salva, and answers the complaint alleging as follows:

1–4. Admitted.

5–6. Admitted upon information and belief.

  7. Admitted.

  8. Admitted upon information and belief.

  9. Admitted.

10. Admitted upon information and belief.

11. Admitted.

12. Denied.

13. Admitted.

14. Admitted upon information and belief.

Count I

Plaintiff v. Defendant Clemmons

15. No answer is required to the averments set forth in this paragraph.

16. Denied.

17. Denied.

WHEREFORE, Defendant respectfully requests that plaintiff's complaint be dismissed with prejudice.

Paragraphs 18–26. No answer is required as they are addressed to defendants other than Clemmons.

AFFIRMATIVE DEFENSES

27. Defendant Clemmons incorporates by reference his answers to paragraphs 1 through 26.

28. Plaintiff's claims are barred by the statute of limitations.

29. Plaintiff's claims are barred by the doctrine of sovereign immunity.

30. Plaintiff's claims are barred by the doctrine of contributory negligence.

31. Plaintiff's claims against the answering defendant are barred by the doctrine of respondeat superior.

WHEREFORE, Defendant respectfully requests plaintiff's complaint be dismissed.

The plaintiff and the defendant against whom a counter- or cross claim is asserted must file an answer to those pleadings called a **reply**. The reply is in the same format as the answer—with a caption, title of the document, and numbered paragraphs that respond to the numbered paragraphs of the counter- or cross claim.

reply
Response of a plaintiff (or defendant) against whom a counterclaim (or cross claim) is asserted.

■ THIRD-PARTY PRACTICE

LEARNING OBJECTIVE 3
Prepare, file, and serve a third-party complaint and summons.

In some instances, the investigation completed by the defendant will reveal that a third party, a person or entity not presently a party to the lawsuit, is responsible for the harm suffered. In an auto accident, the defendant may determine that a defect in the manufacture of the car's brakes was the cause of the accident. The defendant will want to add the manufacturer of the brakes to the lawsuit. This pleading is referred to as **joinder,** or **third-party practice.**

Third-Party Complaint

joinder
Inclusion in the lawsuit of a third party, not presently a party to the lawsuit, who is or may be responsible for the harm suffered.

third-party practice
The process and procedure for including or joining a previously undisclosed party to the lawsuit.

third-party plaintiff
Defendant who intends to file a complaint against a third party.

third-party defendant
Third party against whom a complaint is prepared, filed, and served along with a summons.

third-party complaint
Follows the same format as the complaint that initiated the lawsuit.

The defendant who intends to file a complaint against a third party is called a **third-party plaintiff.** The third-party plaintiff prepares, files, and serves a complaint, along with a summons, against the **third-party defendant.** The **third-party complaint** follows the same format as the complaint that initiated the lawsuit. It states the claims the defendant, now the third-party plaintiff, has against the third-party defendant and includes a copy of the initial complaint as an exhibit. Under the federal rules, so long as the third-party complaint is filed within ten days of the answer to the initial complaint, court permission to join the third party is not required.

There are times when the existence of a third-party defendant will be discovered much later in the litigation. At that time, any effort to make a third party a part of the litigation will require permission of the court by the filing of a motion. The motion will include the identification of the third party, the reason he or she was not discovered earlier, and a proposed complaint against the third party. Unless the statute of limitations has passed, courts are generous in granting the joinder of a third party to promote just resolution of the dispute and avoid multiple lawsuits.

Third-Party Answer

Like the complaint that initiated the lawsuit, the third-party complaint must be answered under the time constraints determined by court rules. The rules for a third-party answer are the same as those for an answer to the complaint, including the time for response, the ability to request an extension of time to respond, and the right to file a Rule 12 motion to dismiss the action. The third-party answer is prepared using the same format as an answer, responding to each of the numbered paragraphs of the third-party complaint and asserting affirmative defenses, counterclaims, and cross claims.

■ FAILURE TO RESPOND TO COMPLAINT

LEARNING OBJECTIVE 4
Explain the result of not properly responding to the complaint.

default
Failure to file a timely response, whether to a motion or an answer.

Failure to file a timely response, whether as a motion to dismiss or as an answer, can result in a **default** judgment being entered against the defendant (Fed. R. Civ. P. 12). Entry of default is not automatic on the part of the court; the plaintiff's counsel must file the appropriate documents with the court to have the default entered. In the federal court system, this is a two-step process: entering default on the docket, which prevents the defendant from filing a late answer, and entering judgment, which usually will include some calculation of damages or a request for a hearing to determine damages.

CONCEPT REVIEW AND REINFORCEMENT

KEY TERMS

defendant   258
responsive pleading   258
answer   258
default judgment   259
extension of time to
  respond   260
admit   262
deny   262

general denial   262
affirmative defenses   262
assumption of risk   263
contributory negligence   263
comparative negligence   263
counterclaim   263
mandatory counterclaim   264
permissive counterclaim   264

cross claim   264
reply   267
joinder   268
third-party practice   268
third-party plaintiff   268
third-party defendant   268
third-party complaint   268
default   268

CHAPTER SUMMARY

PLEADINGS: RESPONSES TO COMPLAINT

Introduction to Responses to Complaint	The party who is sued is called the defendant, not because of any indication of guilt, but merely as a party called upon to respond to the claims of the plaintiff. The defendant must file a responsive pleading or risk having a judgment entered for failure to respond. The response must be filed within the time frame required under court rules.
Responses to the Complaint	The defendant has a limited time within which to file a response, unless granted an extension of time from opposing counsel or by order of the court. The response may be an answer admitting or denying the allegations of the complaint. A motion to dismiss may be filed, alleging a lack of jurisdiction or other defect in the plaintiff's complaint.
Answer to the Complaint	Answers to the complaint must contain an admission or a denial to each of the numbered paragraphs of the plaintiff's complaint. Use of just the term "Denied" may be treated as a general denial, which has the effect of admitting the allegation. The answer also contains a prayer for relief asking that the case be dismissed. The defendant may assert in the answer affirmative defenses, legal theories that would serve to bar the plaintiff's case. The statute of limitations is an affirmative defense in which the time frame within which the plaintiff must institute suit or have his right to use the courts to obtain a resolution is barred. Additional affirmative defenses include assumption of the risk (that the plaintiff knew the risks and assumed them) or, depending upon the jurisdiction, contributory negligence or comparative negligence. Contributory negligence theory denies recovery if the plaintiff has in any way contributed to the harm. Comparative negligence jurisdictions allow for a percentage of recovery based upon the percentage of fault.

(continued)

	The defendant may state any claims against the plaintiff that arise under the same factual pattern; these are mandatory counterclaims. Permissive counterclaims are those claims against the plaintiff that arise from some other event for which the defendant has a claim against the plaintiff. A cross claim is a claim that one defendant may have against another defendant in the same action.
Third-Party Practice	In some instances, the defendant may believe that a third party, not presently a party to the lawsuit, is responsible for the harm caused to the plaintiff. The defendant may join this additional third party by filing a third-party complaint. The party named or joined in this suit as a defendant files a response in the form of a third-party answer responding to each of the numbered paragraphs of the third-party complaint.
Failure to Respond to a Complaint	Failing to respond to the complaint may result in a default judgment being entered against the defendant. The entry is not automatic but must be requested by the plaintiff.

REVIEW QUESTIONS AND EXERCISES

1. What are the terms used to describe the parties to a lawsuit?
2. Is the defendant the guilty party? Explain.
3. What are the permissible responsive pleadings to a complaint?
4. What is the penalty for not filing a responsive pleading within the time frame required by court rule?
5. What is meant by a *default judgment*?
6. Under the federal rules, if a defendant is personally served with a complaint, how much time does he or she have to respond to the complaint?
7. What is the effect of a general denial to an allegation in a complaint?
8. What is meant by an *affirmative defense*? Give an example.
9. What is the difference between contributory negligence and comparative negligence?
10. What is meant by a *permissive counterclaim*?
11. What is a *cross claim*?
12. What are *mandatory counterclaims*?
13. What is meant by *third-party practice*?
14. What is the purpose of filing a third-party complaint?
15. What is the appropriate pleading in response to a third-party complaint?

BUILDING YOUR PARALEGAL SKILLS

INTERNET AND TECHNOLOGY EXERCISES

1. How can use of LawToolBox prevent ethical problems for the litigation team?
2. How can office management software, like AbacusLaw, be used to avoid missed deadlines?
3. Can basic calendaring software, like Microsoft Outlook, be used efficiently for deadline calculation? What are the pros and cons?

CIVIL LITIGATION VIDEO CASE STUDIES

Truck Driver's Deposition

The truck driver who was driving at the time of the accident is deposed.

After viewing the video at www.pearsonhighered.com/careersresources, answer the following questions.

1. May a fact witness give an opinion of the cause of the accident?
2. What happens to objections made during a deposition?

CHAPTER OPENING SCENARIO CASE STUDY

Use the Opening Scenario for this chapter to answer the following questions.

1. What procedures should the office have to ensure that no deadlines are missed?

2. Should the paralegal assigned to the case prepare a time line for filing dates and response dates? Why or why not?

COMPREHENSIVE CASE STUDY

SCHOOL BUS–TRUCK ACCIDENT CASE

Review the assigned case study in Appendix 2.

1. Assuming a complaint has been filed against the driver of the bus in the assigned case:
   a. Prepare all of the necessary pleadings as the attorney for the bus driver.

   b. Prepare a third-party complaint that might be filed by the driver of the bus against the manufacturer of the tractor-trailer and its brakes in the assigned case study in Appendix 2.

BUILDING YOUR PROFESSIONAL PORTFOLIO AND REFERENCE MANUAL

CIVIL LITIGATION TEAM AT WORK

See page 18 for instructions on Building Your Professional Portfolio.

Policy Manual

Policy and procedures to ensure that no deadlines are missed.

Forms

Form necessary in your jurisdiction to toll the statute of limitations.

LEARNING OBJECTIVES

After studying this chapter, you should be able to:

1. Define *discovery* and explain its purposes in litigation.

2. Describe how the Federal Rules of Civil Procedure and Rules of Evidence define the scope of discovery in federal court.

3. Describe the forms of discovery permitted under the Federal Rules of Civil Procedure.

4. Explain the sequence and timing of discovery under the mandatory disclosure Rules in Federal Court.

5. Describe the court methods for ensuring compliance with discovery rules.

Introduction to Discovery | CHAPTER 11

CHAPTER 11

OPENING SCENARIO

 The partners had carefully considered what the most appropriate court would be for filing their lawsuit on behalf of the group of clients injured in the motor vehicle accident. They decided to bring suit in the federal court on the basis of diversity of citizenship. Ethan Benjamin was assigned as the supervising attorney because his office was the closest to the federal courthouse, and Roy Saunders was named lead trial counsel. Mr. Benjamin was reminded by his partner, who had been a clerk to a federal court judge, that the Federal Rules of Civil Procedure pose a burden (from a time management standpoint) on the process of litigation but result in faster trial dates. Mr. Benjamin and Caitlin, his paralegal, were concerned that they might not be able to gather all of the necessary information under the accelerated time frame for discovery before the scheduling conference. This was not the firm's first case under the federal e-discovery rules, but there were concerns related to the number of defendants and the potentially large amount of electronically stored information. He wanted to ensure that the scheduling conference would go well.

OPENING SCENARIO LEARNING OBJECTIVE

Explain the discovery timeline and requirements in federal court civil cases.

■ INTRODUCTION TO DISCOVERY

Discovery is a step in the litigation process in which the plaintiff and the defendant share information relevant to their dispute. The discovery process can be a time-consuming and sometimes frustrating phase in litigation. Successful discovery requires an organized approach and a familiarity with the rules of court that apply to discovery. Paralegals on the litigation team are often charged with coordinating discovery requests (including responses from clients and opposing parties) and working with information technology experts.

■ PURPOSE OF DISCOVERY

LEARNING OBJECTIVE 1
Define *discovery* and explain its purposes in litigation.

Discovery is a court-sanctioned process during which the parties engage in various activities to elicit facts of the case prior to trial. Discovery serves a number of purposes: understanding and evaluating the client's case; focusing the legal team on the strengths and weaknesses of its case; understanding and evaluating the strengths and weaknesses of the opponent's case; preparing for trial; preserving testimony; and potentially facilitating settlement.

Evaluating Your Client's Case

PRACTICE TIP
PURPOSES OF DISCOVERY

- Understand and evaluate the client's case
- Understand and evaluate the opposing party's case
- Trial preparation
- Preserve testimony
- Impeach witness testimony
- Facilitate settlement

By answering each other's questions, the plaintiff and defendant share information about the facts, documents, statements of fact, and the identity of expert witnesses related to the legal dispute. By openly sharing information that may be used at trial, each side is forced to evaluate its own case and the opponent's case and determine the ability to meet its burdens of proof. With each side fully aware of the potential evidence to be presented, including potential damages, the legal team can, based on prior experience or reported similar cases, put a potential value on a trial outcome. In many cases, the decision to try a case or settle a case is a business decision. Is the cost of a trial outweighed by the potential recovery? With two well-prepared legal teams, the evaluation is surprisingly close, and settlement is more likely than not.

Evaluating Your Opponent's Case

When reviewing the discovery responses received from the opposing party, you will evaluate the documents supplied as potential evidence and, more importantly, the credibility of potential witnesses who will be used to present the evidence. If the defense witness is calm and appears authoritative and believable, even a questionable document may be accepted by the trier of fact as important.

Preparing for Trial

Properly completed discovery eliminates the potential for surprises in the evidence presented at trial. In fact, many of the "surprises" one sees on television trial dramas are not possible under discovery rules that are designed to prevent trial by surprise.

Preserving Oral Testimony

Discovery is also a method for preserving oral testimony. There are times when witnesses may not be available to attend trial to testify. Examples include witnesses who are gravely ill and not expected to live until trial, those who are elderly or incapacitated and physically unable to come to the courthouse, and those who are outside the geographical jurisdiction of the court. Under limited circumstances, the deposition testimony of these unavailable witnesses may be presented at trial. The deposition of these witnesses is given the same treatment as if the witness was in court, testifying in person.

Impeaching Witness Testimony

Closely related to preserving testimony is the concept of challenging the credibility of a witness who testifies at trial. If the witness has given a deposition or other recorded statement and at trial says something different, then that difference can be brought to the attention of the fact finder, whether judge or jury. We expect a statement made closer in time to the incident to be accurate and if different from what is said at trial, which may occur years after the incident, the truthfulness of the witness is called into doubt or impeached.

Facilitating Settlement

Properly conducted discovery facilitates settlements. Careful analysis of the evidence revealed through discovery enables the legal team to evaluate the relative strengths and weaknesses of their client's case and those of the opposing side's case. When discovery is conducted properly, both sides are in a better position to evaluate their chances of success before the trier of fact; they can judge the likelihood of success based on the weight of evidence and the perceived credibility of witnesses.

■ RULES OF COURT AND RULES OF EVIDENCE

What is permitted and what is not permitted in civil litigation is, with some variation of style of counsel and permission of the judge assigned to the case, set out in the rules of the particular court and the related rules of evidence. Each court system, state and federal, has a set of rules, the rules of civil procedure, that control the process of the litigation. Each court system also has a set of rules, the rules of evidence, that define what evidence is admissible in court proceedings. The rules of evidence are similar from jurisdiction to jurisdiction and court to court. However, a court may have a set of local rules, and an individual judge may have rules setting standards for conducting proceedings in his/her court.

In the federal courts, the Federal Rules of Civil Procedure provide the framework for conducting litigation. Local district court rules may supplement these rules, as will the particular requirements and procedures, if any, of the assigned judge. The conduct of the trial is largely a matter of what evidence is and is not permitted to be introduced and admitted at trial. The Federal Rules of Evidence provide the guidelines for use of evidence in federal courts.

Civil litigation is serious business. The rules of court and the rules of evidence provide a level playing field. Like the participants in a professional baseball or football game, both sides need to know what the rules are and see that they are fairly applied. The judge becomes the interpreter and enforcer of the rules, similar to the role of the umpire or referee. With a well-understood set of rules evenly and fairly applied, justice may be served with each side feeling it had its day in court.

Scope of Discovery

Under the Federal Rules of Civil Procedure, everything is discoverable that is not privileged or attorney work product and is relevant or may lead to **relevant evidence.** Documents and information that may be obtained through the discovery

LEARNING OBJECTIVE 2
Describe how the Federal Rules of Civil Procedure and Rules of Evidence define the scope of discovery in federal court.

relevant evidence
Evidence that tends to prove the existence of facts important to the resolution of a case.

process are considerably broader than that which may be used or admissible at trial under the Federal Rules of Evidence. An item or information is relevant for purposes of discovery if it has a relationship to evidence about the litigation and is likely to lead to admissible evidence. An item of information sought in discovery is not required to meet the requirements of the Rules of Evidence for admission at trial; real, reliable, relevant, and probative value outweighs prejudice (Fed. R. Civ. P. 26 (b)). Thus, many more items may be available to the legal team through discovery.

FRCP 26 (b) Discovery Scope and Limits

(1) Scope in General. Unless otherwise limited by court order, the scope of discovery is as follows: Parties may obtain discovery regarding any nonprivileged matter that is relevant to any party's claim or defense—including the existence, description, nature, custody, condition, and location of any documents or other tangible things and the identity and location of persons who know of any discoverable matter. For good cause, the court may order discovery of any matter relevant to the subject matter involved in the action. Relevant information need not be admissible at the trial if the discovery appears reasonably calculated to lead to the discovery of admissible evidence. All discovery is subject to the limitations imposed by Rule 26(b)(2)(C).

Privilege

privilege
A rule of evidence that prohibits certain types of communication from being disclosed at trial. The recognized privileged communications include attorney–client, physician–patient, priest–penitent, and spousal. The privilege may also apply to documents via the work product or trade secrets doctrine.

Under ordinary circumstances, some information is not required to be shared, nor may it be demanded in court or under oath. Any item, whether testimonial or tangible, that falls under one of the recognized **privileges** found in the rules of evidence will be protected from discovery. These privileges are typically thought of in terms of oral communications. But a client could deliver a gun to his attorney in the course of his representation. The gun—and its existence, ownership, and whereabouts—could be protected from discovery because of the attorney–client privilege.

The "privilege" belongs to the client, not to the attorney. The client may waive the privilege and allow the attorney or paralegal to reveal the information; however, the attorneys or paralegals may not by themselves waive the privilege when asked what the client has told them. In a court proceeding, an appropriate answer to the question of what the client said would be: "I decline to answer because of the attorney–client privilege." If, however, the client had revealed or released the same information to someone else, the privilege is lost. Thus, the client must really keep the information secret for the privilege to apply.

The concept of privilege also extends to persons while they are acting within certain roles such as:

1. spouse;
2. clergy–penitent;
3. doctor–patient;
4. psychotherapist–patient; and
5. participants in settlement negotiations.

Claim of Privilege

claim of privilege
The person claiming the privilege—usually the client—has the burden to establish its existence.

Privilege is not automatically invoked. The person claiming the privilege—usually the client—has the burden to establish its existence, called **claim of privilege.**

"To sustain a claim of privilege, the party invoking it must demonstrate that the information at issue was a communication between client and counsel or his employee, that it was intended to be and was in fact kept confidential, and that it was made in order to assist in obtaining or providing legal advice or services to the client." *SR International Bus. Ins. Co. v. World Trade Center Prop. No. 1 Civ. 9291* (S.D.N.Y. 2002) quoting *Browne of New York City, Inc. v. Ambrose Corp.*

IN THE WORDS OF THE COURT…

Privilege

Trammell v. United States, 445 U.S. 40 (1980).

"The privileges between priest and penitent, attorney and client, and physician and patient limit protection to private communication. These privileges are rooted in the imperative need for confidence and trust. The priest–penitent privilege recognizes the human need to disclose to a spiritual counselor, in total and absolute confidence, what are believed to be flawed acts or thoughts and to receive priestly consolation and guidance in return. The lawyer–client privilege rests on the need for the advocate and counselor to know all that relates to the client's reasons for seeking representation if the professional mission is to be carried out. Similarly, the physician must know all that a patient can articulate in order to identify and to treat disease; barriers to full disclosure would impair diagnosis and treatment."

Extension of Attorney–Client Privilege to Others

It is now accepted that the efficient administration of justice requires lawyers to engage others, such as legal assistants, accountants, information technologists, and other experts. This would not be possible if the privilege did not extend to these agents of the attorney, including, most recently, public relations firms.

The U.S. District Court for the Southern District of New York summarized the law, stating:

"…the privilege in appropriate circumstances extends to otherwise privileged communications that involve persons assisting the lawyer in the rendition of legal services. This principle has been applied universally to cover office personnel, such as secretaries and law clerks, who assist lawyers in performing their tasks. But it has been applied more broadly as well. For example, in United States v. Kovel, the Second Circuit held that a client's communication with an accountant employed by his attorney were privileged where made for the purpose of enabling the attorney to understand the client situation in order to provide legal advice." (IN RE Grand Jury Subpoenas dated March 24, 2003 directed to (A) Grand Jury Witness Firm and (B) Grand Jury Witness, M11-188 (USDC, S.D.N.Y.) (June 2, 2003).)

Common Interest Privilege

Another variation of privilege is the **common interest privilege.**

"The purpose of the common interest privilege is to permit a client to share confidential information with the attorney for another who shares a common legal

common interest privilege
To permit a client to share confidential information with the attorney for another who shares a common legal interest.

interest. The key consideration is that the nature of the interest be identical, not similar [emphasis added], and be legal, not solely commercial. *SR International Bus. Ins. Co. v. World Trade Center Prop. No. 1 Civ 9291* (S.D.N.Y. 2002) quoting *North River Insurance Co. v. Columbia Casualty Company No. 9 Civ 2518, 1995 WL 5792.*

Work Product Doctrine

duty of confidentiality
An ethical obligation to not reveal any information about a client's affairs regardless of the source of the information.

work product doctrine
A limited protection for material prepared by the attorney, or those working for the attorney, in anticipation of litigation or for trial.

The work product doctrine is different from both the attorney–client privilege and the **duty of confidentiality.** The attorney–client privilege and the duty of confidentiality relate to the information provided by the clients regardless of whether they involve potential litigation. The **work product doctrine** provides a limited protection for material prepared by the attorney (or those working for the attorney) in anticipation of litigation or for trial, such as research on theories of law, defenses that may be raised in the trial, trial strategy for the order of presentations, or methods of impeaching the credibility of witnesses for the other side. "The work product doctrine is narrower than the attorney–client privilege in that it protects only materials prepared 'in anticipation of litigation,' Fed. R. Civ. P. 26(b) (3), whereas the attorney–client privilege protects confidential legal communications between an attorney and client regardless of whether they involve possible litigation." *Electronic Data Systems Corporation v. Steingraber Case* 4:02 CV 225 USDC, E.D. Texas (2003).

The work product doctrine is codified in the Federal Rules of Civil Procedure Rule 26 (b)(3)(B) and in Rule 16(b)(2)(A) of the Federal Rules of Criminal Procedure.

IN THE WORDS OF THE COURT...

Hickman v. Tayler, 329 U.S. 495 (1947) at page 511

The U.S. Supreme Court recognized the work product doctrine and its importance saying:

"Proper preparation of a client's case demands that he assemble information, sift what he considers to be the relevant from the irrelevant facts, prepare his legal theories and plan his strategy without undue and needless interference. That is the historical and the necessary way in which lawyers act within the framework of our system of jurisprudence to promote justice and to protect their clients' interest.

This work is reflected, of course, in interviews, statements, memoranda, correspondence, briefs, mental impressions, personal beliefs, and countless other tangible and intangible ways—aptly though roughly termed by the Circuit Court of Appeals in this case as the 'work product of the lawyer.' Were such materials open to opposing counsel on mere demand, much of what is now put down in writing would remain unwritten.

An attorney's thoughts, heretofore inviolate, would not be his own. Inefficiency, unfairness and sharp practices would inevitably develop in the giving of legal advice and in the preparation of cases for trial. The effect on the legal profession would be demoralizing. And the interests of the clients and the cause of justice would be poorly served.

...where relevant and non-privileged facts remain hidden in an attorney's file and where production of those facts is essential to the preparation of one's case, discovery may be properly had."

ETHICAL Perspectives

> ## RHODE ISLAND RULES OF PROFESSIONAL CONDUCT
> ## RULE 1.6 CONFIDENTIALITY OF INFORMATION
>
> (a) A lawyer shall not reveal information relating to the representation of a client unless the client gives informed consent, except for disclosures that are impliedly authorized in order to carry out the representation, and except as stated in paragraph (b).
> (b) A lawyer may reveal such information to the extent the lawyer reasonably believes necessary:
>   (1) to prevent the client from committing a criminal act that the lawyer believes is likely to result in imminent death or substantial bodily harm;
>   (2) to establish a claim or defense on behalf of the lawyer in a controversy between the lawyer and the client, to establish a defense to a criminal charge or civil claim against the lawyer based upon conduct in which the client was involved, or to respond to allegations in any proceeding concerning the lawyer's representation of the client;
>   (3) to secure legal advice about the lawyer's compliance with these Rules; or
>   (4) to comply with other law or a court order.
>
> *Source:* http://www.courts.ri.gov/supreme/pdf-files/Rules_Of_Professional_Conduct.pdf

Exceptions and Limitations to the Work Product Doctrine

The work product doctrine has some exceptions. It does not cover documents prepared in the normal operation of the client's business, such as sales reports, data analysis, or summaries of business operations.

> The work product doctrine does not extend to documents in an attorney's possession that were prepared by a third party in the ordinary course of business and that would have been created in essentially similar form irrespective of any litigation anticipated by counsel. In Re Grand Jury Subpoenas, 318 F.3d 379 (2nd Cir 2002) at page 385.

In other words, the client cannot obtain protection for internal business documents by giving them to the attorney (and thereby protect them from discovery by the other side because they are in the possession of the attorney).

Exception to the Third-Party Document Exception

The courts have made an exception to the exception in which a lawyer is trying to find out the other party's strategy by asking about documents already in his/her possession that would not be protected under the third-party exception. To protect the lawyer's trial strategy, the court may impose a privilege where it would not otherwise exist.

> ...Where a request is made for documents already in the possession of requesting party, with precise goal of warning what the opposing attorney's thinking or strategy may be, even **third-party documents** may be protected. Id. page 385

third-party documents
Documents prepared by a third party in the ordinary course of business that would have been prepared in similar form even if there was no litigation.

Internal Investigations and Evidentiary Privileges

Businesses, and particularly corporations with publicly traded securities, are under state and federal law and regulation requirements to take a proactive approach to determine wrongdoing and identify violations of statutes and regulations. These investigations and "audits" create a body of documents. All, some, or none of these documents may be subject to evidentiary privilege. Without the protection of the privilege, businesses would be hesitant to conduct audits for fear of prosecution.

■ FORMS OF DISCOVERY

LEARNING OBJECTIVE 3
Describe the forms of discovery permitted under the Federal Rules of Civil Procedure.

There are five forms of discovery permitted under the Federal Rules of Civil Procedure:

1. depositions;
2. written interrogatories;
3. production of documents or things or permission to enter upon land or property of another for inspection;
4. physical and mental examinations; and
5. requests for admissions.

Depositions

deposition
A form of discovery available to ask questions and obtain oral answers under oath from a witness or party to a lawsuit. Questions and answers are recorded stenographically.

perjury
Deliberately making a false or misleading statement while under oath; is potentially subject to court sanction, including incarceration.

Depositions are questions asked of a witness or party to the lawsuit that are required to be answered under oath subject to penalties of perjury. **Perjury** is deliberately making a false or misleading statement while under oath. Perjurers are potentially subject to court sanction, including incarceration. The questions may be asked orally in person before a court reporter and stenographically recorded. In some cases, depositions may also be videotaped and recorded in written form.

Depositions are the only method of discovery that can be used to question witnesses identified by the opposing party as potential witnesses at trial. Because depositions provide an opportunity for each side to personally question and assess the reliability of each party and witness that is expected to testify at trial, depositions are considered the most valuable part of the discovery process.

Interrogatories

interrogatories
A form of discovery in which written questions are addressed to a party to a lawsuit requiring written answers made under oath.

Interrogatories are written questions addressed to the opposing party in a lawsuit that must be answered in writing, under oath. Typically, the questions seek factual information, such as names, addresses, identification of witnesses, and documents relevant to the lawsuit. As a way of expediting the discovery process and eliminating objections and lost court time hearing motions on discovery matters, many courts have issued or approved sets of standard form interrogatories for different areas of law that must be answered. Exhibit 11.1 shows a portion of the standard set of interrogatories for use in a motor vehicle case in the Court of Common Pleas of Philadelphia (a trial court).

WEB RESOURCES

Use the Internet to find any standard form interrogatories used in your jurisdiction.

production of documents or things
A form of discovery in which written requests for documents and things to be made available for inspection are sent to the opposing party. A written response made under oath is required.

Production of Documents or Things

Production of documents or things makes available for discovery documents and other physical objects, like defective products, relevant to the lawsuit. The process of production of documents is a written request addressed to a party to

Exhibit 11.1 Standard Form Interrogatories for Motor Vehicle Liability Cases

---

FIRST JUDICIAL DISTRICT OF PENNSYLVANIA

IN THE COURT OF COMMON PLEAS OF PHILADELPHIA COUNTY

PLAINTIFF'S NAME	:	Civil Trial Division
	:	
	:	Compulsory Arbitration
	:	Program
vs.	:	
	:	_____ Term, 20
	:	
DEFENDANT'S NAME	:	No. _____

PLAINTIFF'S INTERROGATORIES DIRECTED TO DEFENDANT(S)

Motor Vehicle Liability Cases

Plaintiff(s) hereby make demand that the Defendant(s) answer the following Interrogatories pursuant to the Pennsylvania Rules of Civil Procedure 4001 et seq. These Interrogatories must be answered as provided in Pa. R.C.P. 4006 and the Answers must be served on all other parties within thirty (30) days after the Interrogatories are deemed served.

These Interrogatories are deemed to be continuing as to require the filing of Supplemental Answers promptly in the event Defendant(s) or their representatives (including counsel) learn additional facts not set forth in its original Answers or discover that information provided in the Answers is erroneous. Such Supplemental Answers may be filed from time to time, but not later than 30 days after such further information is received, pursuant to Pa. R.C.P. 4007.4.

These Interrogatories are addressed to you as a party to this action; your answers shall be based upon information known to you or in the possession, custody or control of you, your attorney or other representative acting on your behalf whether in preparation for litigation or otherwise. These Interrogatories must be answered completely and specifically by you in writing and must be verified. The fact that investigation is continuing or that discovery is not complete shall not be used as an excuse for failure to answer each interrogatory as completely as possible. The omission of any name, fact, or other item of information from the Answers shall be deemed a representation that such name, fact, or other item was not known to Defendant(s), their counsel, or other representatives at the time of service of the Answers. If another motor vehicle was not involved in the alleged accident, then interpret any questions to include a non-motor vehicle (i.e. pedestrian, bicycle, etc.).

(1) State:

    (a) If an individual: Full name (maiden name, if applicable), alias(es), date of birth, marital status (name of spouse) at the time the cause of action arose and currently, residence and business addresses at time of cause of action and currently and Social Security Number.

    (b) If a corporation: registered corporation name, principal place of business and registered address for service of process at the time the cause of action arose and currently.

    (c) If a partnership: registered partnership name, principal place of business and registered address for service of process at the time the cause of action arose and currently as well as the identities and residence addresses of each partner at the time the cause of action arose and currently.

(2) If you (and/or your operator) were/are employed, state:

    (a) By whom, at the time the cause of action arose and currently;

    (b) Your title or position and accompanying duties and responsibilities at the time the cause of action arose and currently;

    (c) The length of your employment as of the time the cause of action arose and currently.

Source: http://courts.phila.gov/pdf/regs/2005/cptad02-2005.pdf

the litigation. The party must respond in writing to each request. The response may also include a paper (hard copy) or electronic copy of the documents or the items requested. Examples include medical records of an injured plaintiff, a copy of a liability insurance policy, a police accident report, an e-mail, or an employee personnel file.

Where the "thing" is not capable of delivery, such as a building, tractor-trailer/stone truck combination, or other large object, this discovery tool includes the right of entry onto the land of another for purposes of inspection. This discovery tool may also be used in cases where the volume of documentary evidence or electronic records is too large for practical delivery, such as a warehouse with thousands of cartons of paper files.

Example

The parties dispute the condition of goods shipped by the plaintiff to the defendant. Defendant holds those goods at his warehouse. Copies of the documents associated with the manufacture, shipment, and storage of the goods would be appropriate to request through production. Additionally, entry to the defendant's warehouse to inspect the storage conditions in the warehouse and the condition of the goods would be permissible under the rules.

Physical and Mental Examinations

physical and mental examinations
A form of discovery that permits the physical or mental examination of a party by a qualified expert of the opposing party's choosing when the physical or mental condition of the party is at issue in the lawsuit.

Physical and mental examinations of the parties to the lawsuit are permitted where the physical or mental condition of one of the parties is an element of the cause of action. In a personal injury action, the physical injuries suffered and the damages that result from those injuries are elements of the cause of action for negligence. Thus, the defense team may obtain a physical examination of the plaintiff from a doctor of its choosing. In a guardianship proceeding, the plaintiff seeks to be appointed guardian over someone who lacks mental capacity to handle financial and other matters. The cause of action is dependent on the mental state of the individual. Therefore, a mental examination would be appropriate.

Requests for Admission

request for admission
A form of discovery in which written requests are made to the opposing party, asking him to admit the truth of certain facts or liability.

Requests for admission are written requests issued by one party to the lawsuit to the other asking that certain facts or legal issues be admitted as true. Properly used, requests for admission can narrow the focus of trial and streamline the testimony. Some facts are generally not in controversy, such as names, addresses, and other personal information. Locations of accidents, time of day, and related facts may also be admitted without calling witnesses. Who was speeding, not observant, or otherwise negligent are facts rarely admitted because they represent an admission of liability. However, if liability is admitted, the only issue left is damages. Where the damages are minimal, parties may admit to the facts of liability to avoid the time and cost of trial to obtain a finding of fact of something obvious. The remaining issue, determining the monetary value of the injuries or damages sustained, may be agreed upon between the parties or determined by the trier of fact in very short order at little time or expense.

Example

If the defendant admits as true his liability for the auto accident, then that issue is no longer in dispute. No evidence as to the cause of the accident will be required at trial. The trial will then be limited to determining damages only, making a more focused and streamlined case.

■ SEQUENCE OF DISCOVERY

There is no predetermined method or order in which the five discovery methods should be used. From a strategic standpoint, practitioners may have determined a preferred order, such as obtaining written answers to interrogatories before taking oral depositions. Either party may conduct its discovery at any time. The rules contemplate that the discovery of the plaintiff and the defendant should occur simultaneously. In many cases, counsel will schedule and take depositions of parties on the same day and in the same location, utilizing the same stenographic service or videotape operators, to save time and costs.

LEARNING OBJECTIVE 4
Explain the sequence and timing of discovery under the mandatory disclosure Rules in Federal Court.

Under the federal rules of court, discovery may not begin until the lawyers for the parties have conferred and developed a proposed discovery plan, as required in Fed. R. Civ. P. 26(f),(Fed. R. Civ. P. 26(d)).

Discovery Timing

Certain events must take place before discovery may begin. For example, discovery cannot begin until attorneys for the litigants have discussed the case, including the discovery issues. In federal court cases, this meet and confer step must occur before the required scheduling conference with the assigned judge. The scheduling conference occurs within ninety days after the **entry of appearance** by the attorney who will represent the defendant (or 120 days after the defendant is served with the complaint). The meet and confer must occur at least twenty-one days before the scheduling conference with the judge. Following the meet and confer between opposing attorneys, a written statement memorializing the items discussed must be submitted to the court within fourteen days. It is this statement that the judge will review and rely on in discussing the issues at the scheduling conference.

entry of appearance
An attorney for one of the litigants files papers officially identifying himself as representing the client before the court.

The required meet and confer is between the attorneys without a judge. It affords them the opportunity to amicably agree to and propose to the judge a schedule to manage the discovery phase of the litigation. This process of discussing and planning discovery is particularly important in complex litigation and in those cases involving large amounts of electronically stored information. The goal of the conference between counsel is to discuss the nature of the claims and the likelihood of settlement, arrange for mandatory disclosure under Rule 26(a), and develop a discovery plan in the event one is necessary.

The meet and confer of the attorneys is linked in time and responsibility to the Rule 16(b) scheduling conference with the judge. Under the federal rules, a judge is assigned to the case from the time of filing the complaint. The judge will usually take an active role in setting a time line for discovery and trial (see Exhibit 11.2). The attorneys have an opportunity to participate in that process by issuing the report of their meet and confer conference and participating in the scheduling conference with the judge. The judge will usually give great deference to the recommendations of the attorneys in scheduling deadlines for discovery.

Rule 26(a) Disclosure Requirements

Rule 26(a) makes mandatory the initial disclosure of certain information that for years was available only after a formal written discovery request was issued. For many cases, no action was taken on a file until one side moved the case forward with a formal discovery request. Under current rules, everything the legal team intends to rely upon to prove its claims must be disclosed early in the litigation.

Exhibit 11.2 Time Line From the Filing of the Complaint to the Scheduling Conference

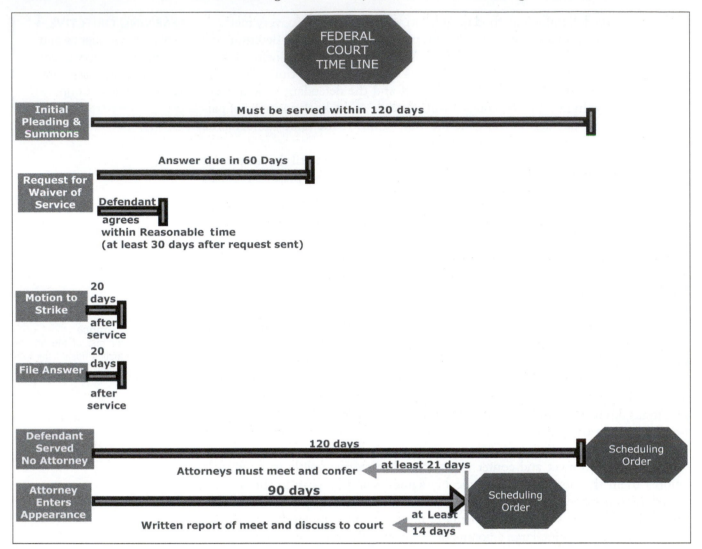

Insufficient time to investigate the claim is not a valid excuse for failure to comply. The benefits of mandatory disclosure are twofold:

1. It provides for the early evaluation and settlement of claims; and
2. it reduces the amount, nature, and time necessary to conduct formal discovery.

From a practical standpoint, the plaintiff's legal team must be prepared for initial disclosure at or shortly after filing the complaint.

The federal rules set a minimum time frame for this initial disclosure to occur at the meet and confer but no later than 14 days thereafter. Although the attorneys have authority to agree to extend that time, the judge at the scheduling conference may encourage them to conclude the disclosure at a faster pace.

Thus, the plaintiff's thorough investigation of the case, including obtaining a report of any expert witness, must be complete before filing suit. For the defense team, the time to investigate and comply is very short. There is no time for procrastination in investigating and establishing the grounds to defend the claims.

Information Subject to Mandatory Disclosure

Almost anything relied upon in developing the claim, regardless of whether it is admissible at trial, must be disclosed. This disclosure includes the identity of witnesses, copies of documents, a computation of damages, and a copy of any insurance policy that may be used to satisfy a judgment obtained in the litigation.

Prior to the adoption of Rule 26(a) mandatory initial disclosure, information used to compute damages represented the plaintiff attorney's thought process and was not released as part of discovery under the work product doctrine. Under the current rule, however, the attorney's value on the case is made known within months of the complaint being filed.

From the defense standpoint, the disclosure of insurance coverage, which is not admissible at trial, is significant. A key element in settling most cases is the existence of and limitations on insurance coverage. With both the plaintiff's calculation of damages and the defendant's ability to pay based upon disclosure of insurance coverage known within months of filing the lawsuit, the chances for fruitful settlement discussions are enhanced.

Experts and Witnesses

Expert witnesses expected to be called at trial must also be identified. A copy of the expert's qualifications as an expert (including a list of publications for which the witness has written from the preceding ten years, a statement of compensation, and a list of other cases in which the witness has testified) must also be provided under the disclosure rule. The most critical element to be shared is the written report of the expert's opinion. The report represents what the expert is expected to say at trial. The written report must include the opinion of the expert and the basis of that opinion, including the information relied upon and any assumptions made. The disclosure of the expert and his report must be made at least ninety days prior to trial. Some courts require the disclosure of the expert at the time of the initial disclosure or within thirty days of receipt of the expert's report. Many lawsuits become a battle of the experts. The early disclosure of the expert and his opinion often leads to early resolution of the case.

expert witness
A person qualified by education, training, or experience to render an opinion based on a set of facts that are outside the scope of knowledge of the fact finder.

■ COMPLIANCE AND COURT INTERVENTION

From the perspective of the bench, the attorneys should be able to complete the initial disclosure and discovery without the court's assistance. Often, that is not the case. Whatever the reason, the legal team's response to discovery requests can be delayed or, worse, forgotten. No matter which side of the discovery request you are on, the issuer's or the responder's, the legal team must have a system in place to comply with discovery deadlines; that means establishing an internal calendaring system, observing the deadlines the team creates for itself, and obtaining client cooperation. There will be times when it is not possible to comply, and the paralegal then needs to know the steps to take to obtain an extension of time to comply. Alternatively, the paralegal must also know the manner in which to use court intervention to have the opposing party come into compliance.

Most judges disfavor judicial involvement in the discovery process. The mindset of the bench is that counsel should anticipate and resolve discovery problems through the planning tools available under the Rules, including the Rule 26(f) meet and confer, the Rule 16(b) scheduling conference with the judge, and the scheduling order that the conference produces.

LEARNING OBJECTIVE 5
Describe the court methods for ensuring compliance with discovery rules.

Seeking Compliance as the Issuer of Discovery Requests

The response date for the discovery requests can be the time limit set forth in the rules (typically 30 days), or it can be based on an enlargement of time agreed to and incorporated into the scheduling order. When the deadline has passed and no response is received, the paralegal should, as a matter of professional courtesy, contact the opposing counsel's office. The goal of this initial contact is to determine the cause of the delay and to determine a date when the responses will be completed. Typically, the attorneys will agree to an extension, which should be memorialized with a stipulation filed with the court.

If opposing counsel fails to respond, a follow-up telephone call or letter may be appropriate to encourage compliance. When the amicable attempts at encouraging compliance fail, the legal team must seek the assistance of the court via a **motion to compel.** From a practical standpoint, the motion will result in an order compelling the party to respond to the discovery request within a certain time period (usually 20 days from the date of the order) and instructing that party to pay the attorney's fees and costs associated with the motion. If the responses are not provided in accordance with the court-ordered deadline, a **motion for sanctions** can be filed to seek the court's intervention. As the non-responding party has violated a court order, sanctions for contempt are applied. Typical sanctions can include a prohibition from introducing evidence, a dismissal of claims, and an award of attorney's fees.

motion to compel
Motion seeking the opposing party's cooperation and compliance in responding to discovery requests.

motion for sanctions
Where an order compelling a party to cooperate is not complied with, the next step is to request that the court impose a penalty against the non-compliant party.

Seeking Compliance as the Recipient of Discovery Requests

The litigation paralegal will have primary responsibility for preparation of responses within the specified time frame. Developing a procedure that ensures client participation and cooperation in the preparation of responses is crucial to the success of the paralegal assisting with discovery. Upon receipt of the discovery request, two working copies should be made. One copy should be sent to the client with a letter of instruction describing the document and the time limitation the legal team and client are working under. The client should be asked to answer the questions and gather documents to the best of his ability. A caution is in order with regard to electronically stored information: Certainly by the time discovery requests have been issued, a litigation hold will be in place preventing the tampering and/or destruction of electronically stored information. How that information is gathered, sorted, and provided in response to a discovery request may be best handled by an information technologist to avoid a potential spoliation claim.

A firm date is set for a meeting to review responses and documents with the client. The date must allow sufficient time to review and complete the process in the time allotted. Before meeting with the client, the legal team should be sure to review the file and the documents in the firm's possession and prepare responses based on that information. The meeting with the client should serve two purposes: (1) to determine whether the file is complete and (2) to prepare final answers to the discovery requests. After preparing the formal response, the attorney should review the responses and make any changes. As most discovery is answered under oath, one more meeting with the client to review and sign the final responses will be required before they are sent to the opposing counsel.

In some instances, the information or documents sought through discovery may be inappropriate. Questions that ask for attorney notes would be protected under the work product doctrine. The paralegal must be prepared to respond to the interrogatory or other request with an objection to the question or request and must be able to set forth the specific grounds for that objection. When sub-mitting the response, a **motion for protective order** should be filed with the court to determine whether the request should be answered or an order protecting the material from discovery is appropriate.

CONCEPT REVIEW AND REINFORCEMENT

KEY TERMS

discovery   274
relevant evidence   275
privilege   276
claim of privilege   276
common interest privilege   277
duty of confidentiality   278
work product doctrine   278
third-party document   279

depositions   280
perjury   280
interrogatories   280
production of documents or
    things   280
physical and mental
    examinations   282
request for admission   282

entry of appearance   283
expert witness   285
motion to compel   286
motion for sanctions   286
motion for protective
    order   287

CHAPTER SUMMARY

INTRODUCTION TO DISCOVERY

Introduction to Discovery	Discovery is a step in the litigation process where the plaintiff and defen-dant share information relevant to their dispute. The discovery process can be a time-consuming and sometimes frustrating phase in litigation. Successful discovery requires an organized approach and familiarity with the rules of court that apply to discovery.
Purpose of Discovery	Discovery may be used for case evaluation, to aid in potential settlement, to prepare for trial, and to preserve oral testimony of witnesses who may not be able to attend trial.
Rules of Court and Rules of Evidence	The rules of court and the rules of evidence provide a level playing field for conducting a trial.
Forms of Discovery	There are five forms of discovery under the federal rules: 1. depositions; 2. written interrogatories; 3. production of documents or things or permission to enter onto the land or property of another for inspection; 4. physical and mental examinations; and 5. request for admissions.
Sequence of Discovery	There is no predetermined order in which the five discovery tools must be used. Preference, strategy, and convenience will influence which tools are used and when. However, discovery may not begin until a scheduling conference is held and the materials subject to mandatory disclosure are exchanged.

(continued)

Compliance and Court Intervention	Discovery should be a cooperative effort. When counsel fails to deliver requested items, opposing counsel may file a motion to compel and seek court intervention.
	If the court order is not obeyed, a motion for sanctions may be filed, seeking a punishment for the contempt of the court's order.
	The legal team must develop a discovery plan that ensures client participation and timely responses.

REVIEW QUESTIONS AND EXERCISES

1. Define *discovery* and describe the purposes of discovery.
2. What is the scope of discovery?
3. How is discoverable information different from admissible information?
4. Who may claim that communication is protected by privilege? Who may waive privilege?
5. Describe exceptions and limitations to privilege.
6. Describe the types of discovery.
7. What time constraints are imposed on the discovery process?
8. What is *mandatory initial disclosure*? How has it changed civil litigation in federal court?
9. Describe how you would gain compliance in responding to a discovery request.

BUILDING YOUR PARALEGAL SKILLS

INTERNET AND TECHNOLOGY EXERCISE

1. Use the Internet or a library to find copies of the most current version of the Federal Rules of Civil Procedure, Rules 16, 26, 33, 34, 37, and 45.

CIVIL LITIGATION VIDEO CASE STUDIES

Confidentiality Issue: Need-to-Know Circle

Two paralegals meet in the law office coffee room and discuss a case on which only one of them is working.

After viewing the video at www.pearsonhighered.com/ careersresources, answer the following questions.

1. Can all the facts about a client or case be discussed with anyone in the law firm, or is doing so a breach of the ethical obligation of confidentiality?
2. Do conversations about the facts or confidential information breach the attorney–client privilege or the ethical obligation of confidentiality?

Attorney Meet and Confer: Electronic Discovery Issues

Two attorneys meet to discuss the management of the case, the exchange of information under mandatory disclosure rules, discovery, and deadlines.

After viewing the video at www.pearsonhighered.com/ careersresources, answer the following questions.

1. Are the attorneys appropriately prepared for their conference? How could they be better prepared?
2. Would the meet and confer be more effective if mandatory disclosure had already been accomplished?
3. Would the presence of an information technologist have made the meeting more successful?

CHAPTER OPENING SCENARIO CASE STUDY

Use the Opening Scenario for this chapter to answer the following questions.

1. As defense counsel, draw up a document discovery agreement for plaintiff's counsel. Is the language the same for both plaintiff and defendant? Explain.

2. Prepare a list of mandatory disclosure materials to be delivered electronically to the opponent.

COMPREHENSIVE CASE STUDY

SCHOOL BUS–TRUCK ACCIDENT CASE

Review the assigned case study in Appendix 2.
Prepare a form (template) Motion to Compel and a Motion for Sanctions for use in a future case.

BUILDING YOUR PROFESSIONAL PORTFOLIO AND REFERENCE MANUAL

CIVIL LITIGATION TEAM AT WORK

See page 18 for instructions on Building Your Professional Portfolio.

Forms

1. Draft a form letter to send to the opposing party, who has failed to respond to discovery in a timely fashion.

2. Prepare a form (template) Motion to Compel and a Motion for Sanctions for use in a future case.

3. Obtain standard form interrogatories for civil cases for your local court.

Procedures

1. Mandatory disclosure rules for your jurisdiction.

LEARNING OBJECTIVES

After studying this chapter, you should be able to:

1. Define *electronic discovery*; explain how technology has changed the discovery process.

2. Describe the different electronic document formats and the reasons for using them in litigation.

3. Describe the electronic discovery process.

4. Explain how the courts have implemented the federal rules on electronic discovery.

5. Explain how predictive coding technology can ease the burden of electronic discovery.

6. Understand the ethical issues and the procedures in protecting confidential or privileged information.

7. Explain the effect of inadvertent disclosure of confidential information.

Issues in Electronic Discovery | CHAPTER 12

OPENING SCENARIO

The discussion in the firm meeting turned to the continuing legal education course on electronic discovery that the partners had attended. The paralegal in the suburban office mentioned in the conference call that clients were asking for advice on document retention policies for their businesses. The attorneys were concerned that they did not have a good handle on what advice to give to clients. They suggested having another firm meeting to discuss individual clients in their respective situations and any pending or active litigation. The initial feeling was that it was not wise to generally tell clients they could destroy all documents that exceeded a certain age, including electronic records.

Someone mentioned she wasn't sure that the rules were absolute and that there might be situations in which sanctions might be imposed for destroying documents if the clients knew that litigation was more than just probable. The partner with the prosecution background indicated that the whole area of electronic discovery was evolving and that rules were still in an evolutionary phase as more cases were brought before judges for ruling. Certainly, they did not want to get into a situation of advising destruction of records if the client knew or should have known of a potential suit. The paralegals asked for guidance, as they were handling these matters while acting as litigation support. Some suggested that the current rules seemed to follow the thinking and logic in the *Zubulake* and Pension Committee cases and that everyone should read the opinions in those cases and be prepared to discuss them at the next firm teleconference.

Describe the impact of improperly advising clients on e-discovery policies and procedure.

■ INTRODUCTION TO ELECTRONIC DISCOVERY

Computer usage in the law office has created a number of changes in the practice of law and in litigation. The practice of law has long been based on tradition, with change coming slowly and only as needed. Computers have, to some in the profession, "burst" upon the scene. Suddenly, everyone is using word processing, sending e-mails, converting to paperless offices, and being required to file documents electronically. For many practitioners, recognizing and accepting the role of electronic documents have come slowly and with great reluctance. Many lawyers who did not grow up in the computer age have resisted the change to electronic documentation and its impact on their practice of law and how they handle and try cases in court. It may seem to some that the changes have happened overnight. In reality, they have evolved, but admittedly at an increasing pace and over a relatively short period of time. A few major cases have forced the profession to acknowledge that electronic copies have replaced hard copies and that the procedures, policies, and methods have changed. To maintain the orderly administration of justice and case management, the courts also have had to face the issue of electronic discovery.

The federal rules now in place are a response to the change, from paper-based to electronic systems, in the way that people, businesses, government, and organizations communicate. For hundreds of years of legal practice, the traditional source of documentation in legal cases was in the form of paper documents. Documents were written by hand, then with typewriters, and later with word processors, fax machines, and other mechanical reproduction machines like blueprint machines. In a relatively short period of time, the computer and other computerized devices have enabled the electronic creation of documents that formerly were created only in paper form. Documents that were once printed and placed in file folders and filing cabinets are now created and saved in electronic files and folders. Documents that were sent in paper form are now sent electronically, in some cases to hundreds of recipients without a paper copy ever being printed.

■ DISCOVERY IN THE TECHNOLOGICAL AGE

LEARNING OBJECTIVE 1
Define *electronic discovery*; explain how technology has changed the discovery process.

In the paper-based world, a single copy of a document might have been the only copy; at most, a document existed in duplicate or triplicate. These documents would be obtained via interrogatories that sought the identification and physical location of relevant documents. A request to produce those identified documents would result in reproduced photocopies of the paper documents. Before delivering requested documents, lawyers, paralegals, and law clerks routinely scanned every document to find and remove or redact anything considered confidential, privileged, or work product.

In the electronic world, a single keystroke may result in the creation of tens or hundreds of copies of a single document. Along with the ease of creation and distribution of documents comes the ability to delete, with a keystroke, a single copy or an entire backup system file of all the copies distributed in a company.

Obtaining, retaining, preserving, and restoring electronic documents is a new and constantly evolving area that the legal team must address, whether representing a plaintiff, a defendant, or just a client asking for advice on establishing a retention policy for electronically stored documents. The identification and

Exhibit 12.1 Comments by the Advisory Committee on Civil Rules of the Judicial Conference
Committee on Rules of Practice and Procedure

The Advisory Committee on Civil Rules of the Judicial Conference Committee on Rules of Practice and Procedure comments explain the reason for the change:

"The amendment to Rule 16(b) is designed to alert the court to the possible need to address the handling of discovery of electronically stored information early in the litigation if such discovery is expected to occur. Rule 26(f) is amended to direct the parties to discuss discovery of electronically stored information if such discovery is contemplated in the action. Form 35 is amended to call for a report to the court about the results of this discussion. In many instances, the court's involvement early in the litigation will help avoid difficulties that might otherwise arise."

---

production of documents created electronically remain much the same as in the traditional, paper-based world. The difference is the magnitude of the task of individually reviewing limitless numbers of documents that exist in electronic format.

In a suit by shareholders, Tyco International Ltd. provided 80 million e-mails, spreadsheets, and other documents as part of discovery where plaintiffs were looking for evidence of fraud that caused the stock price to drop.

E-Discovery under the Federal Rules of Civil Procedure

Before the adoption of recent revisions to the federal rules, the opinions written in the *Zubulake* case, discussed throughout the chapter, raised many of the issues surrounding the emergence of e-discovery: duty to preserve evidence, duty to produce, cost of production, and the need for early awareness in the case of potential e-discovery issues. The Federal Rules of Civil Procedure (Fed. R. Civ. P.) effective December 2006 and restated December 2007 addressed many of these issues, as indicated by the comments of the Advisory Committee on Civil Rules of the Judicial Conference Committee on Rules of Practice and Procedure, as shown in Exhibit 12.1.

WEB RESOURCES

For additional e-discovery information, sample forms, and case lists, go to the Kroll Ontrack website at www.krollontrack .com/legalresources/.

Amendments to the Federal Rules of Civil Procedure

The original changes, effective in December 2006, amended six rules and provided one new form:

Rule 16 Pretrial Conferences; Scheduling; Management

"...amendment to Rule 16(b) is designed to alert the court to the possible need to address the handling of discovery of electronically stored information early in the litigation if such discovery is expected to occur..."

Rule 26 General Provisions Governing Discovery; Duty of Disclosure

"...amended to direct the parties to discuss discovery of electronically stored information if such discovery is contemplated in the action....a party must disclose electronically stored information as well as documents that it may use to support its claims or defenses..."

Rule 33 Interrogatories to Parties

"...recognizing the importance of electronically stored information....the Rule 33(d) option should be available with respect to such records as well."

"...Special difficulties may arise in using electronically stored information, either due to its form or because it is dependent on a particular computer system.

Rule 33(d) allows a responding party to substitute access to documents or electronically stored information for an answer only if the burden of deriving the answer will be substantially the same for either party..."

Rule 34 Production of Documents, Electronically Stored Information, and Things and Entry Upon Land for Inspection and Other Purposes

"...amended to include discovery of data compilations, anticipating that the use of computerized information would increase..."

Rule 37 Failure to Make Disclosures or Cooperate in Discovery; Sanction

"...absent exceptional circumstances, sanctions cannot be imposed for loss of electronically stored information resulting from the routine, good-faith operation of an electronic information system."

Rule 45 Subpoena

"...amended to recognize that electronically stored information, as defined in Rule 34(a), can also be sought by subpoena...."

Form 35 Report of Parties' Planning Meeting

"...a report to the court about the results of this discussion." (under Rule 26)

Comments of the Advisory Committee on Civil Rules of the Judicial Conference
Committee on Rules of Practice and Procedure.

The full text of the new rules and the comments of the Advisory Committee on Civil Rules of the Judicial Conference Committee on Rules of Practice and Procedure are included in Appendix D. The committee notes give insight to the intent and reasons for the changes.

Changes in Traditional Discovery

e-discovery
Discovery of documents created, disseminated, and stored via electronic means.

WEB RESOURCES

Learn more about the e-discovery process at the e-discovery road map on the LAW.COM website at http://www.law.com/jsp/legaltechnology/eDiscoveryRoadmap.jsp.

E-discovery is the term used to describe discovery of ESI (Electronically Stored Information), that is, documents created, disseminated, and stored via electronic means. Until adoption of the federal rules on electronic discovery, lawyers and the courts relied on the traditional Request for Production of Documents used to obtain paper copies to obtain electronic documentation. From a practical standpoint, a request to produce all copies of a document that may exist in electronic format could be problematic. The new rules address three specific concerns: (1) preserving electronic materials, (2) producing electronic materials, and (3) destroying electronic materials.

Lawyers and paralegals are concerned about their responsibilities and how to advise clients of the impact of the rules on business practices such as policies for electronic data retention. This concern extends not just to complex cases but also to small-scale litigation, which represents the majority of litigation cases, and to any client who creates and maintains documents electronically. For example, in a typical construction case, blueprints and construction documents are now in the form of electronic files created with computer graphics programs and sent electronically to architects, builders, subcontractors, suppliers, and clients. When written documentation in the form of e-mails and other word processing documents is added, the number and location of individual documents needed in the litigation process may number in the thousands or more. How do the client and the legal team know how long to keep these documents? How do they review documents in response to a request for production? Who bears the cost of retrieval?

Ethical Issues in Document Delivery

Federal rules and case law provide sanctions for failing to properly deliver documents under a discovery request. The sanction ordered or imposed by the court may be as slight as an extension of the date for trial or as extreme as a jury instruction that the inference to be drawn from the failure to produce is that the information was not favorable to the side failing to deliver the information or, even worse, a charge of contempt or criminal charges for destruction of evidence.

Under appropriate rules of ethics, the legal team has a duty to protect the documents and comply with the discovery request in compliance with court discovery orders. A major issue is the clients' handling of the documents before they are produced to the legal team. Clients must be advised to preserve evidence and not destroy it if litigation is pending. But, what about before litigation is pending? There may be legitimate reasons to purge files and to strip **metadata** from electronic files. However, removing or changing metadata can lead to court-ordered sanctions. On the other hand, if there is a legitimate reason, and a company has a standing policy on document retention and destruction, it is unlikely any sanction will occur. But, as soon as notice of impending litigation is given, clients must be advised to cease all scrubbing of metadata and suspend the destruction or erasing of applicable electronic files. Nevertheless, there are no hard-and-fast rules on preservation and retention; each case must be reviewed on its own unique facts.

metadata
Information about a particular data set that may describe, for example, how, when, and by whom it was received, created, accessed, and/or modified and how it is formatted.

Preserving Electronic Materials

At what point should an individual or business save materials about a particular matter? This distinctive issue arises out of the concern over destruction of electronic materials with a single keystroke, whether intentionally or inadvertently. A company that is concerned about a potential lawsuit could easily destroy evidence contained in electronic files. The amendments to the rules seem to suggest that once a client has a reasonable belief that litigation may arise from a dispute, a duty to preserve all documents related to that dispute also arises. Note that the requirement is not that a lawsuit has been filed or a complaint served; it is a reasonable belief that litigation may arise. An emerging thread of cases suggests that there may be a requirement if the party knows or should have known of the possibility of litigation—for example, when others in the same industry have been sued. The need for preservation may require placing a matter and all documents related to it on **litigation hold.** This term or some equivalent serves as a red flag to the company and its employees not to destroy or alter but instead to save, in their present condition, all documents related to the dispute. Attorneys are obligated to notify clients of the litigation hold and to follow up with them to ensure that they have in fact honored the hold and not destroyed any documentation that might potentially relate to the claim.

litigation hold
A process whereby a company or individual determines that an unresolved dispute may result in litigation and that, as a result, electronically created and stored documents should not be destroyed or altered.

Documents in Litigation

In the past, there was little choice in how to handle document requests or document processing when received in response to interrogatories. The responding party would have to search manually through each document to find the requested documentation, a process that in large, complex cases could take large teams of paralegals, law students, and lawyers searching days, weeks, and months. Upon receipt by the requesting party, the documents would have to be reviewed for relevancy and materiality and potential clues to other documentation to be requested.

Advances in copier technology made it easier to make multiple copies, using high-speed copy machines, for multiple people to review. Additional advances in software technology permitted electronic copies to be printed out directly from computers in a variety of image formats, and ultimately to be produced not in a paper form but in a computer-readable image format, like a photograph of the document that allowed reviewers to review the documents on a computer screen instead of in paper form.

At some point in this technological development process, technology-savvy litigation counsel realized that data about the creation and changes to the underlying documents (like dates of creation, changes, and persons who worked on the document), called metadata, could be viewed using the same programs that had been originally used to create the documentation when the documents had been supplied in electronic forms. Depending on whether they were providing documentation or requesting documentation, counsel would either ask for delivery in electronic format, with the underlying metadata included, or, if asked to produce documentation, would do so in a format that did not allow review of the underlying metadata: either the metadata had been removed or the document had been provided in a printed or hard-copy, paper form. This underlying metadata about documents has become an area of interest when the authenticity and genuineness of a document are questioned. For example, did someone, after the institution of suit or after receiving notice of the lawsuit or discovery requests, make changes to the original document?

Native Format

native format
Electronic files in the format of the original program used to create the file.

With an appreciation that there might be "hidden data" about the document, technology-knowledgeable counsel wanted the original files, or at least copies of the files in their original format, called **native format.** The problem with using native file delivery is that being able to open and read a document usually requires a copy of the program used to create the document. Historically, there has not been a universal set of operating systems or standard software. As computer technology has developed, many companies have competed for business using proprietary computer systems, operating systems, and programs to capture and create electronic documents. There have been many failed efforts to develop and gain acceptance of a universal computer operating system and its programs—for example, Apple, Microsoft, and Linux operating systems and related software suites of programs using those operating systems are not compatible. Even within the same operating systems, there continue to be competing programs, such as Microsoft Word and Corel WordPerfect for the Windows operating system. In the area of accounting and database software, there are also competing systems, each of which has its own format for the creation, storage, and retrieval of electronic files. For the litigator without access to the original computer or copies of the software originally used in creating the ESI, paper copies or image copies readable on other available computers are the only solution.

Computer Format

In cases with large amounts of data, finding the relevant information is critical. Records, documents, and data files that are in a computer-usable format are easier to search and analyze using computer programs that have word search capabilities. When documents are not delivered in a computer-usable format, they can usually be processed and saved in one of the other usable computer formats, but without the metadata about the original files. In computer-friendly formats, documents may be searched for key words, terms, or names as part of a records review. Where documents are not provided in usable electronic formats, service bureaus may be used to convert the paper to a searchable electronic format, with some service bureaus coding the document by the key words contained and providing indexes by key word, creator, recipient, and similar characteristics.

Subject to time and cost-effectiveness, advances in computer technology now allow some of this conversion from paper to electronic form to take place within the law office. In many law offices, some of the most used software programs are imaging and optical character recognition (OCR) programs. OCR programs allow the litigation team to convert paper documents into searchable electronic documents and, after conversion, to store them within litigation support programs for easy recovery.

Metadata

When documents are converted from paper copies to computer-usable formats, the original, hidden electronic file information about the document, called metadata, is lost. Metadata is frequently referred to as data about data, and every electronic document has that information about the document—such as who created it; the date it was created, modified, or accessed; and other information related to its creation and location—contained within the document's electronic file.

Metadata is divided into two areas. The resource or system metadata is data about the content or application information. The resource metadata is used to track or locate the file containing the data such as file names, size, and location. Content (application) metadata is the data in the file itself, such as the author of the document, any tracked changes, and the version. An example of the metadata for the word processing file for this chapter in Microsoft Word 2010 is shown in Exhibit 12.2.

Exhibit 12.2 Metadata for the Word Processing File for This Chapter in Microsoft Word 2010

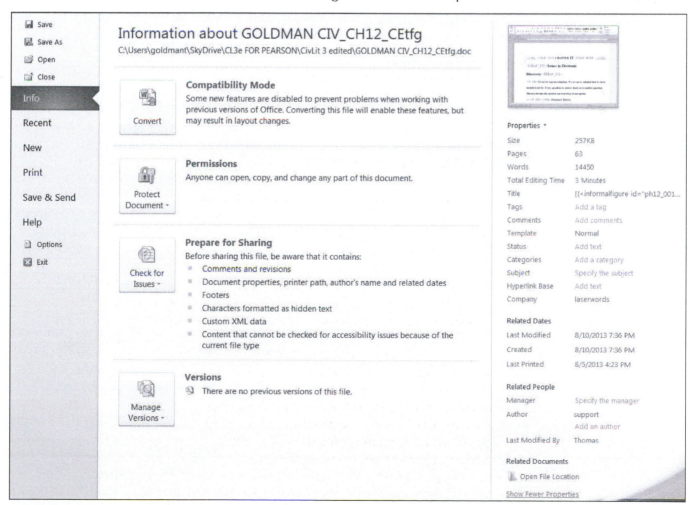

Each time a file is sent as an e-mail or an attachment to an e-mail, metadata is part of the transmission. The recipient can frequently see the content or application metadata like the author and version by using a function in the program used to view the documents, such as Word or WordPerfect for word processing documents.

Access to the metadata provides some ability to verify some of the issues related to authentication, such as the last date a change was made or who actually created the document. Some form of delivery may have the metadata included, such as delivery of documents in native format. However, it is also possible to remove the metadata before delivery, even in native format, by using features of the original program like the Microsoft Word 2010 Document Inspector (Exhibit 12.3), which reviews the document for metadata and allows its removal before saving the document.

Exhibit 12.3 Example of Metadata in a Microsoft Word Document

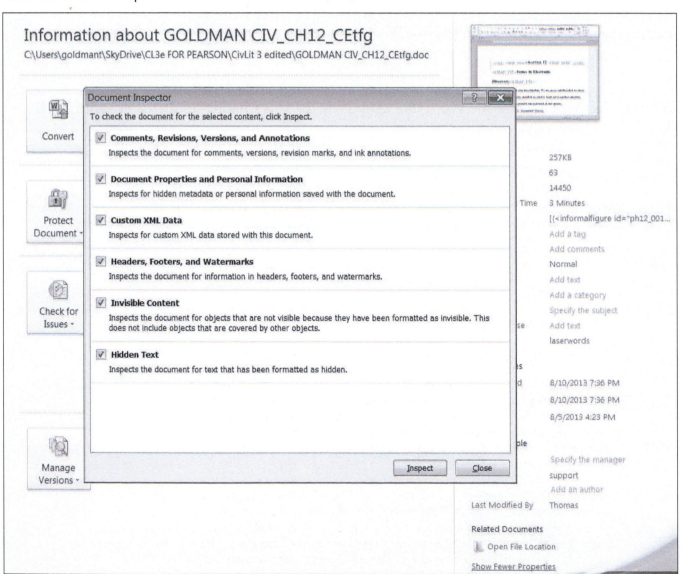

Producing Electronic Materials

The production of documents created and stored electronically falls under the traditional production of documents discovery tool. The unique issues that arise with the production of electronic documents are review for privileged information and the costs of that review and retrieval. Practitioners can use a search engine to locate and review documents containing key terms. But if 100 employees have received a single e-mail containing those key words, all 100 e-mails will be part of the search result. The amendments to the rules attempt to address the time and cost of sifting through thousands of documents. When opposing counsels confer under Fed. R. Civ. P. Rule 26(f), they must discuss electronic discovery and how they intend to address documents produced that include privileged information. They must be sufficiently knowledgeable of the methods and techniques used in electronic discovery to establish an electronic discovery plan, including appropriate search terms or methods and proper ways to ensure that the search will produce the desired results.

IN THE WORDS OF THE COURT...

United States District Court,

S.D. New York.

The PENSION COMMITTEE OF the UNIVERSITY OF MONTREAL PENSION PLAN, et al., Plaintiffs,

v.

BANC OF AMERICA SECURITIES, LLC, Citco Fund Services (Curacao) N.V., the Citco Group Limited, International Fund Services (Ireland) Limited, Pricewaterhousecoopers (Netherland Antilles), John W. Bendall, Jr., Richard Geist, Anthony Stocks, Kieran Conroy, and Declan Quilligan, Defendants.

No. 05 Civ. 9016(SAS).

Jan. 15, 2010.

SHIRA A. SCHEINDLIN, District Judge.

I. INTRODUCTION

In an era where vast amounts of electronic information is available for review, discovery in certain cases has become increasingly complex and expensive. Courts cannot and do not expect that any party can meet a standard of perfection. Nonetheless, the courts have a right to expect that litigants and counsel will take the necessary steps to ensure that relevant records are preserved when litigation is reasonably anticipated, and that such records are collected, reviewed, and produced to the opposing party. As discussed six years ago in the *Zubulake* opinions, when this does not happen, the integrity of the judicial process is harmed and the courts are required to fashion a remedy. Once again, I have been compelled to closely review the discovery efforts of parties in a litigation, and once again have found that those efforts were flawed. As famously noted, "[t]hose who cannot remember the past are condemned to repeat it." By now, it should be abundantly clear that the duty to preserve means what it says and that a failure to preserve records—paper or electronic—and to search in the right places for those records, will inevitably result in the spoliation of evidence....

(continued)

Proceeding chronologically, the first step in any discovery effort is the preservation of relevant information. A failure to preserve evidence resulting in the loss or destruction of relevant information is surely negligent, and, depending on the circumstances, may be grossly negligent or willful. For example, the intentional destruction of relevant records, either paper or electronic, after the duty to preserve has attached, is willful. Possibly after October, 2003, when *Zubulake IV* was issued, and definitely after July, 2004, when the final relevant *Zubulake* opinion was issued, the failure to issue a *written* litigation hold constitutes gross negligence because that failure is likely to result in the destruction of relevant information....

The next step in the discovery process is collection and review. Once again, depending on the extent of the failure to collect evidence, or the sloppiness of the review, the resulting loss or destruction of evidence is surely negligent, and, depending on the circumstances may be grossly negligent or willful. For example, the failure to collect records—either paper or electronic—from key players constitutes gross negligence or willfulness as does the destruction of email or certain backup tapes after the duty to preserve has attached. By contrast, the failure to obtain records from *all* employees (some of whom may have had only a passing encounter with the issues in the litigation), as opposed to key players, likely constitutes negligence as opposed to a higher degree of culpability. Similarly, the failure to take all appropriate measures to preserve ESI likely falls in the negligence category.

Cost of Producing Electronic Materials

A major concern in the production of electronic materials is the cost associated with review and production as well as the costs of retrieval and restoration of archived, corrupted, or deleted computer files. Traditionally, costs of production of records were the responsibility of the producing party; in the case of an extraordinary item, the cost would be shifted to the requester. The same appears to apply in e-discovery. However, where the costs become excessive due to retrieval and recovery of corrupted and deleted files, the court may reassess the costs. If corrupted or deleted files exist because a litigant intentionally and without good faith destroyed or altered them, the court will assign the cost to reconstruct and resurrect that data to that litigant.

What is the cost to recover and produce a tape backup? And of what value is it unless reproduced in some usable form for manual review or electronic scan and review?

As an example, in the *Zubulake* case, UBS was billed:

31.5 hours for restoration services at an hourly rate of $245 ($7,717.50);
6 hours for the development, refinement, and execution of a search script at $245 an hour ($1,470);
101.5 hours of "CPU Bench Utilization" time for use of the forensic consultants' computer systems at a rate of $18.50 per hour ($1,877.75);
plus a 5 percent "administrative overhead fee" of $459.38.

Thus, the total cost of restoration and search was $11,524.63. In addition, UBS incurred the following costs:

$4,633 in attorney time for the document review (11.3 hours at $410 per hour); and
$2,845.80 in paralegal time for tasks related to document production (16.74 hours at $170 per hour).

The total cost of restoration and production from the five backup tapes was $19,003.43 less $432.60 in photocopying costs, paid by Zubulake and not part of the cost. The cost of additional production was estimated by UBS to be $273,649.39, based on the cost incurred in restoring five tapes and producing responsive documents from those tapes, the total figure including $165,954.67 to restore and search the tapes and $107,694.72 in attorney and paralegal review costs [*Zubulake v. UBS Warburg* (S.D.N.Y. 2003) *216 F.R.D. 280, July 24, 2003*].

Destruction of Electronic Records

Spoliation is the destruction of evidence when the party knows or should know there is pending litigation. It is punishable by sanctions against the party who destroyed the evidence. Typical sanctions include (1) advising the jury of the destruction, which may be interpreted negatively, or (2) denying the party an opportunity to defend the claims that arise out of the destroyed document. With such serious consequences for destruction of information, the question becomes, "Must we save everything?" The legal team working with electronic materials must advise a client to put in place a procedure that will allow the destruction of records without penalty. Clients often ask their legal counsel, "How long do I have to keep the records or documents?" *Forever* is one answer. If no litigation is contemplated or is pending, there is some support for the position that if a company has a regular destruction policy in place, that company may destroy its files safely. But once a case is filed or pending, the duty exists to preserve evidence.

When companies store paper or other physical evidence, file cabinets and boxes of paper take up valuable and costly storage space, and there is a constant concern of fire if the materials are not stored in rooms that are fireproof or equipped with sprinklers. The electronic era has changed some of these concerns. Paper is still important, but electronic documents and e-mails are becoming more prevalent as the source of business records. With tape and CD storage of electronic documents, thousands of documents can be saved and stored in the space formerly taken up by a few sheets of paper.

First, the client must institute a standard operating procedure for the retention and destruction of records. In a perfect world, clients would have some system in place long before a dispute arises or a lawsuit is filed. In a medical practice, for example, all files with no activity for a period of three years are destroyed. Instituting and consistently implementing this type of retention policy will demonstrate the good faith, ordinary-course-of-business destruction the court views favorably. Where there is good faith, it is unlikely sanctions will be imposed.

Second, and in conjunction with the retention policy, is adopting a litigation hold policy. Here, the client needs to establish a rubric to assess those matters that may result in litigation so that the records will not be destroyed under the retention policy. In the medical practice example just described, the rubric might include patients who have expressed dissatisfaction with the results of their medical treatment and those who have failed to pay their bills. A file that meets either of these criteria would be placed on a litigation hold so that it would not be destroyed. Exhibit 12.4 is the first page of a sample letter to a client to preserve electronic evidence.

General Provisions

There are some additional general limitations on discovery that are imposed by the rules. The rules seek to eliminate duplicative, burdensome, and oppressive

Exhibit 12.4 Page 1 of Sample Letter to Client to Preserve Electronic Evidence

---

SAMPLE PRESERVATION LETTER—TO CLIENT

[Date]

RE: [Case Name]—Data Preservation

Dear:

Please be advised that the Office of General Counsel assistance believes electronically stored information to be an important and irreplaceable source of discovery and/or evidence in [description of event, transaction, business unit, product, etc.]. The lawsuit requires preservation of all information from [Corporation's] computer systems, removable electronic media and other locations relating to [description of event, transaction, business unit, product, etc.]. This includes, but is not limited to, email and other electronic communication, word processing documents, spreadsheets, databases, calendars, telephone logs, contact manager information, Internet usage files, and network access information.

[Corporation] should also preserve the following platforms in the possession of the [Corporation] or a third party under the control of the [Corporation] (such as an employee or outside vendor under contract): databases, networks, computer systems, including legacy systems (hardware and software), servers, archives, backup or disaster recovery systems, tapes, discs, drives, cartridges and other storage media, laptops, personal computers, internet data, personal digital assistants, handheld wireless devices, mobile telephones, paging devices, and audio systems (including voicemail).

Employees must take every reasonable step to preserve this information until further notice from the Office of General Counsel. *Failure to do so could result in extreme penalties against [Corporation].*

All of the information contained in the letter should be preserved for the following dates and time periods: [List dates and times].

PRESERVATION OBLIGATIONS

The laws and rules prohibiting destruction of evidence apply to electronically stored information in the same manner that they apply to other evidence. Due to its format, electronic information is easily deleted, modified or corrupted. Accordingly, [Corporation] must take every reasonable step to preserve this information until the final resolution of this matter.

This includes, but is not limited to, an obligation to:

- Discontinue all data destruction and backup tape recycling policies;
- Preserve and not dispose of relevant hardware unless an exact replica of the file (a mirror image) is made;

Source: Sample letter to client to preserve electronic evidence, Sample Forms and Pleadings, 2007. Reproduced by the permission of Kroll Ontrack Inc.

discovery requests. Requests are duplicative or burdensome when the information sought has already been provided or is more easily obtained from another source.

Another obligation that continues throughout the litigation is the duty to supplement or revise responses should additional or different information become known. A typical example is an answer to an interrogatory that indicates the identity and address of a witness. At some later point in time, counsel learns that the witness has relocated. That information must be shared with opposing counsel.

Information Technologists as Members of the Legal Team

The legal team can no longer depend only on the skill and time of lawyers and paralegals in preparing and executing a discovery plan or, for that matter, advising clients on maintenance and methods of document retention. With the constant changes and advancements in ESI, the lawyer and the paralegal would be remiss to rely on their own experiences. Rather, the technology of electronically maintained records requires the input of information technology (IT) specialists.

Like forensic accountants, IT specialists can become valued members of the legal team because they understand the electronic format of the documentation, the efforts required in producing or reproducing it, the problems involved, and the latest developments in the field.

Electronically stored data are created and stored in many formats using many different software programs. While there are some commonly used protocols, formats, and methods for creation and storage, the lawyers and paralegals on the legal team cannot be expected to have the specialized technical knowledge of an information technologist. Even the IT specialist may need to engage the assistance of additional specialists in rarely used methods, software, or hardware. In some cases, like those involving erased data or damaged storage media, a forensic expert may have to be consulted.

The lawyer may need the expertise of the IT specialist to advise clients on matters of data preservation and archiving in order to avoid potential claims of spoliation or delay of trials because of the inability to produce the required documents in the required format.

Internal, or in-house, IT personnel should not be used as experts in the discovery process. As with any expert, they may be subject to a requirement that they be available for deposition and trial. To preserve the confidentiality of the trial preparation effort and work product, IT personnel should be considered part of the litigation team. If an expert is needed, an outside expert should be brought in, just as other experts are used in cases where their access to information is limited to that needed to prepare the expert opinion.

■ ELECTRONIC DOCUMENT FORMATS— COMPARISON OF PDF AND TIFF

In addition to the native format, documents may now be saved in a graphic image format or a portable document format (PDF). These graphic images may not be easily or readily changed by the recipient. The two formats competing for use as a common format for large-scale case use are the TIFF and the PDF formats. The up-front costs to convert from the native file format to TIFF or PDF formats are about the same. Many programs used to create the original documents, like WordPerfect and Word, have a built-in feature allowing files to be saved automatically as PDF files. In addition, most litigation support software programs, such as AD Summation and LexisNexis Concordance, support both TIFF and PDF formats. The advantage of conversion to either format is that the new files can be searched across different computer platforms.

TIFF was developed in the 1980s as a format for scanning paper documents. Adobe Systems now holds the copyright for the TIFF specification. Many lawyers latched onto this format and continue to prefer it. Some attorneys prefer the TIFF format because TIFF files cannot be altered. Adobe invented PDF in 1992 as a replacement for the TIFF format and has not supported any new activity for TIFF since then. PDF files have the advantage of being usable across many different platforms (computer systems) and software programs regardless of how the files were originally created.

One of the differences between TIFF and PDF is the amount of memory required to store one document. Because of the built-in file compression in the PDF format, PDF files are normally about one-tenth the size of TIFF files. The actual file size will vary depending on which of the many compression methods is used in saving the TIFF file. If you have ever sent an e-mail with an attachment,

LEARNING OBJECTIVE 2
Describe the different electronic document formats and the reasons for using them in litigation.

consider the additional time it took to send a TIFF file rather than a PDF file of the same document.

The disadvantage from the receiving party's point of view is that hidden data (or metadata) of the original (or native) format document cannot be seen in TIFF files.

The ability to save documents in a format that cannot be easily changed through the use of a computer is one of the basic requirements of a system that allows for electronic documentation. Anyone who has received a word processing document file knows that he or she may change it, save it, and present it as an original unless access has been restricted, such as by use of password restriction.

The creation of documents in PDF format requires specialty software such as Adobe Acrobat. To encourage use of the PDF format as a standard, Adobe Systems, the developer of the PDF format, allows everyone to download a free Adobe Reader to view these documents, adding to the acceptance of the PDF format. With the acceptance of this format has come a willingness to scan and store documents electronically and eliminate or return to the client the original paper copies. Companies like Adobe Systems frequently provide free, limited versions of their programs, downloadable from their websites, that allow the opening and reading of files created using their proprietary software formats, such as Adobe's PDF file format. Many websites that provide programs using these proprietary formats, such as the forms website of the Internal Revenue Service, contain links to these programs. These programs are limited in that they allow the user to open and read files but do not allow the creation of new document files, which requires the full version of the program.

Adobe Acrobat

Adobe Acrobat has become a standard software tool in many paperless offices for creating PDF files. With each new version or update to the original program, additional features have been added to allow greater sharing of documents, a higher level of security, and better collaboration on document preparation.

Creators of PDF documents using the newer versions of Adobe Acrobat (versions 5 and above) can limit the ability of the receiver to print the document by requiring a password to allow printing. This password feature allows the legal team to send documents that others on the legal team can view, and about which they can make and submit comments to the documents' originator, but cannot make changes to.

In typical use, the attorney or paralegal creates the document in a word processor such as Word or WordPerfect and uses Adobe Acrobat to convert the document to a PDF. The PDF format reduces the risk of sending the document metadata found in the native or original word processor document.

PDF Converter

Nuance's PDF Converter is a lower-cost alternative to the widely used Adobe Acrobat. In addition to creating PDF documents, the PDF converter also provides a number of other options. For instance, the converter feature can be used to convert PDF files into fully formatted Word, WordPerfect, and Excel documents.

An interesting additional feature of PDF Converter is its ability to convert documents into audio files that can be played back through a computer or an MP3 player, like an Apple iPod. Anyone who has tried to proofread, by herself, technical language in a document or the legal description in a real estate agreement or deed will appreciate the ability to have the language "read to her" while following the written language in the document to verify accuracy.

As with Acrobat, PDF Converter allows the same type of security settings for documents created with the program, including password limitations for changes and printing.

Examining a PDF for Hidden Content

People who create PDF format documents sometimes have the mistaken belief that the file does not have metadata. Every document has metadata—data about the document—as part of the document file.

In the Preference selections window, one of the options in Acrobat is to set the preference to Examine Documents. Two options exist: (1) examining *before* sending the e-document electronically and (2) examining *before* saving. Both practices might prevent information being sent that is not intended for the recipient.

■ SCANNING

Documents may be copied by scanning the original and then saving the scanned image in a desired electronic format such as a PDF, an image, or, with OCR software, a word processing document format. Originally, scanning hardware was costly and frequently unreliable. However, modern scanners provide double-sided (front and back) scanning of documents with a high degree of accuracy at a relatively low cost. Scanning today has also become a common feature of office printers and copy machines. Double-sided scanning is also found today in multifunction devices containing printing, scanning, copying, and faxing features, at prices sometimes under $100. These devices, when coupled with document management software such as Nuance's PaperPort, allow virtually anyone to convert paper to electronic forms as well as create electronic documents. An automatic document feed scanner allows for single or multiple sheet-fed scanning, which is a time-saver when scanning multiple-page documents. A flatbed scanner allows for scanning sheets as well as documents that can't be fed through a page feeder, such as books or labels on packages.

Scanning Software

The process of scanning large numbers of documents requires the ability to organize the scanned documents. Scanning, organizing, and storing paper documents have become easier with the development of document management software such as PaperPort by Nuance. This software provides easy-to-use, high-speed scanning and document capture. As a document management software application, it allows for organizing, finding, and sharing paper and digital documents, permitting the elimination of paper documents, as shown in Exhibit 12.5.

Optical Character Recognition

There are obviously times when documents need to be converted from graphic images to a format that allows for editing or other use in an office suite of applications. These software applications have come to be referred to as **OCR,** or **optical character recognition** applications. Products such as OmniPage, by Nuance, provide document conversion solutions by permitting any scanned page, PDF file, or other image or document file to be converted quickly and accurately into one of a number of different editable formats, including Microsoft Word or Corel WordPerfect.

OCR—optical character recognition
Software used to convert documents in graphic format to a format that allows for editing or other use in office suite applications.

Exhibit 12.5 Document Management Software Application

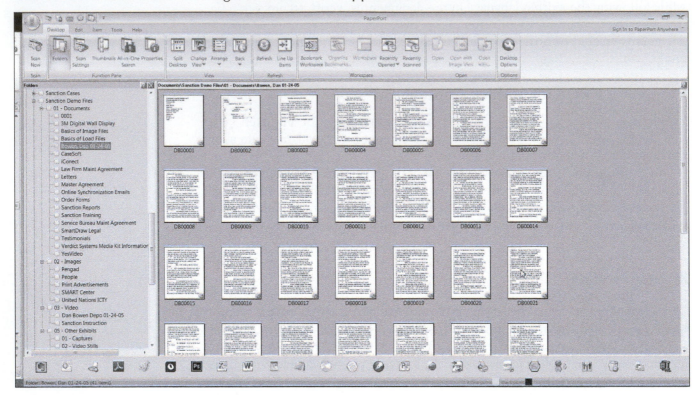

ELECTRONIC DISCOVERY IN LITIGATION

LEARNING OBJECTIVE 3
Describe the electronic discovery process.

Not every lawsuit will require the use of all of the tools available for electronic discovery. Many cases may involve limited numbers of documents in both paper and electronic forms. It is important to know what documents are available in electronic form and how to secure them. For example, in uncomplicated cases, you can request paperless medical records from a doctor's office in PDF format. Or, you can agree to file delivery on a DVD in the original MS Word format (native format). This will require the law office to have a PDF viewer like Adobe Reader or a copy of MS Word in order to view the documents.

VIDEO ADVICE FROM THE FIELD

ELECTRONIC DISCOVERY PROCESS

Don Swanson President, Five Star Legal Services
A discussion of electronic discovery as a process and not as a static activity and an explanation of the role of the paralegal in conducting the electronic search.

After watching the video at www.pearsonhighered.com/careersresources, answer the following questions.

1. How has technology changed the discovery process?
2. Why is it important for the paralegal to understand the new technology?
3. Why must the paralegal know how to conduct a comprehensive electronic search?

In complex cases, like one involving a concern that records may have been intentionally erased or "lost," the costs of using the electronic discovery tools may be an issue in deciding whether to accept or pursue a case. Corporate clients will frequently be sophisticated enough to ask for a discovery budget as part of a cost-benefit analysis. Clients less knowledgeable or not experienced in litigation need to be properly advised as to the costs associated with the potential discovery issues. It will frequently be the role of the paralegal to determine what outside discovery experts and vendors, like forensic experts, will charge. Clients do not like surprises when it comes to the costs that they will be expected to pay. Good client relationship management requires a discussion of the discovery budget.

Reviewing Electronic Documents

One of the biggest costs in electronic discovery is incurred in reviewing the electronic material to find relevant items and to identify privileged, confidential, or protected documents. In small cases, making copies of the files using the original programs used to create the files (like the process for making a backup copy) may be the easiest method for delivery. The client delivers the files after copying them from the computer onto a portable storage device like a CD, DVD, flash drive, or tape. File review is completed by using the program used to create the file, such as Word, Excel, or Access; the material could be viewed on a computer screen or printed out.

When documents are delivered in a number of different formats, such as word processor, database, or spreadsheet formats, review usually requires multiple programs to view the originals. When the number of documents is in the thousands or tens of thousands, this process can be very time consuming. One solution is to convert all of the documents into one common program format that can then be searched and indexed.

Obtaining Documents via Paper Discovery

Not all documents are in electronic form. Many public agencies, like police and fire departments, still file paper-based reports. Litigation that involves a time frame prior to the age of electronic document preparation also requires paper-based documents. These cases often involve a large volume of material that must be processed by the legal team. Converting the paper documents to electronic form may be a solution.

Converting Documents

The typical response to a paper document request is the delivery of a photocopy of the requested items. As with electronic discovery, the number of documents can be in the thousands or even millions (for example, a class action suit involving tobacco companies). Before the computer era, these documents had to be reviewed manually, which provided work for many law students and paralegals. Computer technology now allows these paper documents to be converted into electronic files that can be processed like other electronic files. Typically, the documents are copied or scanned and saved in an electronic file format.

■ EMERGING CASE LAW AND COURT RULES

The Federal Rules of Civil Procedure now provide a framework for requesting and satisfying requests for documents in electronic format such as e-mails, electronically stored word processor documents, and information in electronic databases.

LEARNING OBJECTIVE 4
Explain how the courts have implemented the federal rules on electronic discovery.

One of the first cases to offer guidance on the issues surrounding electronic storage and electronic discovery was *Laura Zubulake v. UBS Warburg, LLC, UBS Warburg, and UBS AG.* In a series of opinions, Judge Shira Scheindlin addressed many of the issues in this area.

The *Zubulake* case was initially filed in the Federal District Court for the Southern District of New York, February 2002 (02 CV. 1243) after Zubulake had received a right-to-sue letter from the Equal Employment Opportunity Commission (EEOC) based on her initial filing with the EEOC on August 16, 2001. The issues raised, primarily concerning electronic discovery, have resulted in a number of notable opinions, decisions, and orders by Judge Shira Scheindlin:

Zubulake I May 13, 2003
Zubulake II May 13, 2003   217 F.R.D. 309
Zubulake III July 24, 2003   216 F.R.D. 280
Zubulake IV October 22, 2003   220 F.R.D. 212
Zubulake V July 20, 2004   229 F.R.D. 422
Zubulake VI February 2, 2005
Zubulake VII March 16, 2005

Laura Zubulake sued her former employer, UBS Warburg LLC, for sex discrimination (including disparate treatment and wrongful termination) and retaliation in violation of Title VII of the Civil Rights Act of 1964. As with many cases, the needed proof was in electronically stored documents and e-mails. The court in the case was required to address the significance of electronically stored documentation, the required procedures for its disclosure, and the question of who should pay the costs associated with production.

Spoliation of Evidence

spoliation of evidence
Destruction of records that may be relevant to ongoing or anticipated litigation, government investigation, or audit. Courts differ in their interpretations of the level of intent required before sanctions may be warranted.

Many court opinions have addressed the issue of **spoliation of evidence.** Spoliation is "the destruction or significant alteration of evidence or the failure to preserve property for another's use as evidence in pending or reasonably foreseeable litigation" *West v. Goodyear Tire & Rubber Co.,* 167 F.3d 776, 779 (2d Cir. 1999).

Spoliation may be the destruction of physical evidence such as the disposal, crushing, or other destruction of a motor vehicle that shows evidence of an accident. It may be the shredding or burning of a letter or handwritten note that confirms the existence of a promise or other obligation. In the electronic world, it may be the deletion of documents on a computer or the erasing of backup tapes of e-mails.

Spoliation of evidence may result in sanctions by the court. There is no uniform standard for imposition of sanctions, which can range from an adverse inference instruction to the jury to dismissal of the case. The degree of the sanction is usually dependent on the bad conduct of the party and the relevance of the documents lost.

As state by Judge Scheindlin in the Pension Committee case cited above:

"For less severe sanctions—such as fines and cost-shifting—the inquiry focuses more on the conduct of the spoliating party than on whether documents were lost, and, if so, whether those documents were relevant and resulted in prejudice to the innocent party. As explained more thoroughly below, for more severe sanctions—such as dismissal, preclusion, or the imposition of an adverse inference—the court must consider, in addition to the conduct of the spoliating party, whether any missing evidence was relevant and whether the innocent party has suffered prejudice as a result of the loss of evidence."

IN THE WORDS OF THE COURT...

Standard for Electronically Stored Information

Zubulake v. Ubs Warburg LLC, (S.D.N.Y. 2004)
229 F.R.D. 422
Laura Zubulake, Plaintiff, v. UBS Warburg LlC, UBS Warburg, and
UBS AG, Defendants. 02 Civ. 1243 (SAS).
United States District Court, S.D. New York.
July 20, 2004
Shira Scheindlin, District Judge.

VI. Postscript

The subject of the discovery of electronically stored information is rapidly evolving. When this case began more than two years ago, there was little guidance from the judiciary, bar associations, or the academy as to the governing standards. Much has changed in that time. There have been a flood of recent opinions—including a number from appellate courts—and there are now several treatises on the subject.... In addition, professional groups such as the American Bar Association and the Sedona Conference have provided very useful guidance on thorny issues relating to the discovery of electronically stored information.... Many courts have adopted, or are considering adopting, local rules addressing the subject.... Most recently, the Standing Committee on Rules and Procedures has approved for publication and public comment a proposal for revisions to the Federal Rules of Civil Procedure designed to address many of the issues raised by the discovery of electronically stored information....

Now that the key issues have been addressed and national standards are developing, parties and their counsel are fully on notice of their responsibility to preserve and produce electronically stored information. The tedious and difficult fact finding encompassed in this opinion and others like it is a great burden on a court's limited resources. The time and effort spent by counsel to litigate these issues has also been time consuming and distracting. This Court, for one, is optimistic that with the guidance now provided it will not be necessary to spend this amount of time again. It is hoped that counsel will heed the guidance provided by these resources and will work to ensure that preservation, production, and spoliation issues are limited, if not eliminated.

SO ORDERED.

IN THE WORDS OF THE COURT...

Sanctions

IN RE: Telxon Corporation Securities Litigation, (N.D. Ohio 2004)
In Re: Telxon Corporation Securities Litigation. William S. Hayman, et al.,
Plaintiffs, v.
Pricewaterhousecoopers, LLP, Defendant.
Case Nos. 5:98CV2876, 1:01CV1078.
United States District Court, N.D. Ohio,
Eastern Division. July 16, 2004.

...Finally, the magistrate judge has considered, but cannot recommend, any lesser sanction than the entry of default judgment against PwC. Lesser sanctions would

(continued)

result in "unwinding" over three years of litigation. This would require the re-taking of many depositions and the taking of new depositions, the conduct of additional expert analyses and the production of new reports, and the propounding of new interrogatories. But four considerations militate against this solution to the problem.

First, beginning discovery again would mean additional lengthy delay before the case reaches a resolution. Telxon and plaintiffs have already suffered sufficient delay because of PwC's bad-faith conduct; to allow PwC's misbehavior to impose substantial new delays to reaching a resolution of this litigation would be unfair to Telxon and plaintiffs.

Second, because PwC failed to archive the 1998 workpapers which are at the heart of this case until late January of 1999, those workpapers were vulnerable to undetectable alteration while the Telxon litigation was pending. The Ennis case in particular creates strong suspicions that this has been done to at least one document. Third, PwC's production of still more documents after April 21, 2004 undercuts any belief that PwC has now or will ever produce all relevant material in its possession. Fourth, and most critical, there is strong evidence that documents have been destroyed, placing plaintiffs and Telxon in a situation which cannot be remedied.

Because PwC's conduct has made it impossible to try this case with any confidence in the justice of the outcome, PwC should bear the burden created by its conduct. For this reason, the magistrate judge recommends that the court grant Telxon's and plaintiffs' motions and enter default judgment against PwC and in favor of Telxon and plaintiffs in cases 5:98CV2876 and 1:01CV1078.

IN THE WORDS OF THE COURT...

Sanctions for Nonproduction of Evidence

**Residential Funding Corp. v. De[G]eorge Financial, 306 F.3d 99
(2nd Cir. 2002)
Residential Funding Corporation, Plaintiff-Appellee, v. De[G]eorge Financial
Corp., De[G]eorge Home Alliance, Inc. and De[G]eorge Capital Corp.,
Defendants-Appellants.
No. 01-9282.
United States Court of Appeals, Second Circuit.
Argued: August 8, 2002.
Decided: September 26, 2002.**

Appeal from the United States District Court for the District of Connecticut, Arterton, J.

...[T]his is not a typical spoliation case. It does not appear that RFC *destroyed* the e-mails on the back-up tapes. Rather, RFC failed to produce the e-mails in time for trial. Accordingly, this case is more akin to those in which a party breaches a discovery obligation or fails to comply with a court order regarding discovery.

...Where, as here, the nature of the alleged breach of a discovery obligation is the non-production of evidence, a district court has broad discretion in fashioning an appropriate sanction, including the discretion to delay the start of a trial (at the expense of the party that breached its obligation), to declare a mistrial if trial has already commenced, or to proceed with a trial and give an adverse inference instruction. See *Reilly v. Natwest Markets Group Inc.*, 181 F.3d 253, 267 (2d Cir. 1999).

(continued)

...Where a party destroys evidence in bad faith, that bad faith alone is sufficient circumstantial evidence from which a reasonable fact finder could conclude that the missing evidence was unfavorable to that party. See, e.g., *Kronisch*, 150 F.3d at 126 ("It is a well-established and long-standing principle of law that a party's intentional destruction of evidence relevant to proof of an issue at trial can support an inference that the evidence would have been unfavorable to the party responsible for its destruction."). Similarly, a showing of gross negligence in the destruction or untimely production of evidence will in some circumstances suffice, standing alone, to support a finding that the evidence was unfavorable to the grossly negligent party. See *Reilly*, 81 F.3d at 267-68. Accordingly, where a party seeking an adverse inference adduces evidence that its opponent destroyed potential evidence (or otherwise rendered it unavailable) in bad faith or through gross negligence (satisfying the "culpable state of mind" factor), that same evidence of the opponent's state of mind will frequently also be sufficient to permit a jury to conclude that the missing evidence is favorable to the party (satisfying the "relevance" factor)....

...In this case, the District Court stated that the only evidence DeGeorge had adduced "suggesting that [the unproduced e-mails] would likely have been harmful to RFC" was the nonproduction itself. Trial Tr. at 1377. It also stated, however, that RFC's actions after it retained EED, "including representation that e-mails would be produced, without mentioning the absence of any from the critical time period, a missed Federal Express deadline for sending backup tapes so they could be forwarded to DeGeorge's vendors, and resistance to responding to technical questions about the tapes, suggest [a somewhat purposeful] sluggishness on RFC's part." Trial Tr. at 1376 (*emphasis added*).

...In sum, we hold that:

1. where, as here, the nature of the alleged breach of a discovery obligation is the non-production of evidence, a District Court has broad discretion in fashioning an appropriate sanction, including the discretion to delay the start of a trial (at the expense of the party that breached its obligation), to declare a mistrial if trial has already commenced, or to proceed with a trial with an adverse inference instruction;

2. discovery sanctions, including an adverse inference instruction, may be imposed upon a party that has breached a discovery obligation not only through bad faith or gross negligence, but also through ordinary negligence;

3. a judge's finding that a party acted with gross negligence or in bad faith with respect to discovery obligations is ordinarily sufficient to support a finding that the missing or destroyed evidence would have been harmful to that party, even if the destruction or unavailability of the evidence was not caused by the acts constituting bad faith or gross negligence;...

■ PREDICTIVE CODING/TECHNOLOGY ASSISTED REVIEW

Electronic tools are replacing manual examination of electronically stored documents. As the volume of documents increases, the cost to manually review them has increased to such a point that courts are weighing the cost of the review versus the value of the documents as evidence determinative of the case outcome. The balancing of cost versus value is often referred to as proportionality. In an effort to reduce cost and obtain the relevant documents, computers are used to conduct

LEARNING OBJECTIVE 5
Explain how predictive coding technology can ease the burden of electronic discovery.

searches similar to any computerized search query. Keyword searches are useful when the set of documents is small enough to manually check the results. But when the volume increases into the millions as in the Biomet case shown below, a more automated process is required to reduce cost and deliver relevant documents. Increasingly, counsel are using a set of software tools collectively referred to as **predictive coding programs** or **technology assisted review.** These programs use search algorithms to search a small set of documents that have already been manually reviewed. A comparison of the result generated by the search to the manual result is made to determine the rate of success of the search parameters. The search parameters and algorithms are then refined and modified until the desired percentage of successful search is attained. Then the search parameters are applied to the entire set of documents. In the Biomet case, application of this process took in excess of 19.5 million documents and reduced them to 3.9 million relevant documents.

predictive coding programs or technology assisted review
Computer programs that use search algorithms to search a small set of documents that are manually reviewed for accuracy in selecting the desired terms before the search is applied to a larger set of electronic files.

IN THE WORDS OF THE COURT...

UNITED STATES DISTRICT COURT NORTHERN DISTRICT OF INDIANA SOUTH BEND DIVISION
IN RE: BIOMET M2a MAGNUM HIP
IMPLANT PRODUCTS LIABILITY
LITIGATION (MDL 2391) CAUSE NO. 3:12-MD-2391

This Document Relates to All Cases

ORDER REGARDING DISCOVERY OF ESI

Biomet has produced 2.5 million documents to plaintiffs in this docket's constituent cases, and the Plaintiffs' Steering Committee believes production should run to something closer to 10 million documents. The parties have set forth their positions on the procedures or protocols that should be used to facilitate identification, retrieval, and production of electronically stored information in submissions filed on April 1 and 5. The parties seek my guidance as to the direction discovery of ESI should take, and I believe the parties need a prompt ruling more than they need extensive discussion of each point they raise. Biomet began producing documents in cases eventually centralized here in the summer of 2012. Some plaintiffs' counsel, anticipating this docket's formation, told Biomet (occasionally in forceful terms) not to begin document production until the Judicial Panel on Multidistrict Litigation decided whether to centralize. Biomet, neither sold on centralization nor free of judicial exhortations in other Cases against it, started the process of identifying and producing documents. Biomet used a combination of electronic search functions to identify relevant documents. Keyword culling was used first, reducing the universe of documents and attachments from 19.5 million documents to 3.9 million documents, comprising 1.5 terabytes of data. Removal of duplicates left 2.5 million documents and attachments. Statistical sampling tests of a random sample projected, with a 99 percent confidence rate, that between .55 and 1.33 percent of the unselected documents would be responsive and (with the same confidence level) that between 1.37 and 2.47 percent of the original 19.5 million documents were responsive. In comparison, Biomet's keyword/deduplication approach had identified 16 percent of the original 19.5 million.

Biomet then employed technology-assisted review, or predictive coding, to identify the relevant documents to be produced from the 2.5 million that
(continued)

emerged from the keyword and deduplication processes. Predictive coding has found many uses on the Internet. Under predictive coding, the software "learns" a user's preferences or goals; as it learns, the software identifies with greater accuracy just which items the user wants, whether it be a song, a product, or a search topic. Biomet used a predictive coding service called Axelerate and eight contract attorneys to review a sampling of the 2.5 million documents. After one round of "find more like this" interaction between the attorneys and the software, the contract attorneys (together with other software recommended by Biomet's ediscovery Vendor) reviewed documents for relevancy, confidentiality, and privilege.

...It might well be that predictive coding, instead of a keyword search, at Stage Two of the process would unearth additional relevant documents. But it would cost Biomet a million, or millions, of dollars to test the Steering Committee's theory that predictive coding would produce a significantly greater number of relevant documents. Even in light of the needs of the hundreds of plaintiffs in this case, the very large amount in controversy, the parties' resources, the importance of the issues at stake, and the importance of this discovery in resolving the issues, I can't find that the likely benefits of the discovery proposed by the Steering Committee equals or outweighs its additional burden on, and additional expense to, [B]iomet. Fed. R. Civ. P. 26(b)(2)(c).

WEB RESOURCES
Review Rule 1.6 of the ABA Model Rules of Professional Conduct at the ABA website: http://www.abanet.org/cpr/mrpc/rule_1_6 .html.

LEARNING OBJECTIVE 6
Understand the ethical issues and the procedures in protecting confidential or privileged information.

■ PROTECTING CONFIDENTIAL OR PRIVILEGED MATERIALS

As previously discussed, the attorney has an obligation to preserve the confidences of clients (see Rule 1.6 of the ABA Model Rules of Professional Conduct).

The Fed. R. Civ. P., in Rule 26, specifically recognizes that parties may withhold information, otherwise discoverable, and it provides within the rule a framework for the process, as shown in Exhibit 12.6.

Exhibit 12.6 Fed. R. Civ. P. 26(5) (A) and (B) Procedures for Claiming Protection for Privileged or Work Product Materials

---

Rule 26. General Provisions Governing Discovery; Duty of Disclosure

(5) Claims of Privilege or Protection of Trial Preparation Materials.

(A) Information Withheld.
When a party withholds information otherwise discoverable under these rules by claiming that it is privileged or subject to protection as trial-preparation material, the party shall make the claim expressly and shall describe the nature of the documents, communications, or things not produced or disclosed in a manner that, without revealing information itself privileged or protected, will enable other parties to assess the applicability of the privilege or protection.

(B) Information Produced.
If information is produced in discovery that is subject to a claim of privilege or of protection as trial-preparation material, the party making the claim may notify any party that received the information of the claim and the basis for it. After being notified, a party must promptly return, sequester, or destroy the specified information and any copies it has and may not use or disclose the information until the claim is resolved. A receiving party may promptly present the information to the court under seal for a determination of the claim. If the receiving party disclosed the information before being notified, it must take reasonable steps to retrieve it. The producing party must preserve the information until the claim is resolved.

When vast numbers of electronic files are delivered as part of the discovery process, it may not always be possible, within the limited time frames required for compliance, to check every document before handing it over to opposing counsel. Many times the documents will be part of an answer to a request for electronically stored documents that will be delivered on computer tape, CD, DVD, or other computer storage media. The electronic documents may contain confidential material, like e-mails between attorney and client, work product materials, or a client's proprietary information or trade secret.

The rules provide for a "claw-back" provision as part of the discovery plan. A **claw-back provision,** under Fed. R. Civ. P. 16(b)(6), is "any agreements the parties reach for asserting claims of privilege or of protection as trial-preparation material after production."

In theory, if privileged or confidential material is inadvertently disclosed, the material may be recovered. Different courts have applied different interpretations and rules regarding the inadvertent disclosure of confidential material. State courts are still split in their approaches, from those courts barring its use to the courts allowing it as if the disclosure were intentional (and therefore the privilege waived). Under the new federal rules, at the least, the legal team must include a claw-back clause to prevent a potential claim of malpractice for not attempting to protect the material. However, the use of a claw-back agreement alone does not relieve the attorney of his or her obligations regarding confidential client information. The legal team must still take necessary steps to protect the confidences of clients. The claw-back provision is only a safety device for inadvertent disclosure after reasonable methods, under the circumstances, have been used to otherwise protect and preserve confidential material.

Committee notes to Rule 26 indicate the intention to recognize "that a party must disclose electronically stored information as well as documents that it may use to support its claims or defenses." The Committee notes to Rule 16 indicate recognition of the need in electronic discovery to protect privileged and confidential material, which the parties can do by agreement as part of the discovery plan (Fed. R. Civ. P. 16(b)(3)). Under Rule 16, the intention is to cause the parties to alert the court to the possible need to address the handling of electronically stored information early in the litigation as part of case management.

■ INADVERTENT DISCLOSURE OF CONFIDENTIAL INFORMATION

Inadvertent or accidental disclosure of confidential or privileged information does happen. It may be the slip of a finger in sending an e-mail, an accidental pushing of the wrong number on the speed dial of a fax machine, or the sending of a misaddressed envelope. In large-scale electronic document submissions in response to discovery requests, it may be the inadvertent inclusion of or failure to **redact** work product, attorney–client privileged material, or confidential documents. The admissibility of the inadvertently disclosed documents may hinge on the steps the legal team takes before and after the disclosure. Having a proper screening policy in place and monitoring this policy may prevent a claim of negligence (VLT Inc Lucent Technologies No 00-11049-PBS (D. Mass 01-21-2003)). The treatment will depend on the individual jurisdiction. The courts follow no single policy.

---

claw-back provision
A provision contained in the report of counsels' meet and confer and included in the court's scheduling order that describes what to do with privileged materials that are disclosed inadvertently through e-discovery. The provision should address return of the materials and waiver of the privilege.

LEARNING OBJECTIVE 7
Explain the effect of inadvertent disclosure of confidential information.

redaction
The removal of confidential information (or at least that which is claimed to be confidential) or material prepared for trial under the work product doctrine.

State Courts

State courts have used four different tests—Strict Liability, Multi-factor, Intentional Waiver, and the Significant Party—as described by the court in the case of *Alldread v. City of Grenada:*

> …a voluntary disclosure of information which is inconsistent with the confidential nature of the attorney–client relationship waives the privilege….There is no consensus, however, as to the effect of inadvertent disclosures of confidential communications. A few courts hold that where there has been a disclosure of privileged communications to third parties, the privilege is lost, even if the disclosure is unintentional or inadvertent….The courts subscribing to this view place the risk of inadvertent disclosure on the producing party, reasoning that "the amount of care taken to ensure confidentiality to the holder of the privilege reflects the importance of that confidentiality to the holder of the privilege."…The majority of courts, though, while recognizing that inadvertent disclosure may result in a waiver of the privilege, have declined to apply this "strict responsibility" rule of waiver and have opted instead for an approach which takes into account the facts surrounding a particular disclosure….In our view, an analysis which permits the court to consider the circumstances surrounding a disclosure on a case-by-case basis is preferable to a per se rule of waiver. This analysis serves the purpose of the attorney–client privilege, the protection of communications which the client fully intended would remain confidential, yet at the same time will not relieve those claiming the privilege of the consequences of their carelessness if the circumstances surrounding the disclosure do not clearly demonstrate that continued protection is warranted.

> 988 F2d 1425, 125 Lab.Cas. P 35, 803, 25 Fed.R.Serv.3d 786, 1 Wage & Hour Cas.2d (BNA) 629 United States Court of Appeals, Fifth Circuit. April 27, 1993.

Federal Courts

As of September 19, 2008, Federal Rule of Evidence 502(b) was enacted by Congress and signed into law by the President providing that a disclosure made in a federal proceeding does not operate as a waiver if:

1. the disclosure is inadvertent;
2. the holder of the privilege or protection took reasonable steps to prevent disclosure; and
3. the holder promptly took reasonable steps to rectify the error, including (if applicable) following Federal Rule of Civil Procedure 26(b)(5)(B).

Rule 502 is a change in the substantive law of privilege and waiver. Rule 502 (as shown below) provides a uniform standard for all federal proceedings. As with any new law, it has not been fully tested to determine every possible outcome when it is challenged; therefore, it does not provide an absolute answer to inadvertent disclosure. For example, what is meant by "reasonable precautions to prevent disclosure" or "prompt measures" is still undetermined in some jurisdictions.

Federal Rules of Evidence

> **Rule 502. Attorney–Client Privilege and Work Product; Limitations on Waiver** http://www.law.cornell.edu/rules/fre/rule_502
>
> (a) **Disclosure Made in a Federal Proceeding or to a Federal Office or Agency; Scope of a Waiver.** When the disclosure is made in a federal proceeding or to a federal office or agency and waives the attorney-client privilege or work-product protection, the waiver extends to an

undisclosed communication or information in a federal or state proceeding only if:

(1) the waiver is intentional;

(2) the disclosed and undisclosed communications or information concern the same subject matter; and

(3) they ought in fairness to be considered together.

(b) **Inadvertent Disclosure.** When made in a federal proceeding or to a federal office or agency, the disclosure does not operate as a waiver in a federal or state proceeding if:

(1) the disclosure is inadvertent;

(2) the holder of the privilege or protection took reasonable steps to prevent disclosure; and

(3) the holder promptly took reasonable steps to rectify the error, including (if applicable) following Federal Rule of Civil Procedure 26(b)(5)(B).

(c) **Disclosure Made in a State Proceeding.** When the disclosure is made in a state proceeding and is not the subject of a state-court order concerning waiver, the disclosure does not operate as a waiver in a federal proceeding if the disclosure:

(1) would not be a waiver under this rule if it had been made in a federal proceeding; or

(2) is not a waiver under the law of the state where the disclosure occurred.

(d) **Controlling Effect of a Court Order.** A federal court may order that the privilege or protection is not waived by disclosure connected with the litigation pending before the court—in which event the disclosure is also not a waiver in any other federal or state proceeding.

(e) **Controlling Effect of a Party Agreement.** An agreement on the effect of disclosure in a federal proceeding is binding only on the parties to the agreement, unless it is incorporated into a court order.

(f) **Controlling Effect of this Rule.** Notwithstanding Rules 101 and 1101, this rule applies to state proceedings and to federal court-annexed and federal court-mandated arbitration proceedings, in the circumstances set out in the rule. And notwithstanding Rule 501, this rule applies even if state law provides the rule of decision.

(g) **Definitions.** In this rule:

(1) "attorney-client privilege" means the protection that applicable law provides for confidential attorney-client communications; and

(2) "work-product protection" means the protection that applicable law provides for tangible material (or its intangible equivalent) prepared in anticipation of litigation or for trial.

ABA Ethics Opinion

The American Bar Association has issued a formal opinion modifying the longstanding opinion 92-368, which advocated for confidentiality of privileged materials to protect the client. The ABA imposed a burden upon receiving attorneys not to review privileged material and to return it following instructions given to them by the disclosing attorney. Clarifying formal opinion 05-437 states:

> A lawyer who receives a document from opposing parties or their lawyers and knows or reasonably should know that the document was inadvertently sent should promptly notify the sender in order to permit the sender to take protective measures. To the extent that Formal Opinion 92-368 opined otherwise, it is hereby withdrawn.

WEB RESOURCES

Find the complete version of Fed. R. Civ. P. 26 at the Cornell University Law School Legal Information Institute at www.law.cornell.edu/rules/frcp/rule26.htm.

CONCEPT REVIEW AND REINFORCEMENT

KEY TERMS

e-discovery   294
metadata   295
litigation hold   295
native format   296

OCR—optical character
   recognition   305
spoliation of evidence   308
predictive coding   312

technology assisted
   review   312
claw-back provision   314
redaction   314

CHAPTER SUMMARY

ISSUES IN ELECTRONIC DISCOVERY

Introduction to Electronic Discovery	The Federal Rules of Civil Procedure (Fed. R. Civ. P.), in place since December 2006, have addressed the change from paper-based to electronic-based documentation. Lawyers and paralegals are concerned about their responsibilities and how they should advise clients of the impact of the rules on business practices like retention policies of electronic data. Information technology (IT) staffs for law firms are concerned about making available the needed computer and technology resources.
Discovery in the Technological Age	For hundreds of years of legal practice, documentation in legal cases was in the form of paper. The computer and other computerized devices have enabled the creation of documents that formerly were in paper form to be created and viewed solely in electronic form. In the paper world, interrogatories (formal written discovery requests) sought the identification and physical location of relevant documents and requested hard copies. With the increasing use of electronic alternatives for the creation and storage of documents of all types, the number of paper copies has been reduced.
Amendments to the Federal Rules of Civil Procedure	The federal courts amended six rules specifically applicable to electronic discovery: Rule 16 Pretrial conferences; scheduling; management Rule 26 General provisions governing discovery; duty of disclosure Rule 33 Interrogatories to parties Rule 34 Production of documents, electronically stored information, and things and entry upon land for inspection and other purposes Rule 37 Failure to make disclosure or cooperate in discovery; sanction Rule 45 Subpoenas In addition, one new form was introduced: Form 35 Report of parties' planning meeting

(continued)

Changes in Traditional Discovery	Electronic discovery is a process and not a single event. The process includes obtaining the documents, filtering the documents for relevant terms, removing duplicates, and converting the documents into electronic files that can be processed like other electronic files.
Ethical Issues in Document Delivery	Federal rules and case law provide sanctions for failing to properly deliver documents under a discovery request. Under the rules of ethics, the legal team has a duty to protect the documents and comply with the discovery requests in compliance with court discovery orders.
Preserving Electronic Materials	Because of the ease of destruction of electronically stored materials by a single keystroke, whether intentional or inadvertent, parties concerned about potential litigation have an obligation to avoid destruction of potential evidence and may be required to place all documents related to a matter on a litigation hold.
Documents in Litigation	In the past, request for documents in response to interrogatories was met with the delivery of paper documents. During the transition period from paper to electronic documentation, issues have arisen with regard to the proper format for the delivery of requested documentation.
Native Format	Native format, the format in which the original files were created and saved, contains hidden data about the document known as metadata.
Computer Format	Documents that are delivered in computer-usable formats are easier to search and analyze using computer programs designed for those purposes. When documents are not delivered in computer-usable format, they can usually be processed and saved in such a format. However, the documents will no longer have any of the hidden data that is present in the original files.
Metadata	Metadata is frequently referred to as data about data. Metadata is divided into two types. Resource or system metadata is information about the content or application. This is used to track or locate the files and contains information such as file names, sizes, and locations. Content metadata is in the file itself, such as who the author of the document is and any changes that have been made to the document.
Producing Electronic Materials	The production of documents created and stored electronically falls under the traditional production of document discovery rule. The unique issues that arise with the production of electronic documents are the review for privileged information and the cost of that review and retrieval.
Cost of Producing Electronic Materials	A major concern in the production of electronic materials is the costs associated with review and production as well as the cost of retrieval and restoration of archived, corrupted, or deleted computer files.
Destruction of Electronic Records	Spoliation is the destruction of evidence when the party knows or should know that there is pending litigation. It is punishable by sanctions against the party who destroyed the evidence, which include the potential of an adverse instruction to the jury on the destruction or denying the party a right to defend the claim arising out of the destruction.
Information Technologists as Members of the Legal Team	The increased complexity of litigation involving electronically maintained records requires input from multiple experts, as seen in the increased use of information technologists as members of the legal team.

Electronic Document Formats—Comparison of PDF and TIFF	The two most common formats for large-scale document delivery are the TIFF and PDF formats. Neither of these formats contains the original metadata of the native format document. It is for this reason that some counsel prefer to deliver documents in these formats to avoid revealing the associated metadata.
Scanning	Scanning software today permits the scanning of documents and the conversion of documents into computer-readable formats by the use of optical character recognition software. This conversion enables the documents to be searched by other computer programs.
Electronic Discovery in Litigation	Not every lawsuit requires the use of all of the electronic discovery tools available. Many cases involve only limited numbers of documents in both paper and electronic forms.
Reviewing Electronic Documents	The biggest costs in electronic discovery come from reviewing electronic materials to find relevant items; identifying privileged, confidential, or protected documents; and delivering the relevant responses to discovery requests in appropriate formats.
Emerging Case Law and Court Rules	There are few cases to refer to for guidance about electronic discovery issues. The leading case is that of *Zubulake v. UBS*, in which the court issued a number of notable opinions, decisions, and orders concerning every aspect of electronic discovery. Among the issues addressed by the court was that of the destruction of evidence, referred to as spoliation of evidence. The court also addressed the issue of costs of discovery, including laying basic ground rules for when that cost should be shared by the parties and when it should be assigned to a specific party.
Predictive Coding/ Technology Assisted Review	Predictive coding programs or technology assisted review programs use algorithms to search a small set of documents that are representative of the entire, larger set to determine if the search terms are sufficiently locating the desired documents before applying the search to the entire date set.
Protecting Confidential or Privileged Materials	The attorney has an obligation to preserve the confidences of clients. It may not always be possible, within the limited time frames required for compliance, to check all documents before handing them over to opposing counsel.
Inadvertent Disclosure of Confidential Information	The new rules provide for a "claw-back" provision as part of the discovery plan. A claw-back provision, under Fed. R. Civ. P. 16(b)(6), is "any agreements the parties reach for asserting claims of privilege or of protection as trial-preparation material after production." State courts are still split in their approaches; some courts bar inadvertently disclosed data use, and some allow it as if the disclosure were intentional. The use of the claw-back agreement alone does not relieve the attorney of obligations regarding confidential client information.

REVIEW QUESTIONS AND EXERCISES

1. What is the impact of the Federal Rules of Civil Procedure on the timetable for discovery requests?
2. What types of electronic information might be requested in litigation today that did not exist twenty years ago?
3. What is meant by *spoliation* of evidence?
4. What are the possible sanctions for spoliation of evidence?
5. What are the possible costs associated with electronic discovery?
6. What are the ethical issues in protecting confidential or privileged information in this age of electronic documents?
7. What is meant by a *claw-back provision* in a discovery plan? How important is it ethically?
8. What role does cost play in electronic discovery plans?
9. May a firm or client regularly destroy the firm's records? Explain fully.
10. What is *inadvertent disclosure*? How does the court deal with it?
11. Why is electronic discovery not an issue in all cases?
12. What is the biggest cost in electronic discovery? Explain fully.
13. Why is electronic discovery a process? What are the steps in the process?
14. What is meant by *redaction*? When would it be used?
15. Why would a litigation team use an outside consultant in litigating a case?
16. What is the role of the information technologist on the legal team in the area of electronic discovery?
17. What is meant by *native format*?
18. How can paper documents be converted to electronically searchable formats?
19. What is metadata and why is it important in the litigation process?
20. What is the difference between system metadata and content metadata?
21. What is the disadvantage of receiving documents in TIFF or PDF format?
22. What is the value of optical character recognition software to the litigation team?

BUILDING YOUR PARALEGAL SKILLS

INTERNET AND TECHNOLOGY EXERCISES

1. Conduct an Internet search to locate software that can be used in the e-discovery process. What resources do the individual companies offer to help you learn and use the software?
2. Search the web for service bureaus that provide e-discovery services.
3. Locate and download a current case on spoliation of evidence.
4. Use the Internet to prepare a list of resources on electronic discovery for the legal community. List the services offered and the contact information.

CIVIL LITIGATION VIDEO CASE STUDIES

Zealous Representation Issue: Handling Evidence

A paralegal has discovered a document that is detrimental to the law firm's client. No one else is aware of its existence.

After viewing the video at www.pearsonhighered.com/ careersresources, answer the following questions.

1. Does the law firm have any duty to make available to the opposing side evidence that is detrimental to their case?

2. Is there any ethical or legal reason not to hide or destroy a document if no one else knows of its existence?

Privilege Issue: Misdirected E-Mail

The paralegal working on a case accidentally sends a confidential memo to opposing counsel.

After viewing the video at www.pearsonhighered.com/careersresources, answer the following questions.

1. Who is ultimately responsible for inadvertent disclosure of confidential information or work product?
2. What steps should be taken in your jurisdiction when confidential information is inadvertently sent to the wrong party?

CHAPTER OPENING SCENARIO CASE STUDY

Use the Opening Scenario for this chapter to answer the following questions.

1. Prepare a summary for the attorney to use in advising clients on the basic rules of spoliation and its potential impact on litigation.
2. Prepare a memo to the IT staff or outside consultant explaining what the trial team needs in a case of this type.
3. Prepare a memo from the IT staff to the trial team explaining what issues they should be aware of and giving suggestions for obtaining and protecting the needed data.

COMPREHENSIVE CASE STUDY

SCHOOL BUS–TRUCK ACCIDENT CASE

Review the assigned case study in Appendix 2.

1. Prepare an electronic document discovery request, under the applicable Federal Rules of Civil Procedure, for the accident case in Appendix 1.
2. As defense counsel, draw up a document discovery agreement for plaintiff's counsel. Is the language the same for both plaintiff and defendant? Explain.
3. Prepare a memo to the supervising attorney concerning electronic discovery issues that must be discussed with opposing counsel and resolved in advance of the Rule 16(b) scheduling conference.

BUILDING YOUR PROFESSIONAL PORTFOLIO AND REFERENCE MANUAL

CIVIL LITIGATION TEAM AT WORK

See page 18 for instructions on Building Your Professional Portfolio and Reference Manual.

Policy Manual

Create an office policy on litigation hold procedures.

Forms

1. Create a litigation hold template letter to send to a client.

2. Create a checklist for obtaining and protecting client data that might be subject to discovery disclosure.

Procedures

Local court policy on spoliation of evidence.

Contacts and Resources

Find business and web addresses of computer forensic consultants in your jurisdiction.

LEARNING OBJECTIVES

After studying this chapter, you should be able to:

1. Define *interrogatories* and *requests for production of documents and things* and understand the best use of each.

2. Discuss the discovery time frame and how it may be modified.

3. Draft questions and answers for interrogatories.

4. Prepare requests and responses to requests for production.

5. Understand the new requirements related to electronic discovery.

Interrogatories and Requests for Production

CHAPTER 13

OPENING SCENARIO

All of the interrogatories and requests for production in the school bus accident case had been forwarded to the paralegal in the suburban office for processing and logging into the calendar system. There did not appear to be any unusual requests in the initial set of interrogatories addressed to the clients. The main concern was how the parents of the children would relay the children's answers.

Caitlin, the paralegal in the downtown office, was asked to prepare the initial draft of the interrogatories to be submitted to the defendants. It was obvious that not much would be learned except the most basic information. But Caitlin wanted to be certain that all of the underlying information was obtained to allow for continuing investigation. She would also use the information to prepare questions to ask various witnesses and parties involved at depositions. It appeared there might be some allegations of wrongdoing by corporate defendants that might be documented in e-mails and other electronically stored documents, such as those about potential negligent design or poor maintenance of the braking systems. There had been no initial disclosure of these files, and Caitlin wanted to draft additional interrogatories to discover the potential sources without revealing the trial strategy.

OPENING SCENARIO LEARNING OBJECTIVE

Draft a cover letter for interrogatories to be sent to a client, outlining the obligations and limitations permitted in answering interrogatories including the right to destroy potential evidence.

■ INTRODUCTION TO INTERROGATORIES AND REQUESTS FOR PRODUCTION

interrogatories
A form of discovery in which written questions are addressed to a party to a lawsuit requiring written answers made under oath.

requests for production of documents
The shorthand name for production of documents and things.

Interrogatories and **requests for production of documents** are methods of discovery that are used early in the discovery phase. The initial sets of interrogatories and requests for production are often submitted to the opposing party at the same time. There are similarities between interrogatories and requests for production—both are written requests for information addressed to a party to the lawsuit. Both require written answers or responses within a fixed period of time, usually thirty days. The answers frequently provide information that is the basis of additional requests for production or other discovery, including oral depositions and requests for admissions.

■ INTERROGATORIES AND REQUESTS FOR PRODUCTION OF DOCUMENTS AND THINGS

LEARNING OBJECTIVE 1
Define *interrogatories* and *requests for production of documents and things* and understand the best use of each.

An interrogatory is a formal request for written answers to written questions addressed to another party to the lawsuit (Fed. R. Civ. P. 33). The answering party is required to prepare complete answers or objections to each question, in writing, within thirty days of service of the interrogatories. Answers are made under oath by the answering party, which subjects the answering party to a potential charge of perjury for providing false answers under oath. Objections to answering the interrogatory questions may be made if the questions seek information subject to a recognized evidentiary privilege, such as the attorney–client privilege, or because they are not relevant to the issues in the current lawsuit. If the response is an objection to the interrogatory question based on a legally recognized reason, the attorney for the answering party also signs the answer to the interrogatory.

movable items
Documents, photographs, recordings, and similar tangible items.

non-movable items
Real property or large goods that are not readily movable but remain at the heart of the lawsuit.

The full title in the federal rules for requests for production is *Producing Documents, Electronically Stored Information, and Tangible Things, or Entering onto Land, for Inspection and Other Purposes* (Fed. R. Civ. P. 34). It includes provisions for the production of **movable items** and **non-movable items** for copying, testing, and sampling. Movable items include documents, photographs, recordings, electronically stored items and the media on which they are stored, and similar items. Non-movable items are such things as real property or large goods that are not readily movable but remain at the heart of the lawsuit. All relevant movable

VIDEO ADVICE FROM THE FIELD

INTERVIEW: WORKING WITH IT

Charlotte Harris, Manager, Litigation Support, Hess Corporation

A discussion emphasizing the relationship between the paralegal and the information technologist and the skills necessary to be successful in the litigation support profession. The differences in the roles

of the paralegal and the litigation support person are explained.

After watching the video at www.pearsonhighered.com/ careersresources, answer the following questions.

1. What are the skills of a successful litigation support specialist?
2. How does the role of the paralegal differ from that of the litigation support specialist?

and non-movable items may be requested. Requests for production are similar to interrogatories—they are formal written requests issued to another party to the lawsuit. The answering party must respond, in writing, within thirty days after being served with the request for production, indicating whether inspection will be permitted and how it will be accomplished; if inspection is not permitted, the answering party must state the specific grounds for any objection to the request. Using a subpoena issued by the clerk of court, a request for inspection or copying of documents may also be made by either party on those who are not parties to the action. The subpoena may also include a command to appear at a deposition, hearing, or trial, as shown in Exhibit 13.1 (Fed. R. Civ. P. 45).

Exhibit 13.1 Subpoena Issued to a Nonparty to the Action to Produce Documents

AO88 (Rev. 12/06) Subpoena in a Civil Case

Issued by the
UNITED STATES DISTRICT COURT

DISTRICT OF _____

SUBPOENA IN A CIVIL CASE

V.

Case Number:[1]

TO:

☐ YOU ARE COMMANDED to appear in the United States District court at the place, date, and time specified below to testify in the above case.

PLACE OF TESTIMONY	COURTROOM
	DATE AND TIME

☐ YOU ARE COMMANDED to appear at the place, date, and time specified below to testify at the taking of a deposition in the above case.

PLACE OF DEPOSITION	DATE AND TIME

☐ YOU ARE COMMANDED to produce and permit inspection and copying of the following documents or objects at the place, date, and time specified below (list documents or objects):

PLACE	DATE AND TIME

☐ YOU ARE COMMANDED to permit inspection of the following premises at the date and time specified below.

PREMISES	DATE AND TIME

Any organization not a party to this suit that is subpoenaed for the taking of a deposition shall designate one or more officers, directors, or managing agents, or other persons who consent to testify on its behalf, and may set forth, for each person designated, the matters on which the person will testify. Federal Rules of Civil Procedure, 30(b)(6).

ISSUING OFFICER'S SIGNATURE AND TITLE (INDICATE IF ATTORNEY FOR PLAINTIFF OR DEFENDANT)	DATE

ISSUING OFFICER'S NAME, ADDRESS AND PHONE NUMBER

(See Rule 45, Federal Rules of Civil Procedure, Subdivisions (c), (d), and (e), on next page)

[1] If action is pending in district other than district of issuance, state district under case number.

WEB RESOURCES

For a complete set of sample interrogatories and to obtain the latest version of the sample pages in Exhibit 13.2, visit www.krollontrack.com.

As shown in Exhibits 13.2 and 13.3, interrogatories and requests for production contain:

1. the caption of the case;
2. identification of the document;
3. introductory paragraph further identifying the document;
4. the party serving it;
5. the action required of the recipient;
6. a list of definitions;
7. the interrogatory questions, or documents or things requested to be produced;
8. the signature of the attorney;
9. certification of service; and
10. verification page for the signature of the answering party.

Exhibit 13.2 Sample Interrogatories in Federal Court for Cases Involving Electronic Discovery

---

SAMPLE INTERROGATORIES

UNITED STATES DISTRICT COURT
DISTRICT OF [Jurisdiction]

Court File No.:

,
Plaintiff,

v.

,
Defendant.

INTERROGATORIES TO [Party Name]

I. DEFINITIONS. The definitions below will apply to the interrogatories requested in this document.

A. APPLICATION: An application is a collection of one or more related software programs that enable a user to enter, store, view, modify or extract information from files or databases. The term is commonly used in place of "program," or "software." Applications may include word processors, Internet browsing tools and spreadsheets.

B. BACKUP: To create a copy of data as a precaution against the loss or damage of the original data. Most users backup some of their files, and many computer networks utilize automatic backup software to make regular copies of some or all of the data on the network. Some backup systems use digital audio tape (DAT) as a storage medium. Backup Data is information that is not presently in use by an organization and is routinely stored separately upon portable media, to free up space and permit data recovery in the event of disaster.

C. DELETED DATA: Deleted Data is data that, in the past, existed on the computer as live data and which has been deleted by the computer system or end-user activity. Deleted data remains on storage media in whole or in part until it is overwritten by ongoing usage or "wiped" with a software program specifically designed to remove deleted data. Even after the data itself has been wiped, directory entries, pointers, or other metadata relating to the deleted data may remain on the computer.

D. DOCUMENT. Fed.R.Civ.P. 34(a) defines a document as "including writings, drawings, graphs, charts, photographs, phone records, and other data compilations." In the electronic discovery world, a document also refers to a collection of pages representing an electronic file. Emails, attachments, databases, word documents, spreadsheets, and graphic files are all examples of electronic documents.

Exhibit 13.2 (*continued*)

E. HARD DRIVE: The primary storage unit on PCs, consisting of one or more magnetic media platters on which digital data can be written and erased magnetically.

F. MIRROR IMAGE: Used in computer forensic investigations and some electronic discovery investigations, a mirror image is a bit-by-bit copy of a computer hard drive that ensures the operating system is not altered during the forensic examination.

G. NETWORK: A group of computers or devices that is connected together for the exchange of data and sharing of resources.

H. OPERATING SYSTEM (OS): The software that the rest of the software depends on to make the computer functional. On most PCs this is Windows or the Macintosh OS. Unix and Linux are other operating systems often found in scientific and technical environments.

I. SPOLIATION: Spoliation is the destruction of records which may be relevant to ongoing or anticipated litigation, government investigations or audits. Courts differ in their interpretation of the level of intent required before sanctions may be warranted.

J. SOFTWARE: Coded instructions (programs) that make a computer do useful work.

II. Documents and Data.

A. *Individuals/organizations responsible*. Identify and attach copies of all company organizational and policy information including:

1. Organizational charts;
2. A list of the names, titles, contact information, and job description/duties for all individuals (or organizations) responsible for maintaining electronic processing systems, networks, servers, and data security measures; and
3. A list of the names, titles, contact information, and job description/duties for all individuals employed in the following departments (or their equivalents) for [Plaintiffs/Defendants/Third Party]:
   a. Information Technology;
   b. Information Services;
   c. Incident Response Teams;
   d. Data Recovery Units; and
   e. Computer Forensic or Audit/Investigation Teams.

B. *Relevant Products/Services*. Identify and attach copies of all documents related to (including marketing, selling, leasing, sharing or giving to another party) the computer system, programs, software, hardware, materials, tools or information that [Plaintiffs/Defendants/Third Party] uses or has used in relation to the sale or use of [Product/Service]. This includes all electronic data and necessary instructions for accessing such data relating to:

1. The pricing of [Product/Service] in the United States and internationally;
2. Customer invoices for [Product/Service], including the customer names/addresses, purchase volume, prices, discounts, transportation charges and production information;
3. Email sent or received by [Plaintiffs/Defendants/Third Party] to customers relating to [Product/Service];
4. Accounting records relating to [Product/Service], including work-in-progress reports, billing records, vendor invoices, time and material records, cost completion reports for each of [Plaintiffs/Defendants/Third Party] customers;

Source: From Sample Interrogatories in Federal Court for Cases involving Electronic Discovery, Sample Forms and Pleadings, 2006. Reproduced by the permission of Kroll Ontrack Inc.

Exhibit 13.3 Request for Production of Documents

SUPERIOR COURT OF THE STATE OF CALIFORNIA
COUNTY OF _____

[PLAINTIFF(S) NAMES] **Plaintiffs,** **v.** **[DEFENDANT(S) NAMES]** **Defendants**	))))))))))))	**CASE NO: _____** **DEMAND FOR PRODUCTION** **AND INSPECTION OF** **DOCUMENTS**

_____

Demanding Party: _____

Inspection Demand Set _____

Responding Party: _____

To _____ [responding party],

Demand is hereby made that you produce for inspection and copying the following documents or categories of document in your possession, custody, or control. The documents or categories of documents must be produced within 30 days after service of this demand the office of demanding party's counsel. Pursuant to section 2031(h) of the Code of Civil Procedure, a written response to this inspection demand with 20 days from the date of service of this demand.

1. _____ [List and number each document or category of documents separately, describing each in enough detail to allow responding party to easily identify items demanded, for instance:

   a. Every written statement or transcription of a recorded statement, and all notes of conversation made by any witness to the accident that is the subject of this suit.

   b. Every report, photograph, recording, or other writing prepared by investigator _____ (invesigator name), based on _____ (investigator his or her) investigation of _____ (accident scene) located at _____ (address), _____ (accident scene city), _____ (accident scene county)County, California.

   c. Every photograph that shows any personal injuries sustained by _____ (responding party) in the accident that is the subject of this suit.

   d. Every bill, statement, report, record, or other writing that pertains to personal injuries sustained by _____ (responding party) in the accident that is the subject of this suit.]

2. _____ [Specify manner in which activities other than inspection will be performed, for example: The items produced by _____ (responding party) will be subjected to inspection, photographing, testing, and sampling as follows:

   a. Photographic enlargement of each document produced.

   b. Handwriting analysis of each handwritten document.]

DATED:

_____

_____

(Signature)

Definitions of standard or specific terms and nomenclature that relate to the particular facts of the case or are defined in a way unique to a particular field, industry, or business may be included. For example, the term "barrel" in the oil industry means a container of 42 gallons; in the beer industry, 31.5 gallons; and if used as an equivalent term to "drum," 55 gallons. If the issue is one of how many gallons are covered by a contract, the correct equivalent barrel volume must be defined before asking how many barrels were delivered.

■ TIME FRAME FOR DISCOVERY

Most rules of court provide a time frame within which discovery may occur without permission from the court—both a starting point after the lawsuit is filed and an ending point so that the trial or other ADR hearing is not delayed. Within these starting and ending points, there are time limits imposed to compel answers. On a motion or request to the court, if there is a good reason, parties may be able to start discovery earlier (prefiling) and continue longer, closer to trial. Deadlines for filing or returning the answers to discovery may also be extended, both informally by agreement of the attorneys and formally by motion to the court, again for "good cause."

LEARNING OBJECTIVE 2
Discuss the discovery time frame and how it may be modified.

Initial Discovery Requests

In federal court, in general, discovery may not begin until the attorneys have conferred about the case, prepared a plan for discovery, and issued a report to the court containing a plan for the timing of the discovery (Fed. R. Civ. P. 26). The discovery plan may become part of the court's scheduling order, which sets the deadlines for motions, discovery, and trial. There are no other limitations on when interrogatories, requests for production, or other discovery methods can be used or in what order.

Extension of Time for Responding

The parties, through their counsel, may enlarge or extend the normal thirty-day time period for responding to the interrogatories or requests to produce.

Experienced attorneys anticipate that additional time will be necessary to respond to discovery requests, and they allow for that in the initial conference planning report submitted to the court before the required scheduling conference with the trial judge. The scheduling order that governs the case may include a universal time extension (for example, sixty days to answer all discovery requests). The scheduling order that appears in Exhibit 13.4 requires that discovery be completed by a date certain, September 14, 2014.

Counsel may also enlarge the time to respond to discovery by a stipulation. Extension by stipulation of counsel is permitted as long as that extension does not violate the discovery deadline imposed under the court's scheduling order or interfere with another hearing or proceeding. These time constraints, whether thirty days or some agreed-to extension, may be critical where the answering party objects to the question or request and must file a timely objection to avoid the objection being considered waived.

Exhibit 13.4 Final Scheduling Order

IN THE UNITED STATES DISTRICT COURT
FOR THE NORTHERN DISTRICT OF FLORIDA
PENSACOLA DIVISION

STATE OF FLORIDA, by and
through Bill McCollum, et al.,

Plaintiffs,

v.   **Case No.: 3:10-cv-91-RV/EMT**

UNITED STATES DEPARTMENT OF
HEALTH AND HUMAN SERVICES,
et al.,

Defendants.

_____/

FINAL SCHEDULING ORDER

A Rule 16 pre-trial scheduling conference was held in this matter today, April 14, 2014. Present were the attorneys for the plaintiffs: Blaine H. Winship, Florida Attorney's General Office; Joseph W. Jacquot, Florida Attorney General's Office; Chesterfield Smith, Jr., Florida Attorney General's Office; and David B. Rivkin, Jr., Baker & Hostetler; and attorneys for the defendants: Ian Gershengorn, Deputy Assistant Attorney General, Civil Division; Brian Kennedy, Department of Justice Civil Division's Federal Programs Branch; Eric Beckenhauer, Department of Justice Civil Division's Federal Programs Branch; and Pamela Monie, Assistant United States Attorney. Also appearing via telephone were the named plaintiffs or their representatives for the states of Alabama, Arizona, Colorado, Florida, Indiana, Michigan, Nebraska, Nevada, Pennsylvania, South Carolina, South Dakota, Texas, Utah, Washington.

After discussion with the attorneys of record, and the court otherwise being fully advised in the premises, it is hereby ORDERED:

A. The following schedule and dates are hereby set and approved for pretrial proceedings in this case:

May 14, 2014	Plaintiffs' date for filing an amended complaint;
June 16, 2014	Defendant s' date for filling a motion to dismiss;
August 6, 2014	Plaintiffs' date for filing a brief in opposition to the motion to dismiss;
August 27, 2014	Defendant s' date for filling a reply to Plaintiffs' opposition brief;
September 14, 2014 at 9:00 a.m.	Oral argument on Defendants' motion to dismiss.

Case No.: 3: 10-cv-91-RV/EMT

Exhibit 13.4 *(continued)*

Case 3:10-cv-00091-RV-EMT   Document 26   Filled 04/14/10

The plaintiffs may, but they are not required to, file their motion for summary judgment at or after the time they file their response in opposition to defendants' motion to dismiss (August 6th). The plaintiffs' motion for summary judgment, if filed prior to resolution of the motion to dismiss, will be held in abeyance until the court rules on the motion to dismiss. If this case survives dismissal, in whole or in part, the defendants will then have forty (40) days from the date of the order ruling on the motion to dismiss (or from the filing of the plaintiffs' motion for summary judgment, whichever is later) to respond to the motion of summary judgment. The plaintiffs will have twenty-one (21) days to reply to that response. An oral argument date will be set by the Court on the summary judgment motion once the briefing dates become fixed.

B. The briefing with regard to the motions described above will be limited to fifty (50) pages for the initial and responsive briefs, and twenty-five (25) pages for reply briefs.

C. The deadline for joining parties will be the same date for the amended compliant (May 14, 2014).

D. To the extent that any discovery may be required in this case, the discovery deadline is September 14, 2014.

E. The parties are hereby excused from compliance with the initial disclosure provisions under Rule 26, Federal Rules of Civil Procedure, and the other reporting requirements under Rule 16 of those rules, as well as the corresponding Local Rules, pending further Order from this Court.

DONE and ORDERED this 14th day of April, 2014.

/S/ *Roger Vinson*

ROGER VINSON
Senior United States District Judge

■ DRAFTING QUESTIONS AND ANSWERS TO INTERROGATORIES

More than any other discovery tool, interrogatories have traditionally been the largest source of objections and motions for relief. Many court rule changes are designed to eliminate some of the objections and remove the need for court involvement. Many judges in motions court routinely limit the number of interrogatory questions to which counsel may raise objections. Interrogatories generally provide only a limited insight into the other party's case. In practice, the questions provide information that may be used to frame other discovery requests. Federal court rules limit the number of questions (including subparts of questions) that may be asked in interrogatories to twenty-five (Fed. R. Civ. P. 33).

LEARNING OBJECTIVE 3
Draft questions and answers for interrogatories.

Initial Disclosures

In addition to the twenty-five interrogatory questions permitted, parties are required to make certain additional information available as part of the initial disclosures under federal rules. This includes the identity of individuals having discoverable information, the location of discoverable information, computation of damages, and insurance agreements (Fed. R. Civ. P. 26). Although not part of the initial disclosure, identification of expert witnesses, a statement of their qualifications, and their reports, including their opinions, must also be shared. In many jurisdictions, mandatory form interrogatories that must be answered by the litigants may have already been approved by the court. These mandatory interrogatories serve the same purpose as the mandatory disclosure requirements.

Drafting Questions

Drafting questions for interrogatories is an important skill. Most of the information that the legal team needs, such as identification of witnesses (and the substance of their testimony), exhibits, and experts, will be shared under the Rule 26 mandatory disclosure. With all of this information already shared, it may appear unnecessary to conduct additional discovery with interrogatories. However, areas of additional inquiry should be explored.

Standard interrogatories, or form interrogatories, may be sufficient for routine cases, and no additional questions may need to be asked. In complex or unusual cases, however, it may be necessary to ask additional questions to obtain the information necessary to further investigate the case or prepare for other forms of discovery.

Determining what to ask and how to ask it is a process that includes analysis of the underlying claims, the needed evidentiary proof, and strategy.

Claims, Defenses, and Issues

The first step is to review the pleadings and identify the claims made, the legal issues involved, and the defenses asserted. The elements required to establish the claims and defenses must be identified, and potential sources of evidence for each must also be identified. For example, a defendant may assert assumption of the risk as a defense, which requires proof that the plaintiff (1) knew, understood, and appreciated the risks associated with a particular activity; (2) had full knowledge of that risk; and (3) freely and voluntarily proceeded with the activity. If the mandatory initial disclosure does not reveal anyone with evidence of assumption of the risk, additional interrogatories may be needed to identify those who might have witnessed or might have evidence of the assumption of the risk in the form of a document, such as a release signed by the plaintiff before skydiving.

Evidentiary Proof

An analysis of the disclosed information should focus on whether the information will satisfy the evidentiary requirements at trial. In the assumption of risk example, the defendant identifies witnesses and provides copies of documents, but there is no reference to the assumption of risk defense, the witnesses who may testify, or the evidence that may be presented in support of the defense. Thus, an area of inquiry appropriate for interrogatory questions has been discovered, such as that shown in Exhibit 13.5.

Strategy

The final consideration before including a question in the interrogatories is one related to strategy. This analysis is based on the amount of time the answering party has to develop a response to a written question versus the lack of time to think before answering an oral question (and follow-up questions) presented under oath in a deposition. Some questions may be better left to the deposition, where there is no time to craft a response.

Exhibit 13.5 Sample Assumption of the Risk Interrogatory

Interrogatory No. 3

With regard to the affirmative defense of assumption of the risk which appears in paragraph 15 of your Answer to the Complaint, kindly:

    a. identify each witness upon whom you rely and a summary of each identified witness's knowledge with regard to the plaintiff's assumption of the risk

    b. identify the documents, if any, upon which you rely to establish that the plaintiff assumed the risk

---

Checklist ✔

PREPARING INTERROGATORIES

- Review pleadings for claims and defenses.
- Prepare a list of claims/defenses.
- Add the elements required to establish each claim/defense to the list.
- Review the initial disclosure information required under Fed. R. Civ. P. 26(a).
- Look for claims/defenses where there is a lack of supporting information.

Serving Interrogatories

Interrogatories may be served upon any other party to the action without request of or leave of court. Copies may be served upon represented parties by sending a set of interrogatories to their counsel. Rules of ethical conduct preclude counsel from communicating directly with anyone who is represented, except through his or her attorney. The manner and time of service should be noted for the file, and the date the answers are due should be entered into the firm's calendar system for follow-up.

Preparing Responses

Responding to interrogatories follows a process similar to creating interrogatories. Before giving any consideration to responding to interrogatories, the due date should be calendared to avoid missing the deadline. It is also good practice

ETHICAL Perspectives

INDIANA RULES OF COURT
RULES OF PROFESSIONAL CONDUCT RULE 4.2.
COMMUNICATION WITH PERSON REPRESENTED
BY COUNSEL

In representing a client, a lawyer shall not communicate about the subject of the representation with a person the lawyer knows to be represented by another lawyer in the matter, unless the lawyer has the consent of the other lawyer or is authorized by law or a court order.

WEB RESOURCES

Contrast and compare the Indiana Rules of Court at http://www.state.in.us/judiciary/rules/prof_conduct/index.html#_Rule_4.2._Communication_with_Person with the American Bar Association Model Rules of Professional Responsibility at and the ethical rules in your jurisdiction.

to include several reminder dates, such as three weeks, two weeks, ten days, seven days, four days, and the day before the answers are due. Under this type of reminder system, the paralegal who has been drawn into other projects will not forget to complete and prepare the interrogatories for signature and service within the required time frame.

The interrogatories are sent to counsel but are addressed to the client and are intended to be completed and signed by the client, though in reality, most of the information is completed from the law office file. A copy of the interrogatories must be sent to the client with a letter explaining what interrogatories are and the time limitations imposed on answering them. The letter also should ask the client to prepare answers to the best of his ability and to contact the law office staff to schedule a definite time to meet with the attorney or paralegal to review the answers. Exhibit 13.6 is a sample cover letter to accompany interrogatories sent to a client.

Exhibit 13.6 Sample Letter to Client to Send with Interrogatories

Mason, Marshall and Benjamin
Attorneys at Law

Owen Mason

Arial Marshall

Ethan Benjamin

Cary Eden

July 18, 2014

Mr. & Mrs. Steven Knowles
1234 Asbury Avenue
Bennington, VT

Re: Knowles v. Clemmons *et.al*

Dear Mr. and Mrs. Knowles:

Enclosed you will find a copy of Interrogatories that have been served on us by the Defendants Smith and Ace Trucking in the lawsuit filed on behalf of your daughter.

Interrogatories are written questions about the lawsuit that require written responses. Your responses are made under oath as to their truth. We are required to complete the responses to the enclosed Interrogatories and return them to Attorney Morris by August 15, 2014.

In order to assist us in the process, kindly review and answer each question with your daughter. You may mark the answers directly on the copy of Interrogatories enclosed. Feel free to consult any documents, records, or other items that may help recall the events of the accident.

I have scheduled an appointment for us to meet and review the answers on August 1, 2014, at 11:00 a.m. in our suburban office. Please bring your copy of the Interrogatories with the answers completed to the best of your ability and any documents you referred to in preparing the answers to our appointment on August 1.

Should you have any questions or concerns, please feel free to call.

Sincerely,

Caitlin Gordon

Paralegal

Review for Objections to Questions

The interrogatories should be carefully reviewed to determine if any questions are **objectionable.** There are several grounds to object to interrogatories. The questions may be objectionable for several reasons, including:

1. They seek information protected from disclosure by privilege, the work product doctrine, trade secrets, or a similar rule.
2. The question might be duplicative, or materials answering the question may have been shared through disclosure, and it is just as easy for the requesting party to review those documents as it is for the answering party to do so.
3. The questions may be vague, overly broad, or burdensome.
4. The questions may be unlikely to lead to admissible evidence.

The supervising attorney makes the final decision concerning any objections. The answer will state specifically the grounds for the objection. Often, the problem with objectionable questions is how the question was drafted, as shown in Exhibit 13.7.

An objectionable question may be both objected to (by stating the grounds for the objection) and answered (by providing the information the answering party believes the opposing party was seeking), or some combination of the two. One answer to Interrogatory No. 8 shown in Exhibit 13.7 is shown in Exhibit 13.8. An example of a more carefully drafted interrogatory question seeking the same information is shown in Exhibit 13.9.

Motion for Protective Order

When an interrogatory is objectionable, a decision must be made whether to object or ignore the objection and provide an answer. Poorly drafted questions sometimes are a strategic advantage. They may reveal that the other side doesn't understand the issues or may be willing to accept the information provided. If the question is one to which an objection must be filed, a **motion for protective order**

objectionable
In discovery, items that are not discoverable because the information is protected by privilege, the work product doctrine, trade secrets, or a similar rule; the question might be duplicative; materials answering the questions may have been shared through disclosure; or the questions may be vague, overly broad, burdensome, or unlikely to lead to admissible evidence.

motion for protective order
Motion that asks the court to determine whether certain information must be disclosed in discovery.

Exhibit 13.7 An Interrogatory Objectionable as Vague, Overly Broad, and Unduly Burdensome

---

Interrogatory No. 8

List every phone call and describe the nature of the conversation.

Exhibit 13.8 Possible Answer to Objectionable Interrogatory

Answer

Objection. The Interrogatory is vague, overly broad, and unduly burdensome in that it is not limited as to time, the parties to, or subject matter of the litigation. To the extent the question seeks information regarding telephone calls between the defendant and plaintiff during the relevant times set forth in the complaint, they are listed below.

DATE	CONTACT	NATURE OF DISCUSSION
1/3/14	plaintiff called defendant	plaintiff advised goods were damaged
1/5/14	plaintiff called defendant	plaintiff requested defendant inspect goods
1/10/14	plaintiff called defendant	plaintiff requested instructions for return of goods and refund

---

must be prepared and filed with the court simultaneously with sending the answers with objections to opposing counsel.

A motion for protective order asks the court to determine whether the objection to the interrogatory or other discovery request is appropriate. The court may determine whether the objection should be sustained and the material protected from discovery, or it may overrule the objection, directing that the question be answered within a certain time frame, usually ten days.

Meeting with the Client to Answer Interrogatories

Before meeting with the client to review the answers to the interrogatories, the contents of the case file should be carefully reviewed. Answers to most questions asked in interrogatories can be based on the information in the file. During the meeting with the client, it will be important to note discrepancies between the information contained in the file and the information the client provides. Sometimes these differences are negligible or easily explained. A fact initially reported by the client based upon memory may differ from the answer to an interrogatory because the client has had the opportunity to review records and prepare a written response. For example, a client who reported going to the doctor one week following an accident may realize, after looking at a personal calendar and bill from the doctor, that it was really three weeks after the injury.

Some discrepancies are not so easily explained and may change the client's case or even result in withdrawing the claim. For example, a client claims he

Exhibit 13.9 Sample of a more carefully written interrogatory asking for information sought in the interrogatory in Exhibit 13.7

Interrogatory No. 8

List the date, time, individuals who participated in, and substance of any telephone conversations that took place between the plaintiff and the defendant, or their representatives.

---

was overcharged for unauthorized home construction work. After he reviews his documents, he finds the work change order form listing the work. The form, signed by the client's spouse, authorizes and agrees to pay for additional work. These discrepancies should be brought to the attention of the supervising attorney immediately, as they may change the entire outcome of the case. The paralegal may be the one to work with the client to prepare answers for review, revision, and correction by the supervising attorney. The client will be required to sign the verification stating the answers are true and accurate to the best of his knowledge. The attorney will also sign the answers wherever objections have been raised. The final task is to prepare a certificate of service indicating that the answer to interrogatories was served on all interested parties, as shown in Exhibit 13.10.

PRACTICE TIP

Paying attention to objectionable questions from others will help you become a better drafter of properly worded, non-objectionable interrogatory questions.

Exhibit 13.10 Sample Certificate of Service

UNITED STATES DISTRICT COURT - NORTHERN DISTRICT OF NEW YORK

B.K., a minor by her
Parents and Guardians,
Janice Knowles and
Steven Knowles,
Plaintiff

v.

Ronald Clemmons,
Lower Council School District,
Bud Smith, and
Ace Trucking Company,
Defendants

:   No.: _____

:

:   PLAINTIFF'S ANSWER
        TO DEFENDANTS
:   SMITH AND ACE TRUCKING
        INTERROGATORIES
:

:

:   Attorney ID No. 124987

CERTIFICATE OF SERVICE

The undersigned certifies that the document described below was served on the parties listed below by first class mail postage prepaid delivered at the post office in Albany, New York 05432 on August 15, 2014.

Document served: Plaintiff's Answers to Defendants Smith and Ace Trucking
                            Company Interrogatories

Parties Served: John Morris, Esquire
                            Counsel for Defendants Smith and Ace Trucking
                            Street address
                            Albany, New York

                            William Buchter, Esquire
                            Counsel for Defendants Clemmons and Lower Council School
                            District
                            Street Address
                            Albany, New York

Date: _____   _____

                                                         Ethan Benjamin, Esquire
                                                         Roy Saunders, Esquire
                                                         Mason, Marshall and Benjamin
                                                          Street Address

Checklist  PREPARING ANSWERS TO INTERROGATORIES

- ■ Enter calendar due dates and reminder dates.
- ■ Send a work copy of the interrogatories to the client with a letter of instruction.
- ■ Complete a work copy based on the contents of the client's file.
- ■ Present objectionable questions to the attorney for determination.
- ■ If questions are determined objectionable, prepare motion for protective order.
- ■ Meet with client to review answers.
- ■ Prepare final answers for review by supervising attorney.
- ■ Meet with client to sign interrogatories.
- ■ Serve answers on all interested parties.

Reviewing Answers to Interrogatories

When the answers to interrogatories are received, they must be reviewed to be certain all the interrogatories have been fully answered or, if there are objections, a motion for protective order must be included with the answers submitted. If a motion has been filed, the response and hearing dates must be entered onto the calendar and a reply to the motion prepared and filed.

The answers provided to interrogatories may reveal new areas for discovery. Documents, witnesses, and legal theories may be all revealed. The best method to obtain discovery in these new areas, such as requests for production or depositions, must be determined by the supervising attorney.

■ DRAFTING REQUESTS FOR PRODUCTION OF DOCUMENTS AND PREPARING RESPONSES

LEARNING OBJECTIVE 4
Prepare requests and responses to requests for production.

Requests for production are designed to obtain all tangible materials regardless of how they were created or are stored, including electronic information. The process of preparing a request or response serves other purposes for the legal team. This process forces the legal team to obtain original documents from the client and preserve them. It also forces the legal team to read and evaluate the contents of those documents to determine their relevance to the litigation and to determine whether a privilege applies that prevents disclosure. Finally, it forces the legal team to organize the information, whether provided by the client or the opposing party, in a manner that will permit easy retrieval during additional discovery and at trial.

Preparing a Request for Documents

The process for preparing a request for production of documents is almost identical to the process for preparing questions for interrogatories. The pleadings must be carefully reviewed to look for claims asserted and defenses raised. An analysis of the elements of the claims and defenses (and the evidence that may be used to establish those elements at trial) is crucial, as is a review of the exhibits identified and provided through the initial mandatory disclosure (Fed. R. Civ. P. 26(a)). The answers to interrogatories may yield other documents, exhibits, or tangible evidence referred to or relied upon by the opposing party in meeting its burden of proof. For example, in the telephone conversation answer to the interrogatory shown in Exhibit 13.8, a listing of telephone calls may include a call to or from a cell phone from another jurisdiction or service provider. Based on this, additional phone records may be sought in a request for production, as shown in Exhibit 13.11.

Responding to Requests for Production

The procedure for preparing and gathering documents for the response to a request for production is very similar to the procedure for answering interrogatories: Send a copy to the client with a letter of instruction; review requests that may be objectionable; and gather documents that are already a part of the file. Each document must be reviewed and a decision made regarding its relevance and any applicable privilege. The attorney will make the final decision, but the paralegal can assist by bringing things to the attorney's attention.

Exhibit 13.11 Request for Production Based Upon Answer to Interrogatory Question

---

UNITED STATES DISTRICT COURT - NORTHERN DISTRICT OF NEW YORK

B.K., a minor by her Parents and Guardians, Janice Knowles and Steven Knowles, Plaintiff	: : :	No.: _____ PLAINTIFF'S REQUEST FOR PRODUCTION TO DEFENDANT ACE TRUCKING
v.	:	
Ronald Clemmons, Lower Council School District, Bud Smith, and Ace Trucking Company, Defendants	: :	 Attorney ID No. 124987

Request for Production under Fed. R. Civ. P. 26

TO: Ace Trucking Company
c/o John Morris, Esquire
Street Address

Demand is made that you produce for inspection and copying the following documents or categories of documents in your possession, custody or control within 30 days of the date of service of this demand.

(1) In your Answer to Interrogatory 8 you provided a summary list of telephone conversations. Provide all documents, including but not limited to, telephone logs, telephone messages, voice mail messages and notes upon which you relied to create that summary of conversations.

(2) Provide order forms, receipts and invoices for brake pads purchased for your fleet of dump trucks for the period of twelve months immediately preceding the accident.

(3) Provide the driver's log for your employee Bud Smith for the 90 day period immediately preceding the accident.

(4) Provide the medical records including but not limited to the annual Department of Transportation physical and results of random drug testing on your employee Bud Smith.

Respectfully Submitted,

The federal rules require a written answer to each request (Fed. R. Civ. P. 34(b)). The answer may simply refer to documents attached and labeled, usually with a numbered tab that matches the number of the request. Another option is for the answer to indicate how, when, and where the documents will be made available for inspection and copying. This answer will typically be used when there are large volumes of documents being produced or stored electronically. The documents may be available in paper or electronic format. Rather than going to the expense and time of copying each item, everything not claimed as privileged is made available for review and copying by the reviewing party. The answer may state the specific grounds for objection to production and inspection of the requested items. As with answers to interrogatories, if an objection is raised, a motion for protective order may be filed with the court, unless the legal team decides to waive the objection as part of the trial strategy.

Reviewing Responses to Requests for Production

Even in smaller cases, a lot of time may be spent reviewing the answers and documents produced in response to a request for production. Boxes of paper documents and business records may have to be scanned manually in the hope of finding the one bit of evidence that will show the defendant was at fault or the plaintiff really is not suffering from a permanent disability. As discussed next, records can be converted to electronic form by scanning them into a computer. This can be a time-consuming and tedious process, but scanned documents do provide useful information. The legal team must be prepared to follow through on those areas where privilege has been asserted as the basis for not answering the request. If the responding party has not filed a motion for protective order for the court to rule on the privilege, a motion to compel may be prepared and filed seeking the desired records.

■ ELECTRONIC DISCOVERY—THE PROCESS

LEARNING OBJECTIVE 5
Understand the new requirements related to electronic discovery.

e-discovery
Discovery of documents created, disseminated, and stored via electronic means.

Electronic discovery, or **e-discovery,** is a process. The initial phase in the e-discovery process is determining what documents are desired, who has those documents, what format the documents are in, what their value is, and what it would cost to retrieve them. Many different types of documents are considered "records" by the court and may be part of the discovery request. A properly prepared electronic document request, based on the federal or local rules, can then be prepared.

The legal team must keep in mind that the area of electronically created, stored, and retrieved documents is in transition. There is no single method used by all parties to create, store, or retrieve electronic information. As the computer information industry has matured, some standards have emerged, such as the dominant use of programs like MS Outlook, SQL databases, and the hard disk drive for storage. However, many documents are still created using nonstandard programs and saved or stored on magnetic media such as tapes. Some of these devices use proprietary software and hardware that may not be readily available.

Costs of recovery and delivery may be a major issue in producing electronic records. Legal teams will need to decide who will bear the cost of delivery of nonstandard data, if it is worth the cost to obtain this evidence, and whether the client can afford to pay the cost.

Evidence in electronic form may be from the more traditional, paperless office sources of word processing, electronic spreadsheets, and electronic databases. It may also be in the less traditional forms of e-mails, text messages, instant messages, podcasts, and voice mail sources.

Meet and Discuss

The primary purpose of the meet and discuss conference between the attorneys before the scheduling conference with the judge is to discuss and resolve issues pertaining to discovery, particularly electronic discovery. The meet and confer must, at minimum, result in decisions about how to produce electronic information, how preliminary screenings will be conducted to locate and distinguish relevant from privileged materials, and how to protect inadvertently disclosed privileged materials. The results of this meeting must be provided to the judge overseeing the case at least fourteen days before the scheduling conference.

It would be foolish to meet with the opposing counsel, who may be very knowledgeable in electronic discovery, without a thorough knowledge of the types and formats of the electronic information that might be sought by the other side. This may require the legal team to schedule time with the client's technical support staff sufficiently in advance of the meeting to allow time for sampling the data sources. It may also be strategically important to hire an expert to advise the legal team on the practical aspects and costs for the demands by the opposite side.

Know Your Client

The first step for the legal team is to know the client. Whether a Fortune 500 company or a Mom-and-Pop cleaning service, much of what is accomplished within a business is done electronically. Before they can prepare for the meet and confer with opposing counsel and make a recommendation for handling electronic discovery, the legal team must have a thorough understanding of the client's information technology (IT) structure. The following checklist provides a representative list of questions that will help the legal team understand the creation, storage, and retrieval of documents within the client's business.

The answers to these and many other questions will assist the legal team in determining how discovery of electronic materials will best be accomplished. The IT structure will also impact the process of screening documents for privilege and relevancy. For example, communication via instant messaging typically is not stored on computer systems—once transmitted, the message is gone. However, communication via e-mail is stored on the hard drive of a computer. Even after it has been deleted or sent to a recycle bin, e-mail may still be retrievable from the hard drive. One e-mail sent to 100 employees means 100 documents stored on the computer system. Add to that the responses that include the original message or forwarded copies of the message, and the number of documents can grow exponentially.

Checklist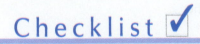

- Who manages the computers, networks, and other electronic devices used by the firm?
- What programs and software are used?
- How does communication take place, such as instant messaging or internal e-mail?
- How are documents created, transmitted, and stored?
- What system is used to back up the firm's critical information?
- Who within the company structure has access to which programs, files, and other information?
- Who outside the firm has access to this information?
- What security features are in place to limit access?
- Who performs maintenance and repair services?
- What is the document retention and destruction policy?

A crucial inquiry is whether the client has a retention and destruction policy. A firm may have a daily backup system with a device that saves data for a set period of time, say, three years. Or a firm may simply delete all materials when a business deal is concluded. Understanding what policy is in place for retention of information may impact the electronic discovery process as well. It could be that all relevant documents, paper and electronic, have been completely destroyed. On the other hand, there may be backup copies archived that can be used to re-create the files and data. Or the client may think that everything is destroyed, but there may be employees who have, in violation of company policy, retained copies on personal computers or even on iPods used as portable storage devices. This information may impact the time and cost to conduct discovery (especially if employee depositions are necessary to locate relevant data sources) and should be included in the discovery plan that results from the Fed. R. Civ. P. 26(f) conference.

Screening Clients' Documents

In traditional paper discovery, the paralegal, the associates, the law clerk, and the attorney may screen the client's documents manually to determine whether they are relevant or protected by some privilege and, therefore, are not discoverable. The same screening process must take place with electronic documents. Sorting and culling through all the electronic documents can be accomplished by the use of a search engine set up to look for words, phrases, or combinations, just as search parameters are set up for legal or factual research on the computer. A first-level screening might begin with searching the easily accessible information for relevant documents based on date, author, recipient, subject matter, or some combination of these elements. Then a process to eliminate the duplicates, called de-duping, will eliminate duplicate copies of the same document, like the multiple copies of the company vacation schedule sent to a long list of e-mail recipients. The search result can be reduced even further by searching the results for specific terms and excluding certain words.

This screening process can be discussed at the meet and confer as part of the plan to uncover relevant documents from the opposing party's records as part of the request to produce documents. If your legal team has already been through this process with your client, the attorney will be in a better position to form a plan that best aids in the discovery process. Transparency and cooperation will be critical in determining that the parties have devised a discovery plan in good faith. If it appears that one or both have devised a scheme to hide the proverbial smoking gun, the court will likely penalize the litigants.

Privileged Materials

Despite the best efforts to electronically screen documents and even with the additional examination by human eyes, as the volume of documents increases, so too does the chance for inadvertent disclosure of privileged material. This is particularly true when documents are produced electronically. Attorneys must address the issue of inadvertent disclosure and propose how to deal with privileged materials. Methods for dealing with these inadvertent disclosures may depend on what position, if any, your jurisdiction has adopted. The privileged materials, once discovered, can be immediately returned and treated as though they were never disclosed. Alternatively, the materials may be treated as though the client waived the privilege and made them available to the client's opponent for use at trial. Rather than being subjected to the court rule within the jurisdiction, the legal team can anticipate the event and limit its impact by including language in the proposed discovery plan to the effect that all inadvertently disclosed materials will not lose their status as privileged and that such information may not be used by the other side. This is called a "claw-back provision." The provision states specifically what the parties are obligated to do with inadvertently disclosed privileged materials.

Producing Electronic Documents

Electronic files can be made available in a number of formats. With a small company, producing the files in their native (original) format may be acceptable—that is, files are shared in the format in which they were created. The disadvantages are that the recipient must have a copy of the program used to create the files to be able to open and view them. Files produced in this manner can be altered, and proprietary data (metadata) may also be revealed. The advantage is that production in native file format t is an inexpensive way of delivering the files.

Another option is to have all files, no matter what the native format, converted to PDF or TIFF format. The recipient needs only a freely available PDF reader program to be able to open and view all the documents provided.

No matter which format for production is selected, the attorneys will be expected to resolve this issue at the meet and confer. For the small company where all documents are in MS Word, native format may be fine. That may not be true for the larger company, however. Knowing the client, its IT system, the volume of documents, and the programs in which they were created will put the legal team in the best position to make appropriate recommendations for an effective discovery plan.

How to Advise Clients

The legal team will be in a position to advise the client involved in litigation and to help to develop a plan for all other clients concerning the use of technology and its impact on litigation. Clients must establish and observe a good faith retention and destruction policy. That policy must include a mechanism to prevent the destruction of materials where the potential for litigation exists. Destruction of documents can be used against a litigant at trial. The jury can be instructed that the documents destroyed may be considered to have held information unfavorable to the one who destroyed them. The client with a good faith policy for destruction of records, which includes a policy for retaining records where the possibility of litigation exists, will not be penalized for the destruction of records.

CONCEPT REVIEW AND REINFORCEMENT

KEY TERMS

interrogatories 324	movable items 324	motion for protective
requests for production of	non-movable items 324	order 335
documents 324	objectionable 335	e-discovery 340

CHAPTER SUMMARY

INTERROGATORIES AND REQUESTS FOR PRODUCTION

Introduction to Interrogatories and Requests for Production	Interrogatories and requests for production of documents are the two most frequently used methods of discovery. They are similar in that they are written requests to the opposing party to the lawsuit and must be answered within a fixed period of time.
Interrogatories and Requests for Production of Documents and Things	An interrogatory is a formal written request for answers to questions, answered under oath, generally within thirty days of service.
	"Requests for production" is the shorthand way of referring to producing documents, electronically stored information, and tangible things, or entering onto land, for inspection and other purposes under the federal rules. It provides for the production of both movable and non-movable items for copying, testing, and sampling. Written answers must be provided within a limited time frame, generally thirty days from service.
	Requests for the same information can be made to a nonparty to the action but only by use of a subpoena issued by the court.
Time Frame for Discovery	Most federal and state rules of civil procedure provide a time frame within which discovery may occur, generally starting after the filing of the lawsuit and terminating prior to the commencement of trial. For good cause shown, the court may extend or modify the time frames.
	Counsel may also agree to extensions of time by agreement or stipulation.

Drafting Questions and Answers to Interrogatories	Courts have tried to simplify the process for interrogatories to avoid wasting the court's time ruling on objections and motions. Most courts have some limitations. The federal courts limit the number of interrogatory questions to twenty-five. The information that must be provided to the other party by initial disclosures includes the identity of individuals having discoverable information, the location of that information, the computation of damages, and any insurance agreements. Standard interrogatory questions are used to avoid having objections raised to the form or the nature of the questions. Additional questions may be asked that are not covered by standard interrogatories because of the nature of the case. Interrogatories must be served upon the other party to the action and may be done so without leave of court. Answers to most interrogatories may be found within the case file. That information should always be reviewed with the client, who must sign the affidavit attesting to the accuracy of the answers. Objections may be filed and a motion for protective order served with the answers when the questions are objectionable. Objections arise from poor draftsmanship or questions that seek information that is not relevant or likely to lead to admissible evidence.
Drafting Requests for Production of Documents and Preparing Responses	Requests for production of documents are designed to obtain all tangible materials regardless of how they were created or are stored, including electronically stored information. The process for making a request is similar to that for interrogatories. Each request must be answered in writing, and any objections must be raised as part of the answer. Where large amounts of documents are requested, the answer may be to provide the time and place for review and copying by the requesting party.
Electronic Discovery— The Process	Electronic discovery is the process of determining what documents are wanted, who has the documents, and in what format the documents are stored. Because there is no single method used by all parties for creating, storing, or retrieving electronic information, the costs of recovery and delivery may be a major issue, including the question of who will bear the cost of delivery of nonstandard data. The federal rules require counsel to meet and discuss issues with regard to discovery, particularly electronic discovery, before they have their scheduling conference with the trial judge. The purpose is to eliminate conflict and come to an agreement as to how discovery will be handled. Preparation for the meet and confer requires that the attorney meet with the client and determine the client's methods of creating and storing documentation. Any issues that may be involved in the preservation or retention of the records should be discussed at that time. Privileged material may also be identified during the meet and confer; provision should be made for protecting the privilege in the event of inadvertent disclosure.

REVIEW QUESTIONS AND EXERCISES

1. How are interrogatories and requests for production similar?
2. How are interrogatories and requests for production different?
3. What types of items may be inspected under a request for production?
4. How and why is the number of interrogatories limited in federal court?
5. When may interrogatories or requests to produce be used?
6. How long does a party have to respond to interrogatories and requests to produce? How can that time be altered?
7. What steps must the paralegal follow to draft questions or requests?
8. Describe the procedure that should be followed in obtaining client involvement and cooperation in preparing answers to interrogatories and requests to produce.
9. On what grounds may an interrogatory or request for production be objectionable?
10. Where objectionable questions or requests exist, what steps must be followed by the paralegal preparing the answers? What should the paralegal receiving the answer with objections do?
11. What is electronic discovery?
12. What must the legal team do differently in cases where clients create, store, and retrieve documents electronically?
13. Must the method of creation and production of documents be the same? Different? Why?
14. Compare the process of screening traditional paper documents with the process of screening electronically created documents. How are these processes the same? How are they different?
15. What is a claw-back provision? What is it designed to protect?
16. What is a retention and destruction policy?
17. Why is it important for a client to have and follow the terms of a retention and destruction policy?

BUILDING YOUR PARALEGAL SKILLS

INTERNET AND TECHNOLOGY EXERCISES

1. Check your state and federal courts' websites for standard form interrogatories for a breach of contract action and a personal injury action.
2. Locate a website that has a local court version of subpoenas.
3. What are the issues that must be considered in making discovery requests for electronic records?
4. Should a technically knowledgeable person accompany a lawyer to a meet and confer session under the federal rules? Why or why not? What are the ethical issues?

CIVIL LITIGATION VIDEO CASE STUDIES

Confidentiality Issue: Disclosure of Damaging Information

A paralegal meets with a client to review answers to discovery requests that must be sent to opposing counsel. While they are reviewing the answers, the client tells the paralegal about a prior fraudulent insurance claim.

After viewing the video at www.pearsonhighered.com/careersresources, answer the following questions.

1. May paralegals release confidential information about a client in answers to interrogatories?
2. What if the opposing counsel leaks information to the press about a client's conviction in order to bias potential jurors? Why isn't this a violation of the duty of confidentiality?
3. If the information can be found in public documents such as court files, is it still confidential?

UPL Issue: Improper Supervision

A paralegal attempts to have his supervising attorney review and sign documents in a case. The attorney offers the paralegal her signature stamp to use instead of personally signing the documents.

After viewing the video at www.pearsonhighered.com/careersresources, answer the following questions.

1. What are the alternatives to obtaining supervision?
2. Did the supervising attorney act in an unreasonable manner?
3. What are the alternatives for paralegals who believe they are not being properly supervised?

CHAPTER OPENING SCENARIO CASE STUDY

Use the Opening Scenario for this chapter to answer the following questions.

1. What role should the attorney play in the preparation of interrogatories?
2. What guidelines should the attorneys in the office provide to the paralegals to help in preparing the interrogatories?

COMPREHENSIVE CASE STUDY

SCHOOL BUS–TRUCK ACCIDENT CASE

Review the assigned case study in Appendix 2.

1. Using your state's standard form of interrogatories (or, if none, the standard interrogatories included in the chapter materials), prepare interrogatories addressed to the employer of the bus driver in the bus accident case in Appendix 2.
2. Exchange your interrogatories with another student and prepare answers to the other student's interrogatories.

BUILDING YOUR PROFESSIONAL PORTFOLIO

CIVIL LITIGATION TEAM AT WORK

See page 18 for instructions on Building Your Professional Portfolio.

Policy Manual

1. Create guidelines for paralegals to use in preparing interrogatories.
2. Include a personal prepared statement to use when confronted with a lack of proper legal supervision.

Forms

1. Your local jurisdiction's state and federal courts standard form interrogatories for personal injury and motor vehicle cases.

2. Form letter to a client to obtain timely responses to interrogatories.
3. Form letter to opposing counsel seeking compliance with discovery requests.
4. Form letter to a client that addresses the concerns of "document hold" when the potential for litigation arises with the client's business.

Procedures

Local court limitations on number of interrogatories.

LEARNING OBJECTIVES

After studying this chapter, you should be able to:

1. Identify the types of depositions.

2. Understand the ways in which deposition testimony can be used.

3. Schedule depositions of parties and witnesses.

4. Prepare a case file, clients, and witnesses for depositions.

5. Describe how to review a deposition transcript and prepare a digest of the testimony.

CHAPTER 14

Depositions

OPENING SCENARIO

The attorneys and paralegals in the suburban and center city offices had been working diligently as they prepared to take depositions of the other side. At the same time, they were preparing for potential depositions of their own clients. In addition to the information they gained from the answers provided in interrogatories, they consulted the investigation file, which included articles and other documents retrieved via Internet searches for accidents involving the same defendants and vehicles. There were some serious questions to be asked with regard to potential underlying causes.

For the plaintiff's side of the case, there were some strategic issues regarding videotaped depositions of the minor plaintiffs. It was clear that having the children tell this story to a jury would be the best approach to gain sympathy from the jury; however, there was concern as to the psychological effect that testifying might have on the children. Hence, the legal team discussed videotaping that testimony. Of course, cost was always a factor in these types of cases. With the firm's limited resources, the team needed to think carefully about videotaping its experts to save the cost of having the experts attend trial, where the usual daily rate would be double or triple the cost of having the experts testify via videotape. This was a significant enough case that the strategy of how to present witnesses and testimony was of paramount concern in order to maximize the potential reward from a favorable jury verdict. Owen Mason, the partner with the most experience, believed there was still an opportunity to settle the case if the depositions went well; if so, the other side would see the strength of the plaintiffs' case and the potential impact the sympathetic plaintiffs would have on a jury, many of whom might be parents or grandparents themselves.

Prepare the necessary documentation to set up a deposition of a fact witness and an expert witness in your jurisdiction.

■ INTRODUCTION TO DEPOSITIONS

deposition
A form of discovery available to ask questions and obtain oral answers under oath from a witness or party to a lawsuit. Questions and answers are recorded stenographically.

Depositions are a unique form of discovery. A deposition is an opportunity to ask questions of parties and witnesses under oath, out of court. Each side has the opportunity, if it wishes, to face the witness and observe his or her demeanor under questioning, and to have the benefit of a transcript of the session for later review. Depositions are the only discovery tool that is not limited to questions to the parties to the litigation; rather, questions may be asked of parties, lay witnesses, and expert witnesses. The ability to assess the demeanor and credibility of witnesses before trial gives the trial team an opportunity to evaluate the strengths and weaknesses of the presentations of both sides, to adjust trial strategy, and to attempt settlement or an alternative dispute resolution method.

Paralegals assist in scheduling depositions, reviewing the files for areas of inquiry, and preparing clients and witnesses. Paralegals frequently attend depositions to assist the attorney, as they do at trial, and then prepare annotated digests or summaries with page references for quick reference at trial.

■ TYPES OF DEPOSITIONS

LEANING OBJECTIVE 1
Identify the types of depositions.

Depositions are conducted by attorneys to determine what the opposing party and its witnesses will say about the event in question. Rarely does an attorney conduct a deposition of his or her own client or witnesses; the legal team learns what its client and witnesses know through the interview and investigation process. Through depositions, the legal team hears the story from the opposing party and its witnesses' viewpoints without the editing or revisions that might be made to the written answers given to interrogatories. Thus, depositions allow for assessment of the opposing party's and witnesses' demeanor and credibility: Are they likely to be sympathetic and believable and win the jury over with their personalities and manners of speech? There are four types of depositions:

1. depositions before filing a complaint;
2. depositions on written questions;
3. oral depositions; and
4. videotaped depositions.

Deposition before Filing a Complaint

motion
Formal request to the court seeking some type of relief during the course of the litigation.

prefiling depositions
Depositions used to obtain information necessary to file an action.

In limited circumstances, courts will permit depositions to be conducted before a complaint is filed. Permission is requested from the court by filing a **motion**—a request to the court—with supporting reasons for conducting the depositions. The primary reason for **prefiling depositions** is when the information necessary to prepare the complaint is in the sole or exclusive possession of another. When another party is in sole possession of all the relevant information, documents, and evidence, little information can be obtained using traditional means of investigation. Without the evidence discoverable through the prefiling deposition, the attorney may not be able to determine if there is, in fact, the basis for filing the lawsuit. An example is a beneficiary who seeks to challenge the validity of a will based on the **diminished capacity** of the decedent at the time the will was written and signed. Under current privacy laws, that beneficiary will be unable to obtain medical records. However, by the legal team's conducting a deposition prior to filing the lawsuit, the beneficiary will be able to determine if the medical evidence shows a lack of mental capacity. If it does, the case may be filed; if not, time, money, and effort are saved by not filing the suit.

diminished capacity
An impaired mental condition caused by intoxication, trauma, or disease that prevents one from understanding the nature and effect of his or her actions.

Deposition on Written Questions

This form of deposition is unusual. It represents a hybrid of two discovery methods: interrogatories and depositions. Written questions are served with the notice of deposition, identifying the witness to be deposed, and the date, time, location, and manner of recording the oral answers. All of the parties or their counsel have the opportunity to object to or add questions to those originally submitted by the party scheduling the deposition. As with interrogatories, the witness receives the questions in advance and has the opportunity to think about and plan responses. At the time of the deposition, the court reporter will swear in the witness, ask the questions submitted by the attorneys, and stenographically or otherwise record the oral responses of the witness. Because the attorneys are not present, they do not have the ability to ask follow-up questions or to observe the demeanor and credibility of the witness. This type of deposition may be used in situations where travel is limited or access to the witnesses is prohibited.

Oral Deposition

Oral depositions are what we traditionally think of when we hear the term *deposition*. The plaintiff and the defendant, their lawyers, the witness, and a court reporter are all present in a conference room, and the witness is asked questions by one or both of the attorneys and responds spontaneously. The court reporter stenographically records what is said. Oral depositions are used by one attorney to interview, on the record, the witnesses for the opposing party. The plaintiff's attorney will conduct a deposition of the defendant and defense witnesses, both lay and expert, identified in the initial disclosure and responses to written discovery (interrogatories). The defendant's attorney will depose the plaintiff and the plaintiff's lay and expert witnesses previously identified in the initial disclosure and written discovery.

oral deposition
Plaintiff, defendant, their lawyers, the witness, and a court stenographer are together in a conference room. The witness, asked questions by one or both attorneys, responds spontaneously, and the court stenographer records what is said.

In the typical deposition, the attorney will question the opposing party and witnesses, as though on cross-examination at trial, using leading questions. Opposing counsel usually will not ask questions of his client or witnesses. However, counsel may ask a follow-up question of his own witness or client if he feels the answer will aid in an out-of-court settlement or will show how the witness will present additional facts to the trier of fact that show a much stronger case than the deposition's answers demonstrate. It is all a matter of settlement and trial strategy.

How the deposition is conducted is a matter of discovery strategy and attorney style. Some attorneys will use a friendly manner to disarm the witness, hoping the witness will reveal facts that actually help the attorney's client rather than the opposing party. Other attorneys will use a contentious, antagonistic, or threatening manner in hopes that the witness will fall apart under the pressure. Some attorneys use a combination of the two styles; when the "good cop" strategy fails, the attorney will switch to the "bad cop" questioning technique. The typical deposition begins with the court reporter or the attorney giving instructions and basic guidelines for how the deposition is conducted. For example, the court reporter can record the testimony of only one person at a time; therefore, each person should wait until the other has spoken before speaking. The attorneys may agree to certain procedures for handling objections, formal signing of the deposition documents, and admission of documents during the deposition. The attorneys will also instruct the witness that all responses must be verbal—no nodding or shaking of heads as answers—because the court reporter can record only what is said. Similarly, the attorneys will caution to not talk over one another as only one person's words can be recorded at a time. Then the attorney will ask "warm-up" questions. These are questions used to put the witness at ease by asking basic questions about the person that are not in dispute, such as having the witness state his or her name and spell it for the record, give the home address, identify the name and location of employment, and indicate whether the witness knows the parties to the lawsuit. These questions serve to develop a comfortable environment for the witness and establish a rapport for the remainder of the deposition. Once some level of comfort has been established, the questioning about the matter in litigation will begin.

Knowing the variety of questioning styles and understanding their purposes will assist the paralegal in preparing clients and witnesses for deposition. Where the depositions are held can also be a part of attorney strategy. For clients, the comfort of their attorney's office, as opposed to the unfamiliarity of the opposing attorney's office, may impact the testimony. In some cases, the solution is a neutral location like a courthouse deposition room or a room provided by the court reporting service. Some attorneys go so far as to bring refreshments to make the witness feel comfortable and thus perceive the attorney as a friendly and trustworthy person.

Just as parties may object to written discovery questions or requests, deposition questions and testimony may also be subject to objections. The scope of discovery is much broader than what the court rules of evidence allow for the admission of testimony. Generally, any questions that are likely to lead to admissible evidence are allowed to be asked. However, if a question is objectionable, the attorney must raise that objection in the deposition record and the question must be answered. In the interest of concluding the deposition, attorneys will usually stipulate that a court ruling on any objection raised as to admissibility be deferred until the time of trial. An additional stipulation may be that any objection to a question or to the form of a question not raised during the deposition is waived, in conformity with the well-established rule of evidence that an objection must be raised in a timely manner or otherwise will be waived. An attorney who objects to a question or response must state the reason during the deposition and on the record. Failure to raise the objection means losing the right to raise that objection at some later time. After the objection is made, the witness being deposed will be instructed to answer the question for the stenographic record. Before that deposition testimony can be used at trial, the judge will be asked to rule on the objections raised at the deposition. Under the federal rules, each litigant is limited to conducting ten depositions without obtaining *leave* of court (permission) to conduct more depositions (Fed. R. Civ. P. 30(2)(A)(i)).

Videotaped Depositions

videotaped deposition
A type of oral deposition where testimony is recorded stenographically and videotaped for presentation at trial.

Videotaped depositions are a type of oral deposition. The deposition testimony is recorded stenographically and videotaped for presentation at trial. Videotaped depositions are typically taken when a witness is not expected to be available to testify at trial. Frequently, videotaped depositions are used for expert witnesses, such as physicians, for whom the requirement to appear in court to testify is an onerous burden or the cost is prohibitive—that is, the cost would be a financial burden on the party presenting the expert witness. Expert witnesses calculate their appearance fee based on the time they must be away from their practices. This fee, in addition to any fee for reviewing records and issuing a written report, can be in the thousands of dollars. Thus, a deposition videotaped at a convenient time and location for the expert will significantly reduce the cost of live testimony and usually will be just as effective with a jury.

Videotaped depositions also allow the use of testimony of witnesses for whom travel is not an option for reasons of disability or geography, such as a scientific expert in a remote part of the world.

Video Guidelines — U.S. DISTRICT COURT FOR THE EASTERN DISTRICT OF PENNSYLVANIA CHAMBERS' POLICIES AND PROCEDURES

Bruce W. Kauffman, J.

13. VIDEOTAPED TESTIMONY

All videotape recordings should be conducted with an acute sensitivity that the videotape may be shown to a jury. Skillful organization of the testimony, elimination of unnecessary objections, and conservation of time are strongly urged. Videotaped testimony should begin with the witness being sworn. Whenever a deposition or videotape is to be used, a transcript of the testimony and all exhibits should be furnished to the Court in advance. Objections should be submitted to the Court well in advance of the tapes being offered so that the tapes may be appropriately edited.

Source: www.paed.uscourts.gov/documents/procedures/kaupol.pdf

■ USES OF DEPOSITIONS

Witnesses' Versions of the Events

Depositions provide an opportunity to hear the other side's version of the events and issues in the litigation. When the legal team conducts a deposition of the opposing party or their witnesses, they are not only listening to the facts but also evaluating the manner in which those witnesses testify. Seeing how one's own client will react to hostile questioning also presents an opportunity to evaluate how the client might respond to the pressures of cross-examination at trial. Although depositions are conducted in an atmosphere that is less formal than a courtroom, the questions are asked in the same manner. Occasionally, lawyers may question more aggressively in depositions because there is no judge to moderate or because they are evaluating opposing counsel for reaction and skill in the trial process. If the witness is uneasy in the deposition format, the legal team must be honest in evaluating the witness's possible impact at trial: Is the witness credible or lacking in believability? Will the witness easily lose control under intense questioning? One witness may appear more confident and better able to present the facts in a highly credible way than another who was thought to be a star witness. After observing the witnesses from both sides, counsel may feel that settlement is a better option than trial.

LEARNING OBJECTIVE 2
Understand the ways in which deposition testimony can be used.

Preserving Testimony

preserving testimony
When a witness is unavailable or unable to testify at trial, the deposition testimony can be presented at trial so long as both parties to the litigation had the opportunity to pose questions to the witness at the time of the deposition.

Deposition testimony is also used to **preserve the testimony** of a witness. Many unexpected events can occur that prevent a witness from testifying. For example, a witness may be in a fatal accident or develop a medical condition that limits memory or speech. In that event, the deposition testimony can still be presented at trial, so long as both parties to the litigation had the opportunity to pose questions to the witness at the time of the deposition.

Sometimes the legal team knows that a witness will not be available for trial. The typical situation is the need for videotaped deposition of an expert, as discussed previously. Another example is an elderly witness or a witness with a terminal disease. Again, so long as both attorneys had the opportunity to question the witness, the deposition transcript can be admitted as evidence at trial.

Impeachment

impeach
Questioning the witness on cross-examination to demonstrate to the jury that the witness is not reliable.

Deposition testimony can also be used to **impeach,** or challenge the credibility of, a witness. For example, at trial, a witness who was previously deposed is called to testify on direct examination. During direct, the witness says something that conflicts with or contradicts what he said at deposition. On cross-examination, opposing counsel will confront the witness and use the deposition testimony to imply that the witness is not truthful. Even though the witness will be given a chance to explain why the testimony at trial is different from what he said at his deposition, the jury will have the impression, "Either the witness was lying then or he is lying now. In either event, the witness is a liar and his testimony is not to be believed." In this manner, impeachment can raise doubts about the reliability of the witness's testimony. The threat of impeachment is a key component to trial preparation; it is why paralegals prepare deposition digests and why witnesses are encouraged to review their prior recorded testimony and statements.

PRACTICE TIP

Prepare a visual timeline showing the range of dates the parties and respective counsel are available. Where the time frames line up, you can see the dates that work for everyone. This is easier than trying to work with a list of dates written on a notepad.

LEARNING OBJECTIVE 3
Schedule depositions of parties and witnesses.

■ SCHEDULING DEPOSITIONS

Scheduling depositions seems like it should be an easy task for the paralegal, but it can be grueling to coordinate the schedules of multiple attorneys, the plaintiff, the defendant, and the witness. Sometimes it will make sense to simply consult your supervising attorney's calendar and schedule the deposition. More likely than not, you'll receive at least one phone call advising that the date does not work, but you will have gotten the opposing side's attention. In other instances, it makes sense to circulate a calendar that includes the next month or so. Ask the attorneys, parties, and witness to indicate the dates that work. From that list, you will be able to schedule the deposition.

Notice of Deposition

notice of deposition
Notice to all interested parties of the date, time, location, and identification of the individual to be deposed; has power over parties only.

subpoena duces tecum
A court order compelling a witness to attend, testify, and bring with him documents; must accompany a notice of deposition served on a nonparty witness.

The legal team must give notice to all interested parties of the date, time, location, and identification of the individual to be deposed. The interested parties include the plaintiff, the defendant, their attorneys, the witness to be deposed, and the court reporting service that has been engaged to record the deposition. If the person to be deposed is a party to the lawsuit, nothing more is required. If, however, the person who is being deposed is a nonparty witness, the **notice of deposition** should be accompanied by a *subpoena duces tecum*—an order to attend and bring relevant documents to the deposition. Exhibit 14.1 is a notice of deposition.

Exhibit 14.1 Notice of Deposition

STATE OF NEW YORK

SUPREME COURT: COUNTY OF MONROE _____

TINA A. BIDEN,

             Plaintiff,

FLASH DATA SYSTEMS, INC.

             Defendant.

_____

NOTICE TO TAKE DEPOSITION UPON ORAL EXAMINATION

Index Number: WC-3324-10

RJI _____

Hon. _____

Sir: **PLEASE TAKE NOTICE**, that pursuant to Article 31 of the Civil Practice Law and Rules, the testimony, upon oral examination of Tina A. Biden, will be taken before a notary public who is not an attorney, or employee of an attorney, for any party or prospective party herein and is not a person who would be disqualified to act as a juror because of interest or because of consanguinity or affinity to any party herein, at

411 Main Street, Rochester, New York 14600

on the 3rd day of July, 2011 at 10:00 o'clock in the forenoon of that day with respect to evidence material and necessary in the defense of this action:

That the said person to be examined is required to produce at such examination the following:

The circumstances or reasons such notice is sought or required are as follows:

_____

Dated: _____, 2015

RICHARD A. WALMART, ESQ
Worth & Walmart
411 Main Street
Rochester, New York 14600
585-555-2102

To:

    Eleanor W. Handy, Esq.
    Handy, Twist & Handy
    699 Franklin Street, Suite 9000
    Buffalo, NY 14200
    716-555-9889

Subpoena

A notice of deposition alone has no force to compel the attendance of a witness at a deposition. The notice has power over the litigants only. Thus, all other witnesses must be served with a **subpoena** and the notice of deposition. The subpoena is an order of court commanding the person named to appear and testify. A *subpoena duces tecum* orders the person to appear and bring with him any documents or things relevant to the lawsuit. As an order of court, the subpoena

subpoena

A court order compelling a witness to attend and testify; must accompany a notice of deposition served on a non-party witness.

Exhibit 14.2 Filable Subpoena and Return of Service Available Online

AO 88 (Rev. 07/10) Subpoena to Appear and Testify at a Hearing or Trial in a Civil Action

UNITED STATES DISTRICT COURT
for the

_____ _____ ▾

_____	)
Plaintiff	)
v.	) Civil Action No.
_____	)
Defendant	)

SUBPOENA TO APPEAR AND TESTIFY
AT A HEARING OR TRIAL IN A CIVIL ACTION

To:

    YOU ARE COMMANDED to appear in the United States district court at the time, date, and place set forth below to testify at a hearing or trial in this civil action. When you arrive, you must remain at the court until the judge or a court officer allows you to leave.

Place:	Courtroom No.:
	Date and Time:

    You must also bring with you the following documents, electronically stored information, or objects *(blank if not applicable)*:

    The provisions of Fed. R. Civ. P. 45(c), relating to your protection as a person subject to a subpoena, and Fed. R. Civ. P. 45 (d) and (e), relating to your duty to respond to this subpoena and the potential consequences of not doing so, are attached.

Date: _____

      CLERK OF COURT

                               OR

_____   _____
    Signature of Clerk or Deputy Clerk   *Attorney's signature*

The name, address, e-mail, and telephone number of the attorney representing *(name of party)* _____
_____, who issues or requests this subpoena, are:

must be obeyed or the witness may be subject to penalties for contempt of court. Exhibit 14.2 is a form of subpoena available online from the federal court.

Service

Service of the notice of deposition can be accomplished by regular mail, or electronic mail if the parties have agreed to that, and goes to the parties, their counsel, and the court reporting service. Personal service on a nonparty

Exhibit 14.2 *(continued)*

AO 88 (Rev.07/10) Subpoena to Appear and Testify at a Hearing or Trial in a Civil Action (page 2)

Civil Action No.

PROOF OF SERVICE
(This section should not be filed with the court unless required by Fed. R. Civ. P. 45.)

This subpoena for *(name of individual and title, if any)* _____
was received by me on *(date)* _____ .

☐ I served the subpoena by delivering a copy to the named person as follows: _____

_____

_____ on *(date)* _____ ; or

☐ I returned the subpoena unexecuted because: _____

_____ .

Unless the subpoena was issued on behalf of the United States, or one of its officers or agents, I have also
tendered to the witness the fees for one day's attendance, and the mileage allowed by law, in the amount of

$ _____ .

My fees are $ _____ for travel and $ _____ for services, for a total of $ 0.00   .

I declare under penalty of perjury that this information is true.

Date: _____   _____
                                                            Server's signature

                                                     _____
                                                            Printed name and title

                                                     _____
                                                            Server's address

Additional information regarding attempted service, etc:

witness is required by the Federal Rules of Civil Procedure and can be accomplished in the same manner as personal service of a complaint. An adult individual who is not a party to the lawsuit may personally deliver the notice of deposition and subpoena on the witness at his or her residence or usual place of business. When dealing with a friendly witness, the paralegal should alert him or her to the forthcoming personal service. In some jurisdictions, a witness fee to compensate for travel may be required to accompany the subpoena. A check of the local rules is necessary to determine what constitutes valid service of a subpoena. Court penalties for failure to appear will be imposed only where service is in compliance with the rules of the particular court issuing the subpoena.

Notifying Court Reporter/Videographer

It is not unusual to arrive at a carefully planned deposition only to discover that someone forgot to notify the court reporting service. While these oversights are not unexpected, they reflect poorly on the legal team. Thus, the paralegal should be certain that the court reporting service has been notified of the date, time, location, and type of recording that is requested—written or video. Whether it is a simple stenographic transcription or an audio and/or video deposition, the court reporter cannot bring the correct equipment if he or she has not been notified of the type of deposition being conducted. Also, if depositions are to be videotaped, a larger room may be necessary to accommodate the additional videotape operator and equipment.

■ PREPARING FOR DEPOSITION

LEARNING OBJECTIVE 4
Prepare a case file, clients, and witnesses for deposition.

Preparing for deposition begins with a review of the file. A review of the facts alleged in the pleadings, the evidence obtained as part of the investigation of the case, and other discovery conducted provide areas where additional information and explanation may be needed.

Special Instructions for Clients and Witnesses

Preparing witnesses or clients for deposition is very similar to preparing them for testifying at trial. Much of the information shared and instructions given are the same. In fact, it may be helpful for the witness to think of the deposition as a practice run for trial.

The client or witness should review all prior statements made to police, accident or insurance investigators, medical personnel, and the law firm. Memories do fade with time, and the person may not remember the incident as originally stated or shown in the reports. The police report and other reports prepared at the time of the incident are more likely to be accurate than memories that have faded or been altered through recounting the incident to friends.

Depending on the style of the supervising attorney, the paralegal might be able to suggest areas of questioning, such as, "Be prepared to answer questions about how your life has changed since the accident." The paralegal can also explain the use of **leading questions**—questions that suggest a response. These are used by opposing counsel on cross-examination; an example is the classic "Have you stopped kicking your dog?" Answering the question "yes" implies that the witness kicked the dog in the past. Answering the question "no" implies that the witness is currently abusing the animal. Neither response is what the witness intends to say, and both show the witness in a poor light. Knowing the types and manner of the potential questions allows the witness to be prepared to give accurate answers and not be bullied into an inaccurate answer.

leading questions
Questions that suggest the answer, usually calling for a "yes" or "no" response.

Checklist ✓  DEPOSITION

✓ Dress appropriately.
✓ Be on time.
✓ Don't talk over the attorney or anyone else; the court stenographer can record only one person's words at a time.
✓ Listen to the question.
✓ If you don't understand a question, say so and ask for the question to be rephrased.

✓ When you answer a question, it is assumed you understand and are responding to the question asked.

✓ Don't guess.

✓ If you don't know, say so. It's OK to say, "I don't know."

✓ Don't argue.

✓ Tell the truth.

Witnesses must be instructed to listen carefully and answer the question that has actually been asked and not the one they think they are being asked.

Some lawyers conduct a mock deposition to prepare the client or witness for what to expect. This can help the witness understand the process and questions, or it can make the witness seem too stiff and rehearsed. A balanced approach may be to describe the areas of questioning and pick one area in which to conduct a mock deposition.

Lay witnesses and parties may have no experience with depositions; as a result, they might not understand the process for raising objections or their obligation to answer after the objection is made for the record. The paralegal should thus explain that the deposition may be interrupted by the lawyer saying, "Objection." They should remain silent until told what to do by their lawyer, and they should then expect to hear "The witness is instructed to answer."

Preparation to Depose the Opposing Party or Witness

The deposition of the opposing party and witnesses is the opportunity to complete the investigation of the facts that could not be done either because of the prohibition of talking to a represented party or because of a hostile witness's refusal to cooperate. Everything that could be asked at trial and more may be asked. In addition to the potentially admissible evidence, questions may be asked that will probably be objectionable in trial, but that might lead to admissible evidence. There is little downside to asking all the questions and probing deeply into the facts. The counsel who is asking the questions may try to make the witness comfortable and act with openness and friendliness as a tactic to obtain information. One of the comments frequently heard after a deposition is the client saying that she could not believe how nice counsel was to the other side. It may be the paralegal who needs to reassure the client that this tactic was taken to better obtain the needed information and was not a sign of betrayal.

Just as the legal team prepares other forms of discovery to issue to the opponent, the team will review the file, the investigative materials, the pleadings, the material provided through mandatory disclosure, and the responses to written discovery requests in order to develop areas of questioning and specific questions.

Basic information about the witnesses and parties is provided as part of the interrogatories to allow the deposition to be scheduled. Use of computer search engines like Google, Bing, Ask.com, and others permits the legal team to delve deeper into the person's life, and may result in useful information, such as a history of being a fact witness or victim in other cases not reported or revealed by the other side. Details of the incident reported in newspapers or blogs may also be of use in preparing questions for the witness.

Paralegal Functions at Deposition

The functions of the paralegal at deposition are not significantly different from their responsibilities at trial. The paralegal can take notes, listen, and observe the nonverbal cues of the witnesses. The paralegal can also make sure people get where they are supposed to be, greet clients and witnesses, and help them to feel comfortable by offering water, coffee, or other refreshments. Giving a deposition is stressful, and many people feel dehydrated and need something to drink before testifying. Also, it's a good idea to learn the location of the restrooms and let the client or witness know where they are.

Paralegals sitting outside the deposition room may also observe the conduct of the other side's witnesses and overhear information that may be of interest or value. As long as the paralegal does not misrepresent herself as being with the opposing side, anything observed may be reported to the supervising attorney.

■ REVIEWING TRANSCRIPTS AND PREPARING DIGESTS

LEARNING OBJECTIVE 5
Describe how to review a deposition transcript and prepare a digest of the testimony.

Deposition transcripts are prepared by the court reporter. They may be in written form, electronic form, or both. Many stenographic services offer a variety of forms for a fee. An electronic format can be easily searched on a computer using standard search queries to locate specific information. Whether to file the transcript away or review it immediately may be a function of time and other pressing matters of the paralegal and the legal team. If at all possible, the transcript should be reviewed on receipt and deposition summaries prepared while the information is fresh in the minds of those who attended the deposition. Completion of this time-consuming task can ease the burden when time seems limited in the weeks just before a trial. A **deposition digest** is a summary of the testimony that identifies the corresponding locations in the written transcript and/or the video footage; a sample is shown in Exhibit 14.3. The summary will also point out objections raised during the testimony, which the trial attorney can use to make arguments to the court for inclusion or exclusion of the testimony. If the paralegal attended the deposition, a comparison with or reference to notes taken at the deposition may also be included with the digest.

deposition digest
A summary of deposition testimony with reference to the location in the transcript and/or in the video footage.

WEB RESOURCES

For additional samples of deposition summaries for different types of cases, visit the DepoSums.com website at www.deposum.com.

PRACTICE TIP

There is a difference between the spoken and the written word. The impact of body language, tone, inflection, and nonverbal cues is eliminated when reading words from a page in black and white.

Witness' Right to Review and Sign

At the beginning of the deposition, in many jurisdictions the court reporter will ask the following question of counsel: "Usual stipulations?" What the **usual stipulations** are depends on local practice or court rules. In some cases, it means the attorneys stipulate or agree that all objections will be resolved at the time of trial and failure to raise a particular objection on the record serves to waive the

usual stipulations
Agreements between the attorneys about how the deposition will be conducted; will vary by jurisdiction.

Exhibit 14.3 Sample Deposition Summary

CONFIDENTIAL ATTORNEY WORK PRODUCT
Deposition Summary
of
Jackson Robert Ludlum
Taken November 7, 2005
Re: Bonds v. Santa Fe Pacific Railroad, a corporation, and related actions.
Case No.: CIV-J-07-866053-2

Page:Line	Testimony EXAMINATION BY MR. EISENHOWER
	Deponent's name and employment
6:11 6:24	Deponent states that his full name is Jackson Robert Ludlum. He is employed with the California Highway Patrol (CHP) in the Sacramento area. He has worked for the CHP for sixteen years.
	Education
6:25 7:12	Ludlum received a bachelor's degree from Pepperdine University in Malibu, CA in Public Administration with an emphasis on criminal justice. He has done some post-graduate work at UCLA but has received no degree. He has no additional training in accident reconstruction.
	Prior expert qualification
7:13 7:21	Ludlum has been qualified as an expert in the area of accident reconstruction on one occasion in a civil matter in Los Angeles County. He testified regarding the collision sequence and damage to the vehicle.
	Police academy training
7:22 8:3	Ludlum attended a six-month academy in Long Beach. This included training in accident investigation, among other topics.
	Ludlum was one of investigating officers at subject accident site
8:4 8:11	Ludlum was one of the officers who investigated the accident at the crossing of Almond Avenue and the railroad tracks near Auburn Boulevard on December 24, 2004.
	Exhibit A: Traffic Collision Report
8:12 8:21	Exhibit A is a copy of a four-page traffic collision report prepared by CHP Officer Steven Parker.

Attorney Work Product

Source: Used by permission from West Coast Paralegal Services & DepoSums.com.

objection. The usual stipulations may also mean that the deposed witnesses is waiving his/her rights to review the transcript and make any corrections so that the transcript accurately reflects what was said. Court reporters make mistakes in taking and transcribing the testimony; this may be caused by lack of experience, or by trying to record what is being said when more than one person (e.g., both the witness and opposing counsel) is talking. It may also be an attempt to capture a head movement indicating yes or no.

If the "usual stipulations" are not agreed to, the transcript will need to be reviewed with the witness and the witness' signature obtained after all corrections are made.

CONCEPT REVIEW AND REINFORCEMENT

KEY TERMS

deposition 350	videotaped deposition 352	subpoena 355
motion 350	preserving testimony 354	leading question 358
prefiling depositions 350	impeach 354	deposition digest 360
diminished capacity 351	notice of deposition 354	usual stipulations 360
oral deposition 351	*subpoena duces tecum* 354	

CHAPTER SUMMARY

DEPOSITIONS

Introduction to Depositions	A deposition is an opportunity to ask questions of both parties and witnesses under oath.
Types of Depositions	Depositions are generally taken only of the other party and their witnesses.
	Depositions may be taken before filing a complaint by filing a motion with the court seeking approval. This is done primarily to obtain the necessary information to prepare the complaint when that information is solely within the control of another party.
	Depositions may also be taken on written questions. In this situation, the parties receive the questions in advance, but the answers will be taken orally by a court reporter after the person is placed under oath.
	Oral depositions are the traditional form of deposition; each party is permitted to ask questions and follow-up questions of parties, lay witnesses, and experts.
	Videotaped depositions are a form of oral deposition in which a record is made stenographically and is recorded by videotape. Videotaped depositions are used when a witness is not expected to be available to testify at trial, such as a terminally ill patient or an expert for whom attending trial might be too costly.
Uses of Depositions	Depositions provide each side with an opportunity to observe the opposing parties and their witnesses; both sides can determine issues of credibility and learn the facts as they will be presented at the time of trial.
	Depositions may also be used at the time of trial for a witness who is suddenly unavailable. As long as both sides have had an opportunity to question the individual, the testimony will be allowed by having it read into the record.
	Statements made at trial that are inconsistent with statements made in the depositions may be used to impeach or challenge the credibility of a witness.
Scheduling Depositions	Notice must be given to all interested parties of the date, time, location, and individuals to be deposed. The attendance of non-witnesses may be achieved by the use of a subpoena issued by the court, which compels a person to attend, or a *subpoena duces tecum*, which commands the witness to attend and bring documents relevant to the dispute.

Preparing for Deposition	The legal team prepares witnesses and clients for depositions in the same way they prepare witnesses and clients for trial: They are requested to review all prior statements and refresh their recollections as to the events previously related. Depositions are likely to be the first time the legal team sees the other side's client and is able to evaluate the client's credibility and the possible impact of the client's testimony on a jury or other finder of fact. Clients must be properly advised and instructed on appropriate attire and behavior during and following the deposition. Preparation for deposing the opposite side or its witnesses includes eliciting all of the testimony that may be offered in support of the opposite side's position. It may also include questions that will probably not be admissible at trial but that might lead to other relevant, admissible evidence.
Reviewing Transcripts and Preparing Digests	Court reporters prepare a written deposition transcript for the attorneys. Many also provide a copy in electronic form that can be used for electronic searching and processing. A deposition digest is a summary of the testimony with appropriate citations so that a specific item may be found during trial if needed for impeachment purposes. Depending upon the stipulation agreed to, the witnesses may have the right to review and correct the transcript. If the attorneys agree to the "usual stipulations," however, that right is effectively waived.

REVIEW QUESTIONS AND EXERCISES

1. What is a deposition?
2. Describe the four types of depositions.
3. What is the disadvantage of the deposition on written questions?
4. Why would an attorney need to conduct a deposition before filing a lawsuit?
5. How is an oral deposition different from a videotaped deposition?
6. What are the purposes of depositions?
7. How are depositions different from other forms of discovery?
8. Under what circumstances would a deposition be used to preserve testimony?
9. What is impeachment? How are depositions used for impeachment?
10. How do paralegals schedule depositions?
11. Is arranging the deposition of a witness the same as arranging the deposition of a party to the lawsuit? Why? If different, how so?
12. What is the purpose of a *subpoena duces tecum*?
13. How can the paralegal help prepare the client for a deposition?
14. How can the paralegal help the supervising attorney prepare to depose the opponent's witnesses?
15. What things can a paralegal do at a deposition?
16. What is a deposition digest?
17. How is a deposition digest used?

BUILDING YOUR PARALEGAL SKILLS

INTERNET AND TECHNOLOGY EXERCISES

1. Use the Internet to obtain a *subpoena duces tecum* for your local federal and state courts.
2. Use the Internet to determine if your state requires a witness fee to accompany a subpoena and, if so, the amount of the fee.
3. Search the Internet and prepare a list of court reporter services in your area that provide video deposition service, Real Time Certified reporters, and Livenotes service.
4. What ethical issues exist in the taking of depositions remotely, with parties and attorneys at different locations?

CIVIL LITIGATION VIDEO CASE STUDIES

UPL Issue: Working with Experts—Deposition of a Medical Expert, Dr. Galo

After viewing the video at www.pearsonhighered.com/careersresources, answer the following questions.

1. Did the paralegal properly introduce herself to the expert and in the video deposition?
2. Was the purpose of the video deposition for trial preparation or for use in trial?
3. What differences are there in each case?
4. Why would the opposing counsel stipulate that the doctor is an expert?
5. Do you see any ethical concerns in the video?

Remote Videoconference: Taking Fact Witness' Video Deposition

Attorneys use videoconferencing to depose the father of an injured child, who will be a fact witness at trial. The father is not in the jurisdiction.

After viewing the video at www.pearsonhighered.com/careersresources, answer the following questions.

1. What is the purpose of deposing a fact witness?
2. What issues might arise when the plaintiff's counsel is not onsite for the deposition?

Real-Time Reporting of Witness Testimony: Deposing a Minor

One of the children injured on the school bus is deposed.

After viewing the video at www.pearsonhighered.com/careersresources, answer the following questions.

1. What is the purpose of a stipulation in a deposition?
2. Should a minor be treated differently than an adult in a deposition?

Video Deposition of a Treating Doctor, Dr. Lee

The testimony of the treating physician of a student injured on the school bus is being taken by videotaped deposition because the doctor will not be available to testify at the time of the trial.

After viewing the video at www.pearsonhighered.com/careersresources, answer the following questions.

1. What is the role of an expert witness?
2. What are the qualifications to be an expert witness?
3. Is a physician an expert in all aspects of medicine?
4. What is the proper method of qualifying an expert witness?
5. Do the rules of evidence require experts to be identified before depositions?

CHAPTER OPENING SCENARIO CASE STUDY

Use the Opening Scenario for this chapter to answer the following questions.

1. What should the legal team consider when taking depositions of children? How is this different from deposing adults?

2. What information should the paralegal organize for the attorney in preparation for the taking of depositions?

COMPREHENSIVE CASE STUDY

SCHOOL BUS–TRUCK ACCIDENT CASE

Review the assigned case study in Appendix 2.

1. Prepare a *subpoena duces tecum* for a nonparty witness for a deposition in your jurisdiction.
2. Prepare a Notice of Deposition for a nonparty witness with instructions for service in your jurisdiction.
3. Prepare deposition questions to ask the bus company's expert witness concerning the elderly bus driver.
4. Review the deposition transcript and videotape of the expert witness on the truck brakes. Prepare a digest of the deposition that identifies corresponding page numbers and locations in the video footage.

BUILDING YOUR PROFESSIONAL PORTFOLIO AND REFERENCE MANUAL

CIVIL LITIGATION TEAM AT WORK

See page 18 for instructions on Building Your Professional Portfolio.

Forms

1. Notice of Deposition
2. *Subpoena duces tecum*

Procedures

1. Create a procedure for serving parties and witnesses.
2. Determine any required witness fees and how they must be paid.

Contacts and Resources

1. Local court reporting services in your jurisdiction
2. Local video deposition services in your jurisdiction

LEARNING OBJECTIVES

After studying this chapter, you should be able to:

1. Explain the purpose of and procedure for obtaining a physical or mental examination of a party to the lawsuit.

2. Prepare for attending a defense medical evaluation.

3. Describe the purpose of and procedure for making and responding to requests for admissions.

Other Forms of Discovery | CHAPTER 15

OPENING SCENARIO

 Ethan and his legal team were handling the liability portion of the school bus accident cases. The police reports and the statements of the parties to the school bus accident made it clear that there were some areas of agreement. It was possible the other side would agree to some of the facts if a request for admissions were filed. The issue of trial strategy needed to be discussed with the other members of the firm. Maybe it would be better to lay everything out for the jury with live testimony and make a fuller showing of the negligent conduct. The team concentrating on the physical injuries had already received an informal request to have all the surviving children examined by the defense medical expert. Some of the parents expressed concern about the effect this might have on the children, who had already been traumatized in the accident. There were strategic issues for the firm partners in recommending that the parents agree instead of having the other side make a discovery motion. The injuries were so obvious that any defense examination would only reaffirm the finding of the children's primary treating doctors; with that presented to the jury, it could only reinforce the damages issue.

OPENING SCENARIO LEARNING OBJECTIVE

Prepare the documentation necessary to request an defense medical examination of a plaintiff in your jurisdiction.

■ INTRODUCTION TO OTHER FORMS OF DISCOVERY

Request for physical or mental examination and the request for admissions are two additional tools of discovery available to the legal team. While the use of these discovery methods is limited, they are no less important than interrogatories, requests for production, and depositions. Requesting physical or mental examinations of the other parties is not always appropriate as a trial strategy, but when necessary, it is important to understand how to obtain the examinations and how they are conducted. Understanding these discovery tools from both the defense's and the plaintiff's perspectives is a key element to the use of these tools of discovery.

■ REQUEST FOR PHYSICAL OR MENTAL EXAMINATION

LEARNING OBJECTIVE 1

Explain the purpose of and procedure for obtaining a physical or mental examination of a party to the lawsuit.

The request for a physical or mental examination is an important discovery tool for those cases in which the physical or mental state of a party to the litigation is in question. Physical and mental exams may be ordered by the court upon motion for good cause (Fed. R. Civ. P. 35). Where the physical or mental state of a litigant is at the heart of the lawsuit, the opposing party may file a motion requesting that the litigant to the lawsuit submit to the examination, and the court will order that party to submit to the exam (Exhibit 15.1).

In a personal injury lawsuit, the nature of physical injuries and the treatment of, recovery from, and permanency of those injuries will be a component of the **causation** and damages elements of the cause of action. In a breach of contract case, the mental capacity of the parties at the time the contract was entered into is an element of the cause of action. To be appointed as a guardian of someone who lacks the mental capacity to handle financial and other matters requires the testimony of a qualified physician. The cause of action is dependent on the mental state of the individual, who may not voluntarily submit to such an examination for that purpose. Where medical testimony for physical or mental status is required in order to meet the burden of proof, the court will, on proper motion, order the examination. In most cases, the attorneys know and understand that documentation of the person's mental and physical condition and prognosis are necessary to sustain the cause of action and recover damages; therefore, they will agree to permit the client to submit to the examination. Ideally, the attorney or paralegal will accompany the client to the examination.

The examination promotes fairness by permitting litigants to verify the accuracy and extent of injuries claimed in the reports and documents submitted. In personal injury cases, plaintiffs have treating physicians who have examined them for purposes of determining the cause of the medical complaint and for prescribing a course of treatment. Ultimately, it is the reports of these examinations for the purpose of treatment and follow-up treatment that become the basis for the damage claim made. The initial examination is made for the purpose of **diagnosis**—that is, to determine the source of the medical complaint. Follow-up examinations provide the information for the reports on **treatment**—what was performed to cure or alleviate the symptoms. An important part of the treating physician's report is the **prognosis,** which is how the medical complaint will resolve: full recovery, persistent problems, or permanent disability. The demand in a personal injury case in which the plaintiff will never recover fully but will always have pain (such as a lower back disk herniation) has a higher value for

causation
The link between the injury suffered by the plaintiff and the action or inaction of the defendant; includes causation in fact (actual cause) and proximate cause (legal cause).

PRACTICE TIP

With health care privacy laws, the attendance by the lawyer or the paralegal is not ensured unless the client signs a release required by the defense medical expert.

diagnosis
A determination of the source of a medical complaint.

treatment
A course of medical services designed to heal, correct, alleviate, or resolve a medical complaint.

prognosis
How the medical complaint will resolve: full recovery, persistent problems, or permanent disability.

Exhibit 15.1 Motion for Physical Examination

UNITED STATES DISTRICT COURT _____   DISTRICT OF _____

Mandy Stein, a minor by her Father and guardian, Larry Stein, Plaintiff v. Lower Council School District Defendant	: : : : : :	No.: _____ **DEFENDANT LOWER COUNCIL SCHOOL DISTRICT MOTION FOR PHYSICAL EXAMINATION** CIVIL ACTION - NEGLIGENCE Attorney ID No. 124987

Defendant, Lower Council School District, pursuant to Fed. R. Civ. P. 35, moves this Court to order plaintiff, Mandy Stein, to submit to a physical examination and avers the following in support of its motion:

(1) Fed. R. Civ. P. 35 provides, in pertinent part, that whenever the physical or mental condition of a party is in controversy, the court may order a physical or mental examination of that party by a physician on motion for good cause shown.

(2) Plaintiff alleges in her complaint that she suffered personal injuries in the incident giving rise to the underlying civil action, including but not limited to those set forth in Exhibit A.

(3) Plaintiff's Answers to Interrogatories detail alleged injuries and resultant permanent damages. See in particular Plaintiff's response to Interrogatories 3 through 7, copies of which are attached as Exhibit B.

(4) Defendant has denied that Plaintiff was so injured as a result of the alleged incident.

(5) In view of the above, it is clear that Plaintiff's physical condition is in controversy in this action and a physical examination of Plaintiff's present condition is relevant and essential for Defendant to properly prepare a defense of the underlying civil action.

(6) Defendant desires to have Plaintiff examined by Dr. Michael Moritz, a plastic surgeon specializing in the area of facial lacerations and the impact of infection on healing and scarring of facial lacerations.

(7) Defendant has, through counsel, requested informally to have the Plaintiff examined. Efforts to conduct a physical examination by agreement have included seven phone calls and three letters over a period of six months. Copies of the letters are attached as Exhibit C.

WHEREFORE, Defendant respectfully requests this Honorable court enter an order directing the Plaintiff to attend and undergo a physical examination by Dr. Moritz at his offices on November 26, 2014 at 8:00 a.m. for the purposes of inquiring into the Plaintiff's alleged physical condition and injuries suffered or suffer sanctions upon further order of this court.

Respectfully submitted,

settlement than one in which the injury self-heals in a few days or weeks, like a bruise that will never be seen again.

The treating physician or some other expert selected by the plaintiff or (counsel for the plaintiff) will issue an opinion that the accident was the cause of the injuries and will describe the extent of the injuries, the long-term effect of the injuries, the diagnosis, and the prognosis. Pain is a subjective thing; some people suffer more than others from the same injuries. How much treatment is required is based in some part on the patient's own pain threshold; for the physician, some diagnoses are dependent on the medical history and symptoms related by the patient. Soft tissue injuries and those involving muscle strains are hard to diagnose independent of the statements of the patient. It is not unknown for patients to exaggerate their injuries and pain and suffering or for a family or treating physician to accommodate the complaints of the patient, knowing that longer treatments mean higher fees.

defense medical evaluation (DME)

Medical examination of the plaintiff performed by a physician selected by the defendant.

independent medical examinations (IMEs)

Term formerly used to describe a defense medical evaluation.

From the defense side, it is the uncertainty in some cases that dictates a need for a **defense medical evaluation (DME).** With this discovery tool, the defense also has the opportunity to select its own expert to examine and issue a report with an opinion about the condition of the plaintiff. These examinations are frequently called **independent medical examinations (IMEs);** however, these exams are no more independent than those of the treating physician or a doctor hired by the plaintiff to give an opinion. They are thus more properly called *defense medical evaluations*, whether physical or mental in nature. Their purpose is to determine for the defense the cause of the injury, the propriety of the treatment, and the prognosis.

Where it is clear the court will order the examination, counsel will generally agree to voluntarily allow the examination of a client. In some cases, the legal team will request a list of physicians acceptable to the defense from which to select a doctor to conduct the DME. This permits the attorney to eliminate those doctors who, in the attorney's experience, do not have the expertise or the reputation for objectivity that is necessary; doctors who may not be appropriate for a particular client, such as a male doctor for a female client in certain cultures or religions, can also be eliminated.

Judges do not want to be bothered with motions concerning discovery where there is no real issue. It is better for both sides to agree than to risk creating a negative impression with the trial judge. If not, your side might be wasting time and money on a motion that will easily be granted, giving the other side a moral victory and an opportunity to tell the judge on another important motion that your side is always objecting.

Litigation paralegals frequently prepare the client for the DME, explaining the purpose and what can be expected. Clients need to be advised of the differences between a normal visit to their own doctor for the purpose of treatment and the nature and purpose of the DME, an examination that has the potential to help the other side argue against the injuries and damages the client claims.

DME reports detail the examination, including the history given by the client, any reluctance or negative reactions on the part of the client, and the level of the client's cooperation. Failing to cooperate in all phases of the exam makes the client appear to be withholding valuable information that might be needed for a proper medical evaluation.

In some instances, the paralegal or other member of the legal team may be allowed to attend with the client. By attending the examination, the paralegal or other team member can observe the manner in which the exam is conducted: how much time is spent taking the client's history, for example, and how long the physician took to perform the examination. These types of observations can be helpful when it comes time to review the DME report.

The DME report will need to be reviewed, as will the credentials of the expert who issued it. In reviewing the report, the paralegal (or the person who attended the DME with the client) has an advantage. The DME report should be consistent with the observations and notes taken that describe what was happening and what was being asked and answered. The client's medical history and the findings upon physical examination should be accurate and consistent. This information, as well as any opinions or recommendations in the report, should be compared with the records and reports from the client's treating physicians. The purpose of the review is to find areas within the report to attack the credibility of the physician. For example, whereas the defense medical evaluation is performed based upon a review of the records only, the resulting report could easily be attacked if the client was never physically examined.

Another area of review for the paralegal is the credentials of the physician who conducted the exam. A physician whose practice is limited to pediatrics is easily attacked for issuing a report and opinion on loss of hearing in an elderly client. Whether the paralegal is evaluating a physician for selection for the client's case or evaluating the opposing legal team's selection, the credentials of the physician can significantly impact the case.

◼ PREPARING FOR AND ATTENDING A DEFENSE MEDICAL EVALUATION

Defense counsel and insurance companies regularly use the same doctors to perform DMEs for them. Although the doctors are professionals, they are looking to discredit the findings of the treating physician, minimize the impact of the accident or injury, or find a preexisting cause that reduces their client's liability. As with every science, there are gradations of possible findings and potential causes.

LEARNING OBJECTIVE 2
Prepare for attending a defense medical evaluation.

People generally act with great deference to doctors. In seeking treatment, they are more likely than not to tell doctors things they would not tell anyone else. In a DME, a client who has not been properly prepared may think the doctor is asking questions in order to help and advise. This is clearly not true in almost all cases. The doctor has a job to do for the defense side and may use the position of physician to ask questions of a limited nature, focusing solely on some alternate theory that exculpates the defendant, rather than questioning that would lead to a correct diagnosis. Because of the concern for the methods of conducting the DME and the nature of the questions designed to give a basis for a negative finding, someone from the legal team generally accompanies the client to the DME and frequently sits in on the examination. It is desirable to have someone of the same gender as the client, but this is not always possible nor necessary, depending on the nature of the examination. For example, a dentist examining the jaw for Temporomandibular (TMJ) injury will not reveal any embarrassing or sensitive physical conditions.

Where there is a more personal examination or possible removal of clothing, the accompanying person from the legal team may be asked to face away from the client. It is always essential that the client be consulted about his or her feelings in this regard. Some may be very embarrassed at anyone being present for anything, and others will insist that the person from the legal team observe exactly what is done.

The paralegal who attends the DME must make a report of the DME to the trial counsel. This includes the length of the examination, the questions that were asked, the tests that were performed, and the comments that were made. In some cases, the doctor will dictate the findings as she proceeds. There are standard tests and terminology that are used. For example, for an injury to the shoulder, one of the tests is a **range of motion** test. How far can the person rotate the shoulder now, immediately after the injury, and just before the injury? The degree of rotation is reported from 0 to 180 degrees, based on the chart shown in Exhibit 15.2. What may be observed during the DME is a test for rotation in which the doctor pushes the patient beyond the comfort zone. The report might read that the person was able to rotate through the full range of motion, but the observation of the paralegal attending the DME is that the person called out in pain and asked the doctor to stop.

range of motion
The ability to move—for example, the arm—through a variety of motions.

Exhibit 15.2 Range of Motion for Human Shoulder

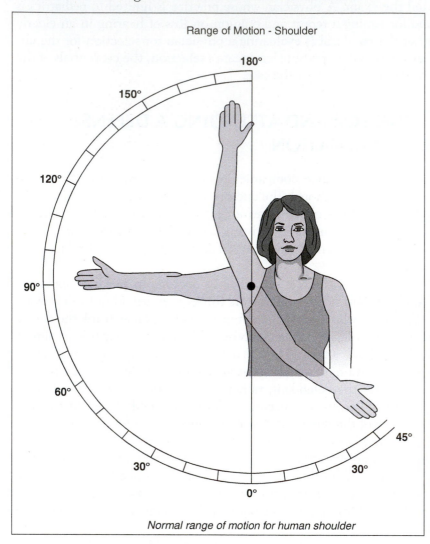

Range of Motion - Shoulder

Normal range of motion for human shoulder

Anyone working in the civil litigation areas involving personal injury or medical malpractice must become familiar with at least some of the common medical terminology used, such as the skeletal structure of the body shown in Exhibit 15.3.

In many cases when medical records are used, nurse consultants or nurse paralegals are asked to review the records. Some have worked in areas of medical specialty, such as cardiac care, emergency medicine, orthopedics, or another specialty. The specialized knowledge of the medical issues and the practice issues in that specialty enable them to review medical records more efficiently than a paralegal or attorney without medical training.

In appropriate cases it may be beneficial to have a nurse paralegal attend the DME. For some patients, having a nurse in attendance makes the presence of an outsider more acceptable.

When children are the clients, a parent should always accompany the child to the DME. In these cases, it may also be advisable to have a medical professional, such as a nurse paralegal, present to avoid any issues of lack of privacy or impropriety if the child is undressed in any way for the examination.

Exhibit 15.3 Human Skeletal Structure

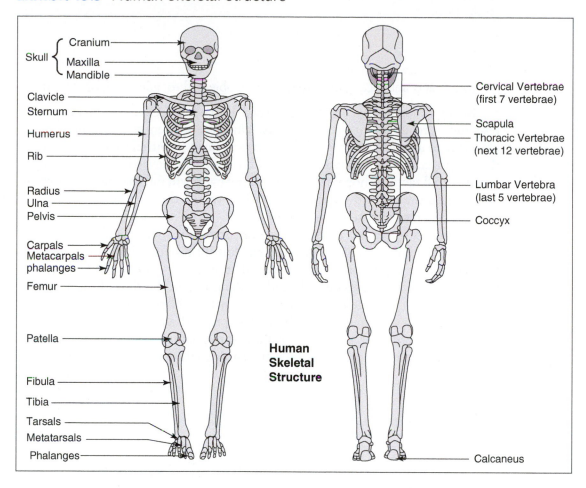

Skull { Cranium
Maxilla
Mandible

Clavicle
Sternum
Humerus
Rib
Radius
Ulna
Pelvis
Carpals
Metacarpals
phalanges
Femur
Patella
Fibula
Tibia
Tarsals
Metatarsals
Phalanges

Cervical Vertebrae
(first 7 vertebrae)

Scapula
Thoracic Vertebrae
(next 12 vertebrae)

Lumbar Vertebra
(last 5 vertebrae)

Coccyx

Calcaneus

**Human
Skeletal
Structure**

■ REQUESTS FOR ADMISSIONS

Requests for admissions are requests to agree to certain facts that, once established, do not need to be proven through evidence or testimony at trial. If all of the relevant facts are admitted, there are no disputed material facts, and all that remains is to apply the law to the facts, then a motion for summary judgment could be filed.

A request for admissions is not always appropriate, as this request is more likely to involve case or trial strategy than the more frequently used discovery tools of depositions and interrogatories. There are times when trial strategy calls for presenting parts of the case for the jury with witness testimony or exhibits that are so compelling that one side wants the jury to observe it firsthand rather than simply be presented with a cold statement of fact. An example is the plaintiff who suffered the loss of a leg when the defendant drove a car into the plaintiff, who had been standing at the rear of a car loading grocery bags into the trunk. Requests for admissions are written requests submitted to the opposing party, asking him to admit the truthfulness of facts, opinions of fact, the law applicable to the dispute, or the application of the law to the facts of the case. Requests for admissions are valuable tools for determining areas of agreement and focusing the legal team on facts and issues that must be presented to the jury for resolution.

LEARNING OBJECTIVE 3
Describe the purpose of and procedure for making and responding to requests for admissions.

The format of the request is similar to that of interrogatories and requests for production:

1. caption;
2. title;
3. introductory materials; and
4. list of facts and legal claims that must be objected to, admitted, or denied.

Requests for admissions are governed by Fed. R. Civ. P. 36. A written response is required within thirty days. Unless a written response denying or objecting to a matter is served, the matter is deemed admitted for the purposes of the litigation. It is not unusual for experienced legal teams to use this discovery tool as a trial tactic in hopes that the opposing party will fail to meet the response deadline. In the event the opponent fails to respond, the legal team will find its case has become easier to present and win.

Exhibit 15.4 contains a list of proposed admissions that could be included in a request for admissions in a personal injury lawsuit resulting from an automobile accident. Some admissions relate to facts that are easily established and perhaps agreed upon, such as the date and weather conditions at the time of the accident. Failure to respond to these requested admissions would not harm the defendant. Others are facts that must be established to prove the case, such as the defendant's failure to stop at a red light. Failing to respond to that request for admission would result in establishing the defendant's liability for the accident.

Exhibit 15.4 Request for Admissions

UNITED STATES DISTRICT COURT _____   DISTRICT OF _____

Suzanne Roper	:	No.: _____
Plaintiff	:	REQUEST FOR ADMISSIONS
v.	:	
Joel Wilkenson and Mary Smith,	:	Civil Action – Negligence
Defendants	:	Attorney #097351

TO: Joel Wilkenson
    c/o Roy Saunders, Esquire
    Street Address
    Anytown State

You are requested to admit or deny the facts listed below in the time permitted under Fed. R. Civ. P. 36.

(1) The accident occurred on April 15, 2014 at approximately 10:30 a.m. at the intersection of 14th and Market Streets.
(2) The weather conditions at the time of the accident were clear, dry, sunny with a temperature of 72° F.
(3) Plaintiff was crossing the street in the designated crosswalk.
(4) Plaintiff was crossing the street and had the right of way because of a green light in her direction.
(5) Defendant Wilkenson was operating a white, four-door 2007 Toyota Camry.
(6) Defendant struck Plaintiff while she was crossing the street.
(7) Defendant Mary Smith was operating a tan, four door 2010 Ford Explorer.
(8) Defendant Mary Smith failed to stop at the red light.
(9) Defendant Mary Smith struck Defendant Wilkenson's vehicle causing his to strike Plaintiff.
(10) Plaintiff was injured as a result of being struck by the vehicle operated by Defendant Wilkenson.

A fact that is admitted or deemed admitted for failure to deny or object is conclusively established for the purposes of trial. Contrary evidence cannot be presented for consideration by the jury.

The best advice for the legal team is to include on the calendar the due date of the response along with sufficient reminders to get the response completed in a timely fashion.

There are three acceptable responses to a request for admissions:

1. admit the truth of the matter stated;
2. deny the matter stated and set forth alternate facts or law; or
3. object to the matter requested, setting forth the specific grounds for the objection.

It is generally unacceptable for the responding party to state that he/she lacks knowledge, information, or belief as to the truth of the matter. Because requests for admissions are typically used as a concluding discovery tool to aid in the preparation of trial, it is unlikely that the litigants would lack knowledge of the facts of the case. Where there remain disputed facts, it might be appropriate to state that the request asks for a conclusion of law or an application of the law to the facts, which is the function of the jury. Exhibit 15.5 provides proposed responses to the requested admissions that appear in Exhibit 15.4.

Exhibit 15.5 Answer to Request for Admissions

UNITED STATES DISTRICT COURT _____   DISTRICT OF _____

Suzanne Roper Plaintiff	:	No.: _____
	:	DEFENDANT WILKENSON'S ANSWER TO REQUEST
v.	:	FOR ADMISSIONS
Joel Wilkenson and Mary Smith,	:	Civil Action – Negligence
Defendants	:	Attorney #097351

(1) Admitted.

(2) Admitted.

(3) It is admitted that Plaintiff was crossing the street. It is denied that the Plaintiff was crossing within the designated crosswalk. To the contrary, there is no designated, delineated, or marked crosswalk at the intersection.

(4) It is denied that Plaintiff had the right of way and the light was green. To the contrary, the light was not operating properly at the time of the accident.

(5) Admitted that Defendant was operating the vehicle described. However, it should be noted that Defendant Wilkenson's vehicle was at a complete stop waiting to make a left turn and waiting for the Plaintiff to cross the street before attempting that turn.

(6) Admitted that Defendant Wilkenson's vehicle struck the Plaintiff but only after first being struck by a vehicle operated by Defendant Smith.

(7) Admitted.

(8) Denied that Defendant Smith failed to stop at the red light. The light was not red. The light was not operating properly at the time of the accident.

(9) Admitted.

(10) Denied that Plaintiff was injured as a result of being struck by the vehicle operated by Defendant Wilkenson. To the contrary, Plaintiff was injured as a result of her failing to be alert and observe the conditions at the time she crossed the street and because her view was blocked by the transit bus at the corner. Any injury the Plaintiff sustained was a direct result of her own negligence. Further, as there remain disputed material facts, the matter must be submitted to the jury for determination.

CONCEPT REVIEW AND REINFORCEMENT

KEY TERMS

causation   368
diagnosis   368
treatment   368

prognosis   368
defense medical evaluation
   (DME)   370

independent medical examination
   (IME)   370
range of motion   371

CHAPTER SUMMARY

OTHER FORMS OF DISCOVERY

Introduction to Other Forms of Discovery	A request for examination of a party is limited to those situations where the physical or mental condition of the person is at issue in the case.
	Requests for admissions are used to obtain agreement to certain facts to avoid the need to present evidence to prove those facts in trial.
Requests for Physical or Mental Examination	Where the physical or mental health of a party is at issue, a defense medical examination may be agreed to or may be ordered by the court upon good cause shown. In personal injury cases, the examination is typically agreed to, and the plaintiff may have some control over the choice of expert to conduct the examination.
	Where the mental state of the party is at issue, a defense medical examination generally requires a court order after a hearing before the court, except in the most obvious cases of mental disability.
Preparing for and Attending a Defense Medical Evaluation	The defense medical evaluation is an attempt by the defense to determine the legitimacy of the claims being made for personal injuries. Typically, the client will be taken to the DME by a member of a legal team, who will then observe and take notes on the methods and comments of the physician during the examination.
	It is important for those attending medical evaluations to understand the terminology used, including knowledge of the basic human skeletal structure and terms used with regard to the type of injury claimed, such as range of motion.
Requests for Admissions	A request for admissions is a written request submitted to the opposing side asking for agreement to stipulate to certain facts without the need for a formal proof at trial. Failure to deny a request or file an objection to the request conclusively establishes those facts for purposes of trial.

REVIEW QUESTIONS AND EXERCISES

1. Why is a request for physical or mental examination a discovery tool with limited use?
2. What is the purpose of using requests for admissions?
3. When would trial counsel not want to use requests for admissions with regard to easily agreed-upon facts?

4. When is a request for mental examination an appropriate discovery request?
5. Why might a mental examination be requested in a breach of contract action?
6. Why would a court order be required for a mental examination?
7. What is the relationship between a diagnosis and a prognosis?
8. What is the purpose of medical treatment?
9. Why is the term *defense medical evaluation* a more accurate term than *independent medical examination*?
10. What is the advantage of attending a defense medical evaluation with the client?
11. Prepare a list of items that should be looked for when doing a review of the defense medical evaluation report.
12. What advice should be given to a client before attending a defense medical evaluation?
13. What is the advantage of having a nurse paralegal attend a defense medical evaluation?
14. What is the advantage of having a nurse paralegal in a personal injury case?
15. What are the advantages in making requests for admissions?
16. What is the effect of not objecting to or denying a request for admissions?

BUILDING YOUR PROFESSIONAL PORTFOLIO

INTERNET AND TECHNOLOGY EXERCISES

1. What medical resources are available for lawyers who are preparing to attend a defense medical evaluation? Prepare a list for future use.
2. What resources exist on the Internet for validating the credentials of doctors and other experts?
3. Locate an online medical dictionary. Prepare a list of online medical services for future reference.

CIVIL LITIGATION VIDEO CASE STUDIES

Mechanic's Deposition

The mechanic who purchased and installed the brake pads on the truck involved in the accident is asked a question about the reason for purchasing brake pads that were not rated top of the line.

After viewing the video at www.pearsonhighered.com/ careersresources, answer the following questions.

1. What affirmative duties does the attorney have to prevent spoliation?
2. What are the potential penalties for causing or permitting spoliation of evidence?
3. Is there a conflict in having the same lawyer represent the insurance company, the employer, and the mechanic?
4. Is the principal-employer liable for the actions of the agent-employee?

CHAPTER OPENING SCENARIO CASE STUDY

Use the Opening Scenario for this chapter to answer the following questions.

1. Who should be involved in the trial strategy discussions?

2. How should the final decisions be made regarding the strategic decision on presenting the case?

3. Who should make the ultimate decision on the presentation of the case in trial?

COMPREHENSIVE CASE STUDY

SCHOOL BUS–TRUCK ACCIDENT CASE

Review the assigned case study in Appendix 2.

1. List facts and/or law that would be appropriate for a request for admissions.

2. Prepare a list of medical terminology and definitions that would be useful for attending the DME of the child plaintiff.

3. Prepare a form for the paralegal attending the DME to record observations of the exam.

BUILDING YOUR PROFESSIONAL PORTFOLIO

CIVIL LITIGATION TEAM AT WORK

See page 18 for instructions on Building Your Professional Portfolio.

Forms

1. Create a template of a letter to a client in a personal injury case whom you will be accompanying to a defense medical evaluation. Include an explanation of the defense medical exam.

2. Create a form for the paralegal attending the DME to record observations of the exam.

Contacts and Resources

1. List of medical resources available for lawyers preparing to attend a defense medical evaluation

2. List of Internet sites for validating the credentials of doctors and other experts

3. Web address of an online medical dictionary

LEARNING OBJECTIVES

After studying this chapter, you should be able to:

1. Identify and distinguish between legal and factual issues for trial.

2. Prepare a pretrial memorandum.

3. Describe the purpose of a trial brief.

4. Describe the purpose of doing a cost-benefit analysis of a lawsuit.

5. Explain how to prepare clients and witnesses for trial.

6. Prepare exhibits for trial presentation.

7. Explain the purpose and procedure of jury investigation.

8. Organize a trial notebook.

9. Obtain a continuance of a trial date.

Trial Preparation— Postdiscovery to Pretrial

CHAPTER 16

OPENING SCENARIO

With everyone in both offices involved with the school bus cases, the offices began to hold weekly meetings as the trial date got closer. The division of work between the liability issues and the damage issues had enabled each office to concentrate on the specifics of each client's claims. Discovery had helped to frame many of the remaining legal issues that might come up during trial regarding procedural matters of admission of certain evidence, like the graphic photographs of the injuries suffered by some of the children and the issues of liability of third parties who manufactured parts that had failed on the truck. Everyone agreed that Roy Saunders, their co-counsel, should be the lead attorney in the trial because of his broader trial experience. He asked his paralegal, Emily, to prepare a draft of the comprehensive pretrial memorandum that the trial judge required; he then suggested that each of the other attorneys review the first draft. He was particularly concerned that Mr. Benjamin, who was responsible for the damage issues, review the valuations listed for each client for pain and suffering and special damages. Mr. Benjamin and his paralegal were asked to be certain that all the electronic devices they intended to use during the trial, including the laptop and projectors, were working. They also had to ensure that they had adequate backups in the event something happened to the laptop, which held the electronic trial notebook they would depend on to present an organized presentation.

OPENING SCENARIO LEARNING OBJECTIVE

Compile a list of the tasks necessary for preparation for trial.

■ INTRODUCTION TO TRIAL PREPARATION

Trial preparation begins the moment the legal team meets the client. Initial determinations must be made that the client has a valid cause of action and that the statute of limitations has not expired. The legal team must then determine the likelihood of success and the perceived credibility of the client and other witnesses, and deal with other evidentiary issues. Because of the time limits imposed by court rules once a case has been filed, careful investigations and evaluation of the case must be done before the case is filed and the clock starts ticking toward the trial date. Under current federal court rules, a trial date is set at the scheduling conference with the trial judge, which takes place approximately ninety days after the defense counsel enters its appearance, or 120 days after the defendant is served. Many state courts assign a trial date early in the litigation process as well. With the trial deadline clock running, preparation time is limited. The accelerated trial deadlines are designed to reduce court backlogs and offer speedy justice, but they add to the stress of the legal team, requiring them to be organized and efficient as well as effective. Having well-thought-out trial preparation and case-handling procedures for litigation helps minimize the stress and anxiety.

■ IDENTIFYING ISSUES FOR TRIAL

LEARNING OBJECTIVE 1
Identify and distinguish between legal and factual issues for trial.

The first phase of trial preparation involves focusing on the legal issues and the evidence of the essential facts of the case, which will be decided by the trier of fact—the jury or a judge in a bench trial. During the discovery phase, the litigants share all the information they intend to present at trial to support or defend the lawsuit. A result of the sharing of information may be agreement between counsel on some facts or legal issues. These areas of agreement, whether factual or legal, represent things that will not have to be argued or presented at trial. The result is a more focused and potentially shorter trial and, in some instances, settlement of the case before the commencement of the trial.

Legal Issues

legal issue
Points of dispute on which law is applicable and/or how the law should be applied.

Legal issues in a case are points of dispute about which law is applicable and/or how the law should be applied. Those issues that arise out of the manner in which the case is managed or the trial is conducted are called **procedural issues;** examples include rulings on the admissibility of evidence and proposed jury instructions. Those issues that arise over how the law on the subject matter of the case is applied are called **substantive issues.** For example, liability is a substantive legal issue: Do the facts as alleged satisfy the statutory or case law elements for imposing responsibility on the defendant for the plaintiff's injuries? **Claims** are the allegations that all the necessary facts exist to satisfy the legal requirements for liability. An automobile accident may lead to a number of claims for personal injury and property damage by more than one person. In a contracts case, breach of contract is a legal issue. The facts necessary to prove a claim are the existence of a valid contract and the failure to perform as required by the terms of the contract. The first legal issue would be a finding that all the necessary elements of a valid contract are present.

procedural issue
Issues that arise from the presentation of the trial, such as those involving the application of the Federal Rules of Evidence.

substantive issue
Issue that arises from which law is applicable or how the law is applied to the dispute.

claim
A right asserted against another for which a remedy is sought in a lawsuit.

Discovery allows the litigants to assess the claims made. Some claims may not hold up once all the facts are revealed. Other claims may have uncontroverted facts that demonstrate that every element of the legal requirement has been met. The discovery process thus allows the legal team to focus on proving the facts that support the claims made.

When investigation and discovery show that the facts do not support a claim, the attorney may voluntarily **withdraw the claim** (Fed. R. Civ. P. 41). A more likely consequence is for the opposing counsel, having had the benefit of the same discovery, to file a **motion for summary judgment** (Fed. R. Civ. P. 56). Typically, after discovery and before trial, both attorneys will file a motion for summary judgment on behalf of their clients. This motion forces each legal team to focus on the legal issues and the elements required to prove those issues; each team then compares the elements with the facts developed through discovery. If the legal teams have thoroughly and properly investigated their clients' claims and defenses, there should be few surprises. When filing the motion for summary judgment, the legal teams tell the court there are no disputed material facts; all that remains is the application of the law to the facts and a representation that when the law is applied to the facts, there can be just one outcome—in their client's favor.

Few lawsuits involve only a single legal issue. For example, in a construction contract lawsuit, there may be multiple claims, each having separate legal issues—for example, claims based on breach of contract, breach of warranties related to the workmanship or goods used, or fraud and misrepresentation as to the quality of workmanship and goods provided. The facts developed through discovery may disclose a work change order that the client's spouse signed, authorizing the use of substitute goods of a lesser quality. With that document, the legal issues and claims related to fraud or breach of warranty as to the quality of goods would be appropriate for a motion for summary judgment. The evaluation of the legal claims for purposes of preparing a motion for summary judgment is a crucial element of trial preparation because a successful motion for summary judgment will resolve one or more legal issues presented to the court for consideration. That issue, along with the witnesses and evidence necessary to prove it, will then not need to be part of the trial presentation.

Facts

Facts are actual or alleged events and occurrences. The location of the incident, the parties involved, the time of the accident, and what or how something happened are all facts of the case. Beginning steps in understanding a case are to create a time line of the facts as related by the client, to supplement those facts with the facts obtained from witnesses, and to contrast them with the facts described by the opposing party. Exhibit 16.1 is a fact time line showing contrasting facts of a case.

After the parties review the documents supplied as a result of discovery and deposition transcripts, there may be facts that are not disputed. For example, there may be agreement as to the date and time of the accident or the authenticity of repair receipts or bank records. If the parties agree to facts, they may formally **stipulate to facts.** That is, those facts will be presented by both sides to the trier of fact—the jury or the judge acting as trier of fact—as not contested. With agreement, there is no need to have documents authenticated by the person who created them (or under whose supervision they were created).

If areas of agreement are found, fewer witnesses will need to testify. Having fewer witnesses results in shorter trials and more attentive jurors. Finding areas of agreement also results in learning the areas of disagreement, where evidence will have to be presented. The legal team can then focus on which witnesses and exhibits are most persuasive and determine the strategy for the best way to present those witnesses and exhibits.

---

withdraw the claim
Process by which a party to the lawsuit voluntarily withdraws or terminates one or more of his claims.

motion for summary judgment
A motion by which a party seeks to terminate the lawsuit prior to trial, alleging there are no disputed material facts and all that remains is in the application of the law to the facts.

facts
Actual or alleged events and occurrences.

stipulate to facts
Facts presented by both sides to the trier of fact—jury or judge acting as trier of fact—as not contested.

Exhibit 16.1 Contrasting Fact Time Line

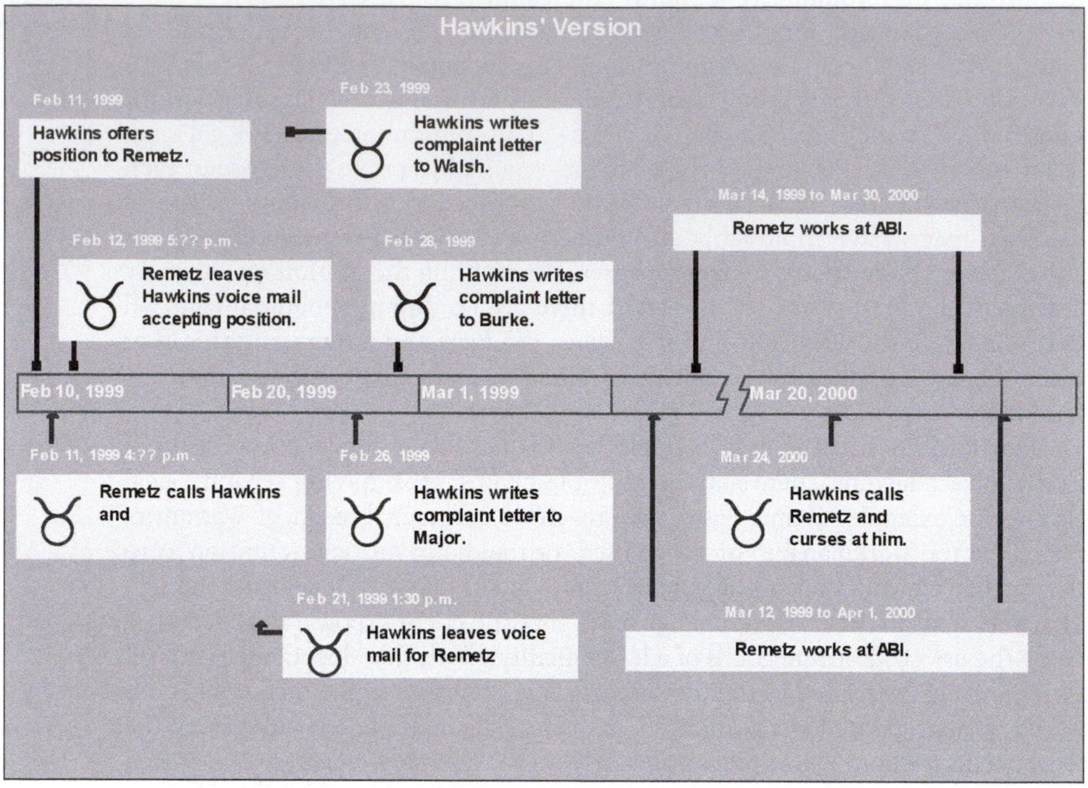

Source: Reproduced with permission from Lexis Nexis.

A time line of the facts, as shown in Exhibit 16.2, graphically shows what elements of the case must be proven at trial and who the best witnesses may be to testify concerning those facts. If the time line is allowed as an exhibit, it also represents a potentially persuasive visual message to the jury of what had to be shown and what was shown by the evidence presented.

Psychological Advantages of Stipulations

In a bench trial there is no jury; instead, the judge sits as the fact finder replacing a jury and hears the evidence, applies the law to the facts, and makes a finding of facts, which is equivalent to a jury verdict. Judges favorably view stipulations and every effort of the parties and their attorneys to streamline the case because it can save substantial judicial time. Many judges maintain a good poker face in the courtroom, but when meeting in chambers the same judges may show some favoritism to the attorney who seems to be moving the case along and disdain for the attorney who is dragging out the process.

In a jury trial, the judge acts as the facilitator of the process, applying the law to the procedural aspects of the trial and ultimately to the finding of facts made by the jury in its deliberations. Jurors have certain expectations of what a trial is like from having seen television and movie depictions of courtroom action. For example, juries expect to watch an adversarial, contentious dispute unfold before them. However, the announcement in court of facts that are presented by agreement of the parties demonstrates to the jury that while the litigants have

Exhibit 16.2 Time Line of Facts

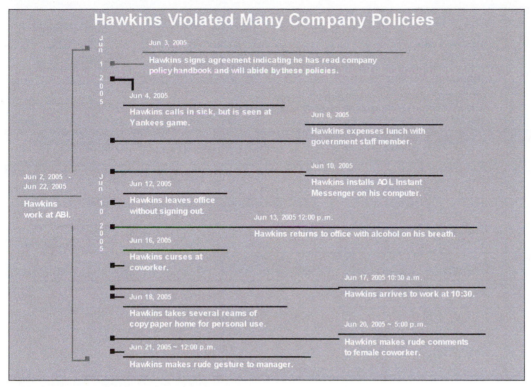

Source: Reproduced with permission from Lexis Nexis.

a dispute, they are not so unreasonable as to be unable to agree on some issues. This may serve to diminish any negative notions the jurors have about those who bring lawsuits. It can also result in the belief that the parties tried to resolve as much of their dispute as possible. The determination of the unresolved facts is left to the jury.

■ PRETRIAL MEMORANDUM

A **pretrial memorandum** is the lawyer's summary of the case prepared as a guide for the trial judge. The memo includes the substantive, procedural, and factual issues; the areas of agreement of counsel; and how long the trial will take. As shown in Exhibit 16.3, it can be a simple form.

A more comprehensive pretrial memorandum may include a comprehensive list, as shown in the pretrial memorandum format used in the U.S. District Court for the Middle District of Pennsylvania shown in Exhibit 16.4.

A more formalized document is the pretrial order prepared and submitted jointly by opposing trial counsel and signed by the trial judge as an order of court, shown in Exhibit 16.5. It includes proposed questions for jury selection, proposed jury instructions, stipulated and disputed facts, legal issues, evidentiary issues, deposition testimony that will be read into the record, and other procedural matters. The required details vary from court to court and even among judges in the same jurisdiction. Therefore, before submission, local rules must be checked

LEARNING OBJECTIVE 2
Prepare a pretrial memorandum.

pretrial memorandum
A summary of the case prepared as a guide for the trial judge on what the issues are, what the areas of agreement of counsel are, and how long the trial will take.

Exhibit 16.3 Pretrial Memo Form Used in Connecticut

PRETRIAL MEMO

JD-ES-47 Rev. 10-08
P.B. §§ 14-13, 14-14
www.jud.ct.gov

INSTRUCTIONS

*Each party claiming damages or that party's attorney shall complete
Part I below and at the commencement of the pretrial session give
a copy to the judge or judge trial referee and to each other party.
Attach additional sheets if necessary.*

**NOTICE: This memo is intended for pretrial purposes only
and shall not be construed as an admission against any party.**

COURT USE ONLY
PRETMEM

DOCKET NUMBER

DATE

PART I *(To be completed by attorney/pro se party)*

PLAINTIFF		DEFENDANT #1	DEFENDANT'S TRIAL COUNSEL	PHONE NO.
PLAINTIFF'S TRIAL COUNSEL	PHONE NO.	DEFENDANT #2	DEFENDANT'S TRIAL COUNSEL	PHONE NO.
INTERVENING TRIAL COUNSEL	PHONE NO.	DEFENDANT #3	DEFENDANT'S TRIAL COUNSEL	PHONE NO.

RETURN DATE	DATE CERT. OF CLOSED PLEADINGS FILED	TYPE OF CLAIM		TRIAL DATE

HAVE YOU DISCUSSED APPROPRIATE A.D.R. WITH YOUR CLIENT? ☐ YES ☐ NO   DOES YOUR CLIENT HAVE ANY OBJECTION TO A REFERRAL TO NON-BINDING A.D.R.? ☐ YES ☐ NO

CLAIM
(e.g. Accident)

DATE AND TIME OF ACCIDENT *(if applicable)*

INTERVENOR'S CLAIM

DAMAGES OR DEMAND
(e.g. Injuries)

NATURE OF DAMAGES OR DEMAND

IF APPLICABLE

LAST MEDICAL EXAM	PERMANENCY OF INJURIES/LIFE EXPECTANCY	AGE OF PARTY

	REASON	COST	EXPLANATION
SPECIALS	1. Doctor(s)		
	2. Hospital(s)		
	3. Subtotal *(Add 1 & 2)*		
	4. Future Medical		
	5. Wages — LOST WAGES		
	5. Wages — FUTURE CAPACITY		
	6. OTHER *(Prop. Dam., etc.)*		
	7. TOTAL		Copies of all medical bills and reports have been furnished to the Defendant(s) ☐ YES ☐ NO

(Page 1 of 2)

Exhibit 16.4 Pretrial Memorandum Format, U.S. District Court for the Middle District of Pennsylvania

APPENDIX B

PRETRIAL MEMORANDUM FORMAT

UNITED STATES DISTRICT COURT

FOR THE MIDDLE DISTRICT OF PENNSYLVANIA

:

:

:

v.   : CIVIL ACTION NO.

:

:

PRETRIAL MEMORANDUM

Date conference was held by counsel:

A. A brief statement as to federal court jurisdiction.

B. A summary statement of facts and contentions as to liability.

C. A comprehensive statement of undisputed facts as agreed to by counsel at the conference of attorneys required by Local Rule 16.3. No facts should be denied unless opposing counsel expects to present contrary evidence or genuinely challenges the fact on credibility grounds. The parties must reach agreement on uncontested facts even though relevancy is disputed.

D. A brief description of damages, including, where applicable:

(1) Principal injuries sustained:

(2) Hospitalization and convalescence:

(3) Present disability:

(4) Special monetary damages, loss of past earnings, medical expenses, property damages, etc.:

(5) Estimated value of pain and suffering, etc.:

(6) Special damage claims:

E. Names and addresses of witnesses, along with the specialties and qualifications of experts to be called.

F. Summary of testimony of each expert witness.

G. Special comment about pleadings and discovery, including depositions and the exchange of medical reports.

H. A summary of legal issues involved and legal authorities relied upon.

I. Stipulations desired.

J. Estimated number of trial days.

K. Any other matter pertinent to the case to be tried.

L. Pursuant to Local Rule 16.3 append to this memorandum a prenumbered schedule of exhibits, with brief identification of each, on the clerk's Exhibit Form.

M. Append any special verdict questions which counsel desires to submit.

N. Defense counsel must file a statement that the person or committee with settlement authority has been notified of the requirements of and possible sanctions under Local Rule 16.2.

O. Certificate must be filed as required under Local Rule 30.10 that counsel have met and reviewed depositions and videotapes in an effort to eliminate irrelevancies, side comments, resolved objections, and other matters not necessary for consideration by the trier of fact.

P. In all trials without a jury, requests for findings of both fact and law shall be submitted with this Memorandum as required under Local Rule 48.2.

Exhibit 16.5 Final Pretrial Order for the United States District Court for the Northern District of Illinois

<u>**United States District Court**</u>
For The Northern District of Illinois
Eastern Division

Austin Bennaza

Plaintiff[1],

           Civil Action No. 04-CIV-004578

     v.

           Judge Caroline S. Cascino

Buddy Smith,

Defendant.

FINAL PRETRIAL ORDER

This matter having come before the court at a pretrial conference held pursuant to Fed. R. Civ. P. ("Rule") 16, and Jennifer L. Abernathy, 565 West Adams St., Chicago, IL, 312 906-5000, Jay C. Carle, 565 West Adams St., Chicago, IL, 312 906-5000, and Kathryn M. Smith, 565 West Adams St., Chicago, IL, 312 906-5000, having appeared as counsel for plaintiff(s) and J. Justin Boyd, 565 West Adams St., Chicago, IL, 312 906-5000, and John G. New, 565 West Adams St., Chicago, IL, 312 906-5000, having appeared as counsel for defendant(s), the following actions were taken:

(1) This is an action for battery and assault and the jurisdiction of the court is invoked under 28 U.S.C. § 1332. Jurisdiction is disputed. The claim against the Village of Kenilworth was dismissed without prejudice.

(2) The following stipulations and statements were submitted and are made a part of this Order:

(a) a comprehensive stipulation or statement of all uncontested facts, which will become a part of the evidentiary record in the case (and which may be read to the jury by the court or any party):

(i) Plaintiff Bennaza is a citizen of Illinois;

(ii) Defendant Smith is a citizen of Wisconsin;

(iii) Plaintiff Bennaza's medical treatments after the incident in litigation cost $75,100, of which $60,000 was paid by insurance, and the remainder paid by plaintiff himself;

(iv) Plaintiff Bennaza was stopped by Defendant Smith for an allegedtraffic violation in the Village of Kenilworth on September 21, 2004;

(v) Defendant Smith is employed by the Village of Kenilworth Police Department as a Patrolman;

(vi) Illinois law applies to the substantive claims by plaintiff;

(continued)

Exhibit 16.5 (continued)

(b) an agreed statement or statements by each party of the contested issues of fact and law and a statement or statements of contested issues of fact or law not agreed to:

(i) whether plaintiff has satisfied the jurisdictional minimum for diversity jurisdiction as a matter of law;

(ii) whether the conduct by Defendant Smith constitutes the tort of battery;

(iii) whether the conduct by Defendant Smith constitutes the tort of assault;

(iv) whether the conduct by Defendant Smith was privileged under Illinois law or within an immunity conferred by Illinois law.

(c) except for rebuttal exhibits, neither party will offer exhibits, demonstrative evidence or experiments into evidence, except for the following:

(i) flashlight used by Defendant Smith

(ii) demonstration by Defendant Smith of his movements and those of Plaintiff

(iii) Defendant Smith's personnel records or summaries thereof, the authenticity of which will be stipulated before trial

(d) a list or lists of names of the potential witnesses to be called by each party, with a statement of any objections to calling, or to the qualifications of, any witness identified on the list:

Plaintiff: Austin Bennaza

Defendant: William H. "Buddy" Smith

Treating physician or bartender (Frank Salinas, 565 West Adams St., Chicago, IL, 312 906-5000) (expert, if physician)

Anger management witness (Patricia A. Culliton, 565 West Adams St., Chicago, IL, 312 906-5000) (expert)

Ambulance driver or attendant (Nathan B. Hinch, 565 West Adams St., Chicago, IL, 312 906-5000)

(e) no expert witnesses will be called by either party, except as indicated in subsection (d); qualifications of experts identified in subsection (d) are stipulated

(f) a list of all depositions, or portions thereof, to be read into evidence and statements of any objections thereto: none, except as may be used for impeachment;

Exhibit 16.5 *(continued)*

(g) special damages have been stipulated;

(h) no claims or defenses have been abandoned by any party except for those covered by the stipulations set forth above;

(i) each party has provided the following:

(i) trial briefs except as otherwise ordered by the court (none, pursuant to court order);

(ii) one set of marked proposed jury instructions, verdict forms and special interrogatories, if any; and

(iii) a list of the questions the party requests the court to ask prospective jurors in accordance with Fed.R.Civ.P. 47(a);

(k) the parties have engaged in settlement negotiations, but further negotiations are not likely to be productive;

(l) each party has completed discovery. Absent good cause shown, no further discovery shall be permitted; and

(m) no motions in limine are anticipated.

(3) Trial of this case is expected to take one hour and forty minutes. Trial will commence at 6:00 PM.

(a) Plaintiff shall have five minutes for an opening statement, 15 minutes to present his case in chief, 15 minutes to cross examine Defendant's witnesses, and five minutes for closing argument;

(b) Defendant shall have five minutes for an opening statement, 15 minutes to cross examine Plaintiff's witness, 15 minutes to present his case in chief and five minutes for closing argument;

(4) [*Indicate the type of trial by placing an X in the appropriate box*]

[X] Jury   [_] Non-jury

(5) The parties recommend that 75 jurors be selected; the jurors will have been selected and will be seated at the commencement of the trial.

(6) The parties agree that the issues of liability and damages should not be bifurcated for trial.

(7) [*Pursuant to 28 U.S.C. § 636(c), parties may consent to the reassignment of this case to a magistrate judge who may conduct any or all proceedings in a jury or nonjury civil matter and order the entry of judgment in the case. Indicate below if the parties consent to such a reassignment.*]

[_] The parties consent to this case being reassigned to a magistrate judge for trial.

(8) This Order will control the course of the trial and may not be amended except by consent of the parties and the court, or by order of the court to prevent manifest injustice.

(continued)

Exhibit 16.5 (*continued*)

(9) Possibility of settlement of this case was considered by the parties.

(10) One photographer (Henry H. Perritt, Jr.) shall be allowed to photograph the trial.

_____
United States District Judge[15]

Date: 1 December 2004

[*Attorneys are to sign the form before presenting it to the court.*]

_____   _____
     Attorney for Plaintiff   Attorney for Defendant

Exhibit 16.6 Standing Order of Judge Hart from the Eastern District of Pennsylvania

---

JUDGE HART'S STANDING ORDER RE PRETRIAL STIPULATION

(JURY TRIAL)

In lieu of pretrial memoranda or a Final Pretrial Order, under Local Rules 16.1(d)(1) and (2), a Pretrial Stipulation shall be submitted, containing the following:

1. **Agreed facts.** A conscientious effort should be made to narrow the areas of dispute.

2. **Each party's disputed facts.**

3. **Each party's exhibits, as marked for trial.** (Any objections to authenticity should be noted or will be considered waived. Exhibits shall be provided to the Court in the form of two, jointly prepared, loose leaf Exhibit Books, each separately numbering Joint Exhibits, Plaintiff's Exhibits, and Defendant's Exhibits.)

4. **Each party's witnesses and the subject matter of the witness's testimony.** (PLEASE NOTE: IF YOU WILL BE USING VIDEO EQUIPMENT TO PRESENT THE TESTIMONY OF A WITNESS, YOU MUST EITHER SUPPLY THAT EQUIPMENT OR REQUEST AT LEAST TWO WEEKS BEFORE TRIAL THAT THE COURT RESERVE EQUIPMENT FOR YOU)

5. **Unusual issues—contentions and authority.**

6. **Proposed voir dire questions, requests for jury instructions, and a proposed jury verdict form.** Counsel shall make a good faith effort to agree upon as many of these items as possible. (THESE ITEMS ARE TO BE SUBMITTED ON DISK—WORDPERFECT IF POSSIBLE—AS WELL AS IN HARD COPY.)

7. **The signed approval of trial counsel for each party.**

IT SHALL BE THE RESPONSIBILITY OF PLAINTIFF'S COUNSEL TO CIRCULATE A DRAFT OF THIS PRETRIAL STIPULATION AT LEAST ONE WEEK BEFORE IT IS DUE.

---

trial brief
Document presented to the court setting forth a legal argument to persuade the court to rule in a particular way on a procedural or substantive legal issue.

LEARNING OBJECTIVE 3
Describe the purpose of a trial brief.

WEB RESOURCES
Contrast and compare the Wyoming Rules of Professional Conduct for Attorneys at Law, Rule 3.3. Candor toward the tribunal, at http://courts.state.wy.us/CourtRules_Entities.aspx?RulesPage=AttorneysConduct.xml, with the ABA Model Rules of Professional Conduct, 3.3 Candor to the Tribunal, at http://www.abanet.org/cpr/mrpc/rule_3_3.html, and the ethical rules in your jurisdiction.

for compliance with the standing orders of the trial judge; for example, see the requirements of Judge Hart shown in Exhibit 16.6.

■ TRIAL BRIEF

A **trial brief** is a document presented to the court that sets forth a legal argument and attempts to persuade the court to rule in a particular way on a procedural or substantive legal issue. In some courts, trial briefs are included as part of the pretrial memorandum. In others, trial briefs are submitted at the commencement of trial and others during the trial itself when an issue arises. The trial brief submitted by each attorney presents the statutes and case law that support each attorney's legal position.

For example, an area of frequent disagreement is the admissibility of evidence. The attorneys may disagree over the admission of photographs that depict the scene of an accident. Some of the photographs may be explicit, showing blood pools and severed body parts. One attorney will want the jury to see the photos because they depict what the plaintiff experienced; the other will argue that the photos should be excluded because they will cause the jurors to react emotionally. The judge will then be required to resolve the issue. The trial brief submitted by each attorney will present the statutes and case law that support the position for admission or exclusion of the evidence. Local rules and the standing orders of the particular trial judge should be consulted to determine the form and content required for a trial brief.

ETHICAL Perspectives

ETHICAL DUTY OF CANDOR

In preparing any submission to the court, the attorney is under an ethical obligation of candor toward the court. It is not acceptable to fail to submit a controlling case or statute simply because it does not favor the position being argued. It must be revealed even if the opposing attorney has not discovered it.

Wyoming Rules of Professional Conduct for Attorneys at Law

Rule 3.3. Candor toward the tribunal.

A lawyer shall not knowingly:

(1) make a false statement of fact or law to a tribunal or fail to correct a false statement of material fact or law previously made to the tribunal by the lawyer;

(2) fail to disclose to the tribunal legal authority in the controlling jurisdiction known to the lawyer to be directly adverse to the position of the client and not disclosed by opposing counsel; or

   (a) offer evidence that the lawyer knows to be false. If a lawyer, the lawyer's client, or a witness called by the lawyer, has offered material evidence and the lawyer comes to know of its falsity, the lawyer shall take reasonable remedial measures, including, if necessary, disclosure to the tribunal. A lawyer may refuse to offer evidence, other than the testimony of a defendant in a criminal matter, that the lawyer reasonably believes is false.

   (b) A lawyer who represents a client in an adjudicative proceeding and who knows that a person intends to engage, is engaging or has engaged in criminal or fraudulent conduct related to the proceeding shall take reasonable remedial measures, including, if necessary, disclosure to the tribunal.

   (c) The duties stated in paragraphs (a) and (b) continue to the conclusion of the proceeding, and apply even if compliance requires disclosure of information otherwise protected by Rule 1.6.

   (d) In an ex parte proceeding, a lawyer shall inform the tribunal of all material facts known to the lawyer that will enable the tribunal to make an informed decision, whether or not the facts are adverse.

With a streamlined trial in mind, judges prefer to rule on as many of the procedural, substantive, and factual stipulation issues as possible before the trial begins. Raising the issues during trial, in the presence of the jury, takes time and may draw attention away from the actual issues being litigated. Once a trial begins, judges want to keep these non-fact-finding issues from the jury to avoid any potential influence on their fact-finding obligation.

■ COST-BENEFIT ANALYSIS OF A LAWSUIT

In most civil lawsuits, each party is responsible for paying his own attorney's fees, win or lose. This is called the "American rule." The court can award lawyer's fees to the winning party if there is statutory authorization or if the parties have agreed to this arrangement; for example, a contract may include a clause that requires the losing party to pay the litigation costs of the winner. If a party has

LEARNING OBJECTIVE 4
Describe the purpose of doing a cost-benefit analysis of a lawsuit.

acted maliciously or pursued a frivolous case, that party may be required to pay the legal fees of the other party.

An attorney in a civil lawsuit may represent the plaintiff on an hourly, project, or contingency-fee basis. Hourly fees may range from $100 to $2,000 per hour, depending on the type of case, the lawyer's expertise, and the locality of the lawsuit. Under a **contingency-fee agreement,** the lawyer receives a percentage of the amount recovered for the plaintiff. Contingency fees may range from 20 to 50 percent of the award or settlement. Courts may limit the contingency fee in cases involving minors or other incompetent parties, and in some jurisdictions, the percentage fee is reduced as the amount of the award increases; for example, one-third on the first $100,000 and 20 percent on the next $150,000, with some caps as low as 10 to 15 percent of the remainder. Lawyers for defendants in lawsuits are typically paid on an hourly basis.

The choice of whether to bring or defend a lawsuit should be analyzed like any other business decision. This includes performing a **cost-benefit analysis** of the lawsuit—calculating what can be gained at what cost. For the plaintiff, it may be wise not to sue. For the defendant, it may be wise to settle. In deciding whether to bring or settle a lawsuit, the following factors should be considered:

- the probability of winning or losing;
- the amount of money to be won or lost;
- lawyers' fees and other costs of litigation;
- loss of time by managers and other personnel;
- the long-term effects on the relationship and reputation of the parties;
- the amount of prejudgment interest provided by law;
- the aggravation and psychological costs associated with a lawsuit;
- the unpredictability of the legal system and the possibility of error; and
- other factors unique to the parties and lawsuit.

■ CLIENT AND WITNESS PREPARATION

Paralegals work with the trial attorney in preparing clients and witnesses for trial. The difficult discussions with clients and witnesses relate to personal style and include such things as the appropriate attire, hair, makeup, and demeanor for court. Without being judgmental, the paralegal may need to ask the person to wear a long-sleeved blouse to cover tattoos or slacks with a traditional waistband so undergarments are not visible. A good approach for this sensitive topic is to describe the courtroom, the judge, jury, and other staff in the courtroom. It may also help to describe what takes place in the courtroom. Sometimes using an analogy will be enough for the client or witness to understand that he or she must be dressed to impress and on his or her best behavior. Judges and jurors will be making decisions of credibility and, potentially, will arrive at a verdict based in part on their perception of the people who appear before them; after all, they have no knowledge of the people's prior behavior or belief systems except as they relate to the trial.

Clients and witnesses also need to be reminded of the difference between conversing and giving sworn testimony in court. In court, when witnesses speak, they are responding to a question they have been asked that is being stenographically recorded by a court reporter. Because the court stenographer is taking down the words being spoken, only one person may speak at a time. The

---

contingency-fee agreement
Fee agreement whereby the lawyer receives a percentage of the amount recovered for the plaintiff.

cost-benefit analysis
Process by which a litigant determines the costs of pursuing litigation and compares them to what is likely to be gained.

LEARNING OBJECTIVE 5
Explain how to prepare clients and witnesses for trial.

PRACTICE TIP
If at all possible, arrange for the clients and witnesses to arrive early enough to enter the courtroom and see the space while court is in recess. Anxiety about testifying in court can be reduced if everyone has had a chance to see, feel, and become comfortable in the courtroom before testifying.

witness may not talk at the same time as the other person, as frequently occurs in daily conversation when people anticipate what another will say and respond before that person finishes speaking.

Checklist ✔   PRETRIAL INSTRUCTIONS

- Tell the truth.
- If you don't understand the question, say so; otherwise, the answer given will be assumed to be your response to the question asked.
- If you don't know or can't remember, say so.
- Never guess.
- When you hear the word *objection*, stop talking and wait for instruction from the attorney or the judge.

The process of direct and cross-examination should be explained. Give specific examples of leading questions asked on cross-examination to demonstrate the importance of listening to and responding to the questions. Encourage clients or witnesses to think before responding, pause momentarily to allow their attorney to make any objections to the question, and wait until the judge decides to sustain or overrule the objection before saying anything—*and if the objection is sustained, not to answer but to wait for another question.*

Provide witnesses with copies of their prior statements and depositions. It is important for clients and witnesses to review these statements and deposition testimony. The testimony given at trial will usually cover the same areas as in the deposition and be measured against those prior statements. Explain that any inconsistency will be used to impeach them or attack their credibility.

The paralegal can also review the types of questions that will be asked of the client and the witness. Some think it is good practice to rehearse questions and answers with clients and witnesses. Others think too much rehearsal results in testimony that sounds scripted and overprepared, which may cause the jury to doubt the witness's sincerity. Follow the supervising attorney's guide, but in no event should the paralegal instruct the client or witness how to testify.

Some special preparation applies to use of subpoenas. Typically, all witnesses will be served with a subpoena to compel their attendance at trial. However, to keep friendly witnesses friendly, it is wise to advise them that a subpoena is going to be personally served on them and to explain why it is important to do so. Nothing changes a friendly witness to a hostile one more quickly than unexpectedly being served with a subpoena in the workplace.

Jurors may feel that a witness has more credibility if the person is there involuntarily instead of as a cooperating witness. Some trial attorneys may attempt to call the credibility of the witness into doubt with questions like, "Isn't it true you gave up a day of work to travel all this way to court to help your friend?" The witness can respond, truthfully, "No, I was ordered to attend by subpoena." Exhibit 16.7 is a standard form subpoena from the Southern District of Texas. Note that subpoenas generally require the witness to appear on the first day of trial and remain until called.

Exhibit 16.7 *Subpoena Duces Tecum* in Fillable PDF Format Available Online

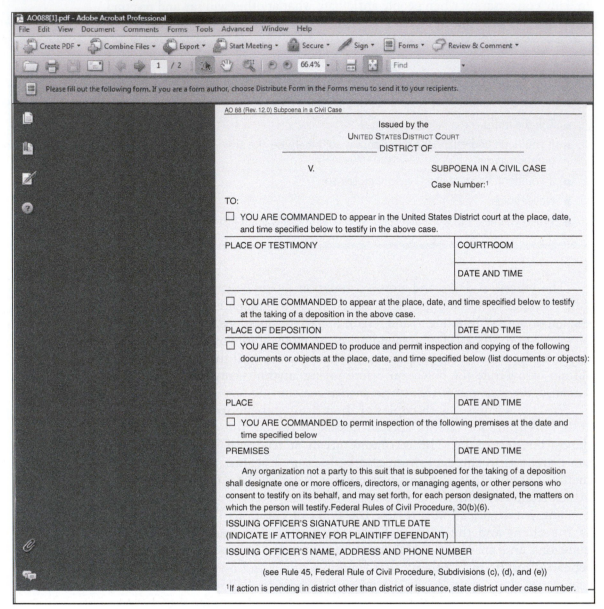

Source: Courtesy of U.S.D.C.

Placing Witnesses on Call

Depending on the length of the trial, the potential of settlement early in the trial, and the willingness of the court to accommodate, witnesses available on short notice may be placed on call. Before placing witnesses on call, consult with the court to determine the judge's policy. Some courts are agreeable to a potential delay to allow a witness to be called in, while others insist on all witnesses being in the courthouse from the start. The impact of a delayed witness on potential trial strategy should also be considered. Opposing counsel, knowing that key witnesses are on call, may move more quickly to the conclusion of their presentation in an attempt to block the appearance of the witness on another day.

Trial preparation includes preparing a telephone on-call list for witnesses who can get to the courthouse in thirty minutes or less.

■ PREPARATION OF EXHIBITS

Models, photographic enlargements, and other demonstrative evidence that will be used at trial and will require time to create must be ordered early enough to be available well in advance of trial. The legal team will want an opportunity to review the model, diagram, or photographic enlargements to check for accuracy and presentation effect. The legal team should also give the witness who is expected to use the exhibits in testimony an opportunity to review the items before trial. For his testimony to have the desired impact on the jury, the witness must be able to explain the exhibit with confidence. This is particularly true of the use of elaborate models and simulation videos.

Documents and Things

Whether exhibited as a PowerPoint presentation, overhead projection, or poster on an easel, the item must be large enough for the judge, jury, witness, and opposing party to see clearly.

Copies of original documents should be made for opposing counsel and the court. If original documents are not available, copies must be prepared that are acceptable under the rules of evidence. All exhibits should be premarked if they have not already been marked in the discovery process.

Exhibits should be organized so that the legal team need not shuffle through files and papers. Doing so distracts the jury and gives the impression that the legal team is not prepared.

Electronic Presentations

Where the jurisdiction has converted to (or is in the process of converting to) electronic courtrooms, the paralegal will have to determine what is available within the courtroom, what audiovisual equipment can be provided by the courthouse staff upon request, and what the legal team may bring to court to assist in presenting the evidence.

■ JURY INVESTIGATION

Jury investigation is the ability to investigate the **jury pool**—all individuals called to serve for jury duty—before trial begins. Jury investigation begins with the legal team's analysis of the personality profile of individuals likely to be sympathetic toward their client. This type of analysis might be based on the personal or trial experiences of the supervising attorney. In complex litigation, an expert might be hired to provide an assessment of the types of persons likely to be sympathetic to the client's situation. The result may be a recommendation that the most sympathetic jurors would be professional women between the ages of 50 and 65 who work outside the home.

The next step is to review the persons in the jury pool, identifying those who match the desired criteria. In most jurisdictions, the list of potential jurors called for a particular trial week or term is available from the court clerk or jury commissioner. All members of the jury pool complete a preliminary questionnaire that includes name, age, education, and employment. If available prior to trial, further information to determine which members of the pool may be appropriate to serve on the jury may be obtained through personal investigations; from Internet searches, such as through Google.com; or from a public records search conducted

LEARNING OBJECTIVE 6
Prepare exhibits for trial presentation.

PRACTICE TIP

No matter what type of exhibit is used, the paralegal should prepare a backup plan. Electricity fails and jurors forget their eyeglasses; for the trial to proceed (and it will), prepare paper copies that can be distributed.

LEARNING OBJECTIVE 7
Explain the purpose and procedure of jury investigation.

jury investigation
The ability to investigate the jury pool.

jury pool
All individuals called to serve for jury duty before trial begins.

at the local courthouse or online. Information such as voter registration and party affiliation, real estate ownership, vehicle registration, and judgments or liens against an individual are easily obtainable and can help in deciding if the person fits the desired juror profile.

Mock Jury Trial

mock jury trial
Process that allows the legal team to create a mock jury with similar socio-economic factors as those in the jury pool; the team presents its case, and the mock jury returns a verdict and a critique.

A **mock jury trial** is a costly process, but it allows the legal team to create a mock jury with similar socioeconomic factors as those in the jury pool. The legal team presents its case, and the mock jury returns a verdict. The mock jury then provides a critique of the strengths and weaknesses of the witness testimony and case presentation. The benefits to the legal team are twofold: being able to investigate the jury and being able to test the case presentation.

■ TRIAL NOTEBOOK

LEARNING OBJECTIVE 8
Organize a trial notebook.

trial notebook
Summary of the case, usually contained in a tabbed, three-ring binder with sections such as Pleadings, Motions, Law, Pretrial memo, and Witnesses.

The legal team may use a manual or a computerized system to organize the case for trial. Exhibits and appropriate portions of deposition transcripts must be easily accessible when a witness is testifying. Most trial attorneys have a preferred method of organizing the information for use in trial. The traditional method has been the **trial notebook,** usually a tabbed, three-ring binder with sections such as Pleadings, Motions, Law, Pretrial memo, and Witnesses. In more complex cases, the litigation team will have boxes of trial notebooks and related evidentiary documents. Whether a notebook, box, or computerized system, each section contains the relevant materials that may be required at trial with regard to a particular issue. There may be copies of the statutes and case law that relate to the legal issues expected to come up at trial. In the Witnesses tab or folder, there is usually a section for each individual witness with questions to be asked, the subpoena issued to the witness, the deposition transcript, other statements of the witness, and exhibits about which the witness will testify.

With the growth of the use of computer technology in litigation, the traditional paper trial notebook may be replaced with a laptop computer on which electronic files replace all but the evidence needed in hard-copy form for use with the witnesses. Deposition transcripts and documentary evidence in electronic form on the computer are almost instantly searchable and available for electronic presentation using presentation software. The responsibility for running the computer and electronic presentation software may fall on the paralegal. Pretrial preparation should include verification that all the needed items are on the laptop and that there is a backup immediately available in case of loss or equipment failure; for many, that includes a paper backup for the contents of the laptop. Preparation should also include a session with trial counsel in which the coordination among the trial team members is worked out so the appearance in court is one of confidence and preparedness.

■ CONTINUANCES

LEARNING OBJECTIVE 9
Obtain a continuance of a trial date.

Trial dates are usually known well in advance. Some courts assign a trial date upon the filing of the complaint or after a scheduling conference with the trial or calendar judge. It is not unusual for a litigation team to find it is scheduled

Exhibit 16.8 Rule of the Federal District Court for the Northern District of California for Continuances

---

40-1. CONTINUANCE OF TRIAL DATE; SANCTIONS FOR FAILURE TO PROCEED.

No continuance of a scheduled trial date will be granted except by order of the Court issued in response to a motion made in accordance with the provisions of Civil L.R. 7. Failure of a party to proceed with the trial on the scheduled trial date may result in the imposition of appropriate sanctions, including dismissal or entry of default. Jury costs may be assessed as sanctions against a party or the party's attorney for failure to proceed with a scheduled trial or failure to provide the Court with timely written notice of a settlement.

Northern District of California

---

to be in two places at the same time. When that happens, one of the matters must be deferred and rescheduled. The process of rescheduling a matter is called requesting a **continuance.** Continuances are granted at the discretion of the judge and are normally granted within reason. Courts have been known to grant continuances when a preplanned vacation interferes. There should be a valid, good faith basis for the request, such as another case previously scheduled in another court or more recently scheduled in an appellate court with a limited schedule for hearing appeals. Some jurisdictions use a system under which an attorney is **attached** for trial, placing a restriction on the attorney's accepting another case for the same time. Usually, notice of attachment is sufficient grounds for a continuance, though a higher-level court (trial court) may not recognize attachment by a lower court (minor judiciary or small claims court). If a **"date certain"** is set, usually no further continuances will be permitted. Continuances are requested by way of a written motion. Local rules and standing orders of the individual judge should be consulted before filing the motion. Exhibit 16.8 is a local rule from the Federal District Court for the Northern District of California for continuances. Note that continuances are granted by order of court only, and that failure to appear and proceed on the date scheduled for trial can result in serious consequences.

continuance
Request made to the court to change the date scheduled for trial.

attached
A restriction by the trial court that prohibits an attorney from accepting another trial for the same time.

date certain
Date set by the judge for trial to begin; it cannot be changed.

CONCEPT REVIEW AND REINFORCEMENT

KEY TERMS

CHAPTER SUMMARY

TRIAL PREPARATION—POSTDISCOVERY TO PRETRIAL

Introduction to Trial Preparation	Trial preparation begins with the first meeting with the client, when a determination must be made of the validity of the claims being made by the client and the ability to prove the case.
	Shortened time lines utilized by courts put additional pressure on the legal team to move effectively, efficiently, and quickly through trial preparation.
Identifying Issues for Trial	Legal issues are points of dispute on the application of procedural and substantive law. Procedural issues are those arising from the presentation of the trial, such as those involving the application of the Federal Rules of Evidence. Substantive issues are those that arise from the statutory and case law that applies to the particular area out of which the claim of the client arose, such as the elements of the law of negligence.
	Facts are the actual or alleged events and occurrences that gave rise to the claim of the plaintiff or some wrongdoing by the defendant for which a remedy is provided by statutory or case law.
	A motion for summary judgment tests the legal sufficiency of the claims of the parties. The motion will be granted if, after accepting all of the facts as alleged, there is no recognizable legal right for redress.
Pretrial Memorandum	Each court sets its own standards for the pretrial memorandum that it requests from trial counsel. A pretrial memorandum typically summarizes the case that will be presented at trial, including areas of agreement and disagreement, witnesses, and time frames for conducting the trial.
Trial Brief	A trial brief is a document presented to the court that makes a legal argument in an attempt to persuade the court to take a particular point of view. Trial briefs are typically prepared on those issues of law for which there is a likelihood of disagreement requiring a decision by the judge, such as the admissibility of certain types of evidence.
Cost-Benefit Analysis of a Lawsuit	Each side should prepare an analysis of the potential cost of trial versus the expected outcome. When costs vastly exceed the potential outcome, it may not be viable, except as a matter of principle, to proceed. For the defendant, it may be a matter of settling for a dollar amount that is less than it would cost to defend the action.
Client and Witness Preparation	Few clients or witnesses have had experience with the litigation process except for what they have seen on television or in the movies. Therefore, the process needs to be explained to them. The paralegal also needs to stress the importance of their appearance and conduct during the trial as they relate to seeming credible and likable to the jury.
	Potential witnesses need to understand the procedural aspects of examination and cross-examination in terms of what to expect and how to act in the event of objections raised by the other side's counsel.
Preparation of Exhibits	Demonstrative evidence in the form of models, photographic enlargements, and other documents should be prepared sufficiently in advance to allow the witnesses to become familiar with the exhibits that will be used during their examination.
	Where electronic presentations are to be used, local court rules, procedures, and availability need to be verified early enough to allow for alternatives in the event the equipment is not available or must be rented.

Jury Investigation	Jury investigation is the investigation of the jury pool, the group of people from whom a jury may be selected, to determine the potential jurors who fit the profile of those most likely to be sympathetic to the case presented, or those who might be antagonistic and therefore undesirable as jurors. In significant cases where resources are available, the legal team may conduct a mock jury trial using a representative sample of individuals of similar backgrounds to the potential jury pool to determine how the case will be received by the jury.
Trial Notebook	A trial notebook may be a three-ring binder with tabs for items such as Pleadings, Motions, Law, and Witnesses. Or a trial notebook may be an electronic set of files on a computer or laptop that is taken to court and used for retrieving information needed during the examination of witnesses and the cross-examination of witnesses for the other side.
Continuances	A continuance is a request to reschedule a trial or hearing. When good cause is shown, most continuances are granted. However, courts may not agree to a continuance once a date certain is set on which the case must begin.

REVIEW QUESTIONS AND EXERCISES

1. When does trial preparation begin? Explain fully.
2. What is involved in trial preparation?
3. Why might some of the factual and legal issues not need to be tried?
4. What is meant by *facts*, in a legal sense?
5. What is meant by *legal issues*?
6. What is the difference between claims and legal issues?
7. How might a contrasting fact time line be used by the litigation team?
8. What is the advantage in stipulating to the facts?
9. What question is the court asked to decide on a motion for summary judgment?
10. What advantages are there to presenting stipulated facts to the fact finder?
11. What purposes does a motion for summary judgment serve?
12. Why would a litigant withdraw a claim? What impact will that have on the lawsuit?
13. What is a *pretrial memorandum*?
14. What controls the form and content of the pretrial memorandum?
15. What is a *trial brief*?
16. How is a trial brief different from a pretrial memorandum?
17. What is a *trial notebook*?
18. What is a *subpoena*?
19. Should a friendly witness be served with a subpoena to attend trial? Why or why not?
20. What advice can the paralegal give the client or witness in preparing for trial?
21. What is the purpose of jury investigation?
22. What is a *mock jury trial*? What purposes does it serve?
23. What is a *continuance*?
24. Are continuances easily obtained? On what grounds might a continuance be denied?
25. What is meant by a *date certain*?

BUILDING YOUR PARALEGAL SKILLS

INTERNET AND TECHNOLOGY EXERCISES

1. Can any computer software be used to organize the case for trial?
2. Can text messaging and instant messaging be used as notification systems for witnesses and parties in trial? What are the pros and cons?

CIVIL LITIGATION VIDEO CASE STUDIES

Final Pretrial Conference: Resolving Evidentiary Issues

The trial judge and opposing counsel meet in the judge's chambers for the final conference before trial of the case. The judge needs to decide certain evidentiary issues involving the use of graphic photographs and the use of children as witnesses.

After viewing the video at www.pearsonhighered.com/careersresources, answer the following questions.

1. Is the pretrial conference the appropriate place to make arguments to the judge?
2. Does a pretrial conference eliminate all the surprise for counsel at trial?
3. Does the court always issue evidentiary rulings before the start of the trial? Does such an issuance have an effect on the preparation for trial?

Preparing for Trial: Preparing for Deposition and Trial

A paralegal prepares a nervous witness to have her testimony taken under oath.

After viewing the video at www.pearsonhighered.com/careersresources, answer the following questions.

1. Should the paralegal conduct a mock question and answer session as if it were a deposition? Why or why not?

2. Should the paralegal tell the witness how to testify?
3. What role should the attorney play in witness preparation?
4. Is there a difference in how a witness is prepared for a deposition and for a trial?

Fact or Expert: Resolving Objection in Videotaped Deposition Discussions

The lawyers meet with the trial judge to resolve the issue of whether the plaintiff's doctor, who was called as a fact witness, can be used as an expert witness by the defense without having previously identified the doctor as an expert witness.

After viewing the video at www.pearsonhighered.com/careersresources, answer the following questions.

1. What is the difference in the role of a fact witness and that of an expert witness?
2. What are the qualifications to be an expert witness?
3. Is there a difference in the compensation paid to a fact witness and that paid to an expert witness?

CHAPTER OPENING SCENARIO CASE STUDY

Use the Opening Scenario for this chapter to answer the following questions.

1. What policies and procedures should the offices have regarding the technology that will be used in preparation of the case and in the presentation in court?

2. What procedures should be followed to ensure proper communication between the offices on the case?

COMPREHENSIVE CASE STUDY

SCHOOL BUS–TRUCK ACCIDENT CASE

Review the assigned case study in Appendix 2.

1. Prepare a list of the sections and subsections to be included in a trial notebook for the case study found in Appendix 2. To the extent you have obtained or prepared documents that should be included in the trial notebook, incorporate them.
2. Use the official website for your federal or state court to obtain standard civil jury instructions for motor vehicle accidents.
3. Prepare exhibits for trial. Include a determination as to which exhibits are appropriate for electronic display.
4. Prepare a trial brief on the use of photographic evidence that is graphic in nature and that shows physical injuries sustained by a child in a motor vehicle accident.
5. Prepare subpoenas for witnesses who will be called to testify at trial.

BUILDING YOUR PROFESSIONAL PORTFOLIO AND REFERENCE MANUAL

CIVIL LITIGATION TEAM AT WORK

See page 18 for instructions on Building Your Professional Portfolio.

Policy Manual

1. Create policies and procedures regarding the technology that will be used in preparation of the case and in the presentation in court.
2. Create a procedure to use to place witnesses on call.

Forms

1. Pretrial memorandum form template for your jurisdiction
2. Local judge's standing orders

3. Local civil jury instructions
4. A memo or brochure for clients and witnesses on what to expect at trial

Procedures

Specific standing orders of the trial judges in your local jurisdiction regarding trial

Contacts and Resources

1. Courthouse electronic presentation resource personnel in the trial courtrooms in your local jurisdiction
2. Trial presentation consultants

LEARNING OBJECTIVES

After studying this chapter, you should be able to:

1. Distinguish between evidentiary and non-evidentiary phases of a trial.

2. Describe the early trial proceedings.

3. Describe the presentation-of-evidence phase of a trial and the role of the paralegal in this phase of the trial.

4. Describe the concluding phase of a trial.

CHAPTER 17

Trial

OPENING SCENARIO

The litigation team, with Mr. Saunders as trial counsel and Mr. Benjamin as the second chair, was reviewing the list of potential members of the jury pool that the court had selected to appear that day. The paralegals had obtained the list a few days earlier and had already conducted a number of searches of public records using the Internet. They also performed a Google search to discover any additional information that might be useful. The team had an idea of the type of juror who would be most sympathetic to its case—parents and grandparents of young children. Based on the nature of the cause of the accident, the general opinion was that professional truck drivers would be less sympathetic jurors than people who were accustomed to seeing injured children, such as hospital workers and emergency medical personnel.

The paralegals, Emily and Caitlin, were asked to look after the clients and witnesses, ensuring that they were in the courtroom when needed. From prior experience, the team planned to request that the witnesses not be allowed in the courtroom except when they were testifying. They did not want the children who were their clients and, potentially, their best witnesses to have to listen to all of the other testimony given in the courtroom and become bored while waiting to be called. They therefore intended to advise the court that they would have all the witnesses available in their office across the street from the courthouse and could have any of them available to testify within fifteen to twenty minutes. They thought the court would allow this, as opposed to having the witnesses wait on hard wooden benches outside the courtroom.

The attorneys practiced the opening statement that they intended to make to the jury and felt they had a good case. Mr. Benjamin had spoken the previous week with the clerk of court and had made arrangements for the electronic presentation equipment they would need. To avoid any possibilities of problems, he had duplicated all of the files on three separate laptops—one for each lawyer to use during trial and one as a backup.

OPENING SCENARIO LEARNING OBJECTIVE

Prepare a list of voir dire questions to be used in selecting appropriate members of the jury.

■ INTRODUCTION TO TRIAL PROCEEDINGS

Laypeople think trials are conducted as depicted on prime-time television shows. When faced with an actual trial as participants, witnesses, or jurors, they might be disappointed that the entire case does not unfold and come to a conclusion in an hour. Civil trials, however, are not scripted events controlled by a director, with mistakes and miscues edited out of the final product.

The legal team must be aware of these preconceived notions when planning its trial strategy. If jurors' expectations are not met, they may not be favorably inclined toward the client and the claim or defense presented.

■ PHASES OF CIVIL TRIALS

LEARNING OBJECTIVE 1

Distinguish between evidentiary and non-evidentiary phases of a trial.

evidentiary phase
Phase of the trial where testimony and evidence are presented to the jury or judge.

There are two phases in civil trials. The **evidentiary phase** is where testimony and evidence are presented to the jury or judge. The second is the non-evidentiary phase, which includes everything else that occurs at trial. The **non-evidentiary phase** has two components:

1. early proceedings, such as jury selection, and
2. concluding events, such as jury deliberation.

Jury selection and deliberation are important components of the trial; however, neither is evidentiary in nature. The evidentiary phase takes place between these two non-evidentiary elements.

■ EARLY TRIAL PROCEEDINGS

LEARNING OBJECTIVE 2

Describe the early trial proceedings.

non-evidentiary phase
Phase of trial that includes early proceedings, such as jury selection, and concluding events, such as jury deliberation. The non-evidentiary phase includes everything that is not considered the presentation of evidence at trial.

Before putting that first witness on the stand, the legal team is involved in early proceedings that will set the stage for the evidentiary phase of the trial.

Final Pretrial Conference with Judge

Most judges require a pretrial conference with the trial attorneys. This meeting is independent of any pretrial conference that was conducted days or weeks earlier to discuss and resolve the issues raised in pretrial memoranda. This final meeting, which usually occurs on the morning a trial is set to begin, allows the judge and the attorneys to discuss how the trial will unfold. The judge may advise the amount of available court time in the coming days. The judge might give some final instructions or rulings on jury selection or evidence. The judge may make one final attempt to settle the case. The attorneys might advise of the limited availability of a particular witness and seek cooperation in the order of presenting that witness's testimony. The attorneys may have reached further agreement on facts or law, thus eliminating the need to present that evidence to the jury. The goal of the final pretrial conference is twofold: (1) to facilitate open communication between the judge and the attorneys about how the trial will proceed and (2) to streamline, as much as possible, the trial itself. This list of events, while representative, is neither exclusive nor exhaustive when describing what can take place at the final conference.

Jury Selection

Jury selection is the process by which a group of six or more people is chosen to serve on the jury; the jury will hear a dispute, be instructed in the applicable law, and render a decision. In most jurisdictions, a civil trial jury consists of twelve members plus two **alternate jurors.** The Federal Rules of Civil Procedure permit the size of the jury panel to include as few as six people.

Alternate jurors hear the case with the rest of the jury. In the event one member of the jury becomes ill or, for some other unforeseen reason, is unable to complete service as a juror, the alternate juror will take his or her place. This procedure saves the court from having to declare a **mistrial** and conduct a new trial.

Those eligible to serve on a jury are the residents living within the court's geographic boundary. The larger the geographic boundary, the wider the diversity of individuals in the jury pool available to sit on a jury. For example, Chicago is part of Cook County, Illinois. For the trial court in the state court system, the jury pool comes from Cook County residents only. By contrast, for the United States District Court for the Northern District of Illinois, Eastern Division, the jury comes not only residents of Chicago and Cook County, but also residents of the seven surrounding counties. The result is a greater diversity of men and women available to serve on the jury in the federal trial. Exhibit 17.1 is a map from the U.S. District Court for the Northern District of Illinois depicting the location of the court for the Eastern and Western divisions, as well as the counties from which potential jurors are drawn. The members of the jury pool are drawn from driver's license or voter registration records. Many jurisdictions have shifted to using driver's license registration records because more people are licensed to drive than are registered to vote.

Prior to arriving for jury duty, potential jurors complete and return a questionnaire to the clerk of court. This questionnaire represents the first level of screening of the jury pool. It seeks basic information such as name, age, occupation, and highest level of education. Exhibit 17.2 is the Summons for Jury Service and Juror Qualification Questionnaire used in the United States District Court for the Northern District of Illinois.

On any given day, hundreds of individuals will arrive at the courthouse, anticipating serving on a jury. Generally, groups of twenty to fifty individuals are brought into the courtroom for the next level of screening.

Voir Dire

The screening of jurors is called **voir dire.** The term comes from the French and literally translates as, "to speak the truth." The purpose of conducting voir dire is to determine whether individuals will be able to serve on a jury and render a verdict based solely on the evidence presented at trial and the instructions given by the judge. The questions asked of potential jurors are determined during the

jury selection
Process by which a group of six or more people is chosen to serve on a jury.

alternate jurors
Jurors selected to hear the case with the rest of the jury but who participate in rendering a decision only when another juror is unable to complete the service.

mistrial
Trial ending without a verdict being determined and requiring that a new trial be conducted.

voir dire
Process whereby prospective jurors are asked questions by the judge or attorneys to determine if they would be biased in their decisions.

Exhibit 17.1 Map from the U.S. District Court for the Northern District of Illinois

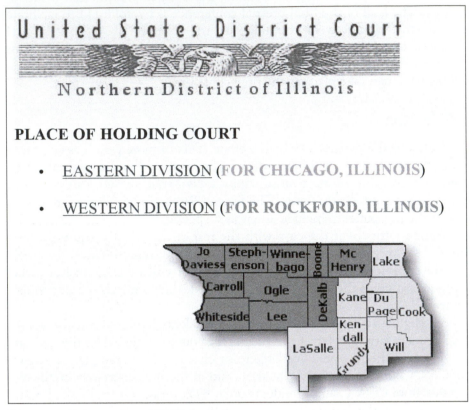

Source: www.ilnd.uscourts.gov/JURY/index.html

pretrial phase, and are often included in the pretrial memorandum or order. The questions are designed to expose any bias or prejudice of the individual that might affect his or her ability to decide the case.

For example, in a medical malpractice lawsuit that involves the diagnosis of and treatment for cancer, members of the jury pool who have had cancer or who work in the health care profession may have a bias. Based upon personal experiences and knowledge, a potential juror may be unable to hear the evidence and render a decision independent of those experiences and that knowledge. In theory, those are exactly the jurors who should not serve on the jury. In reality, however, those are exactly the jurors one of the parties *does* want to serve because of a perceived favorable bias. Part of the trial strategy is attempting to get favorable jurors selected. Exhibit 17.3 shows some questions that may be asked of potential jurors in voir dire.

How the voir dire is conducted is entirely at the judge's discretion. Some judges ask the voir dire questions; others allow the attorneys to ask the questions.

The manner in which voir dire will be conducted is resolved in the pretrial conference. The questions to be used are also discussed during the conference. In some instances, a panel of 24 potential jurors will be brought into the courtroom and seated in the public seating area. When questions are directed to a large panel of 12 or more potential jurors, most questions can be answered with a "yes" or "no" response. In some instances, the judge will ask the questions; this allows the attorneys to observe and record the responses of the potential

Exhibit 17.2 Summons for Jury Service and Juror Qualification Questionnaire Used in the United States District Court for the Northern District of Illinois

From:	**UNITED STATES DISTRICT COURT** **NORTHERN DISTRICT OF ILLINOIS** **219 SOUTH DEARBORN STREET, ROOM 250** **CHICAGO, ILLINOIS 60604**	FOR OFFICIAL USE ONLY 1
TO:	ARE YOUR NAME AND PERMANENT ADDRESS CORRECT? YES NO IF "NO", MAKE CORRECTIONS HERE. ☐ ☐	JUROR PARTICIPANT NUMBER:

SUMMONS FOR JURY SERVICE

PLEASE BRING THIS FORM WITH YOU ON YOUR 1ST DAY

YOU ARE HEREBY SUMMONED FOR A TWO WEEK TERM OF JURY SERVICE BEGINNING ON:

▶

PLEASE READ THE SUPPLEMENTAL INFORMATION SHEET

You must call 1-800-572-4210 after 5:00 p.m. on
or all day Saturday or Sunday to determine if you are required to appear. **If your juror participant number is not ordered to appear, you must continue to call the 1-800 number each night after 5:00 p.m. throughout the two week term. Please have your summons handy when placing this call.** (See item #2 below for additional & important call-in instructions.)

IMPORTANT INSTRUCTIONS

1 **HARDSHIP EXCUSE**	If the jury term for which you are summoned will result in undue or extreme inconvenience because of illness in your family or a similar serious problem, and you want to ask for a temporary excuse, you must notify the Clerk of Court immediately in writing upon receipt of this summons or immediately upon learning of any such serious problem which arises before your appearance date. A request for temporary excuse must be made in writing USING THE ENCLOSED POSTAGE PAID ENVELOPE or using the address at the top of this form. Include a statement of the facts relating to the hardship and the earliest date in the near future when you can serve. If you fail to notify the Court immediately of a hardship and ask for a temporary hardship excuse when you report for jury duty, you will not be paid an attendance fee or travel allowance if you are excused or deferred.
2 **RECORDED MESSAGE**	This Court uses an automated telephone system to advise jurors if they are expected to serve, are postponed or excused. Upon receipt of your juror information form, your status will be updated in this system. To receive information regarding your status, call 1-800-572-4210 before the summons date listed above. Please allow a week for delivery and processing. The system will ask you to enter your nine digit participant number located to the right of your name on this form. The system does not take messages. The 1-800 number functions only from the 224, 312, 630, 708, 773, 815, and 847 area codes. Please dial 1-800-572-4210 after 5:00 p.m. on the evening of the last work day before the day you are to appear.
3 **PENALTY**	Unless you receive a notice from this Court granting a requested temporary excuse, or unless the Court notifies you in writing or by phone to report at a different time, you must attend as directed in this summons. Failure to obey this summons may be punishable by fine and/or imprisonment.
4 **ATTENDANCE FEE/MILEAGE**	Jurors will receive a daily attendance fee of $40.00 plus mileage. U.S. Government employees, instead of the attendance fee, will receive their regular pay without deduction from authorized leave.

PLEASE COMPLETE THE JUROR INFORMATION FORM ENCLOSED AND RETURN IT AT ONCE IN THE POSTAGE-PAID ENVELOPE EVEN IF YOU ARE REQUESTING AN EXCUSE

(continued)

Exhibit 17.2 (continued)

United States District Court

JUROR ID

Important Directions for Marking Answers & Signing This Form Use A No. 2 Pencil

USE NO. 2 PENCIL ONLY

- Do not use ink or ballpoint
- Fill out form on hard surface
- Make heavy black marks that fill in the circle completely
- Erase any changes completely
- Make no stray marks
- Do not write in margins nor in official use only areas

Right ●
Wrong ⊗

FOR OFFICIAL USE Jurors Please Do Not Write In This Space

Q ○
X ○
E ○
D ○

TO: If your name and permanent address are not correct, please make corrections here.

Provide Your Phone Number(s)
Home   Work (Incl. extension)
County You Now Live In
Area Code   Number   Area Code   Number & Ext.

JUROR QUALIFICATION QUESTIONNAIRE
Please Read Letter On Other Side Before Completing

If another person fills out the form, please indicate that person's name, address and reason why in the "Remarks" section.

Fill In Completely Your Response To Each Question.

Yes / No

1. Are you a citizen of the United States? ○ ○

2. Are you 18 years of age or older? Yes / No ○ ○
Date of Birth: Give your age _____
Month _____ Day _____ Year _____

3. Has your primary residence for the past year been in this state? Yes / No ○ ○
If "No", show under Remarks on reverse the names of other counties or states of primary residence during the past year and show dates.   in the same county? Yes / No ○ ○

4. Do you read, write, speak and understand the English language? Yes / No ○ ○

If your answer to No. 5 or 6 is "Yes" please see notes to Questions 5 and 6 on reverse side.

5. Are any charges now pending against you for a violation of state or federal law punishable by imprisonment for more than one year? Yes / No ○ ○

6. Have you ever been convicted, either by your guilty or nolo contendere plea or by a court or jury trial, of a state or federal crime for which punishment could have been more than one year in prison? Yes / No ○ ○

7. (If "Yes"), Were your civil rights restored? (If "Yes", explain on the reverse side) Yes / No ○ ○

8. Do you have any physical or mental disability that would interfere with or prevent you from serving as a juror? (If "Yes", please see notes to Question 8 on reverse side). Yes / No ○ ○

9. ——— EXEMPTIONS ———
Are you employed on a full time basis as a:

Public official of the United States, state, or local government who is elected to public office or directly appointed by one elected to office Yes / No ○ ○

Member of any governmental police or regular fire dept. (not including volunteer or non-governmental departments) Yes / No ○ ○

Member in active service of the armed forces of the United States. Yes / No ○ ○

10. ——— RACE/ETHNICITY ———
a. To assist in ensuring that all people are represented on juries, please fill in completely one or more circles which describe you. (See note on reverse side.) Nothing disclosed will affect your selection for jury service.
○ Black/African American ○ Asian ○ American Indian/Alaska Native
○ White ○ Native Hawaiian/Pacific Islander
○ Other (specify)
b. Are you Hispanic or Latino? Yes ○ No ○

11. ——— SEX ———
Male ○
Female ○

12. ——— OCCUPATION (See reverse side) ———
Are you now employed? Yes ○ No ○
Are you a salaried employee of the U.S. gov't? Yes ○ No ○
Your Usual Occupation, Trade, Or Business
Your Employer's Name
Business Or Employer's Address

13. ——— EDUCATION ———
Show the extent of your education above grade school   Yes No
High school/ GED equivalent ○ ○
Trade/Vocational school ○ ○
Above high school ○ ○

14. **Grounds For Requesting Excuse** (see Notes to Question 14 on other side).

This section describes certain categories of persons who may be excused from service as a juror. If you are a person in one of these categories listed below and you wish to be excused, fill in completely the circle for the number of your category listed below here:

Or, if you wish to serve, do not show anything here. Persons showing a category of excuse which requires more information must give it on the other side under "Remarks".

1 ○   2 ○
3 ○   4 ○
5 ○   6 ○
7 ○   8 ○
9 ○   10 ○

FOR OFFICIAL USE

15. MARITAL STATUS: ○ Single ○ Married ○ Widowed ○ Separated or Divorced
16. I declare under penalty of perjury that all answers are true to the best of my knowledge and belief

SIGN HERE ▶ _____   Date _____

If your address changes after you have returned the questionnaire, please notify the court promptly by letter or post card, addressing it to **"Attention: Jury Administrator."**

Source: http://www.uscourts.gov/uscourts/FormsAndFees/Forms/AO205.pdf

jurors. In other courtrooms, the judge may prefer that the attorneys ask some or all of the questions. In that event, the paralegal assisting at trial is essential to the legal team's jury selection process. The paralegal will be responsible for observing and recording the responses of the potential jurors. To assist in that process, the legal team typically uses a jury chart to record information about the jury pool. One method involves preparing a chart with twelve blocks, each representing a seat in the jury box, such as the one that appears in Exhibit 17.4. A similar chart can be arranged for large pools of 24 potential jurors. Questions

Exhibit 17.3 Sample Voir Dire Questions

Sample Questions for Voir Dire

1. The parties in this lawsuit are Joan Smith and William Doe. They are seated at the counsel tables in front of you. If you know either Ms. Smith or Mr. Doe, please raise your hand.

2. The attorneys who will be presenting evidence to you in this case are Cary Moritz and Elaine Martin. If you know either of these attorneys, kindly raise your hand.

3. This lawsuit involves a claim about cancer. Do you have cancer? Have you been treated for cancer? Do you have a close family member who currently has cancer or was treated for cancer in the past?

4. Are you a doctor? Do you work in a health-care profession?

are asked and potential jurors raise their hands if their response is "yes." Using the chart, the paralegal or attorney can quickly record the question number to indicate an affirmative response by a potential juror seated in a particular spot. When a juror answers "yes," the judge or one of the attorneys may question the juror directly on the matter. This questioning can take place in the presence of the entire panel, or the panel can be dismissed and the individual juror questioned. Suppose juror no. 3 responds "yes" to the question about a family member having cancer. The judge may ask what relation, the type of cancer, and the outcome of the treatment. The answers of juror no. 3 will indicate whether the juror is potentially biased because of his life experience. A juror whose spouse died from cancer will have stronger feelings and more personal knowledge than a juror whose adult cousin was treated for and survived a form of cancer in childhood. The judge may question the juror further as to whether that life experience will impact his ability to impartially hear and decide the dispute.

At the conclusion of questioning, the lawyers must decide whether to accept the person as a member of the jury. Individuals can be rejected for jury service based on a **challenge for cause.** Or an attorney can make a strategic decision that a juror is undesirable by making a **peremptory challenge.** A potential juror can be challenged for cause when his answers to voir dire questions indicate bias. There is no limit on the number of jurors who can be stricken from the jury for cause. In a medical malpractice case, one or both of the attorneys may request that juror no. 3 be stricken for cause. The judge will

challenge for cause
A potential juror may be struck from the jury when his answers to voir dire questions indicate bias.

peremptory challenge
A potential juror may be struck from the jury without the attorney stating a reason.

Exhibit 17.4 Jury Chart for Recording Responses of Potential Jurors during Voir Dire

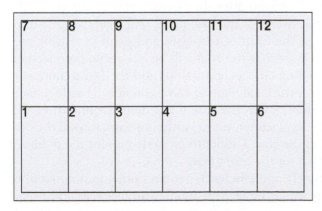

rule on the request: "Yes" means the juror is stricken, and "no" means the juror remains eligible to serve on the jury.

The federal rules permit each side three (3) peremptory challenges, which allow the attorney to strike a potential juror at his discretion without stating a reason. At the pretrial conference, the parties may request additional peremptory challenges because of multiple defendants, a large amount of pretrial publicity, or a complex case. The judge has discretion to increase the number of peremptory challenges.

Jurors who are not stricken for cause or on a peremptory challenge are **seated,** or selected, for jury service. Those potential jurors who are stricken are excused, and another group is brought to the courtroom for the voir dire process to begin again. The process continues until twelve suitable jurors are selected. The jury panel, with alternates, is then seated. Members of the jury are sworn to serve to the best of their abilities.

seated
Term used to describe a juror who has been selected to serve on a jury.

Jury Charge

The judge instructs the panel on how the trial will proceed and how jurors should conduct themselves. These instructions to the jury are called the **jury charge.** Instructions may include a direction to avoid looking at newspaper, television, or other media accounts of the trial, and may also describe the operation of the courtroom. Judges advise the jurors that they must not discuss the case among themselves and should not rush to make a decision about the dispute until they have heard all the evidence.

jury charge
Instructions to the jury given by the judge at the beginning of trial to describe how the trial will be conducted or at the end of the trial to inform of the law to be applied in the case.

Opening Statements

The final event to occur before the evidentiary phase begins is the **opening statements** of the attorneys. Opening statements are the first opportunity for the attorneys to address the jury. First impressions count and the opening statement can be crucial. The purpose of the opening statement is to give the jury a brief synopsis of the client's case. This introduction is also designed to get the jurors' attention, encourage their interest in the trial, and establish rapport and credibility. However, the opening statements must be limited to a recitation of the facts. Emotional pleas to tug at the heartstrings of the jury cannot be part of the opening statement. Ideally, the opening statement should be like a movie preview—providing enough information to get the jury interested in the client's story that they are about to hear.

opening statements
The first opportunity for the attorneys to address the jury and describe the nature of the lawsuit.

■ PRESENTATION OF EVIDENCE

LEARNING OBJECTIVE 3
Describe the presentation-of-evidence phase of a trial and the role of the paralegal in this phase of the trial.

The evidentiary phase of the trial begins after the opening statements are made. Whether because of novels, television, or movies, jurors will likely already have an idea of how the evidence in the form of witnesses and exhibits will be presented. They are also likely to hope that the trial will be like those portrayed on television—with dramatic, grueling cross-examinations and the last-minute witness who saves the day. Thus, for the legal team, it can be an uphill battle to fight for the jury's attention, particularly when the case is not dramatic and there will be no last-minute witness. The legal team must nevertheless work toward the best presentation of the evidence in the case. Failure to properly present the merits of the case might result in a verdict for the other side.

Presenting the case effectively and efficiently requires organization. Neither judges nor jurors want to wait while the lawyers shuffle through files and papers looking for exhibits; request delays to wait for a witness to arrive in court to testify; or repair or replace a malfunctioning video player. Delays and technical problems can create a negative view that may cause the jury to not appreciate the merits of the case. However, these distractions during the presentation of the client's case can be avoided with careful planning, and the judge's and jury's impatience resulting from an occasional delay can be diminished with a sincere apology.

Plaintiff's Case-in-Chief

In civil cases, the plaintiff presents his or her case first. The plaintiff's **case-in-chief** is presented with the testimony of the plaintiff, fact and expert witnesses, and exhibits. In the civil case, the plaintiff has the **burden of proof** to establish the existence of the **elements of a cause of action.** The plaintiff must prove each element of the cause of action by a **preponderance of the evidence.** A preponderance of the evidence is that amount of proof that tips the scales of justice ever so slightly in one direction or the other. This is in contrast to the prosecution's burden of proof in a criminal matter, which is beyond a reasonable doubt, a much higher standard.

For example, in a negligence action, each element of the cause of action of negligence must be proved by the preponderance-of-evidence standard—(1) that a duty of care existed; (2) that the defendant failed to adhere that duty; (3) that the defendant's failure to adhere to the duty of care was the cause of the accident; and (4) that the plaintiff suffered damages as a result of the accident.

Direct Examination

The presentation of evidence starts with the **direct examination** of each of the plaintiff's witnesses. Direct examination refers to questions addressed to a witness by the attorney who has called that witness to testify on behalf of his client. In a medical malpractice action, witnesses for the plaintiff's case-in-chief might include the plaintiff, the physicians who treated the plaintiff and/or diagnosed the earlier malpractice, family members who cared for the plaintiff, and an economist, who might testify about the plaintiff's lost earnings and earning capacity.

An important strategic decision that the trial counsel must make is the order in which witnesses are called. This decision is made based on the nature of the testimony, timing and the availability of the witness, or some other strategy. Some lawyers base their choice on the belief that most people are more likely to remember either what they heard first or what they heard last. Depending on the view held by trial counsel, the most persuasive witness might therefore be placed on the witness stand first or last. In a medical malpractice action, a physician—whether the treating physician or an expert—may be used for the purpose of educating the jury. An early explanation of the medical condition and terminology, if this information is vital to jurors' understanding of the case, is an effective way to gain the confidence of the jury for the remainder of the trial. The final witness for the plaintiff's case-in-chief may be someone who can leave a lasting impression on the jury. Often that means the plaintiff will be the last to testify so that the emotional impact of the plaintiff's description of the incident, the injuries sustained, and the recovery can have its greatest effect on the jury. If, however, the attorney believes the case can still be settled before it is decided by the jury, trial counsel may have the strongest witness to sway the jury testify first to show the other side why it should make a settlement offer before the case proceeds any further. There are many strategies and beliefs that determine how a lawyer will try the case. For

case-in-chief
The portion of the trial where one side presents all of its evidence to the jury through direct and cross-examination.

burden of proof
Level of proof required to establish an entitlement to recovery.

elements of a cause of action
The components of a legal claim that must be established by the burden of proof.

preponderance of the evidence
The burden of proof in most civil litigation cases; the amount of proof that tips the scales of justice ever so slightly in one direction or the other.

direct examination
Questions addressed to a witness by the attorney who has called that witness to testify on behalf of his client.

example, some lawyers put their most important witnesses on the stand only in the morning in the belief that after lunch, most people are tired and tend to be less attentive than earlier in the day and are thus less likely to pay attention.

Cross-Examination

cross-examination
Opportunity of defense (opposing) counsel to question a witness after the direct examination of the witness.

Following each witness's direct examination, he or she will be subject to **cross-examination.** Cross-examination is the opportunity for the defense counsel to question a witness after the direct examination of the witness. The purpose of cross-examination is to test or challenge what the witness has said. This testing of testimony is a key component of the adversarial system. Truthful testimony of witnesses will withstand testing by the opponent. The questions asked on cross-examination are designed to **impeach the credibility** of the witness. The goal of impeachment is to convince the jury that what the witness just testified to on direct examination should not be trusted or believed. For example, questions might reveal the witness's desire to help the plaintiff or the existence of a special relationship between the plaintiff and the witness. Testimony might show that the witness is forgetful, or that the witness was not positioned to be able to clearly observe the accident. Prior recorded deposition testimony of a witness is also used to impeach when the witness says something different at trial.

impeach the credibility
Questioning the witness on cross-examination to demonstrate to the jury that the witness is not reliable.

Redirect Examination

rehabilitate
During redirect examination, the attorney will ask questions to allow the witness to explain her answers on cross-examination.

redirect examination
After cross-examination, the counsel who originally called the witness on direct examination may ask the witness additional questions.

Following cross-examination, the counsel who originally called the witness on direct examination has an opportunity to **rehabilitate** the witness by asking questions on **redirect examination.** In redirect examination, an effort is made to ask questions that, when answered, will provide a plausible reason for the witness's faulty memory. A typical question will give the witness a chance to explain, for example, that the special relationship with the plaintiff would not cause the witness' testimony to be untruthful. It is important to note that the scope of questions permitted on redirect examination is severely limited and that it is not a second chance for the witness to add new testimony. Rather, it is an opportunity to clarify what was previously asked and answered on cross-examination.

Recross Examination

recross examination
Permits opposing counsel to again challenge the credibility of the witness but only as to the matters questioned on redirect examination.

Recross examination permits opposing counsel to again challenge the credibility of the witness but only as to matters questioned on redirect examination.

Objections

objections
The method by which an attorney orally advises the court that the evidence being presented is not admissible.

overruled
A judge's ruling on an objection that the evidence challenged is admissible.

sustained
A judge's ruling on an objection that the evidence challenged is not admissible.

A witness's testimony is rarely able to be given without interruption. The testimony, or an exhibit that is offered, may not be admissible because it fails to satisfy the requirement of admissibility or is offered in violation of a preexisting ruling on admissibility made by the court as part of the pretrial decisions. The rules of evidence are designed to ensure that the information presented to the jury for consideration is real, reliable, and relevant to the resolution of the dispute. When the testimony or evidence fails to satisfy those requirements, the opposing attorney will object to its admission into evidence. In many courtrooms, the judge will require the attorney to state the reasons for the **objection,** occasionally including the rule number from the rules of evidence. The judge makes a ruling on the objection. When the judge does not believe the objection is valid, he or she states that the objection is **overruled;** the witness may then answer or the exhibit is then admitted as evidence, and the testimony may continue. When the testimony violates the rules of evidence and may not be presented, the judge states the objection is **sustained.**

Motion for Directed Verdict

At the conclusion of the plaintiff's case-in-chief, the plaintiff will **rest** his case. Both plaintiff and defendant may make an oral **motion for directed verdict.** A motion for directed verdict is made when one party believes the other has failed to meet its burden of proof. Basically, the plaintiff is saying that he has met the burden of proving the elements of his cause of action by a preponderance of the evidence, and the defendant has no defense. The defendant makes the argument that the plaintiff failed to meet the burden of proof or failed to prove a necessary element of the case. The purpose of these motions is to conclude the trial.

Defendant's Case-in-Chief

The next phase of the trial is the defendant's case-in-chief. The defendant must establish any defenses raised in the answer to the complaint by the same preponderance of the evidence, tipping the scales of justice slightly in his favor. If the defendant asserts a counterclaim against the plaintiff, it is during the defendant's case-in-chief that the elements of that cause of action are presented.

The defendant's case-in-chief is presented in the same manner as the plaintiff's case-in-chief: direct examination, cross-examination, redirect and recross, and motions for directed verdict at the conclusion of the presentation of the defense case.

Direct examination is conducted by defense counsel of defense witnesses. Each of those defense witnesses will be subject to cross-examination by the opposing (plaintiff's) counsel. Defense counsel will have an opportunity to rehabilitate the defense witnesses through redirect examination, which is followed by recross by the plaintiff's counsel. The testimony and evidence presented are subject to the same objections related to the admissibility of evidence as the plaintiff's. At the conclusion of the defendant's case-in-chief, both sides may make an oral motion for directed verdict. In either case, the parties are asking the judge to enter judgment in their favor as a matter of law. For the plaintiff, the motion for directed verdict says the defendant has failed to set out any defenses to liability and/or has failed to prove the elements of the counterclaim asserted. For the defendant, the motion asserts that now that the defense side of the dispute has been told, it is clear the plaintiff is not entitled to relief.

Rebuttal

The **rebuttal** phase of the trial gives the plaintiff the chance to address or respond to information contained in the defendant's case-in-chief. During the plaintiff's case-in-chief, evidence is presented to support the claims for relief. However, evidence is not presented in anticipation of what the defense might say—that would confuse the jury. Instead, the plaintiff presents the case, and the defendant challenges the plaintiff's witnesses on cross-examination. Through the presentation of the defendant's case-in-chief, the defense presents its version of the facts and claims against the plaintiff. The plaintiff may then rebut the defendant's presentation of evidence. As in redirect and recross, the scope of questions on rebuttal is limited to those new items brought out in the defendant's case-in-chief that the plaintiff has not previously addressed. For example, in a medical malpractice case, the defendant might claim that the plaintiff failed to participate in post-operative physical therapy and that that failure, rather than something the physician did, was the cause of her injury. In rebuttal, the plaintiff might present expert testimony to show that physical therapy would have had no impact on the plaintiff's recovery from the surgical procedure.

rest
The party has concluded the presentation of its case-in-chief.

motion for directed verdict
Motion made at the conclusion of a party's case-in-chief that states that the other side has failed to meet its burden of proof.

rebuttal
Phase of the trial that gives the plaintiff the chance to address or respond to information contained in the defendant's case-in-chief.

Sur Rebuttal

Sur rebuttal allows the defense to respond to the evidence presented by the plaintiff during rebuttal. The evidence presented is limited to that which directly addresses the claims made by the plaintiff in rebuttal and is not an opportunity for the defense to present the same evidence again, just in a different way. Only new evidence or testimony that responds to the rebuttal is permitted. At the conclusion of rebuttal and sur rebuttal, the parties may again make motions for directed verdict.

Sidebars and Conferences with the Judge

During trial, the judge may wish to confer with the attorneys. The purpose of these conferences can vary; anything from scheduling an afternoon recess to discussing the admissibility of an exhibit or the form of jury instructions can take place. Sometimes one or both of the attorneys will request the conference. When these conferences take place in the courtroom with the jury seated in the jury box, they are called **sidebar conferences.** This term refers to the fact that the conference takes place at the judge's bench in hushed or whispered voices so the jury cannot hear what is being said. Because sidebar conferences are distracting, to the extent possible, they should be avoided. In addition, the jury might resent the sidebar and think information important to the case and their deliberation is being withheld. The better approach is for these conferences to take place when the jury is dismissed in the ordinary course of the trial proceedings (for their mid-morning, lunch, mid-afternoon, or end-of-day break). In that scenario, the attorneys and the judge remain in the courtroom to discuss and resolve the issue, and the jury is not distracted.

How the Paralegal Can Assist in the Presentation of Evidence

Because so much of what happens at trial is the function of the trial attorney, paralegals sometimes doubt they can make a contribution. However, the paralegal can provide invaluable assistance at trial, and this is particularly true in the evidentiary phase. Much of what the paralegal does at trial is an extension of trial preparation. To the extent the paralegal manages this aspect of the trial, the attorney can focus on the presentation of evidence.

Paralegals are typically responsible for organizing exhibits for presentation at trial and communicating with witnesses about when they need to be at the courthouse to testify. Another task of the paralegal is to be sure the exhibits are available when the attorney wants them. This includes having the correct number of copies, having the exhibits premarked if required by the judge, and anticipating when the attorney will ask for the exhibits. Seeing the paralegal shuffling through files or papers on counsel's table gives the jury the wrong impression about the legal team. Additionally, the paralegal may be responsible for keeping an exhibit list indicating that an exhibit has been offered and received into evidence. Attorneys have been known to be so preoccupied with the direct and cross-examination of witnesses that they neglect to make a motion to have the exhibits received into evidence. As a result, the exhibits are not part of the record of the proceedings, and the jury is unable to consider them in their deliberations.

During trial preparation, paralegals frequently review deposition transcripts and prepare digests. Thus, paralegals are very familiar with the deposition testimony of witnesses. If inconsistent testimony is offered at trial, paralegals will notice it and will be able to pinpoint the deposition testimony for the attorney. This is a vital role in cross-examination.

Paralegals assisting at trial also serve as watchful eyes. They observe and report to the attorney what is happening in the courtroom. When the attorney is focused on the cross-examination of a witness, the paralegal is in a position to observe the jury for their reactions to testimony and body language. Sometimes the paralegal may observe and report that the judge was napping during the afternoon session. While this seems like trivial information, it is not. It tells the attorney about the judge's level of interest, which can impact the jury. It may change the way the attorney conducts the next portion of the trial.

Paralegals are often asked to take notes of what is taking place at trial. This could include notes about the witness testimony, objections on evidence and rulings by the judge, and conferences that take place while the jury is out of the courtroom. The goal here is to provide another set of eyes and ears to observe while the attorney focuses on examination of a witness or argument over a legal issue.

The paralegal may also be expected to be responsible for the electronic presentation equipment or material, including laptop computers or display equipment. The paralegal must determine *before* trial if the assigned courtroom is equipped electronically. When the courtroom is not equipped with the necessary electronics, the paralegal must be certain the appropriate equipment is available when needed and that it is operational.

■ CONCLUSION OF TRIAL

The third and final phase of the trial involves the concluding activities—the closing arguments, the jury charge and deliberations, and the entry of a verdict. No evidence is presented during the concluding phase of the trial. This phase, which brings the trial to its conclusion, can be dramatic and can significantly impact the outcome of the case.

LEARNING OBJECTIVE 4
Describe the concluding phase of a trial.

Closing Arguments

Closing arguments are the last opportunity for the attorneys to address the jury. Each attorney will have the chance to sum up his client's case and persuade the jury to decide in his client's favor. Once again, because of the influence of television and movies, members of the jury are likely to expect the closing argument to be thrilling, direct, and brief.

closing arguments
The last opportunity for the attorneys to address the jury, sum up their client's case, and persuade the jury to decide in their client's favor.

> **PRACTICE TIP**
>
> It is important to note that the opening is a statement and the closing is an argument. When making the opening statement to the jury, the facts must be shared in a neutral way so as to avoid creating a bias before the jury hears the testimony and receives the evidence. When making the closing argument, attorneys seek to argue the merits of the case and why the jury should decide in their client's favor.

Attorneys may seek the paralegal's assistance in developing a strong closing argument. Paralegals can serve as a sounding board—listening and providing comments to help the attorney make his argument more direct. Paralegals can also help by reminding the attorney of the reactions the jury displayed during the trial.

Jury Instructions

jury instructions (charge)
Instructions given by the judge to the jury informing them of the law to be applied in the case.

The next element is the judge instructing the jury on the law, called the **jury instructions,** or jury charge, such as that shown in Exhibit 17.5. At this point, all of the evidence has been received and the attorneys have each made one last plea on behalf of their clients. Now the judge instructs the jury in the law that controls the case. The jury instructions usually include an explanation of the burden of proof, the specific cause of action and its individual elements, and whether the verdict must be unanimous or a majority vote.

The jury instructions are generally agreed to by the attorneys and the judge during the pretrial activities. In many instances, proposed jury instructions are included in the pretrial memorandum. Prior to giving the jury the instructions, the judge and attorneys will meet again to review the instructions the judge intends to give. The goal is to make certain that no error is made in the law in which the jury will be instructed. If the instructions are incorrect, the jury's verdict may be meaningless.

Jury Deliberations

jury deliberations
Process wherein the jury meets to discuss and reach a decision on the case.

Having heard all the evidence and been instructed in the law, the jury is ready to begin its **jury deliberations.** Jurors are sent from the courtroom to a room to deliberate. They then select a foreperson to oversee the deliberation process, and the jurors discuss the evidence and vote on an outcome. The jury is also permitted to send written questions to the judge during its deliberative process. These questions may request that a portion of testimony be read back to them or that the judge explain a law. Usually the jury will return to the courtroom for the court stenographer to read back testimony or for the judge to provide additional instruction in the law. The deliberations of the jury are concluded when they determine whether the defendant is liable to the plaintiff, and, if so the damages to which the plaintiff is entitled.

Jury Verdict

jury verdict
Decision reached by the jury that concludes the case.

Deliberations of the jury continue until it reaches a verdict. The **jury verdict** is the decision the jury reaches to conclude the case. In criminal trials, the jury will rule that the defendant is "guilty" or "not guilty." In civil trials, the jury will

Exhibit 17.5 Sample Jury Instructions in a Negligence Case

1.01 FUNCTIONS OF THE COURT AND THE JURY

Members of the jury, you have seen and heard all the evidence and arguments of the attorneys. Now I will instruct you on the law.

You have two duties as a jury. Your first duty is to decide the facts from the evidence in the case. This is your job, and yours alone.

Your second duty is to apply the law that I give you to the facts. You must follow these instructions, even if you disagree with them. Each of the instructions is important, and you must follow all of them.

Perform these duties fairly and impartially. [Do not allow (sympathy/prejudice /fear/public opinion) to influence you.] [You should not be influenced by any person's race, color, religion, national ancestry, or sex.]

Nothing I say now, and nothing I said or did during the trial, is meant to indicate any opinion on my part about what the facts are or about what your verdict should be.

Source: Pattern Civil Jury Instructions for the Seventh Circuit.

find the defendant "liable to the plaintiff for her injuries" or that the defendant "breached the contract." The verdict is announced orally in court and usually is read from the jury verdict slip by the jury foreman.

Verdict Slip

One of the important instructions the jury is given is on the use of the jury **verdict slip.** A jury verdict slip is a written document that asks the jury to answer specific questions about its decision. The verdict slip usually follows a logical progression; for example, finding a duty of care existed and was breached, and then calculating an award of damages. Exhibit 17.6 shows a jury verdict slip for a personal injury case.

verdict slip

A written document that asks the jury to answer specific questions about its decision.

Exhibit 17.6 Jury Verdict Slip for a Personal Injury Case

UNITED STATES DISTRICT COURT - NORTHERN DISTRICT OF NEW YORK

B.K., a minor by her	:	No.: _____
Parents and Guardians,		
Janice Knowles and	:	
Seven Knowles, Plaintiff	:	Civil Action – Negligence
v.		
Ronald Clemmons,	:	Jury Trial Demanded
Lower Council School District,		
Bud Smith, and	:	
Ace Trucking Company,		Attorney ID No. 124987
Defendants		

JURY VERDICT SLIP

On the First Count

1. Do you find that the Defendant Clemmons breached the duty to operate his vehicle in accordance with the rules controlling traffic on the roads of the State of New York?
   ____ Yes   ____ No

2. Do you find that Defendant Clemmons breach of the duty of care to operate his vehicle in accordance with the rules controlling traffic resulted in an accident?
   ____ Yes   ____ No

3. If you answered Yes to number 2 above, do you find that the Plaintiff was injured as a result of the accident?
   ____ Yes   ____ No

4. Do you find that action or inaction of the Plaintiff was a cause of her injury?
   ____ Yes   ____ No

5. If you answered YES to question 4 please determine the percentage of liability.
   ____ % to Plaintiff
   ____ % to Defendant

Please assess a dollar value as to the damages sustained by the Plaintiff.
$_____

After announcing the verdict, the work of the jury is complete. Members of the jury are then traditionally thanked by the judge for their service and excused from the courtroom. Many lawyers will attempt to speak with the jurors after the verdict, wanting to know why the jurors ruled as they did, and also hoping to obtain feedback on their presentation of the case.

Posttrial Motions

posttrial motions
Motions made orally asking the judge to overturn the verdict of the jury.

Even though the announcement of the verdict concludes the trial for the members of the jury, the attorneys may not be finished. The attorneys may make **posttrial motions** asking the judge to overturn the verdict of the jury. The attorneys may argue that the evidence presented does not support the verdict. They may also argue that the judge made a mistake in the legal instructions given to the jury.

Entry of Judgment

entry of judgment
Taking the verdict announced by the jury and converting it to a legally enforceable judgment.

The final component of trial is the **entry of judgment** by the judge; that is, taking the verdict announced by the jury and converting it to a legally enforceable judgment. This happens when the judge states, for example, "Judgment entered in favor of the plaintiff and against the defendant in the sum of $300,000." However, in addition to the verbal statement, the judgment must also be placed in the written record of the docket entries maintained in the clerk's office.

CONCEPT REVIEW AND REINFORCEMENT

KEY TERMS

evidentiary phase   406
non-evidentiary phase   406
jury selection   407
alternate juror   407
mistrial   407
voir dire   407
challenge for cause   411
peremptory challenge   411
seated   412
jury charge   412
opening statement   412
case-in-chief   413
burden of proof   413

elements of a cause of action   413
preponderance of the
   evidence   413
direct examination   413
cross-examination   414
impeach the credibility   414
rehabilitate   414
redirect examination   414
recross examination   414
objections   414
overruled   414
sustained   414
rest   415

motion for directed
   verdict   415
rebuttal   415
sur rebuttal   416
sidebar conference   416
closing arguments   417
jury instructions
   (charge)   418
jury deliberations   418
jury verdict   418
verdict slip   419
posttrial motions   420
entry of judgment   420

CHAPTER SUMMARY

TRIAL

Introduction to Trial Proceedings	Civil trials can be divided into the evidentiary phase of the trial, where testimony and evidence are presented, and the non-evidentiary phase, which includes everything else, such as the early proceedings of jury selection and the concluding events of jury deliberation.
Early Trial Proceedings	Typically, a pretrial conference is held before the start of the trial to resolve basic housekeeping issues, including the court schedule and how it chooses to proceed with the various procedural steps.
	Before the beginning of the trial, the jury is selected from a pool of prospective jurors drawn from voter registration and motor vehicle license lists within the court's geographic boundaries. There may be as few as six or as many as twelve jurors; alternate jurors are selected in case one of the regular jurors becomes ill or cannot continue his or her jury service.
	The process for questioning the jurors to determine their suitability to hear the case is called voir dire. The questioning may be done by the court or by the attorneys. Jurors who demonstrate a bias may be excused for cause by the court. Each attorney is given an opportunity to exclude jurors without giving a reason using peremptory challenges, which are limited in number.
	Once a jury has been selected, the court instructs them about their obligations as jurors and explains how the case will proceed; this is called a jury charge.
	Opening statements of the attorneys addressed to the jury are not considered evidence in this part of the non-evidentiary phase of the trial.
Presentation of Evidence	The presentation of evidence begins the evidentiary phase of the trial. The plaintiff in a civil case has the burden of proof and is first in presenting his case, known as the case-in-chief.
	In a civil case, the burden of proof is proof by a preponderance of the evidence, which is that amount of proof that tips the scale slightly to one side or the other, unlike the proof that is required in a criminal case, which is proof beyond a reasonable doubt.
	The presentation of one's case by questioning witnesses is called direct examination. On completion of the direct examination, the opposing party is given the opportunity to cross-examine the witness for the purpose of impeachment or to raise questions of credibility or accuracy. Questions asked on cross-examination are limited to areas covered during the direct examination.
	Redirect examination gives the plaintiff's counsel an opportunity to rehabilitate the witness she originally called by asking additional questions based on those asked during cross-examination. New questions or new areas of inquiry may not be raised during redirect examination.
	Opposing counsel may then use recross examination to clarify any issues raised during the redirect examination.

(continued)

Objections are legal challenges to the admissibility of evidence based on the question asked or the exhibit offered. Admissibility of evidence is a procedural rule that the court must decide before the witness may answer or the evidence may be admitted. If the objection is proper, a court will sustain the objection, and the witness may not answer the question. If the objection is not accepted, it is overruled, and the witness is directed to answer that question.

On conclusion of the plaintiff's case-in-chief, the defense presents its case-in-chief. Evidence is presented through the use of witnesses called to testify for the defense by direct examination followed by cross-examination, redirect examination, and recross examination, just as in the plaintiff's presentation of its case-in-chief.

In the rebuttal phase of the trial, the plaintiff is given the opportunity to respond or address information that was presented during the defendant's case-in-chief. For example, evidence that was presented that varies from the facts and claims of the plaintiff may be addressed by the plaintiff in rebuttal. The defense is then given the opportunity in sur rebuttal to address new evidence presented during rebuttal by the plaintiff.

Conclusion of Trial

Closing arguments are the last opportunity for the parties to address the jury and refresh the jury member's recollections of what the attorneys presented as evidence.

Following the closing arguments, the court will instruct the jury—the jury charge—by reviewing for the jury the legal issues that they are to decide based on the facts they have heard. The jury charge is usually agreed to by counsel before the beginning of the trial (during the pretrial conference or as part of the pretrial memorandum).

The jury returns its verdict in a written form called a jury verdict slip, which sets forth each of the findings of fact of the jury and lists any damages or damage awards. The jury made these determinations during jury deliberations out of the courtroom and behind closed doors.

Following the jury verdict announcement, counsel may argue that the evidence does not support the finding or may raise other issues with regard to the procedural decisions of the court in asking for relief from the verdict. Once the court has entered the judgment, it becomes a legally enforceable judgment that must be entered on the docket of the court.

REVIEW QUESTIONS AND EXERCISES

1. What are the phases of a trial? What occurs during these phases?
2. What is the purpose of the final pretrial conference?
3. Provide a list of items that might be discussed or resolved at the final pretrial conference.
4. What is jury selection?
5. What is the purpose of voir dire? How is that purpose achieved?
6. Who conducts voir dire?
7. How can a paralegal assist in the jury selection process?
8. How does the jury pool in state trial court differ from that in federal trial court? Why would one be preferable to the other?
9. Describe the difference between a challenge for cause and a peremptory challenge.

10. What purpose does the opening statement serve?
11. Describe the plaintiff's case-in-chief.
12. What is the difference between direct examination and cross-examination?
13. What is the purpose of redirect examination? Of recross?
14. What are objections? What rulings can be made on objections?
15. What is a motion for directed verdict? When is it raised?

16. What is the defendant's case-in-chief? How is it different from the plaintiff's case-in-chief?
17. What is rebuttal? Sur rebuttal?
18. Why should sidebar conferences be avoided?
19. Describe the tasks a paralegal may perform at trial.
20. How are closing arguments different from opening statements?
21. What is a jury charge or jury instruction?
22. How are jury deliberations conducted?
23. What is a verdict slip?

BUILDING YOUR PARALEGAL SKILLS

INTERNET AND TECHNOLOGY EXERCISES

1. What are the advantages and disadvantages of using technology in the presentation of a civil case?
2. Do you think television shows about the law, criminal investigation, and police have any impact on jurors' expectations? Can you locate an article on the Internet suggesting that these shows have an impact?
3. Does your local jurisdiction court have any rules on the use of technology in trial presentation?

CIVIL LITIGATION VIDEO CASE STUDIES

Jury Selection: Potential Juror Challenged for Cause

A truck driver who has been called as a potential juror is asked about his ability to serve on a jury for a case involving a truck accident.

After viewing the video at www.pearsonhighered.com/ careersresources, answer the following questions.

1. What is the purpose of voir dire, or asking jurors questions?
2. What are the reasons to exclude a potential juror?
3. May a lawyer exclude a potential juror without any just cause?

A Salesman's Courtroom Testimony

A salesman for Acme Brake Company is providing courtroom testimony regarding his sale of unlabeled, "seconds"-quality brake pads to the truck mechanic for Ace Trucking Company.

After viewing the video at www.pearsonhighered.com/ careersresources, answer the following questions.

1. If you were opposing counsel, on what areas might you consider cross-examining this witness?
2. How would you prepare for cross-examination of a witness?

Trial: Direct and Cross-Examination of a Witness

An eyewitness to the school bus–stone truck accident is examined by the plaintiffs' attorney and cross-examined by defense counsel.

After viewing the video at www.pearsonhighered.com/careersresources, answer the following questions.

1. Why is the witness sworn? Does it make a difference that she affirms rather than swears?
2. Is there any limit on the questions that may be asked in cross-examination or on redirect examination?
3. How effective is a hostile cross-examination likely to be? Does it depend on the particular witness? Whether it's used in a jury case or a trial by judge?

Preliminary Jury Instructions before Trial

The judge explains the role of the judge and the jury during the civil trial.

After viewing the video at www.pearsonhighered.com/careersresources, answer the following question.

– What is the purpose of the judge's preliminary instructions to the jury?

Closing Argument: A Lawyer's Last Chance

The lawyer is making his closing argument to the jury.

After viewing the video at www.pearsonhighered.com/careersresources, answer the following questions.

1. What is the purpose of the lawyers' closing arguments, and what may be included in the statement of the law and facts?
2. How would the arguments of the plaintiff's lawyer and the defendant's lawyer differ on the issue of damages?

Judge Charges the Jury

The trial judge gives the jurors instructions on the law at the conclusion of the presentation of evidence and closing statements.

After viewing the video at www.pearsonhighered.com/careersresources, answer the following questions.

1. Why does the judge "wait" to instruct the jury on the law as it applies to the case until the end of the trial, just before the jurors start deliberations?
2. Would it make sense to instruct the jury on the law before the trial begins?

CHAPTER OPENING SCENARIO CASE STUDY

Use the Opening Scenario for this chapter to answer the following questions.

1. Prepare a list of activities and tasks that paralegals should do in preparation for the trial and on the day of trial.
2. What should the paralegals do to get the parties and the witnesses ready for the trial? What should they do to prepare the parties and witnesses on the day of trial?
3. Should the paralegals expect to entertain the clients and witnesses while they wait to be called to testify?

COMPREHENSIVE CASE STUDY

SCHOOL BUS–TRUCK ACCIDENT CASE

Review the assigned case study in Appendix 2.

1. Prepare a list of proposed questions to be used in voir dire to uncover bias, including bias that is both helpful and harmful to the client's case. Include these questions in the Forms section of your portfolio.

2. Prepare the pretrial memorandum using the rules for your state trial court and the rules for the federal district court in your jurisdiction.

BUILDING YOUR PROFESSIONAL PORTFOLIO AND REFERENCE MANUAL

CIVIL LITIGATION TEAM AT WORK

See page 18 for instructions on Building Your Professional Portfolio.

Forms

1. Pretrial memorandum formats for local and federal courts
2. Checklist of items that might be discussed or resolved at the final pretrial conference

Procedures

1. Local jurisdiction court rules on the use of technology in trial presentation
2. Procedure for obtaining daily trial transcript copies
3. Process for obtaining jury pool information

Contacts and Resources

Jury commissioner

LEARNING OBJECTIVES

After studying this chapter, you should be able to:

1. Describe the electronic courtroom.

2. Interact with courthouse information technologists to plan for the use of equipment at trial.

3. Understand the use of presentation graphics programs.

4. Create a basic electronic presentation.

5. Explain the use of trial presentation programs.

The Electronic Courtroom and Trial Presentation

CHAPTER 18

OPENING SCENARIO

Ethan Benjamin and his partner, Ariel Marshall, had been working on the presentation of the case for months. Slowly, the realization of the magnitude of the trial was hitting home. It was a new experience for Ethan as the trial attorney and not the litigation paralegal, his former career. While he was preparing for the trial, his paralegal had taken over the role of litigation support paralegal. The overall concern of the trial team was to make the best possible presentation to the jury and obtain a favorable verdict. With the large number of medical witnesses, it was not possible to get everyone to appear in court at the same time; in addition, many of the injured plaintiffs would be physically unable to attend the trial on a daily basis. The firm had thus incurred considerable expense in taking videotaped depositions of all the medical experts and the plaintiffs because the reality was that in the high-technology electronic courtroom in federal court, the entire case could be presented with graphics and videotape. However, strategy decisions still had to be made on how to present the case.

OPENING SCENARIO LEARNING OBJECTIVE

Obtain the local court rules or a list of available electronic technology tools in your jurisdiction's trial courts.

■ INTRODUCTION TO THE ELECTRONIC COURTHOUSE

Computer technology has changed the way law offices and court systems perform traditional functions. The shift from paper to electronic documents and electronic communications in the form of e-mails has resulted in an explosion in the volume of electronically created and stored files. At the same time, cases are coming to trial faster, allowing less time to prepare and present a case in court. The result has been growth in the use of electronic documentation, computerized case management, and computers in litigation.

■ THE ELECTRONIC COURTROOM

LEARNING OBJECTIVE 1
Describe the electronic courtroom.

Increasingly, courts are embracing the use of online and computer-based systems in court administration and in the courtroom. As a result, courts are switching to a paperless system for litigation, which requires the electronic filing of pleadings and allows the use of computer-based systems for trial presentations.

Getting experts to testify is difficult when the time and day for presenting their testimony can't be set in stone because of the uncertainty of trial schedules. Many experts, such as noted surgeons and medical forensics experts, have active, lucrative practices and demand compensation that can go as high as thousands of dollars per hour for the time lost while waiting to testify. The average litigant can rarely afford this cost. Luckily, an electronic recording of a deposition can be used in trial as a cost-effective method of presenting expert witnesses; this strategy is also useful when witnesses are in poor health or live a great distance from the trial venue.

electronic courtroom
Courtroom equipped with electronic equipment for use in trial presentations.

As judicial budgets allow, courtrooms are being outfitted with computers and audiovisual recording and presentation systems and being turned into **electronic courtrooms**. Exhibit 18.1 shows the U.S. Tax Court's electronic courtroom in Virginia. The extent to which courtrooms are set up for technology ranges from the basic—wall outlets for power—to the advanced—installed wiring and equipment. Some courts have started the process of transitioning into a wired courtroom by eliminating traditional court reporters and replacing them with technology in the form of an audio-wired courtroom that has microphones at each needed location—witness box, counsel table, judge's bench—and a recording system located either in the courtroom or at a remote location. For example, the Delaware County courthouse in Pennsylvania has wired all of its courtrooms with microphones and playback equipment that is monitored from a separate location in the courthouse. Requests to repeat what was just said are handled by a request to the audio operator to play back an audio segment.

Computerized courtrooms can be seen frequently on TRUTV (formerly Court TV) televised trials, where computer terminals are present at each lawyer's table, at the judge's bench, and for each of the court support personnel, with monitors for the jury.

Litigation support software is used in trial to display documentary evidence, graphic presentations, and simulations of accidents. Relevant portions of documents can be displayed as a witness testifies and identifies the document for everyone in the courtroom to see at the same time, without the need to pass paper copies to everyone. Lawyers can rapidly search depositions and documents, sometimes in the tens of thousands of pages, on their laptop computer to find pertinent material for examination or cross-examination of a witness. Exhibit 18.2 shows another way in which litigation support software—in

Exhibit 18.1 U.S. Tax Court Electronic (North) Courtroom

Source: Courtesy of U.S. Tax Court.

Exhibit 18.2 Sanction Presentation of Videotape Deposition

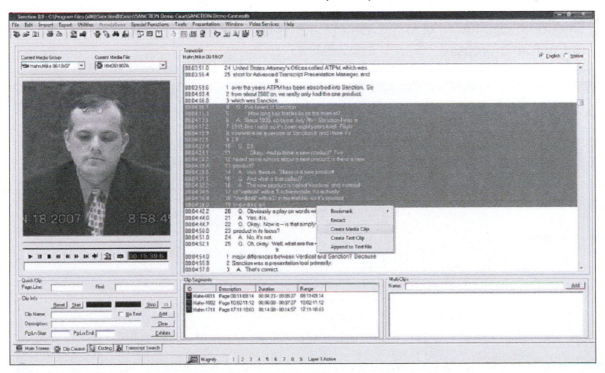

this case, Sanction from LexisNexis—is used to display part of a transcript and the video presentation at the same time.

■ WORKING WITH COURTHOUSE TECHNOLOGY STAFF

Within each courthouse and each courtroom are numerous people more than willing to help the legal team if they are properly approached and consulted. The people working in these areas have a substantial amount of technical knowledge because they work in their area of expertise on a daily basis. Occasional users of technology, like members of a litigation trial team, cannot expect to have the same amount of expertise, unless they also spend considerable time learning the ropes. And even then, courthouse technology staffers can make the process flow smoothly because they are familiar with the idiosyncrasies peculiar to their courthouse's installation.

Exhibit 18.3 shows an example of how the U.S. District Court for the Eastern District of California invites users to become familiar with the electronic support in the courtroom. The IT or technical support office should be the first place to go or contact if any technology will be needed or used in the courtroom, whether it be in a deposition or a trial. Find out what the procedures are first. Members of the support staff usually know how the different judges feel about the use of technology. Some may not approve of large-screen displays, whereas others may think that a single large-projection screen is appropriate. Some may have individual monitors all over the courtroom and yet not want them used for things like presenting a video deposition, preferring instead a single monitor placed for the judge and the jury to view.

The technical support person may also be the one to help clear the hardware through security, saving time and stress on the day of trial by getting everything into

Exhibit 18.3 Electronic Courtroom of U.S. District Court for the Eastern District of California Website

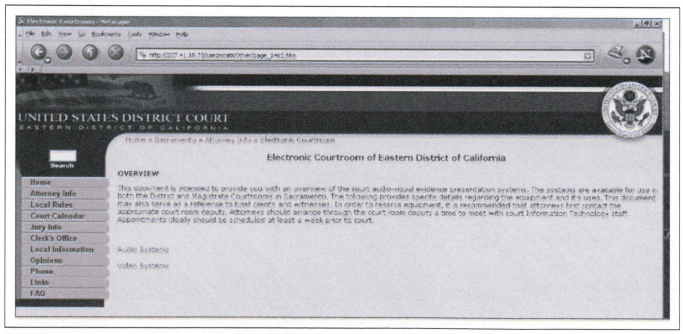

the building in time to set it up and try it out beforehand. Remember, courtroom IT staffers usually hold the master keys to unlock the courtroom. It is also an advantage for the legal team to have someone who speaks the same technical jargon and can interface at the same knowledge level. A little goodwill can go a long way.

Clearing the Right to Bring in the Equipment Beforehand

Anyone who has been in a courthouse in the past few years knows of the increased security measures in place: metal scanners, X-ray machines, and briefcase searches. Anything out of the ordinary, particularly electronic equipment, can result in special scrutiny. In the ideal setting, the only thing the legal team needs to bring is the pertinent CD, videotape, or other electronic storage media—all the equipment is provided by the courthouse.

Rarely does everything work so smoothly as the ideal. Most attorneys carry the electronic files on their laptops. The trial presentation plan might be to use the software and files on a laptop by connecting it to the courtroom equipment with a cable. Where the court system is not compatible or the equipment is not provided, the legal team must bring all the needed equipment into the courthouse. It is highly recommended that the security office be contacted ahead of time to learn the policy and procedures for bringing equipment into the courthouse and setting it up. In a number of courthouses, it means using the loading dock of the courthouse or other alternate entrance and waiting for clearance. Pre-clearing equipment can save valuable time on the day of trial, not to mention ensuring that everything will work as planned.

What Happens When the Lights Go Out

Even the best plans can be sidetracked when the equipment fails or when the power needed is not available. In many parts of the country, the power company's reaction to excess power demand is to reduce the power (sometimes called a *brownout*) when the voltage is reduced. Some equipment will work at a lower-than-optimum voltage, while other items must have a constant power supply. For example, many homeowners have found their refrigerators not working after a brownout because the motors, unable to operate at the lower voltage supplied by the power company, have burned out. While there are options like battery-powered backup systems, these may not be practical. Therefore, in anticipation of "when all else fails," it is always good to have backup hard copies of graphs and charts.

Many legal teams bring backups of important files and software on extra laptop computers, just in case. Particularly well-prepared or overly concerned legal teams check the equipment in advance and bring extra bulbs for the computer projector; they may even bring backup projectors, monitors, and, in some cases, printers. To paraphrase an old adage, if anything can go wrong, it will, at the worst possible moment—and in the middle of trial.

> **PRACTICE TIP**
> All programs in the Microsoft Office Suite, including PowerPoint, offer online tutorials to help users learn how to use the programs.

■ USING TECHNOLOGY TO PRESENT THE CASE

Presentation and Trial Graphics

It has been said, one picture is worth ten thousand words. Properly prepared graphics are an excellent way of telling a story and making a point, whether it be to a jury, a client, or a group of concerned residents in a public meeting. Conversely, poorly prepared graphics can be boring and can distract from the main message.

> **LEARNING OBJECTIVE 3**
> Understand the use of presentation graphics programs.

presentation graphics
Visual aids used to enhance an oral presentation.

Nearly everyone has seen PowerPoint slides used as part of a presentation. Some slides hit home and make everyone in the audience wish they had copies. Others convey a confused message at best or offer a few minutes of sleep to the audience at worst. More and more people use graphics in presentations as the software to create them becomes more affordable and easier to use.

Among the most available **presentation graphics** software programs are those included as part of the office suites of programs from Microsoft PowerPoint and Corel Presentation. These programs are used in many law offices to create high-quality slide shows and drawings that include text, data charts, and graphic objects.

One of the advantages of these programs is their flexibility. They can be used to prepare and present the graphic presentation electronically, using a computer with or without a projector, and they're also capable of printing out paper copies for distribution. Presentation programs typically provide stock templates of graphics, artwork, and layouts as samples that the user can easily modify. More advanced users can add sound or video clips to the presentation, include still photos, and incorporate custom graphics from other programs.

■ ELECTRONIC GRAPHICS CREATION

LEARNING OBJECTIVE 4
Create a basic electronic presentation.

It used to be that when you walked into a courthouse, you knew who was trying a case by the armload of poster board graphics and easels being carried by the legal support staff. The use of photographs has always been a common form of exhibit. In fact, the use of photographs is a good lesson in what is appropriate for a presentation graphic. While some lawyers carry snapshot-sized photos (4 × 5 in.) and others carry larger photos (8 × 10 in.), it is a good idea to remember the words of a wise old judge to a novice trial attorney: If it's important enough to use a photo, make sure the last person in the jury box and the judge can see it at the same time. With the introduction of overhead projectors and slide and computer projectors, many wiser trial attorneys have given up larger (30 × 40 in.) blow-ups of photos in favor of computer-projected versions (where size is limited only by the size of the screen or wall). The same is true of drawings and diagrams. But always remember the advice about poorly prepared graphics—do not use them.

Graphic creation programs are used to create visuals either as stand-alone graphics or as part of a presentation, such as a PowerPoint presentation. One of the newer classes of graphic software programs that offer templates is SmartDraw. Exhibit 18.4 shows examples of a graphic created for trial. The obvious advantage to this class of software is the ability of the legal team to create its own graphics without the need of artists and outside consultants. It is possible to create **trial graphics** in court on a laptop computer to meet an unexpected factual twist and to display the image using the laptop and projection unit. Even when the graphics are printed out, these programs provide an electronic backup if the large display boards are delayed in transit or damaged by an overzealous cleaning staff.

trial graphics
Visual aids used to enhance a trial presentation.

PowerPoint has become the standard for making electronic presentations of all types to all types of audiences, from grade schools (see Exhibit 18.5) to corporations to courtrooms.

A good PowerPoint presentation can reinforce and highlight the speaker's ideas and concepts. A poor PowerPoint presentation can undermine all the hard work that went into the presentation. While some presentations are designed for only intermittent viewing, in the legal community they are typically used

Exhibit 18.4 Intersection of Accident Scene Created with SmartDraw

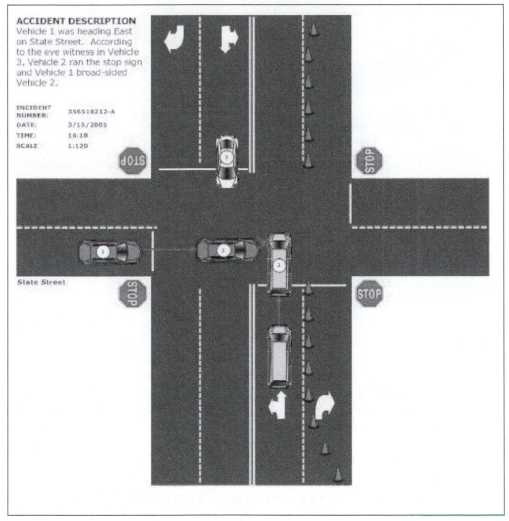

Source: Reprinted with permission from SmartDraw.

to reinforce ideas, concepts, and thoughts the presenter wants to make to the audience.

A few pointers on presentations using PowerPoint:

- *Viewability.* Use background and text color combinations that can be read by everyone in the room. Be aware of the issue of colorblindness and the effects of some colors, like soothing pastel colors and vivid, wake-up colors like red.
- *Density.* Slides should support ideas in as few words as possible; no one wants to read a full page of text.
- *Sounds.* Sounds can be very effective when used appropriately; overdo it, however, and their impact is lost. Also, inappropriate sound effects, like gunshots, may be unacceptable or not permitted to be used in a courtroom.
- *Stand aside.* Even the best presentation is worthless if the presenter is standing in front of it, blocking the viewers' ability to see it.
- *Imagery.* Choose the picture wisely. What is the lasting impression you want to leave in the minds of, say, the jury members when they go into deliberations? Among the most effective pictures in a personal injury case may be a photo of the victim sitting in a wheelchair or lying in a hospital bed—no words are necessary.

Exhibit 18.5 PowerPoint Sample Slide

Source: Screen shot reprinted by permission from Microsoft Corporation.

SmartDraw

SmartDraw is a graphics creation program that can be used to create stand-alone images, both in print form and in computer slide presentations. In addition to its intuitive user interface, one of its biggest advantages for the legal team is the thousands of templates and icons available for creating graphics quickly. Many of the graphics included in the program anticipate the needs of the legal community and require only minor modification.

■ ELECTRONIC TRIAL PRESENTATION PROGRAMS

LEARNING OBJECTIVE 5
Explain the use of trial presentation programs.

More and more courtrooms are providing, or allowing litigants to bring for their trial, computer-based electronic display systems. Some see this as nothing more than a logical outgrowth of the multimedia presentations that started with the use of chalkboards, movie clips, and slide projectors.

Modern trial presentations frequently include videotaped depositions and the presentation of images, photos, videos, and portions of documents. These may be exhibited on personal monitors or large-screen displays.

Managing the hundreds of individual case components to be displayed in the courtroom can be a trial nightmare unless they are organized and easily accessed for presentation. Litigation presentation programs, like Sanction by LexisNexis and TrialDirector by inData, are multifaceted trial presentation programs that provide a comprehensive approach to presenting all types of exhibits in the courtroom, including documents, photographs, graphic images, video presentations, and recorded depositions. Unlike PowerPoint, which requires the creation of individual slides, these programs allow existing documents and files to be presented by simply copying them into the program data file and making a selection for presentation. Trial presentation programs, like Sanction, are thus databases of the documents either in a case file or on a computer.

The selection of the individual items for presentation is facilitated by a panel that allows a preview of the item selected. The final presentation is usually

Exhibit 18.6   Sanction Dual-Monitor Mode for Courtroom Presentation Allows the Trial Team to see the Image before it is Projected on the Courtroom and Individual Monitors

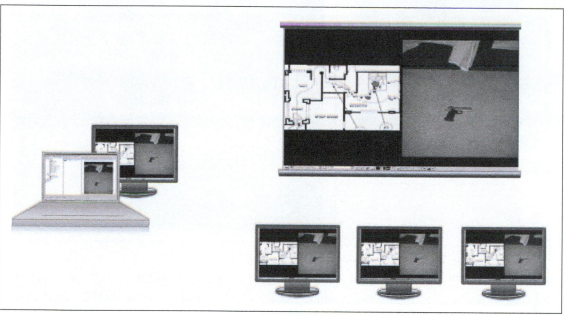

Source: Sanction LexisNexis. Reprinted with permission.

previewable on a computer or on a laptop screen using the dual-monitor mode before being projected, as shown in Exhibit 18.6.

Sanction, TrialDirector, and similar **trial presentation programs** allow the legal team to organize and manage the documents, depositions, photographs, and other data as exhibits for trial and then display them as evidence when needed in depositions and trial.

trial presentation program
Computer program that organizes and manages documents, depositions, photographs, and other data used as exhibits for trial and displays them as evidence when needed.

PRACTICE TIP
SUPPORTED FORMATS

Not all native formats can be used in all trial presentation programs, just as not all music files can be played on every brand of portable music player. Early in the preparation process, it is wise to check the formats supported by the trial presentation program selected for trial to ensure compatibility and avoid scrambling near the trial date to convert or find suitable replacements.

Limitations on Presentation Graphics

Any limitations on using presentation graphics are determined by the equipment in the courtroom. If the courtroom is not set up with appropriate power sources, screens, or monitors, computer presentations will not work, and print exhibits may still be needed. A key issue for the legal support staff is to determine well in advance of trial the availability of technical resources in the courtroom in which the trial will take place. If the courtroom is not equipped for computer presentations, will the court allow the installation and use of computer presentation equipment? And, if all of the equipment must be supplied, will the client be willing to pay the costs associated with acquiring or renting and installing the needed hardware?

Exhibit 18.7 Judge's Bench

Exhibit 18.8 Counsel Tables

![globe icon] **WEB RESOURCES**

WEB RESOURCES

For complete information and documentation on the Matthew J. Perry, Jr. Courthouse in Columbia, South Carolina, go to the United States District Court for the District of South Carolina website: http://www.scd.uscourts.gov/.

large-screen monitor
A video monitor conveniently located in the courtroom that is large enough for all to see the graphics displayed.

The following information and the photographs in Exhibits 18.7, 18.8, and 18.9 are from online material available at the U.S. District Court for the District of South Carolina website, which opened its first fully electronic courtrooms at the Matthew J. Perry, Jr. Federal Courthouse in Columbia, South Carolina. They offer a glimpse into the features and equipment that might be found in other courtrooms and courthouses.

Video monitors are strategically placed around the courtroom. The judge's bench (Exhibit 18.7), the witness stand, the courtroom deputy, each of the counsel tables (Exhibit 18.8), and the jury box (Exhibit 18.9) have a video monitor to display the evidence.

The jury box has one flat-panel monitor placed between every two juror chairs.

There are also **large-screen monitors** for displaying evidence using a document camera or other electronic media (Exhibit 18.10) just inside the

Exhibit 18.10 Counsel Lectern with Document Camera and Large-Screen Display

Exhibit 18.9 Jury box

well of the court, so those in the gallery can view evidence displayed through the system.

At the heart of the electronic courtroom is the **visual presentation cart,** or media center, which contains most of the presentation electronics, including:

> **document camera,**
> **annotation monitor,**
> **interpreter box,**
> **infrared headphones,**
> **laptop port,**
> **VCR,** and
> **dual-cassette player.**

In addition to the electronic courtroom capabilities, videoconferencing technology is available in any courtroom at the Matthew J. Perry, Jr. Courthouse.

Electronic Equipment in the Courtroom

Document Camera

The document camera (Exhibit 18.11) is an easy-to-operate, portable evidence-presentation system. This unit is equipped with a high-resolution camera and features a 12:1 magnification zoom lens with a high-accuracy, auto-focusing system. The document camera can present evidence (e.g., 3-D objects, paper documents, transparencies, X-rays, etc.) for display on monitors throughout the courtroom.

Annotation Monitor

Annotation monitors (Exhibit 18.12) allow a witness to easily make on-screen annotations with the touch of a finger. Annotations can be made by pressing lightly and dragging your finger as you would a pen.

visual presentation cart
A media center located in the courtroom.

document camera
A portable evidence-presentation system equipped with a high-resolution camera.

annotation monitor
A monitor that allows a witness to easily make on-screen annotations with the touch of a finger.

infrared headphones
An assisted listening device for the hearing impaired.

interpreter box
Routes language translations from an interpreter to the witness/defendant's headphones or the courtroom's public address system.

laptop port
A connection into which a laptop may be plugged.

VCR
Equipment that plays back video and audio.

dual-cassette player
Equipment that plays back audio.

Exhibit 18.11 Document camera

Exhibit 18.12 Annotation monitor

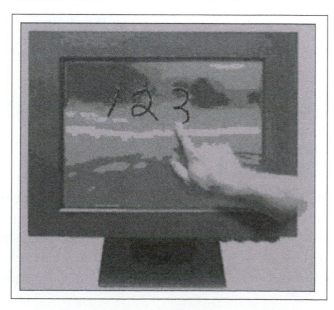

Exhibit 18.13 Interpreter box

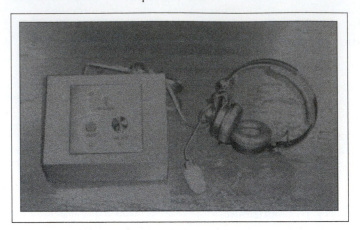

Exhibit 18.14 Infrared headphones

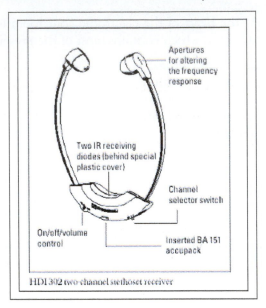

Interpreter Box

The interpreter box (Exhibit 18.13) routes language translations from an interpreter to the witness/defendant's headphones or to the courtroom's public address system.

Infrared Headphones

Infrared headphones (Exhibit 18.14) are used as an assisted listening device for the hearing impaired. The Americans with Disabilities Act requires this type of device to be available for any individual needing it. It can also be used in conjunction with the interpreter box for language interpretations.

> **PRACTICE TIP**
>
> **GETTING TECHNOLOGY TO WORK IN THE COURTROOM—A PRESENTATION APPROACH**
>
> Try it out ahead of time.
>
> Have backup equipment.
>
> Have a separate operator.
>
> Know the passwords.

CONCEPT REVIEW AND REINFORCEMENT

KEY TERMS

electronic courtroom 428	visual presentation cart 437	laptop port 437
presentation graphic 432	document camera 437	VCR 437
trial graphics 432	annotation monitor 437	dual-cassette player 437
trial presentation program 435	interpreter box 437	
large-screen monitor 436	infrared headphones 437	

CHAPTER SUMMARY

THE ELECTRONIC COURTROOM AND TRIAL PRESENTATION

Introduction to the Electronic Courthouse	Technology has changed the way that courts perform their traditional functions, recognizing the demand for swift justice.
The Electronic Courtroom	Electronic and court-based systems are increasingly being used in the courts. As budgets allow, courtrooms are being outfitted with computers and audiovisual presentation systems. Courtrooms are being wired with technology ranging from the very basic to highly sophisticated technology, with monitors and computers at every workstation for the lawyers, the judge, and the jury.
Working with Courthouse Technology Staff	Courtrooms generally have support personnel who are available to assist the members of the litigation team in the use of the technology available in the courtroom or the courthouse. They are also the key people to contact when permission is needed to bring equipment into the courthouse on the day of trial. Good working relations with the technical support staff can be invaluable when everything goes wrong and backup equipment is needed on an emergency basis.
Using Technology to Present the Case	Properly prepared graphics are an excellent way of telling a story and making a point. The most accessible presentation software programs are Microsoft PowerPoint, Corel Presentation, and SmartDraw. Courtrooms are providing, or allowing litigants to provide for their trial, computer-based electronic display systems. Trial presentations frequently include videotaped depositions and the display of images, photos, videos, and portions of documents. Trial presentation programs allow the legal team to organize and manage the documents, depositions, photographs, and other data used as exhibits for trial and then display them as evidence when needed. ■ Sanction and TrialDirector—These trial presentation programs are electronic trial presentation software applications. ■ Supported formats—Not all native formats can be used in all trial presentation programs. It is wise, early in the preparation process, to check the formats supported by the trial presentation program selected for trial to ensure compatibility.
Electronic Graphics Creation	Properly prepared graphic presentations assist in presenting a case. Graphic software like SmartDraw makes the creation of trial graphics quick and easy.

REVIEW QUESTIONS AND EXERCISES

1. List and explain some of the advantages of the use of technology in litigation.
2. What are the functions for which a litigation team uses litigation presentation programs?
3. How can PowerPoint be used as a litigation presentation program?
4. How can the legal team use presentation graphics programs? Give examples of both litigation and nonlitigation uses.

5. Explain the use of trial presentation programs.
6. What can you do when the power fails during a trial?
7. List and explain considerations in the creation of presentation graphics.
8. List and explain limitations on presentation graphics used at trial.
9. Why is the courthouse technology team important to the legal team?

BUILDING YOUR PARALEGAL SKILLS

INTERNET AND TECHNOLOGY EXERCISES

1. Use the Internet to locate resources for learning how to use Microsoft PowerPoint. List the topics available and the web address for accessing this information.
2. What Internet resources are available for obtaining maps and aerial views that might be used for trial preparation?
3. Using the court you selected to file the lawsuit in the exercise in Chapter 4, find out what information is available online about the procedural aspects and the electronic capabilities of the courtrooms.
4. Create an accident scene exhibit using a graphics software program.

5. Create a basic PowerPoint presentation on the use of PowerPoint in litigation.
6. Create a basic PowerPoint presentation on the use of PowerPoint by the legal team, including an explanation of how to make a slide.
7. Prepare a PowerPoint presentation for use in trial using the exhibits in the comprehensive tort case study in Appendix 1 and the graphics prepared using SmartDraw Legal Edition and LexisNexis TimeMap.
8. Create a presentation for use in court using Sanction for the comprehensive tort case study in Appendix 1.

CIVIL LITIGATION VIDEO CASE STUDIES

Expert Witness Video Deposition

An expert witness has his deposition videotaped.

After viewing the video at www.pearsonhighered.com/ careersresources, answer the following questions.

1. How may a videotaped deposition of an expert witness be used in trial?
2. What are the advantages and disadvantages to using videotaped depositions?

CHAPTER OPENING SCENARIO CASE STUDY

Use the Opening Scenario for this chapter to answer the following questions.

1. How can all the needed equipment be used in court without having to use a truck to carry all the documents and exhibits?
2. How can graphics be used in the trial?
3. What are the advantages and disadvantages of the different trial graphics options, in software cost and the time needed for preparation? Explain, using specific software costs.
4. What are the possible methods of presenting expert testimony? Describe the advantages and disadvantages of each.
5. What cautions should the trial attorney consider in using graphics at trial?
6. What pretrial measures should be taken if trial graphics are going to be used?

COMPREHENSIVE CASE STUDY

SCHOOL BUS–TRUCK ACCIDENT CASE

Review the assigned case study in Appendix 2.

1. Prepare a PowerPoint presentation for use in trial using the exhibits in the comprehensive case study in Appendix 2 and the graphics prepared using SmartDraw and LexisNexis TimeMap.
2. Create a presentation for use in court using Sanction for the comprehensive case study in Appendix 2.

BUILDING YOUR PROFESSIONAL PORTFOLIO AND LITIGATION REFERENCE MANUAL

CIVIL LITIGATION TEAM AT WORK

See page 18 for instructions on Building Your Professional Portfolio.

Form

Prepare a form engagement letter for all outside consultants who work on a case, stating their obligation to keep everything confidential.

Contacts and Resources

1. Internet address of resources for learning how to use Microsoft PowerPoint
2. Internet resources for obtaining maps and aerial views of locations
3. Technology contact or court technology office in your local and federal courts

LEARNING OBJECTIVES

After studying this chapter, you should be able to:

1. Describe the procedure and purpose of entering a judgment of record.

2. Identify the types of errors made at trial.

3. Describe the procedures available to seek relief from the trial court for errors made at trial.

4. List the requirements for perfecting an appeal.

5. Describe the appeal process in the United States Court of Appeals and the United States Supreme Court.

Posttrial Procedures | CHAPTER 19

OPENING SCENARIO

The entire legal team—attorneys and staff from both offices—waited anxiously in the downtown office conference room for the judge's law clerk to call and let them know the jury had reached a verdict. With so many claims and issues, it was likely to be some time before they would get the call to return to the courtroom. Mr. Saunders, Mr. Benjamin, Ms. Eden, and their paralegal, Caitlin, gathered at one end of the conference room while Mr. Mason, Ms. Marshall, and their paralegal, Emily, were at the other. There was no sense in wasting time. They were going over the trial while the events were fresh in their minds, comparing notes and looking for potential areas of procedural error that could be used for reconsideration or appeal, if necessary. They did not have a transcript because the costs to obtain it on a daily basis far exceeded their or their clients' ability to pay for one. Based on the hoped-for verdicts, the paralegals were asked to prepare draft orders for the judge to sign as well as to start preparation of any motions that might be needed.

OPENING SCENARIO LEARNING OBJECTIVE

Prepare an appeal of an adverse decision in a civil trial court for filing in your jurisdiction.

■ INTRODUCTION TO POSTTRIAL PROCEDURES

After the jury has rendered its verdict, win or lose, the legal team needs to anticipate the next step in the civil litigation process—posttrial procedures and relief. If errors are alleged to have been made by the court in the conduct of the trial, depending upon the nature and effect on the client's case, steps may need to be taken to correct those errors. If a verdict was entered in favor of the client, it must be procedurally turned into an enforceable judgment. Time limits on posttrial motions, appeals to higher courts, and action on judgments must be investigated and carefully observed to avoid losing rights to posttrial relief.

■ ENTERING JUDGMENT

LEARNING OBJECTIVE 1
Describe the procedure and purpose of entering a judgment of record.

There are several ways in which litigation might terminate, resulting in judgment entered on the official court record, the docket:

1. motion for judgment on the pleadings,
2. motion for summary judgment,
3. default judgment,
4. bench trial verdict,
5. jury verdict, or
6. final ruling of an appellate court verdict.

motion for judgment on the pleadings
A motion filed at the conclusion of the pleadings phase of the litigation by either the plaintiff or the defendant in order to end the lawsuit.

Motion for a Judgment on the Pleadings.   After the conclusion of the pleadings phase of the litigation, either the plaintiff or the defendant may file a **motion for a judgment on the pleadings,** claiming that he is entitled to judgment in his favor as a matter of law. The motion asks the court to consider everything contained in the pleadings (and not any outside matters) in the light most favorable to the non-moving party (the opposing party). If there are no disputed material facts, the moving party is entitled to judgment. "Undisputed facts," in this context, means that any fact denied by the opposing party is considered as not true, and all of the opposing party's allegations are treated as true. Because either party can bring the motion, judgment may be entered in either's favor.

motion for summary judgment
A motion by which a party seeks to terminate the lawsuit prior to trial, alleging there are no disputed material facts and all that remains is the application of the law to the facts.

Motion for Summary Judgment.   At any time, any of the parties to the litigation may file a **motion for summary judgment.** A motion for summary judgment is decided in the same way as the motion for judgment on the pleadings, except that the court can look at items outside the pleadings. As with the motion for a judgment on the pleadings, the court views the pleadings in the light most favorable to the non-moving party. All that remains is the application of the law to the facts, which requires entry of judgment in favor of the moving party. The difference is that in the motion for summary judgment, the court can consider more than just the pleadings. For example, the court can look at responses to written discovery requests, deposition transcripts, and affidavits.

Both of these motions determine, as a matter of law, whether one of the parties is entitled to judgment in its favor. At trial, attorneys make oral motions for directed verdict, asking the judge to dismiss the lawsuit or enter judgment in favor of their client.

An entry of default judgment occurs when a party fails to respond to a pleading containing claims against him or her—for example, if the defendant fails to file an answer to the complaint or the plaintiff fails to respond to affirmative defenses and counterclaims raised by the defendant.

Verdict.   At the conclusion of trial, the jury or a judge sitting in a bench trial returns a **verdict,** which results in a determination of liability or fault and an award of damages.

Although all of these end the litigation, none has any effect on the litigants until judgment is entered on the written record of the docket in the office of the court that maintains the court records—sometimes called the clerk of court or prothonotary. This is particularly true of a jury verdict and an oral motion granted at trial. The force of law accompanies these only after they are reduced to a written court order, the judgment, and it is entered on the docket. The date of the **entry of judgment** is the date from which all dates for posttrial proceedings are calculated.

In many instances, the judge will orally enter judgment following completion of the case or announcement of the jury verdict. It is incumbent upon the litigants to make sure the judge's oral statements from the bench become part of the written record and are entered on the docket. If the judge has not previously been provided with a blank copy of the order of court to sign, one that conforms to the verdict of judgment rendered may need to be prepared and submitted for the judge's signature.

Entry of judgment in the federal courts requires that a separate written document be filed with the clerk of court. Although Fed. R. Civ. P. 58 specifies some instances where a separate document is not required, the better practice is to be prepared to offer the judge the necessary documents to sign for entry of judgment. Many local rules require the attorneys to take the steps necessary to ensure that the judgment has been entered into record.

Whether the judgment is prepared by the judge on his own or by the attorneys at the judge's direction, the form is the same. Exhibit 19.1 shows a form for entry of judgment on jury verdict. The form is found as Form 70 in the Appendix of Forms to the Federal Rules of Civil Procedure. The form may be adapted to meet the circumstances of the particular case.

verdict
The decision reached by the jury, or judge in a bench trial, that concludes the case.

entry of judgment
Taking the verdict announced by the jury and converting it to a legally enforceable judgment.

Exhibit 19.1 Sample form for entry of judgment in Federal District Court

---

IN THE UNITED STATES DISTRICT COURT FOR THE EASTERN DISTRICT OF PENNSYLVANIA

John Smith,
Plaintiff   :   Civil Action #

v.   :

Mack Truck Company,   :   Judgment
Defendant   :

This action came for trial before the Court and a jury, Honorable Norma Shapiro, District Judge, presiding, and the issues having been duly tried and the jury having duly rendered its verdict,

It is Ordered and Adjudged

That the Plaintiff, Smith recover of the Defendant Mack Truck Company the sum of $250,000 with interest thereon at the rate of six (6%) percent as provided by law, and his costs of action.

Dated at Philadelphia, Pennsylvania, this _____ day of _____ 20_____.

_____
Clerk of Court

■ ERRORS MADE AT TRIAL

LEARNING OBJECTIVE 2
Identify the types of errors made at trial.

posttrial relief
Action, such as an appeal to a higher court, taken by one of the litigants to correct errors made at trial.

error made in evidentiary ruling
An error made at trial by the judge with regard to the admission or exclusion of evidence.

error made in instructions to jury
An error made at trial by the judge with regard to the instructions given to the jury or the recitation of the instructions.

verdict unsupported by evidence
An error made at trial where the verdict of the jury is not supported by the evidence or the verdict disregards the law as presented in the jury instructions.

preserving the record
The obligation of the attorney to raise objection to mistakes made at trial. The objection gives the trial judge notice of an error he may be about to make or may have already made and gives the judge the opportunity to correct that error at trial.

continuing objection
An acknowledgment in the record of the trial that the attorney objects to particular testimony or evidence without her having to object each time the witness answers a question. The purpose is to permit the testimony to be presented seamlessly without the attorney waiving the error of the testimony's admission.

Once judgment is entered on the record, the clock begins to run for the attorney to pursue **posttrial relief.** Posttrial relief includes the identification of errors made at trial that impacted the client's case and its outcome and the procedures needed to correct those errors. Because of the short period of time (usually ten days) to take action and file documents with the court, the determination of the existence of error might have to be made without the benefit of a trial transcript to review. Instead, this determination of error may be made based on the attorney's memory and the notes kept by the paralegal and other members of the trial team during the trial.

Errors made at trial are generally errors made by the judge related to procedure, such as rulings on objections made at trial. These rulings fall into two broad categories: **errors made in evidentiary rulings** and **errors made in instructions to the jury.** A third area of error at trial occurs when the jury **verdict is unsupported by the evidence** or is contrary to the evidence.

Evidentiary Rulings

One type of error made at trial is related to the admission or exclusion of evidence, including the testimony of witnesses or exhibits and other evidence. Disputes concerning known or expected issues of the admission or exclusion of evidence are usually raised in the pretrial memorandum. During the final pretrial conference, the judge will issue a ruling on the admissibility of evidence as raised in the pretrial memorandum. For example, in a contested will case, the parties may have included in their pretrial memoranda an issue related to hearsay: *Are oral statements of the decedent's surviving spouse, who is now incapacitated and unavailable to testify at trial, admissible as an exception to the hearsay rule?* The judge may decide that all statements of the decedent's spouse, even hearsay, are relevant and admissible in determining the decedent's intent. The court may justify this ruling by saying the determination of intent outweighs the potential prejudice created by the unreliability of hearsay evidence. Alternatively, the judge could exclude the testimony of a witness because it is unreliable "double hearsay" (e.g., the witness would testify that the wife told her what the husband had said about the distribution of his estate). With either ruling, one side will be dissatisfied with the judge's admission or exclusion of the testimony.

Assume for the moment that the judge ruled to permit hearsay testimony. When the witness is called to testify at trial, the opposing attorney will object to the testimony. The judge then has a second chance to rule on the admissibility of the testimony. Again, regardless of the ruling made during trial, one side will be dissatisfied with the decision.

A crucial part of the trial is **preserving the record** for appeal. The concept requires counsel to take steps to bring any error to the court's attention and to seek its correction as soon as possible. This obligation is a continuing one, and each time the error arises, the attorney must object in order to preserve the objection on the record for possible appeal. Sometimes the judge will recognize that a party intends to object and, for ease of the presentation of evidence, will permit a **continuing objection** to be placed on the record. The continuing objection applies to all evidence related to that issue and that witness. Failure to object, which draws the court's attention to the error, results in a waiver of the issue—the objection—on appeal. Thus, even though counsel in the preceding example was aware of the judge's pretrial ruling (to permit the hearsay), counsel renewed or again raised her objection to the admissibility of the testimony when it was presented at trial.

Preserving the record applies to all evidence presented at trial, not just testimony of witnesses. Admission of photographs may be an error because they do not depict the scene of the accident accurately. An expert's opinion on the cause of an accident may be admitted in error because the expert assumed facts that are not part of the case or the expert was not properly qualified to render an opinion.

Instructions to the Jury

The second type of error may occur in the instructions given to the jury. The jury hears all the evidence and then is instructed by the judge in the law that is applicable to the case. Proposed jury instructions are usually presented to the judge by both attorneys in their pretrial memoranda and in a conference held by the judge with the trial attorneys at the close of evidence. Although the attorneys may present proposed instructions, the judge makes the ultimate decision as to what instructions the jury should receive. The judge delivers those instructions orally to the jury. Error may be found in the instructions themselves or in the recitation of the instructions to the jury.

For example, the injured passenger in a single-car automobile accident sues the driver. The evidence shows that the injured passenger was intoxicated, but the driver was not. The law states that intoxication of a driver involved in an automobile accident is a factor in assessing liability or fault. The judge instructs the jury, "Intoxication may be considered in finding fault or liability of the driver." This instruction may be made in error because it is an incomplete statement of the law and potentially misleads the jury to consider the intoxication of the passenger, which is not a factor in determining the liability of the driver.

Verdict Unsupported by the Evidence

The third type of error made at trial relates to the actions of the jury. In some cases, the jury fails to consider all of the evidence or misapplies the law. Under these circumstances, there is no error by the judge in admitting or excluding evidence or in instructing the jury. Rather, the jury, as shown by its verdict, has either disregarded evidence or has inaccurately applied the law. Typically, this type of error results from a highly emotional case where the members of the jury strongly identified with one of the parties to the lawsuit or the wrong complained of. A strong emotional reaction can cloud a jury's decision making and result in a verdict that is unsupported by the evidence or is against the law. In some cases, the decision as to liability of the parties to the lawsuit will be supported by the evidence and the law, but the calculation of damages may be out of proportion.

Consider the infamous McDonald's coffee case, where a patron who ordered, received, and paid for a cup of coffee at the drive-through window was burned when the hot coffee spilled in her lap. The jury awarded her $2.9 million—$200,000 represented damages to compensate for her injuries and $2.7 million represented damages to punish McDonald's. The woman was assigned 20 percent comparative negligence, which reduced the compensatory damages to $160,000. Although the evidence supported the liability of McDonald's for serving coffee at a temperature that was too high, the punitive damages were determined by the trial judge to be unsupported by the evidence and disproportionate to the compensatory award. Thus, the judge reduced the punitive damages to $480,000, or three times the compensatory award. The multimillion-dollar verdict was highly publicized. However, the judge's reduction of the jury award was not, nor was the fact that the parties ultimately settled out of court for an undisclosed sum believed to be significantly lower than the judge's ruling. Exhibit 19.2 is an article describing the specifics of the case.

Exhibit 19.2 The McDonald's scalding coffee case

THE MCDONALD'S SCALDING COFFEE CASE

Stella Liebeck of Albuquerque, New Mexico, was in the passenger seat of her grandson's car when she was severely burned by McDonald's coffee in February 1992. Liebeck, now 81, ordered coffee that was served in a styrofoam cup at the drive-through window of a local McDonald's.

After receiving the order, the grandson pulled his car forward and stopped momentarily so that Liebeck could add cream and sugar to her coffee. (Critics of civil justice, who have pounced on this case, often charge that Liebeck was driving the car or that the vehicle was in motion when she spilled the coffee; neither is true.) Liebeck placed the cup between her knees and attempted to remove the plastic lid from the cup. As she removed the lid, the entire contents of the cup spilled into her lap.

The sweatpants Liebeck was wearing absorbed the coffee and held it next to her skin. A vascular surgeon determined that Liebeck suffered full thickness burns (or third-degree burns) over 6 percent of her body, including her inner thighs, perineum, buttocks, and genital and groin areas. She was hospitalized for eight days, during which time she underwent skin grafting. Liebeck, who also underwent debridement treatments, sought to settle her claim for $20,000, but McDonald's refused.

During discovery, McDonald's produced documents showing more than 700 claims by people burned by its coffee between 1982 and 1992. Some claims involved third-degree burns substantially similar to Liebeck's. This history documented McDonald's knowledge about the extent and nature of this hazard.

McDonald's also said during discovery that, based on a consultant's advice, it held its coffee at between 180 and 190 degrees Fahrenheit to maintain optimum taste. He admitted that he had not evaluated the safety ramifications at this temperature. Other establishments sell coffee at substantially lower temperatures, and coffee served at home is generally 135 to 140 degrees.

Further, McDonald's quality assurance manager testified that the company actively enforces a requirement that coffee be held in the pot at 185 degrees, plus or minus five degrees. He also testified that a burn hazard exists with any food substance served at 140 degree or above, and that McDonald's coffee, at the temperature at which it was poured into styrofoam cups, was not fit for consumption because it would burn the mouth and throat. The quality assurance manager admitted that burns would occur, but testified that McDonald's had no intention of reducing the "holding temperature" of its coffee.

Plaintiff's expert, a scholar in thermodynamics as applied to human skin burns, testified that liquids, at 180 degrees, will cause a full thickness burn to human skin in two to seven seconds. Other testimony showed that as the temperature decreases toward 155 degrees, the extent of the burn relative to that temperature decreases exponentially. Thus, if Liebeck's spill had involved coffee at 155 degrees, the liquid would have cooled and given her time to avoid a serious burn.

McDonald's asserted that customers buy coffee on their way to work or home, intending to consume it there. However, the company's own research showed that customers intend to consume the coffee immediately while driving. McDonald's also argued that consumers know coffee is hot and that its customers want it that way. The company admitted its customers were unaware that they could suffer third-degree burns from the coffee and that a statement on the side of the cup was not a "warning" but a "reminder" since the location of the writing would not warn customers of the hazard.

The jury awarded Liebeck $200,000 in compensatory damages. This amount was reduced to $160,000 because the jury found Liebeck 20 percent at fault in the spill. The jury also awarded Liebeck $2.7 million in punitive damages, which equals about two days of McDonald's coffee sales.

Post-verdict investigation found that the temperature of coffee at the local Albuquerque McDonald's had dropped to 158 degrees Fahrenheit. The trial court subsequently reduced the punitive award to $480,000—or three times compensatory damages—even though the judge called McDonald's conduct reckless, callous and willful. Subsequent to remittitur, the parties entered a post-verdict settlement.

Source: Reprinted with permission from Georgia Trial Lawyers Association (GTLA). Copyright © 2002. All Rights Reserved.

Harmless Error

appealable error
An error made at trial that causes harm or prejudice to a litigant.

Not all mistakes made at trial result in appealable issues. For an error to be the foundation of an appeal, it must have resulted in harm or prejudice to one of the litigants. The **appealable error** made must be one that impacted the outcome of the trial. An example that's easy to understand is the exclusion of an alibi witness in a criminal trial. If the witness were to testify concerning the whereabouts of the defendant, the outcome of the case would go a certain way. If the alibi witness were excluded, the outcome of the case could be entirely different. Exclusion of the testimony harms the defendant and would be an appealable error. A new trial, which includes the testimony of the alibi witness, is the appropriate remedy.

Often, errors are made at trial that do not result in harm to either party. The judge may admit or exclude evidence or give a jury charge that is incorrect. Where that error does not contribute to an unfavorable outcome for either of the litigants, it is considered **harmless error,** and no corrective action (appeal) is required. To illustrate, let's return to the contested will case and the admission of the hearsay statements. For this example, assume the hearsay testimony is admitted into evidence. Also admitted are several handwritten letters that have been authenticated as having been written by the decedent. The letters contain the decedent's intent for the disposition of his assets after his death, essentially the same information given in the oral hearsay testimony. On appeal, the error being reviewed would be the admission of the oral hearsay testimony. The appellate court would hold that it was an error to admit the hearsay, but because the same evidence was available from another source, it is unlikely that the erroneous admission of the hearsay resulted in harm. Thus, the admission of the hearsay is harmless error.

> **harmless error**
> An error made at trial that has no impact on the outcome of the case.

■ MOTIONS SEEKING RELIEF FROM THE TRIAL COURT

Following the entry of the verdict, the jury will be excused and the attorneys offered an opportunity to make any oral motions for relief to the trial court. These motions must also be made in writing within ten days from the entry of judgment. These motions include a motion for judgment as a matter of law, motion for a new trial, and motion to mold the verdict.

> **LEARNING OBJECTIVE 3**
> Describe the procedures available to seek relief from the trial court for errors made at trial.

Motion for Judgment as a Matter of Law

A **motion for a judgment as a matter of law** (also known as judgment notwithstanding the verdict, or judgment n.o.v.), asks the trial judge to review and overturn the jury verdict (Fed. R. Civ. P. 50(b)). This motion addresses errors by the jury and says: (1) the jury's decision is against the weight of the evidence and/or (2) the jury has disregarded the law as instructed by the judge, and after reviewing the record, no reasonable minds could disagree about what the outcome of the case should be. However, the jury did not rule in that manner.

> **motion for judgment as a matter of law**
> A posttrial motion that asks the judge to overturn the jury verdict because it is unsupported by the evidence or disregards the law. (Formerly known as a judgment n.o.v. or judgment notwithstanding the verdict.)

 IN THE WORDS OF THE COURT...

Standard of Clear Error

Parts and Elec. Motors, Inc. v. Sterling Elec., Inc.,
866 F.2d 228, 233 (7th Cir. 1988)
"…To be clearly erroneous, a decision must strike us as more than just maybe or probably wrong; it must, as one member of this court recently stated during oral argument, strike us as wrong with the force of a five-week-old, unrefrigerated dead fish."

Motion for a New Trial

A **motion for a new trial** asserts that an error was made in a trial, whether by the judge or by the jury. The error can be related to the admission of evidence, the instructions to the jury, or a verdict unsupported by the law or evidence. Often the error is related to something that occurred at trial that was so prejudicial that it would be a denial of justice to let the jury verdict stand.

Motion to Mold the Verdict

A **motion to mold the verdict** asks the court to take the jury verdict and calculate the amount that the defendant is obligated to pay the plaintiff. This motion is necessary where the defendant is successful on his counterclaim or where the plaintiff has been assigned some portion of negligence in a comparative negligence jurisdiction. Exhibit 19.3 shows a jury verdict slip that would require a motion to mold the verdict. Exhibit 19.4 shows how the verdict might be molded.

Local Rules

It is important to check the local rules in effect in your jurisdiction. Whether in federal court or state court, there will be a set of local rules for the specific court in which you are litigating your case. In some state courts, a panel of trial judges,

Exhibit 19.3 Sample jury verdict slip that requires motion for a molded verdict

---

(Caption of the Case)

On the First Count

Defendant caused the accident
 <u>X</u> Yes   ____ No

Accident caused the injury
 <u>X</u> Yes   ____ No

Plaintiff injuries resulted in damages.
 <u>X</u> Yes   ____ No

Plaintiff caused the accident
 <u>X</u> Yes   ____ No

If yes to above please assigned percentage of liability
 <u>30</u>% to plaintiff
 <u>70</u>% to defendant

Damages sustained by Plaintiff
<u>$300,000.00</u>   ___

On the Second Count

Plaintiff breached the contract
 <u>X</u> Yes   ____ No

Defendant suffered damages as a result of the Plaintiff's breach
 <u>X</u> Yes   ____ No

Damages sustained by Defendant
<u>$30,000.00</u>

Exhibit 19.4 Molded verdict

Molded Verdict

On Count I
Judgment in favor of the Plaintiff in the sum of $210,000

On Count II
Judgment in favor of the Defendant in the sum on $30,000

Final Judgment in Favor of the Plaintiff and against the Defendant in the sum of $180,000.

usually three, must review the trial proceedings before the judgment of the trial judge is considered final and appealable. This is accomplished by a motion for an **en banc review**. In other courts, where the case is tried by a judge without a jury, the judgment of the judge is not final until a written opinion setting forth the judge's findings of facts and conclusions of law is issued.

en banc review
Term used to describe the entire panel of judges sitting and hearing a case, usually on appeal.

■ APPEAL TO AN APPELLATE COURT

After trial-level remedies have been exhausted, and before the expiration of thirty days from entry of judgment, a party may file an appeal with the appellate court. In the federal court system, litigants have the **right to appeal** from the trial court to the intermediate appellate court. Appeals are heard by the U.S. Court of Appeals for the circuit in which the federal district court sits. Exhibit 19.5 shows the locations of the Federal Circuit Courts of Appeals. These appeals are governed by the Federal Rules of Appellate Procedure. In most state court systems, there is an intermediate appellate court, with its own set of rules, that hears appeals from the state trial courts.

LEARNING OBJECTIVE 4
List the requirements for perfecting an appeal.

right to appeal
The right of a litigant to have the decision of the trial court be reviewed by an appellate court.

Exhibit 19.5 U.S. Federal Courts of Appeals

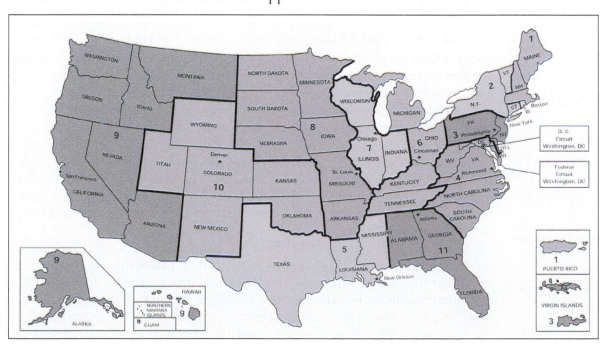

Final Judgment

final judgment
A judgment entered on the docket that ends the litigation, effectively dismissing the litigants from court.

Judgments must be final to be appealable. A **final judgment** is a judgment entered in the docket by the clerk of court that terminates the litigation. Any judgment or ruling of the trial court that does not end the litigation is an **interlocutory order.** Interlocutory orders are not final and are not appealable. For example, a plaintiff's motion for summary judgment to impose liability on the driver in an auto accident case is denied. Even if the court does not make a finding imposing liability, the legal issue may still be litigated in trial. Solely for purposes of the motion for summary judgment, the driver is deemed not liable, leaving the issue of liability subject to further litigation in trial. Because the order does not end the lawsuit, the plaintiff may not appeal the decision.

interlocutory order
Ruling, order, or judgment of the court that affects the rights of the litigants but does not end the litigation.

Alternatively, if the same motion for summary judgment is granted, the driver is held liable, and in that case, the plaintiff has won the lawsuit. The lawsuit is concluded with no further opportunity to litigate the liability issue. This is a final judgment and is appealable by the driver.

Interlocutory Appeals

interlocutory appeal
Appeal from an interlocutory order that requires certification of issue and permission.

In rare instances, interlocutory orders that are not final may be appealed. Where the ruling has the effect of ending the litigation for one of the parties in a multiparty lawsuit, or where the issue involved is a controlling issue of law that is unresolved, the interests of judicial economy may permit the appeal of an interlocutory order. Permission of the court of appeals to hear an **interlocutory appeal** is required. A key component to the acceptance of an interlocutory appeal is certification by the trial judge that the issue involves a controlling question of law to which there is a substantial difference of opinion (Fed. R. App. P. 5).

appellant
The party who asserts that error occurred at trial by filing an appeal for review of the trial proceedings.

petitioner
The party who asserts that error occurred at trial by filing an appeal for review of the trial proceedings.

appellee
The party, usually the verdict winner at trial, who must respond to an appeal for review.

■ PROCEDURE FOR FILING AN APPEAL WITH THE U.S. COURT OF APPEALS

LEARNING OBJECTIVE 5
Describe the appeal process in the United States Court of Appeals and the United States Supreme Court.

The party who is dissatisfied with the outcome at trial and files an appeal is called the **appellant** or **petitioner.** The party who must respond to the appeal is the **appellee** or **respondent.** Typically, the appellant will include several issues that are claimed to represent appealable or reversible error committed by the trial judge or jury. The appellee may argue that the judge did not err or that the error made was harmless error. Sometimes, the appellee may also be dissatisfied with the outcome at trial. Perhaps the jury rendered a verdict for the plaintiff, but the judge reduced the award of damages. The defendant, now the appellant, seeks to overturn the verdict and award of damages. The plaintiff, now the appellee, might file a **cross appeal** seeking to reinstate the jury's original verdict rather than the reduced amount determined by the judge. In that event, the appellee is also the **cross appellant.**

respondent
The party, usually the verdict winner at trial, who must respond to an appeal for review.

cross appeal
Where the appellee also asserts that error occurred at trial and seeks appellate review of the trial proceedings.

cross appellant
The appellee (or respondent) who files a cross appeal.

Court rules are very specific about the procedures for a valid appeal and the form of the documents that must be submitted. Court rules, supplemented by local rules, specify the time deadlines and the particular format of the documents submitted, including such things as the size of the margins, type fonts and type size, type of paper, and the color of the cover attached to the legal brief. Therefore, the rules must be consulted for every detail of an appeal. Not only must the federal rules (or, if filed in a state court, the state appeals rules) be considered, but the local rules must also be consulted for the procedures to **perfect the appeal.** Failure to comply with these rules can result in the appeal being **quashed,** or dismissed, with the client losing her right to appeal the judgment of the trial court. Even when an appeal is not quashed, a law firm's failure to comply with the rules can reflect poorly on the abilities of the legal team. In firms that specialize in appellate practice, paralegals oversee adherence to the timelines, management of the documents, and compliance with the technical requirements of the appellate court, whereas the supervising attorney will be concerned about the legal substance of the argument being made. The paralegal's ability to find the rules (both federal and local), read them, understand them, and apply them to the appeals process will allow the attorney to more completely focus on the legal research and writing the argument.

Notice of Appeal

The filing of an appeal in federal court is governed by the Federal Rules of Appellate Procedure (Fed. R. App. P. 3 and 4). An appeal is commenced by filing a notice of appeal with the clerk of the district court within thirty days of the entry of the judgment. However, in the event posttrial motions have been filed with the district court, the time for filing the **notice of appeal** begins to run out after the last of those motions has been ruled on. The time to file the notice of appeal can also be extended by filing a motion to request an extension with the district court within the thirty-day appeal period. Extension will be granted so long as there is a reasonable basis, rather than someone simply having forgotten to do his or her job. The correct format of the notice of appeal is provided in the rules. Exhibit 19.6 is an example of a notice of appeal.

The procedure for filing the notice of appeal involves paying the filing fee and providing sufficient copies, as required by the rules, of the notice of appeal for the clerk of courts to send to the other parties to the lawsuit. Local rules, such as that of the Second Circuit shown in Exhibit 19.7, should also be consulted.

To prevent efforts to enforce or collect on the judgment entered, the appellant should also file with the court a stay of proceedings.

Record on Appeal

The clerk of court has the responsibility of forwarding to the appellate court the **record on appeal.**

Although it is the duty of the clerk to forward the record, it is the responsibility of the appellant to cooperate in assembling the record so that it can be forwarded. The record on appeal includes the original papers and exhibits filed with the district court, such as the pleadings, motions, and legal briefs. From a practical standpoint, this means the clerk will forward the contents of the file contained in his office for the lawsuit. The clerk must also provide a certified copy of the docket entries. The third and final element of the record to be forwarded by the clerk is the trial transcript. Under Fed. R. App. P. 10(b), the appellant is responsible for requesting and paying for the transcription of the trial. A copy of the Civil Appeal Transcript request form is shown in Exhibit 19.8.

perfect an appeal
A term used to describe compliance with all the procedures necessary for filing a valid appeal.

quashed appeal
Dismissal of an appeal for failure to comply with the rules of procedure.

notice of appeal
Document filed with the clerk of court indicating that a decision of the trial court is being appealed.

PRACTICE TIP

Most of the federal court and many of the state court forms are available online in a PDF form that allows on-screen completion of the forms with fillable areas, such as the example in Exhibit 19.6.

record on appeal
The documents forwarded by the clerk of the district court to the circuit court of appeals for review. The record on appeal includes the original documents filed with the court, the trial transcript with exhibits received into evidence, and the docket entries.

Exhibit 19.6   Notice of appeal

Federal Rules of Appellate Procedure Form 1.   Notice of Appeal to a Court of Appeals From a Judgment or Order of a District Court.

United States District Court for the District of
_____

File Number _____

_____)
Plaintiff,   )
v.   )   Notice of Appeal
)
_____)
)
Defendant.   )

Notice is hereby given that _____, (plaintiffs) (defendants) in the above-named case*, hereby appeal to the United States Court of Appeals for the _____ Circuit (from the final judgment) (from an order (describing it)) entered in this action on the _____ day of _____, 20____.

/s/
_____
Attorney for
_____
Address:
_____

*See Rule 3(c) for permissible ways of identifying appellants

Exhibit 19.7   Second Circuit Rule 3.1

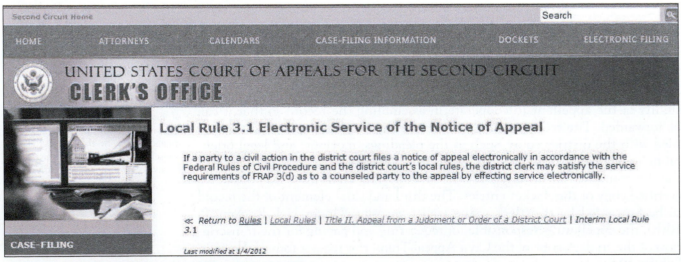

Local Rule 3.1 Electronic Service of the Notice of Appeal

If a party to a civil action in the district court files a notice of appeal electronically in accordance with the Federal Rules of Civil Procedure and the district court's local rules, the district clerk may satisfy the service requirements of FRAP 3(d) as to a counseled party to the appeal by effecting service electronically.

« Return to _Rules_ | _Local Rules_ | _Title II. Appeal from a Judgment or Order of a District Court_ | _Interim Local Rule 3.1_

Last modified at 1/4/2012

Source: www.ca2.uscourts.gov/clerk/Rules/LR/Local_Rule_3_1.htm

Exhibit 19.8 Civil Appeal Transcript form

UNITED STATES COURT OF APPEALS
FOR THE SECOND CIRCUIT

CIVIL APPEAL TRANSCRIPT INFORMATION (FORM D)

NOTICE TO COUNSEL: COUNSEL FOR THE APPELLANT MUST FILE THIS FORM WITH THE CLERK OF THE SECOND CIRCUIT IN ALL CIVIL APPEALS WITHIN 14 CALENDAR DAYS AFTER FILING A NOTICE OF APPEAL.

THIS SECTION MUST BE COMPLETED BY COUNSEL FOR APPELLANT		
CASE TITLE	**DISTRICT**	**DOCKET NUMBER**
	JUDGE	**APPELLANT**
	COURT REPORTER	**COUNSEL FOR APPELLANT**

Check the applicable provision:

☐ I am ordering a transcript.

☐ I am not ordering a transcript

Reason for not ordering a transcript:

☐ Copy is already available

☐ No transcribed proceedings

☐ Other (Specify in the space below):

PROVIDE A DESCRIPTION, INCLUDING DATES, OF THE PROCEEDINGS FOR WHICH A TRANSCRIPT IS REQUIRED (*i.e.*, oral argument, order from the bench, etc.)

METHOD OF PAYMENT ☐ Funds ☐ CJA Voucher (CJA 21)

INSTRUCTIONS TO COURT REPORTER:

☐ PREPARE TRANSCRIPT OF PRE-TRIAL PROCEEDINGS

☐ PREPARE TRANSCRIPT OF TRIAL

☐ PREPARE TRANSCRIPT OF OTHER POST-TRIAL PROCEEDINGS

☐ OTHER (Specify in the space below):

DELIVER TRANSCRIPT TO: (COUNSEL'S NAME, ADDRESS, TELEPHONE)

I certify that I have made satisfactory arrangements with the court reporter for payment of the cost of the transcript. *See* FRAP 10(b). I understand that unless I have already ordered the transcript, I shall order its preparation at the time required by FRAP and the Local Rules.

COUNSEL'S SIGNATURE	DATE

COURT REPORTER ACKNOWLEDGMENT: This section is to be completed by the court reporter. Return one copy to the Clerk of the Second Circuit.

DATE ORDER RECEIVED	ESTIMATED COMPLETION DATE	ESTIMATED NUMBER OF PAGES

SIGNATURE OF COURT REPORTED	DATE

Trial Transcript

Within ten days of filing the notice of appeal, the appellant must order a transcript of the trial from the court reporter and make arrangements to pay for it. It is not necessary to request that the entire trial be transcribed; it is sufficient for the appellant to designate that those portions of the trial that are relevant to the issues on appeal be transcribed. However, the appellee will have the opportunity to review what the appellant has selected for transcription and may request that additional portions of the trial be transcribed.

The court reporter has thirty days to complete the transcription and file it with the clerk of the district court. The court reporter may request an extension of time to complete the transcription. Once the **trial transcript** is received, the clerk of the district court will forward the record on appeal to the clerk of the appellate court.

Scheduling Order

The rules specify the deadlines associated with the appeals process. As previously discussed, there are thirty days to file the appeal and ten days from the filing date to request the transcript. In many of the circuit courts, the clerk, upon receipt of the record on appeal, will issue a **scheduling order.** This order sets specific dates for submission of supplements to the record, briefs, oral arguments, and requests that the matter be submitted for determination without argument. The paralegal must be certain to check the rules as well. Under Fed. R. App. P. Rule 31, the appellant's brief is due forty days after the record on appeal is filed with the clerk of the circuit court. Typically, the scheduling order will include that date, but waiting for the scheduling order to be received may cost the legal team as many as five working days. Thus, familiarity with the rules (rather than waiting to hear from the court) will benefit the legal team. All responsive briefs have due dates under the rules in relation to the date the brief is filed rather than the date the appellate brief is due. Those dates are not listed in the scheduling order and must be calculated from the rules of court.

Briefs

The appellant and the appellee are required to submit to the court written **briefs** setting forth the legal issues presented for review. Each will also include a suggested resolution of those legal issues, based upon well-founded legal research. The paralegal can expect to have a good deal of involvement in the preparation of the appellate brief. Traditionally, legal briefs contain five major components: facts, issues presented, short answer, legal argument, and conclusion. Under the appellate rules, the contents of the brief are more specifically described and must be followed. The requirements for briefs are listed in Fed. R. App. P. 28.

There are three areas where the paralegal will typically be involved in preparing the appellate brief: compliance with the rules, research and writing, and citation checking.

Compliance with Rules

As with all proceedings, the legal team must consult the rules of appellate procedure and the local rules of the particular court. The contents of briefs are governed by Fed. R. App. P. 28 and include all the elements that must be part of the brief. The list is exhaustive, or so it seems, including everything from a table of contents to a conclusion and the components that should be included in the argument. For example, in addition to the rules that dictate the contents, there are also rules that determine the format, including the color of the cover page, how the brief should be held together, the margin and font sizes, and page limitations (Fed. R. App. P. 32), as well the number of copies (e.g., 25) to be submitted to the clerk for filing (Fed. R. App. P. 31).

A brief is not compliant with the rules unless it also satisfies the local rules, as shown in selected portion in Exhibit 19.7. For example, in the Third Circuit, fasteners must have smooth edges; in the Fifth Circuit, only seven copies of the brief need to be filed instead of twenty-five. Failure to comply with the local rules may result in the rejection of the appeal; it also shows a lack of respect for the appellate court.

Research and Writing

The amount of a time a paralegal will have to devote to conducting legal research and writing appellate briefs will be a direct function of the paralegal's experience and the willingness of the attorney to delegate this responsibility. All paralegals should be able to locate a case or statute if requested by the supervising attorney. Additionally, paralegals should be able to locate cases, constitutional provisions, statutes, and administrative law both from traditional book sources and through electronic research methods.

Some paralegals might be entrusted with legal research on a particular topic. The research of a paralegal should always be subject to review by the supervising attorney. Paralegals should be able to write some of the portions of the appellate brief, particularly the preliminary statements such as jurisdiction of the court and the relevant facts. To be complete, the statement of facts must also contain references to the reproduced record. Clearly, the paralegal should be able to read the trial transcript and find the reference to the facts of the case.

It is unlikely that a paralegal would participate in the writing of the legal argument. Legal argument is an area solely within the domain of the supervising attorney. However, the paralegal might assist with checking for grammar and spelling errors and reviewing the overall readability of the argument.

Citation Checking

The final area that paralegals can expect to be involved in is **citation checking.** Citation checking includes verifying that citations to reproduced records and the case and statutory law are accurate. Facts included in the statement of the facts in the brief require a reference or citation to the source of the facts in the reproduced record. Case law and statutes relied upon in the argument section of the brief must also be referenced. At the most fundamental level, the paralegal will be responsible for verifying that the citation, whether to the record or to the law, is in the correct format used by the court. The Rules of Appellate Procedure describe how to refer to the record. The *Bluebook* or *ALWD Book of Legal Citation* will provide the necessary guidance on the proper citation form of legal references. The paralegal will need to check the local rules to determine which method of legal citation has been adopted in the circuit.

Citation checking can also refer to determining whether the reference is correct: Does the citation direct the reader to the correct material? When citing case law, the citation "207 Cal.App.3d 164" should lead the reader to the first page of *Welch v. Metro-Goldwyn-Mayer Film Co.* However, if either the volume or the page number is incorrect, the reader will be unable to find the case relied upon by the writer of the brief.

citation checking
Process by which citations to the record and the law are checked for accuracy.

The next level of checking citations is to determine that the included quotations are accurately quoted.

The final level of cite checking requires the determination that the information, if used to support a legal argument, represents the principle for which it is relied upon. Because this level of cite checking requires legal analysis, it is unlikely that the paralegal will be responsible for it.

However, the paralegal may be responsible for verifying the case law and statutes relied upon to be sure they have not been overturned.

Oral Argument

oral argument
The opportunity for the attorneys to present an oral argument to the panel of appellate judges.

The final step in the appellate procedure is **oral argument.** The paralegal will benefit from understanding the purpose and process of the oral argument even though paralegals rarely attend such proceedings. At oral argument, the attorney is given the opportunity to address the three-member panel of appellate judges. The time for argument is limited—in some instances, to twenty minutes. The expectation is that the attorney will bring to the panel's attention some unique reason why the appeal should be resolved in her client's favor. The attorney should not simply use the oral argument to repeat what is contained in the written brief. Frequently, however, the attorney is not given the opportunity to present the argument planned. Instead, the judges pepper the attorney with questions, perhaps expecting the attorney to defend the weaknesses in the argument set forth in the brief. It is a special talent indeed to be able to appropriately respond to the judges' challenges and stay on point with the argument the attorney had planned to make.

> **PRACTICE TIP**
> **ALTERNATE DISPUTE RESOLUTION (ADR)**
> Many are under the impression that once a jury verdict has been rendered and judgment entered, the potential for alternative dispute resolution no longer exists. In fact, the opposite is true. Even when the parties are contemplating posttrial motions and appellate review, there are opportunities for resolution. The old cliché "A bird in the hand is worth two in the bush" is the motivating factor in settlement discussions at this phase of civil litigation. For example, the defendant may offer some amount less than the judgment amount. For the defendant, the offer to settle not only reduces his liability on the judgment amount but also saves the time and costs associated with an appeal. For the plaintiff, the offer to settle, while resulting in less than the judgment amount, is equivalent to money in her pocket within thirty days, rather than one to three years while the appeals process is fully exhausted.

The paralegal can assist the attorney in preparing for the oral argument by simply listening to the argument. The paralegal can also be proactive by asking questions about the weaknesses in the argument. This gives the attorney a chance to be better prepared for the challenges to the argument the appellate panel might raise to the argument.

Rulings of the Appellate Court

At the close of the oral argument, the appellate panel will take the matter under advisement. This means that the judges will confer about the dispute. Typically, they will discuss and vote on the appropriate outcome. The writing of the opinion, which will contain the legal basis in support of the decision, will be assigned to one of the judges. Once a written opinion is circulated for review and the judges agree on its contents, it will be entered on the docket of the appellate court, sent to the litigants, and made available for review by the public at large.

There are three potential rulings the appellate court can issue: affirm the trial court, reverse the trial court, or reverse and remand for further proceedings consistent with the court's written opinion.

Affirm the Decision. The appellate court can affirm the trial court. To affirm the trial court is to state that no error occurred that requires corrective action. This is the appellate court's approving of the trial court proceedings. The judgment entered in the trial court stands and is now subject to enforcement proceedings.

Reverse the Decision. The appellate court can reverse the trial court. To reverse the trial court is to state that the judgment was entered incorrectly against the appellant at trial, and that the appellant should have won. The trial court's judgment must therefore be stricken from the record of the trial proceedings. Note that reversal is rare and is most likely accompanied by an order for remand.

Remand. The appellate court can remand the case for further proceedings if there has been some reversible error found in the trial proceedings. The appellate court in its written opinion will state clearly the error and what should have been done instead. Then the appellate court will order the matter be reversed and remanded for further trial proceedings based on the instructions contained in the opinion. An example is the admission of hearsay, as discussed at the beginning of the chapter. Assume now that the admission of the hearsay, both the witness testimony and the handwritten letters, is determined by the appellate court to be an error. The decision of the trial court will be reversed and the matter will be remanded, perhaps for a new trial, to determine the decedent's intent without referring to those hearsay elements.

Appeal to the Highest Appellate Court

In some instances, appellants are dissatisfied with the decision of the intermediate appellate court. In the federal court system, as well as in most state court systems, there is another level of review. The highest appellate court in the federal system is the United States Supreme Court. The Supreme Court hears appeals on a permissive basis—a **permissive appeal.** A litigant does not simply file a notice of appeal, as in the circuit court of appeals. Rather, a litigant requests permission to place an appeal on the docket of the Supreme Court. This process is known as a **petition for writ of certiorari.** The Court then decides whether it will consider the issue on appeal. If so, the Court will grant certiorari; if not, the petition is denied.

Once certiorari is granted, the process is similar to an appeal in the court of appeals. That is, there is a schedule for providing the reproduced record and briefs and a date set for argument before the Court. The major difference is that all nine justices of the Supreme Court hear and decide the appeal as an entire panel.

The Court will decide and issue its opinion to affirm, reverse, or remand the case in a similar way as in an appeal in the court of appeals.

 WEB RESOURCES
You can hear oral arguments of selected cases on the U.S. Supreme Court website: http://www.supremecourtus.gov/oral_arguments/oral_arguments.html

permissive appeal
An appellant must obtain the permission of the court to file an appeal.

petition for writ of certiorari
The document requesting that the United States Supreme Court accept a particular matter for review.

CONCEPT REVIEW AND REINFORCEMENT

KEY TERMS

motion for judgment on the pleadings   444

motion for summary judgment   444

verdict   445

entry of judgment   445

posttrial relief   446

errors made in evidentiary ruling   446

errors made in instructions to jury   446

verdict unsupported by the evidence   446

preserving the record   446

continuing objection   446

appealable error   448

harmless error   449

motion for judgment as a matter of law   449

motion for new trial   450

motion to mold the verdict   450

en banc review   451

right to appeal   451

final judgment   452

interlocutory order   452

interlocutory appeal   452

appellant   452

petitioner   452

appellee   452

respondent   452

cross appeal   452

cross appellant   452

perfect an appeal   453

quashed appeal   453

notice of appeal   453

record on appeal   453

trial transcript   456

scheduling order   456

briefs   456

citation checking   457

oral argument   458

permissive appeal   459

petition for writ of certiorari   459

CHAPTER SUMMARY

POSTTRIAL PROCEDURES

Introduction to Posttrial Procedures	Following the jury verdict, posttrial procedures are used to correct any errors alleged to have been made by the court in conducting the trial. Court rules provide for limited time for taking posttrial action.

Entering Judgment	Litigation may terminate by:
	1. motion for judgment on the pleadings;
	2. motion for summary judgment; or
	3. verdict.
	    A motion for judgment on the pleadings can be made by either side based solely on the pleadings submitted, which are considered in the light most favorable to the non-moving party.
	    Motion for summary judgment is similar to a motion for judgment on the pleadings, except that the court may consider documents outside the pleadings, such as written discovery requests, deposition transcripts, and affidavits.
	    A verdict is rendered by the jury or by the judge sitting as the trier of fact.
	    A judgment rendered must be entered on the court docket for it to have any effect on the litigants. In federal court, this requires a written document to be filed with the clerk of court.

Errors Made at Trial	Posttrial relief must be pursued within a short period of time, usually ten days, and usually concerns errors by the judge in ruling on evidentiary admissions or exclusions or in giving the instructions to the jury; posttrial relief might also be pursued where the jury verdict is contrary to or unsupported by the evidence.

The attorney must preserve the record for appeal by making any appropriate objections during the trial. Where the objection will be made repeatedly with regard to the presentation of specific evidence, the court may permit a continuing objection to be placed on the record.

Appealable errors are those that impact the outcome of the trial. Harmless errors are those that did not result in harm to either party and are not appealable.

Motion Seeking Relief from the Trial Court	Following the entry of judgment and within the time period provided for posttrial relief, the attorneys can make a motion for judgment as a matter of law regarding an error of the judge or to overturn the jury verdict when the jury has disregarded the evidence or the law.
	Counsel can also make a motion for a new trial, claiming that the error made by the judge or by the jury is so prejudicial that it would be denial of justice to let the jury verdict stand.
	A motion to mold a verdict asks the court to calculate the amount the defendant is obligated to pay the plaintiff when the defendant has been successful on a counterclaim, in a case in which the plaintiff has been assigned some portion of the negligence, or in a comparative negligence jurisdiction.
Appeal to an Appellate Court	Judgments must be final to be appealable. A final judgment is one that is entered on the court docket, an action that terminates the litigation. A judgment or ruling of the trial court that does not end the litigation is called an interlocutory order. The exception is when one of the parties in a multiparty lawsuit has had an order entered that acts as a termination of the litigation with regard to that party.
Procedure for Filing an Appeal with the U.S. Court of Appeals	The party who appeals is called the appellant or the petitioner. The responding party is called the appellee or the respondent.
	To perfect the appeal, court rules, as supplemented by local court rules, must be carefully followed, or the appeal might be quashed.
	Appeal in federal court is commenced with the filing of a notice of appeal within thirty days of the entry of a judgment. If posttrial motions have been filed, the time begins after the last of the motions has been ruled on by the court.
	For transmission to the appellate court, the appellant must provide the clerk of court with the record on appeal, which includes the court file, certified copies of the docket entries, and the applicable portion of the trial transcript as provided by the appellant. It is the appellant's responsibility to order the transcript from the court reporter and pay for it.
	The clerk of court issues a scheduling order that sets a specified date for submission of supplements to the record, briefs, oral arguments, and requests that the matter be submitted for determination without argument.
	Both parties are required to submit written briefs setting forth the legal issues presented for review to the court. The briefs submitted must comply with all court rules, including local rules, which may specify the number of copies to be supplied and the format of the submission, including paper size, type font, margin sizes, and length.
	An important aspect of the research and writing of the brief is the cite checking, which ensures accuracy of the material quoted and the source of that material. Individual courts and judges might require a specific citation format, which should be determined before submission of the briefs.
	Oral argument may be waived by the attorneys and the case decided by the appellate court on briefs alone. Where oral argument is desired, the time allowed for each attorney is generally limited, in some instances to twenty minutes. Frequently, the court will ask questions during the allotted time and will not allow the attorney to elaborate on her legal arguments.

(continued)

The appellate court may make three potential rulings with regard to the case: to *affirm* and agree that the trial court acted properly and requires no corrective action; to *reverse* and determine that the trial court entered an erroneous judgment, and the judgment should be for the opposing party; to *remand* and determine that there was some error but that the trial court should take additional testimony and correct the errors found.

In each court system, there is an intermediate appellate court and an ultimate, or highest, appellate court. In the federal system, the highest appellate court is the U.S. Supreme Court. The U.S. Supreme Court hears appeals on a permissive basis, selecting only those cases it wishes to hear by granting the appealing party's petition for writ of certiorari.

REVIEW QUESTIONS AND EXERCISES

1. Describe how litigation can be terminated by a judgment.
2. What is the purpose of entering a judgment on the record of the docket?
3. What is meant by the term *posttrial relief*? Explain.
4. What is meant by *appealable error*?
5. What is meant by *harmless error*?
6. Describe the types of reversible error.
7. How is a continuing objection used?
8. What does it mean to preserve the record for appeal?
9. Describe the posttrial relief that is available from the trial court. Explain why seeking relief from the trial court might be unsuccessful.
10. How is the motion to mold the verdict different from other posttrial relief?
11. Explain the difference between the right to an appeal and a permissive appeal.
12. Is an interlocutory appeal a right to appeal or a permissive appeal?
13. Name the party who appeals the result at trial.
14. What is the effect of a final judgment?
15. Is an interlocutory order a final judgment? Are there any exceptions?
16. What does it mean to perfect an appeal? What steps must be taken to perfect an appeal?
17. What is a notice of appeal?
18. What is included in the record on appeal? Who prepares this?
19. Is the trial transcript the record of the entire proceeding that occurred at trial?
20. What is a scheduling order?
21. What is the purpose of an appellate brief?
22. Describe the purposes and types of citation checking.
23. What is the purpose of oral argument? Why would an attorney waive the right to make oral argument?
24. Describe the rulings of the appellate court and the effects of those rulings on the trial court proceedings.
25. What is a petition for certiorari?
26. After termination of litigation by judgment, is settlement of the dispute still a possibility? Why or why not?
27. Should trial evidence be preserved? For how long? Why?

BUILDING YOUR PARALEGAL SKILLS

INTERNET AND TECHNOLOGY EXERCISES

1. Locate the web address of your local federal and state appellate courts.
2. Does your local appellate court publish the local rules on its website?
3. Does your local court support or require electronic filing of appellate filings and briefs? If it does, what are the specific requirements?
4. What online methods can be used to check the latest cases cited in a brief?
5. Prepare a timeline for post-verdict actions.

CIVIL LITIGATION VIDEO CASE STUDIES

Three-Judge Appellate Panel

 On appeal from the trial court, a three-judge panel is hearing and responding to an appellate argument about the scope of strict products liability theory, relevant defenses, and the issue of joint tortfeasors.

After viewing the video at www.pearsonhighered.com/ careersresources, answer the following questions.

1. Will the appellate court allow new testimony?
2. What are the options open to the appellate court in making a decision?
3. Why are only the attorneys present for the presentation to the court?

CHAPTER OPENING SCENARIO CASE STUDY

Use the Opening Scenario for this chapter to answer the following questions.

1. What are the fees charged for transcripts in your local federal court and state court?
2. What motions should the paralegals be ready to prepare? What information will they need?

3. Should the team contact the opposing side to see if the case can be settled before the jury returns its verdict? Why or why not?

COMPREHENSIVE CASE STUDY

SCHOOL BUS–TRUCK ACCIDENT CASE

Review the assigned case study in Appendix 2.

1. Prepare an entry of judgment for the assigned case study in Appendix 2.

2. Prepare a notice of appeal based on the rules in your local federal court for the assigned case study in Appendix 2.

BUILDING YOUR PROFESSIONAL PORTFOLIO AND REFERENCE MANUAL

CIVIL LITIGATION TEAM AT WORK

See page 18 for instructions on Building Your Professional Portfolio.

Forms

1. Required form for entry of judgment in your trial court
2. Required forms for filing appeals in your state and federal courts

Procedures

1. Time limits for filing posttrial motions and entries of judgment
2. Fees for filing

Contacts and Resources

1. Court reporters, along with list of fees charged
2. Court office for filing notice of appeals, along with hours of operation

LEARNING OBJECTIVES

After studying this chapter, you should be able to:

1. Explain the terminology used and the initial timing limitations in collecting judgments.

2. Describe the process of collecting and enforcing judgments.

3. Explain the statutory limitations on collection efforts.

4. Prepare a satisfaction document to file when the judgment is satisfied.

Enforcement of Judgments | CHAPTER 20

OPENING SCENARIO

 The team had been successful in obtaining a very satisfactory award against each of the defendants in the school bus versus truck case. Procedural and other appealable issues had been fully resolved, and there were no more legal challenges except collecting on the judgment. Judgments rendered against multiple defendants on behalf of numerous clients had to be carefully monitored. With the claims of the minor clients, it was necessary to file petitions with the court to confirm the disbursement of funds, the reimbursement of expenses, and the payment of allowable attorney's fees. One of the corporate defendants had quickly offered payment and satisfaction of the judgments against it. Unfortunately, one of the other corporate defendants was in financial difficulty, and obtaining satisfaction of the judgment looked uncertain. In addition, the substantial amounts awarded, when collectively computed, far exceeded the personal assets of the defendant drivers. The team thus needed to be certain that it had investigated every possible opportunity on behalf of its clients to obtain funds to satisfy the judgments and preserve the rights and priorities in the event of any bankruptcy proceedings that might ensue.

OPENING SCENARIO LEARNING OBJECTIVE

Prepare the necessary documentation to enforce a judgment in your jurisdiction.

■ INTRODUCTION TO ENFORCEMENT OF JUDGMENTS

The final and most important step in the civil litigation process is collecting the judgment that was entered on the case. Litigation can conclude with the entry of a judgment on the docket by default judgment, judgment on the pleadings, summary judgment, bench trial verdict, jury verdict, or a final ruling of an appellate court. Regardless of the variety of ways in which a judgment can be obtained, the client and the law firm must enforce that judgment and collect the sums due. The process of judgment enforcement may be as simple as a telephone call to opposing counsel that results in payment from the client; at the other extreme, complex legal proceedings might be necessary to locate assets, formally seize them, and arrange a judicial sale of the seized property.

■ TERMINOLOGY AND TIMING IN JUDGMENT COLLECTION

LEARNING OBJECTIVE 1
Explain the terminology used and the initial timing limitations in collecting judgments.

judgment debtor
The party who lost at trial and now has a judgment entered against him and owes another person money for damages.

judgment creditor
The party who won at trial and is owed money for damages in the amount of the judgment.

debtor
One who owes another a sum of money.

creditor
One to whom money is owed.

judgment
The official decision of the court setting forth the rights and obligations of the parties.

stayed
Holding off for a particular period of time (as in "the collection of a judgment is stayed") until appeals are exhausted.

LEARNING OBJECTIVE 2
Describe the process of collecting and enforcing judgments.

Once judgment is entered, the parties to the underlying lawsuit are identified differently for the purposes of collection and enforcement of the judgment. No longer are they plaintiff and defendant—they now become **judgment debtor** and **judgment creditor.** Think of these terms in their ordinary sense. That is, a **debtor** is ordinarily one who owes money to another; a **creditor** is the one to whom money is owed. The term **judgment** merely describes the nature of the debt owed—a judgment entered in the docket of a court as a result of a legal proceeding. The judgment debtor is the party (whether plaintiff or defendant) who lost at trial and now owes damages in the amount of the judgment. The judgment creditor (whether plaintiff or defendant) is the one who won at trial and is now owed damages in the amount of the judgment.

Under the federal rules, no proceedings to commence the enforcement of judgment may begin until ten days have elapsed from the entry of judgment (Fed. R. Civ. P. 62(a)). Technically speaking, a judgment creditor may begin efforts to collect a judgment ten days after its entry. From a practical standpoint, however, that might not be how the legal team proceeds. Both parties have an opportunity to file posttrial motions within ten days and appeals within thirty days following entry of the judgment. Thus, any efforts toward enforcement will be **stayed,** or held off, during the pendency of posttrial motions and appeals. For many practitioners, the judgment is not considered final and enforceable until these time periods have expired. Therefore, enforcement activities will not normally commence until thirty days following entry of the judgment.

■ COLLECTION OF JUDGMENT PROCESS

In a perfect world, a judgment is entered, and the judgment debtor immediately gives the judgment creditor cash to cover the judgment. More likely, there is an insurance carrier involved that requires certain procedures to be fulfilled before the judgment will be paid. Sometimes there will be no insurance, and the judgment creditor will look directly to the assets of the judgment debtor for payment. While one hopes for the perfect-world result, often the judgment debtor will evade and avoid making payment. In that instance, the legal team must commence legal proceedings to enforce and collect the judgment.

Non-Adversarial Collection Efforts

Where the judgment debtor (or his insurance carrier) is willing and able to pay the judgment amount, the efforts to collect on the judgment are non-adversarial in nature. Typically, a single telephone call or collection letter is enough. A collection letter will include reference to the lawsuit, its docket number, the judgment amount, and the date of entry of the judgment. The collection letter will also request payment in full and indicate a willingness to cooperate with any requirements of the insurance carrier. The collection letter may additionally contain a **satisfaction piece** form intended to be filed with the clerk of court to mark the judgment paid on the docket.

In those cases where the law firm has advanced costs on behalf of the client and/or has deferred payment of its fee until collection of the judgment amount, it is good practice to prepare an **authorization for distribution** for the client to review and sign. This statement will list the anticipated amount of money, the deductions from the gross amount for costs and attorney's fees, and the net amount to be paid to the client. Before preparing the authorization, the paralegal should check the written fee agreement between the client and the law firm to determine who is responsible for the payment of costs; the method of calculation of counsel fees (hourly or contingent on gross or net) should also be verified. The client's file should also be checked to determine what costs are outstanding; if the client paid an advance to cover litigation costs or a retainer against legal fees, a detailed statement of funds and fees must be prepared. One thing that will ruin good client relations is a miscalculation of the fees. Exhibit 20.1 is an authorization for distribution of proceeds of judgment.

satisfaction piece
A document filed with the clerk of court to mark the judgment paid on the docket.

authorization for distribution
Written statement granting permission to accept a sum of money and distribute it in accordance with a schedule of distribution.

Adversarial Proceedings

In those instances where there is no insurance carrier and the judgment debtor fails to respond to the collection letter, the judgment creditor will be required to use the court system to enforce the judgment.

A court must have jurisdiction over the assets (*in rem*) and person (*in personam*) of the judgment debtor to order liquidation of assets for purposes of payment on the judgment. Jurisdiction over the debtor's assets lies with the state court in the state where those assets are located. Thus, enforcing a judgment from the federal court system will require use of state court remedies. The Federal Rules of Civil Procedure acknowledge this limitation of federal court jurisdiction and authorize the use of various state court remedies for the enforcement of judgments (Fed. R. Civ. P. 64).

The Federal Rules of Civil Procedure provide that the rules to enforce a judgment obtained in federal court are the rules of the state court in which the federal district court is located. For example, if the judgment is entered against the debtor in the Eastern District of Pennsylvania, the enforcement of the judgment will be based upon the Pennsylvania Rules of Civil Procedure for such things as execution, levy, garnishment, and replevin.

A legal proceeding must be commenced in the appropriate state court. Under the **Full Faith and Credit clause** of the U.S. Constitution, there is no need for another trial to determine the judgment debtor's liability. The state court must acknowledge the validity of the judgment obtained in federal court. Once the judgment is acknowledged, the state court system and its protections for debtors will be used to enforce the judgment.

in rem
Jurisdiction over the property.

in personam
Jurisdiction over the person.

Full Faith and Credit clause
A provision in the United States Constitution that requires the individual states to honor the judgments entered in other state and federal courts.

Exhibit 20.1 Typical Schedule of Distribution and Authorization

Martin Thomas
112 Schan Drive
Syracuse, New York 13200

Dear Mr. Thomas:

This will confirm that, in accordance with our recent correspondence and discussions, I have conveyed to the insurance carrier your acceptance of the most recent settlement offer. We are currently in the process of drafting the necessary documents to effect a final settlement. Accordingly, I would like to get your authorization to proceed with a settlement in accordance with the following terms:

	$120,000	Total settlement
Less	30,000	Attorney's fees per contingent fee agreement
Less	1,550	Out-of-pocket expenses for filing fees
Less	21,500	Reimbursement for medical expenses to doctors
Total	$ 66,950	Net recovery to you

I believe the foregoing accurately reflects the terms of our retainer agreement. Accordingly, kindly indicate your acceptance of these settlement terms by signing the enclosed duplicate of this correspondence where indicated and returning it to me immediately in the envelope provided.

Sincerely,

Owen Mason

Enclosures

AUTHORIZATION TO SETTLE

I have read the above terms and agree that my counsel may proceed to settle my case in accordance with such terms.

_____ (sign here)

Date_____   Martin Thomas

PRACTICE TIP

Each state that has adopted the Uniform Enforcement of Foreign Judgments Act has made modifications to it so that it complies with that state's specific procedures. Thus, it is important to check your state's version of the Act to determine the particular requirements of your state.

Uniform Enforcement of Foreign Judgments Act

As of 2013, forty-seven states, the District of Columbia, and the U.S. Virgin Islands had adopted the **Uniform Enforcement of Foreign Judgments Act,** with Massachusetts introducing the legislation in 2013, while California and Vermont had not yet adopted or introduced the legislation. The Act provides a simple, uniform procedure for lodging, or entering, **foreign judgments** with a state court. A state court considers a judgment foreign if it originates from any other court—state or federal—of the United States. Thus, a judgment obtained in a federal district court is a foreign judgment that will be registered with the state court and enforced under the state rules of procedure. The Revised Uniform Enforcement of Foreign Judgments Act appears as Exhibit 20.2.

The Act requires that a copy of the foreign judgment (which has been authenticated or certified as true and correct by the clerk of the foreign issuing court) be filed with the clerk of the state court. The authenticated copy is typically accompanied by a complete copy of the docket entries, an affidavit stating the name and last known address of the judgment debtor, and a filing fee. Some states require that the notice of the registration of the foreign judgment, along with a postage-prepaid envelope addressed to the judgment debtor, also be submitted. Once filed, the foreign judgment is now a judgment in the state court. There is a brief time period before further enforcement proceedings can be initiated. This allows the

Exhibit 20.2 Revised Uniform Enforcement of Foreign Judgments Act

SECTION 1. [*Definitions*.] In this Act "foreign judgment" means any judgment, decree, or order of a court of the United States or of any other court which is entitled to full faith and credit in this state.

SECTION 2. [*Filing and Status of Foreign Judgments*.] A copy of any foreign judgment authenticated in accordance with the act of Congress or the statutes of this state may be filed in the office of the Clerk of any [District Court of any city or county] of this state. The Clerk shall treat the foreign judgment in the same manner as a judgment of the [District Court of any city or county] of this state. A judgment so filed has the same effect and is subject to the same procedures, defenses and proceedings for reopening, vacating, or staying as a judgment of a [District Court of any city or county] of this state and may be enforced or satisfied in like manner.

SECTION 3. [*Notice of Filing*.]

(a) At the time of the filing of the foreign judgment, the judgment creditor or his lawyer shall make and file with the Clerk of Court an affidavit setting forth the name and last known post office address of the judgment debtor, and the judgment creditor.

(b) Promptly upon the filing of the foreign judgment and the affidavit, the Clerk shall mail notice of the filing of the foreign judgment to the judgment debtor at the address given and shall make a note of the mailing in the docket. The notice shall include the name and post office address of the judgment creditor and the judgment creditor's lawyer, if any, in this state. In addition, the judgment creditor may mail a notice of the filing of the judgment to the judgment debtor and may file proof of mailing with the Clerk. Lack of mailing notice of filing by the Clerk shall not affect the enforcement proceedings if proof of mailing by the judgment creditor has been filed.

[(c) No execution or other process for enforcement of a foreign judgment filed hereunder shall issue until [_____] days after the date the judgment is filed.]

SECTION 4. [*Stay*.]

(a) If the judgment debtor shows the [District Court of any city or county] that an appeal from the foreign judgment is pending or will be taken, or that a stay of execution has been granted, the court shall stay enforcement of the foreign judgment until the appeal is concluded, the time for appeal expires, or the stay of execution expires or is vacated, upon proof that the judgment debtor has furnished the security for the satisfaction of the judgment required by the state in which it was rendered.

(b) If the judgment debtor shows the [District Court of any city or county] any ground upon which enforcement of a judgment of any [District Court of any city or county] of this state would be stayed, the court shall stay enforcement of the foreign judgment for an appropriate period, upon requiring the same security for satisfaction of the judgment which is required in this state.

[**SECTION 5. [*Fees*.]** Any person filing a foreign judgment shall pay to the clerk of Court _____ dollars. Fees for docketing, transcription or other enforcement proceedings shall be as provided for judgments of the [District Court of any city or county of this state].

SECTION 6. [*Optional Procedure*.] The right of a judgment creditor to bring an action to enforce his judgment instead of proceeding under this Act remains unimpaired.

SECTION 7. [Uniformity of Interpretation.] This Act shall be so interpreted and construed as to effectuate its general purpose to make uniform the law of those states which enact it.

SECTION 8. [*Short Title*.] This Act may be cited as the Uniform Enforcement of Foreign Judgments Act.

SECTION 9. [*Repeal*.] The following Acts and parts of Acts are repealed:

(1)

(2)

(3)

SECTION 10. [*Taking Effect*.] This Act takes effect on _____.

execution
Process whereby the assets of the judgment debtor are collected by the sheriff, sold, and the proceeds used to pay the judgment.

exempt property
Property of the judgment debtor that is set aside for his personal use and is not available for execution.

garnishment
The process wherein a percentage of the judgment debtor's wages is remitted to pay the judgment.

deficiency
The shortfall between the proceeds received at execution and the judgment amount.

schedule of distribution
A schedule that lists the proceeds from the sale, the related expenses, the distribution to the creditor, and any excess collected and returned to the debtor. Also, a written statement that lists a sum of money received and all the distributions that are permitted to be made from the amount received.

debtor the opportunity to file a petition to vacate, open, or stay the judgment. Exhibit 20.3 shows a request to file and index a foreign judgment.

Following the expiration of the waiting period, all remedies in the individual state are available to enforce the judgment. Although each state's remedies might be unique, they all tend to fall into a similar pattern.

The first step in **execution** on the judgment is to obtain a court order authorizing the sheriff or other enforcement agency to take possession of, attach, sequester, or levy against property of the judgment debtor for purposes of satisfying the judgment amount. The property may be real or personal. The procedure includes notifying the judgment debtor of the execution and advising him of his rights to claim certain **property as exempt** from levy and execution. Many states exempt or protect certain types of personal property from execution, like tools of the trade, so that the debtor will not be left destitute or deprived of the tools needed to earn a living. Using the same rationale, many states also limit **garnishment,** or deduction from the judgment debtor's wages, for payment of the judgment. After the necessary time period has expired, a sale of the debtor's non-exempt property can occur, unless the judgment debtor pays the judgment. The costs of sale are then deducted and the balance of the proceeds is distributed to the judgment creditor to satisfy the debt. In the event there is a shortfall, called a **deficiency,** the creditor may execute on other property of the debtor in that jurisdiction or begin the process again in another jurisdiction where the debtor owns property. If there is an overage from the sale of the assets, the debtor will receive those funds. A **schedule of distribution** is then prepared, listing the

Exhibit 20.3 Sample Praecipe to File and Index a Foreign Judgment

COURT OF COMMON PLEAS OF
PHILADELPHIA COUNTY
October Term, 2008

NO. 2008-1234

Dan Thomas, Plaintiff

v.

Stephen Blanca, Defendant

PRAECIPE TO FILE AND INDEX FOREIGN JUDGMENT

To the Prothonotary:

Pursuant to the Uniform Enforcement of Foreign Judgments Act, 42 Pa. Cons. Stat. Ann. § 4306, kindly file and index the attached exemplified and certified copies of the docket entries and the judgment entered in favor of plaintiff and against defendant Stephen Blanca in the total sum of $10,000 in the Supreme Court of the State of New York in and for Albany County, in an action captioned.

Dan Thomas v. Stephen Blanca No. NYS 34-098

Ariel Marshall
Attorney for Plaintiff

proceeds from the sale, the related expenses, the distribution to the creditor, and any excess funds collected and returned to the debtor.

In some jurisdictions, the court allows judgment creditors to issue **interrogatories in aid of execution.** These questions, which are similar to the interrogatories used in the discovery process, are frequently addressed to banks, brokerage houses, and other financial institutions in hopes of locating bank accounts or other assets belonging to the judgment debtor. Exhibit 20.4 shows examples of interrogatories used to locate assets.

interrogatories in aid of execution
Interrogatories issued by the judgment creditor to locate assets of the judgment debtor.

Exhibit 20.4 Interrogatories in Aid of Execution

(Caption of Case)

INTERROGATORIES PROPOUNDED BY PLAINTIFF HARRY ALLEN AND DIRECTED TO DEFENDANT STEPHEN BLANCA IN AID OF EXECUTION

The plaintiff is seeking to collect on the judgment which it has secured against you in this case and needs information about your assets. You are required under the rules of civil procedure to file answers under oath or verification within 30 days after their service on you:

INTERROGATORIES

1. State your full name, address, age, telephone number and Social Security number.

2. What other names do you use, if any?

3. State the name(s), address(es) and age(s) of your present and/or former spouse and your children, if any.

4. With whom do you live?

5. Identify each of your dependents, if any.

6. What is your occupation?

7. If you work for someone else, state the name of your employer, the address where you work, the type of work you do, your gross pay per week and your take-home pay per week. If you receive commissions from your employer, state the average amount of such commissions you receive each week.

8. If you are self-employed, state the nature of your self-employment; the address of your office or place of business; the fictitious name under which you trade, if any; your average gross annual earnings; and your average net annual earnings.

9. Are you associated in a business or professional partnership or joint venture? If so, identify the partnership or joint venture and the members thereof; the nature of the business; the percentage of your interest; the estimated value of your interest; your average gross and net annual compensation; all documents relating to the formation and governance of the partnership or joint venture.

10. Have you, or has anyone on your behalf, conveyed or transferred any interest in any real estate to anyone within the last 5 years? If so, as to each conveyance or transfer state:
    (a) The description of the real estate;
    (b) The interest which you conveyed or transferred;
    (c) The identity of the person to whom you conveyed or transferred that interest;
    (d) The consideration which you received;
    (e) The reason for the conveyance or transfer;
    (f) The fair market value of your interest in the property at the time of its conveyance or transfer by you.

Ariel Marshall
Attorney for Plaintiff

---

post-judgment interest
Interest calculated on unpaid judgments authorized by state statute and added to the amount due the judgment creditor.

Post-judgment interest is permitted in many states. The judgment creditor may receive interest on an unpaid judgment from the date of entry of the judgment until the date of collection. Some states have a statutory flat rate, for example, 6 percent. Other states use a rate that is adjusted annually based on prevailing interest rates in the financial markets. The paralegal might be asked to prepare a statement of the amount due on a judgment at a particular time. It is important to remember to include the judgment amount, costs associated with collection and enforcement efforts, and post-judgment interest, if it is authorized. Exhibit 20.5 shows the calculation of the amount due on a judgment approximately two years after its entry.

The Judgment-Proof Debtor

judgment-proof debtor
A judgment debtor without insurance, cash, assets, or other means of paying a judgment.

The worst-case scenario for the client and the law firm is the **judgment-proof debtor.** A judgment-proof debtor is someone who has no insurance, no assets, and no way of satisfying the judgment. To be awarded a successful judgment at trial only to find there is no way it can be paid can lead to poor client relations and a bad reputation for the law firm. Good investigation skills at the inception of (or early on in) the representation should reveal the existence of insurance, the creditworthiness of the defendant/debtor, and the availability of assets. Investigation of the ability to pay in the event a judgment is obtained will prevent the needless expenditure of time and costs in preparation and trial. If the defendant's penniless situation is discovered at an early stage in the representation, the client will also have the option of dropping the lawsuit for economic reasons.

Faced with a judgment-proof debtor, the legal team must, at a minimum, protect any judgment obtained. Lodging the judgment in the state court where the judgment debtor resides or owns real estate will serve that purpose.

Exhibit 20.5 Calculation of Judgment with Interest Calculation

Judgment entered 3/15/2012	$10,750.00
Costs:	
Obtaining certified copy of Judgment and docket entries	35.00
Sheriff's fees	63.50
Post-judgment Interest	
3/15/12 to 12/31/13 @ 3.5%/year	642.72*
1/1/14 to 7/15/14 @ 4%/year	662.92**
TOTAL DUE through 7/15/2017	**$12,154.14**

* interest calculation for 1 year and 8.5 months
$10,750.00 x 3.5% = $376.25/year interest x 1 year = $376.25
$376.25/12mo = $31.35/mo x 8.5 months = $266.47
Total interest $642.72

** interest calculation for 1 year and 6.5 months
$10,750.00 x 4% = $430.00/year interest x 1 year = $430.00
$430.00/12mo = $35.83/mo x 6.5 months = $232.92
Total interest $662.92

In some jurisdictions, the judgment must be revived every five or so years to preserve its priority.

Being patient is the key to collecting from a judgment-proof debtor. At the time of lodging the judgment, the debtor may not own real estate or may own real estate that has significant mortgage debt. However, at some time in the future, the judgment debtor may seek to buy or sell real estate or refinance the mortgage. When the public records are searched, the judgment will appear. Before the real estate transaction can be concluded, the judgment must be satisfied in order to remove the claim against the title to the property. It may take years, but the client will be paid, and if your state authorizes post-judgment interest, the client's patience will be additionally compensated.

■ STATUTORY LIMITATIONS ON COLLECTION EFFORTS

Debtors are afforded numerous legislative protections in addition to the safeguards built into the court system. Two of the most important, and those that paralegals most frequently encounter, are the Fair Debt Collection Practices Act and Bankruptcy Act.

Fair Debt Collection Practices Act

Congress enacted protections for debtors to limit the activities of creditors' efforts to collect consumer-based debt. The Fair Debt Collection Practices Act, 15 U.S.C. §1692, applies to attorneys who seek to collect and enforce judgment debts on behalf of their clients. To trigger the requirements of the Act, the underlying dispute or debt on which the judgment is based must be a **consumer debt.** Consumer debts are those that are incurred or related to personal, family, or household purposes. A **purchase money mortgage** (a debt created to purchase a home), an automobile loan, an outstanding balance on a credit card, and fees owed to a hospital for a surgical procedure are examples of consumer debt. The Act requires that certain notices be included with all communications to debtors and limits the time and manner of contacting the debtor. The Act also requires that the debtor be advised that he or she may challenge the validity of the debt. Exhibit 20.6 is a standard collection letter issued to a judgment debtor where the underlying debt represents a consumer debt. Failure to comply with the requirements of the Act can result in civil liability for the lawyer attempting to collect the debt on behalf of the client.

Bankruptcy

Lawyers and clients may hear the word "bankruptcy" and believe the judgment obtained is no longer of any value. Although that might sometimes be true, it is not always true. Knowing what rights a judgment creditor has in bankruptcy can be crucial to preserving the client's rights. Depending on the circumstances, the judgment may be collectable in part, if not in whole. There are numerous cases of judgment debtors filing a petition of bankruptcy to hold off creditors only to have the bankruptcy court dismiss the petition, which reopens the opportunity for the judgment enforcement action to be restarted. If that is beyond the training and experience of the attorney and the law firm, it is their ethical obligation to refer the client to a lawyer with that expertise.

LEARNING OBJECTIVE 3
Explain the statutory limitations on collection efforts.

consumer debt
Debts incurred that are related to personal, family, or household purposes.

purchase money mortgage
Debt created to purchase a home.

Exhibit 20.6 Collection Letter with Fair Debt Collection Practices Act Notice

Dear Mr. Blanca,

We have been retained to collect from you the balance of a debt you owe to our client Dan Thomas. As of March 15, 2008 the amount of the debt is $10,000.

Federal law gives you thirty days after you receive this letter to dispute the validity of the debt or any part of it. If you do not dispute it within that period, we will assume that it is valid. If you do dispute it, by notifying us in writing to that effect, we will, as required by the law, obtain and mail to you proof of the debt. And if, within the same period, you request in writing the name and address of your original creditor, if the original creditor is different from the current creditor, Dan Thomas, we will furnish you that information also. The law does not require us to wait until the end of the thirty-day period before suing you to collect this debt. If, however, you request proof of the debt or the name and address of the original creditor within the thirty-day period that begins with your receipt of this letter, the law requires us to suspend our efforts.

This communication is from a debt collector and any information obtained may be used to collect the debt.

Sincerely,

ETHICAL Perspectives

DUTY OF COMPETENCE

Knowing the current laws on collection and bankruptcy, both federal and state, is essential in the collection effort.

Virginia Rules of Professional Conduct

RULE 1.1 Competence

A lawyer shall provide competent representation to a client. Competent representation requires the legal knowledge, skill, thoroughness, and preparation reasonably necessary for the representation.

The federal Bankruptcy Act was designed to give a debtor an opportunity to start over. An in-depth analysis of bankruptcy provisions is worthy of an entire textbook. However, there are certain provisions that should be common knowledge for the paralegal who assists in collecting and enforcing judgments.

There are three common bankruptcy petitions:

Chapter 7—is liquidation bankruptcy, wherein the debtor's non-exempt assets are gathered and liquidated and the proceeds used to pay his debts. Creditors usually receive a percentage of the amount owed, sometimes as little as pennies for every dollar owed.

Chapter 11—is a type of bankruptcy reserved for businesses in which the business is allowed to hold off the collection efforts of creditors while it reorganizes its debt so that it can continue operations. Creditors can expect full payment of their debts but may have to wait to receive it.

IN THE WORDS OF THE COURT...

Debt Collection Activity

Sayyed v. Wolpoff & Abramson, 06-1458, (4th Circuit 2007)

"...The FDCPA clearly defines the parties and activities it regulates. The Act applies to law firms that constitute debt collectors, even where their debt-collecting activity is litigation. W&A asks that we disregard the statutory text in order to imply some sort of common law litigation immunity. We decline to do so. Rather, "where, as here, the statute's language is plain, the sole function of the courts is to enforce it according to its terms." "*United States v. Ron Pair Enters., Inc.*, 489 U.S. 235, 241 (1989) (internal quotation marks omitted)."...

WEB RESOURCES
Contrast and compare the **Virginia Rules of Professional Conduct RULE 1.1 Competence** at http://www.vsb.org/docs/rules-pc_2006-07pg.pdf with the **ABA Model Rules of Professional Conduct ethical duty of competence** at http://www.abanet.org/cpr/mrpc/rule_1_1.html and the ethics rule in your jurisdiction.

Chapter 13—is a debt repayment or personal reorganization plan for individual debtors wherein the individuals are required to pay their debts in full over a particular period of time, usually five years.

The most important bankruptcy provision for the creditor trying to collect on its judgment is the **automatic stay** provision. Upon receipt of notice that a bankruptcy petition has been filed, the judgment creditor must cease all efforts to collect on the judgment. The debtor's filing of the petition causes an automatic stay of all collection efforts, and violation of the stay can result in severe consequences to the creditor.

Many assume a bankruptcy petition is equivalent to the debt being erased. That is not necessarily the case. Creditors may pursue self-help remedies through the bankruptcy court. The creditor must first file a proof of claim, establishing for the bankruptcy court the nature and validity of the debt owed. This step is important because the proofs of claim that are filed are the debts that will be acknowledged by the bankruptcy court and included in the claims to be paid from the bankrupt person's assets. Exhibit 20.7 is a proof of claim form filed with the bankruptcy court.

Based upon these proofs of claim, certain debts will be given priority for payment and others will be designated **non-dischargeable debts,** meaning they will continue to exist as valid debts after the bankruptcy is concluded. Finally, a creditor can file a petition for **relief from the automatic stay,** which, if granted, allows the creditor to continue collection efforts unfettered during the bankruptcy proceedings.

automatic stay
In bankruptcy, a requirement that creditors cease all efforts to collect the debts owed them once a bankruptcy petition has been filed.

non-dischargeable debt
A debt in bankruptcy that must be paid in full.

relief from the automatic stay
A request of a creditor to proceed with his collection efforts outside the jurisdiction of the bankruptcy court.

■ SATISFACTION

The final step of the enforcement process is to ensure that the docket reflects payment by the judgment debtor. This can be accomplished simply by filing the form of satisfaction used in the particular jurisdiction. Satisfactions may need to be filed in more than one place. For example, a satisfaction must be filed in each state court where the judgment was lodged under the Uniform Enforcement of Foreign Judgments Act and also in the federal district court where the judgment was originally entered. Exhibit 20.8 shows a sample of the form used to enter a satisfaction on a judgment.

LEARNING OBJECTIVE 4
Prepare a satisfaction document to file when the judgment is satisfied.

Exhibit 20.7 Proof of Claim

B 10 (Official Form 10) (04/10)

UNITED STATES BANKRUPTCY COURT	PROOF OF CLAIM

Name of Debtor:	Case Number:

NOTE: *This form should not be used to make a claim for an administrative expense arising after the commencement of the case. A reque st for payment of an administrative expense may be filed pursuant to 11 U.S.C. § 503.*

Name of Creditor (the person or other entity to whom the debtor owes money or property):

Name and address where notices should be sent:

Telephone number:

☐ Check this box to indicate that this claim amends a previously filed claim.

Court Claim Number:_____
(*If known*)

Filed on:_____

Name and address where payment should be sent (if different from above):

Telephone number:

☐ Check this box if you are aware that anyone else has filed a proof of claim relating to your claim. Attach copy of statement giving particulars.

☐ Check this box if you are the debtor or trustee in this case.

1. Amount of Claim as of Date Case Filed: $_____

If all or part of your claim is secured, complete item 4 below; however, if all of your claim is unsecured, do not complete item 4.

If all or part of your claim is entitled to priority, complete item 5.

☐ Check this box if claim includes interest or other charges in addition to the principal amount of claim. Attach itemized statement of interest or charges.

2. Basis for Claim: _____
(See instruction #2 on reverse side.)

3. Last four digits of any number by which creditor identifies debtor: _____

    3a. Debtor may have scheduled account as: _____
    (See instruction #3a on reverse side.)

4. Secured Claim (See instruction #4 on reverse side.)
Check the appropriate box if your claim is secured by a lien on property or a right of setoff and provide the requested information.

Nature of property or right of setoff: ☐ Real Estate   ☐ Motor Vehicle   ☐ Other
Describe:

Value of Property:$_____ **Annual Interest Rate**_____%

Amount of arrearage and other charges as of time case filed included in secured claim,

if any: $_____   **Basis for perfection:** _____

Amount of Secured Claim: $_____   **Amount Unsecured:** $_____

6. Credits: The amount of all payments on this claim has been credited for the purpose of making this proof of claim.

7. Documents: Attach redacted copies of any documents that support the claim, such as promissory notes, purchase orders, invoices, itemized statements of running accounts, contracts, judgments, mortgages, and security agreements. You may also attach a summary. Attach redacted copies of documents providing evidence of perfection of a security interest. You may also attach a summary. (*See instruction 7 and definition of "redacted" on reverse side.*)

DO NOT SEND ORIGINAL DOCUMENTS. ATTACHED DOCUMENTS MAY BE DESTROYED AFTER SCANNING.

If the documents are not available, please explain:

5. Amount of Claim Entitled to Priority under 11 U.S.C. §507(a). If any portion of your claim falls in one of the following categories, check the box and state the amount.

Specify the priority of the claim.

☐ Domestic support obligations under 11 U.S.C. §507(a)(1)(A) or (a)(1)(B).

☐ Wages, salaries, or commissions (up to $11,725*) earned within 180 days before filing of the bankruptcy petition or cessation of the debtor's business, whichever is earlier – 11 U.S.C. §507 (a)(4).

☐ Contributions to an employee benefit plan – 11 U.S.C. §507 (a)(5).

☐ Up to $2,600* of deposits toward purchase, lease, or rental of property or services for personal, family, or household use – 11 U.S.C. §507 (a)(7).

☐ Taxes or penalties owed to governmental units – 11 U.S.C. §507 (a)(8).

☐ Other – Specify applicable paragraph of 11 U.S.C. §507 (a)(__).

Amount entitled to priority:

$_____

Amounts are subject to adjustment on 4/1/13 and every 3 years thereafter with respect to cases commenced on or after the date of adjustment.

Date:	**Signature:** The person filing this claim must sign it. Sign and print name and title, if any, of the creditor or other person authorized to file this claim and state address and telephone number if different from the notice address above. Attach copy of power of attorney, if any.	FOR COURT USE ONLY

Penalty for presenting fraudulent claim: Fine of up to $500,000 or imprisonment for up to 5 years, or both. 18 U.S.C. §§ 152 and 3571.

Exhibit 20.8 Satisfaction of Judgment Form

(Caption of Case)

Order to Mark Judgment Satisfied

To the Clerk of Court:

Mark the judgment in the above captioned matter satisfied of record upon payment of your costs only.

_____
Ariel Marshall
Attorney for Plaintiff

CONCEPT REVIEW AND REINFORCEMENT

KEY TERMS

judgment debtor   466
judgment creditor   466
debtor   466
creditor   466
judgment   466
stayed   466
satisfaction piece   467
authorization for
   distribution   467
in rem   467

in personam   467
Full Faith and Credit clause   467
Uniform Enforcement of Foreign
   Judgments Act   468
foreign judgment   468
execution   470
exempt property   470
garnishment   470
deficiency   470
schedule of distribution   470

interrogatories in aid of
   execution   471
post-judgment interest   472
judgment-proof debtor   472
consumer debt   473
purchase money mortgage   473
automatic stay   475
non-dischargeable debt   475
relief from the automatic
   stay   475

CHAPTER SUMMARY

ENFORCEMENT OF JUDGMENTS

Introduction to Enforcement of Judgments	The final step in civil litigation is collecting the amount the client is owed on the judgment entered, regardless of how that judgment was obtained. The process can be simple or complex but is often the responsibility of the paralegal.
Terminology and Timing in Judgment Collection	The judgment debtor is the party (whether plaintiff or defendant) who lost at trial and now owes damages in the amount of the judgment. The judgment creditor (whether plaintiff or defendant) is the party who won at trial and is now owed damages in the amount of the judgment.

(continued)

The rules permit collection efforts to begin as soon as ten days after the entry of the judgment, but practicalities determine that efforts will not begin until all posttrial motions and appeals have been concluded or the time for filing them has expired without the filing of a motion or appeal.

Collection of Judgment Process	Collection on the judgment can be non-adversarial, with payment being the result of a phone call or letter. Paralegals should obtain the client's written authorization for the distribution of the proceeds of the sums collected. This authorization should include payment of costs related to the litigation and attorney's fees, with the balance being distributed to the client. Where there is no insurance and the defendant refuses to pay or lacks the ability to pay, collecting the judgment amount will require adversarial proceedings. Adversarial efforts require use of the rules in effect in the state court where the defendant resides and has assets. The process has been somewhat simplified by the Uniform Enforcement of Foreign Judgments Act, but state procedures must be checked carefully. Execution, attachment, levy, replevin, and sheriff's sale are typically used in most states. Some states also permit the use of interrogatories in aid of execution to assist the judgment creditor in locating assets. Following the procedures to lodge and, if necessary, revive a judgment against the judgment-proof debtor can result in payment of the judgment amount years after the judgment was entered. Patience is often rewarded with the inclusion of post-judgment interest.
Statutory Limitations on Collection Efforts	The Fair Debt Collection Practices Act limits the activities of creditors seeking to enforce and collect consumer debts. Because many judgments are based on consumer transactions, the law firm must comply with the requirements concerning the time and manner of contacting the debtor, the required notices to be sent, and the ability of the debtor to challenge the validity of the debt. The Bankruptcy Act can severely limit efforts to collect on the judgment, but the filing of a bankruptcy petition does not mean the judgment creditor will not be paid. Depending on the type of filing—liquidation or reorganization—the creditor can expect partial or full payment, respectively. There are also procedures within the bankruptcy law that allow the creditor to continue collection efforts while the bankruptcy action is pending. If the legal team is unfamiliar with bankruptcy law, it must refer continuation of the client's collection efforts to a law firm that focuses on this specialized area of law.
Satisfaction	Once paid in full, the judgment must be marked as satisfied on the records of the court. This requires filing the appropriate documents with each court in which the judgment was registered. The legal team should begin with the court in which the judgment was initially obtained and continue with each court where the judgment was registered under the Uniform Enforcement of Foreign Judgments Act. Failure to have the judgment marked satisfied on the dockets of the pertinent courts can negatively impact the judgment debtor and his future financial transactions. It may also subject the law firm to malpractice claims.

REVIEW QUESTIONS AND EXERCISES

1. Why is good investigation at the inception of client representation crucial to later efforts to enforce and collect on a judgment?
2. What is a judgment creditor? A judgment debtor?
3. From a practical standpoint, when will a law firm commence collection efforts? Why?
4. Describe a situation where non-adversarial methods of collection would be appropriate.
5. What is the difference between an authorization for distribution and a schedule of distribution? Why are these documents important to collection efforts?
6. What courts have jurisdiction to enforce a judgment? Why?
7. What is a foreign judgment?
8. How are foreign judgments enforced?
9. What is the Full Faith and Credit clause of the U.S. Constitution? What part does it play in the efforts to collect on a judgment?
10. What are the typical state remedies for collecting and enforcing a judgment?
11. What is post-judgment interest?
12. What is a judgment-proof debtor?
13. What is the Fair Debt Collection Practices Act? Whom does it protect? What actions does it prohibit or require?
14. Describe the effect of a judgment debtor's bankruptcy petition on the collection efforts of the judgment creditor.
15. Compare and contrast the three types of bankruptcy petitions.
16. What is an automatic stay in bankruptcy?
17. Should a judgment creditor give up on collecting his judgment if the judgment debtor files for bankruptcy?
18. Are there remedies for the judgment creditor that will permit continued collection efforts? If so, describe them.
19. What is a satisfaction piece? Where must it be filed? Why?

BUILDING YOUR PARALEGAL SKILLS

INTERNET AND TECHNOLOGY EXERCISES

1. Prepare a list of websites that might be used to verify assets owned by a defendant against whom a judgment has been obtained.
2. Prepare a sample set of search queries for locating information about a corporate party.
3. What are the ethical and legal restrictions on the use of the Internet to obtain information about a civil case defendant and his assets, which might be available for satisfying a judgment?
4. What property records are available online in your jurisdiction?

CIVIL LITIGATION VIDEO CASE STUDIES

A Corporate Officer Seeks Legal Advice

The president of the trucking company that appears to be liable for the school bus accident seeks legal advice on avoiding liability.

After viewing the video at www.pearsonhighered.com/careersresources, answer the following questions.

1. To whom does corporate counsel owe a duty of loyalty—i.e., whom does he represent?
2. Is the conversation with the company president protected under the attorney–client privilege?

3. Does the lawyer have an ethical problem in representing the client and the advice sought?

Deposition in Aid of Execution: Transferring Corporate Assets to Avoid Paying a Judgment

The president of the company held liable is deposed by the plaintiff's lawyer, who is seeking a source of funds to pay the judgment. .

After viewing the video at www.pearsonhighered.com/ careersresources, answer the following questions.

1. Is the corporate officer appearing in his personal or his executive capacity? To whom does corporate counsel owe a duty of loyalty?
2. How often can the plaintiff's lawyer take the deposition to discover assets to satisfy the judgment?

CHAPTER OPENING SCENARIO CASE STUDY

Use the Opening Scenario for this chapter to answer the following questions.

1. Prepare a memo to the paralegal staff assigning the necessary tasks to preserve the rights and priorities of the clients in the event that any of the defendants file for bankruptcy. Include all of the individual steps for each task.

2. How can the legal team be certain it has taken all the necessary steps to collect on the judgments obtained?

BUILDING YOUR PROFESSIONAL PORTFOLIO AND REFERENCE MANUAL

CIVIL LITIGATION TEAM AT WORK

See page 18 for instructions on Building Your Professional Portfolio.

Forms

1. Forms necessary to register with your local state court the judgment obtained in the federal district court
2. Forms and rules for execution on the judgment, including information on any exemptions the judgment debtor might have in your state
3. Proof of claim

Procedures

1. Using your state's Uniform Enforcement of Foreign Judgments Act, prepare a standard procedure for

enforcing a judgment obtained in the federal district court in your state. Include filing fees and any forms available online from the county or parish court.
2. List of exempt property in your state

Contacts and Resources

1. List of websites that can be used to verify assets owned by a defendant against whom a judgment has been obtained
2. Local bankruptcy court
3. Sheriff's office

CHAPTER OPENING CASE STUDY

Each chapter has an Opening Scenario that focuses on the issues presented in the chapter. The scenarios follow the activities of the law firm of Mason, Marshall and Benjamin, Attorneys and Counselors at Law. The firm started in Newtown, a small town near the local state courthouse. With the increased volume of litigation cases, it was determined that a satellite office in the city of Oldtown was essential to service the cases in federal court. A new location was established across the street from the federal district court with Ethan Benjamin, Esq., as the office's managing partner. Benjamin, a former litigation paralegal in the Newtown suburban office, graduated from law school, passed the state bar, and was admitted on the motion of the senior partner, Owen Mason, Esq., to the federal district court. (Owen Mason had been a law clerk to a federal judge in the same court.)

Edith Hannah, an experienced paralegal from a prestigious downtown law firm, was the first employee hired by Mr. Mason to run the original office across from the local state trial court building in the suburban town of Newtown. Ariel Marshall, a former prosecution attorney, and her litigation support paralegal, Emily Gordon, joined the firm in Newtown shortly after its formation, after they had worked on a major multiparty tort action. Ms. Marshall became a partner of Mr. Mason. As the offices grew, Mrs. Hannah became the office manager for both. She soon hired Emily's twin sister, Caitlin, as an additional paralegal to work in the Oldtown office with Mr. Benjamin. Cary Eden, Esq., was hired by Mr. Benjamin as an associate in the Oldtown office to assist him in federal court litigation.

■ LAW OFFICE INFORMATION

Mason, Marshall and Benjamin
Attorneys and Counselors
at Law
Newtown Office
2 South State Street
Newtown, Your State
Office Phone 555-111-2222

Oldtown Office
1 Federal Street
Oldtown, Your State
Office Phone 555-222-1111

Owen Mason, Esquire
138 South Main Street
Newtown, Your State
Social Security Number 123-45-6789
Office Phone 555-111-2222
Home Phone 555-345-3333
Date of Birth 08-19-1961

Ariel Marshall, Esquire
621 Merion Road
Old Station, Your State
Social Security Number 123-45-6792
Office Phone 555-222-2224
Home Phone 555-432-5673
Date of Birth 08-06-1968

Ethan Benjamin, Esquire
138 City Court
Oldtown, Your State
Social Security Number 555-22-7890
Office Phone 555-222-1111
Home Phone 555-987-6543
Date of Birth 06-23-1968

Cary Eden, Esquire
12 Schan Drive
Richboro, Your State
Office Phone 555-222-1111
Home Phone 555-518-9166
Date of Birth 08-12-1964

Mrs. Hannah
43 Washington Avenue
Newtown, Your State
Social Security Number 123-45-6790
Home Phone 555-453-3134
Date of Birth 01-12-1960

Emily Gordon
2916 Boulevard Avenue
Forest Park, Your State and Zip
Social Security Number 123-45-6793
Home Phone 555-468-3335
Date of Birth 01-28-1984

Caitlin Gordon
76 Medford Road
Lawnview, Your State
Social Security Number 999-11-0000
Home Phone 555-444-8888
Date of Birth 01-28-1984

Billing Rates

Owen Marshall, senior partner, attorney—$350 per hour
Ariel Marshall, partner, attorney—$300 per hour
Ethan Benjamin, managing partner, attorney—$250 per hour
Cary Eden, associate attorney—$200 per hour
Mrs. Hannah, paralegal—$90 per hour
Emily Gordon, litigation paralegal—$90 per hour
Caitlin Gordon, paralegal—$90 per hour

YOUR HOURLY BILLING RATE $40 per hour

COMPREHENSIVE CASE STUDY: SCHOOL BUS-TRUCK ACCIDENT CASE STUDY

The Comprehensive Case Study: School Bus-Truck Accident Case is used as the basis for the pleading and forms throughout the text to allow users to follow a single case from beginning to end. Many of the elements of the case are illustrated with videos presented in chapters where appropriate in the video case study material.

The comprehensive case study is based on actual facts as reported in a National Transportation Safety Board (NTSB) report. Though some content has been edited, the words of the report have been reproduced here to provide as much authenticity as possible. NTSB Figures are reproduced from the same report. Some liberty has been taken with the identity of the parties, and none of the names used represent or were actual parties involved in the tragic accident reported. We base this case study on a real incident to give you practice in performing real-world legal and factual research, a skill you will use on the job in the future.

Multi-Vehicle Collision between Truck and School Bus
Near Mountainburg, Arkansas
May 31, 2001

Abstract

On May 31, 2001, near Mountainburg, Arkansas, a Gayle Stuart Trucking, Inc., truck-tractor semitrailer collided with a 65-passenger school bus operated by the Mountainburg, Arkansas, Public Schools. Three school bus passengers were fatally injured; two other passengers received serious injuries. Four passengers, the school bus driver, and the truck driver sustained minor injuries.

Passengers

Refer to seat numbers on National Transportation Safety Board (NTSB) seating chart:

1A Alice Bates ~~Scott~~ *Amanda Bates, 627 Whippoorwill Rd*

2A Amy Francs *Son Francs*

2C Clarisa Howard *Josepha Ethel Howard*

2E Doris Isaacs *Edward & Louise Isaacs*

9A Harry Allen *Douglas Allen*

9C Charles Barley *Brent & Barbara Barley*

10A Dan Thomas *Dan Thomas, Sr. & Jeannie Thomas*

10E David Thompson *Diana Thompson*

11A Thomas Aaron *David & Ella Aaron*

Other Drivers and Parties

School Bus Driver	Robert Howard
Tractor-Trailer Driver	Stephen Blanca
Trucking Company	Gayle Stuart Trucking, Inc

Highway Accident Report

■ EXECUTIVE SUMMARY

On May 31, 2001, about 3:28 P.M. Central Daylight Time, a southbound Gayle Stuart Trucking, Inc., truck-tractor semitrailer exited Interstate 540 at State Highway 282 near Mountainburg, Arkansas. The driver was unable to stop at the stop sign at the bottom of the ramp. The 79,040-pound combination unit was traveling at approximately 48 mph when it entered the intersection and collided with the right side of a westbound vehicle, a 1990 Blue Bird Corporation 65-passenger school bus operated by the Mountainburg, Arkansas, Public Schools. The school bus rotated approximately 300 degrees clockwise and overturned; the body, which partially separated from the chassis, came to rest on its right side on the eastbound shoulder of State Highway 282. The tractor semitrailer continued across the roadway, rotated about 60 degrees clockwise, overturned, and came to rest on its left side.

Three school bus passengers seated across from the impact area were fatally injured; one was partially ejected. Two other passengers (one of whom was seated in the impact area) received serious injuries, and four passengers had minor injuries. The school bus driver and the truck driver both sustained minor injuries.

The Safety Board determines that the probable cause of the accident was the truck driver's inability to stop the tractor semitrailer at the stop sign at the bottom of the ramp due to the reduced braking efficiency of the truck's brakes, which had been poorly maintained and inadequately inspected. Contributing to the school bus passengers' injuries during the side impact were incomplete compartmentalization and the lack of energy-absorbing material on interior surfaces.

NOTE: The complete National Transportation Safety Board report is available and may be downloaded from MyLegalStudiesKit, together with selected exhibits and accident simulations.

CASE FACT SPECIFIC VIDEOS—COMPREHENSIVE CASE STUDY

Chapter 4	Administrative Agency Hearing
Chapter 5	Settlement Conference with Judge
Chapter 9	Scheduling Conference with Judge: Discovery Issue Resolution
Chapter 10	Truck Driver's Deposition
Chapter 11	Attorney Meet and Confer: Electronic Discovery Issues
Chapter 14	Remote Video Conference: Taking Fact Witness Video Deposition
	Real-Time Reporting Witness Testimony: Deposing a Minor
Chapter 15	Mechanic's Deposition
Chapter 16	Final Pretrial Conference: Resolving Evidentiary Issues
	Prepare for Trial: Prepare for Deposition and Trial

APPENDIX 3

SUPPLEMENTAL CASE STUDIES

Additional case studies are provided for independent case analysis using the Comprehensive Case Study: School Bus-Truck Accident Case as an example. Some are based on accident data from the NTSB (National Highway Safety Board).

Two of the additional case studies, New York bus accident and Virginia bus accident, are similar in nature to the Comprehensive Case Study: School Bus-Truck Accident Case. Additional cases are provided: a property damage case, simple personal injury case, a tort action based on a civil assault, a commercial breach of contract, and an airplane crash.

List of Additional Cases:

- Case 1: Simple motor vehicle accident with property damage claim
- Case 2: Student injured on school bus with a delay in treatment
- Case 3: Civil assault on a school bus and failure to protect
- Case 4: Breach of commercial contract
- Case 5: New York school bus accident
- Case 6: Virginia school bus accident
- Case 7: Aircraft fatality

Several of the scenarios and parties in the non-NTSB cases are semi-fictional and loosely based on facts and situations from a number of sources woven together to provide a variety of case types. Some liberty has been taken with the identity of the parties, and none of the names used represent or were actual parties involved in the accidents reported in the NTSB-based case studies.

■ CASE 1: SIMPLE MOTOR VEHICLE PROPERTY DAMAGE CLAIM

Joel Wilkenson is a regular client of the law firm. He recently had a fender bender for which there is no insurance coverage. He was stopped at the traffic light at 14th and Market Streets, waiting to make a left-hand turn, when an SUV driven by a woman talking on her cell phone ran the red light from the other direction. Joel is seeking to sue the woman who hit him in order to recover the costs of his automobile repair.

Parties

Joel Wilkenson

Mary Smith
Mike Pope of Pope's Garage (to testify for damage and repair to car)
Tom Gordon, a fact witness who observed the accident

◼ CASE 2: STUDENT INJURED ON A SCHOOL BUS WITH A DELAY IN TREATMENT

Mandy Stein was returning from a class trip. She was seated in the rear of the school bus. Located directly behind her at the back of the bus were some boxes containing supplies and beverages. The bus stopped suddenly, and a box fell on Mandy's head, injuring her. Mandy was taken to the emergency room, where treatment was provided until her mother arrived at the hospital. Mrs. Stein's religious beliefs do not allow submission to traditional medical treatment; instead, she relies on higher powers for healing and recovery. She insisted that Mandy's treatment be stopped, and she took Mandy home. Mandy's father does not share his wife's religious beliefs, and he sought court permission to have Mandy's injuries treated. Mandy suffered a head/scalp laceration which was stitched in the emergency room, but there was no follow-up treatment or care until her father received court permission to have her treated by Dr. Lee. Because of the delay in treatment, the stitches became infected. As a result, surgery was required to remove the dead and infected skin, facial muscle, and nerves. Mandy has permanent scarring and some loss of the use of her facial muscles.

Parties

Mandy Stein, a minor

Larry Stein, Mandy's father
Samantha Stein, Mandy's mother
Dr. Lee, plastic surgeon
Ron Clemmons, bus driver
Yourtown School District

◼ CASE 3: CIVIL ASSAULT ON A SCHOOL BUS AND FAILURE TO PROTECT

Davis Hilary was riding home from school when Bobby Jones confronted him and prevented Davis from exiting the bus at his regular stop. Bobby held Davis down and threatened to harm him. A girl shouted that Bobby had a knife, and the bus driver stopped the bus to investigate the matter. Bobby was restrained and taken back to school, where an investigation began.

Parties

Bobby Jones, a minor

Robert Jones, Sr., Bobby's father
Davis Hilary, a minor
Katy Hilary, Davis's mother
Lower Council School District
Ron Clemmons, bus driver

CASE FACT SPECIFIC VIDEOS—CASE 3 CIVIL ASSAULT

Chapter 2	Parent and Child Consult the Legal Team
Chapter 4	Administrative Agency Hearing
Chapter 5	Arbitration Before Three-Member Panel
	Preparing For Arbitration
Chapter 6	Altercation on the School Bus
	School Principal Reacts

■ CASE 4: BREACH OF COMMERCIAL CONTRACT

The comprehensive case study is based on facts as reported in public documents. Though some content has been edited, the words of the original documents have been reproduced here to provide as much authenticity as possible. The use of an actual case allows you to practice real-world legal and factual research, a skill that you will use on the job in the future.

Breach of Commercial Contract
Abstract

Melford Olson Honey, Inc. (Mel-O), a Minnesota honey wholesaler, sued Richard Adee (Richard) doing business as Adee Honey Farms (Adee Honey), a South Dakota honey farmer, in Minnesota state court for breach of contract and specific performance, alleging Adee Honey failed to provide the requisite quantity of honey set forth in a June 2002 contract. Adee Honey removed the case to federal court on diversity jurisdiction and counterclaimed for money owed under the same contract. The district court denied both parties' motions for partial summary judgment, and the case proceeded to a jury trial.

Parties

Richard Adee, doing business as Adee Honey Farms

Bruce, SD
with regional offices in Bakersfield, CA, Cedar Rapids, NE, Roscoe, SD, and Woodville, MS USA

Melford Olsen Honey, Inc

Cannon Falls, MN

■ EXECUTIVE SUMMARY

Adee Honey, formed by Richard in 1957, operates honey farms in California, Nebraska, Mississippi, and South Dakota. Adee Honey's principal place of business is in South Dakota. Mel-O is owned by William Sill and Curt and Darcy Riess. They bought the company in 1997 and were referred to Richard by Mel-O's prior owners.

In March 2002, Adee Honey and Mel-O entered into an oral agreement for the sale of honey. At the time, Adee Honey possessed a sufficient inventory of honey and agreed to sell approximately thirty loads, or 1.5 million pounds, to Mel-O for 82¢ per pound. Shortly thereafter, Mel-O sent a purchase order to Adee Honey memorializing the sale of 1.5 million pounds of honey for 82¢ per pound. The purchase order noted it was a contract with a "Good Thru" date of April 11, 2002. It was sent to Adee Honey's South Dakota office although Mel-O allegedly knew Richard was working at the Mississippi facility until mid-June.

At approximately the same time, Adee Honey called Mel-O to discuss the possibility of selling up to twelve loads of its inventoried honey to a competitor. According to Adee Honey, Mel-O agreed, thereby altering the quantity term of the March 2002 contract. According to Mel-O, it permitted Adee Honey to sell twelve loads of inventoried honey to another distributor, provided the terms of the March 2002 contract were fulfilled with other honey. Between the months of May and September 2002, Adee Honey sent Mel-O eighteen loads of honey at 82¢ per pound.

In May 2002, honey prices began to rise due to a contamination in major Chinese honey supplies. In June 2002, Mel-O contacted Adee Honey about purchasing an additional 3.2 million pounds, and the parties agreed on a $1.00 per pound purchase price for the additional quantity. Mel-O sent a contract to Adee Honey detailing the new arrangement, and Richard added a handwritten *force majeure* clause, specifically excusing performance in the event of "an act of God such as a drought or flood."

Later in the summer of 2002, South Dakota was experiencing drought-like conditions, and Adee Honey unilaterally stopped performing its obligations under the June contract. According to Mel-O, Richard contacted it to discuss the possibility of increasing the price of honey by 10¢ per pound to cover losses Adee Honey would suffer due to the production shortage. By the time Mel-O grudgingly decided to accept the terms, Adee Honey instead stated the new price would be $1.55 per pound instead of $1.00 to $1.10 per pound.

In the early fall of 2002, Adee Honey began delivering honey to Mel-O at an invoice price of $1.55 per pound. Mel-O, however, refused to pay for this honey. By November 2002, its account was roughly $1.7 million in arrears. In November and December, Mel-O paid Adee Honey 82¢ per pound for approximately 575,000 pounds received, claiming this honey fulfilled the terms of the March 2002 contract. Mel-O did not pay anything for an additional 602,206 pounds received. Mel-O admits owing $1.00 per pound on this quantity, subject to some adjustments.

Adee Honey admits it contracted with Mel-O for eighteen loads of honey.

Miscellaneous Information

The Minnesota statute of frauds provides oral contracts for the sale of goods for $500.00 or more are unenforceable "unless there is some writing sufficient to indicate that a contract for sale has been made between the parties and signed by the party against whom enforcement is sought." Minn. Stat. § 336.2-201(1).

The statute is applicable because the March 2002 contract for the sale of honey, goods priced over $500.00, was not reduced to writing and signed by Adee Honey, the party against whom enforcement was sought.

Under the merchant exception, Minnesota law provides:

(2) Between merchants if within a reasonable time a writing in confirmation of the contract and sufficient against the sender is received and the party receiving it has reason to know its contents, it satisfies the requirements of subsection

(1) [regarding the general applicability of the statute of frauds] against such party unless written notice of objection to its contents is given within ten days after it is received.

The June 2002 contract contains a handwritten *force majeure* clause. Next to the 3.2 million-pound quantity, Richard added: "provided production of said pounds is NOT impeded by an Act of God such as by drought or flood."

Minnesota law provides:

Except so far as a seller may have assumed a greater obligation and subject to the preceding section on substituted performance:

(a) Delay in delivery or nondelivery in whole or in part by a seller who complies with paragraphs (b) and (c) is not a breach of duty under a contract for sale if performance as agreed has been made impracticable by the occurrence of a contingency the nonoccurrence of which was a basic assumption on which the contract was made or by compliance in good faith with any applicable foreign or domestic governmental regulation or order whether or not it later proves to be invalid.

(b) Where the causes mentioned in paragraph (a) affect only a part of the seller's capacity to perform, the seller must allocate production and deliveries among the seller's customers but may include regular customers not then under contract as well as the seller's own requirements for further manufacture. The seller may so allocate in any manner which is fair and reasonable.

(c) The seller must notify the buyer seasonably that there will be delay or non-delivery and, when allocation is required under paragraph (b), of the estimated quota thus made available for the buyer.

■ CASE 5: NEW YORK SCHOOL BUS ACCIDENT

The comprehensive case study is based on a real accident as reported in a National Transportation Safety Board (NTSB) report. Though some content has been edited, the words of the report have been reproduced here to provide as much authenticity as possible. Figures are reproduced from the same report. Some liberty has been taken with the identity of the parties, and none of the names used represent or were actual parties involved. This case study is based on a real incident to give you practice in performing real-world legal and factual research, a skill you will use on the job in the future.

School Bus and Dump Truck Collision
Central Bridge, New York
October 21, 1999

Abstract

On October 21, 1999, about 10:30 A.M. near Central Bridge, New York, a school bus was transporting 44 students and 8 adults on a field trip. The bus was traveling north on State Route 30A as it approached the intersection with State Route 7. At the same time, a dump truck towing a utility trailer was traveling west on State Route 7. As the bus approached the intersection, it failed to stop as required and was struck by the dump truck. Seven bus passengers sustained serious injuries; 28 bus passengers and the truck driver received minor injuries. Thirteen bus passengers, the bus driver, and the truck passenger were uninjured.

Passengers

Refer to seat numbers on National Transportation Safety Board (NTSB) seating chart (NTSB report Figure 4):

Figure 4 School bus seating and injury diagram

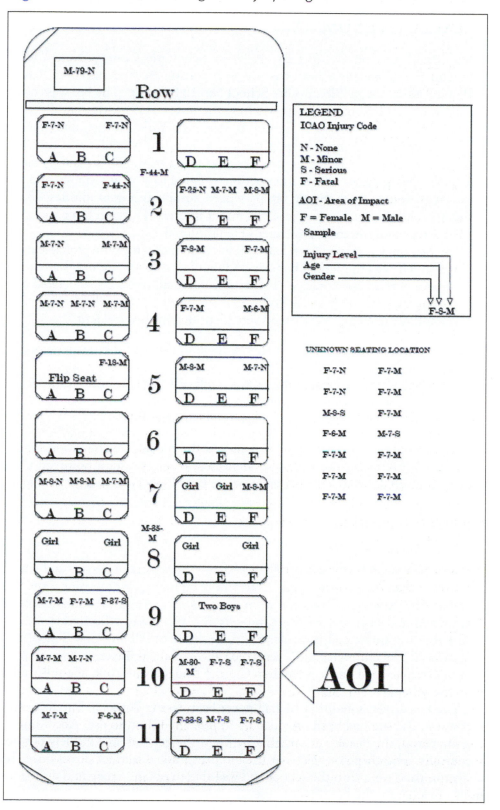

Other Drivers and Parties

School Bus Driver: Sam Carole
School Bus Company: Kinnicutt Bus Company
Tractor-Trailer Driver: Dave Smith
Trucking Company: MVF Construction Company

■ EXECUTIVE SUMMARY

About 10:30 A.M. on October 21, 1999, in Schoharie County, New York, a Kinnicutt Bus Company school bus was transporting 44 students (5 to 9 years old) and 8 adults on an Albany City School No. 18 field trip. The bus was traveling north on State Route 30A, approaching the intersection with State Route 7, which is about 1.5 miles east of Central Bridge, New York. At the same time, an MVF Construction Company dump truck towing a utility trailer was traveling west on State Route 7. The dump truck was occupied by the driver and a passenger. As the bus approached the intersection, it failed to stop as required and was struck by the dump truck. Seven bus passengers sustained serious injuries; 28 bus passengers and the truck driver received minor injuries. Thirteen bus passengers, the bus driver, and the truck passenger were uninjured.

The National Transportation Safety Board determines that the probable cause of this accident was the school bus driver's failure to stop for the stop sign due to his degraded performance or lapse of attention as a result of factors associated with aging or his medical condition or both.

The following major safety issues were identified in this accident:

- the potential for passenger injuries as a result of the school bus emergency exit door design,
- the potential for passenger injuries as a result of school bus seat cushion bottoms that are removable or hinged, and
- the adequacy of commercial vehicle airbrake inspections.

The medical fitness of commercial drivers and the medical examination for the commercial driver's license were also identified as safety issues; however, these issues will be analyzed in a forthcoming Safety Board special investigation report.

Factual Information

Accident Narrative

About 7:20 A.M. on October 21, 1999, in Albany, New York, a 79-year-old school bus driver began transporting students to school on his regular morning route. He drove a 1997 American Transportation Corporation (AmTran) full-size school bus, owned and operated by the Kinnicutt Bus Company (Kinnicutt). About 8:50 A.M., after finishing his regular route, he drove to Albany City School No. 18 and loaded 44 children (5 to 9 years old) and 8 adults (chaperons) for a scheduled field trip to the Pumpkin Patch in Central Bridge, New York, about 40 miles from the school.

The bus driver stated that he had never been to the Pumpkin Patch. No directions to the site had been provided by Kinnicutt for him to use. According to one chaperon, the bus driver said that he knew the general area vaguely but not specifically. The chaperon said that the bus driver asked him for directions. The chaperon then went into the school and was able to obtain a map and directions from a teacher for the bus driver to use.

Each school bus passenger seat was equipped with three color-coded lap belts. These belts were attached to the seat frame at the juncture between the seatback and seat cushion bottom. According to the adult passengers, all of the children were restrained by a lap belt before the trip began. The chaperons said that, to better supervise the children, the adults, except the one seated next to the emergency exit door, were unrestrained.

The bus departed the school about 9:20 A.M. The bus driver took the New York State Thruway west to exit 25A onto Interstate-88 (I-88) and then traveled west on I-88 toward exit 23, the intended exit. The chaperons stated that the bus driver seemed confused about the directions to the Pumpkin Patch and that he turned off at exit 24, the wrong exit.

He ultimately stopped the bus on the exit 24 ramp. One chaperon reported that the driver appeared confused when he stopped on the ramp. She stated that she was concerned about where he positioned the bus on the ramp when he stopped; she feared that it would be struck by another vehicle. After the bus driver

Figure 1 Exterior crush damage of school bus

Figure 3 Final rest position

received directions from a chaperon, the driver returned to I-88 and continued traveling to exit 23, the correct exit.

The bus driver stated that at the top of the exit 23 ramp, he turned right onto State Route 30A (SR-30A) and started looking for State Route 7 (SR-7). About 10:30 A.M., the bus was traveling north on SR-30A between 15 and 25 mph as it approached the intersection with SR-7. The intersection was about 1.5 miles east of Central Bridge. The north- and southbound traffic on SR-30A were controlled by an advance warning sign that indicated a stop ahead, a stop sign, flashing red intersection control beacons, and pavement markings that included the word "stop" and a stop bar.

At the same time, an MVF Construction Company (MVF) dump truck towing a utility trailer was traveling about 45 mph west on SR-7. East- and westbound traffic on SR-7 at the intersection were controlled by flashing yellow intersection control beacons. The dump truck was occupied by its 52-year-old driver and a passenger. As the school bus approached the intersection, according to the chaperons, several children on board saw the sign for the Pumpkin Patch that was beyond the intersection and yelled. These children may also have released the buckles on their lap belts. One child reportedly stood up in the seating compartment. The bus driver, who was looking for SR-7, told investigating police that he saw the posted stop sign and slowed, but did not stop the bus, which then entered the intersection where the dump truck struck it on the right side behind the rear axle. (See Figure 1.)

The school bus, after rotating about 145 degrees clockwise, slid approximately 100 feet and came to rest facing south. The dump truck, after rotating about 150 degrees clockwise, struck three highway guide signs and a utility pole; it then came to rest facing northeast. (See Figure 3.)

The complete National Transportation Safety Board report is available and may be downloaded from www.pearsonhighered.com/goldman or the Technology Resources Website, together with selected exhibits.

SOURCE: http://www.ntsb.gov/publictn/2000/HAR0002.pdf

CASE FACT SPECIFIC VIDEOS—CASE 5 NEW YORK SCHOOL BUS

■ CASE 6: VIRGINIA SCHOOL BUS ACCIDENT

The comprehensive case study is based on a real accident as reported in a National Transportation Safety Board (NTSB) report. Though some of the content has been edited, the words of the report have been reproduced here to provide as much authenticity as possible. Figures are reproduced from the same report. Some liberty has been taken with the identity of the parties, and none of the names used represent or were actual parties involved. We base this case study on a real incident to give you practice in performing real-world legal and factual research, a skill you will use on the job in the future.

Multi-Vehicle Collision between Trash Truck and School Bus
Arlington, Virginia
April 18, 2005

Abstract

A 52-passenger school bus was traveling westbound on Columbia Pike (State Route 244) in Arlington County, Virginia, transporting 15 elementary school children (grades pre-K through 5) to the nearby Hoffman-Boston Elementary School. On approaching the signaled intersection with Courthouse Road, the school bus driver began moving the bus into the left turn lane and slowed it nearly to a stop. As the driver turned the vehicle, its left front encroached slightly into the left lane of the eastbound side of Columbia Pike. A 2003 Mack trash truck was traveling with the flow of traffic in the left eastbound lane on Columbia Pike. The truck reached the intersection with Courthouse Road, continued through it on a green signal, and deviated slightly leftward from its lane toward the yellow centerline. The truck collided with the school bus; the impact involved the front left corners of both vehicles and a sideswipe.

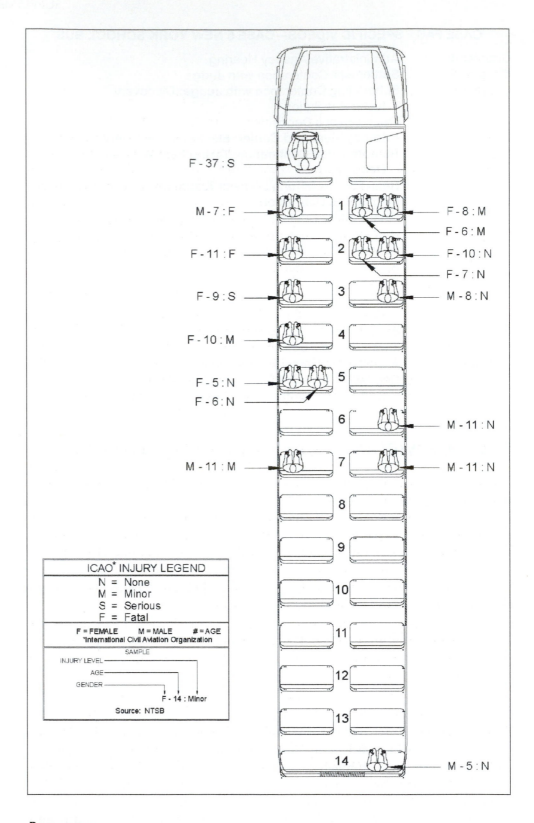

ICAO* INJURY LEGEND

N = None
M = Minor
S = Serious
F = Fatal

F = FEMALE   M = MALE   # = AGE
*International Civil Aviation Organization

SAMPLE

INJURY LEVEL
AGE
GENDER

F - 14 : Minor

Source: NTSB

Passengers

Drivers and Parties

School Bus Driver: Kathryn Salvatore
School Bus Operator: Arlington County School District
Truck Driver: John Gonzales
Trucking Company: AAA Recycling and Trash Removal Services

■ EXECUTIVE SUMMARY

Accident Description

Shortly before 8:40 A.M., on Monday, April 18, 2005, a 52-passenger school bus was traveling westbound on Columbia Pike (State Route 244) in Arlington County, Virginia, transporting 15 elementary school children (grades pre-K through 5) to the nearby Hoffman-Boston Elementary School. On approaching the signaled intersection with Courthouse Road, the school bus driver began moving the bus into the left turn lane (from which it would turn south onto Courthouse Road) and slowed it nearly to a stop. As the driver turned the vehicle, its left front encroached slightly into the left lane of the eastbound side of Columbia Pike. (The driver later stated that distractions inside the bus might have affected her driving at this time. She said her attention was drawn to a student standing on a seat and to a clipboard that fell to the floor at her driving station.)

About 8:40 A.M., a 2003 Mack trash truck was traveling with the flow of traffic in the left eastbound lane on Columbia Pike, at a speed one witness (a driver who was traveling on the road in the same direction) estimated to be approximately 30 mph. The truck reached the intersection with Courthouse Road, continued through it on a green signal and, according to several witnesses, deviated slightly leftward from its lane toward the yellow centerline. The truck collided with the school bus; the impact involved the front left corners of both vehicles and a sideswipe. (See Figures 1 and 2 for a map of the accident location area and a diagram representing the vehicles at the point of impact.)

During the collision, the school bus was pushed backward, but it remained in the left turn lane following the accident. The trash truck continued eastbound about 200 feet, crossed the right eastbound lane, jumped the right curb of Columbia Pike, and came to rest.

One student died at the scene and one student died three days later in the hospital. The truck driver, school bus driver, and one student on the bus sustained serious injuries; four students sustained minor injuries; and the remaining eight students were uninjured. The bus driver, who had been wearing her seat belt, was ejected through the broken windshield when the shoulder portion of the belt was sheared in half. Emergency responders needed approximately one hour to extricate the trash truck driver from the truck cab because his legs were trapped in the wreckage. The students who suffered the most severe injuries were seated behind the driver on the left side, near the front of the bus.

Weather conditions at the time of the accident were clear and dry. The school bus sustained impact damage to its front and left side. (See Figure 5.) The damage continued along the left side of the bus to near the sixth passenger row behind the driver's seat, approximately 20 feet back from the front bumper. Intrusion into the occupant compartment extended inboard to a depth of about 6.5 inches.

Probable Cause

The National Transportation Safety Board determines that the probable cause of this accident was the school bus driver's encroachment into the trash truck's lane and the trash truck driver's failure to maintain proper lane position, for undetermined reasons, causing the front left sides of the two vehicles to collide and the vehicles to sideswipe each other.

Figure 1 Map showing the area of Arlington, Virginia, where the accident occurred

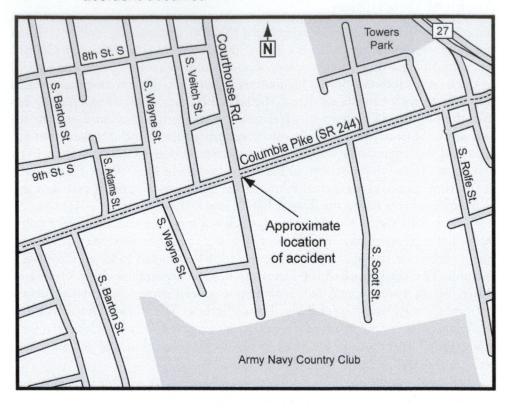

Figure 2 Diagram showing the estimated positions of the school bus and the trash truck at the point of impact

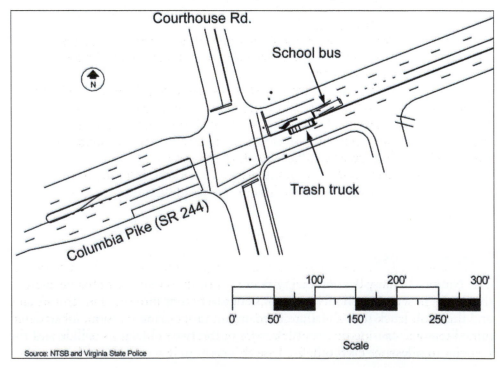

Figure 5 Damage to the school bus

The complete National Transportation Safety Board report is available and may be downloaded from www.pearsonhighered.com/goldman or the Technology Resources Website, together with selected exhibits.

SOURCE: http://www.ntsb.gov/publictn/2008/HAB0801.pdf

CASE FACT SPECIFIC VIDEOS — CASE 6 VIRGINIA SCHOOL BUS

Chapter 4	Administrative Agency Hearing
Chapter 5	Settlement Conference with Judge
Chapter 9	Scheduling Conference with Judge: Discovery Issue Resolution
Chapter 11	Attorney Meet and Confer: Electronic Discovery Issues
Chapter 14	Remote Video Conference/Video: Taking Fact Witness Deposition
	Real-Time Reporting Witness Testimony: Deposing a Minor
Chapter 16	Final Pretrial Conference: Resolving Evidentiary Issues
	Preparing For Trial: Prepare for Deposition and Trial
Chapter 17	Jury Selection: Potential Juror Challenged for Cause
Chapter 20	A Corporate Officer Seeks Legal Advice
	Deposition in Aid of Execution: Transferring Corporate Assets to Avoid Paying a Judgment

■ CASE 7: NEW YORK AIRPLANE CRASH

The comprehensive case study is based on a real accident as reported in a National Transportation Safety Board (NTSB) report. Though some content has been edited, the words of the report have been reproduced here to provide as much authenticity as possible. Figures are reproduced from the same report. Some liberty has been taken with the identity of the parties, and none of the names used represent or were actual parties involved. We base this case study on a real incident to give you practice in performing real-world legal and factual research, a skill you will use on the job in the future.

Aircraft Accident
Clarence Center, New York
February 12, 2009

Abstract

On February 12, 2009, about 2217 (10:17 P.M.) Eastern Standard Time, a Colgan Air, Inc., Bombardier DHC-8-400, N200WQ, operating as Continental Connection Flight 3407, was on an instrument approach to Buffalo-Niagara International Airport, Buffalo, New York, when it crashed into a residence in Clarence Center, New York, about five nautical miles northeast of the airport. The two pilots, two flight attendants, and 45 passengers aboard the airplane were killed, one person on the ground was killed, and the airplane was destroyed by impact forces and a post-crash fire.

■ EXECUTIVE SUMMARY

On February 12, 2009, about 2217 Eastern Standard Time, a Colgan Air, Inc., Bombardier DHC-8-400, N200WQ, operating as Continental Connection Flight 3407, was on an instrument approach to Buffalo-Niagara International Airport, Buffalo, New York, when it crashed into a residence in Clarence Center, New York, about five nautical miles northeast of the airport. The 2 pilots, 2 flight attendants, and 45 passengers aboard the airplane were killed, one person on the ground was killed, and the airplane was destroyed by impact forces and a post-crash fire. The flight was operating under the provisions of 14 *Code of Federal Regulations* Part 121. Night visual meteorological conditions prevailed at the time of the accident.

The home base of operations for both the captain and the first officer was Liberty International Airport (EWR), Newark, New Jersey. On February 11, 2009, the captain had completed a two-day trip sequence, with the final flight of the trip arriving at EWR at 1544. Also that day, the first officer began her commute from her home near Seattle, Washington, to EWR at 1951 Pacific Standard Time (PST), arriving at EWR (via Memphis International Airport [MEM], Memphis, Tennessee) at 0623 on the day of the accident. The captain and the first officer were both observed in Colgan's crew room on February 12 before their scheduled report time of 1330. The flight crew's first two scheduled flights of the day, from EWR to Greater Rochester International Airport (ROC), Rochester, New York, and back, had been canceled because of high winds at EWR and the resulting ground delays at the airport.

The company dispatch release for Flight 3407 was issued at 1800 and showed an estimated departure time of 1910 and an estimated en route time of 53 minutes. The airplane to be used for Flight 3407, N200WQ, arrived at EWR at 1854. A first officer whose flight arrived at EWR at 1853 saw, as he exited his airplane, the Flight 3407 captain and first officer walking toward the accident airplane. The airplane's aircraft communications addressing and reporting system (ACARS) showed a departure clearance request at 1930 and pushback from the gate at 1945. According to the cockpit voice recorder (CVR) recording, the EWR ground controller provided taxi instructions for the flight at 2030:28, which the first officer acknowledged.

About 2041:35, the first officer stated, "I'm ready to be in the hotel room," to which the captain replied, "I feel bad for you." She continued, "this is one of those times that if I felt like this when I was at home there's no way I would have come all the way out here." She then stated, "if I call in sick now, I've got to put myself in a hotel until I feel better...we'll see how...it feels flying. If the pressure's just too much...I could always call in tomorrow. At least I'm in a hotel on the company's buck, but we'll see. I'm pretty tough." The captain responded by stating that the first officer could try an over-the-counter herbal supplement, drink orange juice, or take vitamin C.

The CVR recorded the tower controller clearing the airplane for takeoff about 2118:23. The first officer acknowledged the clearance, and the captain stated, "all right, cleared for takeoff, it's mine." According to the dispatch release, the intended cruise altitude for the flight was 16,000 feet mean sea level (msl) The flight data recorder (FDR) showed that, during the climb to altitude, the propeller deice and airframe deice equipment were turned on (the pitot static deicing equipment had been turned on before takeoff) and the autopilot was engaged.

The airplane reached its cruising altitude of 16,000 feet about 2134:44. The cruise portion of flight was routine and uneventful. The CVR recorded the captain and the first officer engaged in an almost continuous conversation throughout that portion of the flight, but these conversations did not conflict with the sterile cockpit rule, which prohibits nonessential conversations within the cockpit during critical phases of flight. About 2149:18, the CVR recorded the captain making a sound similar to a yawn. About one minute later, the captain interrupted his own conversation to point out, to the first officer, traffic that was crossing left to right. About 2150:42, the first officer reported the winds to be from 250° at 15 knots gusting to 23 knots; afterward, the captain stated that runway 23 would be used for the landing.

About 2153:40, the first officer briefed the airspeeds for landing with the flaps at 15° (flaps 15) as 118 knots (reference landing speed [V_{ref}]) and 114 knots (go-around speed [V_{ga}]), and the captain acknowledged this information. About 2156:26, the first officer stated, "might be easier on my ears if we start going down sooner." About 2156:36, the captain instructed the first officer to "get discretion to twelve [thousand feet]." Less than one minute later, a controller from Cleveland Center cleared the flight to descend to 11,000 feet, and the first officer acknowledged the clearance.

About 2203:38, the Cleveland Center controller instructed the flight crew to contact BUF approach control, and the first officer acknowledged this instruction. The first officer made initial contact with BUF approach control about 2203:53, stating that the flight was descending from 12,000 to 11,000 feet with automatic terminal information service (ATIS) information "romeo," and the approach controller provided the airport altimeter setting and told the crew to plan an instrument landing system (ILS) approach to runway 23.

About 2204:16, the captain began the approach briefing. About 2205:01, the approach controller cleared the flight crew to descend and maintain 6,000 feet, and the first officer acknowledged the clearance. About 30 seconds later, the captain continued the approach briefing, during which he repeated the airspeeds for a flaps 15 landing. FDR data showed that the airplane descended through 10,000 feet about 2206:37. From that point on, the flight crew was required to observe the sterile cockpit rule.

About 2207:14, the CVR recorded the first officer making a sound similar to a yawn. About 2208:41 and 2209:12, the approach controller cleared the flight crew to descend and maintain 5,000 and 4,000 feet, respectively, and the first officer acknowledged the clearances. Afterward, the captain asked the first officer about her ears, and she indicated that they were stuffy and popping.

About 2210:23, the first officer asked whether ice had been accumulating on the windshield, and the captain replied that ice was present on his side of the windshield and asked whether ice was present on her windshield side. The first officer responded, "lots of ice." The captain then stated, "that's the most I've seen—most ice I've seen on the leading edges in a long time. In a while, anyway, I should say." About 10 seconds later, the captain and the first officer began a conversation that was unrelated to their flying duties. During that conversation, the first officer indicated that she had accumulated more actual flight time in icing conditions on her first day of initial operating experience (IOE) with Colgan than she had before her employment with the company. She also stated that, when other company first officers were "complaining" about not yet having upgraded to captain, she was thinking that she "wouldn't mind going through a winter in the northeast before [upgrading] to captain." The first officer explained that, before IOE, she had "never seen icing conditions...never deiced...never experienced any of that."

About 2212:18, the approach controller cleared the flight crew to descend and maintain 2,300 feet, and the first officer acknowledged the clearance. Afterward, the captain and the first officer performed flight-related duties but also continued the conversation that was unrelated to their flying duties. About 2212:44, the approach controller cleared the flight crew to turn left onto a heading of 330°. About 2213:25 and 2213:36, the captain called for the descent and approach checklists, respectively, which the first officer performed. About 2214:09, the approach controller cleared the flight crew to turn left onto a heading of 310°, and the autopilot's altitude hold mode became active about 1 second later as the airplane was approaching the preselected altitude of 2,300 feet. The airplane reached this altitude about 2214:30; the airspeed was about 180 knots at the time.

About 2215:06, the captain called for the flaps to be moved to the 5° position, and the CVR recorded a sound similar to flap handle movement. Afterward, the approach controller cleared the flight crew to turn left onto a heading of 260° and maintain 2,300 feet until established on the localizer for the ILS approach to runway 23. The first officer acknowledged the clearance.

The captain began to slow the airplane less than 3 miles from the outer marker to establish the appropriate airspeed before landing. According to FDR data, the engine power levers were reduced to about 42° (flight idle was 35°) about 2216:00, and both engines' torque values were at minimum thrust about 2216:02. The approach controller then instructed the flight crew to contact the BUF air traffic control tower (ATCT) controller. The first officer acknowledged this instruction, which was the last communication between the flight crew and air traffic control (ATC). Afterward, the CVR recorded sounds similar to landing gear handle deployment and landing gear movement, and the FDR showed that the propeller condition levers had been moved forward to their maximum RPM position and that pitch trim in the airplane-nose-up direction had been applied by the autopilot.

About 2216:21, the first officer told the captain that the gear was down; at that time, the airspeed was about 145 knots. Afterward, FDR data showed that additional pitch trim in the airplane-nose-up direction had been applied by the autopilot and that an "ice detected" message appeared on the engine display in the cockpit. About the same time, the captain called for the flaps to be set to 15° and for the before-landing checklist. The CVR then recorded a sound similar to flap handle movement, and FDR data showed that the flaps had been selected to 10°. FDR data also showed that the airspeed at the time was about 135 knots.

At 2216:27.4, the CVR recorded a sound similar to the stick shaker. (The stick shaker warns a pilot of an impending wing aerodynamic stall through vibrations on the control column, providing tactile and aural cues.) The CVR also recorded a sound similar to the autopilot disconnect horn, which repeated until the end of the recording. FDR data showed that, when the autopilot disengaged, the airplane was at an airspeed of 131 knots. FDR data showed that the control columns moved aft at 2216:27.8 and that the engine power levers were advanced to about 70° (rating detent was 80°) one second later. The CVR then recorded a sound similar to increased engine power, and FDR data showed that engine power had increased to about 75 percent torque.

FDR data also showed that, while engine power was increasing, the airplane pitched up; rolled to the left, reaching a roll angle of 45° left wing down; and then rolled to the right. As the airplane rolled to the right through wings level, the stick pusher activated (about 2216:34), and flaps 0 was selected. (The Q400 stick pusher applies an airplane-nose-down control column input to decrease the wing angle-of-attack [AOA] after an aerodynamic stall.) About 2216:37, the first officer told the captain that she had put the flaps up. FDR data confirmed that the flaps had begun to retract by 2216:38; at that time, the airplane's airspeed was about 100 knots. FDR data also showed that the roll angle reached 105° right wing down before the airplane began to roll back to the left and the stick pusher activated a second time (about 2216:40). At the time, the airplane's pitch angle was −1°.

About 2216:42, the CVR recorded the captain making a grunting sound. FDR data showed that the roll angle had reached about 35° left wing down before the airplane began to roll again to the right. Afterward, the first officer asked whether she should put the landing gear up, and the captain stated "gear up" and an expletive. The airplane's pitch and roll angles had reached about 25° airplane nose down and 100° right wing down, respectively, when the airplane entered a steep descent. The stick pusher activated a third time (about 2216:50). FDR data showed that the flaps were fully retracted about 2216:52. About the same time, the CVR recorded the captain stating, "we're down," and a sound of a thump. The airplane impacted a single-family home (where the ground fatality occurred), and a post-crash fire ensued. The CVR recording ended about 2216:54.

ABBREVIATIONS

AC	advisory circular
ACARS	aircraft communications addressing and reporting system
AFM	airplane flight manual
agl	above ground level
AOA	angle-of-attack
ATC	air traffic control
ATCT	air traffic control tower
ATIS	automatic terminal information service
ATOS	air transportation oversight system
BTV	Burlington International Airport
BUF	Buffalo-Niagara International Airport
CVR	cockpit voice recorder
CWA	Center Weather Advisory
eice	en route ice accumulation
FDR	flight data recorder
IFR	instrument flight rules
ILS	instrument landing system
msl	mean sea level
nm	nautical mile
PIC	pilot-in-command
SIC	second-in-command

The complete National Transportation Safety Board report is available and may be downloaded from www.pearsonhighered.com/goldman or the Technology Resources Website, together with selected exhibits and simulation, or in PDF.

SOURCE: http://www.ntsb.gov/publictn/2010/AAR1001.pdf

APPENDIX 4

GLOSSARY OF SPANISH EQUIVALENTS FOR IMPORTANT LEGAL TERMS

a priori   Desde antes, del pasado.

AAA   Siglas para **American Arbitration Association** Asociación de Arbitraje.

ABA   Siglas para **American Bar Association** Colegio de Abogados Estadounidenses.

accept   Aceptar, admitir, aprobar, recibir reconocer.

accession   Accesión, admisión, aumento, incremento.

accord   Acuerdo, convenio, arreglo, acordar, conceder.

acquittal   Absolución, descargo, veredicto de no culpable.

act   Acto, estatuto, decreto, actuar, funcionar.

actionable   Justiciable, punible, procesable.

adjourn   Levantar, posponer, suspender la sesión.

adjudicate   Adjudicar, decidir, dar fallo a favor de, sentenciar, declarar.

administrative   Administrativo, ejecutivo.

administrative agency   Agencia administrativa.

administrative hearing   Juicio administrativo.

administrative law   Derecho administrativo.

administrative law judge   Juez de derecho, Administrativo.

administrator   Administrador.

admit   Admitir, conceder, reconocer, permitir entrada, confesar, asentir.

adverse   Adverso, contrario, opuesto.

adverse possession   Posesión adversa.

advice   Consejo, asesoramiento, notificación.

affected class   Clase afectada, grupo iscriminado.

affidavit   Declaración voluntaria, escrita y bajo uramento, afidávit, atestiguación, testificata.

affirmative action   Acción positiva.

affirmative defense   Defensa justificativa.

after acquired property   Propiedad adquirida con garantía adicional.

against   En contra.

agency   Agencia, oficina, intervención.

agent   Agente, representante autorizado.

aggrieved party   Parte dañada, agraviada, perjudicada.

agreement   Acuerdo, arreglo, contrato, convenio, pacto.

alibi   Coartada.

alien   Extranjero, extraño, foráneo.

annul   Anular, cancelar, invalidar, revocar, dejar sin efecto.

answer   Contestación, réplica, respuesta, alegato.

antecedent   Antecedente, previo, preexistente.

appeal   Apelar, apelación.

appear   Aparecer, comparecer.

appellate court   Tribunal de apelaciones.

appellate jurisdiction   Competencia de apelación.

applicable   Aplicable, apropiado, pertinente a, lo que puede ser aplicado.

arraign   Denunciar, acusar, procesar, instruir de cargos hechos.

arrears   Retrasos, pagos atrasados, decursas.

arrest   Arresto, arrestar, aprehensión, aprehender, detener.

arson   Incendio intencional.

articles of incorporation   Carta de organización corporativa.

assault   Agresión, asalto, ataque, violencia carnal, agredir, atacar, acometer.

assault and battery   Amenazas y agresión, asalto.

assign   Asignar, ceder, designar, hacer cesión, traspasar, persona asignada un derecho.

attachment   Secuestro judicial.

attorney   Abogado, consejero, apoderado.

award   Fallo, juicio, laudo, premio.

bail   Caución, fianza.

bail bondsman   Fiador, fiador judicial.

bailee   Depositario de bienes.

bailment   Depósito, encargo, depósito mercantil, depósito comercial.

bailment   For hire, depósito oneroso.

bailor   Fiador.

bankruptcy   Bancarrota, quiebra, insolvencia.

battery   Agravio, agresión.

bearer bond   Título mobiliario.

bearer instrument   Título al portador.

bench   Tribunal, los jueces, la magistratura.

beneficiary   Beneficiario, legatario.

bequeath   Legar.

bilateral contract   Contrato bilateral.

bill of lading   Póliza de embarque, boleto de carga, documento de tránsito.

bill of rights   Las primeras diez enmiendas a la Constitución de los Estados Unidos de América.

binder   Resguardo provisional, recibo para garantizar el precio de un bien inmueble.

birth certificate   Acta de nacimiento, partida de nacimiento, certificado de nacimiento.

blue sky laws   Estatutos para prevenir el fraude en la compraventa de valores.

bond   Bono, título, obligación, deuda inversionista, fianza.

booking   Término dado en el cuartel de policía al registro de arresto y los cargos hechos al arrestado.

breach of contract   Violación, rotura, incumplimiento de contrato.

brief   Alegato, escrito memorial.

burglary   Escalamiento, allanamiento de morada.

buyer   Comprador.

bylaws   Estatutos sociales, reglamentos internos.

capacity to contract   Capacidad contractual.

case   Causa, caso, acción legal, proceso, proceso civil, asunto, expediente.

case law   Jurisprudencia.

cashier's check   Cheque bancario.

cease and desist order   Orden judicial de cese.

censure   Censura.

certificate of deposit   Certificado de depósito.

certified check   Cheque certificado.

certify   Certificar, atestiguar.

charge   Cobrar, acusar, imputar.

charitable trust   Fideicomiso caritativo.

chattel   Bienes muebles, bártulos.

cheat   Fraude, engaño, defraudador, trampa, tramposo, estafar.

check   Cheque, talón, comprobación.

cite   Citación, citar, referir, emplazar.

citizenship   Ciudadanía.

civil action   Acción, enjuiciamiento civil, demanda.

civil law   Derecho civil.

claims court   Tribunal federal de reclamaciones.

client   Cliente.

closing arguments   Alegatos de clausura.

closing costs   Gastos ocasionados en la venta de bienes raíces.

clue   Pista, indicio.

codicil   Codicilo.

coercion   Coerción, coacción.

collateral   Colateral, auxiliar, subsidiario, seguridad colateral, garantía prendaria.

collect   Cobrar, recobrar, recaudar.

collision   Choque, colisión.

common law   Derecho consuetudinario.

comparative negligence   Negligencia comparativa.

compensatory damages   Indemnización compensatoria por daños y perjuicios, daños compensatorios.

competency   Competencia, capacidad legal.

concurrent conditions   Condiciones concurrentes.

concurrent jurisdiction   Jurisdicción simultanea, conocimiento acumulativo.

concurrent sentences   Sentencias que se cumplen simultáneamente.

concurring opinion   Opinión coincidente.

condemn   Condenar, confiscar, expropiar.

condition precedent   Condición precedente.

condition subsequent   Condición subsecuente.

confession   Confesión, admisión.

confidential   Confidencial, íntimo, secreto.

confiscation   Confiscación, comiso, decomiso.

consent decree   Decreto por acuerdo mutuo.

consequential damages   Daños especiales.

consideration   Contraprestación.

consolidation   Consolidación, unión, concentración.

constructive delivery   Presunta entrega.

contempt of court   Desacato, contumacia o menosprecio a la corte.

contract   Contrato, convenio, acuerdo, pacto.

contributory negligence   Negligencia contribuyente.

conversion   Conversión, canje.

conviction   Convicción, fallo de culpabilidad, convencimiento, sentencia condenatoria, condena.

copyright   Derecho de autor, propiedad literaria, propiedad intelectual, derecho de impresión.

corroborate   Corroborar, confirmar.

counterclaim   Contrademanda, excepción de compensación.

counteroffer   Contra oferta.

courts   Cortes o tribunales establecidas por la constitución.

covenant for quiet enjoyment   Convenio de disfrute y posesión pacífica.

creditor   Acreedor.

crime   Crimen, delito.

criminal act   Acto criminal.

criminal law   Derecho penal.

cross-examination   Contrainterrogatorio, repregunta.

cure   Curar, corregir.

damages   Daños y perjuicios, indemnización pecuniaria.

DBA   Sigla para **doing business as** En negociación comercial.

deadly force   Fuerza mortífera.

debt   Deuda, débito.

debtor   Deudor.

decision   Decisión judicial, fallo, determinación auto, sentencia.

deed   Escritura, título de propiedad, escritura de traspaso.

defamation   Difamación, infamación.

default Incumplir, faltar, no comparecer, incumplimiento.

defendant Demandado, reo, procesado, acusado.

delinquent Delincuente, atrasado en pagos, delictuoso.

denial Denegación, negación, denegatoria.

deponent Deponente, declarante.

deportation Deportación, destierro.

deposition Deposición, declaración bajo juramento.

detain Detener, retardar, retrasar.

devise Legado de bienes raíces.

direct examination Interrogatorio directo, interrogatorio a testigo propio.

directed verdict Veredicto expedido por el juez, veredicto por falta de pruebas.

disaffirm Negar, rechazar, repudiar, anular.

discharge Descargo, cumplimiento, liberación.

disclose Revelar.

discovery Revelación de prueba, exposición reveladora.

discriminate Discriminar.

dismiss Despedir, desechar, desestimar.

dissenting opinion Opinión en desacuerdo.

dissolution Disolución, liquidación.

diversity of citizenship Diversidad de ciudadanías, ciudadanías diferentes.

dividend Acción librada, dividendo.

divorce Divorcio, divorciar.

docket Orden del día, lista de casos en la corte.

double jeopardy Non bis in idem.

driving under the influence Manejar bajo los efectos de bebidas alcohólicas o drogas.

duress Coacción.

earnest money Arras, señal.

easement Servidumbre.

edict Edicto, decreto, auto.

embezzlement Malversación de fondos.

eminent domain Dominio eminente.

encroachment Intrusión, usurpación, invasión, uso indebido.

encumbrance Gravamen, afectación, cargo.

enforce Hacer cumplir, dar valor, poner en efecto.

entitlement Derecho, título.

equal protection clause Cláusula de protección de igualdad ante la ley.

equal protection of the law Igualdad ante la ley.

equity Equidad. Derecho equitativo.

escheat Reversión al estado al no haber herederos.

estate Bienes, propiedad, caudal hereditario, cuerpo de la herencia, caudal, derecho, título, interés sobre propiedad.

estop Impedir, detener, prevenir.

ethics Sistema ético.

eviction Evicción, desalojo, desalojamiento, desahucio, lanzamiento.

evidence Testimonio, prueba, pruebas documentales, pieza de prueba.

examination Examen, reconocimiento, interrogatorio.

executed contract Contrato firmado, contrato ejecutado.

execution Ejecución, desempeño, cumplimiento.

executory contract Contrato por cumplirse.

executory interests Intereses futuros.

exempt Franquear, exentar, exencionar, eximir, libre, franco, exento, inmune.

exoneration Exoneración, descargo, liberación.

expert witness Testigo perito.

express contract Contrato explícito.

expropriation Expropiación, confiscación.

eyewitness Testigo ocular o presencial.

fact Hecho falsificado.

failure to appear Incomparecencia.

fault Falta, defecto, culpa, negligencia.

fee Honorarios, retribución, cuota, cargo, derecho, dominio, asesoría, propiedad, bienes raíces.

fee simple estate Propiedad en dominio pleno.

felon Felón, autor de un delito.

felony Delito mayor o grave.

fiduciary Fiduciario.

find against Fallar o decidir en contra.

find for Fallar o decidir a favor.

finding Determinación de los hechos.

fine Multa, castigo.

fixture Accesorio fijo.

foreclose Entablar juicio hipotecario, embargar bienes hipotecados.

forgery Falsificación.

franchise Franquicia, privilegio, patente, concesión social, derecho de votar.

fraud Fraude, engaño, estafa, trampa, embuste, defraudación.

full disclosure Revelación completa.

garnishment Embargo de bienes.

gift Regalo, dádiva, donación.

gift causa mortis Donación de propiedad en expectativa de muerte.

gift inter vivos Donación entre vivos.

gift tax Impuesto sobre donaciones.

good and valid consideration Causa contractual válida.

good faith Buena fe.

goods Mercaderías, bienes, productos.

grace period   Período de espera.

grantee   Concesionario, cesionario.

grantor   Otorgante, cesionista.

grievance   Agravio, injuria, ofensa, queja formal.

gross negligence   Negligencia temeraria, negligencia grave.

habitation   Habitación, lugar donde se vive.

harassment   Hostigamiento.

hearing   Audiencia, vista, juicio.

hearsay   Testimonio de oídas.

holder   Tenedor, poseedor.

holding   Decisión, opinión, tenencia posesión, asociación, grupo industrial.

holographic will   Testamento hológrafo.

homeowner   Propietario, dueño de casa.

homestead   Casa, solariega, hogar, heredad, excepción de embargo, bien de familia.

hung jury   Jurado sin veredicto.

identify   Identificar, verificar, autenticar.

illegal   Ilegal, ilícito, ilegítimo.

illegal entry   Entrada ilegal.

illegal search   Registro domiciliario, allanamiento ilegal, cacheo ilegal.

immunity   Inmunidad, exención.

implied warranty   Garantía implícita.

impossibility of performance   Imposibilidad de cumplimiento.

impound   Embargar, incautar, confiscar, secuestrar.

inadmissible   Inadmisible, inaceptable.

income   Ingreso, ganancia, entrada, renta, rédito.

incriminate   Incriminar, acriminar.

indictment   Procesamiento, acusación por jurado acusatorio, inculpatoria.

indorsement   Endose, endoso, respaldo, garantía.

informant   Informador, denunciante, delator.

information   Información, informe, acusación por el fiscal, denuncia.

informed consent   Conformidad por información.

inherit   Heredar, recibir por herencia.

injunction   Mandato judicial, amparo, prohibición judicial, interdicto.

innocent   Inocente, no culpable.

inquiry   Indagatoria judicial, pesquisa.

insufficient evidence   Prueba insuficiente.

interrogation   Interrogación.

interstate commerce   Comercio interestatal.

intestate   Intestado, intestar, sin testamento.

intestate succession   Sucesión hereditaria.

investigation   Investigación, indagación, encuesta.

issue   Emisión, cuestión, punto, edición, número, tirada, sucesión, descendencia, resultado, decisión.

jail   Cárcel, calabozo, encarcelar.

joint tenancy   Condominio.

judge   Magistrado, juez, juzgar, adjudicar, enjuiciar, fallar.

judgment   Sentencia, fallo, juicio, decisión, dictamen, criterio.

judicial proceeding   Proceso o diligencia judicial.

judicial review   Revisión judicial.

jump bail   Fugarse bajo fianza.

jurisdiction   Jurisdicción, fuero competencia.

jury   Jurado

landlord   Arrendatario, propietario.

larceny   Hurto, latrocinio, ladronicio.

law   Ley, derecho.

lease   Contrato de arrendamiento, arrendamiento, arriendo, contrato de locación, arrendar, alquilar.

leasehold estate   Bienes forales.

legatee   Legatario, asignatario.

lender   Prestamista.

lessee   Arrendatario, locatario, inquilino.

lessor   Arrendatario, arrendador, arrendante, locador.

letter of credit   Letra de crédito.

liability   Responsiva, responsabilidad.

libel   Libelo por difamación por escrito.

license   Licencia, permiso, privilegio, matrícula, patente, título, licenciar, permitir.

lien   Gravamen, derecho prendario o de retención, embargo preventivo.

life estate   Hipoteca legal, dominio vitalicio.

limited liability company   Sociedad de responsabilidad limitada.

limited partnership   Sociedad en comandita, sociedad comanditaria.

litigated   Pleiteado, litigado, sujeto a litigación.

majority opinion   Opinión que refleja la mayoría de los miembros de la corte de apelaciones.

maker   Otorgante, girador.

malice   Malicia, malignidad, maldad.

malpractice   Incompetencia profesional.

manslaughter   Homicidio sin premeditación.

material witness   Testigo esencial.

mechanics lien   Gravamen de construcción.

mediation   Mediación, tercería, intervención, interposición.

medical examiner   Médico examinador.

merger   Fusión, incorporación, unión, consolidación.

minor   Menor, insignificante, pequeño, trivial.

misdemeanor   Delito menor, fechoría.

mitigation of damages   Mitigación de daños, minoración, atenuación.

monetary damages   Daños pecuniarios.

mortgage   Hipoteca, gravamen, hipotecar, gravar.

motion to dismiss   Petición para declaración sin lugar.

motion to suppress   Moción para suprimir, reprimir o suspender.

motive   Motivo.

murder   Asesinato, asesinar, homicidio culposo.

naturalization   Naturalización.

negligence   Negligencia, descuido, imprudencia.

negotiable   Negociable.

negotiate   Negociar, agenciar, hacer efectivo, traspasar, tratar.

net assets   Haberes netos.

notice   Aviso, notificación, advertencia, conocimiento.

novation   Novación, delegación de crédito.

nuisance   Daño, molestia, perjuicio.

nuncupative will   Testamento abierto.

oath   Juramento.

objection   Objeción, oposición, disconformidad, recusación, impugnación, excepción, réplica, reclamación.

obstruction of justice   Encubrimiento activo.

offer   Oferta, ofrecimiento, propuesta, ofrecer, proponer.

omission   Omisión, falla, falta.

opinion   Opinión, dictamen, decisión de la corte.

oral argument   Alegato oral.

order instrument   Instrumento de pago a la orden.

owe   Deber, estar en deuda, adeudo.

owner   Dueño, propietario, poseedor.

pain and suffering   Angustia mental y dolor físico.

pardon   Perdón, indulto, absolución, indultar, perdonar.

parol evidence rule   Principio que prohíbe la modificación de un contrato por prueba verbal.

parole   Libertad vigilada.

partnership   Sociedad, compañía colectiva, aparcería, consorcio, sociedad personal.

patent   Patente, obvio, evidente, aparente, privilegio de invención, patentar.

penalty   Pena, multa, castigo, penalidad, condena.

pending   Pendiente, en trámite, pendiente de, hasta que.

per capita   Por cabeza.

performance   Cumplimiento, desempeño, ejecución, rendimiento.

perjury   Perjurio, testimonio falso, juramento falso.

personal property   Bienes personales, bienes mobiliarios.

plea bargain   Declaración de culpabilidad concertada.

plea of guilty   Alegación de culpabilidad.

pleadings   Alegatos, alegaciones, escritos.

pledge   Prenda, caución, empeño, empeñar, dar en prenda, pignorar.

police power   Poder policial.

policy   Póliza, escritura, práctica política.

possession   Posesión, tenencia, goce, disfrute.

possibility of reverter   Posibilidad de reversión.

power of attorney   Poder de representación, poder notarial, procura.

precedent   Precedente, decisión previa por el mismo tribunal.

preemptive right   Derecho de prioridad.

prejudicial   Dañoso, perjudicial.

preliminary hearing   Audiencia preliminar.

premeditation   Premeditación.

presume   Presumir, asumir como hecho basado en la experiencia, suponer.

prevail   Prevalecer, persuadir, predominar, ganar, triunfar.

price discrimination   Discriminación en el precio.

principal   Principal, jefe, de mayor importancia, valor actual.

privileged communication   Comunicación privilegiada.

privity   Coparticipación, intereses comunes.

procedural   Procesal.

proceeds   Ganancias.

profit   Ganancia, utilidad, lucro, beneficio.

prohibited   Prohibido.

promise   Promesa.

promissory estoppel   Impedimento promisorio.

promissory note   Pagaré, vale, nota de pago.

proof   Prueba, comprobación, demostración.

prosecutor   Fiscal, abogado público acusador.

proximate cause   Causa relacionada.

proxy   Poder, delegación, apoderado, mandatario.

punishment   Pena, castigo.

punitive damages   Indemnización punitiva por daños y perjuicios, daños ejemplares.

qualification   Capacidad, calidad, preparación.

qualified indorsement   Endoso limitado endoso con reservas.

quasi contract   Cuasicontrato.

query   Pregunta, interrogación.

question of fact   Cuestión de hecho.

question of law   Cuestión de derecho.

quiet enjoyment   Uso y disfrute.

quitclaim deed   Escritura de traspaso de finiquito.

race discrimination   Discriminación racial.

rape   Estupro, violación, ultraje, rapto, violar.

ratification   Ratificación, aprobación, confirmación.

ratify   Aprobar, confirmar, ratificar, convalidar, adoptar.

real property   Bienes raíces, bienes inmuebles, arraigo.

reasonable doubt   Duda razonable.

rebut   Rebatir, refutar, negar, contradecir.

recognizance   Obligación impuesta judicialmente.

recordation   Inscripción oficial, grabación.

recover   Recobrar, recuperar, obtener como resultado de decreto.

redress   Reparación, compensación, desagravio, compensar, reparar, satisfacer, remediar.

regulatory agency   Agencia reguladora.

reimburse   Reembolsar, repagar, compensar, reintegrar.

rejoinder   Respuesta, réplica, contrarréplica.

release   Descargo, liberación, librar, relevar, descargar, libertar.

relevance   Relevancia.

remainder   Resto, restante, residuo, derecho expectativo a un bien raíz.

remedy   Remedio, recurso.

remuneration   Remuneración, compensación.

reply   Réplica, contestación, contestar, responder.

reprieve   Suspensión de la sentencia, suspensión, indulto, indultar, suspender.

reprimand   Reprender, regañar, reprimenda, represión.

repudiate   Repudiar, renunciar, rechazar.

rescission   Rescisión, abrogación, cancelación de un contrato.

respondeat superior   Responsabilidad civil al supervisor.

respondent   Apelado, demandado.

restitution   Restitución, devolución.

restraining order   Inhibitoria, interdicto, orden de amparo.

retain   Retener, emplear, guardar.

reversion   Reversión, derecho de sucesión.

revocation   Revocación, derogación, anulación.

reward   Premio.

right of first refusal   Retracto arrendaticio.

right of subrogation   Derecho de sustituir.

right of survivorship   Derecho de supervivencia entre dueños de propiedad mancomunada.

right to work laws   Leyes que prohíben la filiación sindical como requisito para poder desempeñar un puesto, derecho de trabajo.

rights   Derechos.

robbery   Robo, atraco.

ruling   Determinación oficial, auto judicial.

sale   Venta.

sale on approval   Venta por aprobación.

satisfaction   Satisfacción, liquidación, cumplimiento, pago, finiquito.

scope of authority   Autoridad explícitamente otorgada o implícitamente concedida.

search and seizure   Allanamiento, registro e incautación.

search warrant   Orden de registro o de allanamiento.

secured party   Persona con interés asegurado.

secured transaction   Transacción con un interés asegurado.

securities   Valores, títulos, obligaciones.

security agreement   Acuerdo que crea la garantía de un interés.

security deposit   Deposito de seguridad.

seize   Arrestar, confiscar, secuestrar, incautar.

settlement   Arreglo, composición, ajuste, liquidación, componenda, acomodo.

sex discrimination   Discriminación sexual.

sexual harassment   Acoso sexual.

shoplifting   Ratería en tiendas.

signature   Firma.

slander   Calumnia, difamación oral, calumniar.

source of income   Fuente de ingresos.

specific performance   Prestación específica contractual.

split decision   Decisión con opiniones mixtas.

spousal abuse   Abuso conyugal.

stare decisis   Vinculación con decisiones judiciales anteriores.

state of mind   Estado de ánimo, estado mental.

statement   Alegación, declaración, relato, estado de cuentas.

statutory foreclosure   Ejecución hipotecaria estatutaria.

statutory law   Derecho estatutario.

statutory rape   Estupro, violación de un menor de edad.

steal   Robar, hurtar, robo, hurto.

stock   Acciones, capital, existencias, semental.

stock option   Opción de comprar o vender acciones.

stop payment order   Suspensión de pago.

strict liability   Responsabilidad rigurosa.

sublease   Subarriendo, sublocación, subarrendar.

subpoena   Citación, citatorio, comparendo, cédula de citación, citación judicial, subpoena.

sue   Demandar, procesar.

summary judgment   Sentencia sumaria.

summon   Convocar, llamar, citar.

suppress   Suprimir, excluir pruebas ilegalmente obtenidas, reprimir, suspender.

surrender   Rendir, entregar, entrega, rendirse, entregarse.

surviving spouse   Cónyuge sobreviviente.

suspect   Sospecha, sospechar, sospechoso.

tangible evidence   Prueba real.

tangible property   Propiedad tangible, bienes tangibles.

tenancy at sufferance   Tenencia o posesión por tolerancia.

tenancy at will   Tenencia o inquilinato sin plazo fijo.

tenancy by the entirety   Tenencia conyugal.

tenancy for life   Tenencia vitalicia.

tenancy for years   Inquilinato por tiempo fijo.

tender   Propuesta, oferta, presentar.

testator   Testador.

testify   Atestar, atestiguar, dar testimonio.

theft   Hurto.

title   Título, derecho de posesión, rango, denominación.

tort   Agravio, torticero, entuerto, daño legal, perjuicio, acto ilícito civil.

Totten trust   Fideicomiso bancario Totten.

trade name   Nombre comercial, marca de fábrica, marca comercial.

trademark   Marca registrada, marca industrial.

transgression   Ofensa, delito, transgresión.

trespass   Transgresión, violación de propiedad ajena, translimitación, traspasar, violar, infringir, transgredir.

trial court   Tribunal de primera instancia.

trust   Fideicomiso, confianza, confidencia, confianza, crédito, combinación, consorcio, grupo industrial.

truth   Verdad, verdadero, veracidad.

try   Probar, juzgar.

ultra vires   Mas allá de la facultad de actuar.

unanimous verdict   Veredicto unánime.

unbiased   Imparcial, neutral.

unconditional pardon   Perdón, amnistía, indulto incondicional.

unconscionable   Reprochable, repugnante, desmedido.

under arrest   Arrestado, bajo arresto.

underwrite   Subscribir, asegurar, firmar.

undisclosed   Escondido, no revelado.

undue influence   Influencia indebida, coacción, abuso de poder.

unenforceable   Inejecutable.

unilateral contract   Contrato unilateral.

unlawful   Ilegal, ilícito, ilegítimo.

unsound mind   Privado de razón, de mente inestable.

usury   Usura, agiotaje, logrería.

vagrancy   Vagancia, vagabundeo.

validity   Validez, vigencia.

valuable consideration   Causa contractual con cierto valor, causa contractual onerosa.

venue   Partido judicial.

verbal contract   Contrato verbal.

verbatim   Al pié de la letra.

verdict   Veredicto, fallo, sentencia, decisión.

victim   Víctima.

voidable   Anulable, cancelable.

wage   Salario, jornal, sueldo.

waive   Renunciar, ceder, suspender, abdicar.

waiver   Renunciar, desistir, ceder, suspender, abdicar, renuncia.

warrant   Autorización, resguardo, comprobante, certificado, justificación, decisión judicial.

warranty   Garantía, seguridad.

warranty of habitability   Garantía de habitabilidad.

welfare   Asistencia pública.

will   Testamento, voluntad.

willful misconduct   Mala conducta intencional.

withhold   Retener, detener.

witness   Testigo, declarante, atestar, testificar, atestiguar.

writ of attachment   Mandamiento de embargo.

writ of certiorari   Pedimento de avocación.

writ of execution   Auto de ejecución, ejecutoria.

GLOSSARY

Admissible evidence   Evidence that is relevant to the case and which the court will allow to be presented.

Admission of a party opponent   A form of non-hearsay; an admission of fact made by one of the parties to the law suit.

Admit   A possible response of the defendant to the complaint which accepts the facts of the averment are true.

Affirm   Ruling of appellate court that agrees with the outcome of trial and can find no error.

Affirmative defense   Those legal theories asserted by the defendant which bar the plaintiff's claim.

Age of majority   The age at which an individual is recognized as an adult, usually 18.

Agent   A person authorized to act on behalf of another.

Alternate jurors   Jurors selected to hear the case with the rest of the jury who participate in rendering a decision only when a juror is unable to complete service.

Alternative dispute resolution   The use of methods other than the judicial system to resolve legal disputes.

American Arbitration Association (AAA)   A private nonprofit organization providing lists of potential arbitrators for parties to select from and a set of rules for conducting the private arbitration.

Analytical skills   Ability to follow a step-by-step process to solve a problem.

Annotation monitor   Monitor which allows a witness to easily make on-screen annotations with the touch of a finger.

Answer   Document by which the defendant responds to the allegations contained in the plaintiff's complaint.

Appealable error   An error made at trial that causes harm or prejudice to a litigant.

Appellant   The party who asserts error occurred at trial by filing an appeal for review of the trial proceedings.

Appellate courts   Courts that review the record from the trial court to determine if the trial judge made an error in applying the procedural or substantive law.

Appellee   The party who must respond to an appeal for review, usually the verdict winner at trial.

Arbitration   The most well-known ADR method which submits a dispute to a third party for binding or non-binding resolution after a hearing in which each side presents evidence and argument of counsel.

Associates   Non-owner lawyers, usually salaried employees of the law firm.

Assumption of risk   An affirmative defense which states plaintiff knew the risks involved with a particular activity and voluntarily proceeded with that activity.

Attached   A restriction by the trial court that prohibits an attorney from accepting another trial for the same time.

Attorney work product   Material prepared for litigation by the attorney.

Attorney-client privilege   Rule of evidence that protects the client from the attorney being required to reveal the confidential information.

Authorization for distribution   A written statement granting permission to accept a sum of money and distribute it in accordance with a schedule of distribution.

Automatic stay   In bankruptcy, a requirement that creditors cease all efforts to collect the debts owed them once a bankruptcy petition has been filed.

Bates production numbering   A Bates production number is a tracking number assigned to each page of each document in the production set.

Best evidence rule   Court preference for original writings, recordings, or photographs.

Bookmarks   Netscape term for saved URL's.

Briefs   Documents submitted by the parties' attorneys to the court that contain legal support for their side of the case.

Burden of proof   The level of proof required to establish an entitlement to recovery.

Calendar maintenance   Adding critical deadlines, appointments, and reminders to the calendar for each member of the legal team.

Candor   Ethical obligation to not mislead the court or opposing counsel with false statements of law or of facts which the lawyer knows to be false.

Caption   Identity of the parties, the court, and the court-identifying information on the complaint.

Case-in-chief   The portion of the trial where one side presents all its evidence to the jury through direct and cross–examination.

Case law   Law created by written decisions issued by the judicial branch; decisions resolve the dispute before the court and serve as precedent or guidance for similar future disputes.

Case management system   Software for organizing the parts of a case in a central repository that can be shared by all members of the legal team.

Cases   Issues that a client has presented to a legal team to handle and resolve.

Certificate of service   Form required by the court certifying the manner and method in which service is made; used after personal service of the complaint for all other pleadings.

Causation   The link between the injury suffered by the plaintiff and the action or inaction of the defendant; includes causation in fact (actual cause) and proximate cause (legal cause).

Cause of action   A wrong that is legally recognized as a basis for compensating one for the harms suffered.

Chain of custody   A written record showing the identity of everyone accessing evidence and showing that the evidence was not altered while in possession of the law firm.

Challenge for cause   A potential juror may be struck from the jury when his answers to voir dire questions indicate bias.

Citation checking   Process by which citation to the record and the law are checked for accuracy.

Civil cover sheet   A summary page of information about a case.

Civil litigation   Resolution of legal disputes between parties seeking a remedy for a civil wrong or to enforce a contract.

Claim   A right asserted against another for which a remedy is sought in a lawsuit.

Claim of privilege   The person claiming the privilege—usually the client—has the burden to establish its existence.

Claw-back provision   A provision contained in the report of counsel's meet and confer and included in the court's scheduling order that describes what to do with privileged materials that are disclosed inadvertently through e-discovery. The provision should address return of the materials and waiver of the privilege.

Closing arguments   The last opportunity for the attorneys to address the jury, summing up the client's case and persuading the jury to decide in their client's favor.

Cloud computing   The access over the Internet of a secure depository by authorized users.

Commitment   Finishing what one starts out to do.

Common interest privilege   To permit a client to share confidential information with the attorney for another who shares a common legal interest.

Communication skills   Ability to express ideas effectively in both spoken and written word.

Comparative negligence   An affirmative defense which reduces an award to the plaintiff by the percentage his own negligence contributed to his injuries.

Compensatory damages   Damages which calculate a monetary value for the actual loss suffered by the plaintiff.

Competent   Having the requisite knowledge and skill, thoroughness, and preparation necessary for representation.

Complaint   Initial pleading filed by the plaintiff designed to give notice to the defendant of the claims against them.

Concurrent jurisdiction   Cases where the federal and state court both have subject matter and personal jurisdiction.

Confidentiality   Ethical obligation to keep client information confidential (not disclose) founded on the belief that clients should be able to tell their attorneys everything about their case so the attorney can give proper legal advice to the client.

Conflict of interest   Situations where the interests or loyalties of the lawyer and client may be or may appear to be adverse or divided.

Consent judgment   Document filed with the court to terminate the lawsuit by entering a judgment against the defendant.

Constitution   A document that establishes the conception, character, and organization of a government, the fundamental and organic law.

Consumer debt   Debts incurred that are related to personal, family, or household purposes.

Contingency fee agreement   Fee agreement whereby the lawyer receives a percentage of the amount recovered for the plaintiff.

Continuance   Request made to the court to change the date scheduled for trial.

Continuing objection   An acknowledgment in the record of the trial that the attorney objects to particular testimony or evidence without having to object each time the witness answers a question. The purpose is to permit the testimony to be presented easily without waiving the error of its admission.

Contract   An agreement entered by two parties for valid consideration.

Contributory negligence   An affirmative defense which states there is no recovery where the plaintiff's negligence contributed to his injuries.

Cost-benefit analysis   Process by which a litigant determines the costs of pursuing litigation and compares them to what is likely to be gained.

Counterclaim   Claims the defendant has against the plaintiff.

Courts of record   Courts in which the testimony and evidence presented are recorded and preserved.

Credibility   Truthfulness and believability of the testimony given.

Creditor   One to whom money is owed.

Criminal litigation   Government enforcing of laws or prosecution for breach of a law.

Cross appeal   Where the appellee also asserts error occurred at trial and seeks appellate review of the trial proceedings.

Cross appellant   The appellee or respondent who files a cross appeal.

Cross claim   Claims that one defendant may have against another defendant.

Cross-examination   Opportunity of defense (opposing) counsel to question a witness after the direct examination of the witness.

Cultural sensitivity   Awareness of and sensitivity to the reasons for differences in the way people behave based on religious and ethnic background and belief system.

Damages   A calculation, usually financial, of harm suffered by the plaintiff.

Database   A collection of similar records.

Date certain   Date set by the judge for trial to begin; it cannot be changed.

Debtor   One who owes another a sum of money.

De-duping   The process of comparing electronic records based on their characteristics and removing duplicate records from the data set.

Default   Failure to file a timely response, whether to a motion or an answer.

Default judgment   Judgment obtained by the plaintiff against the defendant where the defendant has failed to respond in a timely fashion to the complaint.

Defendant   The party who is sued in a lawsuit.

Defense medical evaluation (DME)   Medical examination of the plaintiff performed by physician selected by the defendant.

Deficiency   The shortfall between the proceeds received at execution and the judgment amount.

Demonstrative evidence   Tangible item such as a photograph or map that depicts, displays, or demonstrates a fact.

Deny   A possible response of the defendant to the complaint which asserts the facts of the averment are not true.

Deposition   A form of discovery available to ask questions and obtain oral answers under oath from a witness or party to a lawsuit. Questions and answers are recorded stenographically.

Deposition digest   A summary of deposition testimony with reference to the location in the transcript and/or the video foot location.

Diagnosis   A determination of the source of a medical complaint.

Diminished capacity   An impaired mental condition caused by intoxication, trauma, or disease that prevents one from understanding the nature and effect of their actions.

Direct examination   Questions addressed to a witness by the attorney who has called that witness to testify on behalf of his client.

Discovery   A phase of the litigation process in which the plaintiff and defendant share information relevant to the lawsuit.

Diversity of citizenship   A lawsuit permitted in the federal court where the plaintiffs are from states different from the defendants and the amount in controversy exceeds $75,000.

Docket entries   Written record maintained in the clerk of court's office listing documents and things filed with the court.

Docket   A judge's personal list of pending cases.

Document camera   A portable evidence presentation system equipped with a high-resolution camera.

Documentary evidence   Writings, recordings, and photographs, which include X-ray films, electronic recordings, or any other data compilation.

Documents   Word processing files, scanned images, pleadings, correspondence, or Web pages.

Domestic public documents   A type of self-authenticating document; these records are on file with any domestic government office and are admissible evidence if they bear the seal of the office and the signature attesting to the authenticity.

Dual-cassette player   Equipment that plays back audio.

Duty of care   Duty of individuals to use reasonable care to avoid causing harm.

Duty of confidentiality   An ethical obligation to not reveal any information about a client's affairs regardless of the source of the information.

Dying declaration   A hearsay exception for a deathbed statement.

E-discovery   Discovery of documents created, disseminated, and stored via electronic means.

Electronic courtroom   Courtroom equipped with electronic equipment for use in trial presentations.

Electronic filing   Filing court documents by electronic means, such as e-mail.

Electronic repository   A secure protected file server to which everyone authorized has access over the internet.

Elements   Components of a legal claim that must be established by the burden of proof.

Elements of a cause of action   The components of a legal claim that must be established by the burden of proof.

***En banc* review**   Term used to describe the entire panel of judges sitting and hearing a case, usually on appeal.

Encryption   Technology that allows computer users to put a "lock" around information to prevent discovery by others.

Entry of appearance   An attorney for one of the litigants files papers officially identifying himself as representing the client before the court.

Entry of judgment   Taking the verdict announced by the jury and converting it to a legally enforceable judgment.

Equitable remedy   Used where no amount of monetary damages can make the injured party whole.

E-repository (online document repository)   An electronic data storage facility accessed using the Internet.

Error in instructions to jury   An error made at trial by the judge with regard to the instructions given to the jury or the recitation of the instruction.

Ethical wall   An environment in which an attorney or a paralegal is isolated from a particular case or client to avoid a conflict of interest or to protect a client's confidences and secrets.

Ethics   Minimally acceptable standards of conduct in a profession.

Ethical obligation   A minimum standard of conduct usually within one's profession.

Events   Any appointments, tasks, reminders, or things to do that are scheduled for specific dates.

Evidence   Testimony, documents, and tangible things that tend to prove or disprove a fact.

Error in evidentiary ruling   An error made at trial by the judge with regard to the admission or exclusion of evidence.

Evidentiary phase   Phase of the trial where testimony and evidence are presented to the jury or judge.

Excited utterance   A hearsay exception in which the statement by a declarant about a startling event is admissible.

Exculpatory evidence   Evidence which tends to prove the innocence of the accused or prove the facts of the defendant's case.

Execution   Process whereby the assets of the judgment debtor are collected by the sheriff, sold, and the proceeds used to pay the judgment.

Executive branch   One of the three co-equal branches of the government; represented by the president and administrative agencies.

Exempt property   Property of the judgment debtor that is set aside for his personal use and is not available for execution.

Expert witness   A person qualified by education, training, or experience to render an opinion based on a set of facts that are outside the scope of knowledge of the fact finder.

Extension of time to respond   Request by the defendant to enlarge the time to respond to the complaint beyond that which is permitted under the rules.

Fact pleading   Pleadings required to include all relevant facts in support of all claims asserted.

Fact witness   A witness who testified about facts based upon his observation or has personal knowledge about the matter before the court.

Facts   Actual or alleged events and occurrences.

Factual research   Investigating the facts of the clients case.

Favorites   Internet Explorer term for saved URLs.

Federal Arbitration Act   A federal statute that provides that arbitration agreements in commercial contracts are valid, irrevocable, and enforceable unless some legal or equitable grounds (fraud, duress) exist to invalidate them.

Federal Rules of Civil Procedure   The rules and procedures which control all litigation filed in the federal court system.

Federal Rules of Evidence   Enacted 1975, rules which apply to proceedings in all federal courts to determine what evidence will be admissible in court.

Fiduciary relationship   A relationship where one is under a duty to act for the benefit of another under the scope of the relationship.

Filing fees   A fee charged by the court system that must be paid at the time of filing the complaint.

Filtering   The process used to scan or search the documents for relevant terms in an attempt to narrow the focus, such as a filter to eliminate documents created before or after a certain date.

Final judgment   A judgment entered on the docket which ends the litigation, effectively putting the litigants out of court.

Foreign judgment   Any judgment entered in a court other than a particular state's courts.

Freedom of Information Act   A law that gives the public access to most documents in the possession of federal administrative agencies.

Friendly witness   A witness who cooperates with the party who has called him to testify.

Full Faith and Credit clause   A provision in the United States Constitution which requires the individual states to honor the judgments entered in other state and federal courts.

Garnishment   The process wherein a percentage of the judgment debtor's wages are remitted to pay the judgment.

General damages   Damages related to the injury sustained that can not be calculated with any particular formula or accuracy.

General denial   In some jurisdictions, the word "Denied" alone is insufficient and the averment of the complaint is treated as if it were "Admitted."

General jurisdiction   Power of the court to hear all types of matters so long as the dispute does not fall within the limited jurisdiction of a particular court; it is subject to the court's general jurisdiction.

Harmless error   An error made at trial that has no impact on the outcome of the case.

Hearsay   An out-of-court statement made by someone (declarant) other than the witness testifying; that statement of the declarant is offered for the truth of its contents.

Hearsay exceptions   Hearsay statements that are admissible because they are made under circumstance where they are likely to be true.

Hostile witness   A witness who does not cooperate with the party who called him to testify. A reluctant witness who demonstrates some hostility to the case presented or toward the party who called him to testify.

Human relations skills   Soft skills; ability to work successfully with others and handle oneself appropriately in the working environment.

Impeach   Questioning the witness on cross-examination to demonstrate to the jury that the witness is not reliable.

Impeach the credibility   Questioning the witness on cross-examination to demonstrate to the jury that the witness is not reliable.

Implied attorney-client relationship   Relationship which may result when a prospective client divulges confidential information during a consultation with an attorney for the purpose of retaining the attorney, even if actual employment does not result.

In personam   Jurisdiction over the person.

In rem   Jurisdiction over the property.

In rem jurisdiction   Jurisdiction to hear a case because of jurisdiction over the property of the lawsuit.

Inadmissible evidence   Evidence that either the rules or the court determines is not admissible at trial.

Independent medical evaluation (IMEs)   Term formerly used to describe a defense medical evaluation.

Indispensable party   A part whose interest would be affected by a court's ruling.

Infrared headphones   An assisted listening device for the hearing impaired.

Injunction   A court order that prohibits a person from doing a certain act.

Inside corporate counsel   Lawyer employed by a corporation to provide legal advice and counsel on corporate matters.

Insufficiency of process   Failure to properly service another party.

Interlocutory appeal   Appeal from an interlocutory order that requires certification of issue and permission.

Interlocutory order   Ruling, order, or judgment of the court that affects the rights of the litigants but does not end the litigation.

Interpersonal skills   Ability to work well with all types of people.

Interpreter box   Routes language translations from an interpreter to the witness/defendant's headphones or the courtroom's public address system.

Interrogatories   A form of discovery in which written questions are addressed to a party to a lawsuit requiring written answers made under oath.

Interrogatories in aid of execution   Interrogatories issued by the judgment creditor to locate assets of the judgment debtor.

IT   In larger law offices, corporate legal departments, and government offices, the technical support staff or information technology department.

Joinder   Inclusion in the lawsuit of a third party, not presently a party to the lawsuit, who is or maybe responsible for the harm suffered.

Judgment   The official decision of the court setting forth the rights and obligations of the parties.

Judgment creditor   The party who won at trial and is owed money for damages in the amount of the judgment.

Judgment debtor   The party who lost at trial; now has a judgment entered against him and owes another person money for damages.

Judgment-proof debtor   A judgment debtor without insurance, cash, assets, or other means of paying a judgment.

Judicial branch   One of the three co-equal branches of the government; represented by the court system.

Judicial notice   A court's acceptance of a fact without requiring a party's proof.

Jurisdiction   The authority of the court to hear disputes and impose resolution of the dispute upon the litigants.

Jurisdictional facts   Allegations demonstrating the court's jurisdiction over the persons and subject matter required in a complaint.

Jury charge   Instructions given by the judge at the beginning of trial to describe how the trial will be conducted or at the end of the trial to inform of the law to be applied in the case.

Jury deliberations   The process wherein the jury meets to discuss and reach a decision on the case.

Jury instructions (charge)   Instructions given by the judge to the jury, informing them of the law to be applied in the case.

Jury investigation   The ability to investigate the jury pool.

Jury pool   All individuals called to serve for jury duty before trial begins.

Jury selection   Process by which a group of six or more people is chosen to serve on the jury.

Jury verdict   The decision reached by the jury that concludes the case.

Laptop port   A connection into which a laptop may be plugged.

Large-screen monitor   A video monitor conveniently located in the courtroom and large enough for all to see the graphics displayed.

Lawyers   Law school graduates who have passed the bar examination, hold a license to practice law, and have met the minimum qualifications established by the individual jurisdictions or courts for obtaining a license to practice and represent clients.

Lay witness   A person who has personal knowledge about the matter before the court.

Leading questions   Questions which suggest the answer usually calling for a "yes" or "no" response.

Legal issue   Points of dispute on which law is applicable and/or how the law should be applied.

Legal support staff   Members of the law office who provide support functions to the legal team; these include law librarians, legal secretaries, receptionists, information technologists, bookkeepers and mailroom personnel.

Legal team   The collective group of people working on a case or matter under the supervision of an attorney.

Legislative branch   One of the three co-equal branches of the government; represented by Congress, the House of Representatives, and Senate.

Liability   Defendant's legal responsibility for the plaintiff's damages.

Limited jurisdiction   Courts authorized to hear certain types of disputes such as divorce or bankruptcy.

Litigation hold   A process whereby a company or individual determines that an unresolved dispute may result in litigation and as a result, electronically created and stored documents should not be destroyed or altered.

Long arm statutes   A method of obtaining personal jurisdiction over a non-resident defendant based on a statute that extends a state's jurisdiction.

Managing partner   Partner responsible for managing the business operations of a firm, such as taking care of the facilities, management, human resources supervision, and public relations.

Mandatory counterclaim   Claims that arise from the same event which must be included in the answer to the complaint or the defendant loses the right to bring them.

Matters   Any item, case, file, or project that needs to be tracked.

Mediation   A method of ADR process in which a neutral third party (mediator) helps the participants reach a negotiated settlement of their differences.

Metadata   Information about a particular data set which may describe, for example, how, when, and by whom it was received, created, accessed, and/or modified and how it is formatted.

Minimum contacts   A method of obtaining personal jurisdiction over a non-resident defendant based on the defendant having contacts within a state's jurisdiction.

Mini-trial   A method of ADR where each side presents its case to a panel comprising the parties' decision-makers with settlement authority.

Minors   Those individuals who have not reached the legal age, or age of majority, usually 18 years old.

Mistrial   Trial ended without a verdict being determined and requiring a new trial be conducted.

Mock jury trial   Process that allows the legal team to create a mock jury with similar socioeconomic factors as those in the jury pool; team presents its case, and the mock jury returns a verdict and critique.

Model Rules of Professional Conduct   The American Bar Association set of proposed ethical standards for the legal profession.

Monetary remedies   A form of damages that assigns a financial value to the harm suffered by the plaintiff.

Moral obligation   An obligation based on one's own conscience.

Motion   Formal request to the court seeking some type of relief during the course of the litigation.

Motion for directed verdict   Motion made at the conclusion of a party's case-in-chief which states that the other has failed to meet its burden of proof.

Motion for a judgment as a matter of law   A posttrial motion that asks the judge to overturn the jury verdict because it is unsupported by the evidence or disregarded the law. (Formerly known as a judgment n.o.v. or judgment notwithstanding the verdict.)

Motion for a judgment on the pleadings   A request for judgment as a matter of law based only on the contents of the pleadings.

Motion for a new trial   A posttrial motion that asks for a new trial because errors were made during the trial that make the verdict unreliable.

Motion for protective order   Motion which asks the court to determine whether certain information must be disclosed in discovery.

Motion for sanctions   Where an order compelling a party to cooperate is not complied with, the next step is to request that the court impose a penalty against the non-compliant party.

Motion for summary judgment   A motion by which a party seeks to terminate the lawsuit prior to trial alleging there are no disputed material facts and all that remains is in the application of the law to the facts.

Motion to compel   Motion seeking the opposing party's cooperation and compliance in responding to discovery requests.

Motion to extend the time to respond   A request for a court order allowing additional time to respond.

Motion to mold the verdict   Asks the court to take the jury verdict and calculate the amount that the defendant is obligated to pay the plaintiff.

Movable items   Documents, photographs, recordings, and similar tangible items.

Movant   The party who files a motion.

Mutual release   Document signed by both plaintiff and defendant agreeing to release each other from any and all claims arising from the transaction or occurrence that gave rise to the dispute.

Narrative opportunity   Question that encourages an answer requiring a full explanation.

Negligence   A cause of action in which plaintiff claims that another person's failure to act as a reasonable person would have acted under the same or similar circumstances caused injury for which the plaintiff should be awarded damages.

Neutral fact finding   A method of ADR used in cases that involve areas requiring expertise; the neutral fact finder investigates and issues a report about the matter.

Non-hearsay   Items are not hearsay because the declarant, while presently not testifying, is available to be cross-examined about the statement.

Non-dischargeable debt   A debt in bankruptcy that must be paid in full.

Non-evidentiary phase   Phase of trial that includes early proceedings, such as jury selection, and concluding events, such as jury deliberation. Non-evidentiary phase includes everything else that is not considered presentation of evidence at trial.

Non-movable items   Real property or large goods that are not readily movable but remain at the heart of the lawsuit.

Notice and waiver of service   Under the Federal Rules of Civil Procedure, a procedure where formal service of process is waived and service by regular mail is acceptable.

Notice of appeal   Document filed with the court of appeals indicating that a decision of the trial court is being appealed.

Notice of deposition   Notice to all interested parties of the date, time, location, and identification of the individual to be deposed; has power over parties only.

Notice of dismissal   Document filed with the court to terminate the lawsuit when no answer to the complaint was filed, signed by the plaintiff only.

Notice of motion   Form required by the court that the movant sends with the motion to the responding party; it usually provides a summary of the motion and a hearing and response date.

Notice pleading   Pleading required to include sufficient facts to put the parties on notice of the claims asserted against them.

Notice to Plead   A document containing the same information as a summons but often issued in dual languages.

Objectionable   In discovery, items that are not discoverable because the information is protected by privilege, the work product doctrine, trade secrets, or similar rule; the question might be duplicative; materials answering the questions may have been shared through disclosure; or the questions may be vague, overly broad, or burden-some, or unlikely to lead to admissible evidence.

Objections   The method by which an attorney orally advises the court that evidence being presented is not admissible.

Online collaboration   Members of the team use the Internet to work collaboratively using online software that allow each person to see the documents and in some cases each other, and make on screen notes and comments.

Open ended questions   Questions that usually do not have a "yes" or "no" answer but call for a short narrative response.

Opening statements   The first opportunity for the attorneys to address the jury and describe the nature of the lawsuit.

Oral argument   The opportunity for the attorneys to present an oral argument to the panel of appellate judges.

Oral deposition   Plaintiff, defendant, their lawyers, the witness, and a court stenogra-pher are together in a conference room. The witness, asked questions by one or both the attorneys, responds spontaneously, and the court stenographer records what is said.

Overruled   A judge's ruling on an objection that the evidence challenged is admissible.

Paperless office   Office where documents are created, stored, received, and sent electronically.

Paralegal   A person qualified by education, training, or work experience who is em-ployed or retained by a lawyer, law office, corporation, governmental agency, or other entity that performs specifically delegated substantive legal work for which a lawyer is responsible; equivalent term is legal assistant.

Partners   Lawyers who have an ownership interest in a law firm and a stake in the firm's profits.

PDF   Portable Document Format.

Perfect an appeal   A term of art used to describe compliance with all the rules of procedure for filing an appeal to be valid.

Perjury   Deliberately making a false or misleading statement while under oath; is potentially subject to court sanction, including incarceration.

Permissive appeal   An appellant must obtain the permission of the court to file an appeal.

Permissive counterclaim   Claims against the plaintiff that don't arise from the same event but, in the interests of justice, make sense to include with the defendant's answer.

Personal jurisdiction (*in personam*)   Requires the court to have authority over the persons as well as the subject matter of the lawsuit.

Petition for writ of certiorari   The document associated with the United States Supreme Court requesting that the Court accept a particular matter for review.

Petitioner   The party who asserts error occurred at trial by filing an appeal for review of the trial proceedings.

Physical and mental examination   A form of discovery that permits the physical or mental examination of a party by a qualified expert of the opposing party's choosing when the physical or mental condition of the party is at issue in the lawsuit.

Physical evidence   Any tangible physical evidence, usually an item directly related to the litigation.

Plaintiff   The party who files a lawsuit seeking relief for a harm suffered.

Pleadings   Documents filed to commence and respond to a lawsuit.

Post-judgment interest   Interest calculated on unpaid judgments authorized by state statute and added to the amount due the judgment creditor.

Posttrial motions   Motions made orally asking the judge to overturn the verdict of the jury.

Posttrial relief   Action, such as an appeal to a higher court, taken by one of the litigants to correct errors made at trial.

Practice management system   Practice management systems are programs for managing the daily operations and functions of an office.

Prayer for relief   Also known as a wherefore clause, a paragraph which ends each count of the complaint asking the court for the specific relief the plaintiff seeks.

Prerecorded testimony   Testimony that is recorded in advance of trial that may be used at trial in the event the witness is then unavailable to testify.

Precedent   Prior case law that is controlling and used to resolve the present dispute.

Preemptory challenge   A potential juror maybe struck from the jury without the attorney stating a reason.

Prefiling depositions   Depositions used to obtain information necessary to file an action.

Prejudice   In evidence, the probative value must outweigh prejudice which might mislead or confuse the jury, creating an emotional reaction.

Preliminary value   The total of special and general damages.

Preponderance of the evidence   The burden of proof in most civil litigation cases; the amount of proof that tips the scales of justice ever so slightly in one direction or another.

Present sense impression   A hearsay exception where the statement made describes an event that the declarant was then perceiving.

Presentation graphics   Visual aids used to enhance an oral presentation.

Preserving testimony   When a witness is unavailable or unable to testify at trial, the deposition testimony can be presented at trial so long as both parties to the litigation had the opportunity to pose questions to the witness at the time of the deposition.

Preserving the record   The obligation of the attorney to raise objection to mistakes made at trial. The objection gives the trial judge notice of an error he may be about to make or may have already made and gives the judge the opportunity to correct that error at trial.

Pretrial memorandum   A summary of the case prepared as a guide for the trial judge on what the issues are, the areas of agreement of counsel, and how long the trial will take.

Principal   One who authorizes another to act on his or her behalf.

Prior inconsistent statement   Prior statement given by a witness that is inconsistent with the testimony given at trial.

Private ADR   The use of an ADR method without court involvement, such as an arbitration clause contained in a contract.

Privilege   A rule of evidence that prohibits certain types of communication from being disclosed at trial. The recognized privileged communications include attorney–client, physician–patient, priest–penitent, and spousal. The privilege may also apply to documents via the work product or trade secrets doctrine.

Privileged communication   Communication to be kept confidential based on the relationship with the other party, such as attorney and client.

Probative value   Tendency of the evidence to demonstrate a fact important to the resolution of the case.

Procedural issue   Issue which arises from the presentation of the trial, such as those involving the application of the Federal Rules of Evidence.

Procedural laws   Laws that relate to how the trial is conducted and are usually based upon rules of court and rules of evidence.

Production of documents or things   A form of discovery in which written requests for documents and things to be made available for inspection are sent to the opposing party. A written response made under oath is required.

Professionalism   Conduct in accordance with the expectations of a profession.

Prognosis   How the medical complaint will resolve: full recovery, persistent problems, or permanent disability.

Punitive damages   Damages designed to punish the defendant for behavior that shocks the conscience of the finder of fact.

Purchase money mortgage   Debt created to purchase a home.

Quashed appeal   Dismissal of an appeal for failure to comply with the rules of procedure.

Range of motion   Ability to move—for example, the arm—through a variety of motions.

Real evidence   Testimony which is based on real facts, not some imaginary or hypothetical situation.

Rebuttal   Phase of the trial that gives the plaintiff the chance to address or respond to information contained in the defendant's case-in-chief.

Record on appeal   The documents forwarded by the clerk of the district court to the circuit court of appeals for review. The record on appeal includes the original documents filed with the court, the trial transcript with exhibits received into evidence, and the docket entries.

Recorded recollection   A hearsay exception that allows a personal, contemporaneously made statement in order to refresh their recollection about what happened on a particular day.

Recross examination   Permits opposing counsel to again challenge the credibility of the witness but only as to matters questioned on redirect examination.

Redaction   The removal of confidential information (or at least that which is claimed to be confidential) or material prepared for trial under the work product doctrine.

Redirect examination   After cross-examination, counsel who originally called the witness on direct examination may ask the witness additional questions.

Rehabilitate   During redirect examination, the attorney will ask questions to allow the witness to explain her answers on cross-examination.

Release Document signed by plaintiff which releases defendant from all possible claims arising out of a certain contract, accident, or other occurrence in exchange for the payment of a sum of money.

Relevant In litigation, a fact that if changed would change the outcome of the case.

Relevant evidence Evidence which tends to prove the existence of facts important to the resolution of a case.

Reliable evidence Evidence which is trustworthy; for example testimony from a witness who observed the accident is reliable.

Relief from the automatic stay A request of a creditor to proceed with his collection efforts outside the jurisdiction of the bankruptcy court.

Remand When the appellate court disagrees with the outcome of the trial court but sends the matter back to the trial court for further porceeding in accordance with its opinion.

Remote access Access to the law firm's computer and files from a remote location.

Removal Right of the defendant, in cases of concurrent jurisdiction, to have jurisdiction moved from state to federal court.

Reply Response of a plaintiff (or defendant) against whom a counterclaim (or cross) is asserted.

Request for admission A form of discovery in which written requests are made to the opposing party asking him to admit the truth of certain facts or liability.

Request for production of documents The shorthand name for production of documents and things.

Reserve The amount an insurance carrier sets aside for the case; it must show as a contingent or potential liability on the corporate financial statements.

Residual exception Allows hearsay where the hearsay statement being offered is a material fact of the case and there is no better evidence or testimony available to establish the fact.

Resourcefulness Ability to meet and handle a situation and find solutions to problems.

Respondent The party who must respond to an appeal for review, usually the verdict winner at trial.

Responsive pleading A pleading filed in response to a prior pleading.

Rest The party has concluded the presentation of its case-in-chief.

Restatement of The Law Third, Torts A legal treatise with suggested rules of laws relating to torts.

Reverse Ruling of appellate court that disagrees with the outcome of a trial and finds that error was made.

Right to appeal The right of a litigant to have the decision of the trial court reviewed by an appellate court.

Rule 12 Motion to dismiss Certain defenses, namely those that can bring the litigation to a swift conclusion, can be asserted by a motion to dismiss the complaint.

Rules of Civil Procedure A set of rules and procedures in each court which must be followed in all litigation.

Rules of Court Rules governing the practice or procedure in a specific court.

Sanctions Penalties imposed to punish wrongful behavior of litigants and their counsel; can include a monetary fine paid into court, dismissal of a claim, or payment of the reasonable attorney's fees.

Satisfaction piece A document filed with the clerk of court to mark the judgment paid on the docket.

Schedule of distribution   A schedule of distribution lists the proceeds from the sale, the related expenses, and the distribution to the creditor and any excess collected and returned to the debtor. Also, a written statement which lists a sum of money received and all the distributions that are permitted to be made from the amount received.

Scheduling order   A pretrial discovery order.

Screening Interview   Limited first contact with a prospective new client.

Search engines   Services for searching the world wide web using words or phrases.

Search queries   Specific words used in a computerized search.

Seated   Term used to describe a juror who has been selected to serve on the jury.

Self-authenticating   Because of the nature of the document or the circumstances under which it is created or stored an original is not required.

Service of process   Delivery of the complaint and summons to the defendant as required under the rules of civil procedure.

Settlement brochure   A formal statement of the plaintiff's case presented in brochure form to support the plaintiff's position in settlement negotiations.

Settlement demand   Specific amount plaintiff may demand to settle the case, often the starting point of settlement negotiations.

Settlement negotiations   The process whereby the attorneys for the parties calculate, communicate, posture, and settle the lawsuit through negotiations.

Settlement offer   Specific amount defendant may offer to settle the case.

Settlements   Ending the lawsuit by agreement, usually with the exchange of money.

Sidebar conference   Conference between the attorneys and the judge at the judge's bench in hushed voices with the jury in the courtroom.

Smoking gun   A document on which the case hinges that may be introduced into evidence.

Soft skills   Ability to work successfully with others and handle oneself appropriately in the working environment.

Special damages   Damages that can be calculated with some level of accuracy.

Specialty application program   Specialty programs combine many of the basic functions found in software suites, word processing, database management, spreadsheets and graphic presentations to perform law office case, and litigation management.

Specific performance   A remedy that orders the breaching party to perform the acts promised in the contract; usually awarded in cases where the subject matter is unique, such as in contracts involving land, heirlooms, and paintings.

Spoliation of evidence   Destruction of records which may be relevant to ongoing or anticipated litigation, government investigation, or audit. Courts differ in their interpretation of the level of intent required before sanctions may be warranted.

Standing   The right to bring a lawsuit only where the plaintiff has a stake or interest in the outcome of the case.

Stare decisis   Legal principle that prior case law should apply unless there is a substantial change in society necessitating a change in the law.

Statement against interest   A hearsay exception that recognizes human nature dictates that persons do not make statements that are harmful to themselves or against their own best interests.

Statute of frauds   A state statute that requires certain types of contracts to be in writing.

Statute of limitations   The time frame within which an action must be commenced or the party will lose their right to use the courts to seek redress.

Statutes   Enactments by the legislative branch that include provisions to define and regulate the conduct of its citizens; may also regulate the operation of a business or profession.

Stayed   Holding off for a particular period of time (as in "the collection of a judgment is stayed") until appeals are exhausted.

Stipulate to facts   Facts presented by both sides to the trier of fact, jury, or judge acting as trier of fact as not contested.

Stipulation   Document filed with the court to terminate the lawsuit signed by all parties to the lawsuit.

Strict liability   A tort doctrine that makes manufacturers, distributors, wholesalers, retailers, and others in the chain of distribution of a product liable for the damages caused by a defect irrespective of fault.

Subject matter jurisdiction   The authority of a court to hear and decide a particular type of dispute.

Subpoena   A court order compelling a witness to attend and testify; must accompany a notice of deposition served on a nonparty witness.

Subpoena duces tecum   A court order compelling a witness to attend, testify, and bring with him documents; must accompany a notice of deposition served on a nonparty witness.

Substantive issue   Issue which arises from which law is applicable or how the law is applied to the dispute.

Substantive law   Law that relates to the law of the case, such as the law of negligence or contract.

Summons   A document which advises the defendant he has been sued and gives the time within which he must respond; and alerts him that a failure to respond may result in a loss of rights.

Supervising attorney   Member of the legal team to whom all others on the team report and who has the ultimate responsibility for the actions of the legal team.

Sur rebuttal   Phase of the trial that allows defense to respond to the evidence presented by the plaintiff during rebuttal.

Sustained   A judge's ruling on an objection that the evidence challenged is not admissible.

Tangible evidence   Physical objects.

Testimony evidence   Evidence is given by witnesses who usually appear live in the courtroom to testify.

Third-party complaint   Follows the same format as the complaint that initiated the lawsuit.

Third-party defendant   Third party against whom a complaint is prepared, filed, and served along with a summons.

Third-party documents   Documents prepared by a third party in the ordinary course of business that would have been prepared in similar form if there was no litigation.

Third-party plaintiff   Defendant who intends to file a complaint against a third party.

Third-party practice   The process and procedure for including or joining a previously undisclosed party to the lawsuit.

TIFF   Tagged Image File Format, one of the most widely used formats for storing images. TIFF graphics can be black and white, gray-scaled, or color.

Time keeping   Maintaining records of the time spent in performing tasks on a case or matter; may include the recording of costs or expenditure related to the performance of the tasks.

Torts   Civil wrongs, which are not breaches of contract, for which the court can fashion a remedy.

Treatment   A course of medical services designed to heal, correct, alleviate or resolve a medical complaint.

Trial brief   Document presented to the court setting forth a legal argument to persuade the court to rule in a particular way on a procedural or substantive legal issue.

Trial graphics   Visual aids used to enhance a trial presentation.

Trial notebook   A summary of the case, usually contained in a tabbed three-ring binder with sections such as pleadings, motions, law, pretrial memo, and witnesses.

Trial presentation program   Computer program which organizes and controls documents, depositions, photographs, and other data as exhibits for trial and displays them as evidence when needed.

Trial transcript   The portion of the trial proceedings which are transcribed for the purposes of the appeal; not necessarily the entire trial.

Trier of facts   The trier of facts decides what facts are to be accepted and used in making the decision. It is usually a jury, but may be a judge who hears a case without a jury and decides that the facts and applies the law.

Unauthorized practice of law (UPL)   Giving legal advice, if legal rights may be affected, by anyone not licensed to practice law.

Undisputed facts   Failure to deny material facts in a pleading.

Uniform Arbitration Act   A proposed standardized procedure for arbitration, similar to the Federal Arbitration Act, for adoption by states.

Uniform Enforcement of Foreign Judgments Act   A statute that provides a uniform procedure for the enforcement and collection of judgments from other jurisdictions.

Usual stipulations   Agreements between the attorneys about how the deposition will be conducted; will vary by jurisdiction.

VCR   Equipment that plays back video and audio.

Venue   Process of determining in which court to file a lawsuit when more than one court has subject matter and personal jurisdiction.

Verdict   The decision reached by the jury or judge in a bench trial that concludes the case.

Verdict slip   A written document that asks the jury to answer specific questions about its decision.

Verdict unsupported by evidence   An error made at trial where the verdict of the jury is not supported by the evidence or the verdict disregards the law as presented in the jury instructions.

Verification   Statement attached to the end of a pleading, signed by the client and stating the information contained therein is true.

Videotape deposition   A type of oral deposition where testimony is recorded stenographically and videotaped for presentation at trial.

Visual presentation cart   Media center located in the courtroom.

Voir dire   Process whereby prospective jurors are asked questions by the judge and attorneys to determine if they would be biased in their decision.

Wherefore clause   Also known as a prayer for relief, a paragraph which ends each count of the complaint asking the court for the specific relief the plaintiff seeks.

Withdraw the claim   Process by which a party to the lawsuit voluntarily withdraws or terminates one or more of his claims.

Work product doctrine   A limited protection for material prepared by the attorney, or those working for the attorney, in anticipation of litigation or for trial.

CASE INDEX

SUBJECT INDEX

ABA. *See* American Bar Association (ABA)

AbacusLaw (software), 63, 66, 70–72, 260

Accident fact sheet, 63

Accounting functions, 70

Administrative agencies, 81

Administrative tasks, 13–14

Admissible evidence, 140–142

Admission of a party opponent, 151

Admit, 262

Adobe Acrobat, 304

Adobe Reader, 304

ADR. *See* Alternative dispute resolution (ADR)

Advisory Committee on Civil Rules of the Judicial Conference Committee on Rules of Practice and Procedure, 293

Affirm, 90, 459

Affirmative defenses, 262–263

African Americans, 173

Agency law, 36

Agents, 36

Age of majority, 198

Agreement, contracts and, 125, 126

Alternative dispute resolution (ADR)
explanation of, 80, 103–104
limit on appeals and, 104
methods of, 105–106
posttrial, 458
private, 107–109

American Arbitration Association (AAA), 107, 108

American Bar Association (ABA)
Model Code of Professional Responsibility, 37
Model Rules of Professional Conduct, 28, 37, 39, 177
opinion on confidentiality of privileged materials, 316

American rule, 393

Analytical skills, 8–9

Annotation monitors, 437

Answer
to complaint, 258
to fact-pleading complaint, 264–266

to notice-pleading complaint, 266–267

Appealable error, 448–449

Appeals
to appellate court, 451–452
on briefs, 456
cross, 452
interlocutory, 452
notice of, 453, 454
perfect the, 453
permissive, 459
preserving record for, 446–447
record on, 453
right to, 451
to U. S. Supreme Court, 459

Appellant, 452

Appellate court
appeal to, 451–452
explanation of, 89–90
rulings of, 458–459

Arbitration
explanation of, 80, 106
fact analysis for, 180
request through American Arbitration Association for, 107, 108

Arbitrators, 103–104, 106

Asians, 172–173

Assault, 122–123

Associates, 6

Assumption of risk
explanation of, 123, 263
interrogatory, 333

Attached, 399

Attire, 170

Attorneys. *See also* Supervising attorneys
ethical obligations of, 35–36
explanation of, 5
fairness to opposing party and counsel, 39–41

Attorney work product, 95–96

Authorization for distribution, 467, 468

Automatic stay, 475

Bankruptcy, 473–475

Battery, 122, 123

Bench trials, 88

Best Evidence Rule, 144

Billing, 13–14

Bills, in settlement brochures, 94

Boolean search, 57

Breach of contract, 125

Breach of duty of care, 83, 122

Briefs
explanation of, 456
preparation of, 456–458
trial, 392–393

Business and Professional Code (California), 31, 32

Calendars, 69, 70–72

California
Business and Professional Code, 31, 32
regulation of paralegals, 30

Candor, ethical obligation of, 39, 40, 393

Capacity, 125

Caption, 206

Case files
contents of, 64–65
keeping track of, 70
organization and management of, 14, 58–59

Case-in-chief
defendant's, 415
plaintiff's, 413–415

Case law, 81–82

Case management
manual, 61–62
requirements for, 66–67

Case management software
AbacusLaw, 63, 66
CaseMap, 59–60, 67–69
explanation of, 60, 62
manual approaches vs., 60–62
use of, 66–69

CaseMap (software), 59–60, 67–69

Case notebook
explanation of, 58, 61
tabs for, 58, 61–62

Cases, 61

Causation, 83, 122, 368

Causes of action
in complaint, 206–208, 263–264
contracts and, 125–129

537